Sexual Ethics: An Anthology

T0394192

BLACKWELL PHILOSOPHY ANTHOLOGIES

Each volume in this outstanding series provides an authoritative and comprehensive collection of the essential primary readings from philosophy's main fields of study. Designed to complement the Blackwell Companions to Philosophy series, each volume represents an unparalleled resource in its own right and will provide the ideal platform for course use.

Sexual Ethics
An Anthology

Edited by

Patrick D. Hopkins

WILEY Blackwell

Registered Office
John Wiley & Sons, Inc., 111 River Street, Hoboken, NJ 07030, USA

Editorial Office
9600 Garsington Road, Oxford, OX4 2DQ, UK

For details of our global editorial offices, customer services, and more information about Wiley products visit us at www.wiley.com.

Wiley also publishes its books in a variety of electronic formats and by print-on-demand. Some content that appears in standard print versions of this book may not be available in other formats.

Library of Congress Cataloging-in-Publication Data
Names: Hopkins, Patrick D., editor.
Title: Sexual ethics : an anthology / edited by Patrick D. Hopkins.
Description: Hoboken : Wiley-Blackwell, 2023. | Series: Blackwell
    philosophy anthologies | Includes bibliographical references and index.
Identifiers: LCCN 2022036460 (print) | LCCN 2022036461 (ebook) | ISBN
    9781118615867 (paperback) | ISBN 9781119252177 (adobe pdf) | ISBN
    9781119252207 (epub)
Subjects: LCSH: Sexual ethics.
Classification: LCC HQ31 .S515638 2023 (print) | LCC HQ31 (ebook) | DDC
    176/.4–dc23/eng/20221017
LC record available at https://lccn.loc.gov/2022036460
LC ebook record available at https://lccn.loc.gov/2022036461

Cover design: Wiley
Cover images: The Flirtation (1904), by Eugene de Blaas, photographic reproduction, public domain, Wikimedia Commons

Set in 9/11pt Ehrhardt by Straive, Pondicherry, India

SKY10040774_122922

Contents

Contents

Part IV   Homosexuality and Policy   221

Contents

Preface: How This Book Is Organized and How to Use It

History of the Text

Sexual Ethics: An Anthology is an accessible and provocative collection of readings on conceptual, ethical, and policy issues about sex. Designed for students, teachers, and anyone interested in exploring one of the major moral topics of our times, this collection avoids jargon and obscurity in favor of clear, straightforward discussion, covering a wide array of cases from all sides. It is intended to provoke thought, generate discussion, and analytically clarify the definitions, arguments, assumptions, and options of our personal, public, and political treatment of sex.

Unlike many books, which make their way from author to publisher to classroom, this anthology made the trip the other way around. It started in a classroom and then made its way to the publishing house. Now it's coming full circle. Toward the end of the first decade of the 2000s, when I was revamping my department's offerings and putting several applied ethics courses into rotation, I decided to teach a stand-alone course on sexual ethics. Such a course made sense, seeing as how sex was a major moral issue in society, every bit as controversial and publicly debated as medicine, business, and the environment. I assumed, then, that there would be textbooks on sexual ethics, focused on practical problems and organized in the same ways the medical ethics, business ethics, engineering ethics, and environmental ethics books on my shelves were. To my surprise, I found none. There were excellent books on the philosophy of sex and while those included some applied moral and policy

articles, they focused mainly on conceptual, ontological, and epistemological issues. There were also quite a few books from particular sectarian perspectives whose aims were largely about doctrinal clarification or religious training. There were also various books on feminist theory and gender studies, which tended to center on conceptual, historical, and theoretical concerns, often using abstruse vocabulary. Finally, there were anthologies on very specific issues, such as entire books on sexual harassment law. While all useful for their purposes, these books did not address the needs of a wide-ranging, non-sectarian, accessible, applied ethics course. So, I created my own reader from the sizable literature on sexual ethics. When the class was a success, I decided to turn that reader into a book anyone could use. This is that book.

Purpose of the Text

Applied ethics courses have been popular on college campuses for years. Delving into subjects from medicine to business to law to technology to the environment, they tap into an interest and a need people have to talk about, think about, write about, and hopefully learn about issues that grip our moral consciousness as well as our legislatures. Somewhat surprisingly, given the popularity of medical, business, and environmental ethics, sexual ethics courses are less common even though society seems seized at times with debate over sex and sexuality. The public controversies over gay marriage, pornography, premarital sex, sexual harassment, and adultery, just to name a few, have been as prominent and intense as those about abortion, healthcare costs, corporate misconduct, climate change, and endangered species. There could be several reasons why this is case. Perhaps it is because we are still embarrassed to talk about issues that feel as personal as sex, whether from a puritan inheritance or from a worry that others will think we must be talking about ourselves. Perhaps it is because the very act of talking about sex is sometimes part of a moral controversy itself – as with sexual harassment – and teachers worry that some discussions might be interpreted as inappropriate. Perhaps it is because sex is the area in which humans are both most literally and uncomfortably similar to animals – driven by the same powerful instinctual physical desires of beasts rutting in the field – and most anxiously and distancingly different from animals – driven to interpret, judge, and question those desires. Whatever the case, we seem to find it easier to talk about euthanasia than homosexuality in the classroom – although oddly, we seem to find much more talk about homosexuality in the media than euthanasia.

One way to address this asymmetry between public controversy and classroom discussion is to recognize that the passions and euphemisms and furor in public debates over sex should be taken seriously and can be discussed clearly, analytically, explicitly, and respectfully. A book that clearly labels sexual ethics as an academic and policy area worthy of focused, practical, attention can help with that.

Organization of the Text

This book is organized into three levels. The first level is a set of broad categories of concepts that shape various specific issues. For example, the concept of consent is crucial in analyzing the morality and legality of numerous sexual acts. Therefore, the broad category of consent and coercion is the rubric under which issues of sexual harassment, rape, and cognitive maturity are grouped. The second level is a set of applied framing questions that situate the broader conceptual problems with reference to specific issues. These questions do not exhaust the moral terrain but focus on the way the concepts work in real-world moral and legal decisions. For example, under the broad category of marriage and fidelity, one framing question asks whether purely online romances should count as adultery. The third level is the set of articles themselves, arguing for one conclusion over another, one judgment over another, and one policy over

another. For example, under the broad category of homosexuality and policy, and under the framing question of how we should assess attempts to change sexual orientation, one legal brief argues that "conversion therapy" should be criminalized as malpractice and another argues that it is justified by the right of the therapist to free speech.

With any text like this, the editor has a painful time selecting material. There are often so many good articles on a topic, sometimes only a few good articles on an important topic, and always far too many topics to cover at all. There are hard decisions then, as to what to cover and what to leave for another day. Inevitably, some readers will be disappointed that a topic or article important to them is left out. That is entirely understandable, but limitations of space preclude covering all that would be useful. In choosing the articles for this book, then, I had to decide what selection criteria would guide me. I chose topics I considered to be major issues, but "major" was interpreted in two ways. In one sense, "major" meant "amount of controversy in society." Using that criterion, gay marriage had to be included since it has recently been a monumental cultural focus at the level of individual, city, state, nation, legislature, and supreme court. Interracial marriage, though controversial in its own time and important to look at for the history of sexual ethics, was left out because it currently engenders little public outcry. In another sense, however, "major" meant "getting at the conceptual heart of sexual ethics." Using that criterion, the medical treatment of intersexed infants is included, even though it is a rare condition, and the moral analysis of pedophilia is included, even though there is hardly any public demand for decriminalizing sex with children.

Instructional Benefits of the Text

Having been created in the classroom, for college and law students of all levels and all majors, this book has been deliberately designed to be as user-friendly as possible, always in reference to what makes a text most useful for students, teachers, or anyone who wants a clear direction of where to go and a clear explanation of what to expect. The goal has essentially been to create a ready-to-go course. The specific user-friendly design elements include:

(a) *Categorization*: The book is divided into six broad categories that emphasize how conceptual issues shape debates (Consent, Marriage, Homosexuality, Transgender, Commerce, Paraphilia) with a short introduction to the topic at the beginning of the section.

(b) *Framing Questions*: Each major section of the book includes specific framing questions that address a major moral or policy issue, not to limit the issues but to show how various concepts are employed in real-world cases (e.g., How should we define rape? Should we legalize gay marriage? Should pornography be protected as free speech?).

(c) *Introduction*: The book begins with a concise introductory chapter on concepts and definitions of sex, sexuality, and sexual ethics that brings theoretical issues into clear view, providing the philosophical and scientific background for discussing the readings and explicitly showing how these conceptual issues have direct practical application. For example, definitions of sex are not just intellectual puzzles – definitions legally determine whether or not rape has occurred and thus determine whether or not someone goes to prison. The chapter includes recent empirical research on how people define sex and sexuality and recent empirical research on the moral psychology of emotional reactions to sexual issues.

(d) *Discussion Starters*: Each of the three sections in the introductory chapter (what is sex? what is sexuality? what is sexual ethics?) begins with 5 discussion starters, geared toward getting a class or group talking about issues and beginning to tease out conceptual and ethical elements of the issues. Instructors can use these starters early on in each section of the class to get students used to talking and to start fleshing out ideas.

(e) *Decision Cases*: One of the most valuable elements of this book is the set of decision cases that follow each of the three sections in the introductory chapter. Each of those sections conclude with 15 cases (45 cases altogether, almost all based on real-world events, including recent hot-topics) that call for in-depth philosophical analysis and making actual determinations about what should be done or how a person should be judged. Covering a wide variety of issues, the decision cases are perfect for class debate, for research topics, and for class presentations.

(f) *Representativeness*: Every specific issue is addressed with both Pro and Con articles – sometimes in direct response to one another – showcasing areas of moral, conceptual, and empirical disagreement and exposing readers to multiple positions and arguments.

(g) *Article Summaries*: Every article is immediately preceded by a short summary, indicating the topic, major points, argument structure, conclusion, and implications of the piece. This not only helps readers follow and understand but is immensely helpful for teachers planning courses – allowing them to determine which readings are best suited for a class without having to pre-read entire articles.

(h) *Article Variety*: The book contains a variety of types of readings on sex and sexuality, including argumentative essays, court rulings in specific cases, legal briefs in active court proceedings, position statements from medical organizations, government commission reports, and government agency regulations. This coverage provides a useful array of the types of writing that are influential in sexual ethics debates and demonstrates how actual, practical decisions are often made.

Acknowledgements

Thanks

My thanks go to the following people for their help with this volume.

Jeff Dean at Wiley-Blackwell was very helpful and insightful, seeing how a book like this addressed a gap in the practical ethics literature and shepherding the project through the initial process. Lindsay Bourgeois and Allison Kostka at Wiley-Blackwell also helped develop the project, and were consistently efficient, responsive, and supportive. Finally, thanks to Will Croft and Charlie Hamlyn for finalizing the project and being so helpful and efficient.

My student research assistants were invaluable. Nedah Nemati tirelessly, creatively, and systematically helped with the initial research and formation of the book, not only finding material but adding to the perspective and focus. She is a gem. Connor Houlahan also provided very useful research and practical assistance and was admirably unflinching given the eyebrow-raising search terms he had to regularly enter into the college library databases.

My Sexual Ethics class of 2008 – the first time I had ever offered such a class – was the impetus for this project. They signed up for a provocatively titled course and, though there were inevitably giggles and periodic uncomfortable-seat-shifting at first, quickly showed that serious analytic thinking can be brought to bear on a set of issues that normally are both difficult to talk about openly but also grip the social and legal conscience of society. This book is dedicated to them.

P.D.H.
Jackson, Mississippi

Text Credits

The editor and publishers gratefully acknowledge the permission granted to reproduce the copyright material in this book:

Chapter 1
Patrick D. Hopkins, "What is Sex, Sexuality, and Sexual Ethics?" Written for this volume.

Chapter 2
Anita M. Superson, "A Feminist Definition of Sexual Harassment," pp. 46–64 from *Journal of Social Philosophy* 24 (1994). Reproduced with permission of John Wiley & Sons.

Chapter 3
Laurence Thomas, "Lost Innocence," pp. 91–98 from *Stanford Law and Policy Review* 5 (1994). Reproduced with permission of Stanford University.

Chapter 4
Equal Employment Opportunity Commission v. Domino's Pizza, Inc. 909 F. Supp. 1529 United States District Court (M.D. Florida, Tampa Division) (1995). Public Domain.

Chapter 5
Oncale v. Sundowner Offshore Services Inc. (96–568) 83 F.3d 118 (1998). Public Domain.

Acknowledgements

Chapter 6

Joan McGregor, "Force, Consent and the Reasonable Woman," pp. 231–254 from Jules L. Coleman and Allen Buchanan (eds.), *In Harm's Way: Essays in Honor of Joel Feinberg*. Cambridge University Press, 1994. Reproduced with permission of Cambridge University Press.

Chapter 7

Donald Hubin and Karen Healy, "Rape and the Reasonable Man," pp. 113–139 from *Law and Philosophy: An International Journal for Jurisprudence and Legal Philosophy* 18 (1999). Reproduced with permission of Springer Nature.

Chapter 8

United States Department of Justice, "Attorney General Eric Holder Announces Revisions to the Uniform Crime Report's Definition of Rape," Friday, January 6, 2012. Public Domain.

Chapter 9

Steve James, "Romeo and Juliet Were Sex Offenders: An Analysis of the Age of Consent and a Call for Reform," pp. 241–262 from *UMKC Law Review* 78 (2009). Reproduced with permission of Steve James.

Chapter 10

Jennifer Ann Drobac, "A Bee Line in the Wrong Direction: Science, Teenagers, and the Sting to the 'Age of Consent'," pp. 63–96 from *Journal of Law & Policy* 20 (2011). Reproduced with permission of Jennifer Ann Drobac.

Chapter 11

Katherine Shaw Spaht, "Covenant Marriage Seven Years Later: Its As Yet Unfulfilled Promise," pp. 605–634 from *Louisiana Law Review* 65 (2005). Reproduced with permission of Katherine Shaw Spaht.

Chapter 12

Elizabeth F. Emens, "Regulatory Fictions: On Marriage and Countermarriage," pp. 235–269 from *California Law Review* 99 (2011). Reproduced with permission of University of California Berkeley Law.

Chapter 13

Dale Carpenter, "A Traditionalist Case for Gay Marriage," pp. 93–104 from *South Texas Law Review* 50 (2008). Reproduced with permission of Dale Carpenter.

Chapter 14

Lynn D. Wardles, "A Response to the 'Conservative Case' for Same-Sex Marriage: Same-Sex Marriage and the 'Tragedy of the Commons'," pp. 441–473 from *Brigham Young University Law Review* 22 (2008). Reproduced with permission of Brigham Young University.

Chapter 15

United States v. Windsor, Executor of the Estate of Spyer (Syllabus) 570 U.S. No. 12-307 (2013). Public Domain.

Chapter 16

Marci A. Hamilton, "Marriage," pp. 50–77 from *God vs. the Gavel: Religion and the Rule of Law*. Cambridge University Press, 2007. Reproduced with permission of Cambridge University Press.

Chapter 17

Jon Mahoney, "Liberalism and the Polygamy Question," pp. 161–174 from *Social Philosophy Today* 23 (2008). Reproduced with permission of Philosophy Documentation Center.

Chapter 18

Michelle Chihara, "Multi-Player Option," from Nerve.com (June 8, 2004). Reproduced with permission of Nerve.com.

Chapter 19

Richard Wasserstrom, "Is Adultery Immoral?" pp. 513–528 from *The Philosophical Forum: A Quarterly* 5 (1974). Reproduced with permission of John Wiley & Sons.

Chapter 20

Michael J. Wreen, "What's Really Wrong with Adultery?" pp. 45–49 from *International Journal of Applied Philosophy* 3:2 (1986). Reproduced with permission of Philosophy Documentation Center.

Chapter 21

Christine Tavella Hall, "Sex Online: Is This Adultery?" pp. 201–221 from *Hastings Communications and Entertainment Law Journal* 20 (1997). Reproduced with permission of UC Hastings Law.

Chapter 22

Kathryn Pfeiffer, "Virtual Adultery: No Physical Harm, No Foul?" pp. 667–690 from *University of Richmond Law Review* 46 (2012). Reproduced with permission of University of Richmond.

Chapter 23

Michael Levin, "Why Homosexuality Is Abnormal," pp. 251–283 from *The Monist* 67 (1984). Reproduced with permission of Oxford University Press.

Chapter 24

Timothy Murphy, "Homosexuality and Nature: Happiness and the Law at Stake," pp. 195–204 from *Journal of Applied Philosophy* 4 (1987). Reproduced with permission of John Wiley & Sons.

Chapter 25

Bowers v. Hardwick 478 U.S. 186, No. 85-140 (1986). Public domain.

Chapter 26

Lawrence v. Texas 539 U.S. 558, No. 02-102 (2003). Public domain.

Chapter 27

The American Psychiatric Association, "Therapies Focused on Attempts to Change Sexual Orientation (Reparative or Conversion Therapies) COPP Position Statement," APA Document Reference No. 200001 (2000). Reproduced with permission of American Psychiatric Association.

Chapter 28

Robert L. Spitzer, (A) "Can Some Gay Men and Lesbians Change Their Sexual Orientation?: 200 Participants Reporting a Change from Homosexual to Heterosexual Orientation – Abstract," p. 403 from *Archives of Sexual Behavior* 32 (2003); (B) "Spitzer Reassesses His 2003 Study of Reparative Therapy of Homosexuality," p. 757 from *Archives of Sexual Behavior* 41 (2012). Reproduced with permission of Springer Nature.

Chapter 29

Kamala D. Harris, Douglas J. Woods, Tamar Pachter, Daniel J. Powell, Craig J. Konnoth and Alexandra Robert Gordon, "Donald Welch, et al. v. Edmund G. Brown Jr., Governor of the State of California, et al., Appellants' Opening Brief (Preliminary Injunction Appeal)," pp. 1–76 in *The United States Court of Appeals for the Ninth Circuit*, Case No. 13-15023 (2013). Public Domain.

Chapter 30

John A. Eidsmoe and Joshua M. Pendergrass, "Donald Welch, et al. v. Edmund G. Brown Jr., Governor of the State of California, et al., Brief Amicus Curiae of Foundation For Moral law, In Support Of Plaintiffs—Appellees Urging Affirmance," pp. 1–35 in *The United States Court of Appeals for the Ninth Circuit*, Case No. 13-15023 (2013). Public Domain.

Chapter 31

Darryl B. Hill, Christina Rozanski, Jessica Carfagnini, Brian Willoughby, "Gender Identity Disorders in Childhood and Adolescence: A Critical Inquiry," pp. 57–74 from *International Journal of Sexual Health* 19 (2007). Reproduced with permission of Taylor & Francis Group.

Chapter 32

Robert L. Spitzer, "Sexual and Gender Identity Disorders: Discussion of Questions for DSM-V," pp. 111–116 from *Journal of Psychology & Human Sexuality* 17:3–4 (2006). Reproduced with permission of Taylor & Francis Group.

Chapter 33

American Psychiatric Association, "Gender Dysphoria," from *Diagnostic and Statistical Manual of Mental Disorders (DSM–5)*. © 2013 American Psychiatric Association http://www.psychiatry.org/dsm5. Reproduced with permission of American Psychiatric Association.

Chapter 34

Richard P. Fitzgibbons, Philip M. Sutton, and Dale O'Leary, "The Psychopathology of 'Sex Reassignment' Surgery," pp. 97–125 from *The National Catholic Bioethics Quarterly* 9 (2009). Reproduced with permission of The National Catholic Bioethics Center.

Chapter 35

Heather Draper and Neil Evans, "Transsexualism and Gender Reassignment Surgery," pp. 97–110 from David Benatar (ed.), *Cutting to the Core: Exploring the Ethics of Contested Surgeries*. Rowman and Littlefield, 2006. Reproduced with permission of Rowman and Littlefield.

Chapter 36

Cheryl Case, "Surgical Progress is Not the Answer to Intersexuality," pp. 385–392 from *The Journal of Clinical Ethics* 9:4 (1998). Reproduced with permission of Journal of Clinical Ethics.

Chapter 37

Merle Spriggs and Julian Savalescu, "The Ethics of Surgically Assigning Sex for Intersex Children," pp. 79–96 from David Benatar (ed.), *Cutting to the Core: Exploring the Ethics of Contested Surgeries*. Rowman and Littlefield, 2006. Reproduced with permission of Rowman and Littlefield.

Chapter 38

United States. Attorney General's Commission on Pornography, "Chapter 5, The Question of Harm," pp. 299–351 from *Attorney General's Commission on Pornography Final Report*, Volume 1. U.S. Department of Justice, 1986. Public domain.

Chapter 39

Daniel Linz, Edward Donnerstein and Steven Penrod, "The Findings and Recommendations of the Attorney General's Commission on Pornography: Do the Psychological 'Facts' Fit the Political Fury?" pp. 946–953 from *American Psychologist* 42 (1987). Reproduced with permission of American Psychological Association.

Chapter 40

Cass R. Sunstein, "Pornography and the First Amendment," pp. 589–627 from *Duke Law Journal* 1986: 4 (September). Duke University School of Law. Reproduced with permission of Cass R. Sunstein.

Chapter 41

Ashcroft v. Free Speech Coalition 535 U.S. 234 No. 00-795 (2002). Public Domain.

Chapter 42

Igor Primoratz, "What's Wrong with Prostitution?" pp. 159–182 from *Philosophy: The Journal of the Royal Institute of Philosophy* 68 (1993). Reproduced with permission of Cambridge University Press.

Chapter 43

Yolanda Estes, "Moral Reflections on Prostitution," pp. 73–83 from *Essays in Philosophy* 2:2 (2001). Reproduced with permission of Philosophy Documentation Center.

Chapter 44

Charles Moser and Peggy Kleinplatz, "DSM-IV-TR and the Paraphilias: An Argument for Removal," pp. 91–109 from *Journal of Psychology & Human Sexuality* 17: 3–4 (2006). Reproduced with permission of Taylor & Francis Group.

Chapter 45

Robert L. Spitzer, "Sexual and Gender Identity Disorders: Discussion of Questions for DSM-V," pp. 111–116 from *Journal of Psychology & Human Sexuality* 17:3–4 (2006). Reproduced with permission of Taylor & Francis Group.

Chapter 46

American Psychiatric Association, "Paraphilic Disorders," from *Diagnostic and Statistical Manual of Mental Disorders (DSM–5)*. © 2013 American Psychiatric Association http://www.psychiatry.org/dsm5. Reproduced with permission of American Psychiatric Association.

Chapter 47

Patrick Hopkins, "Rethinking Sadomasochism: Feminism, Interpretation, and Simulation," pp. 116–141 from *Hypatia* 9 (1994). Reproduced with permission of Cambridge University Press.

Chapter 48

John Corvino, "Naughty Fantasies," from David Boonin (ed.), The Palgrave Handbook of Sexual Ethics. Palgrave Macmillan, 2022. Reproduced with permission of John Corvino. This is a slightly modified version (with a new postscript) of an article that appeared in *Southwest Philosophy Review: The Journal of the Southwestern Philosophical Society* 18:1 (January 2002), pp. 213–220.

Chapter 49

Neil Levy, "What (if Anything) Is Wrong with Bestiality?" pp. 444–456 from *Journal of Social Philosophy* 34:3 (2003). Reproduced with permission of John Wiley & Sons.

Chapter 50

Wesley J. Smith, "Horse Sense," from *The Weekly Standard* (August 31, 2005) https://web.archive.org/web/20150906222530/http://www.weeklystandard.com/Content/Public/Articles/000/000/005/985pgwjh.asp. Reproduced with permission of The Weekly Standard LLC.

Chapter 51

Igor Primoratz, "Pedophilia," pp. 99–110 from *Public Affairs Quarterly* 13:1 (1999). Reproduced with permission of University of Illinois Press.

Chapter 52

Robert Ehman, "What Really Is Wrong with Pedophilia?" *Public Affairs Quarterly* 14:2 (2000). Reproduced with permission of University of Illinois Press.

PART I

Introduction to Sex, Sexuality, and Sexual Ethics

Introduction

Thinking analytically about the subject matter of a book like this is both important and somewhat more complicated than might be expected. It's not unusual when people hear about sexual ethics that they think it all centers around debating the morality of some particular sexual act. Is it right or wrong? Should it be legal or illegal? Is it good for us or bad? But in many cases we need to back up a bit and ask this question: What is *it*? What is the *it* we are talking about? What makes the action we are going to debate a *sexual* act? Or more broadly, what is sex? This question is not just an intellectual puzzle. It's not just about "semantics." After all, "semantics" refers to what words mean and what we mean by the term "sex" has a huge practical impact on our lives, personally, morally, and legally. A romantic partner might tell you they are a virgin – and yet regularly engage in an act you consider sex but they don't. A friend might be charged with rape – but claim that they never went "all the way" so they never had sex in the first place. A boss might say something to you with a "sexual" innuendo, and then claim later it was totally innocent. How do we know?

Questions about sexuality can be convoluted as well and have just as important practical consequences. If the law says a person's unchangeable, biological characteristics cannot be the basis of discrimination, then it would be crucial to know whether a person's sexual orientation is genetic or not. If sexual discrimination means treating someone unfairly because of their sex, is it possible to be sexually discriminated against by someone the same sex as you? How should we understand a person who appears to be a heterosexual man since they are anatomically male and attracted to women but who nonetheless claims to be a lesbian?

Once we have a better understanding of what we mean by sex and sexuality, then how do we go about making decisions – both moral and legal – about certain actions? Should we worry exclusively about the effects on society? Or not care about social effects at all? Is it entirely individual tastes? Or can individuals be culpably self-destructive and self-degrading? Are some sexual actions just wrong in themselves? Or does it all completely depend on whether or not actions hurt someone? If someone consents to something, is it okay even if they do get hurt?

The First Part of this book helps clarify these questions and sort through possible answers. Organized around the three following framework questions, it will help set the stage for analyzing the specific moral and legal issues to come.

Framing Questions

- *What is sex?*
- *What is sexuality?*
- *What is sexual ethics?*

1

What is Sex? What is Sexuality? What is Sexual Ethics?

Patrick D. Hopkins

Summary

This chapter summarizes the basic problems in defining the central terms in sexual ethics in three sections – What is sex? What is sexuality? What is sexual ethics? Each section begins with five discussion starters, which are useful for eliciting common positions and intuitions and for initially demonstrating some of the complexity of the concepts of sexual ethics. These starters are followed by analytic outlines of the issues and concepts important in discussions of sexual ethics. Each section ends with 15 decision cases (most of which are drawn from real-world examples, common college experiences, and court cases), which are useful for showing the practical consequences of the philosophical analysis of the concepts, for providing cases for debate, and for covering numerous contested contemporary issues that are not dealt with in depth in the following chapters.

Original publication details: Patrick D. Hopkins, "What is Sex, Sexuality, and Sexual Ethics?" Written for this volume.

Sexual Ethics: An Anthology, First Edition. Edited by Patrick D. Hopkins.

Section 1: What is Sex?

1.1 Discussion Starters

1. If your parents asked you if you had had sex yet, what do you think they would mean by that? How would you know how to answer? If a physician asked you when was the last time you were sexually active, what do you think the physician would mean by that? How would you know how to answer? If a police officer asked you if you had had sex with someone they were questioning, what do you think they would mean by that? How would you know how to answer? Do you think your definitions would match theirs? What are the different consequences of having different definitions in each of those cases?

2. What does it mean for a man and a woman to "go all the way"? What does it mean for a woman and a woman to "go all the way?" What does it mean for a man and man to "go all the way"? Are your answers consistent?

3. Sometimes people joke in response to being asked if they have had sex recently: Does having sex with myself count? But is this a joke? Is masturbating having sex with yourself? Or is having sex with yourself impossible? If masturbation is not considered sex, then why has it been looked down on in so many sexual ethics systems? If masturbation is sex, are you cheating on your spouse if you masturbate? If another person masturbated you, would that count as sex or not? Why would another person make the difference? Are your answers consistent?

4. Zorax is an extraterrestrial anthropologist who has been observing human behavior and is confused by this sex thing. Can you help him out? For example, Zorax has stealthily observed one situation where one human male started kissing another human male at a party and the two of them stumbled into a bathroom where one of them slid his finger into the other's rectum and rubbed his prostate. In another situation at a similar party, one male put his finger inside another male's rectum after the second male passed out drunk on his couch. In a third situation, one male physician put his finger inside another male's rectum and felt his prostate during an annual medical exam. To Zorax, these are all instances of the same physical behavior but apparently some are sexual and some are not. He understands there are differences in consent here, but he wants to know about the sex distinctions. Can you explain this to Zorax?

He also wants to know if it would make a difference if the patient undergoing a physical experienced a pleasurable erotic sensation during the examination? And what if the physician was same man in the first party situation?

5. In discussing the problems of defining sex, several bloggers just say we should have a relativist position in which people define sex for themselves, claiming that no one definition is appropriate for everyone. For example:
   - "Of course people have been arguing for years that we should get away from this need to define sex so specifically, but maybe seeing that other people do indeed engage in many activities that they consider sex . . . will help more people feel comfortable defining sex for themselves. Which is really how it should be – not a single definition that everyone uses but a personal one. Sex is whatever you want to do when you get physically intimate with another person." (Pisaster, 2011).
   - "I'd say that for me, at this point, I'd love to be able to define sex by simply saying "Sex could earnestly be absolutely anything for a given person." (Corinna, 2018).
   - "The short answer is that sex can mean many different things to many different people. There's not one universal definition of sex but a variety of perspectives." (GoAskAlice!, 2017).

But are these positions workable? If sex means whatever an individual wants, then what sense could we make of the claims that "sex requires consent" or "she is guilty of having sex with a minor" or "he could be charged with sexual harassment for asking for sexual favors" or "we should offer more sex education" or "she is a victim of sex trafficking" or any of a number of such statements?

1.2 The Problem of Definitions

Thinking analytically about the subject matter of a book on sexual ethics is both important and somewhat more complicated than might be expected. It's not unusual when people hear about sexual ethics that they think it all centers around debating the morality of some particular sexual act. Is it right or wrong? Should it be legal or illegal? Is it good for us or bad? Is it something a good person would do or a bad person would do? Is it consensual or forced? Is it perverted or normal? But in many cases, we need to back up some and ask this question: What is it? What is the *it* we are talking about? What is sex?

Even asking that question can be imprecise. We could be asking a psychological question about the emotional importance of sex in human life. We could be asking a biological question about procreation and how reproductively dimorphic organisms generate offspring. We could be asking an anatomical question about how to distinguish bodies and genitalia. Although all these questions may come into play in the issues debated in this book, ethics is going to be about judging the morality of actions and their related intentions and motivations. *Sexual* ethics then will be about analyzing and judging the morality of actions classified as sexual. So, what makes an action a *sexual* act as distinguished from a *non-sexual* act? When can we correctly claim that sex occurred? Why use the term "sex" to describe some behaviors and not others? When we make laws about sex, what exactly are we covering?

We might start trying to understand these issues by looking up the term "sex" in a dictionary, focusing on the definitions not related to gender or anatomy but rather those about behavior. Wouldn't that help? Here are a few dictionary examples:

- sexual activity, especially sexual intercourse (American Heritage Dictionary, 2016)
- (chiefly with reference to people) sexual activity, including specifically sexual intercourse (Oxford University Press, 2020)
- coitus (Vocabulary.com, nd.)
- physical activity between people involving the sexual organs (Cambridge University Press, 2021).
- physical activity in which people touch each other's bodies, kiss each other, etc.: physical activity that is related to and often includes sexual intercourse; sexually motivated phenomena or behavior (Merriam-Webster, nd.-a)
- the activity in which people kiss and touch each other's sexual organs, which may also include sexual intercourse (Macmillan Dictionary, 2009–2021).

Notice a few things about these definitions (these are just samples but look at a hundred dictionaries and you will find mostly similar entries).

First, they tend to be circular. Sex will be defined as sexual intercourse or sexual behavior or sexual activity or physical activity related to sexual intercourse. That's not going to help. In looking to define sex, we are asking about what makes something sexual.

Second, some definitions, instead of being directly circular, will give synonyms, such as coitus. However,

when you look up the word coitus, you find "sexual intercourse, especially between a man and a woman." (Dictionary.com, nd.). When you look up sexual intercourse, you find "sexual activity between two people; especially: sexual activity in which a man puts his penis into the vagina of a woman." (Merriam-Webster, nd.-b). Now we're back to circular – sex is coitus, coitus is sex. Even the male/female and penis/vagina wording is given as an example of sexual activity or intercourse particularly connoted by "coitus" – suggesting non-coital forms of sex.

Third, there are definitions that are more broadly behavioral, such as "physical activity between people involving the sexual organs or physical activity in which people touch, kiss, etc." This is less circular and would help with some distinctions. These kinds of definitions could help us determine that an asteroid orbiting the sun is not an example of sex (since it doesn't involve people or genitals) but it won't always help us determine more specific things about people. "Activity between people involving the sexual organs" leaves us asking both what makes an organ sexual (are breasts? are fallopian tubes? are anuses? are mouths?) and whether any type of activity counts (is a vasectomy a sexual act since it involves physical activity touching sexual organs?). "Physical activity where people kiss, touch, etc." probably needs no explication as to how unhelpfully broad it is.

Fourth, some definitions get more behaviorally specific, such as a man putting his penis into the vagina of a woman. That could be very helpful in making distinctions because it is much clearer. However, think about the way in which we use the term "sex" in language – which is all that dictionaries record in the first place. Do we use "sex" to describe anything other than penis-in-vagina? If we do, what makes those other activities sex?

Complicating the situation further, these formal dictionary definitions only cover the barest minimum of language dealing with sex. Think not only of formal synonyms for sex but the vast array of slang synonyms (if they are synonyms) for sex (if it is sex): hooked up, messed around, go all the way, third base, fornicate, got physical, were intimate, copulated, made love, screwed, slept together, made out, had relations, carnal knowledge, coupled, fooled around, mated, got some nookie, roll in the hay, hit the sheets, were in sexual union, experience sexual congress, consummated the relationship, bedded, bred, breed, lay together, lay down with, did it, do it, make it, shagged, fucked, got laid, got lucky, got busy, hit a home run, got some tail, got some ass, got some pussy, got some dick, took it up the ass, did the horizontal tango, made babies, got nasty, got naughty, rooted, ravished, sexed up, did the nasty, got some, got down and dirty, humped, scored, banged, bumped uglies, nailed her/him, rode her/him, boned her/him, put the P in the V, pounded, got a dicking, buggered, got into some hanky-panky, one-night stand, bonked, bagged, blew, sucked, ate, had a romp, had a quickie, hopped in the sack, knew in the Biblical sense, shtupped, diddled, hit it, knocked boots, booty call, boffed, dipped the wick, fiddled the flower, hid the sausage, got a hot beef injection, made whoopee, skrog, spank the monkey, hid the cannoli, get some stankie on the hang down, got busy, did the deed, boink, going to the boneyard, made a deposit, balled, and got a bit of the old slap and tickle – just to mention some of the more contemporary ones. You could also add slang from earlier historical periods – make a beast with two backs, give her a green gown, shoot twixt wind and water, get your corn ground, grope for a trout in a peculiar river, get your ashes hauled, and ride a dragon upon St. George (Okrent, 2014; Thorpe, 2015). It seems that it is important in language (these are only English examples here but there are many, many slang terms for sex in most languages) to refer obliquely to sex. But are these in fact all referring to the same thing? Could you substitute "engaged in sex" for every one of them?

It is important to recognize that there is a difference between the terms we use to describe behavior and the behavior itself. There is a difference between the objective fact of what physical action occurred, the objective fact of what psychological state the agent was in when the physical action occurred, and the subjective choice of words used to describe the physical action. A penis entering a vagina to a distance of x either happened or didn't. A vagina pressing against a mouth and tongue either happened or didn't. A finger entering an anus to a distance of x either happened or didn't. Behavioral events a, b, c, . . . either happened or didn't. Whether we call those acts "sex" as a moral and forensic term is a more complicated social process, but the acts stand alone.

We can thus distinguish between behavior or action and the way that behavior is conceptualized or interpreted. In some contexts, the conceptualization and interpretation is the most important thing – for example, whether or not the action counts as ending virginity, or counts as a crime, or counts as a Title IX violation, or counts as adultery. In some contexts, the behavior or action is the most important thing and our social interpretations of the action are irrelevant – for example, whether or not an act provides a physical vector for HIV

transmission or whether or not the act could lead to pregnancy.

Depending on what you are interested in then, it is very important to ask the specific question you want answered. If you are a physician trying to determine the likelihood that someone may have been exposed to HIV, then what you really want to know is whether some specific body-fluid-exchanging actions occurred, not whether someone conceptualizes themselves as sexually active or not. This kind of issue was brought to light in a 2010 study on what sorts of behaviors people described as "having sex" (Sanders et al., 2010). The study (reported by the authors as the first of its kind) was published by researchers from the Kinsey Institute for Research in Sex, Gender, and Reproduction, and several other notable academic institutions. It had been known for some time that there were problems in surveys and polls that tried to investigate sexual behavior – memory error, self-reporting biases, and biased questions. However, not much attention had been paid to the basic question of what counted as "sex" itself. The authors decided to ask about specific behaviors. The stem question for the random phone survey (486 valid responders) was simply: "Would you say you 'had sex' with someone if the most intimate behaviour you engaged in was . . ." followed by 14 specific descriptions of behaviors. Respondents could simply answer "yes" or "no." Behavioral descriptions included "You had oral contact with a partner's genitals?," "Penile–vaginal intercourse?," "Penile–vaginal intercourse with no female orgasm?," "Penile–anal intercourse, but very brief?," and others. While the study revealed a number of very interesting results, for purposes here it is enough to point out just a few things: only about 50% of respondents considered the use of hands on genitals to be "sex"; only about 70% of respondents considered oral contact with genitals to be "sex"; about 5% of those polled thought whether or not a man ejaculated made a difference to whether penis–vagina intercourse was "sex"; 95% of people thought penis–vagina intercourse was "sex" but only 80% of people considered penis–anus intercourse "sex." One hundred percent of males in the 18–29-year-old age group called penile–vaginal intercourse with a condom sex, but only 82% of men age 65 or older considered intercourse with a condom to be sex.

The consequences of these different definitions can be important. It could account for why significant numbers of patients with sexually transmitted diseases report that they have never had sex. It might mean that for 20% of respondents, gay cis-men are not capable of having sex since penis–vagina intercourse cannot happen and penis–anus intercourse doesn't count. It could explain why a "virgin" doesn't consider herself to be lying even though she regularly has penile–anal intercourse. It could explain why a man who regularly has penile–anal intercourse with other men, but never has a penis inserted into his anus doesn't consider himself gay or bisexual because he doesn't have "sex" with other men. In short, it could account for a lot of confusing responses, medical issues, and identity pronouncements.

1.3 Solutions to the Problem of Definitions

Given the complications of defining sex, we might go one of two directions in trying to settle the issue. One option would be to say anything goes – let people define sex however they want, let there be lots of different definitions, and make it all purely subjective. While this may seem tempting at first, there is a very serious and probably fatal downside to going this way. Issues of sexual ethics (and the directly related issues of sexual laws) are not just personal issues – they are social and political issues involving interactions between people. They are part of a public discourse in which we have to rely on shared terminology to make real-world decisions. The issue of definitions is not just an intellectual puzzle or an observation about vocabulary. It can't be dismissed by saying "it's all just semantics" – after all, "semantics" refers to the meaning of words and what we mean by words has a huge practical impact on our lives, personally, morally, medically, and legally. If we are going to make any sense of common claims (whether you are for or against those claims) such as "there should be laws against sexual harassment" or "rape is sex without consent" or "gonorrhea is a sexually transmitted disease" or "he lied to her about having sex with another woman" then we cannot just say "everyone defines sex however they want." We need to share definitions and we need to be clear on what those definitions are when we are in situations where clarity of meaning is important to making a decision.

A second option then would be to say let's just stipulate a definition of sex. Let's just decide, lay out the definition, and agree to that. This is a more promising direction to take because at least it satisfies the requirement that we have definitions to work with in making decisions that are socially and publicly consequential. This is also what we often actually do sometimes when we make laws or regulations or standards (though we also often assume we already have a shared definition of "sex" and don't specify exactly what we mean). However, while the second option may be the direction we have to go, it

does not always settle the issues. Much of what is debated in society is what to include and what not to include under the term "sex." If we already have principles and values regarding the morality of sex, there can be a drive to include more and more under the definition of sex in order to capture more and more under existing restrictions or protections. For example, if there is already a rule against sexual harassment, some people will be motivated to include more actions under the definition of sexual harassment in order to regulate those actions. An original meaning might have just meant quid pro quo sexual favors but later be expanded to include making any statements about a person's sex that someone might perceive as offensive. The US Equal Employment Opportunity Commission, in fact, now explicitly states that "sexual harassment" does not need to be "sexual" in nature but can include making offensive gender-related comments. Sometimes this is referred to as "mission creep" or "definition creep," referring to the continual expansion of what a term refers to past its original meaning.

There is an intellectual and emotional back-and-forth here with regard to definitions. We need definitions to help us make moral and legal judgments, but sometimes prior moral and emotional judgments will inform how we set up our definitions. Both moral judgments using definitions and moral judgments about definitions themselves must then be subject to critical scrutiny.

1.4 Decision Cases

1. *Is she a virgin?* Ashley is a senior in college who is engaged to be married soon after graduation. She has proudly told her fiancé, Brandon, that she is a virgin. However, you know for a fact that Ashley has had penis–anus intercourse many times with several different men on campus. You heard her talking once about how she only defines real sex as vagina–penis intercourse and her primary reason for anal intercourse has been to maintain her status as a virgin. Your friend Darius, who is gay, says Ashley is deceiving herself and her fiancé and that if anal intercourse doesn't count as sex then he must be a virgin too and always will be. So, what would you argue? Is Ashley lying? Is she telling the truth? Is she misleading Brandon? Why hasn't she told Brandon about what she has done? Does she define sex incorrectly? Does she have a suspect motivation for her definition? If Brandon asked you if Ashley has ever had sex with another man, what should you say? If he asked you if Ashley was an honest person, what should you say?

2. *Did he commit adultery?* Hector and Alina are a married couple with a 3-year old daughter. Hector works a solid 9–5 job and on his off time regularly plays a character on a massive multiplayer online role-playing fantasy game. As his character, he begins a relationship with another player. He chats a lot with her. They go on quests together. They share intimate feelings. Eventually, they begin describing their sexual fantasies to each other and write in detail what they (as their characters) would do with each other. She tells him (in character) that she loves him and Hector (in character) says the same to her. They spend on average between 1 and 2 hours a day interacting with each other. They have never met in real life or had any conversation except through the game. Eventually, Hector's character pops the question and they decide to get married at a castle. They invite other characters from the game to the ceremony. Meanwhile, Alina has been getting increasingly frustrated and angry about how much time Hector spends on the game. One night, when Hector is reading a bedtime story to their daughter, Alina logs in to the game as Hector and reads some of the archived exchanges with his in-game wife. She gets furious and hurt, accuses him of cheating on her, and tells him she can't believe he would do this to her. Hector says it's not him, it's his character, it's all online, and it's nothing like cheating. So, what would you argue here? Did Hector cheat? Is Alina's anger justified? Is her hurt justified? Does she have grounds for divorce? Can Hector be a good husband while carrying on the online relationship?

3. *Was he raped?* Carla and Mark have been dating for six months and have a very active sex life. One sex game they have enjoyed includes Carla blindfolding Mark, leading him around, and then touching, sucking, and edging his penis until he orgasms. One night, Carla decides it would be exciting to try something with Mark she has seen in porn. She blindfolds him as usual, goes through the usual foreplay and teasing, but then unknown to Mark, a gay friend of hers named Joel quietly comes into the room and sucks Mark instead of her, while she makes the usual sounds to trick Mark into thinking it is her. When Mark orgasms, Carla pulls off the blindfold to surprise him, saying what she just saw was so hot. Mark, however, is furious and horrified. He says she is sick and he could charge her and Joel with sexual assault. Carla tells him he is overreacting

and just needs to lighten up. Joel gets angry too and says the only reason Mark is upset is because it was a man and if it had been a woman, he wouldn't be acting this way and he certainly wouldn't think of it as sexual assault. Joel also says that if Mark thinks he was raped then he'll have to admit that in the future he has had sex with a man. Mark says he did not do any such thing. Carla says that doesn't make any sense. How should you analyze this situation? Did Mark have sex with a man? Was Mark raped? If so, by whom – Carla or Joel or both? If Carla and Mark had done this before with another woman and Mark was not upset, does that change anything? What would that say about Mark's character? What does it say about Carla's character that she would do this? What does it say about Joels'?

4. *Did she hire a prostitute?* Charlotte has a medical condition called pelvic floor dysfunction that causes serious pain during sexual intercourse. She has seen a physical therapist for several months who has been treating her with a medically recognized treatment called intravaginal massage and this has helped quite a bit. However, her insurance has run out and she needs more therapy. Having heard about a massage parlor where the employees actually bring clients to orgasm for extra money, Charlotte makes an appointment, explains her situation to the masseuse and pays her to do the intravaginal massage. Charlotte does not experience orgasms during these sessions, but it is pleasurable to further release the tight muscles and it costs far, far less than seeing a physical therapist without insurance. One day, during her appointment, the massage parlor is raided by the police and she is arrested. She argues that she was not paying for sex but instead therapy. The police don't believe her but say if that was true, then she might be charged with soliciting someone to practice medicine without a license. If you were Charlotte's lawyer, what argument would you make to defend her against charges of soliciting prostitution? If you were a prosecutor, what argument would you make that she had broken prostitution laws?

5. *Did he lie about having sex?* In 1998, US President Bill Clinton was impeached (only the second president at that time to be so) and brought to trial in the Senate on charges of perjury and obstruction of justice. The charges were connected to a 1994 sexual harassment lawsuit filed against him by former Arkansas state employee Paula Jones related to his

time as Arkansas' governor. Trying to show a pattern of inappropriate sexual behavior with women, Jones' lawyers put Monica Lewinsky (a former intern who had told a friend she had had a "sexual relationship" with the president) on their witness list. Jones' attorneys asked the presiding judge to approve a formal definition of "sexual relations," of which the judge approved only the first part – a narrow description of sexual relations as "contact with the genitalia, anus, groin, breast, inner thigh, or buttocks of a person with an intent to arouse or gratify the sexual desire of any person" (The Washington Post Company, 1998). In his deposition, Clinton stated that he never had "sexual relations" with Lewinsky. That statement was the ground for the perjury charge. However, Clinton's legal team argued that the approved definition did not include certain actions, thus he did not lie, thus there was no perjury. The indirect claim here seemed to be that even if Lewinsky had performed oral sex on Clinton, the deposition question asked if *he* had sexual relations with her, not if *she* had sexual relations with him. The definition of sex the judge approved made it possible that she could have had sexual relations with him and yet he not have had sexual relations with her (notice "mouth" is not in the definition, so putting a mouth on a penis falls under the sex definition because it counts as contacting genitalia but putting a penis on a mouth does not) (Lacayo, 1998; Tiersma, 2004). So, did Clinton perjure himself? How would you judge Clinton's character as a result of him making this argument?

6. *Did they make child pornography?* In 2011, MTV began airing a show titled *Skins* about the drug- and sex-related activities of teenagers. Following its British original, the show hired actors ranging in age from 15 to 19. The show depicted numerous scenes of suggestive poses, exposed breasts, heavy foreplay, and in one case a naked 17-year-old (whose constant erections were an ongoing joke in the show) running down the street (Stelter, 2011). The Parents Television Council asked the Justice Department to investigate whether the program violated federal child pornography laws, which define child pornography (in section 2256 of Title 18, US Code) as "any visual depiction of sexually explicit conduct involving a minor (someone under 18 years of age)." The law elaborates by stating "the legal definition of sexually explicit conduct

does not require that an image depict a child engaging in sexual activity. A picture of a naked child may constitute illegal child pornography if it is sufficiently sexually suggestive" (US Department of Justice, 2020). The show was canceled before a second season. Do the actions of the minor actors in this show meet the standard of "sexually explicit conduct"? Could MTV have been charged with producing child pornography? Should MTV have been charged? Regardless of the legal issues, was MTV doing something good, bad, useful, or shameful by producing this program? Were the actors doing something good, bad, useful, or shameful in participating in it? Should there even be such a law? When, if ever, should adults intervene in minors' sexual activities?

7. *What were they doing?* In 2015, hackers broke into the Ashley Madison website – a site that billed users for helping them set up adulterous affairs. Once things had settled down from the release of users' names, the company revealed that they had used tens of thousands of "fembots" or small computer programs that pretended to be human women in order to make it look like more women were using the site and to help draw in male customers (Pagliery, 2016). Most men had no idea they were chatting with programs. Some stories described these men as believing they were having online affairs when actually they were just alone, talking to code. Do the sexually explicit conversations men had with these programs count as infidelity or even as "conversations" at all? Were they cheating on their wives if no one else was there? How do the motives and beliefs and intentions of the men play into moral judgments of their activities? Can there be honorable motivations in paying for such a site?

8. *Did she commit adultery?* In 2003 in New Hampshire, David Branchflower filed for divorce on the grounds of irreconcilable differences. Later, however, he amended his petition, arguing that that his wife had been engaged in a continuous adulterous affair with another woman – Robin Mayer. Mayer asked the court to dismiss the amended petition, arguing that a homosexual relationship with a person married to someone else cannot constitute adultery under New Hampshire law. The trial court disagreed and allowed the petition, but Mayer appealed. The New Hampshire Supreme Court took up the case. Although the relevant statute allowed for adultery as a ground for divorce, it did

not define adultery. The justices, therefore, in an attempt to apply the "plain and ordinary meaning" of the term, looked to Webster's Third New International Dictionary, which defined adultery as "voluntary sexual intercourse" between a married person and someone other than their spouse. Then, they looked to the definition of "sexual intercourse" which was described as "coitus." Then, they looked to the definition of "coitus," which was itself described as "insertion of the penis into the vagina." Given these definitions, the court ruled that two women cannot engage in sexual intercourse and thus could not commit adultery with each other (and so the women won their case). In the majority's opinion, any other standard used (such as the dissenting opinion's "intimate sexual activity") "would permit a hundred different judges and masters to decide just what individual acts are so sexually intimate as to meet the definition" (Branchflower v. Branchflower, 2003). Did the court decide rightly? Does a principle of respecting LGBTQ sexuality require treating the women's activities as genuine adultery?

9. *Are you masturbating?* A technology company creates a new type of wearable tech – a haptic data suit. The suit reproduces the same kinds of sensations of touch and feeling and pressure that a person would experience if they were actually in physical contact with an object, even though they are not. This lets whoever wears the suit engage in remote operations that feel just like the real thing. Although marketed at first for activities like gaming, remote surgery, remote music performances, simulated computer keyboard use, testing the feel of new clothing, and test-driving a new car, the technology instantly starts getting used for "virtual sex." But this opens up a big set of questions. If you have virtual sex with another person, but, of course, are only being touched by the suit, are you really having sex? Are you being masturbated by someone? If you use a sex program rather than interact with another person are you being masturbated by a machine? Can you have sex with a machine? Is masturbation itself questionable? Is it a perversion of something that is supposed to be shared with another person? What is the motivation for having sex without getting close to another person? What other questions can you come up with and how would you answer them?

10. *Is it adultery if she can't get pregnant?* In many cultures and legal systems, adultery is grounds for divorce (or criminal charges) and can affect alimony, child custody, and inheritance. Adultery has usually been understood to mean voluntary sexual intercourse between a married person and someone he or she is not married to. In one famous Canadian case, however, a judge ruled that the essence of adultery was introducing the possibility of having a child outside the marriage – so, even artificial insemination by donor with no sexual intercourse would count as adultery. "The fact that it has been held that anything short of actual sexual intercourse . . . does not constitute adultery, really tends to strengthen my view that it is not the moral turpitude that is involved, but the invasion of the reproductive function . . . Sexual intercourse is adulterous because in the case of the woman it involves the possibility of introducing into the family of the husband a false strain of blood. Any act on the part of the wife which does that would, therefore, be adulterous" (Orford v. Orford, 1921). This position seems to be held by a number of people who grew up before the birth control pill was common. In one 2010 study, nearly 20% of men over the age of 65 said that using a condom meant penile–vaginal intercourse did not count as sex (Sanders et al., 2010). More recently, in 2020, a man in the UK was sentenced to four years in prison for rape because he poked holes in a condom he used for sex. Although the sexual act itself was consensual, using a sabotaged condom was ruled to be rape and the judge was quoted as saying the man was fortunate that the woman did not get pregnant (Greenway, 2020). So, how important is potential procreation to defining sex and adultery? Is the key element of the wrongness of adultery not "moral turpitude" but reproductive lies? If a married woman secretly stopped using birth control, would that count as raping her husband, to parallel the UK case? If she used sperm from a donor (without any intercourse) to impregnant herself without her husband knowing about it, is she guilty of a kind of adultery? Could he divorce her on the grounds of adultery? If not adultery, then what marital violation did she commit? What exactly is morally objectionable about adultery?

11. *Is this a case of rape?* In 2012, the US Department of Justice changed the definition of rape for purposes of the Uniform Crime Reporting system. Rape was previously defined as "The carnal knowledge of a female forcibly and against her will." The

new definition says rape is "Penetration, no matter how slight, of the vagina or anus with any body part or object, or oral penetration by a sex organ of another person, without the consent of the victim." This new broadened definition allowed for the concept of male rape victims and object rape. Now consider this situation: A man grabs a woman in a parking garage. He drags her into a van, ties her hands, tapes her mouth, holds her down, and vaginally penetrates her with a bottle. After several minutes, he pushes her out of the van and drives away. Did the man rape the woman? Yes, according to the criminal reporting definition. However, notice that the man did not have sex with the woman, in the sense that any of his sex organs were involved. So, it appears that either rape no longer has to involve sex (rape is penetration, not "sex") or that sex can be asymmetrical (with one person having sex and the other person not – the woman experienced forced sex but the perpetrator did not have sex at all). Also, consider a variation of the situation in which the man did not use a bottle to penetrate the woman's vagina, but instead used a dildo to forcibly, involuntarily penetrate the woman's mouth. Did the man rape the woman? No, according to the criminal reporting definition. Oral penetration only counts as rape if a sex organ is used. If he had used his penis, then it would be rape. So, it appears that the penis is important for oral penetration rape, but not for vaginal or anal penetration rape. Why? Are these good definitions? What do we really want from rape laws in the first place? What are we trying to achieve?

12. *Did she have sex, but didn't know it?* Julie, a 17-year-old mentally disabled girl lives in a residential institution run by the state. She has been told by one of the night employees that needs to have "physical therapy" – a term she is familiar with from treatments during the day helping her deal with a congenital spinal curvature. The employee comes to her room each night and put his fingers in her vagina, stimulating her to orgasm, which she enjoys. Although Julie is familiar with the idea that sex is "a penis in a vagina that makes babies," she doesn't think of this as sex and only thinks of it as fun physical therapy. Is Julie having sex but doesn't know she is? Is Julie being harmed? Disrespected? Used? Helped? Forced? What makes the night employee's actions objectionable? If someone were to find out what was happening and put a stop to it

and decided to explain to Julie what happened, what should they say to explain what was actually happening instead of physical therapy?

13. *Did he think he had sex, but didn't?* On the animated Fox television series *Family Guy* (Season 5, episode 1), Peter (an adult male with limited intelligence) goes to see his family physician for a flu vaccine. Dr. Hartman realizes from looking at Peter's medical record that he has never had a prostate examination, which is recommended for a man his age. The doctor tells Peter he needs to have a prostate exam and Peter agrees to it, not knowing what it means. When the doctor inserts his finger, Peter freaks out. He feels sexually violated, says he had no idea that's what a prostate exam was and shows signs of traumatic stress. When he tells his wife that he was raped, she mocks him for being idiotic. Peter then becomes more and more upset and finally takes Dr. Hartman to court for sexual assault. Although intended to be farcical, does Peter have a case? If he didn't know what a prostate exam was and subjectively experienced it as rape, was it rape? Or, as his wife seems to think, is he intellectually responsible for knowing the difference?

14. *Were you sexually harassed?* Sexual harassment is a crime. The US Equal Employment Opportunity Commission states that sexual harassment can include "unwelcome sexual advances, requests for sexual favors, and other verbal or physical harassment of a sexual nature. Harassment does not have to be of a sexual nature, however, and can include offensive remarks about a person's sex . . . it is illegal to harass a woman by making offensive comments about women in general . . . the law doesn't prohibit simple teasing, offhand comments, or isolated incidents that are not very serious" (U.S. Equal Employment Opportunity Commission, nd.). What counts as "sexual," of a "sexual nature," or "offensive" is not agreed on, however. A 2017 national poll showed, for instance, that while most people agreed that "intentionally groping or kissing without consent" was sexual harassment, 80% of women said intentional touching of *any* sort without consent was sexual harassment, 50% of minorities said hugging without consent was sexual harassment, and 56% of minority women said unwanted compliments about their appearance was sexual harassment. As for what did not count as sexual harassment, 44% of respondents said telling dirty jokes did not count, and nearly 20% of

millennials (people born between 1982 and 2004) said sending nude selfies to someone did not count (Kahn, 2017; Huang and Kahn, nd.). So, literally, Alan could tell Kara her new dress really looks great on her and Kara could believe she has been sexually harassed. Kara, on the other hand, could send nude photos of herself to Alan and not believe she was sexually harassing him. How do you know when sexual harassment has happened? Does the attitude or motivation matter?

15. *Did I have sex?* On various forums and advice sites, people post questions asking about whether or not some experience they recently had counts as sex. Sometimes they are just curious. Sometimes they are disagreeing with someone else. Sometimes it is important to them because they want to be able to say they are still a virgin. Sometimes it is important to them to keep track of the number of people they have had sex with, to fit their idea of whether they are a slut or a stud. Here are a few real examples (typos and misspellings left in). How should their questions be answered? How should the motivations for their questions be judged?

(i) so first off my boyfriend and i have never had sex. okay two nights ago my boyfriend and i were messing around on the couch (like he was rubbing himself on me but not going in) and he kind of slipped and went in maybe an inch or so but not all the way and he quickly pulled out without thrusting or anything. but i dont know if i can call it sex because by deffinition sex is when a a penis is put in to a vigina although i would think there would have to be more to it then that. so my question is did my boyfriend and i have sex? do i have to count him now? does he have to count me? (Anonymous, 2011).

(ii) Well awhile ago before I was with my boyfriend, I was fooling around with this guy. I told him point blank no full on sex, not unless we were in a relationship. Well we were messing around and I think he put his penis in me or the tip like once or he at least tried to since I felt a little pressure but I pushed him back and said NO. If anything it was at the most one thrust, but I wasn't sure since this guy was not at all well endowed I don't think it would have been considered sex but it really bothers me since I have already set a strict limit on the number of people I would sleep with in my life and it really bothers me. I want to make sure this wouldn't have been considered sex. Thanks! (Average Joe, 2012).

(iii) Does it count as having sex if you dont come? I was having it last night but i had too much alcohol so i couldnt come . . . it sucked so bad and was embarrasing . . . (Fozzy13, 2009).

(iv) does it count as sex if you put yer dick in only ONCE and dont go back in at all cuz of lack of condom? Ive wondered this for many years and would tell me exactly when I technically lost my virginity or not (Jester78, 2009).

(v) A few weeks ago some friends and I were discussing the recent date of a male member of the group. He said that he did not have sex on his date. But, after he described the encounter (in which both he and his partner had an orgasm, but did not have intercourse) one of our friends disagreed with him and argued that sex did occur. So who's right? (Muise, 2011).

Section 2: What is Sexuality?

2.1 Discussion Starters

1. How would you describe the difference between sexual behavior, sexual identity, sexual attraction, and emotional attraction? To what extent do these phenomena tend to match up? To what extent do they tend to conflict?

2. You have a girlfriend or a boyfriend you have been together with for a while. You are very much in love. You plan to get married. Suddenly, because of something they could not control (a magic spell, a science fiction scenario accident), they change sex. Would you stay in a sexual and romantic relationship with them? Would you still get married? If yes, does that mean sexual anatomy is not important and anyone could fall in love with anyone? If no, does that mean you are sexist or homophobic or heterophobic, or does it just mean that sexual anatomy is important in relationships? What does your answer mean?

3. Sometimes anthropologists claim that some cultures have "third genders" (or more). Famously, these include the Two-Spirits of North America, the Hijra

of South Asia, the Kathoey of Thailand, the Muxe of Zapotecan Mexico, the Khanith of Oman, the Fa'afafine of Samoa, the Mahu of Hawaii, the Femminiello of Naples, the Burrnesha of Albania, and even the Uranians of 19th Century Germany and England. However, these "third genders" are often described as "female souls in male bodies," "feminine men," "masculine women," "people with both male and female souls," "men who take feminine roles," "between women and men," "another kind of woman," "a second type of a man," "men who wear women's clothes," and "women who decide to live as men." In these descriptions, the binary of female and male is very evident. The "third gender" nomenclature can thus seem questionable, since "third" suggests something different altogether while most of the descriptions instead suggest admixtures of two. What would it take for a culture to have a genuine "third gender" that was not a combination or crossover of the two genders? Are there any "third genders" that would meet this standard?

4. The gay social networking app Grindr is extremely popular among gay men, often used for sexual hookups. It is common for men using Grindr to check out statistics and explicit pictures on a profile, meet for no-strings-attached sex, and then move on. Several attempts have been made to create a Grindr for both lesbians and heterosexuals that would allow for similar NSA hookups for women and women, or men and women but none has been successful. Other apps such as Tinder have succeeded but work very differently (with hardly anything comparable to naked torso and genital pictures of women looking for casual hookups). Why does the format of an app like Grindr work so well for gay men but not for lesbians or straight women?

5. Is sexuality on a continuum? For years, bisexuality was seen by many people as an unlikely sexual orientation. Gay people often said "bisexuals" just hadn't come to terms with the fact that they were gay. Straight people often said the same thing, or that "bisexuals" were just straight people trying to be edgy. Bisexuals resented this and it came to be called "bisexual erasure." Then, another claim started to be made – that everyone is really bisexual. Some may be more or less bisexual, but everyone has "tendencies" and there is hardly anyone that is really 100% straight or gay – they just hide their desires. This came to be the idea that sexuality is on a continuum. Some even thought that if there were no social disapprobation for same-sex attraction and behavior, sexuality would be a bell curve, with bisexuality the most common. So, one claim was that there were really no bisexuals. The other claim was that everyone was really bisexual. A recent major study sheds light on the issue, but in a complicated way. The study shows that the large majority of people are completely straight, with their desires, attractions, behavior, and identities all totally straight-consistent. However, a very small proportion of people are not straight, and their sexualities do show a greater variety and fluidity. So, what is the most accurate way to think of the statistical distribution of sexuality?

2.2 Definitions

To say that sexuality can be complicated is an understatement. In fact, the degree to which sexuality is complicated is itself a point of contention. Some describe sexuality as nearly infinitely variable, while some describe sexuality as relatively simple with its variability widely overstated. Any comprehensive discussion of sexuality is beyond the scope of this book, but it is useful to outline the terrain of sexuality, particularly as it bears on sexual ethics and sexual law.

Sexuality can be usefully considered as a cluster concept divided into at least four areas: biology, behavior, attraction, and identity. Biology refers to physical facts about the body – the most obvious being reproductive anatomy and genetics, though this could include neurological, hormonal, and other physiological traits. Behavior refers to the actions people actually engage in – what sexual actions do they perform and with whom or what? Attraction refers to the sexual desire people experience – what types of bodies, personalities, objects, and activities are sexually arousing? Identity refers to how a person thinks of or describes themself – to what extent does any aspect of their sexuality fit into thinking of themselves as a certain kind of person?

There are two important things to realize about these four areas. First, they are not necessarily connected to each other in exclusive ways (although statistically there are very consistent patterns). Second, different areas are more or less important for specific purposes.

Regarding the first realization, the four areas of sexuality can cross over in multiple ways. One's sexual anatomy could be male, but gender identity be female (a transgendered woman). One's gender identity could be female but sexual attraction be toward females (a homosexual woman). One's sexual anatomy and gender identity could be male and have a sexual attraction toward females, but sexual behavior be to engage with other males (prison situations, prostitution, and gay-for-pay pornography). In fact, if you lay out a simple grid with just three categories of sexuality (sexual anatomy, gender identity, and sexual orientation) and had only two possible options (male and female) for anatomy and identity, and had three possible options (male, female, and both) for orientation, you would have 12 possible combinations.

Sexual Anatomy	Gender Identity	Sexual Orientation	Description
M	M	M	Gay man
M	M	F	Straight man
M	M	MF	Bisexual man
M	F	M	Straight transwoman
M	F	F	Lesbian transwoman
M	F	MF	Bisexual transwoman
F	M	M	Gay transman
F	M	F	Straight transman
F	M	MF	Bisexual transman
F	F	M	Straight woman
F	F	F	Lesbian
F	F	MF	Bisexual woman

If you added categories or options, you could increase the possibilities exponentially. For example, if you added the options of intersexed to anatomy and nonbinary to identity, you would have 27 possibilities. If you broke down the sexual orientation category into options for male, female, transgender, intersexed, and nonbinary, then you would have 45 sexual identities. If you added a new category of genetic sex with three distinct options (XX, XY, and other), you would have 135 possibilities, and if affectional orientation were included as a different category, you would have between 405 and 18,225 sexuality options (depending on how elaborately and specifically you separated out concepts).

And this only includes qualities typically associated with sexuality. But what about people who are particularly (or primarily or only) attracted to redheads? Does that count as a sexual orientation? Do we add that in? It's certainly a logical possibility and there are people who say

they have a particular attraction to redheads. If we do that, though, we could also add blondes, brunettes, shaved heads, and literally thousands of other qualities. Is someone attracted to tall people? Short people? Is someone particularly attracted to intelligence (calling themselves sapiosexuals)? What about attraction to strength, to morality, to recklessness, to big feet, to small ears, to gravelly voices, and to being born on a Thursday? Combining the possibilities literally leads to infinitely many possible sexualities (actual sexualities limited only by the number of actual human beings). Upon hearing that, some people may cheer, thinking that the more the better and that having an infinite number of sexualities is somehow freeing or exciting or gloriously variegated. However, thinking in terms of sexuality as infinitely variable is problematic for practical and moral reasons.

Practically speaking, it is important when considering any question about the importance of sex and sexuality that we look at numbers. In the pursuit of respect for diversity, many people will point to a phenomenon (such as self-identified "asexuals" for instance) and claim that this phenomenon shows sexuality is not universal or is merely a social construction. This sort of generalization is made even easier in the current environment where technologically mediated communication and searchable information databases allow for nearly all phenomena to achieve visibility by merely clicking a link (boiled brussels sprouts recipes are just as easy to find on the Internet as cheesecake recipes but that does not indicate the foods are equally popular). While it is true that the existence of one asexual does prove that sexuality is not universal, without an appreciation of numbers, the presence of an asexual tells us virtually nothing usefully generalizable about human beings. So, if the logical possibility of an infinite number of sexualities would lead us to answer the question "What is human sexuality like?", by simply saying "infinitely variable!" we would be ignoring statistically and evolutionarily important information that would be valuable in describing human behavior, explaining human behavior, making predictions about human behavior, and making policies for human behavior. It is true, for example, that there are human beings who are 8 feet tall. Without some statistical situating of those numbers, however, the fact that there are 8-foot-tall humans is nearly useless for predicting the height of people we will come across, for explaining the most common architectural conventions, or for helping us design seats on new airplanes. When we find out that there are only three known living people over 8 feet tall, which is about 0.0000000004% of the world population, we see that people over 8 feet tall are extreme outliers and provide virtually no useful information generalizable to the human population (other than that it is biophysically possible to be that height). That doesn't mean those people are not valuable or shouldn't be treated well – it simply means that when asking questions about human nature, predicting human behavior, or making social spending arrangements, the over-8-feet-tall category is statistically negligible. Similarly, if it turns out that the (limited amount of) research done to determine the frequency of asexuality shows that less than 1% of people are asexual, then its existence will not tell us much about human psychology and sociology at large. It would be statistically unjustified to say "well, then, there are sexual people and asexual people, so sexuality is just one more variation and you can't say that humans are sexual beings." Think of how much human history, human psychology, and human political analysis would be abandoned if we no longer thought of the human species as a sexual species. Asexuality is merely a sample case here. The point is that it is important to take numbers and statistics into account in order to understand human nature.

Morally speaking, this does not mean, of course, that asexual people (or any particular sexual minority) should not be treated equally. There is no direct implication from statistics to moral standing. However, numbers can be morally important. For example, if we are asking whether sex and sexuality are important aspects of human life, important aspects of being human, someone might point to the existence of asexuality as proof that sex cannot be considered a "basic human good" or a "fundamental quality" because there are people who can lead satisfying lives without sexual behavior or perhaps even sexual desire. For any ethical or legal system that bases rights protection on whether or not something is a basic human good, or a fundamental human quality, then, sex and sexuality would not deserve fundamental protection.

2.3 Contextual Categorizations

This leads us back to the second realization mentioned above. Different classifications of sexuality are used for different purposes. Consider an anatomy professor at a medical school. For purposes of training future surgeons, internal medicine specialists, urologists, and gynecologists how to be good at their work, the actual shape of bodies is most important – how structures connect and function. What sexual desires a patient has or what gender identity a patient has may be irrelevant.

Consider an epidemiologist at a public health office. For purposes of predicting the spread of sexually-transmitted diseases, the behavior of people is most important. Surveying local areas to find out who identifies as gay or straight is not nearly as important as surveying local areas to find out who engages in specific physical acts with whom. For example, several studies have shown that there can be significant discordance between self-reported sexual identity and sexual behavior – and this is strongly affected by ethnicity, class, and social group. There are men who have sex with men exclusively, but say they are heterosexual (and are disproportionately racial minorities) (Pathela et al., 2006). There are men who say they are straight but have life-long histories of sex with men (Zellner et al., 2009). Men in this category are significantly less likely to use condoms or to be tested for HIV (Pathela et al., 2006) and more likely to have sexual transmitted diseases (Zellner et al., 2009) than men who report being gay or bisexual. One study on adolescents reported no consistent pattern describing the categories of identity, attraction, and behavior for those who were not exclusively heterosexual, with behavior accounting for only 31% of those who endorsed some form of non-heterosexuality (Igartua et al., 2009). Thus, for public health tracking, the category of MSM (men who have sex with men – a purely behavioral category) is central.

Consider a political scientist. For purposes of predicting voting behavior, one category that might be important would be identity. Since people who describe themselves as LGBT are more likely to vote for Democratic candidates, it may be useful in explaining why a particular municipal area is more likely to vote for one party rather than another to know the percentage of people who identify as LGBT.

Consider a judge. For purposes of ruling on whether or not a state law unduly burdens or unfairly selects a group for certain kinds of treatment under the law, the court will subject the law to a specific level of "scrutiny" – a legal term referring to how high of a standard a state must meet in order to justify the law as constitutional. The highest level of scrutiny (strict scrutiny) often places heavy emphasis on whether the distinguishing characteristics of the group are immutable, meaning that they are innate and unchangeable. The nature of sexual attraction has been held to be very important here. If the attraction that homosexuals feel is immutable, then it may be that the only way for them to achieve a satisfying and important good in society (romantic relationships) is to be free to pursue same-sex relationships. As such, sexual orientation is central, and laws forbidding homosexual relationships have been held unconstitutional.

To say, however, that there are multiple categorizations of sexuality is not to say that all categorizations of sexuality are true. Claims of sexuality, like any other claims, can be true or false. People can be mistaken about sexuality (for example, believing that homosexuality must be a condition not affected by biology but only by childraising practices). It is also true that a person can misunderstand their own sexuality as they might misunderstand someone else's. The notion that whatever someone says about their own sexuality must be true implies a kind of asocial and context-free omniscience that would be highly unlikely for fallible, social creatures such as human beings. For example, a man who claims to be straight but regularly has sex with other men could be confusingly categorized as a "straight man who has sex with men" but could also be much more easily categorized as a closeted homosexual man who has various social, political, and personal reasons not to describe himself or think of himself as gay. People often think of themselves as one thing when they really are another and this has morally analyzable content. Someone may claim not to be a racist, for example, when they really are, and they clearly have motivating reasons to think they are not racist.

The moral content of sexuality for sexual ethics can arise in several ways. The nature of sexuality may be relevant for moral standing (as with the case of immutable characteristics under the law). The character of someone may be in question if they make claims about their sexuality that are at odds with their behavior (as with people who claim to be straight but engage in homosexual acts). The consequences of someone's sexuality may be beneficial or detrimental to themselves and others (being aroused by caring versus being aroused by hurting). The duties related to someone's sexuality may be different (avoiding children if one is a pedophile). In all these cases, sexuality is itself something to be questioned, analyzed, assessed, and understood, with knee-jerk reactions of "reject aberrant sexualities" or "accept all sexualities" as equally insufficient for genuine moral assessment.

2.4 Decision Cases

1. *Is he a pedophile?* In 2017, former Chief Justice of the Alabama Supreme Court Roy Moore ran for Senator of Alabama in a special election. During campaigning, several women accused him of sexual misconduct that occurred years before, including when some of the women were between the ages of 14 and 18 and he was over 30 (Bump, 2017). As a result, Moore was labeled in some media outlets as a "pedophile" (Broverman, 2018) and a "child molester" (Al Jazeera, 2017). However, the notion of what counts as a "child" has changed considerably over time (remember Juliet was 13 years old and Romeo assumed to be around 16 and that it was not uncommon for 13- and 14-year-old girls to marry prior to 1950). The older notion that childhood is largely over at puberty (contrasted to the modern concept of an extended "adolescence") is still somewhat reflected in US marriage laws. The Pew Research Center reports that over 57,000 minors (between 15 and 17) in the United States were married as of 2014 (McClendon and Sandstrom, 2016). Two states even allow 13-year-old girls and 14-year-old boys to marry. So, should Moore be considered a "pedophile"? Or has the creation of a legally extended childhood also created a new class of criminal and pervert that did not exist before? What are the motivations for describing someone as a pedophile?

2. *Is she really bisexual?* Michelle is a professor at a local college. Before graduate school, she only had heterosexual relationships, only expressed romantic and sexual interests in men, and had never been a part of the LGBT community. When she went to graduate school, however, she was in a program that included a large component of women's studies that was critical of heterosexual privilege. While in the program, she decided to date some women and had a couple of sexual experiences with women. She began to call herself bisexual. After she graduated and left to take a college job in another state, however, she never pursued any other romantic or sexual relationships with women, soon married a man, had children, and attends all the standard social functions that her other married, heterosexual colleagues do. She still calls herself bisexual, often asserting this as part of what makes her especially appropriate to direct programs and teach courses in gender and sexuality and be the "out" advisor to the LGBT student group. Straight friends and colleagues never think of her as anything but straight. Gay colleagues dismiss her claims about being bisexual, referring to her as a LUG – Lesbian Until Graduation – a derogatory

term used to imply her graduate school sexual experiences were safe, "cool," and affectations of a particular academic culture rather than expressions of a genuine sexual orientation that they have had to deal with their entire lives. They are also annoyed that she now uses those few experiences to benefit her career. Is this woman bisexual? Is there anything wrong with her using bisexual identity in her career? Are the criticisms of her just or unjust?

3. *Did he do the same thing she did?* At a campus fraternity party, Madison gets somewhat drunk and publicly makes out with another girl. Everyone whoops at them and cheers and laughs. She's never done that before and enjoys the attention but says she's not gay or bi. Her boyfriend, Ethan also thought it was funny and even kind of hot. They laugh about it later and think of it as no big deal. However, later in the semester, they are at another fraternity party, but this time Ethan gets drunk and publicly makes out with another guy. People stare but this time there are no whoops and cheers, just confusion. He's never done that before and thought it was fun but says he's not gay or bi. Madison does *not* think this is funny or hot. She freaks out. Ethan says it's no big deal. He was just drunk and being spontaneous. Madison isn't okay with that. What's going on here? Are the situations different? Does it mean something different when she made out with another girl than when he made out with another guy? Or is she overreacting? Or is she justified in thinking what Ethan did suggests something more than what she did?

4. *Does this violate the rule or not?* The Roman Catholic Church has a rule that only men can be priests. In one parish, it is discovered that one of the priests who has served the church faithfully for 20 years was born female and transitioned to male 25 years ago. Members of the church bring the issue before the Bishop, claiming that the "priest" is not a man, that sex reassignment does not change gender, that "she" lied to the church, that all "her" sacramental actions are invalid, and that "she" should be removed immediately. The priest, however, says that he has not violated Church teachings. He agrees with the church members that sex reassignment surgery did not change his gender, instead arguing that he was always male because what makes a man a man is his neurologically based inner gender identity, and that his earlier female anatomy was just a developmental birth defect now corrected. His

brain and spirit have always been male. Irrespective of your assessment of the Church's position on transgendered people or the male-only priesthood, is this person violating the Church's rule on male-only priests or not? He is not arguing the Church's rule is wrong; he is arguing that he is not violating the rule. What is the most accurate way of looking at it? And if this is what the priest thought, was it dishonest not to share his history with Church authorities?

5. *Is this a sexual orientation?* Kayla is a white woman who says she is only attracted to black men. She only dates black men, only has sex with black men, and only wants to marry a black man. She doesn't think of this as a political stance and she doesn't hate non-black men. She says she doesn't know why she only likes black men – she just does. To her, it is just her sexual orientation, just as some people are only attracted to men and some are only attracted to women. But several people who know Kayla have a hard time believing this and criticize her character. Some people accuse her of being racist. Some accuse her of being a racial fetishist. Some people accuse her of being rebellious. Some people accuse her of trying to prove how liberal she is by only dating black men. Some people say gender-based sexual attraction is biological but race-based attraction is not, so it can't be a true innate sexual orientation. What is most likely to be true? Is this her sexual orientation? Is racial attraction something different from anatomical attraction? Is Kayla's attraction morally neutral or morally valenced?

6. *Is he really straight?* Adam's favorite sexual activity is pegging with his girlfriend (being penetrated anally by a woman wearing a strap-on dildo). He strongly prefers this to all other sexual activity. In fact, he prefers it to vaginal intercourse. His friends think this is kind of strange. Finally, one of his friends flat out tells him that he must be gay, but just hasn't come to terms with it. Adam says no, he isn't. He is only attracted to women. His friend asks him how he can be straight if he doesn't like vaginal sex. Is Adam straight? Or completely straight? Are his friends making a mistake? Or what? How likely is it that Adam is self-deceived? How likely is it that Adam's friend is making some sort of category error? What if his girlfriend sometimes pretends to be a man during pegging? Does that change anything?

7. *Is sexuality important to being human?* Calvin does not want to have any sexual feelings at all. He is

actively online asking for help with finding some treatment, some medication, or surgery that could permanently eliminate all sexual desire, sexual arousal, and sexual feelings of any kind. He has heard about Depo-Provera shots but that seems time-consuming and inconvenient. He's hoping to find something that will erase his sexuality entirely. In some ways, Calvin is seeking what numerous people in history have sought, though for various reasons – people who thought libido was the source of the world's troubles, people who thought the only way to have a truly spiritual life was to extinguish the physical as much as possible, people who thought masturbation and rampant sexual desire caused diseases, and people who thought sexual desire was animalistic and dirty. However, most organized religions and most popular movements have condemned these anti-sexuality views as heretical, inhuman, self-hating, and in conflict with human nature. Indeed, many people in history have also praised human sexuality and argued that it was a crucial part of the human experience. These arguments have been used in various liberation movements (women's liberation, gay liberation, and the sexual revolution) to value sexuality and to free people from socially imposed guilt. So, is Calvin making a mistake? Is he failing to see that sexuality is human and valuable? Or is it false that sexuality is an important human trait that should be valued and cherished, and that in reality it is neither here nor there? The answer that "anyone should be able to do whatever makes them feel good" doesn't get at the problem. If there is no problem with what Calvin wants, then that means sexuality is *not* inherently valuable. And if sexuality is not inherently valuable or crucial, then the claim that all people must be able to explore and express and accept their sexuality *because of sexuality's inherent importance* is wrong. What should Calvin believe about sexuality? What should he do? How would you analyze Calvin's motivations?

8. *Can a bromance be more rewarding than a romance?* Jackson is straight, very conventionally masculine, and has had sex with lots of women. By the time he was a senior in college, he had had sex with close to a hundred women. He had only had a few short-lived romantic relationships with women, however, and felt that every time he was in a relationship, suddenly he had all these obligations to do things he didn't enjoy, hang out with people he didn't care

for, be careful of what he said, make sure to be available all the time, account for his whereabouts, and talk about things he had no interest in. One day, in a class on contemporary moral issues, he told the whole class that he was totally supportive of gay marriage – but not for the typical reasons. He supported same-sex marriage because he thought the ideal family situation would be for him to marry his male best friend, Eric. They had been best friends since 4th grade, always been there for each other, never had any conflicts, liked to hunt and fish and watch football together, and felt totally comfortable. They were just friends – nothing sexual between them, ever. Jackson thought the perfect situation would be to marry Eric, adopt kids, and they could both sleep with however many women they wanted to – sex with women, but not having to deal with romances with women. The class reacted very skeptically to Jackson's plan, thinking there must be something else going on, thinking that either he was closeted, or that he was sexist, or that he was afraid of commitment. However, some recent qualitative research has suggested that Jackson may have company. A study of male college students asked to compare their "bromances" to their heterosexual romances found that the men described their close male friendships as emotionally open, trusting, and stable. They also described the absence of judgment, the lack of boundaries, and the easier conflict resolution with male friends as leading to more socially fulfilling and emotionally stable relationships than relationships with girlfriends (Robinson et al., 2019). So, can a bromance be a viable long-term substitution for marriage? Is there anything to criticize here about Jackson's character or motivations?

9. *Can a campus sexual identity organization possibly be inclusive enough?* A college campus group is in discussion about whether to change their name – again. Years ago, when the group was started, it was just called the Gay and Lesbian Student Union. Then, it was changed later to Campus Pride, in order to include friends and allies. Later it was reorganized by Student Life to be the Campus LGBT group – to make sure it included bisexuals and transgender students. Now, however, new members are demanding that the name be even more inclusive. Some want to change it to LGBTQIA to include intersexed, queer/questioning, and asexual. This had led to quite a

fight. Some members say the whole thing is too unwieldy. Some members say adding "asexuals" to the group makes no sense – it would be like students who claim to have no ethnic or racial identity joining the Campus Students of Color Coalition. Some students want it to be even more inclusive – LGBTQQIP2SAA, including pansexuals, allies, and Native American Two-Spirits. Some students say just use the term "queer" because it includes everyone except heterosexuals. Allies don't like that. When told "queer" can include allied heterosexuals as well, someone asks "so it's just a group for everyone?" Finally, one student, Aaron, stands up and makes the point that he is gay, male, votes Republican, and thinks the most important political goals were opening up the military and marriage to gay people. But, he is aware that the person sitting next to him, Jade, is pagan, socialist, queer, trans, uses the pronoun "they" and thinks marriage and the military are oppressive patriarchal institutions that no one should support. And he knows that the person in front of him – Mara – is an atheist, anarchist, and radical lesbian who opposes allowing transwomen in women-only events. So, Aaron suggests, why don't we just disband? There is nothing we have in common enough to be a group. What should the group do? Rename? Disband? Break into smaller identity groups? What?

10. *If you can self-identify gender, can you also self-identify age?* The term "agefluid" appears to have originally been created by Internet trolls to mock the concept of gender fluidity. The concept (represented by the black silhouette of an adult male bending down and reaching out to a small boy, but with a white silhouette of a young girl inside the adult male) was that if gender can be fluid and people can identify with a gender that does not match their sexual anatomy, then age could also be fluid, with people identifying with an age that does not match their chronological anatomy. The intended mockery was that this would defend what appeared to be child molestation and that there were no limits to what could be "fluid." While the origin of "agefluid" seems to have been satire, however, it was taken seriously (what does it say about our culture that satire is not discernible?). Some people defended it, saying "transage" was on par with "transgender." One YouTube personality responded to a comment making fun of transage by saying: "I'm telling you guys, you better watch out.

You make fun of these things today and tomorrow you're labeled as not so good things because we reacted to transage the way other people reacted to transgender . . ." (Onisionspeaks). Individuals have also acted on the transage concept seriously. Emile Ratelbrand, a Dutch citizen, petitioned to legally change his age from 69 to 49, saying that he feels and identifies as 49, not 69, and argued that his petition was no different than if he were asking to legally change his gender based on how he feels and identifies (Brenoff, 2019). In another case, the person formally known as Paul Wolscht, a father of seven children, transitioned to female after realizing her transgender status at age 46. However, the transition was not to a 46-year-old woman but to a 6-year-old girl, named Stefoknee Wolscht (James, 2015). Stefonknee identifies as a 6-year-old girl and lives as a 6-year-old girl in many ways, including living with friends who function as adoptive parents. So, is being transage just like being transgender? Or is there a fundamental difference? How do we distinguish what traits can be fluid and what traits cannot?

11. *Is there something bad about this sexual desire?* Xavier is an African-American young man who is in college, has good grades, stays active, has a good relationship with his family, and plans to go into business. He is gay and open about it, but he is not open about one big element of his sexual desires. His major turn-on is raceplay. Raceplay is a controversial type of kink sexual practice where the participants role-play (Jones, 2013). It often works with dominant and submissive roles based on historical racist power dynamics. Commonly, one Black partner will play the "slave" to a White partner's "master" and the White partner will use racial epithets, humiliating verbal abuse, and physical roughness to dominate the Black partner while the Black partner will submit, beg, obey, and otherwise serve the White partner. This is the type of raceplay that turns Xavier on. There are many other raceplay forms – Asian women pretending to be subservient geishas to White partners, Native Americans pretending to be captured by Whites, and even "reversals" in which Black dominant partners "conquer" White partners and enforce the superiority of the Black race over weak, effeminate, white males, and so on. Xavier has only told a couple of friends that he is into this and both of them reacted in horror, telling him that he was

sick, or that he had obviously internalized racist self-hatred, or that something else was wrong with him. Xavier insists it is just for fun and is no different than nurse/patient role playing or teacher/student roleplaying. He says his partners are not racist and everyone knows it is just a game. Is there something wrong with Xavier? Are his sexual desires messed up? Perverted? Politically dangerous? Does he have a psychological problem? Is this just another sexual desire and behavior that doesn't hurt anyone? Can Xavier enjoy this sexual activity and still be a strong, honest, person? Can his partners enjoy this sexual activity and be good, non-racist people?

12. *Are they really what they say they are?* Mateo is 23 and describes himself as straight. Yet, he regularly has sex with men. Because he always takes the top position, he seems to think that doesn't count as being gay or bi – because he says the essence of being gay is to be sexually passive. Isaiah is 26 and identifies as straight but is also on the "down-low," having sex with more men than women. He would never say he is bi or gay and thinks of his down-low activities as totally separate from his real life. Brianna is 14 and describes herself as bisexual, although she has never had any sexual or romantic contact with a girl and doesn't pursue any. But most of her friends think of themselves as counterculture and also say they are bi, or pan, and she feels like she must be too or she wouldn't like hanging out with them. Blake identifies as gay, is very out about it, goes to gay pride parades, and has gay rights bumper stickers on his car. He says he is very gay, loves men, and could never think of himself as anything but gay. However, Blake has never dated, made out, or had sex with a man. In fact, he dates women, sleeps with women, and watches straight porn focusing on women. Even when attractive men come on to him, Blake ignores them and hits on women. Is Mateo straight? Is Isaiah straight? Is Brianna bisexual? Is Blake gay? And importantly, does Blake's situation seem stranger than the others? Given various social forces such as high homophobia in certain communities ("down-low") or a coolness factor among trendy teenagers ("bisexual chic") and the virtual non-existence of cases like Blake's, how seriously should we take how someone "identifies"? What are the various psychological and political motivations for identifying one way rather than another?

13. *Is this a "legitimate" sexuality?* Amanda says she is in love with a chandelier, and she means it literally. Sandy was in love with the Twin Towers and felt widowed when they were destroyed. Bill is in love with an iBook. Edward falls in love and lust with cars, writing poetry to them, singing to them, talking to them, and has had sex with over 1,000 of them (typically penis-into-tailpipe or rubbing against them). Joachim used to be in love with a Hammond organ but for the last few years has been in love with a steam locomotive. Eija-Ritta was in love with the Berlin Wall and ritually "married" it, changing her last name to Mauer (German for "wall") and was devastated when it was torn down in 1989 (Thadeusz, 2007). Erika is in love with the Eiffel Tower and also married it. All these people are objectophiles (or objectum sexuals) (Griffiths, 2013). They are not using objects as mere fetishes (the way someone might get turned on by high heels or lingerie). They maintain that the object itself is the desired sexual, and sometimes, romantic partner. Some, but not all, are animists – believing that the objects have spirits and consciousnesses. Some objectophiles have formed organizations to make connections with others, to push for acceptance, and to denounce films and television programs that showcase them as freaks (objectum-sexuality.org) Some sex researchers recommended seeing objectophilia as a legitimate sexual orientation rather than a paraphilia (Marsh, 2010). Some researchers say it should not be considered pathological because objectophiles do not harm anyone (Griffiths, 2013). So, is objectophilia "legitimate" – a true sexual orientation and not a paraphilia? Is harm the only thing to consider, or is delusion an appropriate consideration as well? Are objectophiles missing out on rewarding human relationships? What is the practical result of treating objectophilia as "legitimate"? What would be done that wouldn't be done otherwise? Can a relationship with an object be a genuine or good relationship?

14. *What terms best describe some sexual desires?* In several online forums about sexuality, it has now become considered inappropriate, offensive, or "politically incorrect" to use certain terms. People sexually attracted to children have been called "pedophiles" but now want the term "minor-attracted persons" or "MAPS" to be used. Bestiality has been used to describe people sexually

attracted to animals but now the term "zoophilia" is preferred. Partly, the terminology is trying to indicate the difference between attraction and behavior (MAPS are not necessarily engaging in sexual activity with children). Partly, it is to reduce the stigma ("beasts" as opposed to "other species"). What terms should be used? Is it always important to use terms that don't offend or is it sometimes important to use terms that include a sense of moral disapproval?

15. *Can you change your sexual orientation?* For years, opponents of gay rights often said homosexuality was "just a phase" or a "choice," while many gay people strongly argued that their sexuality was innate and immutable (a position relied on in Obergefell v. Hodges – the US Supreme Court ruling that legalized gay marriage). Lately, however, it has become more popular for a variety of people to say that sexuality is "fluid" or chosen, and can change over time, or even from day to day. At the same time, sexual orientation conversion therapy is often rejected as a legitimate medical treatment by state regulators because medical authorities say it does not work and causes more trouble than it corrects. All of these claims together cannot be right. Sexual orientation cannot be both fixed and fluid, innate and chosen, impossible to change and possible to change. So, how do all these claims relate to each other? What is the difference between sexuality being "fluid" and it being a "phase"? If sexuality can change, why wouldn't conversion therapy work for those motivated to seek it out and be recognized as a legitimate psychotherapy? What about the feeling many LGBT people have that their sexuality was innate from early childhood and impossible for culture to change?

Section 3: What is Sexual Ethics?

3.1 Discussion Starters

1. In Argentina the age of consent is 13 (with some restrictions). In some US states, the age of consent is 18. If a 25-year-old US citizen has sex with a 13-year-old in the US, it is automatically rape (or criminal sexual abuse). If he does it in Argentina, it is not. Presumably this would be legally true even if the 13-year-old were the same person in both cases. Is it immoral for a 25-year-old to have sex with a 13-year-old in the US? Is it immoral for a 25-year-old to have sex with a 13-year-old in Argentina? Does the moral permissibility of sex change when crossing national borders? Why are there different ages of consent to start with? Are people able to consent at different ages in different cultures?

2. The long-running television program Law and Order: Special Victims Unit opens each episode with this line: "In the criminal justice system, sexually based offenses are considered especially heinous." The Special Victims Unit is an entire unit of detectives, sets of laws, and sets of punishments dedicated specifically to sex crimes. But why? Why "special"? Why should sex have its own criminal code? Why wouldn't the crimes of rape, sexual assault, and sexual harassment not already be covered by assault, battery, extortion, and harassment law? If the harm in rape is the violence, then why add extra punishment for sexuality? (Foucault, 1988).

3. There are numerous textbooks and university courses on applied ethics issues, such as medical ethics, environmental ethics, business ethics, sports ethics, and engineering ethics. There are very few dedicated classes and textbooks about sexual ethics, however. But why? Sex and sexuality are huge issues in politics, the law, religion, and in universities. So, why aren't sexual ethics classes more common?

4. In your sexual ethics class, the professor wants to show several pornographic scenes of various sorts when covering the section on pornography. The professor argues that in a class on advertising, students are required to watch actual ads to get a sense of what is being discussed. In a class on drawing, students are required to draw nude models to get a sense of how to sketch human anatomy. In a class on zoology, students are required to dissect fetal pigs to get experience with organ systems. So, why not show pornography, and require watching it, since part of the issue in pornography is defining it and whether it counts as free speech? The Dean is balking, arguing that conservative students will claim they are being forced to pay to watch immoral obscenity and liberal students will claim they are being forced to stay in a sexually hostile environment that could cause trauma. Is there something about pornography that is relevantly different from tasks in the advertising, art, and zoology classes?

5. How morally permissible is it to have sex with the following people (on a scale from totally immoral, somewhat immoral, neutral, somewhat moral, to

totally moral)? Is there a consistent principle that guides your ranking?

- Someone you are in love with.
- Someone you don't know and will never meet again.
- Someone offering you $500 for sex.
- A professor on campus you are currently taking a class from.
- A professor on campus you will never take a class from.
- Someone you don't like romantically but who has a huge romantic crush on you.
- Someone you are not attracted to but feel sorry for because no one else is attracted to them either.
- A 15-year-old.
- Someone 30 years older than you.
- A married couple who occasionally like to have threeways.
- A woman whose husband will watch you have sex with her but not participate.
- Your first cousin.
- A mentally handicapped person who says they want to have sex with you.
- Someone who tells you several times they want to have sex with you, then gets drunk, and passes out on your bed.
- An ex who you know wants to get back together but with whom you don't want to get back together.

3.2 Methods of Ethics

In thinking about sexual ethics, there is first the question of whether there is, or should be, any such thing. Sometimes people take a stance that sexuality and sexual behavior is mostly private and that "what someone does in their own bedroom" is only their business. As long as they aren't hurting anyone, it's consensual, and they are adults, sex is a private matter and not up for discussions of moral judgment by others. Taking that approach, one might think that the answer to nearly every question raised in this book would be some sort of appeal to privacy and the claim that there shouldn't even be a debate. That position would curtail most discussions about many of the alleged issues.

Notice, however, that this is itself an ethical stance. It does not avoid ethical issues; it makes a set of specific, non-neutral, ethical claims. It says that sexual issues have some kind of exceptional status in society by being largely "private" and as such it is beyond the reach of

moral judgment, social approbation, or legal regulation. That carves out a realm of "privacy" that shelters sex from analysis – but why, and except for masturbation, doesn't sex mostly involve interaction with other beings? It also says that within this private realm, most sex is permissible – meaning that it should be allowed and that other people should not try to restrict it. But that is a moral claim. That specifically says that this set of activities has the moral status of being justified in some way and that it would be morally wrong of others to interfere. It also says that the key elements of this morally justified sexual activity is that participants are adults, consent, and that they do not hurt anyone. Those are moral claims as well, appealing to moral rules that defend certain types of activity, and suggest that sexual activity that involved children or was not consensual or that hurt someone would somehow be unjustified, immoral, not protected by privacy. But why is age relevant? Why is consent so important? Why is not hurting others the line to be drawn? And what counts as being old enough, as consenting, and hurting?

You can see then that just saying "as long as they are consenting adults and aren't hurting anyone else" is not a neutral stance and is not avoiding any moral discussion. It is a specific moral stance that opposes others and appeals to specific criteria for justifying actions. These specific moral criteria need explanation and justification and they could be challenged. Imagine someone making a similar kind of exceptionalist claim about business. Sometimes, people will defend their actions by saying "it's not personal, it's just business," and by this they seem to be saying that in the specific realm of business, actions that are normally criticized, such as lying, cheating, misleading, betraying, being selfish, being unfair, and pursuing money above all else, are happening in some kind of special, exempt sphere. If you lied, cheated, betrayed, or were unfair to someone in a "personal" (private) relationship, then you would be doing something wrong, but in the realm of business, these actions are somehow protected, or expected, or a known element of some game. Interestingly, this sort of claim about business seems to be a twist on the claim about sexuality – actions are morally justified in a public (business) arena that would not be justified if they were in the private arena. However, the existence of business ethics classes, business ethics textbooks, business ethics codes, and tons of business ethics regulations attests to the perception that merely being in the area of business does not exempt someone from morality. Neither is sexuality exempt and it can be shown that even the claim of sexual exceptionalism appeals to specific moral principles.

So, if sex is an area where ethical arguments can be made, the next question is how to go about answering the ethical questions that arise. What methods do you use? In this sense, sexual ethics is in the same boat as any other set of applied ethical problems, like medical ethics, or environmental ethics, or engineering ethics. Most applied ethics questions implicitly or explicitly draw on ethical theory, which is a set of principles used to determine what actions are right or wrong. However, there are different ethical theories that disagree with each other on what principles should be used. While the nature and content of ethical theories are important, there isn't space in an introduction like this to go into the depth that theory deserves. What will be useful, and what will have to suffice, for being able to discuss sexual ethics questions is to summarize the basic kinds of values that different ethical theories focus on in answering questions. There are four commonly discussed classes of ethical theories that emphasize different values.

Duty-based ethics: These kinds of ethical theories posit that actions (and/or motivations for action) have some kind of moral quality about them that make the actions right or wrong in themselves. Called "deontological" theories (from the Greek "deon" meaning "duty," "obligation," "necessity"), this kind of ethical theory typically follows some principle of respect for a moral rule. For example, one of the most influential duty-based theories defended by philosopher Immanuel Kant states that we should always treat human beings as ends-in-themselves and never merely as means to some other end. Lying to people, for instance, is a way to manipulate and use people to achieve some other goal and since people are rational beings with their own moral worth, it is always immoral to manipulate and use them merely as a way to accomplish some other goal. That treats them as just an object in the world to be used. You should never lie to people, then. Another type of deontological theory focuses on rights, arguing that people have certain moral qualities called rights (human rights or natural rights or fundamental rights) that impose duties on other people independent of any agreements, contracts, goals, or consequences. As such, we are all obligated (have a duty) to respect those rights. If people have a fundamental right to free speech, it would be wrong for any person or government to obstruct someone's free speech. When it comes to sexual ethics, then, a deontological approach would focus on whether the actions being considered used other people as a means to an end, what rights

people do or do not have, and whether some sexual practice respected human beings as rational beings.

Consequence-based ethics: These kinds of ethical theories posit that actions are right or wrong depending on the consequences the actions tend to produce. Called "teleological ethics" (from the Greek "telos" meaning "purpose," "end," "result") or just consequentialist ethics, this kind of ethical theory typically points to how much good (happiness, satisfaction, reduction of suffering) an action can produce to determine if it is the right thing to do. We are always obligated to perform the action that does (or reasonably appears that it will do) the most good. As such, there is far less emphasis on following specific moral rules and more emphasis on doing the most good. Lying to people, for instance, can be the right or wrong thing to do based on what is accomplished by the lie. If lying ends up creating more pain, suffering, dissatisfaction, or unhappiness than telling the truth (which in general it probably does), then you shouldn't lie. However, if lying can be seen in a particular situation to lead to more good than bad, then lying is not only permissible, but it is the right thing to do. The goal is always to try to figure out how much good or bad an action will likely create. When it comes to sexual ethics, then, a consequentialist approach would focus on the consequences of a sexual action or a law regulating sexual action and go with what does the most good. There is very little interest in rights (and certainly no interest in some kind of innate, fundamental right) because rights are often used to thwart good consequences in the interest of protecting individuals' personal preferences.

Character-based ethics: These kinds of ethical theories focus less on rules of action and more on the character of the agent considering an action. Central to character-based ethics is the concept of virtue, which is a character trait developed to the point of excellence. It is a thorough disposition to consistently act in certain ways so that the motivation is second-nature or fundamental to the person. Typical virtues include generosity, self-discipline, courage, honesty, modesty, friendliness, patience, and temperance. Lying to people, for instance, is typically motivated by selfishness, manipulativeness, cowardice, and unfriendliness and is therefore to be avoided. However, this not for the deontological reason of respecting a rule that says "do not lie" or the consequentialist reason of just producing the most happiness but is rather motivated by the desire to be a good, strong, virtuous person. When it comes to sexual ethics, then, a virtues approach would focus on the character of the person who is making decisions and acting in certain ways. Are they motivated by the desire to be a good person or are they motivated by vices such selfishness, weakness, insecurity, self-indulgence, intolerance, tactlessness, hypocrisy, or laziness?

Natural-law based ethics: These kinds of ethical theories focus on the nature of human beings (biological, psychological, spiritual, and social) and the belief that real, objective moral obligations stem from that nature. Since humans are rational beings – they are not programmed robots but can think, deliberate, and respond to reasons – they are capable of understanding their own natures and acting morally in ways that are consistent with that nature. Historically, natural law ethics has been informed by the concept of God as the creator of human nature and legislator of divine intent. However, unlike the idea that God simply creates rules, the notion here is that humans are a specific kind of creation with a practical rationality that makes acting consistently with our nature both knowable and obligatory (and if God or nature had made us different, then we would have different natures and different moral obligations). Common to natural law ethics is the claim that there are basic goods for human beings (resulting from the kind of beings we are) – a list that typically includes life, health, friendship, knowledge, aesthetic experience, peace, and community (among others). Lying to people, for instance, is typically rejected as morally permissible because lying is directly opposed to knowledge and anything that undermines a basic good is wrong. When it comes to sexual ethics, natural law tends to include sex as an obvious part of human nature but emphasizes that sex and sexuality have purposes related to their function that can be understood from examining the nature of human beings both biologically and socially. Any sexual act that interfered with this nature or perverted or corrupted this nature would be a violation of practical rationality and morality.

3.3 Moral Psychology and Analysis

Another part of thinking about ethical judgments is moral psychology, which is the study of how people make moral decisions. Moral psychology does not typically try to show whether a decision is morally right or wrong but tries to empirically investigate what elements of a situation or elements of human emotion and cognition led to a particular judgment of right or wrong. One thing that moral psychology has discovered that is particularly relevant to sexual ethics is that our emotional reactions to sex tend to be strong and immediate. One

way this phenomenon works is a tendency to believe certain things are morally right or wrong but be swept up in the heat of the moment and engage in activities that intellectually we are morally opposed to. Having sex with someone when you believe it is a bad idea, but passion overtakes you, is a common example – leading to regret and guilt later. Another way moral psychology relates to sexual ethics is by showing that sometimes people have visceral reactions to a sexual event – strongly opposing it or being disgusted by it – but when you try to get them to explain their moral judgment, they are unable to. A famous example of this is a study (multiple variations have been tested) that used the story of a couple who knew each other well and who had sex with each other. Most people judged the sexual activity to be permissible, but when it was revealed that the couple were brother and sister, they changed their view sharply and said it was wrong. When asked why it was wrong, people tended to say that it was because they might have children with birth defects or because they must have been abused as children. The interesting result, however, was that even when the story was changed to make it clear that there would be no pregnancy and that neither person had been abused and that it was consensual, and so on, very few people reversed their position and said it was allowable. They stayed with their judgment that it was wrong. They didn't know why – it just was (Haidt 2001). Moral psychologists tend to use biobehavioral and evolutionary explanations for this – evolutionarily, interbreeding does tend to lead to birth defects and lower genetic variation, so many animals, including humans, developed a strong aversion to mating with close relatives. That aversion is widespread and hard to react against. This does not mean that incest must therefore be morally wrong, but it does give some evidence as to why the incest taboo is so cross-culturally common.

All of the ethical theories mentioned above and aspects of moral psychology will come into play in making judgments about the morality of sexual actions and sexual relationships. It is important, however, for any analysis of sexual ethics to be clear on what is being described, what the agents know or believe, what the likely motivations of the agents are, what the likely consequences of the actions are, whether the actions are going to interfere with basic human goods, and whether the immediate reaction to a situation is based on principles or an instinctual emotional response. Paying attention to all these factors will help with having a civil, clear, discussion about cases.

3.4   Decision Cases

1. *Can it be justified civil disobedience not to report a sexual assault?* Karen comes to her favorite teacher's office – Professor Mills – to talk about an important issue that has been bothering her. She trusts Professor Mills and has talked with him before about personal problems. In this case, she wants to talk about having been aggressively sexually touched by a male student at a college party. She tells Professor Mills that she just wants to talk about what happened and she absolutely does not want any authorities to be told or involved. She says that is really important to her. Professor Mills interrupts her after she has already quickly said that the issue was one of sexual assault to tell her that new Title IX regulations require all college employees to be mandatory reporters – meaning that now Title IX requires professors to report sexual assault situations regardless of what the student wants. The federal government now expressly forbids teachers to be confidantes to students about sexual misconduct matters. Karen bursts into tears and begs Mills to promise that he won't tell anyone. She wasn't raped. She told the guy off. She just needs to talk about it to process it. Then, Karen says in the very class she took with Professor Mills last semester, they had a whole section on civil disobedience. She asks Professor Mills why he can't just do that? What should Professor Mills do? Is Karen's request of Mills itself moral? Does it make a difference if Mills conceives of not reporting the incident as a type of civil disobedience? Is the federal regulation just to begin with?

2. *Should you be able to sue the "other woman"?* The state legislature is debating a bill that would make it legal to sue a person for "alienation of affection" – allowing married people whose spouses cheated on them to sue not only their spouse for divorce and alimony, but also to sue the person they had the affair with for monetary damages (FindLaw 2019). Several other states already have such a law. The main argument for the bill is that the "other woman" or "other man" is just as much a part of the cause of the breakup of the marriage as the cheating spouse, conspiring with the cheating spouse to break their contract, and as such, has harmed the faithful spouse. The main argument against the bill is that spouses have made contractual promises to remain sexually faithful to each other, but the "other man" or "other woman" have made no such promises or contracts, so it is inappropriate to punish them for someone else's promise-breaking. Should the bill be passed or not? What sorts of considerations should come into play?

3. *Who should be allowed in the locker room?* A local commercial gym and fitness center provides large locker rooms for their clients and wants everyone to feel safe and comfortable. One client is a transgendered person who has had no reassignment surgeries and who has a clearly masculine voice and masculine body. This client uses the women's locker room, states that she considers herself female, and says she would feel very uncomfortable using the men's locker room. A cisgendered female client is very upset by this and complains to the management that she feels very uncomfortable and threatened by the presence of a man changing clothes near her in the locker room and that this person should either use the men's locker room or use a private bathroom to change. What should the manager do? Is this an issue of rights? Is this an issue of beliefs? Is this an issue of character? What should the manager take into account?

4. *Should she be charged with child pornography?* The state criminalizes commerce in child pornography and part of the regulatory definition of the act includes "sending pictures of children under the age of 17 that show the children nude or engaged in sexual activity." Ashley, a 15-year-old girl at a local high school is heavily flirting with Omar, a 16-year-old boy at the same school. Several times she sends him selfies of her breasts and once sends him a picture of herself completely nude. A teacher's aide happens to see her sending one of the pics and alerts the principal, who confiscates the phone. The principal is required by law to report any instances of child sexual endangerment to authorities and so calls the police. Should the police arrest Ashley for producing and distributing child pornography? The criminal statute does not mention anything about the age of the person who distributes pictures or the relation of the subject to the sender or the intent of the sender. Does intention matter? Has Ashley done something wrong? Is this what the legislature had in mind? Does that matter?

5. *Should the doctor tell the wife?* Dr. Weathersby is a family physician and the primary healthcare

provider for the entire Robertson family. As a physician, she has at least two obligations to her patients – to keep all personal medical information confidential and to provide her patients with all the necessary information useful to them for the treatment and prevention of illnesses. Dr. Weathersby is in a bind, however. Mr. Robertson just tested positive for HIV. He apparently picked up the STD from a prostitute he paid for sex while on business travel. The doctor strongly recommends that Mr. Robertson tell his wife – who is also Weathersby's patient. He says he will think about it but seems to be unsure and gives no indication that he will stop having sex with his wife. Should Dr. Weathersby tell the wife anything? If so, what?

6. *Is this a faithful act or a loophole to get around religious principles?* On several University campuses, particularly in the UK, some Shia Muslims increasingly make use of nikah mut'ah, the ancient practice of temporary marriage. The contemporary practice consists of an agreed-upon fixed duration of time ranging from one hour to months to 99 years, various optional stipulations, and a dowry followed by a formal dissolution of the marriage. Some college students and other young people use nikah mut'ah to get to know a potential mate before committing to a full marriage. Some use it for dating. Some use it for sex since Shariah (Islamic law) does not permit sex outside marriage. While some Muslims see temporary marriages as a religiously legitimate practice, others – particularly Sunni Muslims – have criticized the way it is practiced by college students as nothing more than a loophole used for violating the spirit of the laws against fornication and prostitution. The prostitution element is particularly germane since even temporary marriages require a dowry to be paid (although some people use a merely symbolic dowry). Is nikah mut'ah being used improperly? Is there a morally important distinction between the spirit and the letter of the law? Are those students who engage in nikah mut'ah virtuously making use of the practice?

7. *Should schools show children sex videos?* Dr. Eastman is a prominent child psychologist who has done lots of serious and well-received academic research. While being interviewed on a morning news show, he suggests that school sex education programs should show children (starting in the first grade) explicit videos of adults having sex. He is quickly denounced as a pervert, a radical university nutcase, and a crazy libertine. However, he later explains that this is not about thinking it is good to be more open about sexuality. Rather, his argument is that studies show that the ubiquity of Internet and computer access and the impossibility of reliable pornography filters means there is a 90% chance a child will see at least one pornographic video online by age 8 and 20 or more by age 10 – and even higher numbers of sexually explicit still images. Many of these videos (commercial and amateur) include scenes of unsafe sex, rough sex, group sex, profanity, sexist language, extreme age differences, and degrading sexual acts of all sorts. In fact, a simple query through some major search engines (such as Microsoft's BING) can quickly and easily produce images and videos of sex with animals, coprophagia, scatology, and bloodletting – even when one doesn't directly search for those terms. Dr. Eastman says that there are two real-world options – either show children healthy, educational, explicit sex videos and explain what is happening and help them understand sex or show them nothing and they will see online porn anyway. What should sex education programs do? Are there other options?

8. *Should a feminist work there?* Samantha is a college student and works at a Hooters restaurant where she is required to wear tight clothing and cleavage-revealing shirts. On campus she actively argues for women's rights and feminist awareness. When confronted by peers who object to her job as inconsistent with her values, Samantha says making huge tips off of stupid sexist men is totally consistent with her feminist values. Her feminist friends criticize her by saying she could say the same thing about stripping or prostitution or a Black person being in a minstrel show. Is Samantha being consistent? Is it moral for her to work at Hooters? Does she have the right attitude? How will her actions affect others? What will her actions do to her own moral character?

9. *Should he be charged with sexual assault?* Jason and Corey met in a class at their college and started dating three years ago. They began the relationship by flirting, watching movies in Jason's dorm room where Jason would lean up against him, and sometimes put his hand on Corey's thigh. Eventually that led to them having sex regularly. They often slept in the same bed in one's or the other's dorm

room and Jason would sometimes wake Corey by kissing him while he was still asleep and continuing to kiss him even when he said he was sleepy and wanted to go back to sleep. A couple for two and half years, Corey eventually broke up with Jason, seemingly amicably. After the breakup, however, Corey began having problems with alcohol and sought counseling. Part of the counseling included attending a session for the University's Title IX sexual assault training, which emphasized the University's requirement of ongoing verbal affirmative consent for all sexual activity. After attending the training program, and talking more with the counselor, Corey reevaluated his previous relationship with Jason and eventually formally accused him of sexual assault. Corey said that Jason putting his hand on his thigh without asking and kissing him while he was still asleep constituted sexual assault. Jason considered this all innocent flirting and affection. The University investigated, agreed with Corey, and placed a notice of a guilty charge of serious sexual transgressions on Jason's transcript. Jason sued the school for defamation, invasion of privacy, and emotional distress, and publicly accused the school of having gone weirdly overboard in its zeal about sexual assault. Was the school's decision correct? Was their policy a good one? Should Jason have been found guilty? Did he receive due process? What was Corey's responsibility in all this? (Note: see Doe v. Brandeis Univ., 2016).

10. *Who should be allowed to play on the team?* Keisha is a college athlete and trained hard to compete in both volleyball and softball, even getting an athletic scholarship. In the most recent volleyball game with her college's main rival, her team was trounced, a loss attributed mainly to the tremendous performance of their rival's newest member, Candice. Candice is a transgender woman. She was recognized and presented as male until her sophomore year in college, when she told everyone she identified as female and was transgender. Both colleges recently adopted regulations stating that students would be classified as whatever gender they identified as. Keisha is now formally protesting Candice's participation in women's sports. Consistent with statistics on average female/male weight and height differences, Candice is 30 pounds heavier than most of the women on her team and 5 inches taller. Candice argues that she is

a woman and should be accepted on the women's team just as any other woman, regardless of her size, just as any larger or taller ciswoman would be. Keisha argues that the whole point of having college women's sports protected by Title IX is to give women the chance to participate in sports. If gender was never considered, and the only things that mattered were size, speed, and skill, then all college sports would be open to everyone, but practically speaking, very few women would get to participate because of their average smaller size, strength, and height. However, since Candice has the same size, strength, and height advantages as an average man, is genetically male, and had higher levels of testosterone during puberty, she has the same advantages an average man would have if he competed against women in volleyball. Keisha has even heard rumors that their rival team's coach is actively recruiting other transgender women to take advantage of their typically greater strength and size. She argues that this is fundamentally unfair and violates Title IX. So, should Candice be allowed to compete in women's volleyball? Should Keisha even be making this complaint? What are the arguments? What is at stake?

11. *Is this just part of doing business?* While managing an important business trip to the Republic of East Nomia, you learn that public physical affection between men is common. During business meetings and business dinners, it is not unusual for the male managers you are working with to place their hand on your male employees' thighs, to rub their backs, or to drape their arm around their shoulders. You learn this has no sexual connotation in the culture at all, having no more significance than a handshake. However, one of the male employees on your team – Jeffrey – is extremely uncomfortable and anxious about this practice. He says it makes him feel like he is being molested and asks to be excused from further meetings, pointing out that he would never be expected to put up with this behavior back at home and he wouldn't be subject to it on this trip if he were female. However, you need Jeffrey because he is the singular expert in certain areas and if any questions about those areas should arise (which is to be expected), he will need to answer them. If he doesn't attend and questions arise, your negotiations will be seriously hampered and you and your company will come across as ill-prepared. You could ask the local male managers not to touch

him, but your cultural advisor says they will certainly be offended and confused because such behavior is entirely innocent to them. Jeffrey's perception of sexual imposition would be perceived as culturally offensive to your clients. So, what should you require of your male employee? What is Jeffrey obligated to do? Are the managers in East Nomian culture obligated to respect Jeffrey's culture? Would it make any difference if Jeffrey were a woman who would be subject to such touching? Does it make a difference that the touching is not intended as sexual?

12. *How much should he be punished?* Police Officer David Rojas was recently charged with fondling the breasts of a dead woman's body. Local television news reported that Rojas and his partner were called to investigate what seemed to be a dead body – which is indeed what they found. While his partner went back to their patrol car to get some paperwork, Rojas turned off his body-cam and fondled the corpse's breast. Unknown to Rojas, a two-minute buffer on the body-cam kept recording and his behavior was discovered (Puente and Winton, 2019). How severely should Officer Rojas be punished? Or should he be punished at all? Should he be fired? Should he be executed? Should he be fined? Should he be imprisoned? Should he be let go? Most of the reasons given for laws against this kind of touching (sexual assault) are about the harm it does the victim, but can a corpse be harmed? In fact, the officer was not charged with sexual assault, but a felony count of having "sexual contact with human remains without authority," which seems to be about the degree society finds touching dead bodies disgusting more than about whether it harms anyone or violates any duties to anyone. Sources familiar with the case were quoted as saying the officer's behavior was "beyond the pale." The police officers union called the behavior "vile," "abhorrent," and "an affront to every law enforcement professional" and said they would not stand with the officer or assist him in any defense. Under current state law, the officer could go to prison for three years. What should happen? What was wrong with what he did? Is what he did unnatural? Is what he did disrespectful? Is what he did harming someone? Is what he did perverse?

13. *Should their honors be removed?* The issue of withdrawing honors or destroying historical monuments has recently become highly contentious. Confederate statues have been pulled down because the people they honored were fighting, in part, to defend slavery. Street and town names have been changed because the people they honored were later discovered to be anti-Semitic. University buildings have had names changed because the people they honored espoused anti-Native American policies. So, what about honors given to people later found to be guilty or suspected of sexual crimes or sexual immorality? For example, Vanessa Williams was the first African-American woman to be crowned Miss America (crowned in 1983 for the year 1984). Shortly before her reign was over, however, Penthouse magazine announced it would publish nude photos of Williams that had been taken two years before while she was working as a photographer's assistant – photos that showed her in "compromising" positions with another nude woman. Williams resigned her position as Miss America, under pressure from the pageant organization. Over 30 years later, however, she was offered a public apology by the Miss America CEO. More recently, openly gay conservative provocateur Milo Yiannopoulos stated in an interview that some of the concerns about alleged child molestation were based on an "arbitrary and oppressive idea of consent" and that in many cases, sexual relationships between minor boys and older men were consensual and emotionally helpful (Hersher, 2017). He also made a joking reference to a sexual act he performed on a priest while he was underaged and expressed gratitude for the experience. Following a backlash, he had to resign from his position as news editor at Breitbart News, his speaking invitation at the American Conservative Union was rescinded, and his book deal with Simon and Schuster was canceled. Even more recently, there have been calls to remove the walk-of-fame stars for Kevin Spacey and Michael Jackson as a result of their apparent sexual molestations of boys. Some have even argued that radio stations should stop playing Michael Jackson's songs. What is the right thing to do in these cases? Does retaining the honor legitimate the actions? Does removing the honor help any victims? 30 years from now could sex between adults and children be seen as morally acceptable and organizations be expected to apologize to Yiannopoulos as they did to Williams?

14. *Is their sexual orientation and behavior morally different from other legal sexual orientations and*

behavior? The desire to have sex with animals used to be called bestiality and people who had sex with animals bestiaphiles (or some variant spelling). However, recently, people who are sexually attracted to animals have begun to be more open and advocate for the moral acceptance of their desires and actions. A German group, ZETA (Zoophiles Engagement fur Toleranze und Aufklärung) advocates for a better of understanding of zoophiles (a preferred term), stating: "There indeed exists – even if this seems to be unimaginable in the flood of (mis-)information – a group of zoosexual people who love and respect their animals as well as honour their volition." (Zeta-Verien, nd.). The German advocacy group may be especially visible since the German government in 2012 passed a tough law against sex with animals. One zoophile advocate – Michael – argues that: "The actions of society are nearly the same as they were against homosexuals 30 years ago . . . We are doing the same things homosexuals did – we go out in public, we show our faces. You have more fear and hatred of things you do not know." (Moore, 2012). Interestingly, one of the main reasons the German government passed a new law was to move away from Biblical and natural law moral prohibitions on sex with animals as "abominations" to a reasoning based on perceived harm to the animal or the lack of consent of the animal. The head of the parliamentary committee seeking the change in the law stated "Sexual interaction is problematic because it can lead to harm and emotional disorder of animals . . . It's not proven that animals would enjoy sexual interaction with humans." (Moore, 2012). But is that the best reason to oppose sex with animals? After all, animals do not consent to be used for food, to be pets, to not be pets, to stay in the wild, to be ridden for transportation, to be used in experiments, or to be killed by other animals. Why is sex special? And regarding harm, is all sex with animals harmful? As one zoophile defender argues, "The accusation

that a dog who licks peanut butter off your hand is getting a treat, while the same dog licking peanut butter off [your genitals] is being sexually abused is absurd." (Moore, 2012). So, should sex with animals be illegal? Why or why not? Do issues of unnaturalness, perversion, and human dignity play a part in the law? If harm and consent are the only issues, how likely is it that zoosexuality will remain illegal in the future?

15. *Should sex with robots be illegal?* Personal robots are just beginning to be commercially available. While some are simple tools, such as vacuum cleaners, others are more anthropomorphic, with faces, limbs, expressions, and voices. For example, the Japanese company Softbank sells a personal robot called Pepper that has a face, arms, fingers, and the ability to move autonomously and respond differently to different human emotions. One of the requirements for purchasing a Pepper is that owners must sign a contract saying they will not use the robot for "the purpose of sexual or indecent behavior" nor will they develop any obscene or sexual apps (Lott-Lavigna, 2015). The reason for this requirement is not entirely clear, though it seems partly to have to do with not using the robot to stalk other people. Others, however, have argued that it should be illegal to have sex with robots – not so much because of the robot's rights but because having sex with robots will supposedly increase the likelihood that women and children will be sexually objectified or abused. Meanwhile, other companies are developing robots specifically for the purpose of sex (e.g., Roxxxy and Rocky by the True Companion company). As robots become more sophisticated, they could be designed for any sexual purpose and designed to resemble any race, age, or gender. Should sex with robots be regulated? Why or why not? How different is this moral issue from others discussed in this book given the differences of harm and consent? Can someone have a good reason for wanting to have sex with a robot? Can they have bad reasons?

References

Al Jazeera. (2017). Trump back accused child molester Roy Moore for Senate. *Al* Jazeera.com. December 4. Retrieved June 1, 2022, from https://www.aljazeera.com/news/2017/12/04/trump-backs-accused-child-molester-roy-moore-for-senate/

American Heritage Dictionary of the English Language, 5th edn. (2016). Retrieved June 1, 2022, from https://www.thefreedictionary.com/sex

Patrick D. Hopkins

Anonymous. (2011, January 2). Does this count as sex? DearCupid.org. Retrieved June 1, 2022, from http://www.dearcupid.org/question/does-this-count-as-sex.html

Average Joe (2012, April 15). Does this count as sex? *TeenHelp*. Retrieved June 1, 2022, from http://www.teenhelp.org/forums/f6-sex-puberty/t99536-does-count-sex-o_o/

Branchflower v. Branchflower, 150 N.H. 226 (2003).

Brenoff, A. (2019). Should people be allowed to legally change their age? AARP.org, February 13. Retrieved June 1, 2022, from https://www.aarp.org/disrupt-aging/stories/info-2019/legally-change-age.html

Broverman, N. (2018). Accused Pedophile Roy Moore suing female accusers. *The Advocate*. May 1 at 1:32 pm EDT. Retrieved June 1, 2022, from https://www.advocate.com/politics/2018/5/01/gall-accused-pedophile-roy-moore-suing-female-accusers

Bump, P. (2017). Timeline: The accusations against Roy Moore. *The Washington Post*, November 16 at 9:03 a.m. CST. Retrieved June 1, 2022, from https://www.washingtonpost.com/news/politics/wp/2017/11/16/timeline-the-accusations-against-roy-moore/

Cambridge University Press (2021). Definition of sex [online]. Retrieved June 1, 2022, from https://dictionary.cambridge.org/dictionary/english/sex

Corinna, H. (2018, November 5). How do we best define sex? *Scarleteen: Sex Ed for the Real World*. Retrieved June 1, 2022, from https://www.scarleteen.com/blog/heather_corinna/2011/02/09/how_do_we_best_define_sex

Dictionary.com (nd.). Definition of coitus [online]. Retrieved June 1, 2022, from https://www.dictionary.com/browse/coitus

Doe v. Brandeis Univ., 177 F. Supp. 3d 561 (D. Mass. 2016).

FindLaw. (2019). Alienation of affection. Retrieved June 1, 2022, from https://www.findlaw.com/injury/torts-and-personal-injuries/alienation-of-affection.html

Foucault, M. (1988). Confinement, psychiatry, prison. In *Politics, Philosophy, Culture. Interviews and Other Writings, 1977-1984*. Ed. L.D. Kritzman, trans. Alan Sheridan, et al. New York: Routledge.

Fozzy13 (2009, June 1). Does it count as having sex if you don't come? Bodybuilding.com *Forum*. Retrieved June 1, 2022, from https://forum.bodybuilding.com/showthread.php?t=116723521

GoAskAlice! (2017, July 14). Definition of sex? *GoAskAlice!* Retrieved June 1, 2022, from https://goaskalice.columbia.edu/answered-questions/definition-sex-0

Greenway, S. (2020, October 3). Worcester man who raped woman by puncturing a hole in condom is jailed. *Worcester News*. Retrieved June 1, 2022, from https://www.worcesternews.co.uk/news/18767987.worcester-man-raped-woman-puncturing-hole-condom-jailed/

Griffiths, M.D. (2013). Intimate and Inanimate: A brief look at object sexuality. PsychologyToday.com. July 25 Retrieved June 1, 2022, from https://www.psychologytoday.com/us/blog/in-excess/201307/intimate-and-inanimate

Haidt, J. (2001). The emotional dog and its rational tail: A social intuitionist approach to moral judgment. *Psychological Review*, 108, 814–834.

Hersher, R. (2017). After comments on Pedophilia, Breitbart Editor Milo Yiannopoulos Resigns. National Public Radio. February 21, 2017 3:40 PM ET. Retrieved June 1, 2022, from https://www.npr.org/sections/thetwo-way/2017/02/21/516473521/after-comments-on-pedophilia-breitbart-editor-milo-yiannopoulos-resigns

Huang, H. and Kahn, C. (nd.). How do you define sexual harassment? *Reuters Graphics*. Retrieved June 1, 2022, from http://fingfx.thomsonreuters.com/gfx/rngs/USA-METOO/0100605B0CC/index.html

Igartua, K., Thombs, B.D., Burgos, G., and Montoro, R. (2009). Concordance and discrepancy in sexual identity, attraction, and behavior among adolescents. *Journal of Adolescent Health*, 45(6): 602–608.

James, E. (2015). 'I've gone back to being a child': Husband and father-of-seven, 52, leaves his wife and kids to live as a transgender SIX-YEAR-OLD girl named Stefonknee. DailyMail.com, 11:52 EDT, 11 December. Retrieved June 1, 2022, from https://www.dailymail.co.uk/femail/article-3356084/I-ve-gone-child-Husband-father-seven-52-leaves-wife-kids-live-transgender-SIX-YEAR-OLD-girl-named-Stefonknee.html

Jester78 (2009, June 1). Does it count as having sex if you don't come? Bodybuilding.com *Forum*. Retrieved January 1, 2021, from https://forum.bodybuilding.com/showthread.php?t=116723521

Jones, F. (2013). Race play ain't for everyone. Ebony.com. Retrieved June 1, 2022, from https://www.ebony.com/love-relationships/talk-like-sex-race-play-aint-for-everyone-911/

Kahn, C. (2017, December 27). Poll: Hugs and dirty jokes – Americans differ on acceptable behavior. *Reuters*. Retrieved June 1, 2022, from https://www.reuters.com/article/us-usa-metoo-poll/poll-hugs-and-dirty-jokes-americans-differ-on-acceptable-behavior-idUSKBN1EL147

Lacayo, R. (1998, August 24). When is sex not "sexual relations"? *CNN-All Politics*. Retrieved June 1, 2022, from https://www.cnn.com/ALLPOLITICS/1998/08/17/time/clinton.html

Lott-Lavigna, R. (2015). Pepper the robot's contract bans users from having sex with it. *Wired*. September 23 2:30 pm. Retrieved June 1, 2022, from https://www.wired.co.uk/article/pepper-robot-sex-banned

Macmillan Dictionary (2009–2021). Definition of sex [online]. Retrieved June 1, 2022, from https://www.macmillandictionary.com/us/dictionary/american/sex_1

Marsh, A. (2010). Love among the objectum sexuals. *Electronic Journal of Human Sexuality*. 13(1). Retrieved June 1, 2022, from http://www.ejhs.org/volume13/ObjSexuals.htm

McClendon, D. and Sandstrom, A. (2016). Child marriage is rare in the U.S., though this varies by state. PewResearchCenter.org. November 1. Retrieved June 1, 2022, from https://www.pewresearch.org/fact-tank/2016/11/01/child-marriage-is-rare-in-the-u-s-though-this-varies-by-state/

Merriam-Webster (nd.-a). Definition of sex [online]. In Merriam-Webster.com *dictionary*. Retrieved June 1, 2022, from https://www.merriam-webster.com/dictionary/sex

Merriam-Webster. (nd.-b). Definition of sexual intercourse. In Merriam-Webster.com *dictionary*. Retrieved June 1, 2022, from https://www.merriam-webster.com/dictionary/sexual%20intercourse

Moore, O. (2012). "Zoophiles" vow fight after Germany re-bans bestiality. *The Globe and Mail*. December 14, 2012. Retrieved June 1, 2022, from https://www.theglobeandmail.com/news/world/zoophiles-vow-fight-after-germany-re-bans-bestiality/article6356367/

Muise, A. (2011, September 30). Does that count? Differing definitions of sex. *Luvze*. Retrieved June 1, 2022, from https://www.luvze.com/does-that-count-differing-definitions-of-sex/

ObjectumSexuality.org. (2021). http://www.objectum-sexuality.org

Okrent, A. (2014, July 10). 31 Adorable slang terms for sex from the last 600 years. *Mental Floss*. Retrieved June 1, 2022, from https://www.mentalfloss.com/article/57872/31-adorable-slang-terms-sexual-intercourse-last-600-years

Onisionspeaks. https://www.youtube.com/watch?v=SjYug2NOesE Video no longer available.

Orford v. Orford 58 DLR 251(1921, Ontario Supreme Court).

Oxford University Press (2020). Definition of sex [online]. Retrieved June 1, 2022, from https://www.lexico.com/en/definition/sex

Pagliery, J. (2016, July 5). Some Ashley Madison women were actually computer "fembots." *CNN-Business*. Retrieved June 1, 2022, from https://money.cnn.com/2016/07/05/technology/ashley-madison-fembots/index.html

Pathela, P., Hajat, A., Schillinger, J. et al. (2006). Discordance between sexual behavior and self-reported sexual identity: A population-based survey of New York City Men. *Annals of Internal Medicine*, 145(6): 416–425.

Pisaster, Dr. (2011, November 10). The problem with defining "sex." *Pajiba*. Retrieved June 1, 2022, from https://www.pajiba.com/pajiba_dirty_talk/the-problem-with-defining-sex.php

Puente, M. and Winton, R. (2019). LAPD officer under investigation for allegedly fondling dead woman's breasts. *Los Angeles Times*, Dec. 3, 2019, 12:28 PM PT. Retrieved June 1, 2022, from https://www.latimes.com/california/story/2019-12-03/lapd-officer-under-investigation-for-fondling-female-corpse

Robinson, S., White, A., and Anderson, E. (2019). Privileging the bromance: A critical appraisal of romantic and bromantic relationships. *Men and Masculinities*, 22(5), 850–871. https://doi.org/10.1177/1097184X17730386

Sanders, S.A., Hill, B.J., Yarber, W.L. et al. (2010). Misclassification bias: Diversity in conceptualisations about having 'had sex'. *Sexual Health*, 7(1), 31–34.

Stelter, B. (2011). A racy show with teenagers steps back from a boundary. *The New York Times*. Retrieved June 1, 2022, from https://www.nytimes.com/2011/01/20/business/media/20mtv.html

Thadeusz, V.F. (2007). Falling in love with things. *Der Spiegel International*. Retrieved June 1, 2022, from https://www.spiegel.de/international/spiegel/objectophilia-fetishism-and-neo-sexuality-falling-in-love-with-things-a-482192.html

The Washington Post Company. (1998). Grounds for impeachment, No. 1. Retrieved June 1, 2022, from https://www.washingtonpost.com/wp-srv/politics/special/clinton/icreport/7groundsi.htm?noredirect=on

Thorpe, J.R. (2015, March 31). All the ridiculous historical euphemisms for sex. *Bustle*. Retrieved June 1, 2022, from https://www.bustle.com/articles/69554-26-amazing-historical-euphemisms-for-sex-because-you-could-stand-to-have-your-corn-ground

Tiersma, P. (2004). Did Clinton lie: Defining sexual relations. *Chicago-Kent Law Review*, 79(927).

U.S. Department of Justice. (2020). Citizen's guide to U.S. Federal Law on Child Pornography. Retrieved June 1, 2022, from https://www.justice.gov/criminal-ceos/citizens-guide-us-federal-law-child-pornography

U.S. Equal Employment Opportunity Commission. (nd.). Sexual harassment. Retrieved June 1, 2022, from https://www.eeoc.gov/sexual-harassment

Vocabulary.com (nd.) Definition of coitus [online]. Retrieved June 1, 2022, from https://www.vocabulary.com/dictionary/coitus

Zellner, J.A., Martinez-Donate, A.P., Sanudo, F. et al. (2009). The interaction of sexual identity with sexual behavior and its influence on HIV risk among Latino men: Results of a community survey in Northern San Diego County, California. *American Journal of Public Health*, 99: 125–132, https://doi.org/10.2105/AJPH.2007.129809

Zeta-Verien. (nd.). Retrieved June 1, 2022, from https://www.zeta-verein.de/en/the-association/

PART II

Consent and Coercion

Introduction

In a liberal democratic society, a great deal of emphasis is placed on the freedom of individuals to make their own decisions, particularly about their own bodies and private activities. As a result, there is a tendency to think that if someone wants to engage in some sexual activity, freely chooses to do so, and does not harm anyone, then they should not be interfered with. The primary moral concerns here (especially from a public policy perspective) are about respecting individualism and determining whether the sex is consensual and harmless.

This take on sex is not immune to moral criticism or to a need for definitional clarity. In terms of morality, the position that honoring individual choice should always be valued over social consequences, or the potential rights of groups, or even the health and welfare of the choosing individual is not incontestable. There are arguments, for example, that society has some claims against individuals even if no specific other person is directly injured by a free choice or that choosing self-destructive behavior is irrational and therefore not to be respected as free in the first place. But even if the correct focus for judging the morality of sex should be on liberty and self-determination, there are still the questions of what genuine consent means and when we can be sure it is given. Is everyone equally capable of consent? Or are there significant differences between people that sharply limit consent to contexts – differences because of age, gender, and social position? Does consent have to be explicit? Or is there such a thing as trustworthy implicit consent? Is coercion only outright physical compulsion? Or does it include threats and insinuation?

Part II examines issues of consent and coercion. Though such issues arise in many contexts, they are explored here by focusing on three major areas where the definitions of these terms have both important moral impact and serious direct legal implications for determining guilt and innocence.

Framing Questions

- *How should we define sexual harassment?*
- *How should we define rape?*
- *How should we assess the age of consent?*

2

A Feminist Definition of Sexual Harassment

Anita M. Superson

Summary

Argues that sexual harassment is defined too subjectively, does not adequately address the social context of gender, and does not address the harm to women as a group. As such, society should adopt an objective feminist definition of sexual harassment as any behavior by a member of the dominant class that expresses an attitude that women are inferior because of their sex. Consequences of this definition include that sexual harassment is a group harm rather than just an individual harm, that women cannot sexually harass men, that unequal power relations are not required for sexual harassment to occur, that a woman can be sexually harassed without knowing it or being bothered by it, and that a harasser's intentions are irrelevant.

Original publication details: Anita M. Superson, "A Feminist Definition of Sexual Harassment," pp. 46–64 from *Journal of Social Philosophy* 24 (1994). Reproduced with permission of John Wiley & Sons.

I. Introduction

By far the most pervasive form of discrimination against women is sexual harassment (SH). Women in every walk of life are subject to it, and I would venture to say, on a daily basis.[1] Even though the law is changing to the benefit of victims of SH, the fact that SH is still so pervasive shows that there is too much tolerance of it, and that victims do not have sufficient legal recourse to be protected.

The main source for this problem is that the way SH is defined by various Titles and other sources does not adequately reflect the social nature of SH, or the harm it causes all women. As a result, SH comes to be defined in subjective ways. One upshot is that when subjective definitions infuse the case law on SH, the more subtle but equally harmful forms of SH do not get counted as SH and thus not afforded legal protection.

My primary aim in this paper is to offer an objective definition of SH that accounts for the group harm all forms of SH have in common. Though my aim is to offer a moral definition of SH, I offer it in hopes that it will effect changes in the law. It is only by defining SH in a way that covers all of its forms and gets at the heart of the problem that legal protection can be given to all victims in all circumstances.

I take this paper to be programmatic. Obviously problems may exist in applying the definition to cases that arise for litigation. In a larger project a lot more could be said to meet those objections. My goal in this paper is merely to defend my definition against the definitions currently appealed to by the courts in order to show how it is more promising for victims of SH.

I define SH in the following way:

> any behavior (verbal or physical) caused by a person, A, in the dominant class directed at another, B, in the subjugated class, that expresses and perpetuates the attitude that B or members of B's sex is/are inferior because of their sex, thereby causing harm to either B and/or members of B's sex.

II. Current Law on Sexual Harassment

Currently, victims of SH have legal recourse under Title VII of the Civil Rights Act of 1964, Title IX of the 1972 Education Amendments, and tort law.

The Civil Rights Act of 1964 states:

> a) It shall be an unlawful employment practice for an employer –

> (1) to fail or refuse to hire or to discharge any individual, or otherwise to discriminate against any individual with respect to his compensation, terms, conditions, or privileges of employment because of such individual's race, color, religion, sex, or national origin. . . .[2]

Over time the courts came to view SH as a form of sex discrimination. The main advocate for this was Catharine MacKinnon, whose book, *Sexual Harassment of Working Women*,[3] greatly influenced court decisions on the issue. Before it was federally legislated, some courts appealed to the Equal Employment Opportunity Commission (EEOC) *Guidelines on Discrimination Because of Sex* to establish that SH was a form of sex discrimination. The *Guidelines* (amended in 1980 to include SH) state that

> Harassment on the basis of sex is a violation of Sec. 703 of Title VII. Unwelcome sexual advances, requests for sexual favors, and other verbal or physical conduct of a sexual nature constitute sexual harassment when (1) submission to such conduct is made either explicitly or implicitly a term or condition of an individual's employment, (2) submission to or rejection of such conduct by an individual is used as the basis for employment decisions affecting such individual, or (3) such conduct has the purpose or effect of unreasonably interfering with an individual's work performance or creating an intimidating, hostile, or offensive working environment.[4]

In a landmark case,[5] *Meritor Savings Bank, FSB v. Vinson* (1986),[6] the Supreme Court, relying on the EEOC *Guidelines*, established that SH was a form of sex discrimination prohibited under Title VII. The case involved Mechelle Vinson, a teller-trainee, who was propositioned by Sidney Taylor, vice president and branch manager of the bank. After initially refusing, she agreed out of fear of losing her job. She allegedly had sexual relations with Taylor 40 or 50 times over a period of four years, and he even forcibly raped her several times, exposed himself to her in a restroom, and fondled her in public.[7]

Sexual harassment extends beyond the workplace. To protect students who are not employees of their learning institution, Congress enacted Title IX of the Education Amendments of 1972, which states:

> No person in the United States shall, on the basis of sex, be excluded from participation in, be denied the

benefits of, or be subjected to discrimination under any educational program or activity receiving federal financial assistance.[8]

Cases of litigation under Title IX have been influenced by *Meritor* so that SH in educational institutions is construed as a form of sex discrimination.[9]

The principles that came about under Title VII apply equally to Title IX. Under either Title, a person can file two different kinds of harassment charges: *quid pro quo*, or hostile environment. *Quid pro quo* means "something for something."[10] *Quid pro quo* harassment occurs when "an employer or his agent explicitly ties the terms, conditions, and privileges of the victim's employment to factors which are arbitrary and unrelated to job performance."[11] Plaintiffs must show they "suffered a tangible economic detriment as a result of the harassment."[12] In contrast, hostile environment harassment occurs when the behavior of supervisors or co-workers has the effect of "unreasonably interfering with an individual's work performance or creates an intimidating, hostile, or offensive environment"[13] Hostile environment harassment established that Title VII (and presumably Title IX) were not limited to economic discrimination, but applied to emotional harm, as well. The EEOC *Guidelines* initiated the principle of hostile environment harassment which was used by the courts in many cases, including *Meritor*.

[. . .]

Despite major advances made in the last few decades in the law on SH, I believe the law is still inadequate. The main problem in my view is that the law, reflecting the view held by the general public, fails to see SH for what it is: an attack on the group of *all* women, not just the immediate victim. Because of this, there is a failure to recognize the group harm that all instances of SH, not just the more blatant ones, cause all women. As a result, the law construes SH as a subjective issue, that is, one that is determined by what the victim feels and (sometimes) what the perpetrator intends. As a result, the burden of proof is wrongly shifted to the victim and off of the perpetrator with the result that many victims are not legally protected.

For instance, victims filing complaints under Title VII (and presumably Title IX) are not protected unless they have a fairly serious case. They have to show under hostile environment harassment that the behavior unreasonably interfered with their work performance, and that there was a pattern of behavior on the defendant's behalf. Regarding the latter point, the EEOC *Guidelines* say that:

In determining whether alleged conduct constitutes sexual harassment, the Commission will look at the record as a whole and at the totality of the circumstances, such as the nature of the sexual advances and the context in which the alleged incidents occurred.[14]

[. . .]

Victims not protected include the worker who is harassed by a number of different people, the worker who suffers harassment but in small doses, the person who is subjected to a slew of catcalls on her two mile walk to work, the female professor who is subjected to leering from one of her male students, and the woman who does not complain out of fear. The number of cases is huge, and many of them are quite common.

To protect all victims in all circumstances, the law ought to treat SH as it is beginning to treat racial discrimination. In her very interesting paper, Mari Matsuda has traced the history of the law regarding racist speech.[15] Article 4 of the International Convention on the Elimination of All Forms of Racial Discrimination which was unanimously adopted by the General Assembly December 21, 1965, prohibits not only acts of violence, but also the "mere dissemination of racist ideas, without requiring proof of incitement."[16] Apparently many states have signed and ratified the signing of the Convention, though the United States has not yet done so because of worries about freedom of speech protected by the Fust Amendment.[17] Aside from the Convention, the United Nations Charter, the Universal Declaration of Human Rights, the European Convention for the Protection of Human Rights and Fundamental Freedoms, the American Declaration of the Rights and Duties of Man, as well as the domestic law of several nations, have all recognized the right to equality and freedom from racism. In these and other codes, racist ideas are banned if they are discriminatory, related to violence, or express inferiority, hatred, or persecution.[18] On my view, some forms of SH are related to violence, and they *all* express inferiority whether or not they express hatred. At the root of the standard on racism that is gaining worldwide recognition is the view that racist speech "interferes with the rights of subordinated-group members to participate equally in society, maintaining their basic sense of security and worth as human beings."[19] Sexual harassment has the same effect, so it, too, should be prohibited. But I think SH can be afforded the best legal protection under antidiscrimination law instead of tort law, as this misses the social nature of SH. The worldwide standard against racist speech recognizes the group harm of racism by realizing that racist speech expresses inferiority; a similar standard against SH should be adopted.

III. The Social Nature of Sexual Harassment

Sexual harassment, a form of sexism, is about domination, in particular, the domination of the group of men over the group of women.[20] Domination involves control or power which can be seen in the economic, political, and social spheres of society. Sexual harassment is not simply an assertion of power, for power can be used in beneficial ways. The power men have over women has been wielded in ways that oppress women. The power expressed in SH is oppression, power used wrongly.

Sexual harassment is integrally related to sex roles. It reveals the belief that a person is to be relegated to certain roles on the basis of her sex, including not only women's being sex objects, but also their being caretakers, motherers, nurturers, sympathizers, etc. In general, the sex roles women are relegated to are associated with the body (v. mind) and emotions (v. reason).

When A sexually harasses B, the comment or behavior is really directed at the group of all women, not just a particular woman, a point often missed by the courts. After all, many derogatory behaviors are issued at women the harasser does not even know (e.g., scanning a stranger's body). Even when the harasser knows his victim, the behavior is directed at the particular woman because she happens to be "available" at the time, though its message is for all women. For instance, a catcall says not (merely) that the perpetrator likes a woman's body but that he thinks women are at least primarily sex objects and he – because of the power he holds by being in the dominant group – gets to rate them according to how much pleasure they give him. The professor who refers to his female students as "chicks" makes a statement that women are intellectually inferior to men as they can be likened to non-rational animals, perhaps even soft, cuddly ones that are to serve as the objects of (men's) pleasure. Physicians' using Playboy centerfolds in medical schools to "spice up their lectures" sends the message that women lack the competence to make it in a "man's world" and should perform the "softer tasks" associated with bearing and raising children.[21]

These and other examples make it clear that SH is not about dislike for a certain person; instead, it expresses a person's beliefs about women as a group on the basis of their sex; namely, that they are primarily emotional and bodily beings. Some theorists – Catharine MacKinnon, John Hughes and Larry May – have recognized the social nature of SH. Hughes and May claim that women

are a disadvantaged group because (1) they are a social group having a distinct identity and existence apart from their individual identities, (2) they occupy a subordinate position in American society, and (3) their political power is severely circumscribed.[22] They continue:

> Once it is established that women qualify for special disadvantaged group status, all practices tending to stigmatize women as a group, or which contribute to the maintenance of their subordinate social status, would become legally suspect.[23]

This last point, I believe, should be central to the definition of SH.

Because SH has as its target the group of all women, this *group* suffers harm as a result of the behavior. Indeed, when any one woman is in any way sexually harassed, all women are harmed. The group harm SH causes is different from the harm suffered by particular women as individuals: it is often more vague in nature as it is not easily causally tied to any particular incident of harassment. The group harm has to do primarily with the fact that the behavior reflects and reinforces sexist attitudes that women are inferior to men and that they do and ought to occupy certain sex roles. For example, comments and behavior that relegate women to the role of sex objects reinforce the belief that women *are* sex objects and that they *ought to* occupy this sex role. Similarly, when a female professor's cogent comments at department colloquia are met with frowns and rolled eyes from her colleagues, this behavior reflects and reinforces the view that women are not fit to occupy positions men arrogate to themselves.

The harm women suffer as a group from any single instance of SH is significant. It takes many forms. A Kantian analysis would show what is wrong with being solely a sex object. Though there is nothing wrong with being a caretaker or nurturer, etc., *per se*, it is sexist – and so wrong – to assign such roles to women. In addition, it is wrong to assign a person to a role she may not want to occupy. Basically women are not allowed to decide for themselves which roles they are to occupy, but this gets decided for them, no matter what they do. Even if some women occupy important positions in society that men traditionally occupy, they are still viewed as being sex objects, caretakers, etc., since all women are thought to be more "bodily" and emotional than men. This is a denial of women's autonomy, and degrading to them. It also contributes to women's oppression. The belief that women must occupy certain sex roles is both a cause and an effect of their oppression. It is a cause because women are believed to be more suited for certain roles given their association with body and emotions. It is an effect because once they occupy these roles and are victims of oppression, the belief that they *must* occupy these sex roles is reinforced.

[. . .]

Another harm SH causes all women is that the particular form sex stereotyping takes promotes two myths: (1) that male behavior is normally and naturally predatory, and (2) that females naturally (because they are taken to be primarily bodily and emotional) and even willingly acquiesce despite the appearance of protest.[24] Because the behavior perpetuated by these myths is taken to be normal, it is not seen as sexist, and in turn is not counted as SH.

The first myth is that men have stronger sexual desires than women, and harassment is just a natural venting of these desires which men are unable to control. The truth is, first, that women are socialized *not* to vent their sexual desires in the way men do, but this does not mean these desires are weaker or less prevalent. Masters and Johnson have "decisively established that women's sexual requirements are no less potent or urgent than those of men."[25] But second, SH has nothing to do with men's sexual desires, nor is it about seduction; instead, it is about oppression of women. Indeed, harassment generally does not lead to sexual satisfaction, but it often gives the harasser a sense of power.

The second myth is that women either welcome, ask for, or deserve the harassing treatment. Case law reveals this mistaken belief. In *Lipsett v. Rive*-Mora[26] (1987), the plaintiff was discharged from a medical residency program because she "did not react favorably to her professor's requests to go out for drinks, his compliments about her hair and legs, or to questions about her personal and romantic life."[27] The court exonerated the defendant because the plaintiff initially reacted favorably by smiling when shown lewd drawings of herself and when called sexual nicknames as she thought she had to appease the physician. The court said that "given the plaintiffs admittedly favorable responses to these flattering comments, there was no way anyone could consider them as 'unwelcome.'"[28] The court in *Swentek v. US Air*[29] (1987) reacted similarly when a flight attendant who was harassed with obscene remarks and gestures was denied legal recourse because previously she used vulgar language and openly discussed her sexual encounters. The court concluded that "she was the kind of

person who could not be offended by such comments and therefore welcomed them generally."[30]

[. . .]

Both myths harm all women as they sanction SH by shifting the burden on the victim and all members of her sex: women must either go out of their way to avoid "natural" male behavior, or establish conclusively that they did not in any way want the behavior. Instead of the behavior being seen as sexist, it is seen as women's problem to rectify.

Last, but certainly not least, women suffer group harm from SH because they come to be stereotyped as victims.[31] Many men see SH as something they can do to women, and in many cases, get away with. Women come to see themselves as victims, and come to believe that the roles they *can* occupy are only the sex roles men have designated for them. Obviously these harms are quite serious for women, so the elimination of all forms of SH is warranted.

I have spoken so far as if it is only men who can sexually harass women, and I am now in a position to defend this controversial view. When a woman engages in the very same behavior harassing men engage in, the underlying message implicit in male-to-female harassment is missing. For example, when a woman scans a man's body, she might be considering him to be a sex object, but all the views about domination and being relegated to certain sex roles are absent. She cannot remind the man that he is inferior because of his sex, since given the way things are in society, he is not. In general, women cannot harm or degrade or dominate men *as a group*, for it is impossible to send the message that one dominates (and so cause group harm) if one does not dominate. Of course, if the sexist roles predominant in our society were reversed, women *could* sexually harass men. The way things are, any bothersome behavior a woman engages in, even though it may be of a sexual nature, does not constitute SH because it lacks the social impact present in male-to-female harassment. Tort law would be sufficient to protect against this behavior, since it is unproblematic in these cases that tort law foils to recognize group harm.

IV.   Subjective v. Objective Definitions of Sexual Harassment

Most definitions of 'sexual harassment' make reference to the behavior's being "unwelcome" or "annoying" to the victim. *Black's law Dictionary* defines 'harassment' as a term used "to describe words, gestures and actions which tend to annoy, alarm and abuse (verbally) another person."[32] The *American Heritage Dictionary* defines 'harass' as "to disturb or irritate persistently," and states further that "[h]arass implies systematic persecution by besetting with annoyances, threats, or demands."[33] The EEOC *Guidelines* state that behavior constituting SH is identified as "unwelcome sexual advances, requests for sexual favors, and other verbal or physical conduct of a sexual nature."[34] In their philosophical account of SH, Hughes and May define 'harassment' as "a class of annoying or unwelcome acts undertaken by one person (or group of persons) against another person (or group of persons)."[35] And Rosemarie Tong takes the feminists' definition of noncoercive SH to be that which "denotes sexual misconduct that merely annoys or offends the person to whom it is directed."[36]

The criterion of "unwelcomeness" or "annoyance" is reflected in the way the courts have handled cases of SH, as in *Lipsett*, *Swentek*, and *Meritor*, though in the latter case the court said that the voluntariness of the victim's submission to the defendant's sexual conduct did not mean that she welcomed the conduct.[37] The criterion of unwelcomeness or annoyance present in these subjective accounts of harassment puts the burden on the victim to establish that she was sexually harassed. There is no doubt that many women *are* bothered by this behavior, often with serious side-effects including anything from anger, fear, and guilt,[38] to lowered self-esteem and decreased feelings of competence and confidence,[39] to anxiety disorders, alcohol and drug abuse, coronary disturbances, and gastro-intestinal disorders.[40]

Though it is true that many women are bothered by the behavior at issue, I think it is seriously mistaken to say that whether the victim is bothered determines whether the behavior constitutes SH. This is so for several reasons.

First, we would have to establish that the victim was bothered by it, either by the victim's complaints, or by examining the victim's response to the behavior. The fact of the matter is that many women are quite hesitant to report being harassed, for a number of reasons. Primary among them is that they fear negative consequences from reporting the conduct. As is often the case, harassment comes from a person in a position of institutional power, whether he be a supervisor, a company president, a member of a dissertation committee, the chair of the department, and so on. Unfortunately for many women, as a review of the case law reveals, their fears are warranted.[41] Women have been fired, their jobs

have been made miserable forcing them to quit, professors have handed out unfair low grades, and so on. Worries about such consequences means that complaints are not filed, or are filed years after the incident, as in the Anita Hill v. Thomas Clarence case. But this should not be taken to imply that the victim was not harassed.

Moreover, women are hesitant to report harassment because they do not want anything to happen to the perpetrator, but just want the behavior to stop.[42] Women do not complain because they do not want to deal with the perpetrator's reaction when faced with the charge. He might claim that he was "only trying to be friendly." Women are fully aware that perpetrators can often clear themselves quite easily, especially in tort law cases where the perpetrator's intentions are directly relevant to whether he is guilty. And most incidents of SH occur without any witnesses – many perpetrators plan it this way. It then becomes the harasser's word against the victim's. To complicate matters, many women are insecure and doubt themselves. Women's insecurity is capitalized upon by harassers whose behavior is in the least bit ambiguous. Clever harassers who fear they might get caught or be reported often attempt to get on the good side of their victim in order to confuse her about the behavior, as well as to have a defense ready in case a charge is made. Harassers might offer special teaching assignments to their graduate students, special help with exams and publications, promotions, generous raises, and the like. Of course, this is all irrelevant to whether he harasses, but the point is that it makes the victim less likely to complain. On top of all this, women's credibility is very often questioned (unfairly) when they bring forth a charge. They are taken to be "hypersensitive." There is an attitude among judges and others that women must "develop a thick skin."[43] Thus, the blame is shifted off the perpetrator and onto the victim. Given this, if a woman thinks she will get no positive response – or, indeed, will get a negative one – from complaining, she is unlikely to do so.

Further, some women do not recognize harassment for what it is, and so will not complain. Sometimes this is because they are not aware of their own oppression, or actually seem to endorse sexist stereotypes. I recall a young woman who received many catcalls on the streets of Daytona Beach, Florida during spring break, and who was quite proud that her body could draw such attention. Given that women are socialized into believing their bodies are the most important feature of themselves, it is no surprise that a fair number of them are complacent about harassing behavior directed at them.

[. . .]

Moreover, women's *behavior* is not an accurate indicator of whether they are bothered. More often than not, women try to ignore the perpetrator's behavior in an attempt not to give the impression they are encouraging it. They often cover up their true feelings so that the perpetrator does not have the satisfaction that his harassing worked. Since women are taught to smile and put up with this behavior, they might actually appear to enjoy it to some extent. Often they have no choice but to continue interacting with the perpetrator, making it very difficult to assert themselves. Women often make up excuses for not "giving in" instead of telling the perpetrator to stop. The fact that their behavior does not indicate they are bothered should not be used to show they were not bothered. In reality, women are fearful of defending themselves in the face of men's power and physical strength. Given the fact that the courts have decided that a lot of this behavior should just be tolerated, it is no wonder that women try to make the best of their situation.

It would be wrong to take a woman's behavior to be a sign that she is bothered also because doing so implies the behavior is permissible if she does not seem to care. This allows the *perpetrator* to be the judge of whether a woman is harassed, which is unjustifiable given the confusion among men about whether their behavior is bothersome or flattering. Sexual harassment should be treated no differently than crimes where harm to the victim is assessed in some objective way, independent of the perpetrator's beliefs. To give men this power in the case of harassment is to perpetuate sexism from all angles.

An *objective* view of SH avoids the problems inherent in a subjective view. According to the objective view defended here, what is decisive in determining whether behavior constitutes SH is not whether the victim is bothered, but whether the behavior is an instance of a practice that expresses and perpetuates the attitude that the victim and members of her sex are inferior because of their sex. Thus the Daytona Beach case counts as a case of SH because the behavior is an instance of a practice that reflects men's domination of women in that it relegates women to the role of sex objects.[44]

The courts have to some extent tried to incorporate an objective notion of SH by invoking the "reasonable person" standard. The EEOC *Guidelines*, as shown earlier, define SH partly as behavior that "has the purpose or effect of *unreasonably* interfering with an individual's work performance. . . ."[45] [. . .]

In various cases the courts have invoked a reasonable man (or person) standard, but *not* to show that women who are not bothered still suffer harassment. Instead, they used the standard to show that even though a particular woman *was* bothered, she would have to tolerate such behavior because it was behavior a reasonable person would not have been affected by. In *Rabidue v. Osceola Refining Co.*[46] (1986), a woman complained that a coworker made obscene comments about women in general and her in particular. The court ruled that "a reasonable person would not have been significantly affected by the same or similar circumstances,"[47] and that "women must expect a certain amount of demeaning conduct in certain work environments."[48]

But the reasonable man standard will not work, since men and women perceive situations involving SH quite differently. The reasonable person standard fares no better as it becomes the reasonable man standard when it is applied by male judges seeing things through male eyes. Studies have shown that sexual overtures that men find flattering are found by women to be insulting. And even when men recognize behavior as harassment, they think women will be flattered by it.[49] The differences in perception only strengthens my point about the group harm that SH causes all women: unlike women, men can take sexual overtures directed at them to be complimentary because the overtures do not signify the stereotyping that underlies SH of women. A reasonable man standard would not succeed as a basis upon which to determine SH, as its objectivity is outweighed by the disparity found in the way the sexes assess what is "reasonable".

Related to this last topic is the issue of the harasser's intentions. In subjective definitions this is the counterpart to the victim's being bothered. Tort law makes reference to the in juror's intentions: in battery tort, the harasser's intent to contact, in assault tort, the harasser's intent to arouse psychic apprehension in the victim, and in the tort of intentional emotional distress, the harasser's intent or recklessness, must be established in order for the victim to win her case.

But like the victim's feelings, the harasser's intentions are irrelevant to whether his behavior is harassment. As I just pointed out, many men do not take their behavior to be bothersome, and sometimes even mistakenly believe that women enjoy crude compliments about their bodies, ogling, pinching, etc. From perusing cases brought before the courts, I have come to believe that many men have psychological feelings of power over women, feelings of being in control of their world, and the like, when they harass. These feelings might be subconscious, but this should not be admitted as a defense of the harasser.

Also, as I have said, many men believe women encourage SH either by their dress or language, or simply by the fact that they tolerate the abuse without protest (usually out of fear of repercussion). In light of these facts, it would be wrongheaded to allow the harasser's intentions to count in assessing harassment, though they might become relevant in determining punishment. I am arguing for an objective definition of SH: it is the attitudes embedded and reflected *in the practice* the behavior is an instance of, not the attitudes or intentions *of the perpetrator*, that makes the behavior SH.

[. . .]

V. Implications of the Objective Definition

One implication of my objective definition is that it reflects the correct way power comes into play in SH. Traditionally, SH has been taken to exist only between persons of unequal power, usually in the workplace or an educational institution. It is believed that SH in universities occurs only when a professor harasses a student, but not *vice versa*. It is said that students can cause "sexual hassle," because they cannot "destroy [the professor's] self-esteem or endanger his intellectual self-confidence," and professors "seldom suffer the complex psychological effects of sexual harassment victims."[50] MacKinnon, in her earlier book, defines SH as "the unwanted imposition of sexual requirements in the context of a relationship of unequal power."[51]

Though it is true that a lot of harassment occurs between unequals, it is false that harassment occurs *only* between unequals: equals and subordinates can harass. [. . .]

The one sense in which it is true that the harasser must have power over his victim is that men have power – social, political, and economic – over women as a group. This cannot be understood by singling out individual men and showing that they have power over women or any particular woman for that matter. It is power that all men have, in virtue of being men. Defining SH in the objective way I do allows us to see that *this* is the sense in which power exists in SH, in *all* of its forms. The benefit of not restricting SH to cases of unequal institutional power is that *all* victims are afforded protection.

A second implication of my definition is that it gives the courts a way of distinguishing SH from sexual attraction. It can be difficult to make this distinction, since "traditional courtship activities" are often quite sexist and frequently involve behavior that is harassment. The key is to examine the practice the behavior is an instance of. If the behavior reflects the attitude that the victim is inferior because of her sex, then it is SH. Sexual harassment is not about a man's attempting to date a woman who is not interested, as the courts have tended to believe; it is about domination, which might be reflected, of course, in the way a man goes about trying to get a date. My definition allows us to separate cases of SH from genuine sexual attraction by forcing the courts to focus on the social nature of SH.

Moreover, defining SH in the objective way I do shifts the burden and the blame off the victim. On the subjective view, the burden is on the victim to prove that she is bothered significantly enough to win a tort case, or under Title VII, to show that the behavior unreasonably interfered with her work. In tort law, where the perpetrator's intentions are allowed to figure in, the blame could easily shift to the victim by showing that she in some way welcomed or even encouraged the behavior thereby relinquishing the perpetrator from responsibility. By focusing on the practice the behavior is an instance of, my definition has nothing to do with proving that the victim responds a certain way to the behavior, nor does it in any way blame the victim for the behavior.

Finally, defining SH in a subjective way means that the victim herself must come forward and complain, as it is her response that must be assessed. But given that most judges, law enforcement officers, and even superiors are men, it is difficult for women to do so. They are embarrassed, afraid to confront someone of the same sex as the harasser who is likely not to see the problem. They do not feel their voices will be heard. Working with my definition will I hope assuage this. Recognizing SH as a group harm will allow women to come to each other's aid as co-complainers, thereby alleviating the problem of reticence. Even if the person the behavior is directed at does not feel bothered, other women can complain, as they suffer the group harm associated with SH.

VI. Conclusion

The definition of SH I have defended in this paper has as its main benefit that it acknowledges the group harm SH causes all women, thereby getting to the heart of what is wrong with SH. By doing so, it protects all victims in all cases from even the most subtle kinds of SH, since all cases of SH have in common group harm.

[. . .]

Notes

1 RosemarieTong, "Sexual Harassment," in *Women and Values*, Marilyn Pearsall, ed. (Belmont, CA: Wadsworth Publishing Company, 1986), pp. 148–166. Tong cites a *Redbook* study that reported 88 percent of 9,000 readers sampled experienced some sort of sexual harassment (p. 149).

2 Civil Rights Act of 1964, 42 U.S.C Sec. 2000e-2(a) (1982).

3 Catharine A. MacKinnon, *Sexual Harassment of Working Women: A Case of Sex Discrimination* (New Haven: Yale University Press, 1979).

4 EEOC *Guidelines on Discrimination Because of Sex*, 29 C.F.R. Sec. 1604.11(a) (1980).

5 The case was a landmark case because it established (1) federal legislation that SH is a form of sex discrimination, (2) that just because the victim "voluntarily" submitted to advances from her employer, it did not mean she welcomed the conduct, (3) that victims could appeal on grounds of emotional harm, not merely economic harm. For an excellent discussion of the history of the case as it went through the courts, see Joel T. Andreesen, "Employment Discrimination—The Expansion in Scope of Title VII to Include Sexual Harassment as a Form of Sex Discrimination: *Meritor Savings Bank, FSB v. Vinson, The Journal of Corporation Law*, Vol. 12, No. 3 (Spring, 1987), pp. 619–638.

6 *Meritor Sowings Bank, FSB v. Vinson*, 477 U.S. 57 (1986).

7 Joyce L. Richard, "Sexual Harassment and Employer Liability," *Southern University Law Review*, Vol. 12 (1986), pp. 251–279. See pp. 272–275 for an excellent discussion of the case.

8 Title IX of the Education Amendments of 1972, 20 U.S.C. Sec. 1681 (1982).

9 For a very good discussion of the case law regarding Title IX, see Walter B. Connolly, Jr., and Alison B. Marshall, "Sexual Harassment of University or College Students by Faculty Members," *The Journal of College and University Law*, Vol. 15 (Spring, 1989), pp. 381–403.

10 *Black's Law Dictionary*, 6th edn. (St. Paul, MN: West Publishing Co., 1990), p. 1248.

11 Michael D. Vhay, "The Harms of Asking: Towards a Comprehensive Treatment of Sexual Harassment," *The University of Chicago Law Review*, Vol. 55 (Winter, 1988), p. 334.

In the case of students, *quid pro quo* harassment can take the form of a professor threatening the student with a lower grade if she does not comply with his demands.

12 Ellen Frankel Paul, "Sexual Harassment as Sex Discrimination: A Defective Paradigm," *Yale Law & Policy Review*, Vol. 8, No. 2 (1990), p. 341.

13 EEOC *Guidelines, Op.cit.*, at Sec. 1604.11(a).

14 EEOC *Guidelines*, 29 C.F.R., Sec. 1604.11(b) (1985).

15 Mari J. Matsuda, "Public Response to Racist Speech: Considering the Victim's Story," *Michigan Low Review*, Vol. 87, No. 8 (August, 1989), pp. 2320–2381.

16 *Ibid.*, pp. 2345, 2344.

17 *Ibid.*, p. 2345.

18 *Ibid.*, p. 2346.

19 *Ibid.*, p. 2348.

20 This suggests that only men can sexually harass women. I will defend this view later in the paper.

21 Frances Conley, a 50-year-old distinguished neurophysician at Stanford University, recently came forward with this story. Conley resigned after years of putting up with sexual harassment from her colleagues. Not only did they use Playboy spreads during their lectures, but they routinely called her 'hon,' invited her to bed, and fondled her legs under the operating table. *Chicago Tribune*, Sunday, June 9, 1991, Section 1, p. 22.

22 Hughes and May, *Op.cit.*, pp. 264–265.

23 *Ibid.*, p. 265.

24 These same myths surround the issue of rape. This is discussed fruitfully by Lois Pineau in "Date Rape: A Feminist Analysis," *Law and Philosophy*, Vol. 8 (1989), pp. 217–243.

25 MacKinnon, *Op.Cit.*, p. 152, is where she cites the study.

26 *Lipsett v. Rive-Mora*, 669 F.Supp. 1188 (D. Puerto Rico 1987).

27 Dawn D. Bennett-Alexander, "Hostile Environment Sexual Harassment: A Clearer View," *Labor Law Journal*, Vol. 42, No. 3 (March, 1991), p. 135.

28 Lipsett, *Ibid.*, Sec. 15.

29 *Swentek v. US Air*, 830 F.2d 552 (4th Cir. 1987).

30 *Swenlek v. US Air, Ibid.*, 44 EPd at 552.

31 This harm is similar to the harm Ann Cudd finds with rape. Since women are the victims of rape, "they come to be seen as in need of protection, as weak and passive, and available to all men." See Ann E. Cudd, "Enforced Pregnancy, Rape, and the Image of Woman," *Philosophical Studies*, Vol. 60 (1990), pp. 47–59.

32 *Black's Law Dictionary, Op.* Cit., p. 717.

33 *American Heritage Dictionary of the English Language* (New York: American Heritage Publishing Co., Inc., 1973), p. 600.

34 EEOC *Guidelines, Op.cit.*, Sec. 1604.11(a).

35 Hughes and May, *Op.cit.*, p. 250.

36 Tong, *Women, Sex, and the Law, Op.cit.* p. 67.

37 *Meritor, Op.cit.*, at 1113–16.

38 MacKinnon, *Op.cit.*, p. 63.

39 Stephanie Riger, "Gender Dilemmas in Sexual Harassment Policies and Procedures," *American Psychologist*, Vol. 46 (1991), pp. 497–505,

40 Martha Sperry, "Hostile Environment Sexual Harassment and the Imposition of Liability Without Notice: A Progressive Approach to Traditional Gender Roles and Power Based Relationships," *New England Law Review*, Vol. 24 (1980), p. 942, fns. 174 & 175.

41 See Catharine MacKinnon, *Feminism Unmodified: Discourses on life and Law* (Cambridge: Harvard University Press, 1987), Chapter Nine, for a nice discussion of the challenges women face in deciding whether

to report harassment. See also Ellen Frankel Paul, *Op.cit.*, for an excellent summary of the case law on sexual harassment.

42 MacKinnon, *Sexual Harassment of Working Women*, *Op.cit.*, p. 83.

43 See Frankel Paul, *Op.cit.*, pp. 335–365. Frankel Paul wants to get away from the "helpless victim syndrome," making women responsible for reporting harassment, and placing the burden on them to develop a tough skin so as to avoid being seen as helpless victims (pp. 362–363). On the contrary, what Frankel Paul fails to understand is that placing these additional burdens on women *detracts* from the truth that they *are* victims, and implies that they deserve the treatment if they do not develop a "tough attitude."

44 This case exemplifies my point that the behavior need not be persistent in order to constitute harassment, despite the view of many courts. One catcall, for example, will constitute SH if catcalling is shown to be a practice reflecting domination.

45 EEOC Guidelines, *Op.cit.*, Sec. 1604.11(a), my emphasis.

46 *Rdbidue v. Osceola Refining Co.*, 805 F2d (1986), Sixth Circuit Court.

47 *Ibid.*, at 622.

48 *Ibid.*, at 620–622.

49 Stephanie Riger, "Gender Dilemmas in Sexual Harassment Policies and Procedures," *American Psychologist*, Vol. 46, No. 5 (May, 1991), p. 499 is where she cites the relevant studies.

50 Wright Dsdech and Weiner, *Opxit.*, p. 24.

51 MacKinnon, *Sexual Harassment of Working Women*, *Op.cit.*, p. 1. It is actually not clear that MacKinnon endorses this definition throughout this book, as what she says seems to suggest that harassment can occur at least between equals. In her most recent book, she recognizes that harassment "also happens among coworkers, from third parties, even by subordinates in the workplace, men who are women's hierarchical inferiors or peers." Catharine A, MacKinnnon, *Feminism Unmodified: Discourses on Life and Law* (Cambridge: Harvard University Press, 1987), p. 107.

3

Lost Innocence

Laurence Thomas

Summary

Argues that sexual harassment should not be defined objectively as requiring specific "harassing speech" (which is notoriously difficult to catalog) and that not all behavior that a woman finds offensive is in fact sexual harassment. Whether or not behavior is considered sexual harassment should depend in part on the intentions and motivations of those engaging in the behavior – a subjectivist approach. While certain language or actions may always be sexually harassing, the same behavior and speech from two different men with different intentions and understandings of the situation may count as sexual harassment from one but not the other. Part of what causes the over-attribution of sexual harassment is "oppression anxiety," in which members of an historically victimized group preemptively interpret most behavior as harassing or discriminatory.

Original publication details: Laurence Thomas, "Lost Innocence," pp. 91–98 from *Stanford Law and Policy Review* 5 (1994). Reproduced with permission of Stanford University.

Sexual Ethics: An Anthology, First Edition. Edited by Patrick D. Hopkins.

We live in an age of lost innocence. To be sure, the world has never been perfect. All the same, there was a time in the workplace when not every offense that a person might came another was seen as flowing from a corrupt and reprehensible character. Indeed, it used to be allowed that a person could in fact be unaware of having caused offense. Or perhaps better: it used to be allowed that a person acted with good will, although the action itself was inappropriate, perhaps even harmful.[1] Not so any more. The prevailing mood seems to be that if a person feels offended or threatened by what another individual has done, then it is as if that individual had willfully set out to offend or threaten. Not only that, the person's objectionable act proceeds from a corresponding corrupt character, it being disallowed that the individual could have offended with non-reprehensible intentions and motives.[2] The utter unwillingness to allow for this possibility is what I mean by lost innocence.

To focus specifically upon men harassing women: is the assumption of lost innocence in the workplace warranted in the interaction between women and men with respect to sexual harassment? When one considers the extent to which men have exploited and sexually harassed women, invaded the personal space of women and referred to them in degrading ways, all in the name of having a little "innocent" fun, and the extent to which men have displayed brazen insensitivity to the feelings of women, it would seem that the answer to this question can be nothing but a resounding "yes."

I would like to challenge the assumption of lost innocence, not because I want to diminish the wrong of sexual harassment, but because I believe that any attempt to assess human behavior independent of motives and character is misguided. Sexual harassment is offensive, but the converse is false. Not all male behavior that a woman finds offensive is rightly construed as sexual harassment. The analogous point holds for any form of "X-ism" (racism, anti-semitism, and so on). Current discussions of sexual [. . .] harassment seem to run roughshod over this truth, as illustrated by the examples offered in the section which follows.[3] What is more, there is the phenomenon of oppression anxiety. This is when prudence makes being wary and suspicious of a person's beliefs and motives a natural way of life, because of the history of oppression of the group to which that person belongs. I develop this point later in the essay.

Throughout this essay, I shall focus upon communication, because it is relatively clear nowadays that, among adults, bodily contact without consent is inappropriate behavior that would constitute sexual harassment, in whatever context such contact might occur, but especially in the workplace.

As a final introductory remark, it should be mentioned that although it is highly unlikely that in the examples which I offer the male could be held legally accountable for his actions, I am interested in the moral climate that prevails among individuals working together. The moral climate of a workplace or institution pertains not just to the letter of the law, but the spirit as well, regarding what is and is not appropriate behavior. There can be substantial differences in policy renderings of the spirit of the law.[4] Thus, whether or not a charge would hold up in the courts, a woman can feel that she has been sexually harassed, and others may share her conviction. Feelings in this regard are not independent of the moral climate in which things occur, with some being far more protective of women than others.[5] I want to shed some light on the issue of where the baseline should be drawn in terms of how we think about sexual harassment.

The Mary and John Scenario

Suppose John tells Mary, a colleague, that she is wearing an absolutely lovely outfit. Wanting desperately to fit in, Mary smiles demurely and says nothing. However, Mary is a person who feels extremely uncomfortable when complimented on her attire by a man. For good reason, Mary considers it nearly axiomatic that a man who compliments a woman on her attire is up to no good. Not knowing that, the next time John sees Mary in an outfit that he considers lovely, he again remarks that she is wearing a lovely outfit. Is John guilty of sexually harassing Mary?

Despite the fact that John would almost certainly not be legally liable for sexual harassment under *Meritor v. Vinson* and the recent *Harris v. Forklift Systems* decision,[6] this does not, as I indicated in my introductory remarks, mean that society does not view John as a harrasor; nor does it mean that there are not serious consequences for John in being labeled such. After all, a charge of sexual harassment that is eventually dropped or thrown out can still do serious damage to a person's reputation.

Consider, for example, Syracuse University's definition of sexual harassment:

Any unwelcome conduct of a sexual nature, on or off campus, that relates to the gender or sexual identity of an individual or group, and that has the purpose or effect of creating an intimidating or hostile environment for work or study.[7]

Since John's remarks make Mary feel uncomfortable, under this policy they create a hostile work environment.

Assume that if a man had worn a suit to work that John judged to be particularly sharp-looking, John would not have complimented him. John's complimenting behavior may then be said to be gender-related. Under the Syracuse definition, then, John is guilty of sexual harassment.

But surely that is too swift. For suppose that John believes Mary has exquisite taste in professional style, and that he had no more than that in mind when he complimented her. Furthermore, he naturally assumed that she would interpret his compliment in just that way, since it was plain that she was not wearing sexually appealing attire to begin with. Indeed, nothing was more obvious than that she was wearing what some would consider to be a woman's version of a man's suit. In any case, had Mary indicated her discomfort in any way, John would have respected her wishes and apologized profusely for having caused her such discomfort. Besides, John does not believe that it is somehow "natural" for a woman to enjoy a compliment from a man. True, John would not have complimented a man who was exquisitely attired, and this may reflect poorly upon John. But how does this differential turn his complimenting Mary into an intentional offense directed at her?

Yet John's behavior either fully satisfies Syracuse University's definition of sexual harassment, or comes dangerously close to doing so. This is precisely because we have a hostile environment generated through gender-linked behavior. But as shown by the Mary-John example, it is possible for a male to unwittingly create such an environment although his motivations are not in the least salacious. A male who causes a woman sincere discomfort in the workplace is not necessarily a male who intended to cause discomfort. Recall that had Mary given John any indication of her discomfort, he would have sincerely apologized and that would have been the end of such [. . .] behavior on his part toward her.

It may be that no court of law in the United States would deem John guilty of sexual harassment if, at Syracuse University, he were brought up on such charges and took the matter to court. But the lack of legal ramifications does not diminish the potential consequences of the university policy.

The Bombastic Macho Male Vs. The Timorous Heterosexual Male

To illustrate further, I would like to offer two crass models of men: Bombastic Macho Male (BMM) and Timorous Heterosexual Male (THM). Both wrestle with their male identities and see having sex with women as an inextricable part of their male identities; accordingly, each is alert to opportunities that present themselves. The difference, however, is in how each conceives of his initial interaction with a woman. BMM supposes that a brazen display of sexual interest, however crude, reveals his manliness and helps to insure his success with a woman. He is often oblivious to how he actually comes across to women, and he has great difficulty understanding why any woman would bristle at being called "a sweet little thing." BMM is insecure and compensates for his insecurity in this bombastic macho manner.

Then there is Timorous Heterosexual Male (THM). He finds BMMs to be about as offensive as women generally do. THM would not dream of expressing his attraction to a woman unless he first noticed that she found him to be sexually attractive. Even then, his remarks are not brazen in any way for he, himself, has never liked being pressured by others. Thus, he is especially careful not to pressure others. In fact, women have been known to get a little frustrated with THM, wondering if he is ever going to pick up on the avalanche of signs that they have left him. Let me be clear: I do not claim that THMs never overstep their bounds. What I do claim is that the motivational structure of THMs differs radically from that of BMMs. Specifically, the motivational structure of the former when it comes to interacting with women is not morally obnoxious.

Most men fall between these two extremes. Importantly, not all men are BMMs. Therefore, it is wrong to treat all men as if they are BMMs or BMMs in-waiting. Morally obnoxious motives are characteristic of the Bombastic Macho Male's behavior towards women. In this regard, he may be incorrigible, and the objective of sexual harassment policies is simply to get him to keep his thoughts, and most certainly his hands, to himself. Nothing short of the arm of the law will suffice.

My fear, however, is that most analyses of sexual harassment assume that all men have the motivational structure associated with the model of the Bombastic Macho Male. But some men, like the Timorous Heterosexual Male, are not like that. The very point of distinguishing between the Bombastic Macho Male and the Timorous Heterosexual Male is to show that all males cannot be assumed to have obnoxious moral motives when it comes to interacting with women. To treat a THM as if he were a BMM is to do the THM an injustice. And to suppose it is justifiable to treat all men as though they belong to the class of men who are particularly obnoxious solely because one finds their words offensive or discomforting is to commit the moral error of reckless disregard.

In this regard, I am reminded of the story once told to me of a man in Australia who strongly disliked a woman and who went on to hit her after a series of very nasty disagreements. She brought him up on charges of sexual harassment rather than assault and battery, since she could make more headway with the former charge. The man's response was that he had been utterly aggravated by her, and that his hitting her could not have been more unrelated to any sexual interest in her on his part or the desire to remind her that she was a woman and he a man. Any view that turns an intense personal dislike into some form of X-ism – be it sexism, anti-semitism or racism – is, thereby, morally suspect. Dislike across various social categories can very well have nothing whatsoever to do with the social category differences.[8] To deny this possibility is an instance of reckless disregard.

A question that naturally arises then is this: To what extent must women (or for that matter members of any historically oppressed group) share the responsibility for diffusing a potentially uncomfortable work environment? I shall offer and develop only one answer.

Oppression Anxiety

With any group that has been the victim of systematic [. . .] oppression, the members of the group will, in general, experience oppression anxiety. There will be the mistreatment (be it verbal or physical) that one can regularly anticipate, and one must somehow manage not to let that very anticipation take too great a toll. And there will be the mistreatment that one must endure from those whom one had hoped would be different, but turn out not to be. Accordingly, prudence makes being suspicious and weary of the other a natural way of life. Finally, though one could go on at considerable length in this vein, there is the weariness that comes from trying to maintain one's integrity in a world that insists on compromising a person, where prudence and integrity seem to be on a collision course most of the time. It will not always be obvious whether one has compromised one's integrity or whether, for the moment, one is simply too bruised to put up a fight. And to add insult to injury, one must often contend with the internalization of the oppression by members of one's own group.[9] This multiplicity of concerns makes being anxiety-ridden a natural way of life for the oppressed.

One of the most important things an oppressed group can do as it becomes empowered, and social attitudes change for the better, is to bear in mind the difference between oppressive behavior and oppression anxiety. Not surprisingly, and quite understandably, oppression anxiety can manifest itself even in contexts where oppressive behavior is absent.[10]

Returning to the Mary and John scenario will be helpful. Recall that John complimented Mary on her outfit, and that this can be seen as gender-related, since he would not have complimented a man on his outfit. It goes without saying that, owing to the prevalence of sexism, women have had to endure lascivious comments from men. So, women are rightly on their guard when it comes to being complimented by men. A lascivious comment is certainly out of order in the workplace.

Now, while it may be that a concern to avoid even the appearance of sexual harassment is a reason why men should avoid complimenting a female colleague on her outfit, there is nonetheless the separate question of whether the compliment is lascivious. Presumably, what the woman is wearing is quite relevant to how "that is a lovely outfit" should be taken. If she is wearing loose-fitting jeans, a baggy discolored blouse, and tennis shoes, then "that is a lovely outfit" is just a bit of sarcastic humor.

Suppose for a moment, however, that Mary is wearing – and she has every right to wear – a low-cut blouse, a very short skirt, and spiked heels. In this case, there is a strong presumption that John's compliment is laced with sexual innuendo. The issue here is not whether Mary has a right to dress in that manner without being sexually harassed by John. As I have just indicated, there can be no question but that she has every right to do so; rather, the issue is what is the reasonable interpretation to put on John's remark, "that is a lovely outfit." Depending upon what she is wearing, some interpretations are more reasonable than others.

On the other hand, suppose that Mary is wearing a full-length pleated skirt, with matching jacket, and a blouse buttoned up to the neck – for I did remark at the beginning that she was attired in an exquisite business outfit. In this case, there is a very good chance that John's compliment "that is a lovely outfit" is about just that – Mary's outfit. It is in instances such as this that it is important to bear in mind the reality of oppression anxiety. At least part of the meaning of remarks is given by the social context in which they are uttered, which includes the attire of the person to whom the remarks are addressed. It is probably inappropriate for any man to tell a nun wearing a full flowing habit – but in maroon, instead of the customary black – that she has on a lovely outfit. All the same, it is quite unlikely, indeed, that such a remark would have any salacious sentiment behind it. And this the nun should recognize, though she might rightly call attention to the inappropriateness of his remark. The situation is much the same when John compliments Mary in her full-length pleated skirt.

[. . .]

I cannot emphasize too much that the point being made in this section applies to all historical victims of oppression. Time was when a black in America could just assume that racism was behind a white's assessment that her or his work was below the desired standards. This is not true nowadays, although in race relations America [. . .] remains quite the imperfect society. But any given situation may be fraught with ambiguity. Oppression anxiety may readily lead a hard working black, who is disappointed with an assessment of his or her work, to conclude that the assessment was fueled by racism. In some instances, this conclusion will surely be false, given the assumption that society has made some progress towards the goal of racial equality. It may turn out that if the black had attended to other factors, as opposed to merely focusing upon the negative assessment, it would have been evident enough that the assumption of racism was implausible.

In the march towards equality, the situation of women is exactly parallel. In the Mary and John scenario, Mary could let oppression anxiety carry the day and focus upon just the fact that John complimented her; and if she does, then his remarks will seem on a par with the salacious comments that women in the workplace have endured in times past, even though she is wearing a full-length pleated skirt rather than a low-cut blouse and a short skirt. On the other hand, if she also attends to both John's words "that is a lovely outfit" and the fact of her attire, then she might have considerably less reason to suppose that John meant anything untoward by his remark. As I told the story of Mary, it is nearly axiomatic that any man complimenting a woman on her attire is up to no good. In race matters, the analog would be that any behavior on the part of a white towards a minority is racist, including helping behavior since that can be paternalistic. Such axioms pretty much insure that the other is in a no-win situation in terms of having wronged the individual in question. Such is the case with oppression anxiety.

[. . .]

The "Fighting Words" Doctrine Revisited in the Hostile Environment Context

At this juncture, a look at the fighting words doctrine would be instructive. As originally set out by the New Hampshire Supreme Court:

The test is what men of common intelligence would understand what would be words likely to cause an average addressee to fight. . . . The English language has a number of words and expressions which by general consent are "fighting words" when said without a disarming smile. . . . Such words, as ordinary men know, are likely to cause a fight. . . . The statute, as construed, does no more than prohibit the face-to-face words plainly likely to cause a breach of the peace by the addressee.[11]

The Supreme Court affirmed the New Hampshire decision in *Chaplinsky v. New Hampshire*.[12] The Court did not deny that one could offend and provoke a person to fight in extremely subtle ways, but rather pointed out that some words could be deemed highly offensive and provoking to any person to whom they were directly addressed. What is more, the Court held that any person could plainly recognize what such words were, which in effect was to say that there could be no excuse for their utterance. Neither a plea of ignorance nor lack of intent was admissible. For it was as if a person had the intent, since it was plain to any speaker what effect the utterance of such words would have upon the listener. The Court drew a distinction; it did not obliterate one. The Court's position, of course, presupposes cultural familiarity and psychological competence. A citizen of England, with no first-hand cultural experience in America, could not be expected to know just what words count as "fighting words" in America, and would not, in the first instance, at least, be held accountable for using them.[13] Nor would a psychologically incompetent person be held accountable for using "fighting words." Any analysis of sexual harassment should take a cue from the reasoning [. . .] behind this doctrine.

Without a doubt, there are "sexual harassment words."[14] In uttering them to a woman colleague, a man straightforwardly engages in inappropriate behavior toward the woman and creates a hostile work environment. More to the point, a man knows or should have known that his behavior is inappropriate. Indeed, even when such utterances were considered permissible, no one denied that they were used to pressure women. There is, therefore, an exceedingly strong presumption that a man acts with objectionable motives when he utters "sexual harassment words" directly to a woman.

Unlike "fighting words," a disarming smile, far from diminishing the force of "sexual harassment words," serves only to seal their horrific offensiveness in the mind of the listener.

I want to emphasize that just as the doctrine of "fighting words" assumes a morally obnoxious motive on the part of the speaker, the idea of "sexual harassment words" assumes a similar morally obnoxious motive on the part of the utterer. That is, the victim's anger and discomfort stem in large measure, if not entirely, from the fact that the speaker is presumed to have spoken with a morally obnoxious motive, and not simply from the fact that the words were spoken. The motives are not secondary to the words being offensive. Thus, any attempt to understand "sexual harassment words" independent of motives is misguided, and any policy or remedy that does so makes an egregious error. Naturally, there is also the issue of being threatened. But this observation only strengthens the point being made, for a threat from a person presupposes a malicious moral motive. A threat is not just a matter of being made worse off.

So, if any man, including the THM referred to earlier, should utter a string of "sexual harassment words," he should be made to feel the full brunt of the law, as with any BMM, for it is agreed that no reasonable speaker can directly utter such words to a woman without realizing the impact that they will have upon her. Hence, when any man utters such words to a woman his motives are presumed to be morally obnoxious. But not all words carry this presumption, though a woman might find them offensive or otherwise experience discomfort over them.

While an offense-free work environment for both women and men would no doubt be ideal, sexual harassment is not about eliminating any and every offense against a woman that might occur. More precisely, while sexual harassment is indeed offensive, not everything that is offensive to a woman or which causes her discomfort is an instance of sexual harassment.

Objections to the Idea of "Sexual Harassment Words"

There are two obvious, perhaps related, objections to my argument. The first is that any list of "sexual harassment words" will fail to be exhaustive, if only because language constantly evolves. The second objection is that a man may engage in sexual harassment without using "sexual harassment words."

The first objection is easily met, as the case of racial harassment shows. Imagine someone arguing that there are no obvious racial slurs against minorities since language is fluid, and what is a racial slur today may not be that tomorrow. Thirty-five years ago, calling a Negro "black" was highly offensive. Today, calling a black a "Negro" can be offensive, although not to the same degree. Tomorrow, "black" may be offensive as "African-American" gains ascendancy.[15] Clearly, the fluidity of language has not been a bar to recognizing racial slurs against blacks. Nor has it diminished the importance of identifying at least some of the words that a minority group generally regards as racial slurs during a given time period. Likewise, the fact that a list of "sexual harassment words" cannot be exhaustive should not prevent us from recognizing some or most of the words that, at any given time, women find most offensive and threatening.

As to the second objection, I have hardly denied that a man may engage in the most egregious displays of verbal sexual harassment without using "sexual harassment words." Suppose, for example, that an employee installs cameras in the women's rest room. One can lynch a black without calling her or him "nigger." This hardly makes it any less meaningful to recognize "nigger" as a very offensive racial slur. So, the fact that there can be sexual harassment without "sexual harassment words" hardly obliterates the need to distinguish between "sexual harassment words" and words that fall outside this category, just as the fact that one may offend mightily without using "fighting words" does not show that "fighting words" do not exist. However, that verbal sexual harassment can occur without the use of "sexual harassment words" is [. . .] hardly a reason to hold a man guilty of sexual harassment whenever a woman finds his gender-linked words to be offensive or discomforting.

Conclusion

Social interaction is rich and complex. In truth, progress towards equality makes it so, precisely because social interaction across changing diversity is necessarily fraught with ambiguity and a mixture of feelings. Not least among these is what I have called oppression anxiety. It is tempting to think that in a diverse world, nothing matters more than that persons behave towards one another just as they should. In the long run, what matters even more is that good will is the basis for such behavior. For good will is the social lubricant without which social interaction between people disintegrates, as hostility increasingly becomes the order of the day. Equality without good will is fragile, indeed. After all, the law itself is only as good as the character of those who interpret and enforce it. But no workplace can be as efficient and as amiable as it should be without good will.

Of course, good will is compatible with a wealth of mistakes and a considerable amount of lethargy. There is nothing like the long arm of the law to galvanize people (without resorting to violence), and to rid them of their moral laziness. I am very much in favor of the law serving that purpose. But the point of this essay is simply

that a certain moral shortsightedness is to be avoided. In the name of insuring that historically oppressed peoples receive their due, we must not as a general strategy assume away the good will that, in the end, is needed if the equality desperately sought after is to survive. For that strategy may prove to be prophetic in that we will not have to assume any more: good will be gone, and so too will be innocence. And when these things are truly gone, or at any rate, sufficiently diminished, equality will be no more.

[. . .]

Notes

1   Katie Roiphe uses the expression "lost innocence" to contrast today's teenagers, whose exposure to sexual matters is in overdrive, with teenagers of an earlier time, who were literally naive about much. Date Rape's Other Victim, *N. Y. TIMES*, June 13, 1993, at 26. She then suggests that much of the talk about date rape is more than a little disingenuous, since today's teenage female cannot plead the sort of ignorance that a teenage female of only two generations ago could plead. Although I think that Roiphe overstates her case, I am not here concerned to argue the matter.

   By lost innocence, I am inspired by Immanuel Kant's idea of a good will, where it is allowed that a person could have good intentions even if his actions fall short of the mark. *See* Immanuel Kant, *The Groundwork of the Metaphysic of Morals* 61–5 (H. J. Paton trans., 1964).

2   Kant held that nothing is good without qualification except a good will. Kant did not suppose that actions were irrelevant in determining whether or not a person had good will. Indeed, on the assumption that the world is such that we can generally succeed in doing the things that are within our power to do, systematic behavior on a person's part is quite revealing. Kant had the perspicacity to see, however, the importance of having some logical space between a person's good will and her or his actions. For sometimes nothing could be more obvious than that a person had the best of intentions and that things went awry in ways that were quite beyond the individual's control. On Kant's view, surely the good will with which the person acted counts for a great deal. *Id.*

3   Nowhere is this more evident than with sexual harassment policies across college campuses. Of course, these sexual harassment policies rightly make for much needed empowerment on the part of women. The issue, though, is whether these policies come with undesirable costs that were perhaps unforeseen.

4   The Supreme Court has recognized two forms of sexual harassment: quid pro quo, which is the conditioning of employment benefits on sexual favors, and hostile environment, which is harassment that, whether or not affecting

economic benefits, creates a hostile or offensive working environment. Meritor v. Vinson. 477 U.S. 57 (1986). This paper deals only with sexual harassment stemming from a hostile environment.

5   *See* Joni Balter, Feminists Can Still Flirt at UW, *Seattle Times*, Nov. 11, 1993, at Bl. (Although University of Washington women still regard equality as important, they do not see themselves as needing the kind of campus regulations that Ohio's Antioch College has).

6   Harris v. Forklift Systems, Inc., 114 S.Ct. 367 (1993), defines a sexually harassing environment as one which "is permeated with 'discriminatory intimidation, ridicule, and insult,' that is 'sufficiently severe or pervasive to alter the conditions of the victim's employment and create an abusive working environment.'" *Id.*, at 370 (*quoting Meritor*, 477 U.S. at 64, 67).

7   This policy was adopted by the Syracuse University Faculty Senate on November 15, 1993, but has not yet been published.

8   For an account of the notion of social category, *see* Laurence Thomas, Moral Deference, *The Philosophical Forum* 24 (1992–93), where I introduced both this and the notion of social configuration.

9   *See id*

10   As I have made clear, some members of every oppressed group suffer from oppression anxiety. A white student applying to graduate school once asked me whether a letter of recommendation from me would be taken seriously by other members of my profession. For just a fleeting moment, I heard this as "Are you, a black man, competent to assess the philosophical abilities of me, a white student?" when, in fact, the student was asking a quite different question: "Is your profession still sufficiently racist that a letter from you, whose judgment I enormously value, would not be taken seriously?" Had I allowed oppression anxiety to run its course, I would never have heard the latter question. Ironically, the latter question proved to be quite painful in its own right, as I could not offer a resounding "No." Not only that, I have since put that

student's question to various well-placed members of my profession, only to find that no one could muster a resounding "No." A non-racist white student in a racist society could make just the distinction that this student made, and doing so would be very much to her or his credit. Alas, a black suffering from oppression anxiety might fail to see that this distinction was being drawn.

11   State v. Chaplinsky, 18 A.2d 754, 762 (N.H. 1941), *aff'd* 315 U.S. 568 (1942). This doctrine is now judged to be rather quaint. One reason might be that there can be no excuse for engaging in physical combat over provocative words. Another might be that it has become far less plain which words have this status. I suggest that the quaintness of the doctrine is owing more to the first than the latter. Time was when it was perfectly acceptable for men to challenge one another to a duel when their dignity had been insulted, but not any longer. What has changed, though, is not the sense that vastly provocative words can be recognized, but the method for settling the insult of being an object of such words.

12   315 U.S. 568 (1942).

13   In England, the everyday usage of "lovely" pretty much corresponds to the everyday use of "great" in America. Americans visiting England discover soon enough that their actions are not as pleasing to the English as they might have initially supposed. And what American has not been amused, perhaps even utterly astonished, at an English chamber maid's request: "What time shall I knock you up?" – merely a request for the time that one would like to be awakened!

14   The following are examples of sexual harassment words. They are said to one who is a mere acquaintance with whom there is no bond, history, or pattern of acceptable and informed banter: 1) "you look good, sweetie"; 2) "that is a very sexy outfit"; or 3) "you have a really great body." A woman's comment to a man would generally be more overtly offensive, such as "you look like you'd be great at oral sex."

15   My own view is that this usage reflects an extraordinarily homogeneous attitude on the part of black Americans toward Africa, the second largest continent – not country – in the world. Sameness of color has been no bar to recognizing a multitude of differences among whites in the smaller continent of Europe – differences over which whites themselves have shed considerable blood. Thus, under what line of reasoning does it turn out that all African peoples turn out to be less diverse than all other peoples? The issue is not about American blacks identifying with the continent of Africa, but how that with which they identify is characterized.

4

Equal Employment Opportunity Commission v. Domino's Pizza, Inc.

United States District Court (M.D. Florida, Tampa Division)

Summary

The US District Court (Middle District of Florida, Tampa Division) ruled in favor of the plaintiff in the first federal case concerning the sexual harassment of a man by a woman. The court argued that a prima facie case of hostile environment sexual harassment requires that the employee belongs to a protected group, was subject to unwelcome sexual harassment, that the harassment was based on sex and was severe enough to create an abusive work environment, and that the employer was liable. All requirements were met in the case. The fact that the victim was male is irrelevant. For purposes of sexual discrimination law, belonging to a "protected group" simply requires that the employee be a man or a woman.

Original publication details: *Equal Employment Opportunity Commission v. Domino's Pizza*, Inc. 909 F. Supp. 1529 United States District Court (M.D. Florida, Tampa Division) (1995). Public Domain.

Sexual Ethics: An Anthology, First Edition. Edited by Patrick D. Hopkins.
© 2023 John Wiley & Sons, Inc. Published 2023 by John Wiley & Sons, Inc.

[. . .]

EQUAL EMPLOYMENT OPPORTUNITY COMMISSION, Plaintiff,
and
David Papa, Intervenor/Plaintiff,
v.
DOMINO'S PIZZA, INC., Defendant.
No. 91–1020–CIV–T–25(A).
Nov. 17, 1995.

Equal Employment Opportunity Commission initiated case against employer for sexual harassment in violation of Title VII. The District Court, Adams, J., held that: (1) female supervisor subjected male subordinate to hostile work environment and quid pro quo sexual harassment; (2) employer was directly liable for supervisor's actions; (3) employee was entitled to back pay; but (4) employee was not entitled to front pay or reinstatement.

[. . .]

Order

ADAMS, District Judge.

This cause was heard by the Court on November 14–17, 1994. Plaintiff ("EEOC") and Intervenor/Plaintiff ("Papa") claim that Defendant ("Domino's") violated Title VII by subjecting Papa to a sexually hostile work environment, engaging in *quid pro quo* harassment, and retaliating against him for lawful actions. Pursuant to the evidence presented at trial, the Court makes the following findings:

*1533 I. Findings of Fact

1. This is an action under §§ 703(a)(1) and 704 of Title VII of the Civil Rights Act of 1964, as amended. This action was filed by Plaintiff, Equal Employment Opportunity Commission ("EEOC") pursuant to § 706(f)(3) of Title VII, 42 U.S.C. S 2000e–5(f)(3). [. . .]
2. David Papa ("Papa") is intervenor/plaintiff herein. Papa was the store manager of the Defendant's Port Richey store in January, 1988.
3. Defendant Domino's Pizza, Inc. (Domino's) employed Papa and is an employer within the meaning of Title VII, 42 U.S.C. § 2000e(b).
4. Beth Carrier ("Carrier") was Papa's immediate supervisor and Defendant's Corporate Area Supervisor. Papa's performance under Carrier was more than satisfactory. In fact, Papa had been promoted at least twice while under her supervision. Just prior to the termination complained of herein, Carrier had nominated Papa as "Manager of the Year."
5. At various times, from January 1988 until May 1988, the following occurred between Carrier and Papa:
   a. Carrier would come into the store and place her hand on Papa and would rub his neck and back.
   b. While standing besides him, Carrier would put her hand around Papa's waist.
   c. At a business meeting at Carrier's residence, Carrier told Papa that he had a "nice ass" and that he shouldn't bend over as he did because it "turns me on."
   d. Carrier told Papa that he had a "nice ass" on one other occasion when the two of them were distributing coupons to local residences.
   e. Carrier stated. "I know you are having trouble with your wife, but you are separated now and would be interested in starting a relationship again."
   f. Carrier told Papa that she loved him and cared about him.
   g. Carrier told Papa that she would never treat him like his estranged wife did and told him "just think Dave, you could become a supervisor and I could stay home and take care of David [Papa's young son]."
   h. On one occasion, Carrier was standing next to Papa in the store and put her arm on his back while talking to him; when he moved away, Carrier moved close, put her arm around his back again, and "reached down with her hand and she grabbed my behind and squeezed it."
   i. On one occasion, Carrier was in the store helping to make pizza when she told him that her bra had slipped off and asked if that turned him on.
   j. In April or May, Carrier came to his store and said, "You know how I feel about you. I care about you, and you and David are more than welcome to come live with me. . . . you know I love you." Papa ordered her from his office and threatened to report the conduct to her supervisor. Upon leaving the store, Carrier told Papa that she would "get him."
6. Papa claims that Carrier's sexual advances embarrassed him and made him feel uncomfortable. His testimony was corroborated by employees who observed several of the incidents described above. There is no evidence that he provoked or encouraged Carrier's sexual overtures.

7. Approximately six days after the incident described in paragraph 5(j) Carrier and Mike Haskins, Carrier's supervisor, came to the store and fired Papa.

8. The reason for termination proffered by Carrier and Haskins at the time they fired Papa, and the reason proffered by the Defendant at trial are the same. That is that Papa was fired for violating company policy. One alleged violation was the payment of an employee, Mr. Whetzel, out of the mileage account rather than the labor account. Defendants also claim that Papa hid coupons and "lates" (discounts for late deliveries) in order to improve the appearance of the store's financial position. Defendant characterizes* 1534 these activities as "manipulation of paperwork."

9. The evidence did not support Defendant's claim that Papa was responsible for hiding coupons or lates, or that he directed Whetzel to seek payment from the mileage fund. Instead, the evidence showed that Carrier instructed employees to hide coupons and lates. Furthermore, months before Papa's firing, Carrier approved Whetzel's idea to rollover the labor cost into his mileage account and directed Whetzel to carry out his idea.

[. . .]

II. Conclusions of Law

A. Hostile Environment

[1] 1. A prima facie case of sexual harassment under the hostile environment theory is established where the Plaintiff shows, by a preponderance of the evidence, that:
(1) the employee belongs to a protected group;
(2) the employee was subjected to unwelcome sexual harassment;
(3) the harassment complained of was based on sex;
(4) the harassment complained of affected a term condition or privilege of employment in that it was sufficiently severe or pervasive to alter the conditions of the victim's employment and create an abusive working environment; and
(5) the employer is liable.

Meritor Savings Bank, FSB v. Vinson, 477 U.S. 57, 106 S.Ct. 2399, 91 L.Ed.2d 49 (1986). *Sparks v. Pilot Freight Carriers, Inc.*, 830 F.2d 1554 (11th Cir. 1987).

[2] 2. Papa is a man, hence for the purposes of a sexual discrimination case he is a member of a protected group. *Henson v. City of Dundee*, 682 F.2d 897, 903 (11th Cir. 1982). 20

(1) The employee belongs to a protected group. As in other cases of sexual discrimination, this requires a simple stipulation that the employee is a man or a woman.] http://openjurist.org/682/f2d/897/henson-v-city-of-dundee

[3][4] 3. Papa was subjected unwelcome sexual harassment. Actions such as "sexual advances, requests for sexual favors, and other verbal or physical conduct of a sexual nature" may be considered by the Court as evidence of sexual harassment. *Henson*, 682 F.2d at 903. Furthermore, the conduct must be unwelcome in that the "employee did not solicit or incite it, and in the sense that the employee regarded the conduct as undesirable or offensive". *Id.* Carrier's conduct, detailed in paragraph 5 of Findings of Fact *infra*, embarrassed Papa and made him feel uncomfortable. His discomfort was so acute that he even took the step of instructing another employee to be present whenever Carrier visited the store. Furthermore, Papa made it clear to Carrier that her sexual advances were unwelcome, yet she persisted in making them.

*1535 [5][6] 4. Carrier's harassment of Papa was based on his sex. "In proving a claim for a hostile work environment due to sexual harassment, the Plaintiff must show that, but for the fact of his sex, he would not have been the object of harassment." *Bundy v. Jackson*, 641 F.2d 934, 942-43. *Phillips v. Martin Marietta Corp. 5.* 400 U.S. 542. 91 S.Ct. 496, 27 L.Ed.2d 613. This case involves a female supervisor making sexual demands of a male subordinate. Carrier's demands were being made of Papa because he is male, hence this element is clearly established. *Henson*, 682 F.2d at 903–04.

5. Carrier's harassment was sufficiently severe enough to create a hostile and abusive work environment which affected a "term, condition or privilege" of Papa's employment.

[7][8] a. "For sexual harassment to be actionable it must be sufficiently severe or pervasive 'to alter the conditions of [the victim's] employment and create an abusive working environment.'" *Meritor Savings*, 477 U.S. at 67, 106 S.Ct. at 2405 *citing Rogers v. EEOC*, 454 F.2d 234 (5th Cir.1971). As the Supreme Court explained in *Harris v. Forklift Systems, Inc.*, 510 U.S. 17, ——, 114 S.Ct. 367, 370, 126 L.Ed.2d 295 (1993), there is no precise test for determining whether conduct created a hostile and

abusive atmosphere. The *Harris* Court did provide guidance however, by stating that "Whether an environment is 'hostile' or 'abusive' can be determined only by looking at all the circumstances. These may include the frequency of the discriminatory conduct: its severity; whether it is physically threatening or humiliating or a mere offensive utterance; and whether it unreasonably interferes with an employee's work performance." *Id*.

[9] b. Papa protested Carrier's harassment and on one occasion explicitly instructed Carrier not to touch him. In order to avoid unwanted contact with Carrier, Papa resorted to asking employees to be present when she was present in his store. Undoubtedly, the terms and conditions of Papa's employment were altered when he had to confer with his superior in the presence of his subordinates. Finally, when Plaintiff ordered Carrier from the Port Richey store and threatened to report her to her boss, her retaliatory response, "David I'll get you" led to his termination several days later – the most severe alteration of the terms of Papa's employment.

6. Domino's is directly liable for Carrier's creation of a hostile and abusive work environment. The Supreme Court touched on employer liability in *Meritor Savings* by holding that employers are neither strictly liable for the actions of its supervisory employees who create a hostile atmosphere, nor exempt from liability when they have not been notified directly. *Meritor Savings*, 477 U.S. at 72, 106 S.Ct. at 2408. The Eleventh Circuit has established more explicit guidelines for determining when an employer can be liable for the actions of employees who have created a hostile work environment. The employer may be either directly liable or indirectly liable via *respondeat superior*. *Sparks v. Pilot Freight Carriers. Inc.*, 830 F.2d 1554 (11th Cir. 1987).

[10] [11] a. Domino's is not liable via *respondeat superior*. In order to hold an employer indirectly liable for the actions of its employees, the plaintiff must establish that the employer knew, or should have known of the harassment and failed to take remedial action. *Vance v. Southern Bell Tel, and Tel. Co.*, 863 F.2d 1503, 1512 (11th Cir. 1989). The plaintiff can meet this burden either by

showing that he "complained to higher management, or that the harassment was pervasive enough to charge the employer with constructive knowledge." *Id*. Papa never made a report of harassment to anyone at Domino's, although he testified that he attempted to contact Haskins about Carrier's conduct. Furthermore, although the harassment was pervasive in the workplace, no one from Domino's management was there to observe Carrier's conduct.

Accordingly, Domino's had neither actual or constructive knowledge of the hostile atmosphere created by Carrier.

[12] [13] b. However, Domino's is directly liable for Carrier's actions. Where the harasser is the employer or an agent of the employer the employer is directly liable. *Vance*, 863 F.2d at 1512. The Eleventh Circuit adopted the EEOC's view that "supervisor acts as an 'agent' of the employer . . . where [the] supervisor exercises the authority* 1536 actually delegated to him by his employer, by making or threatening to make decision affecting the employment status of his subordinates." *Sparks*, 830 F.2d at 1558–59. As his supervisor, Carrier possessed the authority to fire Papa. When she fired Papa, Carrier exercised the authority delegated to her by Domino's. Domino's direct liability is not impaired by the lack of actual or constructive notice of Carrier's harassment. *Id*.

7. Plaintiffs have established a *prima facie* case that Domino's violated Papa's right to be free from a sexually hostile and abusive atmosphere

B. Quid Pro Quo

[14] 8. To establish a prima facie case of *quid pro quo* harassment, the plaintiff must prove:

1. the employee belonged to a protected group;
2. the employee was subject to unwelcome sexual harassment;
3. the harassment complained of was based on sex; and
4. the employee's reaction to the unwelcome behavior affected tangible aspects of the employee's compensation, or terms, conditions or privileges of employment.

Sparks v. Pilot Freight Carriers, Inc. 830 F.2d 1554 (11th Cir.1987);

9. The first three elements listed above are identical to those discussed in paragraphs 2–4 of the Conclusions of Law listed above. The Court need not repeat its analysis, and finds that the first three elements of *quid pro quo* harassment have been met.

[15] [16] 10. Papa's reaction to Carrier's unwelcome sexual advances affected tangible aspects of his compensation, terms, conditions or privileges of employment. The acceptance or rejection of the harassment by an employee must be an express or implied condition to the receipt of a job benefit or the cause of a tangible job detriment in order to create liability under this theory of sexual harassment. *Henson, Supra,* at 908. Only six days prior to Papa's termination, Carrier came to Papa's store, expressed her love for him, and invited him to live with her. Papa ordered her to leave the store and threatened to notify her superior. Carrier threatened to get even. True to her word, Papa's final and most vehement rejection of Carrier's advances resulted in his termination.

11. Plaintiffs have established a *prima facie* case that Domino's[1] violated Papa's right to be free from *quid pro quo* sexual harassment.

[. . .]

D.   *Plaintiffs' Ultimate Burden of Persuasion*

[19] 14. Plaintiffs' having made a *prima facie* case of hostile atmosphere, *quid pro quo*, and retaliatory discharge; the burden of production then shifts to Defendant. The employer is obliged to rebut Plaintiffs' case with "a legitimate, nondiscriminatory reason *1537 for its action. If the defendant carries this burden of production, then the court must inquire whether the stated reason is merely pretextual". *Donnellon v. Fruehauf Corporation,* 794 F.2d at 600. This burden equally applies to the hostile environment and the quid *pro quo* theories of discrimination. *Texas Department of Community Affairs v. Burdine,* 450 U.S. 248, 101 S.Ct. 1089, 67 L.Ed.2d 207 (1981); *McDonnell Douglas Corp. v. Green,* 411 U.S. 792, 93 S.Ct. 1817, 36 L.Ed.2d 668 (1973).

[20] 15. The Court concludes that the reasons proffered by Defendant for Papa's termination were pretextual. The facts of this case lead the Court to conclude that Carrier reported Papa for her **own** misdeeds and not because he was guilty of hiding coupons and lates or for improperly paying Whetzel from the mileage fund. Carrier's report of Papa's alleged misconduct was made out of spite and in retaliation for Papa's rejection of her sexual advances. Without her intervention Papa would not have been fired.[2]

16. Having determined that Defendant's proffered reasons were pretextual, the Court now concludes that Plaintiffs have met their ultimate burden of persuasion. *St. Mary's Honor Center v. Hicks.* 509 U.S. 502, 113 S.Ct, 2742, 125 L.Ed.2d 407 (1992). The Court concludes that Plaintiffs have demonstrated by a preponderance of the evidence that Domino's discriminated against Papa by violating his right to be free from a sexually hostile and abusive atmosphere; *quid pro quo* harassment; and retaliation for exercising a lawful right. Plaintiffs are therefore entitled to a judgment.

[. . .]

Notes

1   Again, Domino's is directly liable for the actions of Carrier, in whom it vested the authority to terminate Papa. See paragraph 6 *supra*.

2   Domino's knowledge of Carrier's motivation or intent in procuring or justifying Papa's termination is irrelevant. As discussed above, for purposes of Title VII liability, Carrier's actions were the actions of Domino's.

5

Oncale v. Sundowner Offshore Services, Inc.

United States Supreme Court

Summary

The US Supreme Court ruled that nothing in Title VII of the 1964 Civil Rights Act necessarily prevents a claim of sexual discrimination and harassment merely because the persons involved are of the same sex. Adjudicating a case in which a man sued his employer claiming that he was harassed by other male employees in a sexually demeaning way, lower courts had ruled that – by definition – sexual harassment between heterosexual men could not occur since sexual harassment was legally based on sex discrimination law. As such, the plaintiff could not sue. The US Supreme Court reversed, saying that neither the sex nor the sexual orientation of the person involved are central, but only the sex-specific terms of harassment and the hostility generated in the specific context. Same-sex sexual harassment is therefore actionable.

Original publication details: Oncale v. *Sundowner Offshore Services Inc.* (96–568) 83 F.3d 118 (1998). Public Domain.

Sexual Ethics: An Anthology, First Edition. Edited by Patrick D. Hopkins.
© 2023 John Wiley & Sons, Inc. Published 2023 by John Wiley & Sons, Inc.

[. . .]

SUPREME COURT OF THE UNITED STATES
No. 96–568
JOSEPH ONCALE, PETITIONER *v.*
SUNDOWNER OFFSHORE SERVICES,
INCORPORATED, ET AL.

ON WRIT OF CERTIORARI TO THE UNITED STATES COURT OF
APPEALS FOR THE FIFTH CIRCUIT

[March 4, 1998]

JUSTICE SCALIA delivered the opinion of the Court.

This case presents the question whether workplace harassment can violate Title VII's prohibition against "discriminat[ion] . . . because of . . . sex," 42 U. S. C. §2000e-2(a)(1), when the harasser and the harassed employee are of the same sex.

I

[. . .]

In late October 1991, Oncale was working for respondent Sundowner Offshore Services on a Chevron U. S. A., Inc., oil platform in the Gulf of Mexico. He was employed as a roustabout on an eight-man crew which included respondents John Lyons, Danny Pippen, and Brandon Johnson. Lyons, the crane operator, and Pippen, the driller, had supervisory authority, App. 41, 77, 43. On several occasions, Oncale was forcibly subjected to sex-related, humiliating actions against him by Lyons, Pippen and Johnson in the presence of the rest of the crew. Pippen and Lyons also physically assaulted Oncale in a sexual manner, and Lyons threatened him with rape.

Oncale's complaints to supervisory personnel produced no remedial action; in fact, the company's Safety Compliance Clerk, Valent Hohen, told Oncale that Lyons and Pippen "picked [on] him all the time too," and called him a name suggesting homosexuality. [. . .] Oncale eventually quit – asking that his pink slip reflect that he "voluntarily left due to sexual harassment and verbal abuse." [. . .] When asked at his deposition why he left Sundowner, Oncale stated "I felt that if I didn't leave my job, that I would be raped or forced to have sex." [. . .]

Oncale filed a complaint against Sundowner in the United States District Court for the Eastern District of Louisiana, alleging that he was discriminated against in his employment because of his sex. Relying on the Fifth Circuit's decision in *Garcia* v. *Elf Atochem North America*, 28 F. 3d 446, 451–452 (CA5 1994), the

district court held that "Mr. Oncale, a male, has no cause of action under Title VII for harassment by male co-workers." [. . .]

II

Title VII of the Civil Rights Act of 1964 provides, in relevant part, that "[i]t shall be an unlawful employment practice for an employer . . . to discriminate against any individual with respect to his compensation, terms, conditions, or privileges of employment, because of such individual's race, color, religion, sex, or national origin." 78 Stat. 255, as amended, 42 U. S. C. §2000e-2(a)(1). We have held that this not only covers "terms" and "conditions" in the narrow contractual sense, but "evinces a congressional intent to strike at the entire spectrum of disparate treatment of men and women in employment." *Meritor Savings Bank, FSB* v. *Vinson*, 477 U. S. 57, 64 (1986) [. . .] "When the workplace is permeated with discriminatory intimidation, ridicule, and insult that is sufficiently severe or pervasive to alter the conditions of the victim's employment and create an abusive working environment, Title VII is violated." *Harris* v. *Forklift Systems, Inc.*, 510 U. S. 17, 21 (1993) [. . .]

Title VII's prohibition of discrimination "because of . . . sex" protects men as well as women, *Newport News Shipbuilding & Dry Dock Co.* v. *EEOC*, 462 U. S. 669, 682 (1983), and in the related context of racial discrimination in the workplace we have rejected any conclusive presumption that an employer will not discriminate against members of his own race. "Because of the many facets of human motivation, it would be unwise to presume as a matter of law that human beings of one definable group will not discriminate against other members of that group." *Castaneda* v. *Partida*, 430 U. S. 482, 499 (1977). See also *id.*, at 515–516 n. 6 (Powell, J., joined by Burger, C. J., and REHNQUIST, J., dissenting). In *Johnson* v. *Transportation Agency, Santa Clara Cty.*, 480 U. S. 616 (1987), a male employee claimed that his employer discriminated against him because of his sex when it preferred a female employee for promotion. Although we ultimately rejected the claim on other grounds, we did not consider it significant that the supervisor who made that decision was also a man. [. . .] If our precedents leave any doubt on the question, we hold today that nothing in Title VII necessarily bars a claim of discrimination "because of . . . sex" merely because the plaintiff and the defendant (or the person charged with acting on behalf of the defendant) are of the same sex.

Courts have had little trouble with that principle in cases like *Johnson*, where an employee claims to have been passed over for a job or promotion. But when the issue arises in the context of a "hostile environment" sexual harassment claim, the state and federal courts have taken a bewildering variety of stances. Some, like the Fifth Circuit in this case, have held that same-sex sexual harassment claims are never cognizable under Title VII. See also, *e.g.*, *Goluszek* v. *H. P. Smith*, 697 F. Supp. 1452 (ND Ill. 1988). Other decisions say that such claims are actionable only if the plaintiff can prove that the harasser is homosexual (and thus presumably motivated by sexual desire). Compare *McWilliams* v. *Fairfax County Board of Supervisors*, 72 F. 3d 1191 (CA4 1996), with *Wrightson* v. *Pizza Hut of America*, 99 F. 3d 138 (CA4 1996). Still others suggest that workplace harassment that is sexual in content is always actionable, regardless of the harasser's sex, sexual orientation, or motivations. See *Doe* v. *Belleville*, 119 F. 3d 563 (CA7 1997).

We see no justification in the statutory language or our precedents for a categorical rule excluding same-sex harassment claims from the coverage of Title VII. As some courts have observed, male-on-male sexual harassment in the workplace was assuredly not the principal evil Congress was concerned with when it enacted Title VII. But statutory prohibitions often go beyond the principal evil to cover reasonably comparable evils, and it is ultimately the provisions of our laws rather than the principal concerns of our legislators by which we are governed. Title VII prohibits "discriminat[ion] . . . because of . . . sex" in the "terms" or "conditions" of employment. Our holding that this includes sexual harassment must extend to sexual harassment of any kind that meets the statutory requirements.

Respondents and their *amici* contend that recognizing liability for same-sex harassment will transform Title VII into a general civility code for the American workplace. But that risk is no greater for same-sex than for opposite-sex harassment, and is adequately met by careful attention to the requirements of the statute. Title VII does not prohibit all verbal or physical harassment in the workplace; it is directed only at "*discriminat[ion]* . . . because of . . . sex." We have never held that workplace harassment, even harassment between men and women, is automatically discrimination because of sex merely because the words used have sexual content or connotations. "The critical issue, Title VII's text indicates, is whether members of one sex are exposed to disadvantageous terms or conditions of employment to which members of the other sex are not exposed." *Harris, supra*, at 25 (GINSBURG, J., concurring).

Courts and juries have found the inference of discrimination easy to draw in most male–female sexual harassment situations, because the challenged conduct typically involves explicit or implicit proposals of sexual activity; it is reasonable to assume those proposals would not have been made to someone of the same sex. The same chain of inference would be available to a plaintiff alleging same-sex harassment, if there were credible evidence that the harasser was homosexual. But harassing conduct need not be motivated by sexual desire to support an inference of discrimination on the basis of sex. A trier of fact might reasonably find such discrimination, for example, if a female victim is harassed in such sex-specific and derogatory terms by another woman as to make it clear that the harasser is motivated by general hostility to the presence of women in the workplace. A same-sex harassment plaintiff may also, of course, offer direct comparative evidence about how the alleged harasser treated members of both sexes in a mixed-sex workplace. Whatever evidentiary route the plaintiff chooses to follow, he or she must always prove that the conduct at issue was not merely tinged with offensive sexual connotations, but actually constituted "*discrimina[tion]* . . . because of . . . sex."

And there is another requirement that prevents Title VII from expanding into a general civility code: As we emphasized in *Meritor* and *Harris*, the statute does not reach genuine but innocuous differences in the ways men and women routinely interact with members of the same sex and of the opposite sex. The prohibition of harassment on the basis of sex requires neither asexuality nor androgyny in the workplace; it forbids only behavior so objectively offensive as to alter the "conditions" of the victim's employment. "Conduct that is not severe or pervasive enough to create an objectively hostile or abusive work environment – an environment that a reasonable person would find hostile or abusive – is beyond Title VII's purview." *Harris*, 510 U. S., at 21, citing *Meritor*, 477 U. S. at 67. We have always regarded that requirement as crucial, and as sufficient to ensure that courts and juries do not mistake ordinary socializing in the workplace – such as male-on-male horseplay or intersexual flirtation – for discriminatory "conditions of employment."

We have emphasized, moreover, that the objective severity of harassment should be judged from the perspective of a reasonable person in the plaintiff's position, considering "all the circumstances." *Harris, supra*, at 23. In same-sex (as in all) harassment cases, that inquiry requires careful consideration of the social context in which particular behavior occurs and is experienced by its target. A professional football player's working environment is not severely or pervasively abusive, for example, if the coach smacks him on the buttocks as he heads onto the field – even if the same behavior would reasonably be experienced as abusive by the coach's secretary (male or female) back at the office. The real social impact of workplace behavior often depends on a constellation of surrounding circumstances, expectations, and relationships which are not fully captured by a simple recitation of the words used or the physical acts performed. Common sense, and an appropriate sensitivity to social context, will enable courts and juries to distinguish between simple teasing or roughhousing among members of the same sex, and conduct which a reasonable person in the plaintiff's position would find severely hostile or abusive.

III

Because we conclude that sex discrimination consisting of same-sex sexual harassment is actionable under Title VII, the judgment of the Court of Appeals for the Fifth Circuit is reversed, and the case is remanded for further proceedings consistent with this opinion.

It is so ordered.

6

Force, Consent, and the Reasonable Woman

Joan McGregor

Summary

Argues that most current laws regarding rape use the "reasonable man" or equivalent "reasonable person" standard in defining consent and force, which fails to account for the perspective of women and works to their detriment. Rape statutes should be changed to require affirmative consent and rules of evidence should rely upon a "reasonable woman" standard that would move the burden of proof in rape cases from the woman proving she did not consent to the man proving she did consent.

Original publication details: Joan McGregor, "Force, Consent and the Reasonable Woman," pp. 231–254 from Jules L. Coleman and Allen Buchanan (eds.), *In Harm's Way: Essays in Honor of Joel Feinberg*. Cambridge University Press, 1994. Reproduced with permission of Cambridge University Press.

Conservative estimates suggest that between 20 and 30 percent of females over the age of twelve experience a violent sexual assault outside of marriage at some point in their lives. Even though women are reporting rape in record numbers, recent studies suggest that rape is the most underreported of all violent crimes.[1] Moreover, the likelihood of a complaint actually ending in conviction is generally estimated at 2 to 5 percent. While most rapes are perpetrated by an acquaintance[2] of the victim these are precisely the type of offenses which criminal justice officials are most unwilling to prosecute.[3] The current laws of rape, based often upon stereotypes about women and female sexuality, do not adequately protect women from serious harms. Consider the following example: *Slate v. Rusk* (289 Md. 230, 424 A.2d 720 (1981)), the prosecutrix gave the defendant a ride home from a bar where they had met through a mutual friend. The defendant invited the prosecutrix up to his apartment; she declined, but after he took her car keys, she reluctantly accompanied him to his apartment. The defendant started to undress her. Before intercourse the prosecutrix said to the defendant: "If I do what you want will you let me go without killing me?" She started to cry and then the defendant, according to the victim, started lightly choking her. The Maryland Court of Special Appeals argued that she had not been raped as she had not been *forced* to have intercourse.[4] "Prohibited force" is defined in terms of the victim's resistance, and resistance is interpreted to mean physical resistance and not merely verbal protests. Failure to resist, according to many courts, must be based on a *reasonable* fear that if she (the victim) resisted, her attacker would visit great physical harm upon her. In *Rusk*, the victim's fear was based upon being isolated, in an unknown part of town, late at night, with a man she hardly knew who had taken her car keys, who intimidated her and whom she felt threatened by. These fears, according to the court, are not *reasonable*. "She may not simply say, 'I was really scared,' and thereby transform *consent* or *mere unwillingness* into submission by force. These words do not transform a seducer into a rapist (emphasis added)."

This opinion illustrates that inherent in the current rape laws are assumptions and standards about rape, consent, force, resistance, and reasonable belief which not only fail to account for the perspective of women but work to their detriment. Rape only occurs when there is "force," and it is only force when it is over a particular threshold with the victim physically resisting; the only excuse for not physically resisting is based upon "reasonable fear." One "consents" if one says nothing and/or one was afraid but it was not "reasonable" to be afraid. This paper will analyze what is the nature of the moral wrong of rape, supposing that the law should reflect whenever possible the moral proscription. Next we will examine some representative current rape laws and show how those fail to capture the variety of contexts in which women are wronged.[5] Finally, I will argue for specific changes which include requiring affirmative consent and relying upon the standard of the *reasonable woman* as evidence in rape cases. The proposed changes will advance the value of individuals' control over their own bodies and sexual self-determination.

[. . .]

What is the Wrong of Rape?

Rape conjures pictures of strangers wielding knifes or guns and threatening to use them if their victims[6] do not submit to sex. There are many variations on this scenario, but most commonly the attacker has no weapon. He forces himself on his victim with threats or superior strength. In a slightly different scenario, which turns out in fact to be the most prevalent form of rape, the victim knows the attacker, he is a date or boss or other acquaintance, and the victim has not agreed to have sexual relations with this person. The sex is against her will – unconsented-to sexual intercourse or sexual contact. All of the above scenarios seriously wrong their victims and strike terror and fear in potential victims. At the baseline what differentiates rape from other crimes is *sexual intercourse or contact without consent – nonconsensual sex is rape*. The guns, knives, threats, beating, intimidation, fear are various ways of having power over one's victim. They are additional wrongs to the victim and they help the attacker to perpetrate the wrong of rape. Many of the difficult issues in rape laws involve cases where there are no "weapons," such as knifes or guns or "excessive" physical force, and the victim was not physically abused beyond the rape itself. These are the kinds of cases where it is extremely difficult to get police and prosecutors to press charges against the aggressor. Yet, according to some surveys, a third of all rapes are documented to involve no weapon whatsoever; and excessive physical force is missing in over half of all rapes. In this paper, I will focus on nonaggravated rape, that is, rape that involves no weapons or excessive physical force.

Without weapons or "excessive" physical force what is the wrong of rape? The wrong of rape has been located by some theorists in the fact that the rape is nonconsensual. According to Shafer and Frye: "We would not want to say that there is anything morally wrong with sexual intercourse per se, we conclude that the wrongness of rape rests with the matter of the woman's *consent*."[7] The fact that the rape victim's consent is overridden is central, yet we shouldn't stop there. In many instances one's consent may be overridden or circumvented and yet the injury is not a serious one. What explains the seriousness of the injury of rape is what the consent *ranges* over.

In general, the scope of one's power of consent ranges over one's "domain." Being a *person* is conceptually linked to having a domain which one controls through one's power of consent. Persons have particular traits and capacities which define personhood. Which exact traits and capacities an individual has to have to qualify as a person is controversial, yet it is generally accepted that a person has to be capable of identifying his/her own interests, making choices which fit into larger life plans based on one's interest, and have the ability to communicate those interests and choices to others. Persons, it is claimed, have autonomy rights over most issues within their domain. A sovereign nation has control over what happens within its country; analogously, an autonomous person has control over his/her borders. Personhood can, however, come in degrees; for example, children, incompetents, and the insane are not total persons in the sense described, that is, they do not have the power to consent over the range of issues which "full persons" have. Others act on their behalf and in their best interest.

Rights carve out a person's domain. The physical body is the physical locus of the person. Competent adults have an interest in what happens to their bodies and in controlling what happens to their bodies through their power of consent. That any unconsented-to touching violates a person's domain is reflected in the criminal laws through the assault laws. Modern liberal theory claims that we have an autonomy right over, among other things, what happens to our bodies. Following from that, even the most minor of unconsented-to touching of another's body violates that right. Just violating one's right to not have one's body touched may not be enough, some crossings may be too minor to warrant the coercive arm of the law.

[. . .]

Although there are some bodily invasions that are trivial, for example, patting another on the back when that person dislikes it, generally, the more "serious" offenses are ones where consent ranges over that part of our domain that concerns our bodies and our sexual lives. Much of our personal identity is tied to our gender and sexual expression and hence to our sexual self-determination. In our society, sexual interactions are regarded as personal, private, intimate relationships. Sexual relationships are not generally performed in public and are usually assumed to be performed by partners who have a close and caring relationship. Moreover, it is commonly believed that sexual relationships are imbued with significance and meaning beyond the physical act. Another reason for the seriousness of offenses that force a person to relinquish control over this aspect of one's life is that most individuals believe that they are most vulnerable and exposed in sexual interactions so in them, unlike in other interactions, it is even more important that we be able to control who we are intimate with, thereby controlling information about ourselves.

Taking away the power to consent to sexual relationships, to control this most personal part of our domain, is an extremely grave and serious injury.[8] All unconsented-to border crossings show disrespect for the victim, but some more than others. It is a function of how close to the center of one's domain the offense is. Rape not only denies the ability to control a central part of one's domain, but also in doing so makes the victim a mere object, an instrument of her attacker's gratification. Rape makes the victim feel dehumanized, denigrated, and humiliated. The victim is made to feel that she has an inferior status, sexually and morally. Furthermore, the terror of the experience of being violated in this way contributes to the gravity of the offense, as does the psychological trauma that lingers as a result. There is a surprising amount of consensus about how "serious" individuals take the crime of rape to be.[9] In a famous study carried out by Thorsten Sellin and Marvin Wolfgang, rape came in second to murder in a test that asked respondents to decide how serious a long list of crimes were.

The moral wrongness of rape consists in violating an individual's autonomy right to control one's own body and one's sexual self-determination and the seriousness of rape derives from the special importance we attach to sexual autonomy. The importance we attach to controlling our sexual lives should have a significant impact on the role of consent in sexual interactions and whether consent should be implied from the circumstances. The wrong and seriousness of rape is understood in terms of unconsented-to sexual relations, and not necessarily the "incidental" assaults that may accompany it. Whereas the law often, as we saw earlier, focuses on the *forceful* nature of the attack, this argument maintains that the focus should be on the nonconsensual aspect of sexual violation.[10] Nonconsensual sex constitutes a serious wrong to a person. The harm of rape may be secured with a weapon or threats of other assaults that compound the wrong done, but those are not required for nonconsensual sex to be wrong.

The Present Criminal Law of Rape

Do present criminal rape laws protect against the harm of rape? In most jurisdictions, the law does not accept a simple "no" as satisfying the requirements for lack of consent which would establish the grounds for rape. Unlike other criminal statutes, where to rightfully cross an individual's border one needs consent, apparently a woman's verbal refusal is not sufficient to prevent the crossing of her border. Normally, unconsented-to border crossings are violations of a person's domain – violations of a person's rights. The standard for rape is quite different from other crimes, for example, those involving money. Most jurisdictions require a show of "force" for sexual assault. Consider the following cases with particular attention not only to the force requirement but also to how different the outcomes would have been if property were being secured through these means rather than sex.

In *State v. Alston* (310 N.C. 399, 312 S.E.2d 470 [1984]) the Supreme Court of North Carolina reversed Alston's rape conviction. The court said that the victim did not consent and the act of sexual intercourse was against her will, but it also claimed that there was no *force*, hence there was no rape. "Although (the victim's) general fear of the defendant may have been justified by conduct on prior occasions (he had beat her on previous occasions), absent evidence that the defendant used force or threats to overcome the will of the victim to resist the intercourse alleged to have been rape, such general fear was not sufficient to show that the defendant used the force required to support a conviction of rape." Moreover, the victim did not "resist," according to the court, meaning she did not physically resist.

In *Goldberg v. State* (41 Md. App. 58, 395 A.2d 1213 [1979]) a high school senior accompanied a man who told her he was a photographer and that she had an excellent prospect of becoming a model. She went with him to his "studio." Once there she engaged in sexual intercourse with the defendant because she was afraid of him. Her reasons for being afraid, were (1) she was alone with the appellant in a house with no buildings close by

and no one to help her if she resisted, and (2) the appellant was much larger than she was. Appellate court said that "in the complete absence of any threatening wards or actions by the appellant, these two factors, as a matter of law, are simply not enough to have created a reasonable fear of harm so as to preclude resistance and be the equivalent of force." The court said that she was "incredibly gullible." Even though the victim refused consent, she told the defendant that she "didn't want to do that [stuff]", the court said that her verbal refusal was not sufficient to make the intercourse rape.

In *People v. Mayberry* (15 Cal. 3d 143, 542 P. 2d 1337 [1975]) the California Supreme Court reversed the conviction of Mayberry saying that he "reasonably" and in "good faith" believed that the prosecutrix was consenting. Prior to intercourse, the defendant kicked, hit, knocked to the ground, threw a bottle and shouted obscenities at the victim, and threatened her with further assault. The victim was covered with bruises and swelling when the police arrived. Lack of consent is established not by verbal protest but by physical resistance. The attack perpetrated by the defendant is not considered "force" unless the victim physically resists. The attention shifts, in these cases, from the wrongful conduct of the transgressor to the conduct of the victim. Susan Estrich correctly argues that "[t]he prohibition of 'force' or 'forcible compulsion' ends up being defined in terms of a woman's resistance."[11] The victim is only permitted to withhold resistance if she can establish that she was "reasonably" afraid that if she resisted she was in danger of even greater physical harm. The victim in *Mayberry* claimed that she was too afraid to physically resist, the court rejected her fear as "unreasonable."[12]

In *Commonwealth v. Minarich* (498 A.2d 395 [Pa. Super. 1985]) the court claimed that "forcible compulsion" requires "physical compulsion or violence," but does not, according to the court, include "psychological duress." Minarich had threatened a fourteen-year-old girl living in his custody with return to a detention home if she refused to engage in intercourse.[13] The court said this was not rape; this was *seduction*.

Had the defendants in the above cases been seeking money instead of sex their actions would have been in plain violations of traditional state criminal prohibitions.[14] What is so different about sex or sexual interactions that makes the outcomes in these cases so at odds with other criminal rules? Indeed, the converse should be true, that is, if we suppose that sexual offenses are some of the most serious wrongs that can be perpetrated against a person then *any* sign of nonconsent should be sufficient to signal that the interaction is unwanted and thereby impermissible. We should, then, require *more care* about the existence of consent, because if one was mistaken about consent in this area it would constitute a very serious offense.

In most jurisdictions, the law requires a show of *force* by the assailant (physical or with explicit threats of physical assault) and physical resistance by the victim for the conviction of rape. What the law means by 'force,' what we will designate force, is sometimes described as "overwhelming physical force or violence"; it is only legally prohibited force if it goes above a certain threshold. Exactly what that threshold is seems to be elastic. Where "normal" sexual behavior turns into unacceptable "force" is not clear; normal sexual relations, from the legal perspective, can include a lot of force. From whose standpoint should we be asking the question? Should we consider what the man thought was an acceptable level or what the victim thought? Glanville Williams's classic textbook on criminal law warns that women often welcome a "masterly advance" and "present a token of resistance."[15] This, of course, further complicates matters. Stereotypes such as Williams's make it virtually impossible for women to withhold consent because even attempts at resistance are taken as "tokens" that is, as signs of acceptance.

Furthermore, the threats which can stand in for the violence must be explicit, immediately given: their content must involve death or grievous bodily harm. Implicit threats are insufficient to establish force. Thus, if an assailant beat you at an earlier time, as in *Alston*, or is much larger than you, as in *Goldberg*, or if there is more than one aggressor, as in *Sherry*[16], none of these facts are sufficient to establish a threat to the victim thereby establishing force. Moreover, explicit threats that don't involve physical violence but do involve other harms, for instance, economic ones, are not sufficient to establish force.[17]

In all the previously mentioned cases there was question of force. Should the *actus reus* of rape include force as a necessary element? What is the connection between the force and the absence of consent? Other criminal offenses have depended on the absence of consent, but those other offenses have not required physical force, nor have they required the victim to respond with physical resistance thereby demanding that the victim risk further harm in order to prove that she in fact is a victim.[18] What does the element of force add to the specification of the crime of rape? Are there some conceptual or normative reasons that necessitate "force" as opposed to mere nonconsent? Why not merely nonconsensual sexual intercourse? Some have argued that the offense of rape should

be defined as "forcible sexual contact" or "sexual penetration with force," and that consent should bear on the culpability of the actor but need not be incorporated as an element of the offense.[19] The reason for this is that using force to gain sexual access is what is condemned in our society. George Fletcher takes this position and argues, then, that the defining elements of rape are "forcible" sexual contact, "with consent functioning as a ground for regarding the sexual act as a shared expression of love rather than as an invasion of bodily integrity."[20]

[. . .]

Another reason that the moral proscription embodied in rape law is against *forcible* sexual interaction may test on the assumption that no one would permit sexual penetration without their consent unless it was forcibly done.[21] Force and resistance thus become the *evidence* that in fact there was no consent to the sexual encounter. There is, however, a continuum of force: If we thought about force in the broadest of terms, including physical and nonphysical power, then the above assumption would be founded. The aggressor must have some power over his victim but it may not necessarily include, for instance, physically holding his victim down while accomplishing penetration. Because the law has adopted a narrower notion of force (overwhelming physical force), we must ask if it is reasonable to assume force is necessary for nonconsensual sexual relations. In other words, is it reasonable to suppose that one might submit to sexual relations without consent where there was no force? Most women are physically weaker and smaller than most men, and many women have been socialized away from using physical force or acting aggressively. Given the strength differential most women fear a physical confrontation with men. The added fact that law enforcement agencies have traditionally counseled women not to resist in order to avoid even greater harm makes it unlikely for women to physically resist a persistent, more powerful attacker. Recognizing all these facts makes it totally *reasonable* for women to be afraid when confronted with an aggressive and demanding man and to submit to sexual contact without consenting. Consider the "four big men" argument used in *People v. Flores* (145 P. 2d 318 [1944]): "If one were met in a lonely place by four big men and told to hold up his hands or do anything else, he would be doing the reasonable thing if he obeyed, even if they did not say what they would do to him if he refused." With a woman it may only take one big man. The notion that no one submits to sexual penetration against his/her will without force assumes parity of physical strength and other assets which contribute to personal power in a situation. There are many circumstances where I would guess that many women would feel threatened and fearful, without displays of excessive physical force or explicit threats, and in which women would submit to a sexual relationship against their will.[22] A genuine violation or wrong would occur, one which the law ought to protect against.

Furthermore, the forceful aspect of any physical contact does not necessarily make it wrongful. Boxing, football, wrestling, surgical operations all involve forceful physical contact, yet where individuals have consented the acts are not wrongful.[23] Even some consented-to sexual relations are engaged in forcefully but we are not willing to assume that they are wrongful. What is objectionable about assaults is that the attacker intentionally "touches," sometimes with great severity, another *without the consent of that person.*

Another defense of the force requirement is that we want to ensure that the defendant himself knew his victim was not consenting. This attempt to justify the force requirement rests on the assumption that in regard to rape "no" does not mean "no"; when women say "no" that it's reasonable to suppose that they mean "yes." In other words, it assumes that a woman's words are not worthy of respect and that men are not obliged to take care in determining whether in fact the woman is freely consenting. Otherwise we would establish what the defendant knew on the basis of what victim said or did not say. On the present standard, the level of force and amount of resistance must be sufficiently great that the aggressor realized he was forcing her. Rape is only committed if the accused forces the victim; the way he determines if his force is over the threshold, making what he is doing force, is if she *resists.* And the victim's resistance must be physical and aggressive enough so that he does not interpret the resistance along Williams's lines. This rationale cannot be accepted. The law must respect and protect the assertions of rational adults. Verbal protests and even failure to assent must be taken at face value. The additional requirement of force puts the crime of rape at odds with other criminal statutes and puts an extra and unreasonable burden on the victims of rape.[24]

[. . .]

Starting Over: What Should the Rules Look Like?

The standard of rape's criminality centers on "excessive force," some level of force which the assailant thinks

goes over what would be "normal" levels. It is only a crime when it goes above the excessive level, and what constitutes that is determined from the male point of view, including what the accused believes. Because rape is usually an offense which happens to women, women's perceptions about the harm should be determinative. The force requirement, as we have seen, does not necessary pick out all the offenses against a person's sexual self-determination. There are a variety of power relationships which compel women to submit to sex without freely consenting. Recognizing that the wrong of rape lies with undermining consent to sexual interaction and not with force means that we need to refocus our attention to the conditions which undermine consent; and, positively, focus on criteria for when consent is expressed or when it is legitimate to infer the existence of consent. Given the circumstances under which the present criminal rape laws have inferred consent, it is absolutely unclear why consent is a morally significant notion. Traditionally, however, from the moral point of view, concern about personal autonomy and self-determination is represented by guaranteeing agents control over their domain through their power of consent. Consent cannot play this role if it is inferred from the mere fact of silence or submission through intimidation or implicit threats. In what follows, I will analyze the notion of consent.

Consent

There are a number of different ways of construing the nature and effect of consent. Consent is always given to the actions of other persons. One common understanding of consent is that one "authorizes" another to act in an area which is part of one's domain, for example, giving power of attorney to another. Another way of thinking about consent is that of giving "permission" to another to cross over a boundary of one's own. "Any act that crosses the boundaries of a sovereign person's zone of autonomy requires that person's 'permission,' otherwise it is wrongful."[25] Conceiving of consent in either of these ways has normative significance because it brings into existence new moral and legal relationships. In the case of rape, as in other areas, *consent* turns a criminal act into a noncriminal one. Consent must, then, be deliberate and voluntary since its "understood purpose is to change the structure of rights of the parties involved and to generate obligations for the consenters."[26]

Within the sovereign zone of our domain, all others have a duty to refrain from crossing over. Consent cancels that duty, at least in regard to the specific acts consented to, and for a specified time. Giving consent to someone does not mean that forever after that person rightfully has access to that part of the person's domain. If I let you use my car today, you are not violating my right by using it today. However, you have no claim over it tomorrow. Giving consent changes a wrongful act into a permissible one. In order for this change to take place, that is, in order for permission to exist, the person must consent. Consent is performative, it is something that an agent does.[27]

Consent can be given, however, in some cases, without explicitly saying "I consent." John Locke's famous discussion in the *Second Treatise on Government* on tacit consent has set the stage for later discussions. The argument is that silence or inaction, in some circumstances, expresses consent. A. John Simmons gives an example of a board meeting in which the chair announces: "We will meet again next Thursday unless there are any objections to that date. Does anyone have any objections?"[28] There is silence for a period and then the chair notes that everyone agreed (or consented) to the time. Consent to the proposal is given by the failure to speak up when one was given the opportunity. Silence can only be taken as a sign of consent under circumstances meeting very specific constraints. The actors must know that by not saying anything they are expressing consent, and they must know the substance of what they are consenting to, that is, they must not be deceived about what they are consenting to. They must intend to consent by their silence. They must be given a reasonable amount of time to respond and put forth their protests. They must not be acting under coercion, that is, they must be able to withhold consent without fear of reprisal. And finally, the means of dissent must be reasonably easy to perform. The following example shows when the means for indicating dissent are not reasonably easy to perform and the consequences of dissent are detrimental to the potential consenter. The Chairman in our previous example now says: "Anyone with an objection to my proposal will kindly so indicate by lopping off his arm at the elbow."[29] A more appropriate example for our topic would be that the consequence of not consenting to sex is a beating.

When the relevant constraints for tacit consent are met and hence when a person's behavior should be construed as consent can be problematic. David Hume raised concerns to Locke's argument that by remaining in residence in a country that persons tacitly consent to the government. Hume points out

Can we seriously say, that a poor peasant or partisan has a free choice to leave his country, when he knows no foreign language or manners, and lives from day to day, by the small wages which he acquires. We may as well assert that a man, by remaining in a vessel, freely consents to the dominion of the master; though he was carried on board while asleep, and must leap into the ocean, and perish, the moment be leaves her.[30]

Similar worries might be raised to tacit consent in other areas.

In discussing consent Feinberg uses the notion of "symbolically appropriate" behavior as a sign of consent. "Symbolically appropriate" behavior suggests that certain behaviors in specified contexts are universally recognized as expressing consent. Feinberg views the following case as one where consent is clear.

A and B have sexual relations. . . . As preliminary caresses are exchanged A finds at each successive stage enthusiastic encouragement from B, who is all coos and smiles, though no words are exchanged, and no permission requested. After the fact he [A] would be rightly astonished at the suggestion that he had acted without B's consent. To fail to dissent when there is every opportunity to do so, while behaving in appropriately cooperative ways, is universally understood in such contexts to express consent.[31]

Though no explicit question was asked and no explicit answer given, Feinberg claims, consent in this circumstance was actually expressed, but not by "silence but by symbolically appropriate conduct in the circumstances." The notion of "symbolically appropriate" behavior as a sign of consent needs to be seriously questioned in sexual encounters, given the number of "misperceptions." Ellen Goodman, in a recent newspaper column discussing the alleged rape by Senator Kennedy's nephew, William Kennedy Smith, asks "How is it possible that there is such a perceptual gap about 'consent' for sex?" The woman in this case claimed that she was raped and the accused claimed they had consensual sex. One or the other might, of course, by lying. Nevertheless, what often happens is that there is a difference of perceptions about the same situation. Goodman claims "The man will portray steamy sexual intercourse in the grass with just a spicy soupcon of rough stuff. The woman will describe sexual assault and a piercing violation of her will." The man doesn't believe that he has used "force," nor does he believe that the woman resisted enough or more than what would be common with "normal seduction." He believes that she acted in "symbolically appropriate" ways. The problem, as Goodman points out, with this difference of perception (when it is that) is that the state is left with the burden of proof that the victim was *violated*. Just saying so is not sufficient.[32] The courts and public claim in many of the nonaggravated cases that the woman is lying or deceiving herself; there was no rape.[33]

So-called "symbolically appropriate" behavior can be radically redescribed in different circumstances. In Feinberg's example, B might be extremely afraid of A, concerned that if she doesn't "go along," A will hurt her. Perhaps on a previous occasion A hurt B or threatened her, as was true in *Alston*, where the defendant had beaten the victim on numerous previous occasions. It may well be doubted that B had "every opportunity" to dissent, every opportunity means an opportunity without fear of reprisals. If A and B had had a long-term caring relationship, then the scenario described in the excerpt from Feinberg could appropriately be one in which consent was expressed. On the other hand, if A and B had just met, and A had made frightening comments to B, then that same behavior would not necessarily express consent. Consent secured through behavior under one description cannot merely be transferred to that behavior under another description.[34] At least legally, in areas where it is known that misunderstandings are prevalent, it is not unfair to require that agents not rely upon "symbolically appropriate" behavior for consent. When the wrong committed if behavior were misinterpretated is serious – as in rape cases – it is proper to require agents to go beyond "symbolically appropriate" behavior to ensure that consent is given.[35]

This analysis of consent – granting permission to do that which would otherwise be impermissible – requires that the consent be given without the presence of coercion, force, or deception. "Consent" received through the later means does not entail permission to act. Consent is normatively significant since it is the method by which we grant others a right to cross our intimate borders. Only if the consent is *freely* given does the newly formed relationship secured through consent come into existence. The fact that "consent" was given is not a sufficient condition until the circumstances under which consent was allegedly given are scrutinized; in other words, a "yes" does not always mean "yes." Remember the *Minarich* case in which the fourteen-year-old girl "consented" to sex only because she was threatened with return to a detention home. Consent under those circumstances is not genuine, but counterfeit. Cooperative behavior should not, in all cases, be taken as expressing consent. A full account of the subtleties of coercion and

deception will provide an accurate picture of the varieties of rape. This account, however, is beyond the scope of this paper.

Consent is vitiated by other factors which incapacitate a person. The fact that a victim was drunk or high on drugs should naturally lead to the conclusion that she was not consenting, as she was incapable of voluntary consent. Showing that the woman was incapacitated should establish the element of the *actus reus* 'without consent.' Consent is the vehicle through which individuals autonomously direct major parts of their lives, poor choices or choices which fail to conform to a person's good often result when choosing without one's full faculties. Hence consent granted at those times is not held as legitimate. It should be noted that we normally do not let others exploit an incapacitated person and use the incapacitated person's condition to their own advantage.

Rape statutes should spell out as essential elements of the offense that there was no freely given affirmative consent to the sexual acts. The statutes should specify exactly what is meant by 'consent,' thereby not leaving its interpretation to the discretion of judges and juries. The offense is knowingly committed, then, whenever the accused fails to secure affirmative consent. We considered earlier, *Alston, Rusk, Goldberg, Mayberry, Sherry*, all the defendants *knew* that the victim had never affirmatively expressed consent, *a fortiori* each defendant knew he was raping his victim. Explicitly stating in the statute what counts as consent, makes mistake defenses, which defeat the *mens rea* requirement, much more difficult to claim. Mistakes about consent, under the present system, are more readily accepted because of the way in which consent is construed; namely, that lack of physical resistance is a sign of consent, or passive submission or consent to previous relationships are signs of consent. Mistake defenses often, in practice, are resolved on the basis of what particular jurors believe it was reasonable for the defendant to believe. If a juror believes that "no" means "yes" then he/she will believe that it was reasonable far the defendant to believe that the prosecutrix was consenting hence the juror will vote to acquit on the ground of reasonable mistake. Or, if a juror believes that women often feign reluctance and disinterest, then again that juror will understand these as signs of consent. Leaving the question of mistake about consent up to juries will likely turn on the individual juror's perceptions, often based on outmoded and detrimental stereotypes, about women. However, with the analysis proposed here, how can the defendant claim that he was mistaken when he disregarded what the victim said or failed to take care and discover whether in fact she was consenting? How, indeed, can he claim to be mistaken when in fact she did not express affirmative consent?

Requiring affirmative consent to a sexual encounter marks a change in which value the law recognizes as more important and hence is going to protect. The current rules protect the value of maximal individual sexual freedom. In so doing, it should be apparent, that promoting that value leads to sacrificing other values, specifically ensuring individuals' control of their own bodies and sexual self-determination. The alternative, proposed here, is that we protect the value of individuals' discretionary control over their own bodies and decisions and choices concerning sexual matters. This alternative holds that it is a greater value to protect individuals' sexual self-determination and bodily integrity than to protect sexual liberty generally.[36] The greater care and caution that come with the change to affirmative consent may have a "chilling effect" on sexual liberty, and mean, for example, less casual sexual encounters. Individuals will need to be wary of circumstances in which the consent may be undermined. And when there are questions about the legitimacy of consent, engaging in sexual activity may involve risk of harm and liability for rape, thereby encouraging agents to take greater precautions about how they exercise their liberty.

Reasonable Woman

The account of consent provided here is not in practice going to eliminate all disputed occasions of consent. Disputed claims about consent should be analyzed by asking whether in the circumstances it would be reasonable for a woman to consent. Would it be reasonable for a woman to be fearful or feel threatened in those circumstances? The fact that the "reasonable man" would not be afraid should not be relevant since what we want to know is when a woman has consented. When interpreting actions or behavior, that is, when it is being used as evidence of consent, the context in which it was performed must be carefully analyzed. If the man had been abusive or violent, if he made intimidating remarks or gestures, if he had undue influence over her, if she hardly knew him,[37] if the woman was isolated and without transportation, these are factors which might make it reasonable for a woman to be fearful and/or that the circumstances were otherwise undesirable, thereby making it unlikely that consent was given. Genuine consent or permission is not secured by intimidation or attempts to frighten the consenter. Standards of consent are based

upon what the choice of a reasonable person would be, because we are trying to determine whether the reasonable or average woman would consent, the relevant question should be what is reasonable from a woman's point of view.

In matters of sexual self-determination, one always has the option of withholding consent. The choice to engage in sexual activity is based upon the pleasure or other goods secured through the activity. In general, a person can consent without wanting to, something that one has reservations about, but it does not follow that consenting is just a matter of choosing amongst disagreeable alternatives, and picking the most "reasonable" choice. The latter view is consistent with coercion. Particularly in sexual matters, the reasons for consenting should be based on positive goods to be received from the encounter and not avoiding evils. Whether the reasonable woman or average woman would find the circumstances and/or the kind of sex attractive and enjoyable is the question that should be asked to determine whether a woman consented to a sexual relationship. This question is neglected in most jurisdictions, and women are held to have consented in circumstances and to acts which most women would be revolted by.

[. . .]

If the defendant claims that a woman did in fact freely consent in circumstances in which the reasonable woman or the average woman would not, he is going to be required to provide evidence supporting his account. When reason tells us that the reasonable woman would not consent, we need a positive argument to rebut that presumption. Instead of requiring the *victim* to prove that she did not in fact consent in circumstances in which the reasonable woman would not, we shift the burden of that argument to the defendant. Consider, *Alston* where the defendant threatened the victim and had physically abused her in past and engaged in sex that denied the victim sexual enjoyment. The reasonable woman would not consent to sex in those circumstances, and so the presumption would be that she was not freely consenting.

Showing that the victim was incapacitated establishes the *actus reus* – nonconsensual sex. The defendant might argue that he was unaware of the victim's incapacitation and hence believed that she was consenting. However, if the circumstances were ones in which the reasonable woman would not consent, then the burden would be on the defendant to show why it was reasonable for him to believe that she was consenting. Here the defendant would have to show why he didn't realize that she was incapacitated, and thus incapable of consenting, and why it was reasonable for him to believe she was freely consenting to acts or in circumstances where the reasonable woman would not consent.

Agents have a duty, before crossing the borders of others, not only to determine whether the other person is consenting but also they are accountable for having an awareness of the sorts of circumstances and actions which might prevent that other person from voluntarily consenting.[38] Clear cases are where, for example in *Alston*, he had on previous occasions beaten his victim and had only minutes earlier threatened to "Fix her face" if she refused his sexual advances. No one should be surprised that submission under those circumstances was less than fully voluntary. Because a person "went along" with the aggressor or acted cooperatively, if the circumstances were ones where it was reasonable for a woman to be fearful for her safety or otherwise threatened, or to find the circumstances undesirable for other reasons (having sex with a number of men), then the presumption in such contexts should be that there was no consent. This view is in line with other areas of the criminal law. If we find an event to which reasonable persons would not normally consent, whether it involves one's own death, transfer of one's money, or for example, a beating, we presume that it was done without one's consent. It is not that a person could not consent to another's doing these things, but rather that it is unlikely. Similar understanding is called for here, keeping in mind what average women are like and what they might find desirable to consent to, if the circumstances are not ones that the reasonable woman would consent to then we should presume that the victim did not.

[. . .]

The benefits to be gained by changing the rape statutes are many. First, dropping the current force requirement and requiring affirmative consent would empower women with control over their sexual lives. Women's word would be taken at face value rather than being undermined by a system which takes away women's ability to choose and assumes that women don't know what they want or that they lie about their choices. In no other area of the criminal law are there such negative assumptions about the victims of crimes. Second, the law will protect against harms which women fear and describe the offense on the basis of women's violation. Thirdly, changing the standards of consent for rape will make it conform to other consensual arrangements. Fourth, establishing new rules should increase the safety of women against sexual assault because it should be much easier to prove rape and thereby to convict and punish more offenders. Ultimately, these changes will deter others from harmful behavior. And finally, these rules should have the effect of articulating the expectation that men have an awareness of women's preferences and respect their choices. This is done by requiring men to conform to standards of consent in sexual encounters that are "reasonable" from a woman's perspective.

[. . .]

Notes

1 Deborah Rhode, *Justice and Gender* (Cambridge: Harvard University Press, 1989).

2 The term 'acquaintance' in this context means that the victim is in some way familiar with the rapist. This could mean very causally, e.g., were briefly introduced, all the way to a family member or "boyfriend." This is to be distinguished from the common assumption that rapists are always people that the victim does not know.

3 This paper is about rape when the victim is a woman. Men are also victims of rape, although the occurrence outside of prison is rare. Why it is so rare is the subject of conjecture only. A study of Philadelphia prisons claimed: "A primary goal of the sexual aggressor, it is clear, is the conquest and degradation of his victim." Alan Davis, "Sexual Assaults in the Philadelphia Prison System and Sheriff's Vans," *Studies in Human Sexual Behavior: The American Scene*, ed. Ailon Shiloh (Springfield, Ill.: Charles C. Thomas, Publisher, 1970), 340.

4 Rape statutes vary from state to state. The claims of this paper are meant to capture the doctrines that are incorporated into most state statutes. American rape statutes are based on common law which defined *rape* as "carnal knowledge [by a male] of a woman forcibly and against her will." Most American criminal statutes describe "rape" as sexual intercourse achieved "forcibly," "against the will" of the woman, and/or "without her consent."

It should be further mentioned that there was quite a bit of rape reform in the early 1980s. Those reforms included dropping the requirement of corroboration, changing the resistance requirement from "utmost resistance" to "physical resistance," and the so-called shield rules. These reforms, however, have not had the effect that was hoped for.

5 Some states, during the reforming of their criminal statutes, dropped "rape" as an offense. They have replaced the crime of rape with "sexual assault." Often these statutes are gender neutral. There are a number of reasons that these

Joan McGregor

changes have not led to the desired reforms. See Susan Estrich, *Real Rape* (Cambridge: Harvard University Press, 1987), 80–ff.

6 In this paper, I will use the term "victim" as opposed to much rape literature which uses the designation "survivor."

7 Shafer and Frye. "Rape and Respect" in Mary Vetterling-Braggin, Frederick Elliston, and Jane English, eds. *Feminism and Philosophy* (Totowa: Rowman and Littlefield, 1977), 337.

8 One reason that criminalizing abortion is such an injury to women is that it also takes away control of one's body. Criminalizing abortion does not permit women to autonomously determine whether or not to become a parent.

9 See, for example, Thorsten Sellin and Marvin Wolfgang, *The Measurement of Delinquency* (New York: John Wiley & Sons, Inc., 1964). "Forcible rape" came in second to murder, well ahead of armed robbery and "aggravated assault."

10 Though I will not directly argue for it, I am assuming that part of the problem with rape laws is that there is often only one level of the offense, namely, aggravated rape, which carries a very stiff penalty. Since juries do not want to see individuals who are guilty of unaggravated offenses, that is, rapes without other serious physical injuries, go to jail for extended periods of time as the "rape" statutes often dictate, the juries will acquit the defendants thereby avoiding that outcome. The way to solve this problem is to have a number of levels of the offense, with penalties appropriate to the various levels.

11 Estrich, 60.

12 It should be noted that the requirement that the fear be reasonable is not without justification. Consider the case of a person who has irrational fears; even though, let us imagine, they were the basis for her consenting to sex if the accused didn't know about those fears then it might be unfair to hold him culpable for the offense. It is often the interpretation of the doctrine of "reasonable fear" which has been unfounded. Presumably, if the goal is to determine whether the victim's fear was reasonable or not, then it is appropriate for the court to focus on what the reasonable woman would fear.

13 This case has an additional complexity, namely, the question whether or not the threat posed by Minarich was sufficient for coercion given he had a right to return her to the detention home. I have argued elsewhere that threatening to do what one has a legal right to do can be coercive, but many theorists disagree. See literature an coercion: Robert Nozick, "Coercion" in *Philosophy, Science and Method*, eds. Sidney Morgenbesser, Patrick Suppes, and Morton White (New York: St. Martin's. 1969), Michael Bayles, "A Concept of Coercion," in *Coercion*, ed. J. Roland Pennock and John W. Chapman (Chicago: Aldine, Atherton, Inc. 1972), Don Vandeveer, "Coercion, Seduction, and Rights," *The Personalist*, 58 (1977), David Zimmerman, "Coercive Wage Offers," *Philosophy and Public Affairs* 10 (1981), Joel Feinberg, *Harm to Self*.

14 Estrich, 70.

15 Other insidious examples of not taking women victims at their word is the famous special instructions derived from the words of Sir Matthew Hale cautioning jurors to be suspicious of the female accuser since rape is a charge easily made but difficult to defend against "be [the accused] ever so innocent."

16 *Commonwealth v. Sherry* 437 N.E. 2d 224 (Mass. 1982). In this case there were three men and one woman.

17 Interestingly, the crime extortion recognizes that threats other than threats to physically harm the person are instances of the crime. Extortion acknowledges that individuals may be intimidated by threats other than those foreboding bodily harm. There is no apparent reason why this is not also true in the sexual case.

18 See Rhode, 247.

19 George Fletcher, *Rethinking Criminal Law* (Boston: Little, Brown and Company, 1978).

20 Fletcher, 705.

21 Most rape statutes have focused on penetration. See Catharine MacKinnon, *Toward a Feminist Theory of the State* (Cambridge: Harvard University Press, 1989), 172.

22 A couple of extreme cases where there was no force are: *R. v. Plummer* ((1975), 31 C.R.N.S. 220 (Ont. C.A.)) where the accused was charged with raping a girl after she had already been raped by another man. He found her naked and crying on the bed and had sexual relations with her. No threats were made but she submitted out of fear of bodily harm. In *R. v. Hallett* ((1841) 9 Car. P. 748) the victim was raped by eight men who attacked her. She did not resist after the initial attack so they were convicted of assault only.

23 See Feinberg's discussion of the legal maxim *Volenti non fit injuria* in *Harm to Self* (Oxford: Oxford University Press, 1986), 173–ff.

24 Another motivation for the force requirement might have come from concerns to protect women from the following kind of decisions. In *Regina v. Morgan* (1976 A.C. 182 [House of Lords]) the defendants were falsely told by the husband of the victim that she liked "kinky" sex and would feign lack of consent; in fact the victim did not consent to the forced sexual acts. The defendants argued that they lacked the *mens rea* for the crime of rape because they honestly believed that she was consenting. The prohibition against "forcible sexual contact" would have forestalled this defense.

25 Feinberg, *Harm to Self*, 177.

26 A. John Simmons, *Moral Principles and Political Obligations* (Princeton: Princeton University Press, 1979), 76.

27 Consent has sometimes been construed in the "attitudinal" sense of having an attitude of approval towards something. Even if this is a true sense of consent, it is not what we would want to say generates rights, that is, grants permission, to do what is otherwise impermissible.

28 Simmons, 77.

29 Simmons, 81.

30 David Hume, "Of the Original Contract" in A. MacIntyre, ed. *Hume's Ethical Writing* (Collier-Macmillan, 1965).

31 Feinberg, *Self*, 184.

32 Catharine MacKinnon has commented on this same phenomenon, saying: "Reality is split – a woman is raped but not by a rapist? – the law tends to conclude that the rape *did not happen*." *Toward a Feminist Theory of the State* (Cambridge: Harvard University Press, 1989).

33 There may be some cases in which the accuser lied (FBI estimate 2 to 4 percent), but that is true with other crimes as well.

34 At auctions certain gestures are taken to signify assent to particular prices. In many instances, individuals new to auctions have been misinterpreted as acting in these symbolically appropriate ways.

35 Something like this is done in contract law with the Statute of Frauds. The Statue of Frauds does not recognize certain agreements, e.g., verbal contracts for real estate exchanges because of the problems of misunderstanding that come out of those circumstances.

36 A good analogy, suggested to me by Peter Cervelli, is the rules pertaining to the possession and use of hand guns.

    Apparently, we believe that the value of permitting individuals to have access to and use hand guns is greater than the security of a society without them. Some harm will result from individuals having the liberty to possess and use guns. We are willing to take those risks and accept those costs because we believe that the value of owning and using hand guns is of greater importance.

37 Assume that sexual relationships are very personal and private and that they are not engaged in casually.

38 This raises the issue of whether criminal liability should be based upon "objective" or "subjective" standards. This dispute often surfaces in determinations of whether a defendant intended to bring about a given result. According to "objectivists," a person intends the natural and probable consequences of his acts and his intention for purposes of imposing criminal liability is established by reference to the "reasonable person." If the reasonable person would have foreseen that a given consequence would follow from his conduct, then the defendant is held to have intended that result. "Subjectivists" contend that what a defendant intends depends only on what he in fact foresees. This debate is crucial in cases in which a reasonable person would have foreseen a given consequence, though the particular defendant did not.

Rape and the Reasonable Man

Donald Hubin and Karen Healy

Summary

Argues that abandoning a "reasonable person" standard in favor of a feminist "reasonable woman" standard in rape law would have unforeseen and unacceptable consequences. If reason is believed to be inherently gendered, then changing the law could not improve men's attitudes since they inherently have a male perspective. If they do not inherently have a male perspective, then a gender-neutral reasonable person standard would not need to be abandoned in the first place. Also, since rape legally consists of both the victim's non-consent and the perpetrator's guilty mind, an accused male perpetrator would have to be judged with a reasonable man standard, in which case the feminist position would actually reinforce male bias in rape cases.

Original publication details: Donald Hubin and Karen Healy, "Rape and the Reasonable Man," pp. 113–139 from *Law and Philosophy: An International Journal for Jurisprudence and Legal Philosophy* 18 (1999). Reproduced with permission of Springer Nature.

The essential difference between rape and ordinary sexual intercourse, we believe, is the presence of consent: the latter is consented to, the former not. This view is not uncontroversial; not all states define 'rape' in terms of non-consensual sexual contact and not all commentators agree that they should.[1] In what follows, we will assume, rather than argue for, the view that rape is to be defined in terms of non-consensual sexual intercourse.[2] For purposes of this paper, then, it is definitionally true that rape requires non-consensual sexual contact. We also assume that force is *not* a defining element of rape.[3] One can be subjected to non-consensual intercourse without the presence (or even the threat) of force and the same violation of the person characteristic of rape is present.[4] And, one can be involved in extremely forceful, and even violent, sexual contact without this characteristic violation of the person being present.[5]

Given our analysis of the defining elements of rape, a person can be guilty of rape even though there is neither force nor the threat of force present. Imagine the case of a man who, having been out drinking with his friend, returns to the friend's house whereupon the friend promptly passes out in the living room. The man realizes that if he quietly slips into his friend's bed with that man's wife, he may be able to have sexual intercourse with her while she is under the impression that he is her husband. Were he to do so, this would be rape – rape by fraud in the act (Morland 1994). On our account, whatever the woman does to comply with any sexual advances he makes does not constitute consent to sexual intercourse *with him,* if she is under the impression that he is her husband. Indeed, even if it is she who makes the sexual advances in a groggy state, believing him to be her husband, she has not consented to sexual intercourse *with him.* That this is a case of rape is, we think, a welcome implication of our understanding of rape as non-consensual sexual intercourse.

[. . .]

The relevant defining element of rape is lack of consent. And, on one plausible understanding, it appears that consent involves a thoroughly "subjective" element.[6] We do not mean by this to deny that there are might be objective elements as well. Even an essentially subjective approach should insist that a state of mind of the victim is not sufficient in itself – that there must also be some outward signification of this state of mind.[7] Some hold that consent, in the legally significant sense, is *entirely* "objective" – constituted completely by what was said and done in the circumstances. But regardless

of how subjectively or objectively one construes consent, it does not appear that the issue of what a *reasonable* person would do, or believe, or consent to in this situation is a material element of the crime of rape; rape is defined in terms of *this* person's *actual consent.* Of course, the situation is not this simple.

Consent involves both knowledge and freedom. The phrase 'informed, voluntary consent' is a useful reminder of this, but it is, strictly speaking, redundant.[8] There is no consent where the agent does not understand to what she is putatively consenting. A person who signs a consent form for a medical operation in a language he does not understand – believing it to say one thing when, in fact, it says quite a different thing – does not consent to the operation in question. Furthermore, there is no consent where the agent is coerced into giving a conventional sign of consent. Acceptance of a "Don Corleone offer" that one "cannot refuse" is not an instance of consent; a teller who turns over bank funds upon the threat of death does not consent to the transfer.

Coercion undermines the claim of consent.[9] And force can be coercive. Thus, while force is not a defining element of rape, it is relevant to the establishment of a charge of rape because nothing an alleged victim of rape said, or did, or failed to do can count as (being or indicating) consent if it was said, done or omitted under coercion. [. . .]

Not all use of force is coercive, though. As a professional boxer does, we may consent to force being used against us. Force may be, even if not consented to in advance, welcome and, therefore, not coercive to the subject. Even force and threats of force that are unwelcome and nonconsensual may not be coercive. A bank teller confronted by a would-be robber obviously armed only with a squirt gun filled with distilled water can hardly claim coercion if he gives the robber money upon being squirted. And the threat, "Give me all the money in your cash drawer or I'll let the air out of your car's tires," would hardly be counted as a *coercive* threat in ordinary circumstances. Turning over the funds, if done, is done voluntarily in these cases. It is an act consented to despite the use of force or the threat of force.[10]

And here is where reasonability enters once again. For the determination of whether a situation is coercive in a way that undermines consent is plausibly understood "objectively" in terms of how a *reasonable* person could be expected to respond in the situation. A reasonable person can be expected to resist the threat of flat tires, but not the threat of death, when the bank's money is demanded. To illustrate this, consider the Maryland case of *State* v. *Rusk*. In this case, a woman, Pat, met Mr. Rusk at a bar through a mutual friend. She gave Rusk a ride home and he invited her into his apartment for a drink. When she declined, she testified, he took her car keys and, at that point, she agreed to go up to his apartment. Once there, Rusk apparently left Pat alone in the living room for a few minutes. The door was unlocked and there was a phone in the room. Pat remained in the room during Rusk's absence. When he returned, he began to undress her. She alleged that she begged him to let her leave, began to cry, and said to him, "If I do what you want, will you let me go without killing me?" He claimed that Pat came willingly to his apartment and began to cry only after intercourse. Rusk was convicted at trial, but the conviction was overturned by the Court of Special Appeals of Maryland on the grounds that the victim's fears were unreasonable:

[T]here are no acts or conduct on the part of the defendant to suggest that these fears were created by the defendant or that he made any objective, identifiable threats to her which would give rise to this woman's failure to flee, summon help, scream or make physical resistance . . . In my judgment the State failed to prove the essential element of force beyond a reasonable doubt and, therefore, the judgement conviction should be reversed . . . (289 Md. 230,424 A. 2d 720 (1981))

If, as we do, one takes absence of consent (rather than the presence of force) to be the relevant feature of rape, a central issue here concerns whether the situation was such that the victim's "failure to flee, summon help, scream, or make physical resistance" should be taken to constitute or indicate consent. And this issue is commonly understood in terms of whether the force employed was such as to make a reasonable person unable to resist – if so, then the failure to resist cannot be taken as a sign of consent. Thus enters the "reasonable person standard".

The reasonable person standard has been challenged as predicated on a myth – the myth that it is possible to have an ideal of reasonableness that is gender neutral.[11] Those who believe that it is not charge that 'reasonable person' means, in practice, 'reasonable *man*', and the appearance of gender neutrality makes the phrase all the more insidious than the (allegedly) blatantly gendered phrase it replaces. Critics have proposed that these terms are essentially "gendered to the ground" (MacKinnon 1989, p. 183). For expository purposes, we shall here refer to the claim that reasonable agent standards are necessarily gendered as '*the gendered reasonability thesis*'.

Our tasks in this paper include an examination of the implications of the view that reasonable person standards are necessarily gendered. We shall be looking at this issue in the context of current rape law and proposed changes in that law. The implications of the conjunction of the view that the law of rape requires reasonable agent standards with the claim that such standards are essentially gendered are surprising and troubling. While we are optimistic about the possibility of a gender neutral standard of a reasonable agent, we conclude by cautiously suggesting that the correct results achieved by appeal to a reasonable person standard would be better achieved by dispensing with reasonable agent standards all together. Some critics of the "reasonable man" standard have charged that such a standard is essentially gendered in a way that cannot be eradicated by such superficial revisions as replacing 'man' with 'person'. Some terminology will help clarify the issue here. Let us understand 'reasonable agent standards' as referring to a genus of standards comprising at least the following three species:[12] reasonable man standards, which we will understand to be gendered (male) standards; reasonable woman standards, which we will understand to be the female counterparts; and reasonable person standards, which we will understand to be a gender neutral species of reasonable agent standards.

According to the gendered reasonability thesis, of course, there is no defensible reasonable person standard since a gender neutral conception of a reasonable agent is vacuous. Those, like Catherine MacKinnon (1989), who accept the gendered reasonability thesis may have no quarrel with reasonable agent standards, but they will deny that there can be any defensible reasonable *person* versions of such standards. All reasonable agent standards must be gendered – they must be either reasonable *woman* standards or reasonable *man* standards. This assertion, which we have called 'the gendered reasonability thesis', seems to us to be a complex claim – partly empirical, partly normative – which isn't well supported by programmatic proclamations. But we will not contest it here, at least not by attacking its assumptions or the arguments offered in its defense. Rather, we accept the gendered reasonability thesis in order to tease out the implications waiting in the wings.

The most obvious implication for rape law is one that advocates of this position have been quick to herald: when we judge the issue of consent – when we seek to determine whether the actions and words of the victim constitute or indicate consent to sexual intercourse – it is the standard of the reasonable *woman* we must employ. We cannot justifiably employ those of the reasonable man nor the bogus standard of the reasonable person.

When we do this, it is urged, what might have appeared to be consent under the reasonable man standard will appear not to be consent under the reasonable woman standard. Since the latter is the appropriate standard, we will conclude that consent has not been given in some cases in which we would come to the opposite conclusion using a different standard of reasonability.

The Rusk case provides a useful example. If we discuss the case in terms of the reasonable agent language, the Maryland Court of Special Appeals held, in effect, that a reasonable person in the circumstances confronting Pat who did not consent to Rusk's actions would have fled, summoned help, screamed or offered physical resistance. In criticizing the Court's decision, Kim Lane Scheppele points out that while "[t]he reasonable man, who doesn't fear city streets the way the reasonable woman does and who can fight physically with the expectation of success, may have tried to leave or fight" (1991, p. 46), this is not true for the reasonable woman. Substituting a reasonable woman standard for the reasonable man standard, or for the counterfeit (gender neutral) reasonable person standard, would have warranted the opposite conclusion in the Rusk case.

Proponents of the reasonable woman standard believe this will have profound effects in the law of rape. Scheppele, for example, claims that employment of the reasonable woman standard would allow "women's views to have a strong impact on the outcome of rape trials" (1991, p. 45). It would also, she believes, have the effect of "putting men on notice that they must consider how women's perceptions of sexualized situations may be very different from their own" (p. 45) and requiring "men to see the world through women's eyes" (p. 46). These are significant claims concerning the effect of employing a reasonable woman standard in determining consent. They are also unjustifiably optimistic.

The *Mens Rea* of Rape

Were it correct that the issue of consent was dependent on a reasonable agent theory in the way proposed and that there can be no gender neutral species of a reasonable agent theory, then, it seems to follow, the law must apply a reasonable *woman* test to determine whether a woman has consented to sexual contact. Then, we might say, where the situation was such that a reasonable *woman* would have believed resistance to be dangerous to her physical or mental well-being, the failure to resist sexual contact does not signify consent.

This makes the reasonable woman's point of view relevant to a defining element of the crime of rape. If the reasonable woman's view is materially different from that of the reasonable man, then this should have a significant effect within the law of rape. It may well allow "women's views to have a strong impact on the outcome of rape trials" (Scheppele 1991, p. 45). It will not, however automatically have the effect of "putting men on notice that they must consider how women's perceptions of sexualized situations may be very different from their own" (p. 45). And it will not necessarily "[require] men to see the world through women's eyes" (p. 46). This is because, absence of consent to an act of sexual intercourse is only one element of the crime of rape. It forms a part of the *actus reus* of that crime. But liability to punishment for the crime of rape requires *mens rea*, a criminal state of mind, as well.[13,14] And, when this element of the crime of rape is considered, the implications of the belief that notions of reasonable agency are "gendered to the ground" seem quite different from those defenders of the claim anticipate.

One could, of course, insist that rape is a strict liability crime, denying the existence of any *mens rea* element.[15] While this proposal may result in a higher rate of convictions, it is unacceptable for a number of reasons. First, it carves out an apparently indefensible area of strict liability crime within the criminal law generally. On grounds of consistency, then, we must demand that, absent a cogent argument to the contrary, rape be treated like other serious crimes against a person. Secondly, it has implications that are quite unpalatable. Treating rape as special in this respect will lead to clearly unacceptable, sometimes barely coherent, judgments. [. . .]

[. . .]

Suppose, owing to some perceived uniqueness in the crime of rape, we *were* to treat it differently, deciding that rape requires only that a person have sexual intercourse with a non-consenting partner. What would the implications be? We think they would be wildly unacceptable. To see why, recall our discussion of rape by fraud. There we said that a person can be guilty of rape without employing force or coercion. In that case, fraud in the act was sufficient for rape. But mere mistake would not have been. Crucial to the charge of rape in the case we gave, is the man's awareness that woman believes him to be her husband.[16]

Imagine now – to get to a case that illustrates the importance of a *mens rea* condition for rape – that two couples, strangers to each other, are vacationing. They currently happen to be staying at the same old Victorian inn – one that has a common bathroom and kitchen separated from the sleeping rooms by a maze of twisty little passages, all alike. In the middle of the night, one wife gets up to go to the bathroom and the other goes to the kitchen for a cup of herbal tea. Each returns to what she sincerely believes to be her own room but, as the reader will have anticipated, is in fact the other's room. Each crawls in bed with the man she mistakenly believes to be her husband. Each husband, still more asleep than awake, believes that it is his own wife who has rejoined him in bed. Each couple begins to have sexual intercourse, only to be most unpleasantly surprised as the activities carry on to such a point that the mistake is recognized.

On the strict liability notion of rape, who has been raped? Who has raped? We have, in this "preposterous case", as we shall unabashedly call it, four individuals who have engaged in sexual intercourse without consenting to do so with the sexual partner. We have, also, four individuals who have engaged in sexual intercourse with a partner who did not consent to sexual intercourse with them. It appears that we have four victims of rape and four rapists. (Presumably, a reciprocal agreement to drop charges would be proposed by someone.)

[. . .]

If "hard cases make bad law" and what sort of law must be produced by preposterous and improbable cases? Were we forced to rely on such cases and to generate problems for the proposal that rape be considered a strict liability crime, we might think rather better of that proposal. However, there are, quite obviously, relatively mundane cases in which the strict liability view would be clearly objectionable. Suppose, for example, that a husband and wife work different shifts so that he regularly comes home while she is asleep. Frequently, he initiates intercourse with her while she is still mostly asleep. She has always encouraged this though never given him "blanket permission" to continue. One night, for whatever reason, she decides that she does not want him to do this. She writes him a note telling him not to disturb her when he comes to bed, but forgets to leave the note where he will see it. When he comes to bed, he initiates intercourse as he often does. This time, she has not consented to have sexual intercourse with him. He is clearly having sexual intercourse with a woman without her consent. He is not guilty of rape, because it would be unreasonable to expect him to know, or even suspect, that she is not, on this night as she has on all other nights, consenting to his actions.[17]

We conclude from these cases (and a host of others that could be generated) that rape includes, as a defining component, some element of *mens rea*,[18] But what element?

The now infamous case of *Director of Public Prosecutions* v. *Morgan* ([1975] 2 All ER 347 Decision of Court of Appeal, see [1975] 1 all ER 8) raised a challenge for those who believed that the *mens rea* required for rape was either the intent to have sexual intercourse without the consent of the victim or the knowledge that one was doing so. Morgan convinced three other men that his wife would like to have intercourse with them. He explained that she would feign resistance but that this was all part of a rough sort of sexual "play" she desired. Upon arriving at Morgan's home, the four men dragged her from a room where she was sleeping and took turns having intercourse with her while restraining her. They admitted that she protested and resisted as best she could, but alleged that they sincerely believed that she was consenting. The three colleagues were charged with rape; Morgan, himself, was charged with aiding and abetting a rape.

At trial, the defense argued that the three men lacked the requisite *mens rea* for rape; that is, they did not intend to have sexual intercourse with a non-consenting person. They were convicted by the jury after being instructed that any belief in consent would have to be a reasonable one. On appeal, the defense argued that the jury was misinstructed in law because even an unreasonable and false belief in consent, if honestly held, is inconsistent with the intent to have intercourse without a person's consent. The House of Lords, highest court of criminal appeal in England, agreed with the defense on the point of law, but declined to reverse the convictions on the grounds that the claim to a sincere belief in consent on the part of the three defendants was not credible.

The legacy of *Morgan* is this: an honest, though mistaken, belief in consent, *however unreasonable*, is a defense for rape. That is, if the accused honestly believed that the victim consented to sexual intercourse, he lacks the *mens rea* necessary for the crime of rape.

We disagree and believe that there is room here, as in other places in the criminal law, for gradations of a crime determined in part by the mental state of the perpetrator. The defendants in the Morgan case acted at best, we believe, with reckless disregard for the existence of consent. E. M. Curley (1976) argues – persuasively, we think – for this conclusion and for the further crucial claim that, given the importance of what was at stake, such recklessness is a sufficient *mens rea* for rape. We agree and prefer to introduce degrees of rape (or sexual assault) to reflect differences between non-consensual sexual intercourse where there are materially different mental states present in the assailant. [. . .]

Mens Rea and Reasonableness

We are here assuming that the *mens rea* for rape may be intent, knowledge, recklessness or even (perhaps) negligence. In either of the first two cases, the issue of *mens rea* seems to be an entirely subjective matter[19] – defined without reference to a standard of reasonableness. Of course, reasonableness enters into the matter evidentially since we may be reluctant to conclude that an individual defendant held a belief that no reasonable person would have had in the circumstances. This is, in effect, the reasoning of the House of Lords in the Morgan case. Their motivation may have been to preserve, in the face of a difficult case, the Morgan rule, which holds that sincere belief in consent is inconsistent with the *mens rea* of rape. But there is nothing to bar this kind of reasoning even if we admit the concept of reckless or negligent rape; we are still free to use our standards of reasonability to help us to determine whether the denial of intent or knowledge on the part of the assailant is credible.

[. . .]

We conclude at this point that the crime of rape (or criminal sexual assault) requires a *mens rea* of intent, knowledge, recklessness or negligence. Further, if reasonable agent standards are to be used in the law of rape, a reasonable agent standard will be evidentially relevant to determination of the intent and knowledge of the assailant and both evidentially and definitionally relevant in the determination of recklessness and negligence. If the gendered reasonability thesis is correct and there are no gender neutral reasonable agent standards, then, in the typical case in which the assailant is a man, the standard to be used in coming to a decision about the presence of the requisite *mens rea* of rape is a reasonable *man standard*. The implications of this fact for those who accept the gendered reasonability thesis are momentous.

In discussing them, we note at the outset that rape, as we understand it, is a crime which neither by definition nor in fact can be perpetrated only by a man and only upon a woman. The existence of male-on-male rape is undisputed and, depending on how 'sexual intercourse' or 'sexual assault' is understood, female-on-female and female-on-male rape is possible. Our preference is for an understanding of these terms that allows for the logical possibility of these latter forms of rape. Our reason for

this is derived from a conception of the characteristic violation present in rape.[20] The violation of the person that accounts for the wrong of rape is no respecter of gender or genitalia. That said, we shall continue to discuss the cases in which the perpetrator is male and the victim female because these are the cases that motivate the special concern for gendered standards of reasonability in rape law.

If the determination of guilt in rape cases requires the employment of a reasonable man standard to determine the *mens rea* of the assailant, then the fact that a reasonable woman standard is employed to determine the presence of consent will not, by itself, ensure that men are put on notice that "they must consider how women's perceptions of sexualized situations may be very different from their own" (Scheppele 1991, p. 45), or that men will be required "to see the world through women's eyes" (Scheppele 1991, p. 46). Whether these consequences obtain will depend on the *content* of the reasonable man standard.

Suppose that the reasonable woman standard is relevant to the issue of consent. Notwithstanding this, if the reasonable *man* standard does not impose a requirement that a man "consider how women's perceptions of sexualized situations may be very different from his own" or that he look at "the world through women's eyes", then there is nothing in the law of rape that will ensure that these things will happen. The content of the reasonable man standard is crucial – more important to reform of the law of rape, we think, than the standard of reasonableness employed in determining consent.

We do not mean by this to minimize the role that the determination of consent plays and, if the reasonable woman standard is appropriate in addressing this question, the role that standard plays in the law of rape.[21] However, it seems that those rape cases that motivate people to propose a reasonable woman standard, turn more on the issue of *mens rea* than on consent.[22] This fact would tend to be masked by the fact that the defendant would testify to his belief concerning the presence of consent and the grounds for that belief. While it is natural, perhaps, to think that what is in dispute is the presence of consent, it seems more plausible (especially if we view consent as involving an essentially subjective element) that the role of this testimony is, in the difficult cases, to establish that the belief in consent was reasonable rather than that consent was present. So, while the standard of consent is an important issue in the law of rape, we think that, as a practical matter, the central issue is usually over the reasonability in the belief in consent.

If we are to ensure that men look at sexualized situations from the point of view of women in these important cases where the claimed differences in perspectives between men and women are crucial, what is needed is an independent argument that the reasonable *man* standard requires men to look at the situation from that standpoint. And, it seems, the very considerations that motivate gendered reasonability thesis undermine the possibility of giving such an argument.

The call for separate reasonable agent tests for men and women is typically, though not necessarily, motivated by the view that there is a fundamental rift between the perspectives of men and women. Many feminist scholars have charged that the perspectives of men and women are "incommensurable", that male and female "versions of the truth" are incomparable, or even that men and women have different, but equally correct, "truths".[23] It is this conception of a fundamentally, and possibly inherently, gendered epistemology (and, on some views, metaphysics) that seems to motivate the gendered reasonability thesis for many of its defenders. (After all, if there is a single reality, knowable in principle by men and women, why should we be forced to deny that there is a single standard of a rational agent?)

But these extreme philosophical claims undermine the assertion that the reasonable man does, and possibly that the reasonable man *could,* understand the very different experiences of women, and *vice versa*. If such views were correct (correct according to which perspective?), then the reasonable man standard cannot require that men see the world from the perspective of women, and there is no objective perspective from which to see it. All they can do, and all they can be required to do, is to see the world from the male perspective.

Furthermore, the attempt to support the gendered reasonability thesis by denying the possibility of objectivity is deeply incoherent. There is no objective reality, no "fact of the matter" about the world, defenders seem to assert; there are only "perspectives" which, paradoxically, are not perspectives *on* anything, The paradox is, of course, very deep because, as many of us are fond of pointing out to our introductory philosophy students, the very denial of an objective reality seems to assert an objective reality. And this paradox manifests itself in the present case quite problematically. If one holds that the reasonable man would view sexualized situations from the woman's point of view, one is committed to there being a fact of the matter about what is the woman's point of view and a fact of the matter about a reasonable man's point of view – about there being an objective

reality at least with respect to points of view. This denial of objectivity is self-refuting and, unsurprisingly, undermines those very practical conclusions it is intended to support.

We think that it makes more sense – and is more plausible – to say that male and female perspectives of reality are often very different and typically "partial" rather than to say that they are incommensurable or represent separate-but-equal "truths".[24] Claiming merely difference, rather than incommensurability or separate "truth", preserves the uniqueness of male and female experiences in our society without destroying the possibility of mutual understanding and communication.[25] Given this, it becomes possible for courts to determine what really happened regarding rape cases, rather than being lost in the haze created by the idea of multiple truths. It also becomes possible, and we think defensible, for the law to presume that reasonable men and women look at sexualized situations from each others' perspective because both of these are part of an objective reality which is, in principle epistemically accessible to both men and women.[26]

If we are, then, to accept the gendered reasonability thesis, we should make two further commitments in order to realize the aims of defenders of such standards, one metaphysical and one epistemic: we should commit ourselves to there being a fact of the matter about what the reasonable woman or man would think and do;[27] and we should commit ourselves to the epistemic accessibility of the female perspective to males and the male perspective to females. Without these two further commitments, the, now fragmented, rational agent standards do not do the job their proponents want them to do.

And if we admit that there is an objective matter of fact about what the reasonable man and what the reasonable woman would do, it is difficult to deny that there is an objective matter of fact about what happened in a rape case. Indeed, we can't defend the appropriateness of applying *any* sort of reasonable agent standard if there is no fact of the matter about what situation the actual agents were in. The reasonable agent standards, after all, ask us to determine how a reasonable agent would act *in the circumstances the agent was in*.[28] We think, then, that it is reasonable to believe that there is an objective fact of the matter about what happened in alleged rape cases and that, while the victim and the purported assailant may well have different perspectives on this reality – perspectives that are shaped by their gender and the way in which gender is influenced by social circumstances – it is nonetheless possible to determine the facts of the matter, including the facts about what the different parties' perspectives of the situation were. Given this, the prospects for what we have called a reasonable *person* standard (a gender neutral reasonable agent standard) are not dim. Of course, what a reasonable person would do may depend in part on that person's strength, experience, social conditioning, and much more. The reasonable person may flee from a threat if physically fit, but not have this as a practical option otherwise. Thus, the practical import of the reasonable person standard will be relativized to various features of the actual agent. Furthermore, physical strength is correlated with gender. Our experience and social conditioning are also so correlated (at least in our society). Therefore, the reasonable person standard will, in some situations, lead to different conclusions for typical men than for typical women. But this is not because the reasonable person standard fails to present a single (gender neutral) standard, but because the standard we are employing is sensitive to features of the agent and the situation that are correlated with gender.

To make this abstract point more concrete, consider what the defender of a (gender neutral) reasonable person standard might say about the Rusk case. While critics of the reasonable person standard rightly decry the conclusion that the victim's "failure to flee, summon help, scream, or make physical resistance" constituted consent, they are quite wrong if they think that this conclusion is mandated by acceptance of a gender neutral

standard of reasonability. For it is quite plausible that a reasonable person who had the strength, experience and social conditioning that the victim in this case had would not do any of these things despite having not consented to sexual intercourse. If the Maryland Court of Special Appeals failed to draw this conclusion, we think it is not because it failed to employ a (gendered) reasonable woman standard, but either because it employed a *flawed* reasonable person standard, which was not sensitive to the appropriate features of the situation, or because it employed a reasonable person standard incorrectly.[29]

[. . .]

Conclusion

[. . .] We have argued that because rape requires a *mens rea* element, the employment of reasonable agent standards, conjoined with the gendered reasonability thesis, has untoward implications that defenders of the gendered reasonability thesis have not acknowledged or defused. We want to ensure that individuals approach in a sensitive way those sexual situations where misunderstandings over the presence of consent might arise. We do this by requiring that people be sensitive to whatever factors might bear on the presence of consent, and gender may plausibly be one of those. If it is, then we must insist on the reasonability of considering gender, but not on the genderization of reasonability.

Notes

1 For useful discussions of this issue, see Estrich (1987, pp. 29–41), Bessmer (1976, pp. 58–64), and Dripps (1992).
2 It might plausibly be argued that rape should be understood to include non-consensual sex acts other than intercourse. We are here neutral on this issue and use "sexual intercourse" only for expository convenience. If the best account of rape includes actions other than sexual intercourse, the exposition may be changed without loss of cogency.
3 We thus decline Catharine MacKinnon's invitation (1989, p. 172) to interpret the phrase "with force and without consent" as redundant.
4 We do not mean to suggest by this that there are no morally or legally relevant differences between forcible and nonforcible rape. Rather, we mean only to be declaring our understanding of rape as a crime which, like theft, admits of both forcible and nonforcible species. For a cogent statement of the essential wrong involved in rape, see McGregor (1994).
5 The force cannot be *coercive* force of course, for, as we shall argue below, coercive force undermines consent. Still, when

coercive force is present, what contributes *definitionally* to the act of rape is the element of coercion not that of force.
6 'Subjective' is a slippery word – used in dangerously different ways. We do not mean to suggest by calling consent a subjective matter that there is no fact of the matter. Quite the contrary. There is a fact of the matter and that fact seems to involve a subjective mental state of the victim. It appears to depend on the content of her consciousness, not on what is happening external to her, nor on what a reasonable person would believe is happening external to her. As we will stress later, of course, what is happening "outside her consciousness" and what a reasonable person would believe in her circumstances, may have *evidential* bearing on what we should conclude about her subjective state of mind.
7 See Joan McGregor's "Why When She Says No She Doesn't Mean Maybe and Doesn't Mean Yes: A Critical Reconstruction of Consent, Sex, and the Law" (unpublished manuscript).

8   At least, we believe this is true of consent *in the morally relevant sense.*

9   In "The Moral Magic of Consent (II)" (1996), Larry Alexander sketches, but does not endorse, an alternative way of looking at situations of coerced "consent": "Threats by the boundary crosser, then, do not vitiate consent; rather, they render the boundary crosser himself morally powerless to take advantage of the consent he has induced. . ... Provisionally, therefore, we appear to be led to the somewhat counterintuitive conclusion that coerced consent is still consent" (p. 171). If one were to take this view, our claims would have to be recast in terms of consent that confers on the threatener a moral power at cross the consenter's moral boundary, but the argument would remain substantially the same.

10 Of course, we would dismiss the claim that the teller was *"forced* to turn over the funds" in these cases, as well as the claim that he was coerced to do so. However, this is because, in this context, 'forced' functions as a near synonym for 'coerced' That the force used or threatened was insufficient to *"force* the agent *to"* perform the action desired by the attacker does not entail that force was not used or threatened, only that it was not coercive.

11 See, for example, Catharine A. MacKinnon (1989) pp. 172–183 and Kim Lane Scheppele (1991).

12 Some may argue for the importance of recognizing other reasonable agent standards. We do not imply that the three listed species are the only important ones.

13 This seems to be a source of complaint for some. Scheppele claims that employment of a reasonable woman standard for consent would constitute a "radical departure" for the law of rape which "privileges the perspective of the defendant through the *mens rea* requirement" (1991, p. 44). MacKinnon suggests that the *mens rea* component of rape raises a "problem" because "the injury of rape lies in the meaning of the act to its victim, but the standard for its criminality lies in the meaning of the act to the assailant" (1989, p. 180).

14 It might be suggested that *mens rea* is a necessary condition for finding a defendant guilty of the crime of rape, but not an element of the crime. This way of talking sounds needlessly paradoxical to us: is there, for example, a rape but no rapist? We prefer to use the language of rape like that of murder; while a homicide may take place without anyone having the *mens rea* required for murder, the absence of such a mental state means not only that no one was a murderer – it also means that no murder took place.

15 Douglas Husak has pointed out to us that some jurisdictions – Massachusetts, for example – apparently construe rape as strict liability crime. See Common-wealth v. Ascolillo, 541 N.E.2d 570 (1989), and Commonwealth v. Simcock, 575 N.E.2d 1137 (1991). However, it is not clear that this view would be maintained were it tested by actual cases having the facts we describe (hypothetically) below.

16 We explicitly deny (later) that knowledge of lack of consent is a defining element of rape. Reckless disregard (or even negligence) with regard to consent is, we believe, a sufficient *mens rea* condition for at least some grade of rape or, at least, criminally wrongful non-consensual sexual conduct. Therefore, in a modified case in which the man acted recklessly with respect to the woman's knowledge of who he was, he may still be guilty of rape or some criminally wrongful non-consensual sexual conduct.

17 While we take it to be clear that a rape did not occur in this case, some might dispute this. It might be held, for example, that any sexual intercourse without explicit, verbal consent is rape. This strict requirement would, we believe, count most Instances of consensual sexual intercourse as double rapes – a result we find problematic.

18 Again, we see the semantics of 'rape' as paralleling those of 'murder'. An act of rape (murder) requires the existence of a rapist (murderer), and that requires someone with the *mens rea* required by rape (murder). However, as with homicide, this does not entail that a victim has not been harmed just as much as if a rape had occurred.

19 See note 6, above.

20 See note 4, above.

21 In addition, it is the absence of consent that results in most of the harm essential to rape. Consider again MacKinnon's claim that "the injury of rape lies in the meaning of the act to its victim, but the standard for its criminality lies in the meaning of the act to the assailant" (1989, p. 180). Perhaps MacKinnon's point is that it is the absence of consent (which involves, we believe, a subjective state of mind of the victim) that makes the act of nonconsensual sex an injury, but it is this together with the presence of an appropriate *mens tea* that makes such an act the crime of rape. If so, she is right. This means that when a rape case is lost (either because the prosecution fails to *establish* that the woman did not consent or because it fails to establish that the accused had the requisite *mens rea*), we should certainly not conclude (if anyone has) that the victim was not injured at all (MacKinnon 1989, p. 181). Injury turns principally on whether, in fact, she did consent, not on whether this fact is proved or on whether the assailant had the appropriate guilty mind (though the presence of a guilty mind may exacerbate the injury). MacKinnon claims that, "Hermeneutically unpacked, the law assumes that, because the rapist did not perceive that the woman did not want him, she was not violated." That certainly would be an incorrect assumption; what is unclear is why we should think that the law makes it.

22 As MacKinnon puts it; "so many rapes involve honest men and violated women" (1989, p. 183).

23 See, for example, Scheppele (1991, pp. 36ff., emphasis added); "A serious problem for the legitimacy of public institutions occurs when *truths become multiple,* when stories proliferate in *incommensurable* versions, when different people with different *ways of seeing* become empowered to be heard in the public debate." See also MacKinnon (1989, p. 183, emphasis added): "The deeper problem is the rape law's assumption that *a single, objective state of affairs*

existed, one that merely needs to be determined by evidence, when so many rapes involve honest men and violated women. When *reality is split,* is the woman raped but not by a rapist?"

24 The *significance* of an act of forced sexual intercourse may well vary rather dramatically along gender lines. Indeed, there may well be a biological basis for such differences in perspective.

25 Scheppele (1991), too, argues for the possibility (albeit, with difficulty) of understanding between the sexes. It is unclear how she squares this with her talk of "multiple truths" and "incommensurable" versions of reality.

26 Joan McGregor has suggested (correspondence) that employment of the reasonable woman standard in determination of consent can make it more difficult for the accused rapist to establish that he was not acting recklessly with regard to consent when he was in a situation in which a reasonable woman would not have consented. There is a hidden danger in this use of the reasonable woman standard: if the assailant has any reason to believe that the victim does not conform to the reasonable woman standard with respect to her consent to sexual activities, that will become a material element in the case. This will tend to undermine the gains made in some jurisdictions by the introduction of "victim shield laws" for the accused should surely be free

to introduce anything he knew or reasonably believed about the victim that would indicate that it was reasonable for him to take her behavior as consent despite the fact that a "reasonable woman" would not have consented.

27 For a subtle and very helpful discussion of when mistakes about consent are reasonable, see Husak and Thomas (1992).

28 We might also want to know how a reasonable agent would act in the circumstances that the actual agent reasonably *believed* herself to be in. This only pushes back the objectivity one step. For what situation it is reasonable to believe oneself to be in depends crucially on what evidence one actually has at one's disposal. If there is no objective matter of fact about this, there can be no determinate answer to the question of what situation one *reasonably* believes oneself to be in.

29 Much of the problem that has led critics to propose the gendered reasonability thesis arises, as Deborah Merritt has suggested to us, from the fact that a mostly male judiciary may well be deficient in determining what a reasonable *person* would do if placed in the situation of the victim in the cases that interest us here. This is indeed a problem, but it is unclear that it is a problem with the *standard* in question, or that it would be corrected by supplanting that standard with a reasonable woman standard.

References

Alexander, L., "The Moral Magic of Consent (II)," *Legal Theory* 2 (1996): 165–174.

Bessmer, S., *The Laws of Rape* (New York: Praeger Publishers, 1976).

Curley, E.M., "Excusing Rape," *Philosophy and Public Affairs* 5 (1976): 325–360.

Dripps, D.A., "Beyond Rape: An Essay on the Difference Between the Presence of Force and the Absence of Consent," *California Law Review* 92 (1992): 1780–1809.

Estrich, S., *Real Rape* (Cambridge: Harvard University Press, 1987).

Husak, D. and Thomas, G., "Date Rape, Social Convention, and Reasonable Mistakes," *Law and Philosophy* 11 (1992): 95–126.

McGregor, J., "Force, Consent, and the Reasonable Woman," in J.L. Coleman and A. Buchanan (eds.), *In Harm's Way: Essays in Honor of Joel Feinberg* (New York: Cambridge University Press, 1994).

MacKinnon, C., *Toward a Feminist Theory of the State* (Cambridge, Massachusetts. Harvard University Press, 1989).

Morland, S.M., "Rape by Fraud," *The Liverpool Law Review* 16 (2) (1994): 115–132.

Scheppele, K.L., "The Reasonable Woman," *The Responsive Community, Rights, and Responsibilities* 1 (4) (1991).

8

Revisions to the Uniform Crime Report's Definition of Rape

United States Department of Justice

Summary

Revises the crime reporting definition of rape to a more expansive standard. Major changes incorporate eliminating gender-specific language for either victim or perpetrator (thus making it clear that men can be raped and women can be rapists), including objects as well as body parts as penetration instruments, and including situations in which victims are incapable of consent due to age, mental or physical incapacity, or chemical influence.

Original publication details: United States Department of Justice, "Attorney General Eric Holder Announces Revisions to the Uniform Crime Report's Definition of Rape," Friday, January 6, 2012. Public Domain.

Sexual Ethics: An Anthology, First Edition. Edited by Patrick D. Hopkins.

Department of Justice
Office of Public Affairs
FOR IMMEDIATE RELEASE
Friday, January 6, 2012
Attorney General Eric Holder Announces Revisions to
the Uniform Crime Report's Definition of Rape
Data Reported on Rape Will Better Reflect State
Criminal Codes, Victim Experiences

Attorney General Eric Holder today announced revisions to the Uniform Crime Report's (UCR) definition of rape, which will lead to a more comprehensive statistical reporting of rape nationwide. The new definition is more inclusive, better reflects state criminal codes and focuses on the various forms of sexual penetration understood to be rape. The new definition of rape is: "The penetration, no matter how slight, of the vagina or anus with any body part or object, or oral penetration by a sex organ of another person, without the consent of the victim." The definition is used by the FBI to collect information from local law enforcement agencies about reported rapes.

"Rape is a devastating crime and we can't solve it unless we know the full extent of it," said Vice President Biden, a leader in the effort to end violence against women for over 20 years and author of the landmark Violence Against Women Act. "This long-awaited change to the definition of rape is a victory for women and men across the country whose suffering has gone unaccounted for over 80 years."

"These long overdue updates to the definition of rape will help ensure justice for those whose lives have been devastated by sexual violence and reflect the Department of Justice's commitment to standing with rape victims," Attorney General Holder said. "This new, more inclusive definition will provide us with a more accurate understanding of the scope and volume of these crimes."

"The FBI's Criminal Justice Information Services (CJIS) Advisory Policy Board recently recommended the adoption of a revised definition of rape within the Summary Reporting System of the Uniform Crime Reporting Program," said David Cuthbertson, FBI Assistant Director, CJIS Division. "This definitional change was recently approved by FBI Director Robert S. Mueller. This change will give law enforcement the ability to report more complete rape offense data, as the new definition reflects the vast majority of state rape statutes. As we implement this change, the FBI is confident that the number of victims of this heinous crime will be more accurately reflected in national crime statistics."

The revised definition includes any gender of victim or perpetrator, and includes instances in which the victim is incapable of giving consent because of temporary or permanent mental or physical incapacity, including due to the influence of drugs or alcohol or because of age. The ability of the victim to give consent must be determined in accordance with state statute. Physical resistance from the victim is not required to demonstrate lack of consent. The new definition does not change federal or state criminal codes or impact charging and prosecution on the local level.

"The revised definition of rape sends an important message to the broad range of rape victims that they are supported and to perpetrators that they will be held accountable," said Justice Department Director of the Office on Violence Against Women Susan B. Carbon. "We are grateful for the dedicated work of all those involved in making and implementing the changes that reflect more accurately the devastating crime of rape."

The longstanding, narrow definition of forcible rape, first established in 1927, is "the carnal knowledge of a female, forcibly and against her will." It thus included only forcible male penile penetration of a female vagina and excluded oral and anal penetration; rape of males; penetration of the vagina and anus with an object or body part other than the penis; rape of females by females; and, non-forcible rape.

Police departments submit data on reported crimes and arrests to the UCR. The UCR data are reported nationally and used to measure and understand crime trends. In addition, the UCR program will also collect data based on the historical definition of rape, enabling law enforcement to track consistent trend data until the statistical differences between the old and new definitions are more fully understood.

The revised definition of rape is within FBI's UCR Summary Reporting System Program. The new definition is supported by leading law enforcement agencies and advocates and reflects the work of the FBI's CJIS Advisory Policy Board.

[. . .]

12-018
Attorney General

9

Romeo and Juliet Were Sex Offenders: An Analysis of the Age of Consent and a Call for Reform

Steve James

Summary

Argues that age of consent laws in the United States are inconsistently written, inconsistently applied, subject to gender and sexual orientation bias, are often unfair in particular circumstances, can result in bizarre consequences, and merit significant reform since teenagers are capable of genuine consent in many contexts. Reforms include creating age gap considerations, requiring victim cooperation for statutory rape cases, creating restraining orders parents could apply to their children's sexual partners, and providing greater punishment discretion for judges and prosecutors.

Original publication details: Steve James, "Romeo and Juliet Were Sex Offenders: An Analysis of the Age of Consent and a Call for Reform," pp. 241–262 from *UMKC Law Review* 78 (2009). Reproduced with permission of Steve James.

I. Introduction

William Shakespeare's *Romeo & Juliet* is familiar to most as the ultimate tale of young love. The story, of course, centers on two teenagers – a thirteen-year-old girl, Juliet, and an older boy, Romeo – who fall madly in love.[1] Ultimately, though, their love faces great challenges and tragedy because of a feud between their families, the Capulets and the Montagues. This seemingly irrational focus on family ties that prevents her from being with Romeo prompts Juliet to famously ask, "[w]hat's in a name?"[2]

Asking about the significance of a name perfectly captured the couple's plight in Shakespeare's time, but if the two were transported to modern day America, a more appropriate question might be "what's in an **age**?" Because Juliet is only thirteen and Romeo is an older teen, their romance would face serious problems regarding the age of consent for sexual activity. In many states, Romeo, and perhaps Juliet, could be arrested and face prosecution because of their ages.[3] When faced with multiple years in prison and a lifetime on the sex offender registry, a family feud may not seem like that big of a deal by comparison. While the idea of Romeo and Juliet being prosecuted as sex offenders may seem absurd, the reality is that it has happened and could happen to many modern teens.

One of these modern day Romeos is Frank Rodriguez. In 1996, Frank was a Texas high school senior and his girlfriend Nikki Prescott was a freshman.[4] At Nikki's suggestion, the couple had consensual **sex**.[5] According to Nikki, and as many can probably imagine, what they did was not out of the ordinary.[6] Many of her friends were having sex and many "were dating older guys."[7] It did not seem like a big deal. According to Texas law, though, it was a big deal.[8] Because Frank was nineteen and Nikki was only fifteen, what Frank had done was illegal even though the two were dating, both parties consented, and Nikki even [. . .] suggested it.[9] After Nikki's mom called the police to scare the young couple, Frank faced two to twenty years in prison for having consensual sex with his girlfriend.[10] Staring at such a serious sentence Frank pled guilty to sexually assaulting a child in exchange for a lesser sentence.[11]

As part of his plea agreement, Frank was placed on seven years probation and his name was placed on the Texas sex offender registry.[12] One of the terms of his probation mandated that Frank "stay away from anyone under the age of [seventeen]."[13] Therefore, Frank had to move out of his house because he could no longer be near his twelve-year-old sister.[14] Frank also could not be near Nikki, but as soon as she turned seventeen the two moved in together.[15] Eventually they married and now have four kids.[16] While on probation, though, Frank could not take his kids to the park and had to get special permission to pick them up from daycare.[17] Although the probation eventually ended, Frank's name and personal information will forever be on the sex offender registry, visible to anyone, alongside serial rapists and pedophiles.[18]

While Frank and Nikki's story may not have quite the same drama as Shakespeare's play, their tale is not all that different from Romeo and Juliet's. At their core, they are both about young love and teenage sexuality. It seems strange then that many consider *Romeo & Juliet* to be "[o]ne of the most famous love stories in all literature"[19] while Frank and Nikki's story is grounds for two to twenty years in prison. What Frank and Nikki did was technically against the law, but should it be? And should people like Frank face such harsh punishments? Frank, the so-called sex offender, certainly does not think so. Frank describes what he has been through as a "nightmare" and contends "[t]here's gotta be another way."[20] Nikki, Frank's alleged victim, also does not think so. At the time, she told the police again and again that the sex was consensual and that Frank did not rape her.[21] Now, as noted above, she and Frank are married and have four kids.[22] Nikki's mom, the original complainant, also does not think that such harsh punishments are the answer.[23] As soon as she [. . .] realized the seriousness of her complaint, she tried to drop the charges, but the police told her she could not.[24] Now she says she loves Frank and it breaks her heart to think about what happened.[25] Even Texas Senator Dan Patrick, a defender of the state's age of consent admits that the law "seems unfair."[26]

While Frank and Nikki's stray "seems unfair," clearly great social utility exists in establishing an age of consent and in prosecutions for statutory rape. According to the United States Department of Justice, sixty-seven percent of all reported victims of sexual assault were juveniles under the age of eighteen.[27] More significantly, perhaps, half of these juvenile victims were under the age of twelve.[28] These numbers show the tremendous need that exists to protect teenagers and children from sexual abuse. This Comment recognizes that laws establishing an age of consent and punishing statutory rape serve an important and necessary function. The aim of this Comment, therefore, is not to eliminate these laws altogether or allow true sex offenders to go unpunished.

Nor does this Comment intend to ignore the problems that teenage sex can cause. According to the Centers for Disease Control and Prevention, one in four teenage girls in the United States "is infected with at least one . . . sexually transmitted disease []."[29] Furthermore, teenage pregnancy is negatively linked to a number of critical social issues, including poverty and income disparity, overall child well-being, out-of-wedlock births, responsible fatherhood, health, education, child welfare, and more.[30]

Accordingly, the goal of this Comment is only to highlight the significant problems that are present in many of the current age of consent laws in the United States while offering suggestions for reform. Particularly, this Comment will look at the punishment of sex between two consenting young people. As illustrated by the case of Frank Rodriguez, the consequences under these laws can be extreme and unfair. While teenage sex can cause problems, the law should not criminalize consensual teenage sex in the same way that it punishes a serial rapist or pedophile. Few would argue that Frank Rodriguez is anything like Larry Don McQuay, a man who has molested more than two hundred [. . .] children.[31] But there they are together on the Texas sex offender registry sharing the same common label: sex offender.[32]

Part II of this Comment will look at the history of the age of consent and the public policy considerations that have driven the existence of these laws. Next, Part III will explore the myriad age of consent laws in the United States today and the variety of problems that arise in applying these laws. Finally, Part IV will offer suggestions for reforming these age of consent laws that, if adopted, will allow for a more uniform and fair administration of justice.

II. Background on the Age of Consent

In the context of sex, "[t]he age of consent is the age at which a young person is legally able to understand and agree to consensual sex."[33] Generally, until a person reaches this age it is illegal for anyone to have sex with him or her regardless of how old the partner is.[34] As this Comment will demonstrate, in certain cases "the law is slightly different when the partners are of a similar age, but there is usually still a minimum age below which sex is always illegal."[35] In general, "[s]tatutory rape is the crime that someone can be charged with [when he or she has] sex with [someone under] the age of consent but

who agrees to have sex."[36] While the terms "age of consent" and "statutory rape" appear in few of the state statutes criminalizing this activity, these are the common terms used when discussing this area of the law.[37]

The establishment of an age of consent for sexual activity and the crime of statutory rape both date back to the earliest ancient systems of law. The crime of statutory rape is "at least as ancient as the 4000-year-old Code of Hammurabi."[38] [. . .] The roots of statutory rape in modern law trace back to the crime's codification in English law in 1275.[39] Under this early English law, the age of consent was twelve, but in 1576 lawmakers lowered the age of consent to ten.[40] These English codes and English common law later served as the basis for modern American age of consent laws.[41] The first age of consent in American law was set at ten years old.[42] Throughout the 19th century, though, individual states gradually raised the age with some states setting it as high as eighteen or twenty-one.[43] Originally, the age of consent only applied to protect "chaste" young women.[44] Therefore, a woman's prior sexual promiscuity operated as a complete defense to a charge of statutory rape.[45] This sexual promiscuity defense and the age of consent laws themselves evolved from the notion that women were "special property in need of special protection."[46]

Age of consent and statutory rape law have come a long way since these early beginnings. For example, a woman no longer has to remain chaste to receive protection, the exact ages of consent have evolved, and the systems of offenses and punishments have become much more complex.[47] Many of the policy reasons behind these laws, though, remain the same.[48] While women are no longer viewed as "special property in need of special protection,"[49] some of the justifications for the modern age of consent are still rooted in this protectionism.[50] Additional policy reasons that drive today's age of consent are rooted in other familiar historical motivations – morality and money.[51]

The results of a recent American Bar Association survey of twenty-one states that were considering proposed legislation to revise age of consent laws exhibits this focus on protectionism, morality, and money.[52] The primary motivations of the legislators included:

General intent to protect minors from sexual intercourse; [d]esire to protect minors below a certain age from predatory: exploitative sexual relationships – for example, with much older partners; [p]revention and/or [. . .] reduction of the incidence of teen pregnancy; [r]eduction of the number of young mothers on welfare; [and r]esponsibility and accountability in sexuality and parenting.[53]

The reasons given by these legislators are similar to the justifications given by other commentators on the subject who have boiled down the public policy behind the age of consent to four similar, but even more basic motives: "[to] protect young people from coerced sexuality activity; enforce morality; prevent teen pregnancy; and reduce welfare dependence."[54]

III.   Problems With age of Consent Laws in Modern America

While the public policy goals behind these laws are important, age of consent laws in modern America have many problems that often overshadow these goals. As the case of Frank Rodriguez illustrates, the laws can end up applying in strange ways to people who, as this Comment contends, are not criminals. This problem of over-inclusion is just one of several problems, however. American age of consent laws also suffer from inconsistent standards, selective prosecution, and biases based on gender and sexual preference. This Section of the Comment will discuss each of these flaws. These problems undermine the legitimacy of age of consent laws, thus preventing the laws from effectively serving society's interests.

A.   Overinclusive Laws

One of the primary problems with many states' current age of consent laws is that they simply reach too many people. In many cases, the laws criminalize conduct that this Comment contends should not be criminalized at all, let alone punished as harshly as extreme cases of sexual abuse. As noted, Frank Rodriguez, is a perfect example of this type of overinclusive reach.

The law punishes people like Frank even though few feel they really deserve it.[55] Frank was punished under Texas' age of consent law even though no one directly involved in the case seemed to think he should be – not his "victim" whom he would later marry, not his "victim's" mother who tried to drop the complaint and not the Texas Senator who admits the law is unfair.[56] In addition to those directly involved in the case opposing prosecution, some district attorneys feel so strongly that consenting teens like Frank should not be prosecuted that they have adopted a policy against doing so even

though the law provides otherwise.[57] Perhaps most significantly, the "majority of Americans no [. . .] longer view premarital intercourse as wrong."[58] Even for those who do see some criminal element in conduct like Frank's, few, if any, would argue that this conduct is equivalent to that of other sex offenders. But the law places Frank and others alongside serious sexual predators on the sex offender registries and these teens will remain there the rest of their lives.[59] This unduly harsh punishment, or punishment when no one thinks there should be a punishment, is the heart of the overinclusive law problem.

If cases like that of Frank Rodriguez were rare and extreme exceptions, the over-inclusiveness of age of consent laws would not necessarily be an issue. As long as these laws operated primarily in situations where society felt the conduct was reprehensible, the laws would maintain their legitimacy. Certainly lawmakers cannot draft a perfect law and it seems inevitable that every law will in rare cases reach people whom much of society feels it should not. The problem, however, is that under many age of consent laws, cases like Frank's are not rare exceptions.

In a 1997 Wisconsin trial, eighteen-year-old Kevin Gillson was prosecuted after he impregnated his fifteen-year-old fiancee.[60] Gillson just wanted to do the right thing by marrying the girl, getting a job, and supporting his child, but instead faced a sentence of as many as forty years in prison because his fiancee was under Wisconsin's age of consent[61]. Despite public outcry, prosecutors convicted Kevin and his name was placed on the national sex offender registry.[62] Even the jurors who voted to convict Gillson did not feel the teen should be punished, but felt Wisconsin law gave them no choice.[63]

The case of Kevin Gillson is another strong example of how strangely and unfairly these overinclusive age of consent laws can end up applying to consenting young people. Again, the Kevin Gillsons and Frank Rodriguezes of the world are not the extreme and rare cases. "Studies show [a large number] of those prosecuted for age of consent violations are in their teens or early twenties."[64] In California alone, data from recent years indicates that thirty percent of defendants prosecuted under these laws were under the age of twenty.[65] Additionally, forty-two percent of defendants were less than five years older than their alleged victim.[66] These studies show that in a large number of [. . .] cases, age of consent laws are not being used to prevent adults from exploiting children, but instead are serving to punish consenting young people.

Examples of this over-inclusiveness and the prosecution of consenting teens are not just limited to situations where one person is above the age of consent and the other is below. Recent cases across the United States have resulted in prosecutions and convictions of teens in situations where both parties consented but were under the age of consent. In Florida, the state prosecuted a sixteen-year-old for having sex with his consenting sixteen-year-old partner.[67] In California, the court of appeals upheld the conviction of another sixteen-year-old for having sex with his consenting fourteen-year-old girlfriend.[68] An Arizona court charged a thirteen-year-old boy who had consensual sex with a fifteen-year-old girl.[69] Another Arizona court found a sixteen-year-old boy guilty of sexual abuse after he touched the breasts of a fourteen-year-old girl with her consent.[70] Furthermore, a Wisconsin investigator told a fifteen-year-old girl, who had consensual sex with her fifteen-year-old boyfriend, that both she and her boyfriend would face prosecution for having sex with a minor.[71] These cases where both parties are under the age of consent highlight the absurd results reached by some of these laws more than the situations where one party is above the age limit and one is below.

In addition to prosecution of alleged offenders, victims themselves can face punishment if they refuse to cooperate. In one state, sixteen-year-old Amanda Winkler found herself in jail for contempt of court after she refused to testify against her boyfriend Jaime who was twenty-one.[72] Amanda eventually got out of jail and the two quickly married, but that did not stop the prosecution of Jaime.[73] While contempt of court and not a violation of a specific age of consent law was technically what jailed Amanda, as a practical matter her state's overzealous application of its age of consent was what put her in prison. This is just one more example of the overly broad reach of these laws and the absurd manner in which they can end up applying.

[. . .]

B. Selective Prosecution and Bias

A second fundamental problem with age of consent laws in America is selective prosecution. Commentators on the subject have correctly pointed out that "the law on the books . . . differs markedly from the law in action."[74] In a 1981 United States Supreme Court case, Justice Brennan famously noted that between 1975 and 1978 an annual average of only 413 men and boys were arrested for statutory rape violations in California, despite roughly 50,000 pregnancies among women aged thirteen to seventeen during 1976 alone.[75] Clearly, Brennan did not intend to imply that these four hundred men had impregnated over 50,000 women. The obvious aim of Brennan's comment was to highlight the difference in the law on the books and the law in action. The selective prosecution of statutory rape that existed in Brennan's time has continued in recent years. A 2007 study revealed that over forty-seven percent of high school students have had sexual intercourse.[76] Based on this type of data and other studies, commentators have suggested that more than seven and a half million incidents of "statutory rape" occur each year.[77] Of course, these are just the cases that fit the definition of statutory rape under the law and not the total number that states actually prosecute.[78]

For a great number of reasons, states would find it impossible to attempt to prosecute all cases that fall within the law's definition of statutory rape. When nearly half of the teen population engages in the prohibited conduct,[79] the resources required to prosecute the crime and the number of criminal offenders created would be staggering. Furthermore, reporting and proving all these violations would be difficult as many of the consenting victims would not report the crime or assist in the prosecution.[80] Additionally, as discussed before, society may not want to criminalize all these offenses.[81]

[. . .] The problem, however, is that with so few prosecutions in relation to the number of offenses, the laws either apply randomly or lend themselves to biased application. When the application of a law seems so random, people will lose respect for that law. If two people both "break the law" and the state only prosecutes one of the offenders, the law seems to lose its sense of justice while people lose faith in the legal system. If people "break the law" and no one is arrested, then people will begin to question what the point is in having laws at all. When and if states finally do apply the laws, their application will appear unfair and be unpopular in certain cases. Furthermore, this selective prosecution, not surprisingly, will lead to biased application of the law. Statutory rape prosecutions are often markedly different based on gender and sexual preference.[82] This combination of random chance application and biased prosecution causes age of consent laws to further lose their legitimacy.

1. Gender Bias The biased manner in which society views age of consent violations and in which states prosecute the crime is perhaps most obvious in regards to gender. States file the vast majority of charges for violations of age of consent laws against males.[83] In fact, data

from a 2000 United States Department of Justice study indicates that ninety-six percent of offenders in reported cases of sexual assault against juveniles were male.[84] The idea that males commit almost every case of statutory rape seems a bit unbelievable. Certainly, it is plausible that males commit more statutory rape that females, but data suggesting that they are responsible for ninety-six percent of the statutory rapes in the United States is surprising to say the least However, when analyzed in light of the different way society and the law view age of consent violations by males and females, the percentage of statutory rape charges against males becomes more comprehensible.

As noted earlier, in the earliest statutory rape laws women were viewed as "special property in need of special protection."[85] The nature of the laws then was to protect young women from corruption at the hands of older males.[86] Therefore, from their earliest inception, age of consent laws have been biased against males. The laws were set up to make older males the offenders and to ignore older females who had sex with younger males. However, even as the laws have evolved to become more generally applicable, the way violations are portrayed and the amount of protection given across genders has remained vastly different.

[. . .] Recent high profile cases involving female offenders exemplify the difference in how society views male and female offenders. Over the past several years, a number of female teachers have faced prosecution for having sexual relationships with younger students. For example, in 2005, former middle school teacher Debra Lafave pled guilty to statutory rape charges after she had sex with a fourteen-year-old student.[87] Also in 2005, Tennessee teacher Pamela Rogers Turner pled no contest to having sex with a thirteen-year-old student.[88] The case that probably received the most media attention, though, was that of Mary Kay Letourneau.[89] Letourneau, a Seattle teacher, had sex with Villi Fualaau, a former student in her sixth grade class.[90] At file time the sexual relationship started, Letourneau was thirty-four and Fualaau was only thirteen.[91] After violating the terms of her plea deal under which she would have only served three months in prison, Letourneau was eventually sentenced to seven and a half years In prison.[92] Despite the prison sentence, it was obvious to many that Letourneau received "far more public sympathy than a man would [have]" who committed the same offense.[93] Some viewed Letourneau as a tragic figure because she claimed her sex act was motivated by love even though a male offering the same excuse would be laughed at.[94]

The perception of Letourneau highlights the stark contrast in the way society views male and female offenders.

While the perceptual variations based on gender are strong, they are not the only area where one can find differential treatment based on gender. Gender bias also exists in the punishment of these crimes.[95] Sentences of female offenders tend to be light and public disapproval of prosecutions is sometimes strong.[96] As noted above, if she had not violated the terms of her plea deal, Mary Kay Letourneau would have served only three months in prison.[97] Additionally, a judge only sentenced Pamela Diehl-Moore to probation after the former teacher [. . .] was convicted of having sex with a male student.[98] The judge insisted on probation even though the sex happened repeatedly and Diehl-Moore was forty while the boy was only thirteen.[99] The judge justified probation by saying that "[it]'s just something between two people that clicked beyond the teacher-student relationship."[100] He went on to say, "I really don't see the harm that was done, and certainly society doesn't need to be worried."[101] In another case, twenty-four-year-old Rachel Glau was sentenced to two years supervision for having sex with a sixteen-year-old boy.[102] While the sentence may seem light, the more surprising part of the case was that "[t]he boy, his mother, and more than twenty of the parents of Glau's first grade students wrote to the state attorney's office asking that the charges be dropped."[103]

In addition to social perceptions and individual punishments, the age of consent statute itself can discriminate based on gender. In the case of *Michael M. v. Superior Court of Sonoma County*, the United States Supreme Court held that age of consent laws targeting only males are constitutional.[104] The case arose after a seventeen-year-old defendant who had been charged with violating California's statutory rape law challenged the law as a violation of the Equal Protection Clause of the Fourteenth Amendment.[105] The California statute defined the crime of statutory rape as "an act of sexual intercourse accomplished with a female not the wife of the perpetrator, where the female is under the age of 18 years."[106] Therefore, the statute made men the only ones who could be liable for the crime.[107] The Court found the law constitutional even though it discriminated on the basis of gender because it was justified by a compelling state interest in protecting young women and preventing teenage pregnancy.[108] California would eventually change its statutory rape law so that it now applies equally to men and women.[109] However, the Supreme Court's ruling in *Michael M.* remains.

As the cases of Mary Kay Letourneau, *Michael M.*, and others demonstrate, the perception, punishment, and criminality of age of consent violations can be heavily biased along gender lines. The Supreme Court made an important point in *Michael M.* when it recognized that girls may need greater protection because of the risk of teen pregnancy.[110] However, if the gender biased application of [. . .] these laws goes too far, male victims may not get the protection they need and selective prosecution can result in male offenders being unfairly or overly targeted. Additionally, the notion that the law can apply differently to two different people based solely on gender still seems unfair in a way. The California legislature seems to have recognized this when it changed its statute and other states should make similar attempts to eliminate this type of gender bias in the prosecution of statutory rape.

2. Sexual Preference Bias

While selective prosecution based on gender plagues this area of the law, this is not the only type of bias causing problems for age of consent laws. Biased functioning and application of age of consent laws in regards to sexual preference also cast doubt on the legitimacy of these laws. The penalties for same-sex violations "of age of consent laws may be much harsher" and prosecutors are more likely to bring charges even when there is no coercion and the parties are very close in age.[111]

A recent case that was eventually resolved by the Kansas Supreme Court illustrates the way in which offenders in same-sex violations can face harsher punishment.[112] When he was eighteen, Matthew Limon performed consensual oral sex on a nearly fifteen-year-old boy who was a fellow resident at a school for the developmentally disabled.[113] Limon was convicted under a Kansas criminal sodomy statute and sentenced to seventeen years and two months in prison.[114] If Limon's partner had been a woman, Kansas' "Romeo & Juliet" law would have applied and capped any criminal sentence at fifteen months.[115] However, because the "Romeo & Juliet" law excluded gay people, Limon faced a sentence of approximately seventeen times what a straight person could have received.[116] With the help of the ACLU, Limon appealed his conviction and eventually the Kansas Supreme Court found that by excluding same-**sex** interactions, the **"Romeo & Juliet"** law violated the Equal Protection Clause.[117] Although Limon eventually won his legal

battle, it serves as an example of how **age** of **consent** laws can apply differently depending on sexual preference.

[. . .]

C. Inconsistent Standards

Another problem with the current age of consent laws in America is the inconsistency of laws across the country. Depending on which state someone is in, what is legal under these laws varies greatly. In Texas, for example, two seventeen-year-olds engaging in consensual sex is perfectly legal.[118] In the state of Washington, however, the same two teenagers would be sex offenders.[119] This discrepancy in the law is not limited to Texas and Washington, though. Nationwide, the age of consent ranges from twelve to eighteen, with the most common age being sixteen.[120] This lack of uniformity raises additional concerns about these laws by highlighting how arbitrary many of the ages set by the laws are.

The problem of inconsistent standards across state lines is exemplified by a recent high profile celebrity teen pregnancy. In December of 2007, Jamie Lynn Spears, younger sister of Britney Spears and star of the show *Zoey 101* on the Nickelodeon network, revealed that she was pregnant.[121] While news of the pregnancy raised a number of concerns, many wondered whether the pregnancy could be grounds for a case of statutory rape after Spears revealed that Casey Aldridge was the father.[122] Media reports indicated that Aldridge was eighteen or nineteen while Spears was only sixteen at the time.[123] Based on these ages, in certain states Aldridge could be prosecuted for statutory rape but in others his [. . .] actions would not violate the law at all.[124] So whether the law would consider Aldridge's consensual sex with Spears a crime depends on where conception took place. If the child were conceived in California, where Spears films her television show, Aldridge would have committed a crime.[125] The same is true if the child were conceived in Louisiana, the state where Spears plans to raise her baby, but only if Aldridge was nineteen at the time of conception.[126] If Aldridge was only eighteen, then according to Louisiana law he committed no crime.[127] However, if conception took place in Aldridge's home state of Mississippi, he committed no crime regardless of his age because in Mississippi "statutory rape only applies to sex with persons [fifteen] . . . or younger."[128] The way Aldridge and Spears' consensual sex wavers between sex crime and legal act as the state of conception changes highlights the absurdity of these inconsistent standards and demonstrates the need for more uniformity across state lines.

[. . .]

IV. Strategies for Reform

Although flaws abound in current American age of consent laws, these laws are not beyond fixing. Revisions to existing law and policy can help to bring legitimacy to age of consent laws. Additionally, society's goals of protecting young people from coerced sexual activity, enforcing morality, preventing teen pregnancy, and reducing welfare dependency can be better served. The use of age gap considerations and victim cooperation requirements can help to focus prosecutions on those whose actions are truly criminal. The use of parental restraining orders and reforms to mandatory reporting requirements will provide parents and teens with greater peace of mind. By making the standards for criminal conduct more consistent while providing greater discretion in punishment, the laws will gain a greater sense of fairness.

A. Age Gap Considerations

Age gap considerations are essentially provisions built into the age of consent law that either make sexual conduct between persons close in age noncriminal or punish it at a substantially reduced level.[129] These provisions recognize that the risk of coercion and exploitation is not as great between people close in age.[130] Therefore, when addressing consensual sex between young people close in age, the provisions ensure that states either do not punish the conduct at all or punish it to a much lesser degree than sex between an adult and a young person.[131] These age gap considerations are one suggested reform that many lawmakers have actually already adopted.[132] In fact, forty-five states, the District of Columbia, and federal law have already enacted some type of age gap consideration.[133] Only Wisconsin, Kansas, Massachusetts, South Carolina and Vermont have yet to adopt some form of age gap consideration in their statutory rape laws.[134]

[. . .]

B. Victim Cooperation Requirements

Along with age gap considerations, victim cooperation requirements are another powerful reform that legislatures can adopt to age of consent laws. These provisions essentially require that the alleged victim participate in the prosecution in order for the case to proceed.[135] All underage sexual activity would still be criminal, but prosecutions would only proceed if the victim consented to the prosecution.[136] Some states have already adopted these types of provisions.[137] Additional states should consider these victim cooperation requirements as a necessary reform for their statutory rape laws.

These victim cooperation requirements present several benefits that many of the current laws lack. With the adoption of these cooperation requirements, prosecutions would no longer take place in cases of consensual sex between young people. If the sex was indeed consensual, then most likely neither partner would cooperate in a criminal prosecution. Under this scheme, people like Frank Rodriguez and Kevin Gillson would never end up on the sex offender registry because their partners would not cooperate with the prosecution. The public outcry over their convictions would never take place and society would have a greater respect for the law. Such a scheme allows for consensual sexual exploration among young people, while still providing strong tools to prosecute truly exploitive relationships.

Although victim cooperation requirements certainly have benefits, they are not without some drawbacks. For example, if both parties are under the age of consent, difficulties arise in determining who is the "victim" whose cooperation is required to proceed.[138] Under this hypothetical, the scheme breaks down because even if the sex is coercive, the true victim would not cooperate out of fear the other "victim" would simply cooperate in a reciprocal prosecution.[139] Additionally, those who are truly being exploited and coerced may have difficulty coming forward or may refuse to cooperate because they are still under the control of their older partner.[140] Even with these drawbacks, though, victim cooperation requirements still provide great benefits and lawmakers should at least consider them if they attempt to reform their statutory rape schemes.

C. Parental Restraining Orders and Reporting Requirements

As noted above, many statutory rape prosecutions arise after parents, unhappy with their son or daughter's relationship, call the police to put a scare [. . .] into the couple or put a stop to the relationship altogether.[141] In some states, the law requires parents to report any relationship that may violate the age of consent.[142] If states adopted the age gap considerations and victim cooperation requirements outlined above, they would effectively decriminalize much of the conduct that parents are trying to prevent. While this would take away one alternative for parents trying to rein in their sexually active teen, it would not necessarily remove the best alternative. As seen in the case of Frank Rodriguez, parents who report their child and partner to the police may get more than they bargain for and regret the harsh results. If states allowed for parental restraining orders, however, parents could maintain some control and the consenting teens could avoid the penalties associated with current age of consent laws.

Parental restraining orders would allow "a disapproving parent who is aware of or suspects sexual conduct . . . to seek a court order enjoining the relationship of their [sic] son or daughter."[143] This novel approach addresses parents' concerns in a more appropriate way than criminal prosecution of all sexually active teens below a set age of consent. The process for parents to obtain these restraining orders could be streamlined and informal to avoid a burden on the parents.[144] The punishment for violating a restraining order could be carefully tailored to each situation.[145] Moreover, it would be the parent who would decide when the sexual conduct had gone too far rather than a law providing a blanket rule.[146] The parents, after all, are probably "in the best position to determine . . . [what] is harmful to their son or daughter."[147] Additionally, the partner of the parent's child would receive notice through the order that his or her conduct was causing problems, rather than being blindsided by an arrest for statutory rape.[148] Finally, unlike arrests or a listing on the sex offender registry, restraining orders eventually expire so the young person would not face a permanent black mark.[149]

[. . .]

D. *Greater Consistency with More Punishment Discretion*

Adding greater consistency across state lines in terms of what the age of consent is and what constitutes criminal conduct are additional positive reforms that legislatures could enact. As discussed in Part III, there is currently a wide variation in the age at which different jurisdictions deem a young person able to consent to sex.[150] In some jurisdictions, the age of consent is as high as eighteen.[151] In other situations, the law deems a twelve-year-old mature enough to consent.[152] These differences cause confusion and add to a sense of arbitrariness and

unfairness that accompany these laws.[153] By adopting consistent standards for the age of consent across the United States, the laws will gain more legitimacy and yield fewer strange results. Obviously, getting all the states to agree on a common scheme would be difficult. But with federal pressure, perhaps, government leaders could adopt a uniform age of consent much the same way that twenty-one is the national drinking age and eighteen is the uniform age to vote.

While providing consistency across state lines is important, allowing for greater discretion in the punishment of statutory rape would be an even more positive reform. Although consistency and discretion may seem like opposite concepts, in the case of age of consent reform they really are not. There needs to be greater consistency in the age itself and in what exactly constitutes a crime. Beyond that though, there needs to be greater discretion in how those prosecuted for statutory rape are punished. If states provided for greater discretion, judges could look at the individual facts and decide whether the defendant really merited punishment as a sex offender or was just a regular teen engaging in a consensual act that happened to be criminalized.

In response to the Kevin Gillson case, the Wisconsin legislature passed legislation that provided for this type of discretion in punishment of consenting teens.[154] Thanks to Gillson, "circuit courts in Wisconsin have . . . the option of keeping juvenile sex offenders off the [sex offender] registry."[155] Following the public outcry over Gillson, on April 17, 1998, Governor Tommy Thompson signed a new law giving judges the power to exempt offenders who are between the ages of twelve and eighteen from registering as sex offenders.[156] Under this law, judges are able to take into account a range of factors including the age and mental maturity of the parties, any coercion, and recommendations of the prosecution and defense in deciding whether a teen belongs on the registry.[157]

[. . .]

V. Conclusion

States clearly have compelling policy goals that they seek to advance through their age of consent laws. Protecting young people from coerced sexual activity, enforcing morality, preventing teen pregnancy, and reducing welfare dependency are all issues that should concern lawmakers. However, while each of these public policy goals is important, states should not use society's interest in furthering these policy goals to overwhelm the rights of individuals to act freely. Although society may want to protect young people, promote morality, and maximize resources, it should not be allowed to do so at the risk of criminalizing conduct between two consenting parties

who are not being exploited. In any case, lawmakers should balance society's interests in these policies against the freedom and liberty interests that are at stake in the punishment of statutory rape.

[. . .]

Notes

1 WILLIAM SHAKESPEARE, ROMEO AND JULIET act 1, sc. 2, *available at* http://shakespeare.mit.edu/romeo_juliet/full.html. The play does not specify Romeo's exact age, only that he is older than Juliet.

2 *Id.* at act 2, sc. 2.

3 *See infra* Part III.A.

4 John Stossel, Gena Binkley & Andrew G. Sullivan, *The Age of Consent: When Young Love Is a Sex Crime*, ABC NEWS, Mar. 7, 2008, http://abcnews.go.com/2020/Stossel/Story?id=4400537.

5 *Id.*

6 *Id.*

7 *Id.*

8 *See* TEX. PENAL CODE ANN. § 21.11 (Vernon 2009).

9 Stossel, Binkley & Sullivan, *supra* note 4.

10 *Id.*

11 *Id.*

12 *Id.*

13 *Id.*

14 *Id.*

15 *Id.*

16 *Id.*

17 *Id.*

18 *Id.*

19 Microsoft Encarta Online Encyclopedia, Romeo and Juliet (play), http://encarta.msn.com/encyclopedia_701765069/Romeo_and_Juliet_(play).html (last visited June 2, 2009).

20 Stossel, Binkley & Sullivan, *supra* note 4.

21 *Id.*

22 *Id.*

23 *Id.*

24 *Id.*

25 *Id.*

26 *Id.*

27 Howard N. Snyder, U.S. Dep't of Justice, Sexual Assault of Young Children as Reported to Law Enforcement: Victim, Incident, and Offender Characteristics 2 (2000), http://www.ojp.usdoj.gov/bjs/pub/pdf/saycrle.pdf.

28 *Id.*

29 Press Release, Centers for Disease Control and Prevention, Nationally Representative CDC Study Finds 1 in 4 Teenage Girls Has a Sexually Transmitted Disease (Mar. 11, 2008), *available at* http://www.cdc.gov/STDConference/2008/media/release-11march2008.pdf.

30 *See* The National Campaign to Prevent Teen and Unplanned Pregnancy, Why it Matters: Teen Pregnancy, http://www.thenationalcampaign.org/why-it-matters/wim_teens.aspx (last visited June 2, 2009).

31 Steve McVicker, *The Trouble with Larry*, HOUSTON PRESS, Aug. 24, 1995, *available at* http://www.houstonpress.com/1995-08-24/news/the-trouble-with-larry/.

32 *Compare* Texas Department of Public Safety, Sex Offender Registry — MC-QUAY, LARRY DON, https://records.txdps.state.tx.us/DPS_WEB/SorNew/PublicSite/index.aspx?PageIndex=Individual&IND_IDN=3278905 (last visited June 2, 2009), *with* Texas Department of Public Safety, Sex Offender Registry — RODRIGUEZ, FRANK JR., https://records.txdps.state.tx.us/DPS_WEB/SorNew/PublicSite/index.aspx?PageIndex=Individual&IND_IDN=6861573&SearchType=Name (last visited June 2, 2009).

33 AVERT, Age of Consent, http://www.avert.org/ageconsent.htm (last visited June 2, 2009) [hereinafter AVERT, Age of Consent].

34 *Id.*

35 AVERT, Teens, Sex and the Law, http://www.avert.org/teens-sex-law.htm (last visited June 13, 2009),

36 AVERT, Age of Consent, *supra* note 33.

37 Sharon G. Elstein & Noy Davis, Am. Bar Assn Ctr. On Children & The Law, *Sexual Relationships Between Adult Males and Young Teen Girls: Exploring the Legal and Social Responses* 15–16 (1997), http://www.abanet.org/child/statutory-rape.pdf.

38 Michelle Oberman, *Turning Girls Into Women: Re-Evaluating Modern Statutory Rape Law*, 85 J. Crim. L. & Criminology 15, 24 (1994) [hereinafter Oberman, *Turning Girls into Women*] (quoting Rita Eidson, Comment, *The Constitutionality of Statutory Rape Laws*, 27 UCLA L. REV. 757, 762 n.35 (1980)).

39 Eidson, *supra* note 38, at 762 (citing the Statute of Westminster I, 1275, 3 Edw. 1, c.13: "[T]he King prohibiteth that none do ravish, nor take away by force, any Maiden within Age.").

40 Oberman, *Turning Girls into Women*, *supra* note 38, at 24.

41 Frances Olsen, *Statutory Rape: A Feminist Critique of Rights Analysis*, 63 TEX. L. REV. 387.403 (1984).

42 *Id.*

43 *Id.* at 403–04.

44 Elstein & Davis, *supra* note 37, at 15–16.

45 Oberman, *Turning Girls into Women*, *supra* note 38, at 26.

46 *Id.* at 25.

47 Elstein & Davis, *supra* note 37, at 15–16.

48 *See* Oberman, *Turning Girls into Women*, *supra* note 38, at 36.

49 *Id.* at 25.

50 *See id.* at 36.

51 *See* Noy S. Davis & Jennifer Twombly, Am. Bar Assn Ctr. On Children & the Law, *State Legislators' Handbook for Statutory Rape Issues, Context and Questions* (2000), available at http://ojp.usdoj.gov/ovc/publications/infores/statutoryrape/handbook/cont.html.

52 *See id.*

53 *Id.*

54 Daryl J. Olszewski, Comment, *Statutory Rape in Wisconsin: History. Rationale, and the Need for Reform.* 89 MARO. L. REV. 693. 698–99 (2006).

55 *See* Stossel, Binkley & Sullivan, *supra* note 4.

56 *Id.*

57 Oberman, *Turning Girls into Women*, *supra* note 38, at 23.

58 *Id.* at 61 (quoting Deborah L. Rhode, Adolescent Pregnancy and Public Policy, *in The Politics Of Pregnancy* 301, 316 (Annette Lawson & Deborah L. Rhode eds., 1993)).

59 *See* Stossel, Binkley & Sullivan, *supra* note 4.

60 State v. Gillson. 587 N.W.2d214 (Wis. Ct. Anp. 1998) (unpublished table decision).

61 Jim Chilsen, *Town Riled By Sexual Assault Case*, ASSOCIATED PRESS, Apr. 27, 1997, *available at* http://www.levellers.org/jrp/orig/jrp.wiscjury.htm.

62 *Id.*

63 *Id.*

64 Kate Sutherland, From Jailbird to Jailbait: Age of Consent Laws and the Construction of Teen-Age Sexualities. 9 WM. & MARY J. WOMEN & L. 313. 316 (2003).

65 CAL. COAL. AGAINST SEXUAL ASSAULT, 2008 REPORT: RESEARCH ON RAPE AND VIOLENCE 51 (2008), http://www.calcasa.org/stat/CALCASA_Stat_2008.pdf.

66 *Id.* at 52.

67 B.B. v. State. 659 So. 2d 256 (Fla. 1995). However, in this case, the Florida Supreme Court eventually held that the statute prohibiting sexual intercourse between minors was unconstitutional as applied to the defendant and his motion to dismiss the petition was granted. Id. at 260.

68 *In re* T.A.J., 73 Cal. Rptr. 2d 331, 333 (Cal. Ct. App. 1998).

69 Gammons v. Berlat 696 P.2d 700, 700, 704 (Ariz. 1985).

70 *In re* Pima County Juvenile Appeal No. 74802-2, 790 P.2d 723, 725 (Ariz. 1990).

71 Megan Twohey, *Teens Who Have Sex Charged With Abuse: DAs Prosecuting Even When Both Consent*, MILWAUKEE J. SENTINEL, Mar. 8, 2004, *available at* 2004 WLNR 4714641.

72 Sutherland, *supra* note 64, at 317.

73 *Id.*

74 Oberman, *Turning Girls into Women*, *supra* note 38, at 36 (quoting Martha Chamallas, Consent, Equality, and the Legal Control of Sexual Conduct, 61 S. Cal. L. Rev. 777, 778 (1988)).

75 Michael M. v. Superior Court of Sonoma County. 450 U.S. 464.494 n.8 (1981) (Brennan, J., dissenting).

76 CTRS. FOR DISEASE CONTROL & PREVENTION, TEEN SEXUAL ACTIVITY IN THE UNITED STATES 1 (2008), http://www.thenationalcampaign.org/nationaldata/pdf/TeenSexActivityOnePagerJune06.pdf [hereinafter TEEN SEXUAL ACTIVITY].

77 Michelle Oberman, Regulating Consensual Sex with Minors: Defining a Role for Statutory Rape, 48 BUFF. L. REV. 703. 704 (2000) [hereinafter Oberman, *Regulating Consensual Sex*].

78 *Id.*

79 *See* TEEN SEXUAL ACTIVITY, *supra* note 76.

80 *See* SHARON G. ELSTEIN & BARBARA E. SMITH, AM. BAR ASSN CTR. ON CHILDREN & THE LAW, VICTIM-ORIENTED MULTIDISCIPLINARY RESPONSES TO STATUTORY RAPE TRAINING GUIDE, INTRODUCTION (2000), *available at* http://www.ojp.usdoj.gov/ovc/publications/infores/statutory-rape/trainguide/intro.html.

81 *See supra* Part III.A.

82 *See infra* Part III.B.1-2.

83 Sutherland, *supra* note 64, at 319.

84 SNYDER, *supra* note 27, at 8.

85 Oberman, *Turning Girls into Women*, *supra* note 34, at 25.

86 *Id.* at 25–26.

87 Thomas W. Krause, *Lafave Signs Plea*, THE TAMPA TRIBUNE, Nov. 23, 2005, *available at* http://news.tbo.com/news/MGBL1FT6DGE.html.

88 Associated Press, *Teacher Jailed After Affair with Student*, THE SYDNEY MORNING HERALD, Aug. 13, 2005, *available at* http://www.smh.com.au/news/world/teacher-jailed-after-affair-with-student/2005/08/12/1123353501628.html.

89 State v. Letourneau. 997 P.2d 436 (Wash. Ct. App. 2000).

90 Denise Noe, *Mary Kay Letourneau: The Romance that Was a Crime, Love in a Van*, TRUTV, http://www.trutv.com/library/crime/criminal_mind/psychology/marykay_letourneau/1.html (last visited June 6, 2009).

91 *Id.*

92 Denise Noe, *Mary Kay Letourneau: The Romance that Was a Crime, The Deal Goes Dud*, TRUTV, http://www.trutv.com/library/crime/criminal_mind/psychology/mary-kay_letourneau/8.html (last visited June 6, 2009) [hereinafter Noe, *The Deal Goes Dud*].

93 Denise Noe, *Mary Kay Letourneau: The Romance that Was a Crime, Sexism or Legit Distinction?*, TRUTV, http://www.trutv.com/library/crime/criminal_mind/psychology/marykay_letourneau/7.html (last visited June 6, 2009).

94 *Id.*

95 *See* Sutherland, *supra* note 64, at 321.

96 *Id.*

97 Noe, *The Deal Goes Dud*, *supra* note 92.

98 Cathy Young, *Double Standard: The Bias Against Male Victims of Sexual Abuse*, REASON MAG., June 4, 2002, *available at* http://www.reason.com/news/show/31929.html.

99 *Id.*

100 *Id.*

101 *Id.*

102 Sutherland, *supra* note 64, at 321.

103 *Id.*

104 450 U.S. 464, 467 (1981).

105 Id. at 466.

106 *Id.*

107 *Id.*

108 *Id.* at 467.

109 CAL. PENAL CODE § 261.5 (a) (Deering 2009).

110 Michael M., 450 U.S. at 470–71.

111 Sutherland, *supra* note 64, at 327.

112 State v. Limon, 122 P.3d 22 (Kan. 2005).

113 American Civil Liberties Union, Limon v. Kansas – Case Background (9/8/2005), http://www.aclu.org/lgbt/discrim/11940res20050908.html (last visited June 6, 2009).

114 *Id.*

115 *Id.*

116 *Id.*

117 Limon, 122 P.3d at 24. 40–41.

118 TEX. PENAL CODE ANN. § 21.11 (Vernon 2009) (age of consent for sexual activity is seventeen).

119 WASH. REV, CODE ANN. § 9A.44.093 (LexisNexis 2009) (age of consent for sexual activity is eighteen).

120 *See* AVERT, Age of Consent, *supra* note 33.

121 OK! Magazine, World Exclusive: Jamie Lynn Spears -- "I'm Pregnant," http://www.ok-magazine.com/news/view/3425 (last visited June 7, 2009).

122 Access Hollywood, Was Jamie Lynn a Victim of Statutory Rape?, http://www.msnbc.msn.com/id/22349906/ (last visited June 7, 2009).

123 *Id.*

124 *Compare* CAL. PENAL CODE § 261.5(a) (Deering 2009), *with* MISS. CODE ANN. § 97-3-65(1) (2008).

125 Access Hollywood, *supra* note 126.

126 *Id.*

127 *Id.*

128 *Id.*

129 Olszewski, *supra* note 54, at 707.

130 *See* Oberman, *Regulating Consensual Sex*, *supra* note 77, at 751; DAVIS & TWOMBLY, *supra* note 51, at 7, 9.

131 *See* DAVIS & TWOMBLY, *supra* note 51, at 2–3.

132 Olszewski, *supra* note 54, at 706.

133 *Id.* at 706 & n.93.

134 *Id.* at 706–07.

135 *Id.* at 707; *see, e.g.,* GA. CODE ANN. § 16-6-3(a) (2008).

136 Olszewski, *supra* note 54, at 707.

137 *See, e.g.,* GA. CODE ANN. § 16-6-3(a).

138 Olszewski, *supra* note 54, at 707.

139 *Id.* at 707–08.

140 Oberman, *Regulating Consensual Sex*, *supra* note 77, at 779.

141 *See supra* Part I.

142 *E.g.,* WIS. STAT. § 948.02(3) (2008).

143 Olszewski, *supra* note 54, at 718.

144 *Id.*

145 *See id.*

146 *Id.* at 718–19.

147 *Id.*

148 *See id.* at 719.

149 *See* Stossel, Binkley & Sullivan, *supra* note 4.

150 *See* AVERT, Age of Consent, *supra* note 33.

151 *See* WASH. REV. CODE ANN. § 9A.44.093 (LexisNexis 2008).

152 *See* 18 U.S.C. § 2241(c) (2000).

153 As evidenced by the reaction to the cases of Frank Rodriguez and Kevin Gillson.

154 *See* WIS. STAT. ANN. § 301.45 (West 2008).

155 Jack Zemlicka, *Wisconsin Judges Have Flexibility Assigning Teens to Registry*, WIS. L.J., Feb. 4, 2008, *available at* 2008 WLNR 25330847.

156 *Id.*

157 *Id.*

A Bee Line in the Wrong Direction: Science, Teenagers, and the "Age of Consent"

Jennifer Ann Drobac

Summary

Argues that there is confusion and inconsistency in the age of consent for purposes of criminal proceedings versus civil proceedings. In many jurisdictions, teenagers are not legally capable of consenting to sex under criminal codes, so a defendant cannot use the teenager's "consent" as a defense. However, in the very same jurisdictions, teenagers are not allowed to sue for damages because their "consent" can be used by the defendant as a defense. Recent neuroscientific and psychological research on minors' cognitive abilities shows that adolescents are not capable in many cases of appreciating their decisions and the law should reflect this consistently. Creating a policy of legally binding but voidable "assent" for adolescents would be more consistent with adolescent cognitive development, remove inconsistencies in criminal and civil law, provide defense for post-adolescent sexual partners in appropriate cases, and provide adolescents with the opportunity to learn and grow from their mistakes.

Original publication details: Jennifer Ann Drobac, "A Bee Line in the Wrong Direction: Science, Teenagers, and the 'Age of Consent'," pp. 63–96 from *Journal of Law & Policy* 20 (2011). Reproduced with permission of Jennifer Ann Drobac.

Most New Yorkers may not know that a 1933 New York case and its precedential line effectively erase "the age of consent" for New York civil cases. In that case, *Barton v. Bee Line, Inc.*, the New York Supreme Court held that fifteen-year-old Grace Barton, who allegedly consented to sex with a male bus driver, could not recover in a civil case for damages brought by Frank Barton, her guardian ad litem.[1] The court arrived at this conclusion even though New York had outlawed sex with a female under eighteen years old and barred all minors from bringing direct suit. The jury had found for Grace in the amount of $3,000 (about $50,500 today).[2] However, "[t]he court [. . .] set the verdict aside on the ground that, if plaintiff consented, the verdict was excessive .. . ."[3] The appellate court ruled that Grace could not recover civilly even though her seducer was criminally prosecuted "to protect the virtue of females and to save society from the ills of promiscuous intercourse."[4] The court reasoned, "It is one thing to say that society will protect itself by punishing those who consort with females under the age of **consent**; it is another to hold that, knowing the nature of her act, such female shall be rewarded for her indiscretion."[5] The court added:

The very object of the statute will be frustrated if by a material return for her fall "we should unwarily put it in the power of the female sex to become seducers in their turn." Instead of incapacity to **consent** being a shield to save, it might be a sword to desecrate.[6] Desecrate what? A society that righteously protects only "virtuous" (but still incapacitated) girls? The court's opinion highlights its disapproval of possibly sexually active, "promiscuous" young women. It also heralded the end of the "age of **consent**" for civil cases in New York.[7]

This civil law evisceration of "the age of **consent**" is not unique to New York. One can trace similar patterns across the nation, particularly in Illinois and California.[8] The *Bee Line* case, juxtaposed against the new neuroscience and psychosocial [. . .] evidence of adolescent development, resurrects the question of whether a minor should be allowed to recover civilly for alleged damages following a violation of criminal law. This Article explores whether minors have the developmental maturity consistent with an assignment of full adult legal capacity. It also questions whether adolescent "**consent**"[9] should insulate alleged tortfeasors from liability. Are we, as a society, taking a *Bee Line* in the wrong direction?

This Article answers that question in the affirmative. It proposes that New York and sister states adopt a new stance in response to adolescent **consent** to sex with an adult. In particular, it offers the notion of *legal assent*, a mechanism that presumes no threshold *legal capacity* but affords teenagers autonomous decision making authority and protection following misguided decisions. Part I of this Article briefly reviews the neuroscience and psychosocial evidence regarding adolescent development to maturity. This research is new and reported conclusions vary, but a snapshot review of current understanding helps guide an evaluation of law first formulated in 1933. Part I concludes that adolescents are not younger, smaller adults but are fundamentally different in the ways they think and behave. Part II explores legal guidance concerning **consent**, assent, and juvenile incapacity. It highlights that legal authority cautions against attributing full legal capacity to minors – whether or not one affords them decision making autonomy. Part III reviews recent cases from New York to show how New York courts treat adolescent **consent** to unlawful sex with an adult inconsistently. It also notes several other cases from across the nation that replicate the New York inconsistencies. This Article concludes in Part IV by recommending a new approach to adolescent **consent** to sex with an adult – *legal assent*.

I. Adolescent Neurological, Cognitive, and Psychosocial Development[10]

While no set biological markers precisely define the beginning and end of adolescence as a stage of human development, most researchers agree that it occurs during the second decade of life.[11] Increasingly, scientists argue that adolescence (or "emerging adulthood") extends to about age twenty-five.[12] Adolescents experience physical, cognitive, sexual, and psychosocial development during this long maturation phase.[13] The survey of changes discussed below indicates that transitional adolescent functioning differs significantly from adult behavior.

A. Neurological Development

In 1999, the National Institute of Mental Health (NIMH) announced that the adolescent brain undergoes dramatic changes not before understood.[14] Dr. Jay Giedd, a NIMH neuroscientist, examined adolescent brains using advanced imaging technology.[15] He discovered that, over the span of a year, gray matter almost doubles in some brain sectors, including the prefrontal cortex.[16] An important element of the central nervous system, the gray matter consists of cells and neuron connections, synapses, which enable high cognitive functioning.[17] Depending upon the brain sector, non-linear increases in gray matter peak between ages eleven and sixteen for girls and about a year later, respectively, for boys. Following the growth period, the body purges connections not required and reorganizes the functioning of the brain.[18] Scientists knew that such growth and reorganization phases occur during gestation and the first eighteen months after birth. They did not know about this second wave of overproduction and winnowing that occurs throughout puberty.[19]

The dramatic changes that occur during puberty influence adolescent reasoning and the ability to formulate **consent** because of the functions of the particular areas of the brain involved.[20] Neuroscientist Dr. Elizabeth Sowell and her colleagues explain, "Neuropsychological studies show that the frontal lobes are essential for such functions as response inhibition, emotional regulation, planning and organization. Many of these aptitudes continue to develop between adolescence and young adulthood."[21] The more mature the frontal cortex, "the area of sober second thought," the better teenagers can reason, control their impulses, and make considered judgments. "Thus, there is fairly widespread agreement that adolescents take more risks at least partly because they have an immature frontal cortex, because this is the area of the brain that takes a second look at something and reasons about a particular behavior."[22] This understanding has serious implications regarding adolescent **consent** and legal capacity.

Other areas of the brain also influence teen judgment and behavior. Similar to the frontal cortex, the cerebellum matures well into adolescence.[23] Dr. Giedd believes that the cerebellum enhances functioning in all forms of higher thought, from mathematics to decision making and social skill.[24] The corpus callosum connects the two hemispheres of the brain and appears to influence creativity and problem solving.[25] A primitive area of the brain, the amygdala, likely governs emotional and "gut" responses during adolescence. While adults rely primarily on the frontal cortex when interpreting emotional information, adolescents tend to use the amygdala.[26] Some scientists hypothesize that the use of the amygdala rather than the frontal cortex explains why teenagers experience trouble regulating their emotional responses.[27]

The pruning and organization of the new neural connections in the brain continue throughout the teen years. Giedd asserts, "Maturation does not stop at age 10, but continues into the teen years and even the 20s."[28] The mechanism of synaptic pruning is not yet well understood. One might think that more gray matter means higher functioning. Not so, says Giedd. "Bigger isn't necessarily better, or else the peak in brain function would occur at age 11 or 12 . . . . The advances come from actually [the] taking away and pruning down of certain connections themselves."[29] Drawing conclusions from the research, some scientists suggest that the pruning occurs on a "'use it or lose it' principle," such that used connections survive.[30] Unused connections "wither and die."[31] "If a teen is doing music or sports or academics, those are the cells and connections that will be hardwired. If [he or she is] lying on the couch or playing videogames or MTV, those are the cells and connections that are going to survive."[32]

During the gray matter priming phase, white matter increases. The white matter supports neural connections in the brain.[33] "A layer of insulation called myelin progressively envelops these nerve fibers, making them more efficient, just like insulation on electric wires improves their conductivity."[34] More recently, scientists discovered that myelin also "modulates the timing and synchrony of the neuronal firing patterns that create functional networks in the brain."[35] Evidence indicates that environmental experiences influence myelination.[36] According to Dr. Francine Benes, myelination levels increase into the early twenties. "During child development, myelination correlates with maturing patterns of behavior."[37]

This new research confirms that adolescent brain development extends into the twenties, beyond "the age of **consent**" set in every state. Critical abilities – including impulse control, emotional regulation, planning, decision making, and organization – may not fully mature until the third decade of life. Additionally, behaviors and experiences may influence myelination and determine the winnowing and reorganization of gray matter during adolescence. It's possible that teenagers subtly hard-wire experiences, such as algebra homework or sex in a Bee Line passenger car, into their brains.

B. Cognitive Development

Adolescents mature cognitively as well as physically. Cognitive changes include the development of the ability to think more abstractly than children do. Adolescents engage in counter-factual reasoning, consider hypothetical situations, and can adopt a variety of perspectives on a subject.[38] They think introspectively, examining their own thoughts and emotions. The evolution of these cognitive skills happens in unpredictable ways. Some teenagers employ advanced reasoning skills earlier and more often than do their peers. Additionally, situational factors influence individual reasoning performance. For example, when they experience familiar environments and situations, teenagers tend to employ more advanced cognitive reasoning.[39] Dr. Linda Spear notes that some transient developmental declines appear for certain tasks, particularly for those involving stressful or anxiety provoking circumstances.[40]

This information, combined with the theory on hardwiring, suggests that we should not shelter teens from experimentation and gradual learning regarding sexuality, workplace relationships, and other concrete skills and abstract issues. Instead, we should facilitate their learning and maturation under circumstances that safeguard their developmental vulnerabilities. Thus, attributing full capacity to minors may not safeguard them, just as insulating them from all experimentation could stunt their development.

One important factor to remember when examining adolescent cognitive development and capacity is context. Adults should not take one developmental or functional milestone and extrapolate to pronounce any given adolescent mature. For example, research from the 1980s suggested that adolescent cognitive development enabled youth to make hypothetical decisions comparable to those of adults.[41] Following the publication of these data and a number of high-profile violent crimes involving youth, prosecutors began trying more children as adults.[42] The increase in the number of adolescents tried in criminal court as adults at the end of the twentieth-century prompted researchers to revisit the issue of adolescent cognitive competence.[43] The MacArthur Juvenile Adjudicative Competence Study investigated whether adolescents are competent, intellectually and emotionally, to stand trial in adult criminal court.[44] Dr. Laurence Steinberg reported, "Our findings indicate that significant numbers of juveniles who are 15 and younger are probably not competent to stand trial as adults."[45] Dr. Steinberg noted that "younger individuals were less likely to recognize the risks inherent in different choices and less likely to think about the long-term consequences of their choices .. . ."[46] This last finding supports the neuroscience evidence regarding maturity in those brain sectors responsible for inhibition and decision making. According to this research, the competence of sixteen- and seventeen-year-olds to stand trial did not differ from the adults.[47] MacArthur researchers were

quick to point out, however, that the functioning of older juveniles was not necessarily equivalent to that of adults.[48] Researchers emphasized that further inquiry into age differences in other capacities and abilities was ongoing for these older teenagers.[49]

[. . .]

C. Psychosocial Development

Evidence of psychosocial maturation supports the notion that adolescents experience significant changes during not only their teenaged years, but also into their early twenties and beyond. Steinberg describes four psychosocial traits that distinguish adolescents from adults: capacity for self-regulation, reward sensitivity, future orientation, and peer influence.[50]

1. Self-Regulation and Reward Sensitivity

Characteristics common in teenagers mark the transition period that ultimately leads to adulthood. We know, for example, that adolescents take more and greater risks than do adults.[51] Such behaviors include unprotected sex, drunk driving, use of illegal drugs, and criminal activity.[52] Scientists once believed that teenagers differed from adults in their ability to perceive or calculate risks.[53] Neither a lack of information nor cognitive capacity explains their risk-taking tendencies, however. Additionally, studies have demonstrated that increasing knowledge does not necessarily lead people to make better decisions.[54] New evidence demonstrates that age differences in reward sensitivity may explain adolescent risk taking. Teens value rewards over risks more highly than do adults.[55]

Dr. Laurence Steinberg explains adolescent risk taking behavior by examining two interacting neurobiological systems: a socioemotional system, which governs the processing of social and emotional information, and a cognitive control system, which directs deliberative thinking, impulse control, foresight, and the evaluation of risks and rewards.[56] He suggests that a dramatic increase in dopaminergic activity within the socioemotional system at puberty leads to reward seeking.[57] This change precedes the structural maturation of the cognitive control system.[58] Steinberg argues that because the cognitive control system matures later in adolescence, the temporal gap in the development of these two systems "creates a period of heightened vulnerability to risk taking during middle adolescence."[59]

2. Future Orientation

Other studies suggest that adolescents hold different priorities than do adults. In particular, teens "view long-term consequences as less important than short-term consequences."[60] For example, teenagers engage in more delay discounting than do adults, preferring smaller immediate awards over larger but delayed rewards.[61] Self-regulation develops "through adolescence, with gains continuing through the high school years and into young adulthood."[62] Research suggests that development of future-time orientation "continues beyond mid-adolescence, at least through the last year of college."[63] New evidence links future orientation with "brain structure and function, especially in the prefrontal cortex."[64]

Teenagers also engage in more impulsive behavior than average adults. Spear defines impulsivity as the "tendency to react spontaneously without thinking much beforehand as to the consequences."[65] Preliminary studies of juvenile impulsivity suggest that it remains relatively stable until age sixteen when it increases and then again stabilizes at age nineteen. Impulsivity declines during adulthood. More investigation is needed regarding the relation between impulsivity, sensation-seeking, and judgmental maturity. Stress and mood state also influence temperate decision making. Studies indicate that older teenagers exhibit greater mood volatility than do adults.[66]

3. Peer Influence

Researchers (and most parents) know that peers heavily influence teenagers. Steinberg reports that as juveniles form a sense of their own identity during adolescence and young adulthood, they "develop a greater capacity for autonomous decision making and begin to resist peer influence."[67] Until a sense of adult identity and autonomy matures, teenagers make choices influenced both directly and indirectly by peers. Direct coercion affects some decisions, but many others result from an adolescent's concern for peer approval and fear of rejection.[68] Evidence confirms that teens are preoccupied with social status.[69] Dr. Elizabeth Cauffman and Dr. Laurence Steinberg report that adolescents are most susceptible to

peer influence at about age fourteen, after which that influence declines. Studies, however, indicate that a coherent sense of identity does not emerge until about age eighteen. Ego development or individuation, according to some studies, increases throughout adolescent years.

[. . .]

As with the new neuroscience, the research regarding psychosocial traits, various specific **ages**, and maturity of judgment is quite new. Understandably, psychologists hesitate to draw specific conclusions for the practical application of what they now know.[70] This new information, however, raises several important questions for our purposes. For example, who influences an adolescent's decision to have sex with an adult bus driver (assuming that she does actually **consent**)? A parent? Her peers? Social media? Only the driver? Moreover, if she has not formed a coherent independent identity, should we consider her "**consent**" to sex with an adult service provider, teacher, or co-worker legally significant? Do adolescent impulsivity and moodiness combine with stress (including pressure for sex) to influence a teen's decision making process? Should the law regard teen "**consent**," given impulsively and under stress, as significant and legally binding? In light of what we know about teen priorities, including social status and immediate rewards, one can see how sex with an adult, for example a teacher, might seem like a good idea. De-emphasizing the long-term academic career, reputation, and health risks, a teen might choose an exciting sexual relationship and the concomitant status increase with an older, more "sophisticated" man offering such a prize.

4. Adolescent Capacity and Physical Appearance

The research regarding adolescent neurological, cognitive, and psychosocial development is new and ongoing. We cannot draw many firm conclusions about physical changes and behavior. Nor do we fully understand the subtle dynamics of behavior, emotions, environment, and physiology. Does any of this really matter, though?

Assume for a moment that adolescent "**consent**" should not be legally binding because adolescents do not have the power, (equal) status, and/or competence to **consent** to sex with an adult. Will jurists account for the adolescent's developing capacity, status, and power in their allocation of rights and liabilities?

Donald Kramer and Jennifer Soper suggest that while many people claim to base the attribution of rights on competency, they often judge competency and assign rights based on physical appearance.[71] Thus, society treats the children who look physically mature as adults, whether or not those adolescents are emotionally, neurologically, or psychosocially mature. According to neuroscientist Dr. Bea Luna, "An adolescent can look so much like an adult, but cognitively, they are not really there yet ... ."[72] Referring to appearances of physical maturity in adolescents, Dr. Yurgelun-Todd cautions, "[T]hey may not appreciate consequences or weigh information the same way as adults do. So we may be mistaken [that someone is emotionally and psychosocially mature. Even though] we think [he or she] looks physically mature, [his or her] brain may in fact not be mature ... ."[73]

For an example of this phenomenal assumption of maturity, examine the statutory rape defenses. Under this criminal scheme, a minor lacks capacity even if she "consents," so her "consent" is no defense. Her physical maturity, however, might constitute one. In California, the perpetrator's mistake of age, particularly of older victims – arguably based on physical maturity – can be a defense.[74]

[. . .]

A brief review of adolescent development permits us to come back to the law's treatment of adolescents with a fresh perspective. At the very least, we can begin to evaluate whether the law takes us in the right direction. I argue that it does not.

II. Applicable Legal Principles and Guidance Relevant to Juveniles

Before examining case law and the factors that might guide legal reform concerning civil law's treatment of adolescent "consent," we should explore the definitions of some key legal terms.

A. Consent, *Assent, and Acquiescence*

Consent means "to give permission for something to happen; agree to do something."[75] Slightly different from **consent**, assent means "to express approval or agreement"[76] By this definition, assent denotes cooperation or secondary status. Both terms arguably include two prerequisites: knowledge regarding the choice, and volition. In the first aspect **consent** and assent must be

informed and correspond to the activity they legitimate. Ignorant cooperation does not indicate **consent** or assent. Additionally, any misrepresentation taints responsive **consent** or assent. The individual must also possess the cognitive ability to reason about a choice. In the second aspect, **consent** and assent must indicate freedom of choice and volition. The individual must be able to guide her own responsive choices. To acquiesce means "to accept something reluctantly but without protest"[77] and indicates neither full **consent** nor assent.

In distinguishing acquiescence, we add a third requirement for **consent** and assent: a measure of power and autonomy. For example, if someone has no opportunity or authority to dissent, can we value that person's **consent**? **Consent** and assent must be free of coercion and duress. Arguably, they assume a level of equality and mutuality between those persons making a bargain or coming to an agreement. **Consent** carries with it a presumption of intellectual, emotional, and developmental capacity. These characteristics are what undergird legal capacity.

B. Legal **Consent** *and Capacity*

This elucidation of **consent** is consistent with its interpretation in Section 892A of the Second Restatement of Torts. Subsection (2)(a) specifies that in order to extinguish tort liability, **consent** must be "by one who has the capacity to **consent**."[78] A comment to this subsection provides:

> If, however, the one who **consents** is not capable of *appreciating the nature, extent or probable consequences of the conduct*, the **consent** is not effective to bar liability unless the parent, guardian, or other person empowered to **consent** for the incompetent has given **consent**, in which case the **consent** of the authorized person will be effective even though the incompetent does not **consent** ... .[79]

This passage clarifies that one who **consents** must understand what he or she is doing and be able to anticipate results. Such appreciation requires counterfactual thinking or "what if" reasoning. This explanation focuses on the cognitive aspects of **consent**.

Contract law has also examined the notions of legal **consent** and capacity. Contract law has long held that minors lack the capacity to **consent**[80] This conclusion results, in part, from the fear that adults may take legal advantage of minors who make contractual agreements. Contract law, therefore, typically makes contracts by minors voidable by those minors.[81]

[. . .]

C. Medical Assent

While this discussion of key terms has highlighted the similarities between **consent** and assent, government regulation of human-subject medical research brings nuanced meaning to assent as it applies to children in that context.[82] The Code of Federal Regulations mandates that Institutional Review Boards (IRBs) may approve research on children if "adequate provisions are made for soliciting the assent of the children and the permission of their parents or guardians."[83] The IRB decides whether the child is even "capable of providing assent" by considering the child's age, maturity, and psychological state.[84] IRBs may waive parental permission only under special circumstances.[85] No additional guidance suggests how IRBs should weigh these factors. Thus, medical assent does not equate with legal **consent** since parental permission – **consent** – typically bolsters a child's assent Moreover, Cauffman and Steinberg caution, "Adolescents who demonstrate that they meet the criteria for informed [medical] **consent** may nevertheless lack the psychosocial maturity required to make consistently mature judgments."[86] Additionally, one might argue that capacity for medical assent does not equate with legal capacity since the decisions contemplated are so narrowly defined and well-informed. The responsibility for any decision to conduct medical research on a minor typically is shared by the researchers, IRB, the parents, and lastly by the juvenile.

D. Juvenile "Consent" and Capacity

People considering juvenile legal autonomy might agree that teenagers are capable of assent and acquiescence. Similarly, even a six-year-old may "know" or recognize Barack Obama and Mitt Romney and may "voluntarily" pick one or the other for President. We do not allow that child to cast a political vote, however.[87] Additionally, we might agree that many juveniles understand the concept of sexual intercourse.[88] Their knowledge of the mechanics of sexual activity does not necessarily qualify them, however, as competent decision makers or as ready to engage in the behavior. Many adults, judges, and courts disagree. For them, relative cognitive maturity, or even apparent physical maturity, equates with adult capacity.

They ignore or are ignorant of the level of psychosocial maturity required for competent decision making.

E. General Legal Principles and the Scientific Research

Common law and legal treatises have guided the law's treatment of teenagers for years. The new science of adolescent development arguably undermines some of this legal "wisdom."

1. The "Rule of Sevens" and the Restatements

Current law, embodied in the "rule of sevens,"[89] explicitly posits that most teenagers have the legal capacity to **consent**. Under this traditional rule, a minor under age seven cannot give **consent**, be held liable for negligent conduct, or formulate the requisite mental state to engage in criminal conduct. From seven- to fourteen-years-old, the law presumes that a minor lacks capacity. From fourteen to twenty-one (now eighteen), courts operate under a rebuttable presumption that minors are competent to **consent** and are responsible for criminal and negligent conduct.[90] Thus, in the context of a civil claim for damages and absent evidence to the contrary, the bright-line rule allows a trier of fact to presume that a child over fourteen consents to sexual contact.

As noted above, legal treatises and guidance also acknowledge that children may lack legal capacity to make binding legal decisions and offer legal **consent**. Section 15 of the Second Restatement of Contracts addresses volitional incapacity, suggesting that some incapacitated persons who cannot conform their behavior to societal norms may void their contracts. Section 892A comment 2(b) of the Second Restatement of Torts explains, however, that "[i]f the person consenting is a child or one of deficient mental capacity, the **consent** may still be effective if he is capable of appreciating the nature, extent and probable consequences of the conduct consented to .. . ."

The new scientific data concerning adolescents calls into question whether young teenagers possess full legal capacity and, in particular, whether most teenagers are capable of knowing and voluntary **consent** to sex with an adult. What neuroscientists and psychologists have said regarding capacity informs this issue. Dr. Abigail Baird, who specializes in adolescent neurological development, suggests that ". . . it may be physically impossible for adolescents to engage in counterfactual reasoning and as a result of this are often unable to effectively foresee the possible consequences of their actions."[91] This statement directly undermines tort guidance that children may have legal capacity.

Dr. Silvia Bunge has compared the prefrontal cortex of children with those adults suffering from injuries, who take more risks than do healthy adults. She has determined that children make riskier choices than adults, in part because they enjoy doing so. She tied these choices to activity in the prefrontal cortex. Bunge suggests that teens are less able to resist the temptation of a new reward. She explains, "If your friend says, 'Hey let's try this drug; it will be fun,' you might not be able to use the information you know about the possible negative consequences to resist ... ."[92] Bunge's research suggests that even knowing participation in an activity might not justify the attribution of full legal capacity.

These legal examples, when viewed side-by-side with science, suggest that we need to pay serious attention to traditional legal presumptions about adolescents and consider incorporating more about what we now know concerning adolescent development. A few federal and state courts are doing just that.

2. Science and the United States Supreme Court Precedents

Even the United States Supreme Court has noticed the importance of the new science on adolescent development.[93] The Supreme Court's recent *Graham v. Florida* opinion, which relied on *amici* briefing regarding adolescent neurological and psychosocial development, provides valuable guidance relevant to adolescent maturity, "consent," and legal capacity.[94] The *Graham* decision holds that a life sentence without the possibility of parole for particular juvenile offenders violates the Eighth Amendment protection against cruel and unusual punishment.[95] This decision also reaffirms evidence regarding adolescent neurological and psychosocial development, discussed in *Roper v. Simmons*,[96] which invalidated the death penalty for minors. The *Graham* Court noted that "developments in psychology and brain science continue to show fundamental differences between juvenile and adult minds. For example, parts of the brain involved in behavior control continue to mature through late adolescence."[97]

The *Graham* Court found that society might still hold a teenager responsible for his behavior but that "his

transgression 'is not as morally reprehensible as that of an adult.'"[98] This distinction between responsibility and moral culpability is important. If a toddler knocks over a vase while stumbling to a table, we might find him responsible but not morally culpable because he did not intend to break the vase and lacked the motor coordination to control his steps and body. Extend this example to a teenager who may be technically "responsible" for saying "yes" to sex, or who may even initiate sexual activity, but who cannot fully anticipate the consequences of her conduct and may lack the psychosocial skills to control her behavior in context.

[. . .]

III. "Consent' Versus Consent in Criminal Law and Civil Law

In *Doe v. Starbucks*,[99] a California federal district court analyzed whether a minor could bring a civil sexual harassment case against her supervisor and employer when she "consented" to some or most of the alleged offensive conduct.[100] While this case arose in California and was decided using California civil law regarding "the age of **consent**," this controversy could have easily arisen at a Starbucks in New York. We will return to *Starbucks* to explore its relevance for the nation after discussing relevant New York law. For now, however, we focus on the legal significance of the "**consent**" that was pivotal in *Starbucks*, as it is in any sexual harassment case involving an adult. In *Faragher v. City of Boca Raton*, the United States Supreme Court emphasized that, in a sexual harassment case under Title VII of the Civil Rights Act of 1964 (Title VII),[101] the "objectionable environment must be both objectively and subjectively offensive, one that a reasonable person would find hostile or abusive and one that the victim in fact did perceive to be so."[102] One might refer to the objective component as the "reasonableness" standard and to the subjective element as the "unwelcomeness" requirement. Every state fair employment practice statute (FEPS) that similarly prohibits sexual harassment also makes "unwelcomeness" an element of the *prima facie* case.[103] Thus, if Doe's "**consent**" garners legal significance, she loses her sexual harassment case because the conduct is not subjectively "unwelcome."

The complicating factor for employers defending sexual harassment cases (or tort claims like the one in *Barton v. Bee Line, Inc.*) and the jurists evaluating those cases arises from state sex crime statutes that specifically prohibit sexual conduct with minors. Typically, "**consent**" provides no defense for the criminally-accused adult. So, what happens when criminal and civil claims stem from the same conduct? Is the minor's "**consent**" treated consistently? Not in all states, including New York and California. A review of several cases decided since *Bee Line* superbly showcases the conflicts that can lead to bizarre results.

A. New York Criminal Law

Section 130.05(3)(a) of the New York Penal Law states, "A person is deemed incapable of **consent** when he or she is: (a) less than 17 years old .. . ."[104] Section 130.25 (2) prohibits sexual intercourse between an adult twenty-one or older and a youth under seventeen.[105] According to the New York Court of Appeals, this code section "creates an irrebuttable presumption that a child less than [seventeen] years of age cannot **consent** to sexual intercourse with an adult .. . ."[106] Other New York criminal statutes similarly prohibit adults from engaging in sexual acts with youth under seventeen years old.[107] New York courts view a juvenile involved in such conduct as "victimized, regardless of whether or not she or he actually **consents** or even initiates the sexual encounter."[108]

In *People v. Gonzalez*,[109] the defendant challenged on constitutional grounds a New York statute that proscribed oral and anal sexual acts with a minor under seventeen. The County Court acknowledged that minors enjoy most constitutional rights afforded adults, including some privacy rights. The court explained, however, that a state's interest in protecting juveniles justifies limitations on certain rights. The court noted in particular that "the state has the authority to regulate the sexual conduct of its minors by setting age limits to establish whether the individual is sufficiently mature to make intelligent and informed decisions and to **consent** to certain activities."[110]

These New York criminal cases lead one to believe that the New York statutory rape laws are relevant and controlling precedent in every New York court. After all, if a juvenile lacks the capacity to **consent** to sex in the criminal context, what would miraculously enable him or her to develop legal capacity in a civil case? If an adult victimizes a minor, even if that youth initiates the conduct, how is the victimization any less cognizable in civil court? Was *Barton v. Bee Line, Inc.* an unfortunate bumble, which has since been overruled? Anyone who thinks so is mistaken.[111]

B. New York Civil Law

New York civil cases since *Bee Line* have held regularly that **consent**, including juvenile **consent**, may insulate alleged tortfeasors from liability. For example, in *O'Connor v. Western Freight Association*, a 1962 civil assault and battery case involving two males in a fight, the court cited *Bee Line* for the proposition that **consent** operates as a complete defense in a tort action.[112] Fast forward to 1993 and *Stavroula S. v. Guerriera*, a civil assault and battery case brought on behalf of a female under fourteen who allegedly consented to sex with the defendant.[113] The court denied a motion for partial summary judgment because the associated statutory rape case had not resolved whether the plaintiff had consented. **Consent** was not at issue or relevant in the criminal case involving the strict liability prosecution under Penal Law section 130.30. The court reasoned that "the doctrine of collateral estoppel does not bar the defendant from litigating the issue of whether he touched the plaintiff without her **consent**, which is the gravamen of the tort of battery."[114] The court did not address the question of how the plaintiff could have consented if she lacked the legal capacity to **consent**.

In *C. Roe v. Barad*, a similar 1996 battery and intentional infliction of emotional distress case, the New York Supreme Court reversed a lower court decision, granting the fifteen-year-old plaintiff partial summary judgment[115] The appellate court ruled that Penal Law section 130.05(3), which declares that a minor cannot **consent** to sex with an adult, had no application in the tort action. The court found that the defendant could argue both **consent** and lack of emotional distress.[116] The court cited to both *Stavroula S.* and *Bee Line* to support its conclusion.[117] Again, the court did not address the apparent conflict between the treatment of legal capacity in the criminal and civil contexts. The court also failed to explain why "Roe" wasn't a named plaintiff. If Roe was such a capable and calculating actor, why allow her to sue under an alias?

More recently, in *Doe v. Board of Education of Penfield School District*,[118] suit was filed on behalf of a fifteen-year-old student against the school district for negligent supervision after a sexual assault perpetrated by a seventeen-year-old fellow student. The court held, "A school may not be liable where older minors, who are capable of understanding and appreciating their conduct, intentionally avoid detection to go to a prohibited and secluded portion of the school building and engage in consensual sex."[119] The court emphasized, "The

Penal Code 130.05 precluding sexual **consent** by children under 17 years of age may not be applicable in a civil suit."[120] The court cited *O'Connor* and *Barad* for support.[121] It cited no scientific journals or articles for the proposition that a fifteen-year-old is capable of understanding and appreciating her conduct concerning sexual activity such that she can give legal **consent**. Doe may have been capable in this case, but we have no information that an evaluation of her capacity to **consent** was even contemplated or attempted. The irony is that society believes her incapable of suing in her own capacity. [. . .]

This review of New York criminal and civil law permits us to return to the *Starbucks* case to evaluate how a teenaged New York franchise worker might fare in a sexual harassment suit against her employer.

C.   *Starbucks New York Style*

Starbucks hired Jane Doe in July 2005 when she was sixteen years old. She worked closely with her supervisor, Timothy Horton, who was then twenty-four years old. After her hire, Horton allegedly asked Doe out on dates repeatedly and she initially rebuffed his advances.[122] In pleadings, Doe declared that Horton made "'perhaps hundreds'" of sexually explicit or profane statements to her at work in front of coworkers concerning his sexual interest in her.[123] Later, she "finally said 'yes,' hoping it would make him stop."[124] They ultimately engaged in sexual activity in November or December 2005.[125] Doe declared,

> [Horton] demanded that I perform oral sex on him, which I did. I felt like I had to – that I had no choice .. . . I felt that, because he had given me marijuana and I had smoked it with him, I had to do what he said, because he was my Supervisor and I didn't want to lose my job.[126]

Horton told Doe not to tell anyone about their relationship.

In February 2006, however, Doe told her mother that she was having sex with Horton. Doe's mother requested an investigation and that Starbucks take steps to protect her daughter. Store Manager Lina Nobel did not ask Horton about a sexual relationship "because she thought it was not her place to do so."[127] Nobel informed Doe's mother that Horton had "denied any wrongdoing with [Doe], . . . and if she

fired him or terminated him, she was afraid that she was going to have a wrongful termination claim on her bands."[128] Thereafter, Doe requested a transfer to a different Starbucks store "because she 'felt like she had to.'"[129] Finally, in 2006, Doe left her job and "enrolled in a treatment facility out of state to address mental and emotional problems .. . ."[130] Horton ultimately pled guilty to criminal unlawful sexual intercourse with a minor under California Penal Code Section 261.5(a).[131] In that associated criminal case, Doe's "**consent**" to sex failed to provide Horton with a legal defense.

In the civil sexual harassment case later filed on behalf of Doe, however, the federal court left open the possibility that Doe's "**consent**" might serve to insulate Starbucks and Horton from civil liability. The *Starbucks* **federal** court relied on California state legal authority, quoting the California Supreme Court decision in *People v. Tobias:*.[132]

> In 1970, the Legislature created the crime of unlawful sexual intercourse with a minor (261.5) and amended the rape statute (261) so that it no longer included sex with a minor in the **definition** of **rape**. As a result, the circumstances surrounding sexual intercourse with a minor became highly relevant, because this conduct might in some cases be a distinct and less serious crime than rape, particularly where the minor engages in the sexual act *knowingly and voluntarily*.[133]

Oddly, neither section 261.5 nor section 261 refers to a minor acting "*knowingly and voluntarily*." The Court continued:

> In making this change [declassifying the behavior as rape], the Legislature implicitly acknowledged that, *in some cases at least, a minor may be capable of giving legal consent to sexual relations*. If that were not so, then every violation of section 261.5 would also constitute rape under section 261, subdivision (a)(1). Of course, a minor might still be found incapable of giving legal **consent** to sexual intercourse in a particular case, but [the legislature] abrogate[ed] the rule that a girl under 18 is in all cases incapable of giving such legal **consent** .. . .[134]

Whether or not the California Court accurately interpreted the legislature's statutory reforms is beyond the scope of this article.[135a] This passage makes clear, however, that Doe's "**consent**" to have sex with her supervisor may bar her sexual harassment and tort claims.[135b]

[. . .]

D.   The Seventh Circuit and Doe v. Oberweis Dairy

The civil law results in California and New York are not coastal aberrations. Other case law involving teen workers indicates that treatment of a minor's **consent** in criminal cases is very different from how it is in civil cases. What explains this discrepancy? The Seventh Circuit Court of Appeals was one of the first to address the conflicts between criminal and civil laws in *Doe v. Oberweis Dairy*.[136]

Starbucks Doe cited *Oberweis* in support of her contention that minors lack the capacity to **consent** to sex with adults. The *Starbucks* court found that *Oberweis* had "little persuasive effect" since it was a Seventh Circuit case that contradicted *Tobias* and did not consider California law. A closer look at *Oberweis*, however, may lead others to believe that it had more to offer in the *Starbucks* sexual harassment case than the *Starbucks* California federal district court determined.

Like *Starbucks*, *Oberweis* was a sexual harassment case involving a sixteen-year-old teenager and her twenty-four-year-old supervisor.[137] Like New York, Illinois prohibits sex between minors under seventeen and adults.[138] The Illinois federal district court in *Oberweis* found that the "unwelcomeness" requirement applies in employment cases involving minors and that the conduct about which Doe complained was not "unwelcome."[139] The court stated:

> It is undisputed that Plaintiff voluntarily visited Nayman's [the supervisor's] apartment alone the day of the encounter. It is also undisputed that Plaintiff asked Nayman to put a **condom** on [which he did not][140] before they had sex. It is further undisputed that after the sexual encounter, Plaintiff voluntarily interacted with Nayman in social situations outside of the workplace. As such, no genuine issue of material fact exists as to whether the sexual harassment was not unwelcome either in fact or law.[141]

The district court clearly equated voluntariness or acquiescence with legal **consent**. Because Doe did not resist or otherwise indicate that the conduct was unwelcome, the court dismissed her sexual harassment case against *Oberweis Dairy*.

The appellate court reversed.[142] It found that while Nayman had not committed forcible rape, he had committed "statutory rape,"[143] "which is made a crime because of a belief that below a certain age a person cannot (more realistically, is unlikely to be able to) make a responsible decision about whether to have sex."[144] The *Oberweis* court emphasized the age disparity between Nayman and Doe. It explained, "In Illinois as elsewhere the crime is considered more serious the greater the disparity in ages between the parties. The theory is that a young girl (or boy) is likely to have particular difficulty resisting the blandishments of a much older man."[145] Note how this recognition of juvenile limitation resembles the incapacity defense enumerated in section 15 of the Second Restatement of Contracts, discussed above.

Because of the belief that minors may not make responsible decisions about sex, the *Oberweis* court devised a plan for dealing with adolescent "**consent**" to sex under Title VII. The court held that litigants should look to the "age of **consent**" set under state law to determine whether the plaintiffs "**consent**" will have legal significance under Title VII.[146] The court explained:

> To avoid undermining valid state policy by reclassifying sex that the state deems nonconsensual as consensual . . . and to avoid intractable inquiries into maturity that legislatures invariably pretermit by basing entitlements to public benefits (right to vote, right to drive, right to drink, right to own a gun, etc.) on specified ages rather than on a standard of "maturity," federal courts, rather than deciding whether a particular Title VII minor plaintiff was capable of "welcoming" the sexual advances of an older man, should defer to the judgment of average maturity in sexual matters that is reflected in the age of **consent** in the state in which the plaintiff is employed. That age of **consent** should thus be the rule of decision in Title VII cases.[147]

In this passage, the *Oberweis* appellate court also referred to the need to avoid maturity evaluations. A serious problem with this plan becomes obvious immediately, though. Which system, criminal or civil, marks the age of **consent**?

In California, a civil case interpreting *Tobias*, *Donaldson v. Department of Real Estate*,[148] arguably gives us the answer. In *Donaldson*, the court considered whether the California Department of Real Estate had wrongfully revoked the real estate license of a twenty-four-year-old licensee who had seduced his sixteen-year-old sister-in-law. Donaldson had pled "no contest" to charges brought under Penal Code section 261.5. When the California Real Estate Commissioner revoked his license, she interpreted his actions to be "[s]exually related conduct causing physical harm or emotional distress to a . . . non-consenting participant in the conduct."[149] In reversing the Commissioner, the *Donaldson* court held, "Just as there is no longer any "statutory rape" in this state, so there is no "age of consent" as concerns sexual relations, and references to such a concept can only muddy the analytical waters."[150] For states such as California, with no "age of consent," adolescent "consent" garners legal significance, whether or not the minor has legal capacity in the criminal context. But what is the age of consent in New York? Is it determined by the criminal code or by the *Bee Line* cases which might necessarily lead to a maturity evaluation of the plaintiff? If the civil cases control, how will judges (or juries) conduct a maturity evaluation of a youth months or even years after the alleged conduct occurred?

The *Oberweis* appellate court acknowledged that its approach would necessarily mean that "the protection that Title VII gives teenage employees will not be uniform throughout the country, since the age of consent is different in different states, though within a fairly narrow band."[151] This federal appellate court clearly did not know in 2006, however, that only a few months earlier in California, the *Donaldson* state district court had declared the end of the "age of consent" in California civil cases.

Thus, the Seventh Circuit court offered the nation a logical, if imperfect, formula for responding to adolescent "consent" in sexual harassment and sexual abuse cases. Conceivably, this standard produces different results in the case of the seduction of a sixteen-year-old Starbucks barista (or, for example, a Bee Line passenger) depending on where she lives. In Indiana, where the age of consent is sixteen, she loses her Title VII sexual harassment case.[152] In Illinois and Wisconsin, where the ages of consent are seventeen and eighteen respectively,[153] she may get beyond the summary judgment phase. Within the Seventh Circuit, Starbucks and other employers of teenagers navigate three different ages of consent. A random age demarcation alone does not make logical or legal sense. Moreover, this formula provides no clear guidance in states where criminal and civil law conflict in the way they treat adolescent non-resistance or "consent."

[. . .]

IV. Civil Law's Treatment of "Consent"

The neuroscience and psychosocial studies regarding adolescent development continue to influence our perceptions of adolescents as legal actors. Society can expect to hear impressive new revelations in the coming years. Our teenagers cannot wait, however, if waiting means a continuation of the legal status quo. Even if we cannot draw clear causal connections between neuroscience and behavior, we can evaluate whether the law is at least congruent with what we know about adolescent development. This Article suggests it is not and that, as a society, we can do better for our teenagers. The question remains; how do we adapt the law regarding adolescent consent to match their developmental capabilities and needs – at least until we know more?

A. Create a National "Age of Consent"

One proposal for dealing with adolescent "consent" involves nationally synchronizing the "age of consent" with the age of majority at eighteen.[154] We might deny juvenile legal capacity until eighteen, even though we may agree that some minors demonstrate sufficient maturity to constitute legal capacity before that age. Several reasons support this move. First, it is more efficient to draw a bright line in a logical place. While we might disagree about where to draw the line, (at 16, 18, or 21), few will dispute that rules are easier to enforce than maturity evaluations are to conduct.

Second, anything but a consistent bright line might lead to a maturity evaluation which puts a minor "on trial." Anticipation of such a trial might cause many minors not to complain later about coercive and exploitative conduct to which they "consented" initially. Third, who knows how to do an effective maturity evaluation? No such fool-proof test exists or every department of motor vehicles might use it before issuing a driver's license to a teenager. As noted above, *Graham* confirmed that psychological evaluations to link behavior and maturity may not produce robust results. Additionally, who can say that a minor who is mature on the test date was mature on the day she "consented"?

Fourth, many adults would rather err on the side of protecting all of our teenagers, even the relatively mature ones, than risk traumatizing or sacrificing the immature ones. The point of the law is to protect those persons who need the protection the most, not to sacrifice those youth because we are concerned about protecting a few who do not really need protection. However, a rule that eighteen marks the beginning of adulthood, such as most states have adopted, makes little sense given the neuroscience of late adolescent development. According to Dr. Ruben Gur, neuropsychologist and Director of the Brain Behavior Laboratory at the University of Pennsylvania:

> The evidence now is strong that the brain does not cease to mature until the early 20s in those relevant parts that govern impulsivity, judgment, planning for the future, foresight of consequences, and other characteristics that make people morally culpable. Therefore, a presumption arises that someone under 20 should be considered to have an underdeveloped brain. Additionally, since brain development in the relevant areas goes in phases that vary in rate and is usually not complete before the early to mid-20s, there is no way to state with any scientific reliability that an individual 17-year-old has a fully matured brain .... Indeed, age 21 or 22 would be closer to the "biological" age of maturity.[155]

This passage highlights that bright line rules sometimes fail to track scientific advances.

Therefore, I join opponents of bright line demarcations for the reservation of most rights because our children need maturing experiences. By setting the "age of consent" at a particular age, we deny younger teenagers many of the experiences that will lead to their neurological and psychosocial development. We also deny them important rights to which they are entitled and which they may need, such as the right to procreate, or not. If we infantilize them until they are eighteen, we may harm the very teenagers we would hope to protect.

B.   Eliminate the "Age of Consent"

While one might craft a variety of solutions to address the concern that adolescent "consent" is different from adult consent, some responses seem patently irrational. The *Tobias* dicta which eliminates the age of consent in the context of civil liability creates more problems than it solves and appears inconsistent with what we know from the expert scientists regarding adolescent development and psychosocial maturity. This chapter's brief review of conflicting laws and United States Supreme Court acceptance of the developmental differences between adults and teenagers suggests that the

elimination of the "age of the consent" places teenagers at risk – of sexual predation, at least.

C.   Create New Multifactor Standards For Legal Consent

Another approach involves a tripartite or multifaceted scheme.[156] Society might use particular age requirements in certain contexts or for particular privileges, such as smoking or gaming, as the law does now. Where juveniles have less familiarity with the activity, where power imbalances exist, and where more serious consequences (than, for example, a financial loss on a lottery ticket) might result for a teenager, the law might set a higher age requirement tied to an objective criterion. Professor R. George Wright notes that a focus on the age of consent might simply be a distraction.[157] He suggests that where no discernible disparity in power or subtle coercion complicates a relationship or situation, we might eliminate age requirements.[158]

The risk of mandated maturity evaluations still poses a problem under this tripartite approach. As the Doe cases demonstrate, when jurists set fixed age barriers, judges make exceptions, sometimes to remain consistent with other legal doctrines. As noted, science does not yet provide definitive, comprehensive guidance on any given adolescent's maturity, and evaluator bias can skew results of psychosocial evaluations. I worry that law makers will eliminate age of consent requirements to the detriment of youth, as I argue was done in *Tobias*. However, I agree that liability for Romeo and Juliet (or Romeo and Romeo) makes no sense and have suggested as much previously.[159]

[. . .]

D.   Legal Assent

Rather than eliminate default guidance or attempt to implement myriad separate rules for the regulation of adolescent activities and "consent," society might give adolescent "consent" legal significance when it is in a minor's best interests to do so. To that end, I recommend a concept I call *legal assent*. Unlike medical assent, it requires no associated parental consent or permission. Unlike legal consent, it carries no associated threshold level of legal capacity. Similar to consent by a minor under contract law, legal assent is voidable by the minor.

However, legal assent operates somewhat differently from traditional, voidable contract consent by a minor. If a minor gives legal assent, that "consent" is legally binding unless the minor voids her assent during her minority, or during a reasonable time thereafter. Parents cannot void a minor's assent for her. If she successfully voids her assent, a court cannot even admit it into evidence or permit discovery on the matter. A criminal prosecutor might still prosecute an adult who has sex with an assenting minor, however, because the legal assent operates only for the benefit of the *minor*. Voters, legislators, and district attorneys might still act in *society's* best interests. Additionally, parents still would have the authority to discipline their children – even in the context of an assent of which the parents disapproved.

Consider an example. Suppose a minor, Doe, assents to sex with her teacher. The district attorney can prosecute him for statutory rape or, in California, unlawful sex with a minor. A successful case results in a vindication for a society that does not want its teachers having sex with students. If Doe reaffirms her assent, there is no parallel civil case; the legal controversy ends. Certainly, Doe's parents can act domestically to comfort, guide, or discipline their daughter, as they see fit.

If on the other hand, Doe determines that she was duped, coerced, or made a mistake in assenting, she can void her legal assent and bring (through her guardian) a sexual harassment or tort claim against her teacher to recover for her injuries. Arguably, sexual intercourse with an adult (teacher, supervisor, or bus driver) is not in her best interests. The court will affirm her revocation, deny any discovery, and exclude admission of evidence (at any phase of trial) regarding Doe's assent if the adult raises it as a civil defense in a Title IX or tort case. Society allows Doe to void her assent and hopes that teachers will take warning and stay away from teenaged girls and boys. Criminal sanctions for adults clearly suggest that sexual activities with an adult are not in a minor's best interests.

Thus, Doe makes the first and second choices: whether to assent and whether to void her assent Society permits her the second choice to protect her from the bad choices we anticipate she might make *and to facilitate her own correction of her mistake*. If an adult (such as Smith, Horton, Donaldson, or the Bee Line driver) challenges the abrogation, the court evaluation focuses not on the moral purity or maturity of the minor but upon whether the *original* assent was in her best interests. The evaluation focuses on the circumstances, not on the individual minor.

[. . .]

This theory of legal assent and its proposed use in sexual harassment or civil tort sex cases is consistent with what we know about adolescent development; teenagers need maturing experiences and the opportunity to practice their skills. They may not have the capacity to make every decision, but this approach permits teenagers to make some and avoid those that they later believe were unwise, foolish, or mistaken.[160]

V. Conclusions

The existing conflicts between criminal and civil law treatment of adolescent "**consent**" leave teenagers vulnerable, especially to sexual predators. Court conflation of acquiescence, **consent**, and capacity highlights the need for legal reform and intervention. The new neuroscience evidence and studies concerning adolescent cognitive and psychosocial development confirm that adolescents are not the physical or functional equivalents of adults. Scientific studies that demonstrate that teenagers are developing capacity support the call for legal reform. Until we can assess adolescent maturity and capacity accurately, we need a way to protect teenagers while affording them some measure of legal autonomy and maturing experiences.

[. . .]

Notes

1   Barton v. Bee Line. Inc., 265 N.Y.S. 284. 284–86 (App. Div. 1933). This case is a classic "he said, she said" case. Grace Barton claimed forcible rape and the driver claimed that she consented to sex. This Article acknowledges the continuing problematic nature of credibility determinations in alleged rape cases and the bias against complaining women who sue for civil damages. I will address this particular bias more directly in another article. *See* Jennifer Ann Drobac, Abandoning Teenage **Consent** for Legal Assent: Harmonizing Developmental Sciences and the Law (unpublished manuscript) (on file with author).

2   Samuel H. Williamson, *Seven Ways to Compute the Relative Value of a U.S. Dollar Amount, 1774 to Present*, MEASURING WORTH, http://www.measuringworth.com/uscompare/ (enter 1933 as the initial year, 3000 as the initial amount, and 2011 as the desired year; then follow "Calculate" hyperlink) (last visited Nov. 13, 2011).

3   Bee Line, 265 N.Y.S. at 284.

4   Id. at 285.

5   *Id.*

6   *Id.* (quoting Smith v. Richards. 29 Conn. 232, 240 (1860)).

7   The "age of **consent**" commonly refers to the age at which a minor (someone under eighteen years old) may legally **consent** to engage in sexual activity with an adult and, thereby, insulate that adult from criminal prosecution. *But see* Donaldson v. Dep't of Real Estate, 36 Cal. Rptr. 3d 577, 588–89 (Ct. App. 2005) (discussing that "the age of **consent**" may refer to the age a minor can legally **consent** to marry).

8   *See, e.g.*, Doe v. Starbucks. Inc., No. SACV 08-0582 AG (CWx), 2009 WL 5183773. at *2, *7-8 (C.D. Cal. Dec. 18, 2009) (granting in part and denying in part motions for summary judgment).

9   I use quotations with adolescent "**consent**" because even explicit verbal agreement by a minor may not constitute legal **consent** and may equate more realistically with acquiescence. *See* Meritor Sav, Bank v. Vinson. 477 U.S. 57, 68 (1986) (holding that acquiescence is not **consent** in an evaluation of the unwelcomeness of sexual conduct under Title VII of the 1964 Civil Rights Act, 42 U.S.C.) 2000e-2(a)(1) (2006)).

10 For a thorough, detailed and updated discussion of the neurological and psychosocial development of teenagers, see Jennifer Ann Drobac, *Worldly But Not Yet Wise* (Univ. of Chi. Press, under contract); see also Drobac, J. A. 2012. Consent, Teenagers, and (un)Civil(ized) Consequences. In *Children, Sexuality, and the Law*. Eds. Sacha M. Coupet and Ellen Marrus (New York University Press: New York), pp. 30–71. Jennifer Ann Drobac, I Can't to I Kant: The Sexual Harassment of Working Adolescents. Competing Theories, and Ethical Dilemmas. 70 ALB. L. REV. 675, 713-17 (2007). *See generally Jennifer Ann Drobac*, "Developing Capacity": Adolescent "Consent" at Work at Law and in the Sciences of the Mind, 10 U.C. DAVIS J. JUV. L. & POL'Y 1 (2006) (discussing new neuroscientific and psychosocial evidence regarding adolescent physical and psychosocial development).

11 *See, e.g.*, Linda Patia Spear, *The Behavioral Neuroscience Of Adolescence* 5 (2010).

12 *Id.* (citing Jeffrey Jensen Arnett, *Emerging Adulthood: The Winding Road from the Late Teens through the Early Twenties* (2004)).

13 *See generally id* at 36-190.

14 Nat'l Inst. of Mental Health, NIH Publication No. 01-4929, *Teenage Brain: A Work In Progress* (2001) [hereinafter NIMH, *Teenage Brain*], *available at* http://www.wvdhhr.org/bhhf/scienceonourminds/NIMH%20PDFs/04%20Teenage.pdf.

15 Jay N. Giedd et al., Brain Development During Childhood and Adolescence: A Longitudinal MRI Study, 2 *Nature Neuroscience* 861, 861-63 (1999).

16 Paul M. Thompson et al., Growth Patterns in the Developing Brain Detected by Using Continuum Mechanical Tensor Maps, 404 *Nature* 190, 192 (2000).

17 NIMH, *Teenage Brain, supra* note 14. *See generally* Judith L. Rapoport et al., Progressive Cortical Change During Adolescence in Childhood-Onset Schizophrenia: A Longitudinal Magnetic Resonance Imaging Study, 56 *Archives Gen. Psychiatry* 649 (1999) (finding that study patients with early-onset schizophrenia have a significant decrease in cortical gray matter during adolescence, suggesting that the gray matter helps enable high cognitive functioning).

18 SPEAR, *supra* note 11, at 81-83.

19 *Interview: Jay Giedd, Inside the Teenage Brain*, PBS FRONTLINE, http://www.pbs.org/wgbh/pages/frontline/shows/teenbrain/interviews/giedd.html (last visited Nov. 13, 2011) [hereinafter *Interview: Jay Giedd*].

20 *See id.*

21 Elizabeth R. Sowell et al., *In Vivo Evidence for Post-Adolescent Brain Maturation in Frontal and Striatal Regions*, 2 NATURE NEUROSCIENCE 859, 860 (1999).

22 Sarah Spinks, *Adolescent Brains Are Works in Progress, Inside the Teenage Brain*, PBS FRONTLINE, http://www.pbs.org/wgbh/pages/frontline/shows/teenbrain/work/adolescent.html (last visited Nov. 13, 2011) [hereinafter Spinks, *Works in Progress*] (focusing on Dr. Giedd's research).

23 *Id.*

24 *Id.; see also Interview: Jay Giedd, supra* note 19. Dr. Geidd notes that the cerebellum, "involved in coordination of our cognitive process, our thinking processes[,]" does not finish changing until the 20s. He adds that "this ability to smooth out all the different intellectual processes to navigate the complicated social life of the teen...seems to be a function of the cerebellum." *Id.* Dr. Todd Preuss commented here that Dr. Giedd's view on the cerebellum is one not widely held by neuroscientists but one "held by a respected minority." *Id.*

25 *Interview: Jay Giedd, supra* note 19.

26 Sarah Spinks, *One Reason Teens Respond Differently to the World: Immature Brain Circuitry, Inside the Teenage Brain*, PBS FRONTLINE, http://www.pbs.org/wgbh/pages/frontline/shows/teenbrain/work/onereason.html (last visited Nov. 13, 2011) (discussing Deborah Yurgelun-Todd's study); *see also Interview: Deborah Yurgelun-Todd, Inside the Teenage Brain*, PBS FRONTLINE, http://www.pbs.org/wgbh/pages/frontline/shows/teenbrain/interviews/todd.html (last visited Nov. 13, 2011) (noting that Yurgelun-Todd's results are from a very small pilot study, and that caution should be used in the interpretation of the results). *See generally* Abigail A. Baird et al., *Functional Magnetic Resonance Imaging of Facial Affect Recognition in Children and Adolescents*, 38 J. AM. ACAD. CHILD & ADOLESCENT PSYCHIATRY 195 (1999) (discussing Deborah Yurgelun-Todd's study).

27 Sowell, *supra* note 21, at 860.

28 Sharon Begley, *Getting Inside a Teen Brain*, NEWSWEEK (Feb. 27, 2000, 7:00 PM), http://www.newsweek.com/2000/02/27/getting-inside-a-teen-brain.html (quoting Dr. Jay Giedd).

29 *Interview: Jay Giedd, supra* note 19.

30 Spinks, *Works in Progress, supra* note 22. Some researchers caution against premature conclusions based on early scientific findings. *See, e.g.,* Monica A. Payne, *"Use-It-or-Lose-It"? Interrogating an Educational Message from Teen Brain Research,* 35 AUSTRALIAN J. TCHR. EDUC., no. 5, 2010 at 79. In particular, Dr. Elizabeth Sowell commented, "'Jay likes to say "use it or lose it" and that we should put kids in enriched environments. That makes perfect intuitive sense, but we just don't have the data to say that.'" Kendall Powell, *How Does the Teenage Brain Work?,* 442 NATURE 865, 866 (2006) (quoting Dr. Sowell).

31 *Interview: Jay Giedd, supra* note 19.

32 Spinks, *Works in Progress, supra* note 22 (quoting Dr. Giedd). Dr. Preuss stressed here that these assertions come from the scientists' interpretations, not from empirically demonstrated fact. *Id.*

33 *Adolescence, Brain Development and Legal Culpability,* JUV. JUST. NEWSL. (AM. BAR ASSOC./JUV. JUST. CTR., D.C.), Jan. 2004, at 2, *available at* http://www.americanbar.org/content/dam/aba/publishing/criminal_Justice_section_newsletter/crimjust_juvjus_Adolescence.authcheckdam.pdf.

34 NIMH, *Teenage Brain, supra* note 14.

35 Jay N. Giedd et al., *Anatomical Brain Magnetic Resonance Imaging of Typically Developing Children and Adolescents,* 48 J. AM. ACAD. CHILD & ADOLESCENT PSYCHIATRY 465, 468 (2009).

36 SPEAR, *supra* note 11, at 85 (citing R. Douglas Fields, *White Matter in Learning, Cognition and Psychiatric Disorders,* 31 TRENDS NEUROSCIENCE 361 (2008)).

37 Elizabeth Gudrais, *Modern Myelination: The Brain at Midlife,* HARV, MAG. (May-June 2001), http://harvardmagazine.com/2001/05/the-brain-at-midlife.html ("Infants, for example, lack the fine motor coordination to move an index finger independently, since their nerves are insufficiently myelinated."). Dr. Franchie Benes has found that myelination growth increased again in the forties, growing an average of fifty percent again by the mid-fifties. *Id.; see also* NIMH, *Teenage Brain, supra* note 14.

38 SPEAR, *supra* note 11, at 101-02 (citing Laurence Steinberg, *Cognitive and Affective Development in Adolescence,* 9 TRENDS COGNITIVE SCI. 69 (2005)).

39 *Id.* at 102.

40 *Id.* at 107-08.

41 *See, e.g.,* Melinda G. Schmidt & N. Dickon Reppucci, *Children's Rights and Capacities, in* CHILDREN, SOCIAL SCIENCE, AND THE LAW 76, 96 (Bette L. Bottoms et al. eds., 2002) (discussing Lois A. Weithorn & Susan B. Campbell, *The Competency of Children and Adolescents to Make Informed Treatment Decisions,* 53 CHILD DEV. 1589 (1982)).

42 *See, e.g.,* Tony Freemantle, *Lawmakers Get Tougher on Juvenile Offenders,* HOUS. CHRON., Apr. 26, 1998, at A26; *see also* Evelyn Nieves, *California's Governor Plays Tough on Crime,* N.Y. TIMES, May 23, 2000, at A16.

43 MACARTHUR FOUND. RESEARCH NETWORK ON ADOLESCENT DEV. & JUVENILE JUSTICE, THE MACARTHUR JUVENILE ADJUDICATIVE COMPETENCE STUDY SUMMARY 1 (2002) [hereinafter MACARTHUR COMPETENCE STUDY SUMMARY], *available at* www.adjj.org/downloads/58competence_study_summary.pdf.

44 *Id.*

45 Press Release, Temple Univ., Many Kids 15 and Younger May Lack Maturity Necessary to be Competent to Stand Trial, Juvenile Justice Study Finds (Mar. 3, 2003) (*available at* https://www.temple.edu/news_media/bb0302_593.html).

46 MACARTHUR COMPETENCE STUDY SUMMARY, *supra* note 43, at 2.

47 *Id.* at 3.

48 *Id.*

49 *Id.*

50 Laurence Steinberg, *Adolescent Development and Juvenile Justice,* 5 ANN. REV. CLINICAL PSYCHOL. 459, 468 (2009).

51 SPEAR, *supra* note 11, at 130-54; *see also* Elizabeth Cauffinan & Laurence Steinberg, *The Cognitive and Affective Influences on Adolescent Decision Making,* 68 TEMP. L. REV. 1763, 1767 (1995) (providing examples of adolescents' frequent participation in dangerous activities).

52 SPEAR, *supra* note 11, at 130.

53 Steinberg, *supra* note 53, at 469.

54 Cauffman & Steinberg, *supra* note 54, at 1771-72.

55 Steinberg, *supra* note 53, at 469; *see also* SPEAR, *supra* note 11, at 140 (defining sensation-seeking as "a complex trait associated with the desire for diverse, novel, complex, and intense experiences and the willingness to engage in risks to attain those experiences").

56 *Id.*

57 *Id.*

58 Steinberg also distinguishes the maturation of the cognitive control system from the maturation of the frontal lobes through synaptic pruning. He notes that both result in improved thinking abilities but that they happen at different times with different implications for cognitive development. Steinberg, *supra* note 53, at 466.

59 *Id.* While risk taking can be problematic or even life threatening, adaptive benefits also exist, including "opportunities to explore adult behaviors and privileges, to face and conquer challenges, to master the developmental difficulties of adolescence, and to increase status and peer affiliation within certain peer groups." SPEAR, *supra* note 11, at 135 (citations omitted).

60 Cauffinan & Steinberg, *supra* note 54, at 1773.

61 SPEAR, *supra* note 11, at 143.

62 Steinberg, *supra* note 53, at 470.

63 Cauffman & Steinberg, *supra* note 54, at 1787.

64 Steinberg, *supra* note 53, at 469.

65 SPEAR, *supra* note 11, at 142.

66 Cauffinan & Steinberg, *supra* note 54, at 1781-82.

67 Steinberg, *supra* note 53, at 468.

68 *Id.* at 469.

69 Cauffinan & Steinberg, *supra* note 54, at 1773.

70 Cauffinan & Steinberg, *supra* note 54, at 1780.

71 Jennifer Soper, Straddling the Line: Adolescent Pregnancy and Questions of Capacity, 23 LAW & PSYCHOL. REV. 195, 199 (1999).

72 Powell, *supra* note 30, at 865 (quoting Dr. Bea Luna) (internal quotation marks omitted).

73 *Adolescence, Brain Development and Legal Culpability, supra* note 33 (quoting Dr. Deborah Yurgelun-Todd) (internal quotation marks omitted).

74 Charles A. Phipps, Children. Adults, Sex and the Criminal Law: In Search of Reason, 22 SETON HALL LEGIS. J. 1, 52 n.219 (1997) (citing People v. Hernandez. 393 P.2d 673 (Cal. 1964)).

75 THE NEW OXFORD AMERICAN DICTIONARY 362 (Erin McKean ed., 2d ed. 2005).

76 *Id.* at 94.

77 *Id.* at 14.

78 RESTATEMENT (SECOND) OF TORTS)892A(2)(a) (1979).

79 *Id.*892A cmt. b (emphasis added).

80 *See* RESTATEMENT (SECOND) OF CONTRACTS) 12(2)(a) (1981).

81 *See, e.g.*, Jones v. Dressel. 623 P.2d 370, 373 (Colo. 1981); JEFF FERRIELL, UNDERSTANDING CONTRACTS 603-04 (2d ed. 2009).

82 I thank Professor Lois Weithorn for her guidance on this topic.

83 45 C.F.R. 46.404 (2010).

84 46.408(a).

85 46.408(c).

86 Cauffman & Steinberg, *supra* note 54, at 1766.

87 I would, however, permit high school students, who have successfully completed a high school U.S. government or civics class and who have passed a basic knowledge test (similar to a written driver's license test), to participate in elections.

88 *See, e.g.*, People v. Hillhouse. 1 Cal. Rptr. 3d 261, 268 (Ct. App. 2003) ("[W]e would not assume – nor would we infer a legislative presumption – that the average 14 year old in our current society does not possess the intelligence capable of understanding the nature and consequences of a sexual act.").

89 In the criminal system, this rule is also known as the infancy defense. *See generally* MARTIN R. GARDNER, UNDERSTANDING JUVENILE LAW 180-81 (1997) (discussing the infancy defense and capacity to commit a crime).

90 *Id.*

91 Abigail Baird & Jonathan Fugelsang, *The Emergence of Consequential Thought: Evidence from Neuroscience, in* LAW & THE BRAIN 254 (Semir Zeki & Oliver Goodenough eds., 2006).

92 *The Adolescent Brain*, SCI. TODAY U.C. (Nov. 17, 2008), http://www.ucop.edu/sciencetoday/article/18977.

93 For the most recent discussion of the science regarding adolescent conduct and behavior, see Brown v. Entm't Merchs. Ass'n. 131 S. Ct. 2729, 2761-79 (2011) (Breyer, J., dissenting) (citing recent scientific research correlating playing violent video games with aggressive behavior in adolescents to support the contention that the first amendment does not disable the government from placing statutory restrictions upon the sale of video games to minors).

94 Graham v. Florida, 130 S. Ct. 2011, 2026-27 (2010).

95 Id. at 2033-34.

96 Roper v. Simmons. 543 U.S. 551. 569-71 (2005).

97 Graham, 130 S. Ct. at 2026 (citations omitted).

98 *Id.* (quoting Thompson v. Oklahoma. 487 U.S. 815, 835 (1988) (plurality opinion)).

99 Doe v. Starbucks. Inc., No. SACV 08-0582 AG (CWx). 2009 WL 5183773. at *1 (C.D. Cal. Dec. 18, 2009) (granting in part and denying in part motions for summary judgment). This case was set to go to trial the week of June 15, 2010. However, according to the court clerk, the case settled. E-mail from Lisa Bredahl, Court Clerk to the Honorable Andrew J, Guilford, to author (Aug. 24, 2010) (on file with author).

100 *Starbucks*, at *4-5, *7-8.

101 Title VII of the 1964 Civil Rights Act, 42 U.S.C.) 2000e-2(a)(1) (2006).

102 Faragher v. City of Boca Raton, 524 U.S. 775, 787 (1998) (citing Harris v. Forklift Sys., Inc., 510 U.S. 17, 21-22 (1993)).

103 *See, e.g.*, CAL. GOV'T CODE 12940-12951 (West 2010): N.Y. EXEC. LAW 290-301 (McKinney 2010).

104 N.Y. PENAL LAW 130.05(3) (McKinney 2009).

105 N.Y. PENAL LAW 130.25(2) (McKinney 2009).

106 People v. Cratsley, 653 N.E.2d 1162, 1165 n.3 (N.Y. 1995).

107 *See, e.g.*, N.Y. PENAL LAW 130.40 (McKinney 2009) (prohibiting an adult over twenty-one from engaging in oral or anal sexual conduct with a minor under seventeen); N.Y. PENAL LAW 263.05 (McKinney 2008) (prohibiting the use by an adult of a child under seventeen in a sexual performance).

108 In re Rosaly S., No. NA-00012, 2010 WL 1493147, at *15 (N.Y. Fam. Ct. Mar. 26, 2010).

109 People v. Gonzalez. 561 N.Y.S.2d 358 (Cnty. Ct. 1990).

110 Id. at 361 (citing People v. Dozier. 417 N.E.2d 1008 (N.Y. 1980); Michael M. v. Superior Court Sonoma Cnty., 450 U.S. 464, 473 n.8 (1981)).

111 *See, e.g.*, Drobac, *supra* note 80, at 508 n.206 (discounting cases decided before 1945 because of the prevailing sexual norms).

112 O'Connor v. W. Freight Ass'n. 202 F. Supp. 561, 565 (S.D.N.Y. 1962).

113 Stavroula S. v. Guerriera. 598 N.Y.S.2d 300, 301 [App. Div. 1993].

114 Stavroula S., 598 N.Y.S.2d at 301 (citations omitted).

115 Roe v. Barad, 647 N.Y.S.2d 14 (App. Div. 1996).

116 Id. at 16. The defendant had pled guilty to a violation of Penal Law 263.05 which prohibited the use of a child under seventeen in a sexual performance. However, that conviction also did not estop defendant from asserting consent. Id.

117 Id.

118 Doe v. Bd. of Educ., No. 04/6902, 2006 WL 2406532 (N.Y. Sup. Ct. Feb. 10, 2006).

119 Id. at *3.

120 Id.

121 Id.

122 Doe v. Starbucks, Inc., No. SACV 08-0582 AG (CWx), 2009 WL 5183773, at *1-5 (C.D. Cal. Dec. 18, 2009).

123 Id. at *2 (quoting Starbucks's Objections to Plaintiffs Evidence at 9:9-10:8, Starbucks, 2009 WL 5183773).

124 Starbucks, 2009 WL 5183773, at *1 (quoting Doe Declaration P 4, Starbucks, 2009 WL 5183773).

125 Id. at *2.

126 Id. at *3 (quoting Doe Declaration, supra note 143, P 20) (internal quotation marks omitted). Doe and Horton engaged in sexual activities regularly through June 2006. In addition to "vaginal intercourse and oral copulation" at work and offsite, "[t]hey exchanged explicit sexual comments and text messages at work." Id. at *5 (internal quotation marks omitted) (quoting Plaintiffs Statement of Material Facts PP 20, 25, Starbucks, 2009 WL 5183773).

127 Id. at *5.

128 Id. at *6 (quoting J.M. Deposition at 187:18-24, Starbucks, 2009 WL 5183773) (internal quotation marks omitted).

129 Id. (quoting Plaintiff's Statement of Material Facts, supra note 145, P 40).

130 Id. (quoting Plaintiff's Statement of Material Facts, supra note 145, P 59).

131 Id. (citations omitted).

132 People v. Tobias, 21 P.3d 758 (Cal. 2001).

133 Starbucks, 2009 WL 5183773. at *7 (emphasis added) (quoting Tobias, 21 P.3d at 761-62) (citations omitted) (comparing CAL. PENAL CODE) 261.5(b)-(d) [offense classification and punishment for unlawful sexual intercourse with a minor], with CAL. PENAL CODE 264(a) [punishment for rape].

134 Starbucks, 2009 WL 5183773, at *7.

135a For a thorough discussion of this case and the controlling California law, see Drobac, supra note 1.

135b In January 2016, California Civil Code section 1708.5.5 took effect to "prohibit the use of a minor's consent in a civil action against an action against an adult in a position of authority." Jennifer Ann Drobac, Sexual Exploitation of Teenagers: Adolescent Development, Discrimination & Consent Law 238 (University of Chicago Press, 2016).

136 Doe v. Oberweis Dairy. 456 F, 3d 704 (7th Cir. 2006).

137 Doe v. Oberweis Dairy, No. 03 C 4774, 2005 WL 782709. at *1 (N.D. Ill. Apr. 6, 2005), rev'd, 456 F.3d 704 (7th Cir. 2006).

138 720 ILL. COMP. STAT. 5/12-15(c), 16 (2011) (defining criminal sexual abuse for victims under seventeen).

139 Oberweis Dairy, 2005 WL 782709, at *6-7. The district court also found the conduct was not severe or pervasive, another requirement of the prima facie case. The court stated:

Here, it is undisputed that through Plaintiffs approximately eight-month employment with Defendant, Nayman only touched Plaintiff on fifteen occasions. As detailed above, these touches included squeezing Plaintiff's arm above her elbow, whereby Nayman would ask Plaintiff how she was doing, or giving Plaintiff nonsexual "side hugs." Once, Nayman gave Plaintiff a hug and kiss in an effort to make Plaintiff happy; and another time, Nayman gave Plaintiff a "happy-to-see-you type of hug" when she came to work. Nayman also "playfully" hit Plaintiff on the behind with a rag on one occasion. On a few occasions, Nayman made allegedly harassing remarks towards Plaintiff, but it is undisputed that Plaintiff found these remarks "flattering." Despite these allegedly harassing workplace events, Plaintiff continued to visit with Nayman socially outside of work, even after Plaintiff's mother prohibited Plaintiff from visiting Nayman. Accordingly, no genuine issue of material fact exists as to whether the conduct which occurred at Plaintiffs workplace was not severe or pervasive.

Id. at *7.

140 E-mail from H. Candace Gorman, Esq., Counsel for Doe, in Oberweis Dairy, to author (Apr. 29, 2010) (on file with the author).

141 Oberweis Dairy, 2005 WL 782709, at *6.

142 Doe v. Oberweis Dairy. 456 F.3d 704 (7th Cir. 2006). The appellate court described in much more detail how Nayman operated:

Construing the evidence as favorably to her [Plaintiff] as the record permits, as we must, we assume that Nayman, the shift supervisor, regularly hit on the girls (most of the employees were teenage girls) and young women employed in the ice cream parlor. He would, as one witness explained, "grope," "kiss," "grab butts," "hug," and give "tittle twisters" to these employees, including the plaintiff. These things he did in the store, but he would also invite the girls to his apartment. He had sexual intercourse in the apartment with two of them, one of them a minor, before it was the plaintiffs turn. He was 25 when he had intercourse with her.

Id. at 712-13.

143 The court cited to the Illinois statutory rape law. 720 ILL. COMP. STAT. 5/12-15(c), 16(d).

144 Oberweis Dairy, 456 F.3d at 713.

145 Id.

146 *Id.*

147 *Id.*

148 Donaldson v. Dep't of Real Estate. 36 Cal. Rptr, 3d 577 (Ct. App. 2005).

149 *Id.* at 583 (quoting CAL. CODE REGS. tit. 10,) 2910(a) (5) (2011).

150 *Id.* at 589. 592.

151 *Oberweis Dairy*, 456 F,3d at 714.

152 IND. CODE 35-42-4-9 (2011) (sexual misconduct with a minor, establishing the age of **consent** at sixteen).

153 720 ILL. COMP. STAT. 5/11-1.50 (2011) (criminal sexual abuse, establishing the age of **consent** at seventeen); WIS. STAT. 948.09 (2011) (sexual intercourse with a child age sixteen or older, establishing the age of **consent** at sixteen).

154 All states but four set the age of majority at eighteen. In Alabama and Nebraska, persons reach their majority at nineteen. In Pennsylvania and Mississippi, the age is twenty-one. Heather Boonstra & Elizabeth Nash, *Minors and the Right To Consent to Health Care*, GUTTMACHER REP. PUB. POL'Y, Aug. 2000, at 4, 7, available at http://www.guttmacher.Org/pubs/tgr/03/4/gr030404.pdf.

155 Declaration of Ruben C. Gur, Ph.D. at 15, Patterson v. Texas. 528 U.S. 826 (1999) (No. 98-8907), *available at* http://www.americanbar.org/content/dam/aba/publishing/criminal_Justice_section_newsletter/crimjust_juvjus_Gur_affidavit.authcheckdam.pdf.

156 I thank Professor R. George Wright for exploring this approach with me.

157 *See* E-mail from Professor R. George Wright, Ind. Sch. of Law-Indianapolis, to author (Apr. 30, 2010) (on file with author).

158 *Id.*

159 *See* Drobac, *supra* note 80, at 543 n.373.

160 Legal assent makes sense for contexts in addition to those involving adolescent **consent** to sexual activity with an adult. Such situations are beyond the scope of this chapter, however, and will be explored in future academic papers. *See, e.g.,* Drobac, *supra* note 1.

PART III

Marriage and Fidelity

Introduction

Marriage is a long-standing institution of society around which much of human interaction is organized. Finances, responsibility, gender roles, child-raising, property rights, religious status, social status, rituals, health, hopes, dreams, and of course, sex, have all been thoroughly interwoven with marriage. Not surprisingly, then, marriage has been fiercely defended at times as a cultural and moral bedrock on which the rest of society's successful functioning depends, and at other times fiercely challenged as a restrictive and stagnant mire on which the rest of society's dysfunction relies.

But what kind of marriage has been defended and what kind challenged? Sometimes the same marriage forms have been subject to both treatments. Conservatives and reformers could both target polygamy, for example. If polygamy was the tradition, then conservatives would be for it and reformers against it. If monogamy was the tradition, then conservatives would be against polygamy and reformers for it. And what kind of relationship is a marriage in the first place? Is it just a legal contract, like any other? Or is it a psychologically powerful public symbol of a special emotional relationship? Or is it a supernatural condition that society does not create but can only

recognize? And for any of these three, what does being married entail? Is it endlessly open to variation or are there key elements of marriage that have to be met in order for it to make sense as a discrete kind of relationship? For both conservatives and reformers, there must be something central to the meaning of marriage and something important about it, otherwise there would be no motivation either to protect it or to alter it.

Part III examines issues of marriage and fidelity. Though the basic elements in historical debates about marriage consistently recur, they are explored here by focusing on contemporary concerns about what structural form marriages should take, who should be allowed to marry, and what counts as a violation of marriage commitments.

Framing Questions

- *Should we provide new options for heterosexual marriage?*
- *Should we legalize gay marriage?*
- *Should we legalize polygamous marriage?*
- *Is adultery necessarily immoral?*
- *How should we define adultery?*

Covenant Marriage Seven Years Later: Its as Yet Unfulfilled Promise

Katherine Shaw Spaht

Summary

Argues that states offering the option of covenant marriage (typically including mandatory pre-marital counseling, the legal obligation to take all reasonable steps to preserve the marriage, allowing only fault-based divorce for adultery, felony convictions, abandonment, or sexual or physical abuse, and requiring a two-year separation) has the potential to reduce divorce rates, improve relationships, and re-sanctify marriage as a serious committed relationship. However, covenant marriage legislation has only been passed in a very few states (even though it only adds a new option to existing marriage) and relatively few people have opted for it. The reasons for this include a fear of restricted divorce, obstructive civil servants who oppose the option, the false belief that covenant marriage is purely a religious movement, the resistance of clergy to embrace the option, the lack of education regarding the option, and the Supreme Court decision in Lawrence (see part IV) that elevated autonomy and personal liberty over the common good of family and society. Given that covenant marriage has numerous benefits, it should be more strongly promoted by government and more often chosen by people who wish to take marriage seriously.

Original publication details: Katherine Shaw Spaht, "Covenant Marriage Seven Years Later: Its As Yet Unfulfilled Promise," pp. 605–634 from *Louisiana Law Review* 65 (2005). Reproduced with permission of Katherine Shaw Spaht.

Sexual Ethics: An Anthology, First Edition. Edited by Patrick D. Hopkins.
© 2023 John Wiley & Sons, Inc. Published 2023 by John Wiley & Sons, Inc.

I. Introduction

Almost seven years have passed since the first covenant marriage legislation was enacted in Louisiana,[1] followed by the enactment of similar legislation in Arizona in 1998[2] and Arkansas in 2001.[3] During the intervening years between its enactment in Louisiana and the present, covenant marriage legislation has been introduced in approximately thirty other states but the bills containing the legislation have failed to pass. Remarkably, the failure of covenant marriage bills to pass has occurred even though the legislation simply offers a couple an alternative to the prevailing legal regime of "no-fault divorce" marriage.

During the same time period, Steve Nock, a sociologist at the University of Virginia, and his research colleagues have studied the proposition, "Can Louisiana's Covenant Marriage Law Solve America's Divorce Problem?" The wealth of information mined from that ongoing study offers a glimpse of the effect of cultural changes on the understanding of marriage, as well as the self-selection effects of this experiment[4] and the *sanctification* of marriage created by the choice of a more committed form of marriage.[5] By virtue of the same study, results from a Gallup poll conducted in 1998 also revealed the attitudes of a random sample of citizens towards covenant marriage legislation in Louisiana, Arizona, and Minnesota.[6] Thereafter, the research team received another grant to consider the implementation of a change in policy through the use of state civil servants; in the case of covenant marriage, the state civil servants would consist of the staff of the local Clerk of Court's office. But the bulk of information gathered by the research team concerns the couples themselves – 300 covenant couples, 300 standard couples.

With the decision of the United States Supreme Court in *Lawrence v. Texas*[7] followed by the Massachusetts case of *Goodridge v. Department of Public Health*,[8] the air and the vigor has been "sucked out" of the nascent national discussion of marriage. Rather than the broader polity discussing the far more pervasive problems of harm done by divorce, the rescue of at-risk marriages by marriage education, and the promotion of "healthy" marriages by the federal government, national attention is currently focused almost entirely on same-sex sexual expression. Same-sex couples marrying in Massachusetts and a proposed amendment to the United States Constitution defining marriage as a union of one man and one woman[9] have literally consumed all of the media attention.

[. . .]

III. What is Covenant Marriage?

A Louisiana covenant marriage differs in three principal respects from other legally recognized "standard" marriages: 1) mandatory pre-marital counseling; 2) the legal obligation to take all reasonable steps to preserve the couple's marriage if marital difficulties arise; and 3) restricted grounds for divorce consisting of *fault* on the part of the other spouse or two years living separate and apart[10] Each of the three components addresses John Witte's observation in *From Sacrament to Contract* that restricting exit rules of marriage by reforming divorce law requires complementary legal restrictions on entry into marriage.[11] Covenant marriage restricts entry into and exit from marriage for those who choose it and attempts to strengthen the marriage itself by imposing a legal obligation upon the covenant spouses which they agree to in advance of their marriage – taking *reasonable* steps to preserve their marriage if difficulties arise.

The mandatory pre-marital counseling under the covenant marriage statute must contain counsel about the seriousness of marriage, the intent of the couple that it be lifelong, and the agreement that the couple will take all reasonable steps to preserve the marriage.[12] Any minister, priest, rabbi, or the secular alternative of a professional marriage counselor is permitted to provide the counseling and sign an attestation form.[13] Of course, many religious counselors require considerably more, especially if they have signed a Community Marriage Covenant (CMC) or Agreement. The CMC, signed by community clergy, ordinarily requires a minimum of counseling sessions with the minister (four, for example), a premarital inventory such as PREPARE or FOCCUS, and the guarantee of a mentoring couple assigned to the engaged couple. In those cities that now have Community Marriage Agreements, the clergy signatories provide counseling that is far more extensive than the covenant marriage legislation requires.[14]

At the end of the mandatory pre-marital counseling, the prospective spouses sign a document called a Declaration of Intent that contains the content of their *covenant*, which includes the agreement to seek counseling if difficulties arise as well as their agreement to be bound by the Louisiana law of covenant marriage (choice of law clause).[15] Both spouses sign the agreement and then execute an affidavit, signed by a notary, attesting to having had counseling as the law requires and having read the Covenant Marriage Act, the pamphlet prepared by the Attorney General that explains the differences between a covenant marriage and a standard marriage, including comparative grounds for divorce.[16] The Declaration of Intent is in essence a special *contract* authorized by the state (Louisiana, Arizona, or Arkansas) that contains legal obligations similar to those in ordinary contracts. Most importantly, it is the agreement of the covenant spouses in advance to take reasonable steps to preserve their marriage which constitutes a legal obligation, the second distinguishing component of a covenant marriage. This obligation to take reasonable steps to preserve the marriage begins at the moment the marital difficulties arise and "should continue" until rendition of the judgment of divorce,[17] the one exception being "when the other spouse has physically or sexually abused the spouse seeking the divorce or a child of one of the spouses."[18]

Lastly, a spouse in a covenant marriage may obtain a divorce only if she can prove adultery, conviction of a felony, abandonment for one year, or physical or sexual abuse of her or a child of the parties.[19] Otherwise, the spouses must live separate and apart for two years.[20] A comparison of the grounds for divorce in a Louisiana "standard" marriage reveals that a covenant marriage commits the spouses in advance to a relinquishment of the easy exit rules in favor of more stringent, morally based exit rules. In a "standard" marriage a spouse may seek a divorce for adultery,[21] conviction of a felony,[22] or living separate and apart for *six months* either before[23] *or* after[24] a suit for divorce is filed. There is an enormous difference between living separate and apart for six months versus living that way for two years. Furthermore, if one considers Paul Amato's research, the vast majority of divorces (his research suggests two-thirds) occur for the "soft" reasons, such as lack of communication and unfulfilled personal needs, rather than adultery or physical violence.[25]

In other research Amato has conducted, the attitudes of the spouses upon entry into marriage ultimately determines the quality of their marriages; if spouses enter marriage with the belief that divorce is the solution to any problems that arise, their marriages are of significantly lower quality and thus often end in divorce.[26] By contrast, if the spouses believe that divorce is not an option, the quality of their marriages tend to be more satisfying and fulfilling. As a consequence fewer couples in the latter category divorce. Covenant couples enter into marriage only after mandatory pre-marital counseling. They sign a "Declaration of Intent" that emphasizes the expectation that their marriage will be lifelong. The solemnity of the preparation and the significance of signing the "Declaration of Intent" place covenant

spouses within the latter category described by Professor Amato.

IV. Obstacles to Its Implementation: Clergy and Civil Servants

In Louisiana, despite a Gallup poll of Louisiana citizens conducted in 1998 that revealed strong support for covenant marriage[27] – especially the pre-divorce counseling,[28] public servants charged with implementation of the covenant marriage legislation and religious clergy throughout the state have failed in different ways to embrace the marital option. Of the 527 respondents to the survey in Louisiana conducted in May 1998,[29]

eighty-one percent of respondents believed that premarital counseling was very or somewhat important compared to nineteen percent who believed that it was not very or not at all important; 92.3% of respondents believed that the couple agreeing in advance to seek counseling if marital difficulties arise during the marriage was very or somewhat important, whereas 7.7% believed that it was not very or not at all important.[30]

Not unexpectedly, the most controversial of the components of covenant marriage – restricted divorce – proved to be the least popular: "'Overall, [only] two thirds (65.7%) agreed that longer waiting periods for a divorce are a good idea.'"[31] The attitudes of one-third of the respondents about waiting periods reflect lack of knowledge about the benefits of longer "cooling off" periods before divorce, reflected in the recent empirical study of the National Survey of Families and Households by Maggie Gallagher and Linda Waite. They report that "'more than 86% of unhappily married couples in the late 1980s who did *not divorce* reported having a happy marriage five years later (about 15% divorced).'"[32]

Despite Louisianans' favorable view of the covenant marriage legislation, the staff of the Clerks' offices throughout the state who issue marriage licenses have obstructed, rather than facilitated, the implementation of the legislation.[33] Although the legislation as enacted was not specific, the legislature assumed that the Attorney General's pamphlet describing the differences between covenant and "standard" marriages would be delivered by the Clerk's staff to applicants for marriage licenses. During a "confederate" study of the implementation of covenant marriage legislation, Steven Nock and his research team found that clerks offered the information in only thirty-five percent of the parishes, and another forty-seven percent only offered the written information when asked to produce it.[34] In fact the team reported that most clerks expressed negativity about covenant marriage:

In 53% of the parishes, clerks made pessimistic or derogatory comments.[35] [. . .]

If staff members were asked about the option, staff in only twelve percent of the parishes gave accurate information, while in fifty-three percent of the parishes, the explanations contained inaccurate or misleading information, and in the remaining thirty-five percent, "clerks gave patently wrong information."[36] Now, by virtue of 2001 legislation, staff in the Clerks' offices are required explicitly to deliver the Attorney General's pamphlet, called the Covenant Marriage Act, to all applicants for marriage licenses.[37]

After conclusion of the "confederate study" conducted by Nock's research team, the staff of selected clerks' offices were asked to give their opinions on covenant marriage in personal interviews. Most "equated Covenant marriage with a religious movement, and felt only couples who learned about it from their church leaders would or could get one."[38] [. . .]

[. . .]

If it is a religious movement, why is it that so few Christians are electing the choice of a covenant marriage? Where are their pastors, ministers, and priests? The Louisiana bishops of the Episcopal and Methodist churches explicitly rejected "covenant marriage" because it would restore "more difficult" divorce law and minimize "standard" marriages performed in a church setting. The Catholic Church until 1999 refused to permit its priests to participate in the counseling required by the statute because the counselor was required to inform the couple of the grounds for divorce in a covenant marriage. That objection was remedied by amendment to the counseling statute[39] and publicly recognized by the bishops' committee as curing their objections. Nonetheless, there is no evidence that the Catholic Church is officially informing its engaged couples during pre-Canaa sessions that covenant marriage is an option in the state of Louisiana, much less that it is more consistent with the Catholic view of marriage (sacramental). Southern Baptists, the second largest denomination in Louisiana after Catholics, make decisions on such matters church by church although the organized Association has featured the option in at least one of its national gatherings. Thus, we have a "religious movement" alluded to by the Clerks' staff without followers. Christian couples are *not* choosing covenant marriage in

significant numbers. Only two to three percent of the newly married couples[40] in Louisiana in any given year are covenant couples.

The ultimate success of covenant marriage and the protection that it offers children depends upon the action of pastors, ministers, and priests. It is the clergy who are usually among the first to be informed of an engagement and pending nuptials, and they have a moral responsibility to inform couples marrying in their church that Louisiana offers two types of marriage. Even staff in the Clerks' offices recognize who bears the ultimate responsibility, noting that most couples interested in covenant marriage learn about it from their religious leaders and come to the clerk's office prepared to ask for one.[41] If, as estimated, over eighty-five percent of couples who marry in Louisiana marry in a house of worship, future empirical research should focus on the attitudes of the clergy toward covenant marriage.

The state of Louisiana is not entirely blameless, of course. The social science research team opined that

"the state, if truly dedicated to reducing divorce or at least encouraging Covenant marriage, would benefit from a mass public education campaign."

without which,

"the likely growth of Covenant marriage is doubtful."[42] [. . .]

If nothing else, the adoption of covenant marriage by Louisiana in 1997 precipitated a broader national discussion of marriage — its purposes, its "health," its decline, its maintenance, and its endurance. Since 1997 and the beginning of this earnest national conversation, marriage education and divorce reform, a myriad of more sophisticated and compelling empirical studies, and the national government's marriage promotion efforts have resulted. A disparate group of leaders from public think tanks, academia, the therapeutic professions (psychology and social work and other similar disciplines), and faith-based organizations birthed the National Marriage Movement, a loose and broadly constructed coalition or network whose principal goal is to see more children grow up in the home of their biological (adoptive) parents in a low-conflict, healthy marriage.[43] For the seven years following the passage of covenant marriage legislation, there was steady, incremental progress in arresting the damaging "revolutions" of the 1960s and 1970s and a reversal of destructive social experiments designed by adults for their own pleasure. These adult experiments fail to calculate the costs for children.[44]

V.   Nock's Research: What Distinguishes Covenant Couples from Other Married Couples?[45]

Women "are the 'leaders' in selecting covenant marriage, particularly women with a vested interest in childbearing who apparently feel the need for the protection of stronger divorce laws."[46] Men lead in selecting "standard" marriage.[47] Covenant couples have a forceful conviction about the importance of the choice they are making that "standard" married couples do not, believing that they are making a powerful statement about marriage as an institution.[48] Surprisingly to some researchers, "covenant married husbands and wives are more educated and hold more traditional attitudes."[49] Couples in a covenant marriage are "far more likely to choose communication strategies that do not revolve around attacking or belittling their partner. They are less likely to respond to conflict with sarcasm or hostility, two communication strategies that [John] Gottman (1994) indicates are particularly strongly associated with poor marriage outcomes."[50]

Two years after marrying, covenant couples "'described their overall marital quality as better than did their Standard counterparts.' . . . Covenant couples were more committed to their marriage two years after the ceremony than at the time of their marriage; whereas, their standard counterparts had changed little in their level of commitment"[51]

> With the growing centrality of marriage for covenant couples, they experienced "higher levels of commitment . . ., higher levels of agreement between partners. . ., fewer worries about having children . . ., and *greater sharing of housework*." It is not too early. . . to conclude that covenant marriages are better marriages. . . . Steven Nock, the director of the study, expresses the view that "internally the [covenant] marriages are vastly better, and covenant couples agree about who does what, the fairness of things, etc. much more than standard couples."[52]

These covenant couples are participants in a "new" form of marriage "that reserves the traditional, conventional, and religious aspects of the traditional institution, but also resolves the various inequities often associated with gender in modern marriages."[53] In his opinion, "a central theme that discriminates between the two types of unions . . . [is]

institutionalization of the marriage."[54] Institutionalization of the marriage simply reflects the couple's view that "the marriage warrants consideration apart from the individualistic concerns of either partner. In regard to some matters, covenant couples appear to defer to the interests of their marriage even when the individual concerns of the partners may appear to conflict. *And this orientation to married life . . . helps resolve the customary problems faced by newly married couples in regard to fairness and equity.*"[55] Couples in a covenant marriage view marriage institutionally which "elevates the normative (expected) model of marriage to prominence in the relationship."[56] What accounts for this institutional view? "[T]he centrality accorded religion by the couple" and "beliefs about the life of marriage independently of the individual."[57] "Two individuals do not easily make a strong marriage. Rather, it takes the presence of a set of guiding principles around which these two individuals orient their behaviors and thinking."[58] "All in all, this is a very nice story and one that is attracting a lot of interest."[59]

VI.   Completing the Vision of Marriage Within Covenant Marriage

During the 2004 regular session, the Louisiana Legislature enacted new provisions that enhance the covenant marriage legislation by more explicitly addressing the content of the covenant marriage relationship. The provisions concern the rights and responsibilities of married persons. All married persons in Louisiana owe to each other fidelity, support and assistance.[60] Yet, this is the only legal regulation of the marital relationship during its existence. Covenant marriage legislation, in particular the grounds for separation and divorce, speak inferentially to the appropriate conduct for spouses during marriage: each spouse is to "yield to the other in sexual matters as long as the request [is] reasonable [positive aspect of fidelity and its breach constitutes cruel treatment entitling a covenant spouse to a separation] and to conduct himself so as not to bring dishonor and shame to the family formed by the marriage, which could occur by adulterous affairs, outrageous or felonious behavior, and constant intemperance."[61] Furthermore, in a covenant marriage neither spouse should leave the other (abandonment) and by doing so deny to the other support and assistance. Nor should either physically or sexually abuse the other or a child of the parties.[62]

Law can and should do more. Law can teach and exhort.[63] It is possible for a statute drafter to "craft a statute which states general principles about the content of marriage, some with legal consequences intended to constrain or punish and others intended to be simply hortatory or examples of the expressive function of the law."[64] The new legislation restores a vision of marriage that has been lost – a vision of marriage and the public's interest in it, as expressed with its collective voice through the law. Each of the provisions has a foreign source: these provisions appear in civil codes in countries around the world.[65]

La. R. S. 9:293. *Spouses in a covenant marriage are subject to all of the laws governing married couples generally and to the special rules governing covenant marriage.*

La. R.S. 9:294. *Spouses owe each other love and respect and they commit to a community of living. Each spouse should attend to the satisfaction of the other's needs.*[66]

La. R.S. 9:295. *Spouses are bound to live together, unless there is a good cause otherwise. The spouses determine the family residence by mutual consent, according to their requirements and those of the family.*[67]

La. R.S. 9:296. *The management of the household shall be the right and the duty of both spouses.*[68]

La. R.S. 9:297. *Spouses by mutual consent after collaboration shall make decisions relating to family life in the best interest of the family.*[69]

La. R.S. 9:298. *The spouses are bound to maintain, to teach, and to educate their children born of the marriage in accordance with their capacities, natural inclinations, and aspirations, and shall prepare them for their future.*[70]

Submitted in the form of a letter as part of the official record of the hearing on this new legislation, researcher Steve Nock of the University of Virginia supported each legal provision proposed with findings from his study of covenant couples, showing that covenant couples' marital behavior conforms to the legal provisions adopted.[71]

VII. The Threat of *Lawrence v. Texas* and the Ability of Covenant Marriage to Withstand the Threat

And then along comes *Lawrence v. Texas*.[72] Although the *Lawrence* case involved a criminal statute punishing sodomy, it has implications for the entire body of law called

family law. Justice Anthony Kennedy attempts to reassure the reader by stating that the decision is narrow in scope and holds no broad implications for state statutes regulating sexual conduct. First, he observes that the statute in *Lawrence* was criminal, not civil, and it punished sexual acts between consenting adults in the privacy of their bedroom. Regardless of the nature of these acts, they fall within the "liberty" interest of the Fourteenth Amendment:

> The Fourteenth Amendment protects the person from unwarranted government intrusions into a dwelling or other private places . . . . Freedom extends [however] beyond spatial bounds. *Liberty presumes an autonomy of self that includes freedom of thought, belief, expression, and certain intimate conduct. The instant case involves liberty of the person both in its spatial* [geographical] *and more transcendent dimensions.*[73]
> [. . .]

The most disturbing portion of the opinion authored by Justice Kennedy is that portion that develops and describes the "liberty" interest of the individual protected from governmental regulation. "Liberty" after *Lawrence* no longer means a fundamental right, "deeply rooted in the history and traditions of our country."[74] The new, unanchored "liberty" interest "presumes an autonomy of self that includes freedom of thought, belief, expression, and certain intimate conduct."[75] The transcendent dimension includes personal decisions relating to marriage, procreation, contraception, family relationships, child rearing and education – decisions "involving the most intimate and personal choices a person may make in a lifetime, choices central to personal dignity and autonomy . . . ."[76] According to Justice Kennedy, no state, acting for its citizens, can "mandate *our own moral code.*"[77] Justice Sandra Day O'Connor, often the "swing" vote and another appointee of a Republican president, attempted in a concurring opinion an impossible distinction between acceptable laws that "preserve the traditions of society" and unacceptable laws that "express moral disapproval."[78] Yet, of all the incredible statements contained in that opinion, the winner is the one which expresses an autonomy of self that virtually knows no boundaries; hence, none that can be imposed by state regulation.

> At the heart of liberty is *the right to define one's own concept of existence*, of meaning, of the universe, and of the mystery of human life.[79]

Within the context of the married family and state law that regulates the intimate decisions made there, such autonomy creates anarchy. Whose "right to autonomy" trumps? What about the relationship of husband and wife or the common good of the family, as a unit? It was the opening salvo in what was to become a more intense and accelerating "culture war" just as Justice Scalia predicted in his dissenting opinion.[80]

Notwithstanding what the *Lawrence* opinion says about the individual's right to "liberty," any "liberty" interest under the Fourteenth Amendment can be *waived* by the individual who possesses the right, as long as the waiver is knowing and voluntary.[81] Although the "waiver" in a covenant marriage is not a one-time event like a search, there is a parallel in the federal jurisprudence involving enlistment in the military; the enlistee voluntarily and knowingly subjects himself to a distinct system of order and justice which modify the "liberty" interests he possesses under the Constitution.[82] In the case of the military, there are significant governmental interests, such as national defense and security, not present in the case of marriage. But, the governmental interest of assuring "healthy, low-conflict" marriages of superior quality in which children are born and reared by their two biological or adoptive parents seems no less compelling to the future of this country than national defense.

[. . .]

The covenant marriage legislation provides a solution to a potential problem that threatens the institution of marriage and any future attempts to strengthen it legally. Originally, marriage suffered from the problem of impermanence, threatened by unilateral "no-fault" divorce; now, it is threatened by the problem of the usurpation of democracy by the United States Supreme Court.[83]

VIII. Conclusion

Often I have argued that covenant marriage "offers to those people of the dissident culture, either those who belong to a religious community or those who adhere to traditional morality, a safe haven from the post-modern, dominant culture."[84] *Lawrence* and the current culture war focused on same-sex "marriage" merely accelerate the necessity of "constructing 'safe havens' for 'all who desire protection from a corrosive culture advanced by an elite, governing caste."[85]

> Within [the] safe haven [of covenant marriage], spouses who desire to restore the institution of marriage *may offer themselves collectively as witnesses to others about sacrificial love and its central role in binding male and female to each other and their offspring.*[86]

Covenant spouses already view marriage as a transcendent reality, distinctly different from the transcendent reality spoken of by Justice Kennedy in the *Lawrence* decision. Covenant marriage "represents a paradigm that is the opposite of post-modern marriage."[87] Covenant spouses defer to marriage, an abstraction representing a third party to the marriage itself, rather than view marriage as a loose union of two radically autonomous selves acting always in each person's own self-interest — some form of joint venture without sufficient remedy for its breach. Which vision serves the rest of society better? Which vision serves our most vulnerable citizens, children, better?

If the answer to both questions is yes, then why isn't government confidently defending the covenant marriage vision, much less not promoting it? And, why aren't more religious citizens choosing it?

[. . .]

Notes

1 La. R.S. 9:272–275.1, 9:307–309 (2002).
2 Ariz. Rev. Stat §§ 25-901 to 25-906 (1998).
3 Ark. Code Ann. §§ 9-11-801 to 9-11-808 (2001).
4 Selection effects often occur when participation in a program is voluntary, producing "the likelihood that those who choose to participate [in a covenant marriage] are different from those who do not in ways that predispose them to better outcomes regardless of program participation." Alan J. Hawkins, Evaluating Covenant Mariage in Louisiana: Early Lessons 1, Speech and Presentation at Smart Marriages Conference, Denver, Colorado (2000) (manuscript on file with author).

The covenant couples, not surprisingly, were more religious and more conservative; were less likely to have cohabited before marriage; were less likely to have experienced pre-marital conflict; talked more before marriage about important issues that can cause marital problems; received more approval of their spouse from their parents; and were less likely to have been previously married or to have a child. Id.

5 Katherine Shaw Spaht, *What's Become of Louisiana Covenant Marriage Through the Eyes of Social Scientists*, 47 Loy. L. Rev. 709 (2001).

6 Id. at 713–17.

7   539 U.S. 558, 123 S. Ct. 2472 (2003) (declaring Texas' sod-omy statute unconstitutional under the Due Process Clause of the Fourteenth Amendment).

8   798 N.E.2d 941 (Mass. 2003).

9   The proposed Federal Marriage Amendment reads as fol-lows:

Marriage in the United States shall consist only of the union of a man and a woman. Neither this Constitution, nor the constitution of any state, shall be construed to require that marriage or the legal incidents thereof be con-ferred upon any union other than the union of a man and a woman. S.J. Res 40, 108th Cong.(2004).

10 See La. R.S. 9:272 (2004); id. 9:273; id. 9:307.

11 John Witte, From Sacrament to Contract: Marriage, Religion and Law in the Western Tradition 217–18(1997). See also Covenant Marriage in Comparative Perspective (John Witte & Michael J. Broyde, eds., 2005). Wm. B. Eerdmans Publishing Company: Cambridge UK.

12 La. R.S. 9:273(A)(2)(a) (2004).

13 Id. 9:273(A)(2).

14 See Paul James Birch, Stan E. Weed, & Joseph A. Olsen, Executive Summary, Assessing the Impact of Community Marriage Policies on U.S. County Divorce Rates (March 2004) (on file with author).

The first, simplest, and most direct question was whether the divorce rate decline was greater after the CMP was signed than the existing decline before the signing. The researchers examined divorce rates for five years before clergy signed Community Marriage Policies and up to seven years after signing – in 114 communities in 122 counties.. . .

In more familiar terms, counties with a Community Marriage Policy® had an 8.6% decline in their divorce rates over four years, while the comparison counties regis-tered a 5.6% decline. If those rates are projected for seven years, CMP communities enjoy a 17.5% decline in the divorce rate vs. 9.4% in comparison counties. Thus, Com-munity Marriage Policies counties have a decline in the divorce rate that is nearly double that of control communi-ties. The levels of impact would likely be greater if more communities had higher levels of participation and imple-mentation – that is, if more churches and synagogues signed on and more mentor couples trained.

The Institute estimates that 31,000 divorces are being avoided in 114 cities/counties with a Community Mar-riage Policy. Since clergy and community leaders have now created 183 Community Marriage Policies, that number could be perhaps 40,000 to 50,000 marriages being saved. Id.

15 See La. R.S. 9:273.1 (2004); see also Katherine Shaw Spaht & Symeon C. Symeonides, Covenant Marriage and the Law of Conflict of Laws, 32 Creighton L. Rev. 1085 (1999). But see Peter Hay, The American "Covenant Marriage" in the Conflict of Laws, 64 La. L. Rev. 43 (2004).

16 See La. R.S. 9:273.1 (2004).

17 La. R.S. 9:307(C) (2004) (as added by 2004 La. Acts No. 490).

18 Id. 9:307(D) (as added by 2004 La. Acts No. 490).

19 Id. 9:307(A).

20 Id. 9:307(A)(6).

21 La. Civ. Code art. 103(2) (2004).

22 Id. art. 103(3).

23 Id. art. 103(1).

24 Id. art. 102.

25 Paul R. Amato & Allan Booth, A Generation at Risk; Growing Up in an Era of Family Upheaval (1997).

26 Paul R. Amato & Stacy J. Rogers, Do Attitudes Toward Divorce Affect Marital Quality?, 20 J. of Family Issues 69 (1999). Amato and Rogers write:

Although most Americans continue to value marriage, the belief that an unrewarding marriage should be jettisoned may lead some people to invest less time and energy in their marriages and make fewer attempts to resolve marital disagreements. In other words, a weak commitment to the general norm of life-long marriage may ultimately under-mine people's commitments to particular relationships. Id. at 70.

27 Spaht, supra note 5, at 713–17.

28 Id. at 714.

29 Id. at 713.

30 Id. at 714.

31 Id.

32 Id. at 715 (emphasis added).

33 Id. at 723–26.

34 Laura Sanchez, et al., The Implementation of Covenant Marriage in Louisiana, 9 Va. J. Soc. Pol'y & L. 192, 206 (2001). The study was conducted in seventeen of the sixty-four Louisiana parishes chosen "by probability propor-tionate to size, based on the number of marriages they registered in 1998." Id. at 203.

35 Id. at 207.

36 Id. at 206.

37 La. R.S. 9:237(A), (C) (2004).

38 Sanchez, supra note 34, at 207.

39 La. R.S. 9:273(A)(2)(a) (2004).

40 Covenant marriage legislation permits the "conversion" of a "standard" marriage to a "covenant" marriage. See id. 9:275.

41 Sanchez, supra note 34, at 212.

42 Spaht, supra note 5, at 726 (quoting prepublication draft of Sanchez, supra note 59).

43 Katherine Shaw Spaht, Revolution and Counter-Revolution: The Future of Marriage in the Law, 49 Loy. L. Rev. 1, 61–64 (2003).

44 Despite the fact that most social scientists agree that there is insufficient research on same-sex parenting to reach a firm conclusion about differences in outcomes "the most appropriate comparison group [is] children of heterosex-ual divorced parents [most children raised by same-sex parents were conceived in the context of a heterosexual

relationship which failed]." Mary Parke, Are Married Parents Really Better for Children? What Research Says About the Effects of Family Structure on Child Well-Being 5 (CLASP Policy Brief, Couples and Marriage Series, Brief No. 3, 2003).

Of the studies already undertaken, a respected family scholar, Steven Nock of the University of Virginia, testified as follows: "Through this analysis I draw my conclusions that 1) all of the articles I reviewed contained at least one fatal flaw of design or execution; and 2) not a single one of those studies was conducted according to general accepted standards of scientific research." Affidavit of Steven Nock at ¶ 3, Halpern v. Attorney General of Canada, [2000] No. 684/00 (Ont Sup. Ct. of Justice). See also Dennis Prager, Children's Needs Not a Factor in the Homosexual Agenda, Wash. Times (Nat'l Weekly Ed.), May 10–16, 2004, at 33.

45 For a comprehensive discussion and comparison, see Brinig & Nock, supra note 34.

46 Spaht, supra note 72, at 43.

47 Id. at 53.

48 See id. at 53.

49 Laura Sanchez, et al., Is Covenant Marriage a Policy that Preaches to the Choir? A Comparison of Covenant and Standard Married Newlywed Couples in Louisiana 30 (Bowling Green State University Working Paper Series, Working Paper No. 02–06), available at http://www.bgsu.edu/organizations/cfdr/research/pdf/2002/2002-06.pdf.

50 Id. at 31.

51 Spaht, supra note 43, at 54 (quoting a draft of Nock, Sanchez, & Wright, infra note 53). "What is interesting is that these couples feel more strongly about the concept three years into marriage, and that the difference in how they feel is significantly greater than the difference in how the standard marriage couples feel about the same statement." Brinig & Nock, see Margaret F. Brinig and Steven L. Nock, What Does Covenant Mean for Relationships?, Notre Dame Journal of Law, Ethics, and Public Policy 137 (2004), at 175. See also Margaret F. Brinig & Steven L. Nock, "I Only Want Trust": Norms, Trust, and Autonomy, 32 J. Socio-Econ. 471 (2003).

52 Spaht supra note 43, at (quoting a draft of Nock, Sanchez, & Wright infra note 82; E-mail from Steven L. Nock to Katherine S. Spaht (Sept. 16, 2002, 6:32 a.m.)) (emphasis added).

53 Steven L. Nock, Laura Sanchez, & James D. Wright Intimate Equity: The Early Years of Covenant and Standard Marriages 7 (Bowling Green State University Working Paper Series, Working Paper No. 03-04), on file with this author (presented at the annual meeting of the Population Assoc. of America, May 2003). See also Steven L. Nock, Laura Sanchez, Julia C. Wilson, & James D. Wright, Covenant Marriage Turns Five Years Old, 10 Mich. J. Gender & L. 169 (2003).

54 Nock, Sanchez, & Wright, supra note 53, at 6 (emphasis added). See also Brinig & Nock, supra note 34.

55 Nock, Sanchez, & Wright, supra note 53, at 6 (emphasis added).

56 Id. at 11.

57 Id. at 7.

58 Id. at 9.

59 E-mail from Steven L. Nock to Katherine S. Spaht (Sept. 16, 2002, 6:32 a.m.) (on file with the author).

60 La. Civ. Code art. 98 (2004).

61 Katherine Shaw Spaht, The Last One Hundred Years: The Incredible Retreat of Law from the Regulation of Marriage, 63 La. L. Rev. 243, 294 (2003).

62 La. R.S. 9:307(A)(3)–(4) (2004).

63 Two newspaper reports of this legislation demonstrate deep misunderstanding by some members of the press, which is unfortunately generally reflective of the American citizenry at large. The news report of the hearing on House Bill No. 252 in House Committee on Civil Law and Procedure was titled: "Bill 'exhorts' covenant harmony." Marsha Shuler, Bill "Exhorts" Covenant Harmony, The Advocate, Apr. 6, 2004, at 4A. The subsequent editorial in The Advocate on Saturday, April 10, 2004, was titled, "The Legislature's marital counsel," and sarcastically urged the Legislature to reject the bill since it legislated "household chores" and was inane. See The Legislature's Marital Counsel, The Advocate, Apr. 10, 2004, at 6B,

64 Katherine Shaw Spaht, How Law Can Reinvigorate a Robust Vision of Marriage and Rival Its Post-Modern Competitor, 2 Georgetown J. L. & Pub. Pol'y 449 (2004).

65 Id. See also Katherine Shaw Spaht, A Proposal: Legal Re-Regulation of the Content of Marriage, 18 Notre Dame J.L. Ethics & Pub. Pol'y 243 (2004).

66 Family Code of the Philippines art. 68; Code civil [C. civ.] art. 392 (Quebec); Código Civil [C.C.] art. 67 (Spain); Código Civil art. 1672 (Portugal); Código Civil art 131 (Chile); Código Civil [C.C.] art 1566(V) (Brazil); Code civil [C. civ.] art 215 (France); § 1353(1) Bürgerliches Gesetzbuch [BGB] (Germany); Código Civ. art 139 (Venezuela); Burgerlijk Wetboek [BW] art. 1:81 (The Netherlands).

67 C. civ. arts. 392, 395 (Quebec); BW art 83(1) (The Netherlands); Family Code of the Philippines art. 68; Código Civ. art. 199 (Argentina); Código Civ. art. 137 (Venezuela); Código Civ. para el Distrito Federal [C.C.D.F.] art. 163 (Mexico); Código Civ. art. 133 (Chile); Codice civile [C.c.] art. 143 (Italy); Código Civ. arts. 1672, 1673(1)(2) (Portugal); Código Civil [C.C.] art. 1566.V (Brazil); BW art. 1:83(1), (2) (The Netherlands); Código Civ. [Cód. Civ.] arts. 199, 200 (Argentina); Código Civ. arts. 138, 140 (Venezuela); Family Code of the Philippines art. 69; C.C. art. 70 (Spain); C. civ. art. 215 (France); Code civil suisse [Cc] art. 162 (Switzerland).

68 Family Code of the Philippines art. 71; § 1356(1) BGB (Germany); C.C.D.F. art. 168.

69 C.c. arts. 143, 144 (Italy); Código Civ. art. 140 (Venezuela); C.C. art 1567 (Brazil); Código Civ. art. 1671(2) (Portugal); C.C.D.F. art. 168; C.C. art. 671 (Spain).

70 C.c. art 147 (Italy); C.C. art. 1566.IV (Brazil); Cc art. 159 (Switzerland); C.C.D.F. art. 164 (Mexico); BW art. 1:82 (The Netherlands); C. civ. art. 213 (France).

71 See Letter from Steven L. Nock to Katherine S. Spaht (May 4, 2004) (attached as Appendix A).

72 539 U.S. 558, 123 S. Ct. 2472 (2003).

73 Id. at 562, 123 S. Ct. at 2475 (emphasis added).

74 Bowers v. Hardwick, 478 U.S. 186, 194, 106 S. Ct. 2841, 2846 (1986).

75 Lawrence, 539 U.S. at 562, 123 S. Ct. at 2475. For an interesting criticism of an individual's "rights" to privacy versus a right that focuses on "relationships," see Nehal A. Patel, The State's Perpetual Protection of Adultery: Examining Koestler v. Pollard and Wisconsin's Faded Adultery Torts, 2003 Wis. L. Rev. 1013. He reviews pro-marriage and feminist critics of the lack of an adequate legal remedy for adultery, such as William Corbett, A Somewhat Modest Proposal to Prevent Adultery and Save Families: Two Old Torts Looking for a New Career, 33 Ariz. St. L.J. 985 (2001), and Linda R. Hirshman & Jane E. Larson, Hard Bargains: The Politics of Sex 283–86 (1998).

76 Lawrence, 539 U.S. at 574, 123 S. CL at 2481.

77 Id. at 571, 123 S. Ct. at 2480. See also Note, Litigating the Defense of Marriage Act: The Next Battleground for Same-Sex Marriage, 117 Harv. L. Rev. 2684 (2004)

(equating morality with animosity); Steven D. Smith, Conciliating Hatred, First Things, June/July 2004, at 17, 19–22 (describing such United States Supreme Court jurisprudence (especially most recently in cases involving homosexuality) as "evil motives" jurisprudence).

78 Lawrence, 539 U.S. at 582–85,123 S. Ct. at 2486–89.

79 Id. at 574, 123 S. Ct. at 2482 (quoting Planned Parenthood of Southeastern Pa. v. Casey, 505 U.S. 833, 851, 112 S. Ct. 2791 (1992)) (emphasis added).

80 Id. at 602, 123 S. Ct. at 2497. See Symposium: Gay Rights After Lawrence v. Texas, 88 Minn. L. Rev 1017 (2004); see also Marie A. Failinger, A Peace Proposal for the Same-Sex Marriage Wars: Restoring the Household to Its Proper Place, 10 Wm. & Mary J.W. & Law 195 (2004).

81 See, e.g., United States v. Knights, 534 U.S. 112, 122 S. Ct. 587 (2001); Illinois v. Rodriguez, 497 U.S. 177, 110 S. Ct. 2793 (1990); Schneckloth v. Bustamonte, 412 U.S. 218, 93 S. Ct. 2041 (1973) (excellent discussion and illustration of voluntariness); Johnson v. Zerbst, 304 U.S. 458, 58 S. Ct. 1019 (1938)

82 See, e.g., Chappell v. Wallace, 462 U.S. 296, 103 S. Ct. 2362 (1983); Rostker v. Goldberg, 453 U.S. 57, 101 S. Ct. 2646 (1981).

83 Michael M. Uhlmann, The Supreme Court Rules, First Things, Oct. 2003, at 26, 31–35.

84 Spaht, supra note 66, at 261.

85 Spaht, supra note 65 (quoting Spaht, supra note 66, at 261).

86 Id. (quoting Spaht, supra note 66, at 261) (emphasis added).

87 Id.

12

Regulatory Fictions: On Marriage and Countermarriage

Elizabeth F. Emens

Summary

Argues that during contemporary debate about the legal and moral nature of marriage, we should take the opportunity to push beyond questions simply about gay marriage and ask broader questions about the widest possible range of marriage regime alternatives – countermarriage regimes. Drawing on fictional literature and legal attempts to outlaw gay marriage, a number of possible countermarriage forms can be considered. Fiction provides examples of marriage schemes altering permanence, contracts, continuity over time, numbers of participants, racial requirements, legal indemnification, and even eliminating marriage altogether. Anti-gay laws provide examples of forbidding marriage-like arrangements, regulating platonic relationships, or even forbidding any contracts between any romantically involved persons.

Original publication details: Elizabeth F. Emens, "Regulatory Fictions: On Marriage and Countermarriage," pp. 235–269 from *California Law Review* 99 (2011). Reproduced with permission of University of California Berkeley Law.

Sexual Ethics: An Anthology, First Edition. Edited by Patrick D. Hopkins.
© 2023 John Wiley & Sons, Inc. Published 2023 by John Wiley & Sons, Inc.

Elizabeth F. Emens

Introduction

The debates in the public sphere over the future of marriage have spurred theoretical debates in the academy over the value of marriage. Even as some scholars debate whether gay people's relationships are worthy of marriage – sometimes before large crowds hosted by student organizations – arguably the most robust theoretical debates have occurred among academics who all fall on the pro-gay side of the political spectrum.[1] Specifically, pro-gay scholars have engaged in heated exchanges over whether marriage should be the political goal of LGBT and leftist thinkers. Some of these scholars want to imagine intimate possibilities apart from marriage, while others think marriage is the most practical way to organize our intimate lives.[2] And several scholars have identified the current period as a rare window for imagining a space beyond marriage – a space where intimate relationships previously deemed illegal are not yet fully embraced by the long regulatory arm of marriage.[3]

Those who question marriage ask: If marriage urges us to organize our lives in certain conventional ways, then what might society look like in its absence?[4] For some of these scholars, a world beyond marriage sounds hopeful, expansive, or at least interesting for its possibilities. This hypothetical world without marriage stands in sharp contrast to the dim, painful, dignity-deprived world that is typically represented – strategically, but no doubt truthfully, for many – by the plaintiffs' briefs in the same-sex marriage cases.[5] In a sense, then, for the pro-gay scholars who seek to look beyond marriage, the argument is not over whether gay people are worthy of marriage but, rather, whether marriage is worthy of gay people-and thus of everyone.[6]

This Essay imagines a world beyond our current marriage regime by looking to some unusual sources: fiction and anti-gay law.[7] Literature seems the obvious place to look when we are trying to imagine new possibilities, but we rarely look to literature as a source for new laws, and we rarely think of law as a prime site of the imagination. Yet fiction and anti-gay law both occupy places beyond our usual regulatory imaginings, places of fantasy and fear. These sources stand outside of – in excess of – our generally applicable laws.[8]

[. . .]

These unusual inquiries yield a variety of intriguing countermarriage possibilities. By countermarriage, I mean the vast range of alternative ways we might regulate intimate relationships, from tweaks of existing marriage law (for instance, assuming marriages automatically expire after a term of years), to wholesale replacement of marriage with some other regime (for instance, obligations that attach based on behavior rather than consent).[9]

[. . .] This Essay urges the reader to think innovatively about marriage. The fanciful exercises presented here thus complement the thoughtful work already underway on this subject. As noted above, debating the merits of marriage as a regulatory apparatus has occupied numerous scholars in recent years.[10] In light of the academic and popular interest in considering marriage's aims, functions, and value to society, this seems a critical moment for sharpening and expanding our thinking in this area. There is work to be done, and we want to be sure we are up to the task.

Of course, we may continue to accept marriage in its current form even after we question our assumptions about it. Considering alternatives to an institution may lead us to embrace a different approach, or, on the contrary, such a process may lead us to conclude that the institution has value, perhaps with greater confidence than if we had remained tied to our assumptions.[11] This Essay offers an array of inventive variations on our current marriage regime to help free our minds for that evaluative process in the rest of our public and scholarly discourse. If this moment between gay decriminalization and legal domestication is already closing – and I am increasingly hopeful that it is – then we should seize this opportunity to look in any remaining directions for new ideas and possibilities. We should make the most of this window before it closes.

[. . .]

Following this Introduction, Part I of the Essay draws on fictional sources to canvass some unusual visions of what marriage might be. These include exploding marriage, three-strikes marriage, line marriage, renewable marriage, self-marriage, and exculpatory marriage. Part II looks to another unlikely source for imagining countermarriage possibilities for all: anti-gay laws, in the form of state Defense of Marriage Acts ("mini-DOMAs"). In particular, this Part considers a law passed in Virginia in 2004 that expressly forbids "partnership contract[s] or other arrangement[s]" between "persons of the same sex" that "purport[] to bestow the privileges or obligations of marriage."[12] This Part reconceives and extends this restriction, imagining what it might mean instead to disallow not only marriage but also all contracts for all intimate partners. After reflecting on these diverse sources, in the Conclusion I offer some observations on the contributions that literature may make to the project of legal innovation.

Before beginning, I offer a caveat for the normatively inclined reader: this Essay explores but does not prescribe. Though discussions of marriage are typically normative, this Essay resists drawing normative conclusions about whether we should have marriage and in what form. The aim here is instead to step away from this prescriptive project and generate a broad range of countermarriage regimes inspired by unlikely sources.

I. Literature as Law

Literature can open up imaginative possibilities. Because it need not comply with existing laws and social conventions, literature can unsettle our usual frame of reference and invite us to consider new worlds. Thus, literature offers a relatively untapped resource for imagining novel legal regimes.[13] [. . .]

A. Exploding Marriage and Three-Strikes Marriage: Playing with Permanence

Goethe's novel Elective Affinities[14] entertains two different countermarriage regimes that play with the permanence of marriage. A core aspiration of marriage is that it last forever: Till death do us part. The reality is of course rather different, with divorce rates for first marriages at 45–50 percent in the United States.[15] And while marriage rates have declined, spouses continue to enter their marriages optimistic about their prospects for staying together, as reflected in their reluctance to sign prenuptial agreements.[16] Goethe's countermarriage regimes play with this assumption of permanence.

Goethe's first countermarriage idea is what we might call exploding marriage. In this regime, marriage expires after a fixed term of years.[17] The character of the Count in Elective Affinities explains to an assembled dinner group that "[o]ne of [his] friends, whose high spirits mostly express themselves in suggestions for new laws, claimed that every marriage should only be contracted for a period of five years."[18] Five years, the friend thought "was a nice odd number, a sacred number, and a period just sufficient to get to know one another, produce a number of children, separate, and, the nicest part of it, become reconciled again."[19] In explaining his proposal, the friend would "exclaim":

How happily the first years would pass! Two or three years would go by very pleasantly. Then one party, eager to see the relationship continue, would become increasingly attentive the closer the end of the contract

approached. The indifferent or even dissatisfied partner would be charmed and won over. They would forget, as we do the hours in good company, that time was passing, and would be most pleasantly surprised to notice, after the deadline was already passed, that the contract had been extended without a word having ever been spoken.[20] The Count's friend implicitly critiqued the ways married people sometimes come to take each other for granted, and cease to invest in the marriage or to appreciate their spouse. Hence the expiration date. The looming deadline forces the partners to consider each other closely again, much as one might energetically consume – or discard – an overlooked item in the refrigerator upon noticing it expires tomorrow. Interestingly, although the friend's proposal seems to imply that the default rule is for the marriage to explode, not continue, at the five-year mark,[21] he also seems to suggest that the couple can opt out of that presumption and silently ratify their relationship through the behavior of renewing their enthusiasm for each other and continuing together past the deadline.[22]

The Count offers another marriage alternative, three-strikes marriage.[23] Here, only marriages involving someone who has been married twice before are legally permanent:

"That same friend," [the Count] went on, "made yet another suggestion for a new law: a marriage should only be regarded as indissoluble when it was the third marriage of one or both. For this was incontrovertible evidence that marriage was something this person could not do without. Now it would also be known how they had behaved in their previous relationships, and whether they had bad habits, which more frequently lead to separations than do bad characters. We should find out about one another; and we should keep an eye on married people as well as unmarried ones, since we could not know what might come to pass."

"That would greatly increase society's interest," said [another character]; "for indeed, when we are married, nobody bothers about our virtues or faults anymore."[24] The suggestion that marriage should be permanent only if at least one party has been married twice before seems, in a way, perverse. It seems to assume the impermanence of marriage, at least of first (and second) marriages.[25] And it emphasizes desire for marriage itself – as "something this person could not do without" – rather than for the individual partner. And where the Count does attend to the individual, he focuses on habits rather than character. Such an account is surprising because a lover is typically expected to adore the essence of the person.

Habit seems superficial, relative to character, though a long tradition of writers has argued otherwise.[26]

Both of these countermarriage possibilities resist the usual sentimentality that presumes some people are meant for each other or even that the heart of marriage is necessarily love. On the other hand, the two alternatives may be read to push in opposite directions, with three-strikes marriage focused on a party's reaffirming their commitment to the institution time and time again, and exploding marriage focused on the parties' reaffirming their commitment to each other time and time again. By contrast to three-strikes marriage, exploding marriage might seem highly romantic in its emphasis on the part-ners' affirmative desires, rather than on other values. Thus, both of these countermarriage possibilities vary our current regime, with one favoring the institutional over the romantic dimensions of marriage and the other favoring the reverse.

[. . .]

B. Line Marriage: Reconceiving the Basic Structure

Robert Heinlein's novel The Moon Is a Harsh Mistress[27] offers us the idea of line marriage. Real-world marriage typically imposes expectations along the dimensions of numerosity (permitting only two persons per marriage) and exclusivity (permitting erotic intimacy only within marriage).[28] Line marriage necessarily violates the numerosity requirement, and it may also depart from the exclusivity requirement:[29] in this fanciful marital form, spouses of both sexes are added to the marriage, one by one, over time. Line marriage bears a similarity to what we generally think of as polygamy, except that it is sym-metrical and (at least structurally) egalitarian, with mul-tiple spouses of both sexes.[30] It is a "line" in its continuity over time: adding new spouses one after the other makes it possible that the marriage could continue intermina-bly, like a corporation.

The form is introduced in the novel by a participant who emphatically characterizes it as "nice" – a high compliment in his distinctively clipped way of speak-ing.[31] He says,

Our marriage nearly a hundred years old. . . . – twenty-one links, nine alive today, never a divorce. Oh, it's a madhouse when our descendants and in-laws and kin-folk get together for birthday or wedding – more kids than seventeen, of course; we don't count 'em after they marry or I'd have 'children' old enough to be my grand-father. Happy way to live, never much pressure. Take me.

Nobody woofs if I stay away a week and don't phone. Welcome when I show up. Line marriages rarely have divorces. How could I do better?[32] His interlocutor con-curs, "I don't think you could."[33]

Their dialogue further elucidates the variation availa-ble within that line structure. The marriage accommo-dates new spouses at any time because "[s]pacing has no rule, just what suits us."[34] And individual families may create their own patterns, and deviations from those pat-terns. For example, one family institutes a requirement to alternate the sex of each new spouse, but treats it flex-ibly: "Been alternation up to latest link, last year. We married a girl when alternation called for boy. But was special."[35] Throughout the book, line marriage repeat-edly engenders praise for its personal and societal vir-tues, including "financial security, fine home life it gives children, fact that death of a spouse, while tragic, could never be tragedy it was in a temporary family, especially for children – children simply could not be orphaned."[36] Such analytic praise is underscored by the emotional context in which it is offered – as in the statement fol-lowing this list of benefits: "Suppose I waxed too enthu-siastic – but my family is most important thing in my life."[37]

[. . .]

C. Who Can Enter: Flipping the Presumptions

In an essay in the Boston Evening Transcript on August 18, 1900, African-American[38] fiction writer Charles Chesnutt imagined a kind of racial utopia.[39] He pre-dicted that "the future American" would be a mixture of the current races, and he hypothesized a legal regime that would speed us to this conclusion:

We will assume . . . that the laws of the whole country were as favorable to . . . amalgamation as the laws of most Southern States are at present against it; i.e., that it were made a misdemeanor for two white or two colored per-sons to marry, so long as it was possible to obtain a mate of the other race – this would be even more favorable than the Southern rule, which makes no such exception.[40]

Even if we erroneously assume two pure races at the start, Chesnutt concluded, "in three generations the pure whites would be entirely eliminated, and there would be no perceptible trace of the blacks left."[41]

This imagined regulatory regime, akin to one elabo-rated in slightly different form by legal scholar Geoffrey Stone a century later,[42] flips the presumption as to who qualifies to enter a marriage. Instead of our historical legal prescription – and ongoing majority social practice – of racially homogamous marriage,[43] Chesnutt's law (partially) prescribes racially heterogamous marriage.

Various works of science fiction alter other conventional expectations of entrants into marriage, such as the widely held presumption of adult age (by [. . .] making the threshold younger out of necessity in a society decimated by plague[44]), or about the sex of the participants (by encouraging, for instance, same-sex relations to stem population growth in a society feeing resource depletion[45]). Unlike the science fiction variations on this theme, which tend to present new presumptions about who should enter marriage in functional terms, Chesnutt and Stone offer political justifications. In both cases, the fictional nature of the work provides an opportunity for variations that challenge assumptions about the entrants to marriage.

Moreover, Chesnutt's version of this altered reality invokes the criminal law, making certain kinds of marriages misdemeanors. This is a strong form of prohibition. Compared with the softer version of a rule presented in Goethe's exploding marriage, Chesnutt's criminal prohibition highlights the ways the form of the rule can vary – from criminal prohibition of one sort or another, to civil fines, to regulatory approval, to default rules (creating a presumption, which parties can overcome by speaking to the contrary), to forced choosing (requiring parties to choose an option, either of their own design or off a menu), to framing rules (framing parties' decisions with particular words or context). A rich literature on default rules explores the different ways that choices can be framed – with some of that work specifically applying these tools to the realm of family law.[46] The Chesnutt essay, though far from inventing these sorts of variations, calls our attention to degrees of regulatory strength through its invocation of the harshest state regime, criminal prohibition.

D. Renewable Marriage: Buying an Option

Shakespeare's The Winter's Tale[47] provides the inspiration for a form of countermarriage that, generalized, we might call renewable marriage (or perhaps, more playfully, take-a-break-from-marriage marriage[48]). This countermarriage form plays with the permanence, not of the marriage commitment, but of its termination. Extrapolating from The Winter's Tale, we can imagine marriage as a renewable resource: mistreatment by one spouse of the other leads to a term of years apart, which, if it leads to remorse, can end with vibrant reunion.

King Leontes, thinking his wife Hermione unfaithful with his friend, and desperately jealous, jails her, holds a trial in which he disregards the oracle that declares her innocent, and then orders the murder of their newborn daughter, Perdita (though she is secretly hidden rather than killed). His actions lead to the death of their fragile son and the eventual proclamation of Hermione's death from grief as well. After sixteen years pass, Perdita is recovered, and Hermione's friend Paulina elicits from the remorseful King both an admission that he effectively killed his wife through his cruelty and a promise that he would never marry again. The King and Perdita come, with other assembled guests, to ask Paulina to show them a statue of the Queen in her possession. Paulina presents the statue to the visitors, and as they admire the likeness, Paulina promises to bring the Queen back to life: "It is requir'd / You do awake your faith. / Then all stand still: / Or – those that think it is unlawful business / I am about, let them depart."[49] The King orders Paulina to proceed:

[. . .]

The play offers language at various points to suggest that Hermione has been in hiding all these years, cared for by Paulina, but it also leaves open the possibility that her statue has truly been brought to life.[50]

Unlike some of our other fictions, which explicitly offer countermarriage regimes, The Winter's Tale offers merely a scenario, an anecdote, of renewable marriage played out between these lovers. The closest we might come to an affirmative regulatory vision comes in the possible element of magic in the play: the suggestion that magic might assist the Queen's return hints at the possibility of an approving universe – a kind of fictional regulatory body – that looks on and enables the reunion.

Extrapolated from Shakespeare's approving frame, the idea of renewable marriage plays with the presumed continuity of marriage, suggesting that marriage could be intermittent, or terminated and then resumed.[51] It suggests a structure for the unfolding of relations between lovers over time, after growth and new appreciation of one for another. One might imagine variations: from the mistreated spouse who eventually forgives and returns, but only after remorse and recuperation by the abusive spouse, to the perhaps more fantastical permanent presumption in favor of a former spouse. Such a permanent presumption might confer privileges, such as ongoing access to a sexual relationship, even in the face of separation and reunion – that is, the former spouse might be an exception to new commitments of exclusivity or monogamy by the ex.[52]

Elizabeth F. Emens

A formal legal version of this is even more implausible, though not impossible. For instance, we might imagine a regime in which relations with a former spouse would not legally constitute adultery.[67] The path of the older relationship worn into the new one would create a kind of sexual easement that persists despite new ownership.

[. . .]

E. Solitary Marriage: Isolating and Self-Marriage

Marriage is generally conceived of as a joining together. It thus seems contrary to, or at least apart from, solitude. But fictional and philosophical sources – low and high – invite us to consider solitude through marriage.

The poet Rilke, writing in an epistolary mode, urges a view of the good marriage as a path to solitude:

It is a question in marriage, to my feeling, not of creating a quick community of spirit by tearing down and destroying all boundaries, but rather a good marriage is that in which each appoints the other guardian of his solitude, and shows him this confidence, the greatest in his power to bestow.[53]

Rilke eschews the idea of a "togetherness" between people, viewing it as hindering "freedom and development."[54] But, Rilke concludes,

[O]nce the realization is accepted that even between the closest human beings infinite distances continue to exist, a wonderful living side by side can grow up, if they succeed in loving the distance between them which makes it possible for each to see the other whole and against a wide sky![55]

Rilke's metaphor of the lovers always appearing to each other against a vast sky is not a form of structural countermarriage. He embraces our standard marital form – of two people facing each other and (presumably) only each other – but his rendition of marriage also imagines each spouse's role in the other's life not as co-entrant into a union but as a protector of the other's isolation: as the "guardian of his solitude."

The relation between marriage and solitude can take a bolder structural form: marriage to oneself. References to self-marriage appear occasionally in parodic criticism of same-sex marriage – as another place on the slippery slope that allegedly runs from same-sex marriage to polygamy.[56] In popular fiction, the idea of marrying oneself is elaborated slightly more seriously in an episode of the HBO series Sex and the City.[57] There, the lead character, Carrie, decides to announce to a friend that she is marrying herself and registering for a particular pair of

shoes. Carrie's intention is to make her friend realize how much Carrie has spent on the friend's life events, from wedding presents to baby showers. The friend had insulted Carrie for spending too much on a pair of Manolo Blahnik shoes that went missing at the friend's baby shower, where guests were required to remove their shoes for the health of their toddler. On learning the shoes were gone, and after some prompting, the friend had offered to pay for the missing shoes. But when she heard they cost nearly $500, she reneged, intimating that her own grown-up married life with children leaves no room for trivial expenditures such as high-end shoes. Carrie fumes as she adds up how much she has spent on her friend's life choices – for her engagement and wedding and babies – expenditures that may never come back to Carrie. So she decides to leave a voicemail for her friend, announcing her marriage to herself and her registry at one place: the shoe store Manolo Blahnik. The friend finally seems to understand Carrie's point of view and buys the shoes for her, sending a note saying she hopes that "you and you will be very happy."

The episode's flirtation with self-marriage has a serious side: the wealth transfer from single people to married people that custom often dictates. That wealth transfer has legal and institutional dimensions, in terms of the state and workplace benefits that marriage provides to (at least some forms of) married couples.[58] Social status also accompanies marriage, as is often noted in contemporary marriage debates; for many it signifies, among other things, entry into stable adult life.[59] In this light, that someone might want to marry herself sounds like less of a joke, if still fanciful.

F. Exculpatory Marriage: The Ultimate Benefit

Before I discuss Never Let Me Go,[60] a warning to the reader: this Section gives away the twist of this wonderful novel, and can be skipped without ruining your reading of the rest of the Essay.

In Never Let Me Go, Kazuo Ishiguro, the author of The Remains of the Day,[61] applies his subtle appreciation of human relations to a subject more typical of science fiction. Ishiguro portrays a dystopic society where the powers that be have created a race of clones. These clones are kept in institutions so that eventually their organs may be harvested for the benefit of the regular citizens. Society exploits some of the clones not only for their bodies but for their labor: these latter clones act as caregivers for others who, as a result of the organ harvesting process, are growing gradually weaker on their road to an early death (or "completion," as the novel puts it).

The novel's poignancy turns on two of its features. One is the gradual unfolding for the narrator, Kathy, of the truth of her own identity as a clone and of this grotesque societal arrangement; she in turn reveals the rules of her world to the reader bit by bit. The other is the love between two of the clones – Kathy and Tommy, a boy with whom she went to "school" before either knew they were clones – and the rumor that emerges about love as a way out of the early death to which clones are consigned. As Kathy cares for a childhood friend before the latter's completion, the friend reveals the underhanded way in which she had long ago come between Kathy and Tommy, who had always loved each other. She urges Kathy to reconnect with Tommy, to pursue their love, and to seek from the authorities a special dispensation rumored among the clones.

The rumor is that clones can have their organ donations, and thus their premature death, "deferred"–"if they're really in love."[62] Tommy and Kathy journey to the authorities who had run their school so many years ago. The lovers plead their case, only to learn that the rumor is false. There is no way to defer their donations; their love cannot save them. The novel thus beautifully renders, and then shatters, a classic and deeply human fantasy: that love can save us from our own mortality.

In so doing, the novel also portrays a fantastical vision of the benefits the state could bestow on deserving lovers. State–recognized relationships – that is, what we currently tend to call marriage – can involve any number of state-sponsored benefits (and burdens).[63] In Ishiguro's rendering, the state is rumored to have a regulatory regime that bestows the ultimate benefit on deserving couples: life. Those scheduled for execution, for an untimely death by order of the state, could be pardoned, spared – if their love takes the right form. We might call this exculpatory marriage. The novel rejects this rumor, but nonetheless leaves us with a striking vision of a state that could select and recognize only a chosen few for a kind of marriage whose benefit is the right to live.

The possibility of exculpatory marriage drawn from Ishiguro's world, though extreme, looks less absurd if we recognize the ways that our current legal system allows people effectively to "contract around" the criminal law. For instance, in some states, the (in some ways contractual) relationship of marriage is a defense to statutory rape.[64] (And of course marriage is a defense to fornication, ex ante if not ex post.) Consent to sex might similarly be understood, though it sounds crass to many ears,

as a form of contract that converts rape into legal sex.[65] Contracting to make pornographic films can allow one to pay others to have sex without running afoul of prostitution laws.[66] The Ishiguro example draws our attention to this feature of existing law and urges us to imagine the broadest possible range of benefits that marriage law could confer.

G. The End of Marriage

Following this brief tour of fictional rewritings of our marriage regime, let us return to Shakespeare for the ultimate countermarriage proposal – Hamlet's call for the end of marriage:

Ham. I have heard of your paintings well enough. God hath given you one face, and you make yourselves another. You jig and amble, and you [lisp,] you nickname God's creatures and make your wantonness [your] ignorance. Go to, I'll no more on't, it hath made me mad. I say we will have no mo[r]e marriage. Those that are married already (all but one) shall live, the rest shall keep as they are. To a nunn'ry, go.[67]

It is hard to read Hamlet's imagined world without marriage as anything positive, given its inclusion in his rant against Ophelia. Hamlet's spiteful railing against the institution may remind us of Goethe's Count, whose own embitterment may be seen to fuel his personal interest in alternatives to marriage.[68] Remember, however, that one of the Count's variations on marriage – exploding marriage – might be read as more romantic than cynical, leaving us with two different versions of what may inspire a turn to marriage alternatives.[69]

We need not linger over the basic idea of ending marriage, as it has been addressed at length in the same-sex marriage debates. Due attention has been paid to the question whether we should get the state out of marriage altogether and just permit adults to organize their intimate affairs through private contract law. Scholars have proposed various rationales for this contractual regime, including refocusing the state's attention and resources on relations of dependency;[70] getting the state out of an institution with historical associations with coverture and other legal impairments for women;[71] paving the way for religions to define marriage more purely according to their faith, rather than having to accept a compromised version through the state;[72] and prompting partners to make more active choices about the kinds of relationship they want to have under law as well as the role they want law to play in their relationship.[73] Since this Essay aims to unearth regulatory possibilities that have not been examined in these debates, I now turn to a source that manages to push the concept of ending marriage yet another step further: to a world not only without marriage, as Hamlet envisioned, but also without any contracts between intimate partners.

II. Law as Science Fiction

[. . .]

This Section explores a regulatory universe even further afield from current marriage law.[74] The inspiration for this brave new world is, perhaps ironically, legal rules generated in the name of preserving marriage against the threat of same-sex relationships: the so-called mini-DOMAs. The mini-DOMAs are the Defense of Marriage Act statutes and amendments passed by many states in recent years to preserve traditional, different-sex marriage against the perceived threat of same-sex relationships.[75] These laws do not merely declare the absence of marriage for same-sex couples. In their most extreme form, these laws threaten to ignore certain types of contracts between same-sex partners. Extrapolating from such laws, we can envision a dramatic alternative to our marriage regime: a world not only without marriage, but without any private contracts between intimate partners.

To imagine the possibilities generated by these laws, I use a particularly sweeping example of a mini-DOMA – a Virginia statute passed in 2004. This statute is one of many intriguing mini-DOMAs, including others passed in the state of Virginia.[76] But this 2004 Virginia statute is of particular interest because it explicitly targets "partnership contracts." Setting aside the law's discriminatory aspect, I focus instead on what it might mean to treat a law like this as the starting point for an alternative regulatory regime for everyone. In so doing, I also show how law opens up imaginative possibilities through what I call "law as science fiction."[77]

Here is the language of the 2004 statute banning, inter alia, same-sex "partnership contracts":

Civil unions between persons of same sex. A civil union, partnership contract or other arrangement between persons of the same sex purporting to bestow the privileges or obligations of marriage is prohibited. Any such civil union, partnership contract or other arrangement entered into by persons of the same sex in another state or jurisdiction shall be void in all respects in Virginia and any contractual rights created thereby shall be void and unenforceable.[78]

The statute is puzzling to say the least. First, what does it cover? What is included in these words: "partnership contract or other arrangement . . . purporting to bestow the privileges or obligations of marriage"? Indeed, the language is so broad that one might ask: What is not included? The scope of the statute is interesting in its own right, so I will pause over it here.

A. The Scope of the Statute

The "privileges or obligations of marriage" are vast. They include benefits and burdens directly bestowed by the state and those granted by third parties, as well as those that partners bestow on one another exclusively or principally. Though state laws vary, state and federal laws affecting marriage broadly include tax benefits and burdens for spouses; immigration benefits; evidentiary privileges; inheritance benefits and obligations; surrogate decision-making responsibilities; parenting presumptions; special forms of property ownership; various veterans' benefits; statutory privileges (such as caretaking leave time under the Family Medical Leave Act); and a legal mechanism and default rules for divorce, inter alia.[79] Beyond these features created by government, marriage entails a wide range of privately bestowed benefits and burdens, such as hospital visitation rights; employment-related health benefits; shared club membership privileges; presumptively shared names (benefit or burden, depending on your view); and often public ceremonies (and the costs, gifts, and status those entail), to name a few. Marriage also comprises various privileges and obligations that spouses grant each other. These typically include presumptive or explicit sexual exclusivity; first or high priority for time, attention, and caretaking in the event of illness; presumptive personal loyalty; completely or partially shared resources; holiday gifts; shared living space; and kin work.[80] The sheer volume of these marital "privileges or obligations" makes the scope of the Virginia statute a puzzle.

Who does the Virginia statute prohibit from making what arrangements under what circumstances? One could speculate endlessly about what the statute might cover. The statute surely does more than prohibit recognition of out-of-state same-sex marriages, since Virginia already had a statute specifically targeting these.[81] Beyond that, the statute's meaning is far from clear.[82] Here are a few possible readings. As I will discuss, the statute invites us to think beyond the end of marriage and imagine countermarriage regimes for all relationships.

1. State-created civil unions only. The statute might be read to refer only to official civil unions formed in other states. [. . .]

   But there are features of the statute that cut against this reading. For instance, there is a superfluity problem if the statute refers only to other states' statuses, since the second sentence of the statute expressly concerns unions from other jurisdictions. Moreover, both the version of the statute first introduced in the House and the amended version the House initially passed contained only language about unions and contracts created in other jurisdictions.[83] Late in the amending process, the Senate Committee for Courts of Justice incorporated the first sentence of the final statute.[84] In light of the statutory superfluity point, and the timing of the introduction of that first sentence, the statute seems to target something broader than merely out-of-state civil unions.

2. All of marriage. Perhaps the statute narrowly covers only those agreements that include all of the rights and obligations of marriage that private contract can confer, that is, those agreements that attempt to replicate marriage as closely as possibly through private contract. This reading would seem consistent with the idea of trying to prevent harm to the institution of marriage by preventing attempts to copy it. It also has the advantage that a court could probably determine from the four corners of an agreement whether the statute covered it. The difficulty with this reading, however, is the statute's reference to the "privileges or obligations" of marriage, rather than the privileges and obligations. Because an exact copy of marriage would include both privileges and obligations, rather than one or the other, this reading strains against the statutory language.

3. Platonic relationships. The statute might, in principle, disregard romantic involvement. On its face the statute says nothing about homosexuality or romantic relationships. Could the statute apply to a partnership agreement between two male doctors that creates a joint medical practice and conveys the practice to the survivor if one of the partners dies? This borders on the absurd. The legislative history[85] makes plain that the statute's concern is homosexuality. Presumably, only a judge wishing to gain popular support for striking the statute down would read the statute this way (though, interestingly, it might also help the statute escape Romer-type problems).[86]

4. Speaking "marriage." Perhaps the word "marriage" matters. Maybe a court could sort those arrangements that purport to bestow the relevant privileges or obligations from those that don't by looking to whether the word "marriage" appears in the agreement. This might seem unduly formalistic, but, like the "all of marriage" reading above, it would simplify coverage determinations. Of course this would also probably mean a great deal of overbreadth (since "marriage" has meanings beyond romantic marriage[87]) and underbreadth (since the M-word might not be used in romantic situations for any number of reasons).[88]

5. Contextualized overlap with marriage. That we can speak of overbreadth and underbreadth suggests we have some idea of the core of the statute. The context – the relationship of the parties, most importantly, and probably their intent in entering the agreement – would seem to matter. The public nature of their relationship and any associated ceremony might be sufficient (but not necessary) to bring any contracts they formed within the statute's scope. And so, in addition to applying to civil unions from other jurisdictions, the statute would apply to any arrangement between romantically involved same-sex partners that concerned most or many of the key privileges or obligations of marriage. And more broadly, the statute might well mean nonenforcement of any individual agreement between same-sex partners that overlaps with a specific privilege or obligation of marriage.[89] This might also reach any third-party agreement that benefitted them, such as a health-insurance policy covering same-sex partners.[90]

6. Any agreement between same-sex intimate partners. Which of the above interpretations a judge would choose could plausibly depend on whether the judge wanted to uphold or strike down the statute, or, otherwise, how the judge sought to resolve the dispute at hand.[91] But in light of the previous interpretation offered, anyone in a same-sex romantic relationship could understandably be concerned that in the context of his relationship, any contract with his partner might not hold up in court.[92]

This final possibility brings us to a very different kind of inquiry.

B. Freedom for All: Applying a Broad Reading Broadly

One thing (and perhaps only one thing) is clear from the Virginia statute: it covers only persons of the same sex. A man and a woman together doing any of the things potentially proscribed by the statute fall outside its purview. But what if that weren't so? What if the statute applied to everyone?

A generalized version of the statute invites us to imagine a starkly different legal regime.[93] It suggests the possibility of a world in which any contract (whether a partnership contract or otherwise) between intimate partners (whether same-sex or opposite-sex) is void and unenforceable.

Taking the Virginia statute's first sentence as our focus, we can imagine a generalized version:

A civil union, contract, or other arrangement purporting to bestow the privileges or obligations of marriage is prohibited. The world of the revised statute could take either of two forms. In one version, all other laws would stay as they are, so marriage would remain in place, and the only difference from our current world would be that no romantically involved couples, either straight or gay, could create enforceable contracts that overlap with marriage's privileges or obligations. Such a regime might comport with the state's interest in promoting traditional marriage and in preventing alternative arrangements from "weakening the institution of marriage which is foundational to this country's history and tradition."[94] But the second version of this alternative legal regime is more interesting.

Under the second imagined regime, there would not only be no marriage, there would be no enforceable contracts between intimate partners. I am not advocating such a world, nor am I predicting it as in any way a plausible eventuality.[95] In this imagined world, though, people in romantic relationships would not be able to marry or to form any legally enforceable agreements with each other.

Although this might seem absurd, it is possible to generate reasons for refusing to enforce contracts between romantic partners, regardless of how unlikely such a refusal is. First, the state might be concerned about bounded rationality among contracting partners.[96] That is, a state might plausibly think that romantic partners are peculiarly bad at making sensible contracting decisions. Such partners may be overly optimistic about the future, as people on the verge of marriage tend to be. As Pollock and Maitland famously said, "[o]f all people in the world lovers are the least likely to distinguish precisely between the present and the future tenses."[97] They therefore may create contracts that do not properly assess risks and eventualities. Optimism and cloudy thinking may override the cautionary function of legal formalities.[98]

An inability to make rational, independent decisions underpins some standard reasons that we decline to enforce otherwise valid contracts. Think here of duress, undue influence, or even incapacity. We might think of lovers as like those whose will is overborne, or like drunk people or children, in their relations with each other.

Second, the state might be unwilling to hold lovers to their contractual obligations because of paternalistic concerns. As with infancy or mental incapacity, we may worry that inequality in the relationship will produce terms more favorable to one party in a way that is substantively unfair.[99] We thus free our most vulnerable citizens from obligations they may unwittingly incur. Of course, to stretch this concern about vulnerability into a refusal to enforce any such contracts seems excessive. But the aim here is to entertain unusual possibilities, not to devise an ideal regime.

Third, if the parties aren't making rational decisions, then their agreements may be less likely to have the features that lead us, under a welfare rationale, to enforce contracts.[100] That is, the parties, by not pursuing their individual self-interest, may not achieve a surplus; the contract they create may not be Pareto optimal.[101] Classic contracting parties are those who stand "at arm's length." Where the parties' judgment is boundedly rational to the extent of lovers', then their contracts may simply be less likely to be welfare-promoting. If so, why would the state waste resources enforcing such agreements?[102]

Related to this welfare rationale for non-enforcement is a separate concern: enhanced enforcement costs. The state might prefer not to enforce contracts between lovers in order to avoid the costs to the state of such enforcement.[103] Contracts formed between lovers could disproportionately result in litigation costs. Picture two sets of contracting parties: AB and CD. Each set creates a business partnership. The only difference between them is that A and B are romantically involved while C and D are not. Which venture seems more likely to fail? The state might plausibly predict AB. In addition, a state might well predict that even if both AB and CD fail, then AB is more likely to end up in litigation. To paraphrase Bob Ellickson, the conflicts that end up in court, and thus in casebooks, disproportionately involve "sociopaths and love triangles."[104] For any number of paternalistic or cost-based reasons, then, a state might prefer not to enforce contracts between lovers.

This alternative world seems obviously implausible, or even impossible. A world where lovers can neither marry nor contract sounds ludicrous – the mad musings of a legal scholar gone awry. But this scheme is not too far removed from the world contemplated for same-sex couples in Virginia. The state of Virginia thus imaginatively forces us all into this alternative legal world – the world of no marriage and no contracts.

[. . .]

Conclusion: Of Law, Literature, and Innovation

Marriage is the triumph of imagination over intelligence. Second marriage is the triumph of hope over experience.[105]

These lines, often mistakenly attributed to Oscar Wilde, present ordinary marriage as an imaginative endeavor. It may be so, at least for some. And it is certainly possible that little should change in our current marriage regime.[106] As I noted at the start, my aim has not been to argue for one or another countermarriage regime, but to excavate possibilities from some unlikely sources. I thus conclude with a few reflections on these sources, and on the relationships among law, literature, and innovation.

Various justifications may be offered for the status quo. For some traditions and thinkers, the way things are is the way they should be – "Whatever is, is right."[107] Burke famously extolled the virtues of tradition as the accumulated wisdom of the centuries.[108] More recently, there's the joke about the (old school) Chicago economist:

A Chicago economist and a friend were walking along the street when they spotted a $20 bill. The economist kept walking. The friend turned to him and asked, "Aren't you going to pick that up?" "Of course not," said

the economist. "It's fake. If there were a real $20 bill on the sidewalk, someone would have picked it up already."[109]

The joke plays off classical economic principles, which suggest that the current state of affairs cannot be improved upon, because the market has already perfected it.[110]

[. . .]

Research in fields ranging from social psychology (on system justification and status quo bias) to organizational theory (for example, on the so-called dark side of organizations) has documented the ways we become stuck in the present configuration of things.[111] What allows us to think beyond the ruts we create for ourselves, to imagine and examine other possibilities?

In their different ways, both law and literature are realms of the imagination, both mechanisms for innovation. Both urge us to expand our thinking beyond the status quo. Literature is obviously a realm of the imagination. Scholars have already written about the political possibilities of the literary imagination, for instance, in helping to facilitate empathy with diverse others.[112] But literature has been underutilized as a source of legal innovation.

[. . .]

None of these considerations show that things should change. Sometimes the way things are is, indeed, the way things should be. But as Justice Holmes famously wrote, "[i]t is revolting to have no better reason for a rule of law than that so it was laid down in the time of Henry IV."[113] As scholars and students, we should at least consider the range of alternatives to the present state of things before reaching a conclusion about the normative merits or demerits of keepings things as they are. [. . .]

Notes

1   Indeed, these theoretical debates are so extensive that this brief Essay will make no attempt to catalogue the relevant work; the texts cited herein are merely exemplary. On terminology in the Essay, note that by "pro-gay" and "anti-gay," I mean something like Janet Halley's definitions. See Janet E. Halley, Sexual Orientation and the Politics of Biology: A Critique of the Argument from Immutability. 46 Stan. L. Rev. 503,516 (1994) ("By anti-gay, I mean to describe those who believe that homosexuality is bad or harmful and should be punished, hidden, or restrained; by pro-gay, I refer to those who believe that homosexuality is good or value neutral and should be celebrated or

tolerated."). I would revise these definitions, for instance, by replacing "tolerated" with "included," for reasons well developed in Wendy Brown's intervening critique of "tolerance." See Wendy Brown, Regulating Aversion: Tolerance in the Age of Identity and Empire (2008). In addition, when applied to laws rather than persons, these terms refer less to beliefs than to the laws' effects or to the discourse surrounding their passage.

2   Compare, e.g., Martha Albertson Fineman, The Neutered Mother, the Sexual Family, and Other Twentieth Century Tragedies (1995) (arguing for vertical parent–child dyads to replace horizontal intimate dyads as the privileged state

relationship, and replacing marriage with contractual arrangements), and Michael Warner, The Trouble with Normal: Sex, Politics, and the Ethics of Queer Life (1999) (arguing against the push to same-sex marriage as a normalizing and exclusive endeavor), and Mary Lyndon Shanley, Afterword, in Just Marriage 109 (Joshua Cohen & Deborah Chasman eds., 2004) (drawing on essays in this volume by Cossman, Fineman, Metz, and Brown to conclude that the state should not sponsor marriage per se but should offer only civil unions) with Carol Sanger, A Case for Civil Marriage. 27 Cardozo L. Rev. 1311 (2006) (expressing skepticism about the ability of a contract law regime to adequately replace marriage law), and Elizabeth S. Scott, A World Without Marriage. 41 Fam. L.Q. 537, 539, 565–66 (2007) (concluding that, while the choice between expanding marriage and replacing it with universal civil unions is a "difficult one," expanding marriage is probably the better choice), and Mary Lyndon Shanley, Just Marriage: On the Public Importance of Private Union, in Just Marriage, supra, at 3 (arguing that marriage should be reformed rather than replaced with a contractarian regime).

3 See, e.g., Katherine M. Franke, Longing for Loving. 76 Fordham L. Rev. 2685 (2008); Elizabeth F. Emens, Monogamy's Law: Compulsory Monogamy and Polyamorous Existence, 29 N.Y.U. Rev. L. & Soc. Change 277 (2004).

4 See, e.g., Patricia A. Cain, Imagine There's No Marriage. 16 Quinnipiac L. Rev. 27 (1996): sources cited supra note 2.

5 See, e.g., Final Reply Brief of Plaintiffs-Appellees at 23, Vamum v, Brien, 763 N.W.2d 862 (Iowa 2008) (No. 07-1499), 2008 WL 5156764 at *23 ("It is an undisputed fact that [plaintiffs'] inability to marry their chosen partners is a painful frustration of their life goals and dreams, their personal happiness and their self-determination.") (internal quotation marks omitted); see also Transcript of Oral Argument at 21, Vamum v. Brien, 763 N.W.2d 862 (Iowa 2008) (No. 07-1499) (plaintiffs' counsel arguing that refusal to extend marriage to same-sex couples shows "lack of respect and dignity and equality"); Seth Hemmelgarn, Kids Feel the Impact of Prop 8, Bay Area Rep., Mar. 5, 2009, available at http://ebar.com/news/article.php?sec=news&article=3770.

6 Cf., e.g., Shanley, Afterword, supra note 2.

7 For an explanation of the term "anti-gay," see supra note 1.

8 Cf. Adam Phillips, On Balance 2, 9 (2010) ("When people are being extreme they push things to their limits; when they are being excessive they push things beyond their limits.... [S]omething as powerful as excess might – if we can suspend our fear – allow us to have thoughts we have never had before.").

9 I focus principally on sexually intimate relationships here. For thoughtful critiques of the legal centrality of intimacy so defined, see, for example, Brenda Cossman, Beyond Marriage, in Just Marriage 93, supra note 2; Laura A. Rosenbury & Jennifer E. Rothman, Beyond Intimacy 2 (Sept 8,2008) (unpublished manuscript) (on file with author).

10 See, e.g., sources cited supra notes 1-4 and infra notes 93-96; Mary Anne Case, Marriage Licenses, 2004 Lockhart Lecture, 89 Minn. L. Rev. 1758.1792–97 (2005); Elizabeth S. Scott & Robert E. Scott, Marriage as Relational Contract, 84 Va. L. Rev. 1225 (1998).

11 Cf. Phillips, supra note 8, at 10 ("Perhaps as part of growing up we need to be excessive – to try to break all the rules just to be able to find out what, if anything, the rules are made of, and why they matter. Perhaps only the road of excess can teach us when enough is enough.").

12 Va. Code Ann. § 20-45.3 (2004).

13 No pun on "novel" is intended here, but it is interesting to note that the term novel meant, in one historical context, new laws. The fifth definition of novel in the Oxford English Dictionary is "Roman Law. A new decree or constitution, supplementary to a codex; esp. any of those enacted by the emperor Justinian. Now hist." See Oxford English Dictionary Online: novel, http://www.oed.com.ezproxy.millsaps.edu/view/Entry/128757?rskey=eTSpZN&result =l&isAdvanced=false # (last visited Mar. 1, 2011) (quoting Gibbon, inter alia, as here: "1788 Gibbon Decline & Fall IV. xliv. 366 The nine collations, the legal standard of modern tribunals, consist of ninety-eight Novels").

14 Johann Wolfgang von Goethe, Elective Affinities, in 11 Goethe: The Collected Works 89 (David E. Wellbery ed., Judith Ryan trans., Princeton University Press 1995) (1809).

15 Linda A. Jacobsen & Mark Mather, U.S. Economic and Social Trends Since 2000, 65 Pop. Bull., 10 (Feb. 2010).

16 See, e.g., Heather Mahar, Why Are There So Few Prenuptial Agreements? 1 (Harvard Law Sch. John M. Olin Center for Law, Econ. & Bus. Discussion Paper Series 2003), available at http://lsr.nellco.org/cgi/viewcontent.cgi?article=1224&context=harvard_olin (estimating that only 5–10 percent of couples sign prenuptial agreements). On U.S. marriage rates, see D'Vera Cohn, The States of Marriage and Divorce, Pew Research Center Social & Demographic Trends (October 15, 2009), http://pewsocialtrends.org/pubs/746/states-of-marriage-and-divorce ("The proportion of Americans who are currently married has been diminishing for decades and is lower than it has been in at least half a century.... Among Americans 18 and older, the proportion currently married, but not separated, is 55% for men and 50% for women.").

17 I thank Martha Nussbaum for directing me to this novel after hearing me talk about exploding marriage, a concept I think I first heard mentioned by Amy Kapczynski, to whom thanks are also due.

18 Goethe, supra note 14, at 139.

19 Id.

20 Id.

21 Default rules are background rules that govern if contracting parties do not contract around them by opting for another rule. . . . For a discussion of the variability of default rules and their possible uses in marriage law, see

Elizabeth F. Emens, Changing Name Changing: Framing Rules and the Future of Marital Names. 74 U. Chi. L. Rev. 761 (2007).

22 Legal analogues include "year-and-a-day marriages, renewable with the consent of the parties, common among the Irish" and a bill introduced into the Maryland Legislature in 1971 titled "Marriage – Contractual Renewal," which provided "that a marriage be considered a contract for three years with an option to renew for three years, renewable forever, upon mutual consent thereto." See Mary Anne Case, A Brief History of Marriage in Anglo-American Law with Special Reference to those Points of Commonality with the Law of Corporations, 4 n.19 (unpublished manuscript, on file with author) (citing H.D. 623, Feb. 26, 1971). The law recently offered a grimmer, mandatory (rather than default) version of exploding marriage to the same-sex couples married in San Francisco from February 12 to March 11, 2004; later that year, the California Supreme Court declared those marriages void. Lockyer v. San Francisco, 33 Cal. 4th 1055, 1120 (2004). And a geographical, rather than chronological, version of this might be extrapolated from the situation of same-sex couples who marry in one of the few states recognizing same-sex marriage, who then move to a state that refuses to give full faith and credit to their marriage (as announced by many of the state mini-DOMAs, see infra Part II). A more voluntary (and playful) version of this hardship could be reimagined as a same-sex couple's traveling state to state on their honeymoon, watching their marriage disappear and reappear. (I thank Suzanne Goldberg for this point.) For those who thought sex was sexier before it was legal, this kind of vacillating marriage might have a certain appeal. See Bernard E. Harcourt, Supreme Court Review, Foreword: "You Are Entering a Gay and Lesbian-Free Zone": On the Radical Dissents of Justice Scalia and Other (Post-) Queers, 94 J. Crim. L. & Criminology 503, 527 (2004) (quoting Sarah Schulman).

23 Third-time's-the-charm marriage might be a warmer name for this one, though harder to say than three-strikes marriage, which also captures the sense in which this regime takes one out of the dating game after the third "swing."

24 Goethe, supra note 14, at 140.

25 A few states have enacted laws that play with the permanence dimension of marriage in a different way: covenant marriage statutes make entry and exit more difficult for those who opt into them (which is apparently a very small group). See Ariz. Rev. Stat. Ann. §§ 25-901 to -906 (2010); Ark. Code Ann. §§ 9-11-801 to -810 (2010); La. Rev. Stat. Ann. §§ 9:272-274, 9:307 (2009); Steven L. Nock et al., Covenant Marriage Turns Five Years Old, 10 Mich. J. Gender & L. 169, 170 (2003) (estimating that "less than two percent of all newly contracted marriages in Louisiana are covenant marriages").

26 For one such argument, and for a history of this vein of thinking, see, for instance, Elaine Scarry, Thinking in an Emergency (forthcoming 2011) (on file with author).

27 Robert A. Heinlein, The Moon Is a Harsh Mistress (Orb ed. 1997) (1966).

28 See Emens, Monogamy's Law, supra note 3, at 308-09.

29 In principle, line marriage could be either exclusive or open, in that the many spouses within a particular line marriage could be permitted sexual intimacy only with one another, or with others outside the marriage as well. As practiced in the novel, spouses apparently permit sexual contact outside the marriage in a freer way than might be expected in a monogamous culture, but such contact is sometimes presented as a violation (however minor or accepted) of some presumed principle of fidelity and sometimes not. Compare, e.g., Heinlein, supra note 27, at 114 (describing how the narrator's senior wife housed his new female friend in a room close to his workshop, "where I slept when slept alone," in effect telling him, "plain as print", "'Go ahead, dear. Don't tell me if you wish to be mean about it. Sneak behind my back.'"), with id. at 279 (explaining with bemusement that a new visitor to their moon culture was worried when the narrator's wife prepared to kiss him vigorously in greeting after a dangerous journey, because the visitor was from Earth where marriage "makes a difference" to such behavior and the visitor therefore foolishly thought the narrator-husband who was standing right there "might take offense!").

30 The novel also contains other forms of multi-party marriage; on the moon, where the novel takes place, the "commonest type" of marriage is a "troika" with two men and a woman (presumably because of the shortage of women). Id. at 134.

31 The narrator generally avoids articles and otherwise abbreviates his speech, almost as one might imagine a computer would speak.

32 Id. at 42.

33 Id.

34 Id.

35 Id.

36 Id. at 260. See also id. at 47, 172, 261–62. One of the ways that the inhabitants of Earth are rendered unsympathetic is through their oppressive response – namely, criminal charges – to the narrator's line marriage back on the moon. Id. at 262.

37 Id. at 260.

38 Chesnutt considered himself African-American, as did the one-drop laws of various jurisdictions, though his paternal grandfather was a white slave owner and he could apparently pass for white (though he chose not to do so). See, e.g., Pauline Carrington Bouvé, An Aboriginal Author, Boston Evening Transcript, Aug. 23, 1899, at 16; David Perlmutt, Stamp Honors Black Author with N.C. Roots, News & Observer (Raleigh, N.C.), Oct. 7, 2007, at B3.

39 Charles W. Chesnutt, The Future American, Boston Evening Transcript, Aug. 18,1900, available at http://www.online-literature.com/charles-chesnutt/wife-of-his-youth/11/. I thank Kevin Maillard for calling my attention to this text.

40 Id.

41 Id.

42 See Geoffrey R. Stone, Commentary, If America Only Had One Mixed Race, Chi. Trib., Mar. 30, 1999, at 17 (reprinting Stone's University of Chicago Centennial Contribution) (setting out a thought experiment, the Mandatory Miscegenation Act of 2100, which provided that "[n]o person who is not genetically certified as a person of mixed race may procreate with another person of the same race") (internal quotation marks omitted).

43 Homogamy refers to pairing within one's own type. For further discussion, see Elizabeth F. Emens, Intimate Discrimination; The State's Role in the Accidents of Sex and Love, 122 Harv. L. Rev. 1307 (2009).

44 See George Stewart, Earth Abides (1949). I thank Alan Fried for pointing me to Stewart and to Haldeman. See infra note 45.

45 See Joe Haldeman, The Forever War (1974).

46 See, e.g., . . . Emens, Changing Name Changing, supra note 21; . . .

47 William Shakespeare, The Winter's Tale (J.H.P. Pafford ed., Arden 2006).

48 With acknowledgements to Janet Halley's Split Decisions: How and Why To Take a Break from Feminism (2008).

49 Shakespeare, supra note 47, at 158 (V.iii.94–97).

50 Much language pushes toward, but does not definitely determine, the reading of Hermione as having been hidden rather than conjured. For instance, Leontes notes how her statue has wrinkles she did not have sixteen years before – which Paulina explains as part of the sculptor's talent in rendering her as she would be now. Id. at 155 (V.iii.27–32). The text further tells us that Paulina has been visiting a remote place, possibly Hermione's hiding place – "for she hath privately twice or thrice a day, ever since the death of Hermione, visited that removed house" – perhaps to care for her. Id. at 151 (V.ii.105–7).

51 Of course, at present, marriages can be terminated and then resumed, but this is done through divorce and remarriage, which follows the usual procedures for any new marriage, rather than invoking any special practice of renewing the first marriage. In principle, the closest legal analogue to renewable marriage might be the recent phenomenon that Jeannie Suk has termed "state-imposed de facto divorce," in which courts issue restraining orders in domestic violence situations, thereby prohibiting contact between the parties for a specified period ranging from two to eight years. See Jeannie Suk, At Home in the Law: How the Domestic Violence Revolution Is Transforming Privacy 40 n.55, 40–50 (2009). In practice, Suk does not think that reunion is likely

if the parties actually separate for the designated period. See id. at 48. Legal separation, which does not dissolve the marriage but determines certain legal rights between the parties, also might be understood as a form of renewable marriage. See, e.g., 27A C.J.S. Divorce § 349 (2010). And as a social matter, people do "renew their vows." Rachel Emma Silverman, "I Do, I Do, I Do, I Do" The Serial Vow Renewal, Wall St. J., Aug. 28, 2003, at D1–D15. Where this is done to repair a rupture in the relationship, rather than to reaffirm a vibrant commitment, it might be understood as an emotional version of renewed marriage.

52 Think here of popular representations of a partner urging that a sexual dalliance doesn't "count" as infidelity because it involves an ex-lover, not a new lover. Of course, the betrayed lover generally does not see this purported exception the same way. See, e.g., Grace N' Glamour, Don at [sic] Justify Your Cheating, Sept. 14, 2009, http://www.gracenglamour.com/dont-justify-your-cheating/. The emotional, rather than sexual, version of this access may be more accepted. That is, some kind of emotional closeness among former lovers – at least among great loves – sometimes persists in one form or another even across subsequent serial monogamy; new lovers may be more inclined to feel they have to accept this kind of intimacy than physical intimacy.

53 Rainer Maria Rilke, On Love and Other Difficulties 28 (John J.L. Mood trans., 1975). Rousseau also depicts love as a place for the discovery of a vital solitude: "[D]uring those few years, loved by a gentle and indulgent woman . . . [t]he taste for solitude and contemplation grew up in my heart along with the expansive and tender feelings which are best able to nourish it." Jean-Jacques Rousseau, Reveries of a Solitary Walker 154 (Peter France trans., 1979) (1782).

54 Rilke, supra note 53, at 28 (emphasis omitted).

55 Id. (emphasis in original).

56 For instance, one comment to the news on New Hampshire's lifting of the ban on same-sex marriage wrote: Marriage is now meaningless in the Granite State. It's only a matter of time before other special interest groups argue for their "rights," and the precedent set here will allow them to get their way. Want to marry two women? Sure. Ten men. Okay! Want to marry yourself? Why not, can't discriminate.
Tom Fahey, Same-Sex Marriage Becomes Law in NH, UnionLeader.com, June 3, 2009, http://www.unionleader.com/article.aspx?headline=Samesex%2Bmarriage%2Bbecomes%C2Blaw%C2Bin%÷NH&articleId=ac4816e1-7ac9-4694-b89c-b6174c8b6a87 (quoting Alex, Nashua).

57 Sex and the City: A Woman's Right to Shoes (HBO August 17,2003).

58 For instance, in the United States, male-female married couples within certain income ranges receive a federal tax benefit if their income disparity is great enough, but not if their incomes are similar. See, e.g., Shari Motro, A New "I Do": Towards a Marriage-Neutral Income Tax, 91 Iowa L.

Rev. 1509 (2006). available at http://papers.ssrn.com/sol3/papers.cfm?abstract_id=894104; Alternatives to Marriage Project, Legal and Financial Issues, http://www.unmarried.org/legal-financial.html (last visited Jan. 2, 2011). Workplaces provide various kinds of family benefits, the costs of which may be borne at least in part by single (or childless) colleagues. See, e.g., Mary Anne Case, How High the Annie Pie?, 76 Chi.-Kent L. Rev. 1753 (2001).

59 See, e.g., Robin Marantz Henig, What Is It About 20-Somethings?, N.Y. Times Mag., Aug. 18, 2010, at MM28, http://www.nytimes.com/2010/08/22/magazine/22Adulthood-t.html. Moreover, some people might relish the potential for marriage to narrow one's social world – to take one "off the market," as it were.

60 Kazuo Ishiguro, Never Let Me Go (2005).

61 Kazuo Ishiguro, The Remains of the Day (1989).

62 Ishiguro, supra note 60, at 174.

63 See infra text accompanying note 103.

64 See, e.g., Ariz. Rev. Stat. Ann. § 13-1407 (2010) ("It is a defense to a prosecution pursuant to § 13-1404 [nonconsensual sexual conduct] or 13-1405 [sexual conduct with minor] that the person was the spouse of the other person at the time of commission of the act.").

65 And of course, to other ears, sex always bears an important relation to rape. See, e.g., Catharine A. MacKinnon, Toward A Feminist Theory of the State 128 (1989).

66 See People v. Freeman, 758 P.2d 1128 (Cal. 1988). Freeman doesn't focus on the contractual point, but the structure of the arrangement seems to be one in which the parties have contracted out by agreeing to this third purpose – beyond the purpose of sexual gratification, which the court focuses on as the thrust of the prostitution statute at issue – of making films. Note that, beyond sex and marriage contexts, other examples of contracting around the criminal law include the practice of plea bargaining and laws exempting sports activities from assault laws. See, e.g., Iowa Code §708.1 (2010).

67 William Shakespeare, The Tragedy of Hamlet, Prince of Denmark act 3, sc. 1 (alterations in original but for "mo[r]e").

68 See supra note 67 and accompanying text.

69 Id. Two rather different readings of Hamlet's world without marriage are also available from his words: a libertine and a celibate one. "Nunnery" had the contemporary sense of "brothel" as well as "convent." See Oxford English Dictionary (draft revision Sept. 2010) (defining "nunnery" as such and offering the following first example: "1593 Christs Teares 79 b, [To] some one Gentleman generally acquainted, they giue..free priuiledge thenceforward in theyr Nunnery, to procure them frequentance.").

70 This position is most notably associated with Martha Fineman. See Martha Albertson Fineman, The Autonomy Myth: A Theory of Dependency (2004); Fineman, supra note 2; see also Nancy D. Polikoff, Ending Marriage As We Know It, 32 Hofstra L. Rev. 201, 204–05 (2004) (criticizing the U.S. focus on narrowly reforming marriage and holding up as a model alternative the 2001 Law Commission of Canada's Report: Beyond Conjugality: Recognizing and Supporting Close Personal Adult Relationships, Dec. 21, 2001, available at http://www.samesexmarriage.ca/docs/beyond_conjugality.pdf); Nancy D. Polikoff, Why Lesbians and Gay Men Should Read Martha Fineman, 8 Am. U. J. Gender Soc. Pol'y & L. 167 (1999).

71 See, e.g., Cain, supra note 4 (discussing these and other arguments); Cass R. Sunstein, The Right to Marry, 26 Cardozo L. Rev. 2081 (2005) (same).

72 Cf. Kmiec Proposes End of Legally Recognized Marriage, Catholic News Agency, May 28, 2009, http://www.catholicnewsagency.com/news/kmiec_proposes_end_of_legally_recognized_marriage/; Douglas W. Kmiec & Shelley Ross Saxer, Equality in Substance and in Name, S.F. Chron., Mar. 2, 2009; cf. also Martha C. Nussbaum, From Disgust to Humanity: Sexual Orientation & Constitutional Law 163 (2010) (noting, without elaborating, her support for this approach).

73 See, e.g., Just Marriage, supra note 2 (various essays); David L. Chambers, For the Best of Friends and for Lovers of All Sorts, 76 Notre Dame L. Rev. 1347 (2001).

74 Anti-gay law also offers material that could be mined for marriage variations more akin to those discussed in Part I. For instance, we could draw out a category akin to those above by looking to cases that find that same-sex relations do not count as adultery. See, e.g., In re Blanchflower, 834 A.2d 1010, 1011 (N.H. 2003) (holding that sex between two women did not constitute adultery under New Hampshire's fault divorce statute, based on the dictionary definition of "sexual intercourse"). We might (inelegantly) call this asymmetrical gender exclusivity. A social version of this structure is suggested by the web site http://www.pomfidelity.com/, in which a married couple has claimed a niche in the porn industry by inviting others into bed with them, invoking slogans like "The couple that plays together, stays together," and yet engaging in sex outside their marriage only with other women. For legal variations on file exploding marriage theme, see supra note 22.

75 See Andrew Koppelman, The Difference the Mini-DOMAs Make, 38 Lov. U. Chi. L.J. 265 (2007) (explaining the term and the status of these acts, inter alia). Mini-DOMA is the term coined to describe a state-level version of the federal Defense of Marriage Act (DOMA), passed in 1996.

76 Virginia first passed a mini-DOMA statute focusing on same-sex marital relationships: A marriage between persons of the same sex is prohibited. Any marriage entered into by persons of the same sex in another state or jurisdiction shall be void in all respects in Virginia and any contractual rights created by such marriage shall be void and unenforceable.

Va. Code Ann. § 20-45.2 (2004). Only a few years later, Virginia passed an expansively worded constitutional amendment:

[O]nly a union between one man and one woman may be a marriage valid in or recognized by this Commonwealth and its political subdivisions.

This Commonwealth and its political subdivisions shall not create or recognize a legal status for relationships of unmarried individuals that intends to approximate the design, qualities, significance, or effects of marriage. Nor shall this Commonwealth or its political subdivisions create or recognize another union, partnership, or other legal status to which is assigned the rights, benefits, obligations, qualities, or effects of marriage.

Va. Const. art. I, § 15-A (2006). My focus in this Essay is a third law passed between the time of the statute and of the amendment.

77 [deleted reference]

78 Va. Code Ann. § 20-45.3.

79 See, e.g., Goodridge v. Dep't of Pub. Health, 798 N.E.2d 941, 955–56 (Mass. 2003); Anita Bernstein, For and Against Marriage: A Revision, 102 Mich, L. Rev. 129 (2003); David L. Chambers, What If? The Legal Consequences of Marriage and the Legal Needs of Lesbian and Gay Male Couples. 95 Mich. L. Rev. 447 (1996); Cass R. Sunstein, The Right To Marry, 26 Cardozo L. Rev. 2081 (2005).

80 Most of these are neither necessary nor unique to marriage, but most are arguably typical.0 For more on kin work, see Micaela di Leonardo, The Female World of Cards and Holidays: Women, Families and the Work of Kinship, 12:3 *Signs* 440,442 (1987) (coining the term "kin work," which refers to "the conception, maintenance, and ritual celebration of cross-household kin ties . . .").

81 See supra note 76.

82 Virginia courts have offered some limited interpretation of the statute thus far. In Stroud v. Stroud, 641 S.E.2d 142 (Va. Ct. App. 2007), a court of appeals held that the two Virginia statutes cited above bore no relevance to its decision to terminate an ex-wife's alimony upon her cohabitation with another woman. Pursuant to a divorce property settlement agreement, the wife's alimony would be terminated upon "the remarriage of Wife and/or her cohabitation with any person to whom she is not related by blood or marriage in a situation analogous to marriage for a period of thirty (30) or more continuous days." Id. at 145 (emphasis in original). In addition, the Attorney General issued an opinion letter when Virginia was considering its mini-DOMA constitutional amendment in 2006, quoted supra note 76, offering a narrow interpretation of existing law along with the pending amendment. The Attorney General essentially read these laws not to interfere with basic contractual and other rights that were not unique to marriage – in other words, he read these mini-DOMAs narrowly to apply only to rights unique to marriage. Opinion Letter

from Attorney General Robert F. McDonnell to the Honorable Stephen D. Newman et al., No. 06-003, 2006 WL 4286442 (2006). As the court pointed out in Stroud, opinion letters by the Attorney General are not binding on the courts. 641 S.E.2d at 151.

83 The main sponsor of the bill, Representative Marshall, initially put forward two versions of the bill: H.B. 750 (which Marshall proposed alone and which contained an additional line declaring a state of emergency), and H.B. 751 (which lacked the state of emergency language and which several other representatives joined). See H.B. 750, 2004 H. Dels., 2004 Sess. (Va. 2004), http://legl.state.va.us/cgi-bin/legp504.exe?041+sum+HB750 (legislative summary for H.B. 750); H.B. 751, 2004 H. Dels., 2004 Sess. (Va. 2004), http://legl.state.va.us/cgi-bin/legp504.exe?041+sum+HB751 (legislative summary for H.B. 751) [hereinafter H.B. 751 Summary]. H.B. 751 eventually underwent revisions and became the final statute. H.B. 751 Summary. The language of H.B. 751, as originally proposed, was as follows:

The General Assembly hereby concludes that the Commonwealth of Virginia is under no constitutional or legal obligation to recognize a marriage, civil union, partnership contract or other arrangement purporting to bestow any of the privileges or obligations of marriage under the laws of another state or territory of the United States unless such marriage conforms to the laws of this Commonwealth.

H.B. 751, 2004 H. Dels., 2004 Sess. (Va. 2004), http://legl.state.va.us/cgi-bin/legp504.exe?041+ful+HB751 [hereinafter H.B. 751 Proposed]. The additional line in Marshall's alternative and ill-fated version read: "That an emergency exists and this act is in force from its passage." H.B. 750, 2004 H. Dels., 2004 Sess. (Va. 2004), http://legl.state.va.us/cgi-bin/legp504.exe? 041+ful+HB750. The version that the House passed, amended by the House Committee for Courts of Justice on Feb. 6, 2004, reads:

The General Assembly declares as its existing public policy that the Commonwealth of Virginia does not recognize a marriage, civil union, partnership contract, or other arrangement purporting to bestow the privileges or obligations of marriage under the laws of another state or territory of the United States unless such marriage conforms to the provisions of Chapter 2 of Title 20 (§§ 20-13 et seq.).

H.B. 751, 2004 H. Dels., 2004 Sess. (Va. 2004), http://legl.state.va,us/cgi-bin/legp504.exe?041+ful+HB751H1. Finally, on March 8, 2004, the Senate Committee for Courts of Justice proposed the amended version of the statute that incorporated the language that was finally enacted. H.B. 751, 2004 H. Dels., 2004 Sess. (Va. 2004), http://legl.state.va.us/cgi-bin/legp504.exe?041+ful+HB751S1.

84 H.B. 751, 2004 H. Dels., 2004 Sess. (Va. 2004), http://leg1.state.va.us/cgi-bin/legp504.exe?041+ful+HB751 ("Whereas, persons who wish to dispose of their property

or assign the power of attorney to another person in case they are sick or disabled are legally authorized to do so at present without regard to any legal impediment or qualification regarding their sexual orientation.").

This aspect of the process helps to make sense of the fact that the only document in the legislative history – a proposers' preamble (an otherwise unheard-of type of legislative document in Virginia, according to librarians at University of Virginia, the VA State Law Library, and the Virginia Assembly, as reported to Beth Williams, librarian at Columbia Law School) – speaks only of the civil unions of other states and even asserts that same-sex couples can obtain enforcement of private agreements just like anyone else.

85 See sources cited supra note 83.

86 Romer v. Evans. 517 U.S. 620 (1996); see infra note 91.

87 For example, what if our platonic male doctor friends discussed above used the word "marriage" in their contract to convey the closeness of their business relationship (perhaps one of them was an avid reader of the OED)? Presumably, under this reading the statute would reach them.

88 For instance, the statute wouldn't affect two women in a long-term sexual partnership who make an agreement tracking marriage law as closely as possible – in order to try to get around the fact that marriage itself is unavailable to them – if they chose not to use the M-word, for instance, because of simple omission, an attempt to evade the statute, or a wish not to be associated with the institution of marriage for feminist or other reasons). Cf. Paula Ettelbrick, Since When Is Marriage a Path to Liberation?, Out/Look Nat'l Lesbian & Gay Q., Fall 1989, at 14.

89 Related to this, a court that thinks the aim of the statute is to get at bundlings of privileges and obligations might still think that any agreement covering just one such privilege or obligation could be an effort to end-run the statute by building up such a bundling gradually.

90 This is even setting aside the question whether "prohibited" might mean something more than legal but not enforceable – for instance, criminal. Cf. Martha A. Field, Surrogate Motherhood: The Legal and Human Issues (1990) (arguing for a treatment of surrogacy contracts as legal but unenforceable). Note, though, that the second sentence of the statute refers to other jurisdictions' contracts being "void" whereas the language in the first sentence is "prohibited," suggesting that "prohibited" in the first sentence was chosen carefully and has some meaning distinct from "void." The language of prohibited rather than void might seem to imply the criminalization of such contracts – much like for prostitution or conspiracy agreements (or in some places, surrogacy agreements). But without any express mention of the criminal law and any penalties, this seems a stretch.

91 Plausible grounds for striking down the statute would include equal protection via Romer v. Evans, 517 U.S. 620 (1996). The broader the scope of the statute, the harder it becomes to say that the statute's sole purpose is to protect the traditional meaning of marriage rather than to single out lesbians and gays for special legal burdens (to the extent that distinction holds at all). The statute is presumably prospective, not retrospective, but if it were read as the latter, it would presumably violate the Contracts clause. Cf. Douglas W. Kmiec & John O. McGinnis, The Contract Clause: A Return to the Original Understanding, 14 Hastings Const. L.Q. 525 (1987); see also supra note 82 (discussing limited interpretation of the statute thus far).

92 Of course, contracts – express or implied – that trade in sex are generally not enforceable. But even Hewitt, which feared that enforcing a cohabitant agreement would diminish the institution of marriage, recognized that "cohabitation by the parties may not prevent them from forming valid contracts about independent matters, for which . . . sexual matters do not form any part of the consideration." Hewitt v, Hewitt, 394 N.E.2d 1204, 1208 (Ill. 1979). What I am discussing here, by contrast, are contracts that do not have sex as any part of the consideration – such as contracts concerning a business partnership – but that, hypothetically, might nonetheless be invalidated simply because the parties are sexually involved.

93 Such a version would also narrow the range of possible constitutional objections to the statute. Cf. supra note 91.

94 H.B. 751 Proposed, supra note 83.

95 Thus, I do not attempt to define the precise contours of such regime, such as how the state would define and prove romantic relationships for these purposes, or how legal relations to children would be determined. Note, though, that this hypothetical regime has historical analogues, for instance, in the situation of mixed-race couples in states with antimiscegenation laws before Loving v. Virginia, 388 U.S. 1 (1967), and Marvin v. Marvin, 557 P.2d 106 (Cal. 1976) . . .

96 Brian H. Bix, Choice of Law and Marriage: A Proposal, 36 Fam. L.Q. 255, 270 (2002) (defining bounded rationality as "people's natural inability to calculate rationally or effectively about certain matters" and observing that "[t]here is some argument that the problem of bounded rationality might be particularly important for parties' bargaining about marriage"); Melvin Aron Eisenberg, The Limits of Cognition and the Limits of Contract, 47 Stan. L. Rev. 211, 254–58 (1995) (arguing, on the basis of bounded rationality concerns, that courts should evaluate prenuptial agreements for "whether, in light of all relevant factors, the parties were likely to have had a mature understanding that the agreement would apply even in the kind of marriage scenario that actually occurred").

97 2 Sir Frederick Pollock & Frederic William Maitland, The History of English Law Before the Time of Edward I 368–69 (photo. reprint 1968) (2d ed. 1898).

98 Cf. Lon L. Fuller, Consideration and Form, 41 Colum. L. Rev. 799 (1941).

99 These were of course among the reasons adduced for not enforcing prenuptial agreements, in addition to the problem that they contemplated the end of marriage. See, e.g., Simeone v. Simeone. 581 A.2d 162 (Pa. 1990).

100 For a thumbnail sketch of a welfare rationale for contract enforcement, see Louis Kaplow & Steven Shavell, Fairness Versus Welfare. 114 Harv. L. Rev. 961, 1102 (2001) ("From the perspective of welfare economics, the purpose of contracts is to promote the well-being of the contracting parties. . . .").

101 "[A] transaction is Pareto optimal if it makes at least one person better off and no one worse off." Richard A. Posner, Utilitarianism, Economics, and Legal Theory, 8 J. Legal Stud. 103, 114 (1979).

102 There are many plausible responses to this question, and many alternative theories of contract enforcement; I mean here only to adumbrate some arguments that might be mustered in favor of the seemingly ludicrous no-contracts/no-marriage regime.0

103 Cf. Examining the Work of State Courts, National Center for State Courts, http://www.ncsconline.org/D_Research/csp/2007B_files/civil.pdf (2007) (reporting that contracts cases have increased sharply and that "[m]any states are struggling to clear their civil caseloads, possibly as a result of . . . tightening resources").

104 See Emens, Intimate Discrimination, supra note 43, at 1384 (quoting exchange with Ellickson and explaining context).

105 This popular phrase has variously been attributed to diverse sources, including Oscar Wilde. The attribution appears to be apocryphal, and the phrase a paraphrase and amalgamation of separate witticisms by Samuel Johnson and H.L. Mencken. See Boswell, 1 Life of Samuel Johnson 376 (Sir Isaac Pitman & Sons 1907) (entry for 1770) ("A gentleman who had been very unhappy in marriage, married immediately after his wife died: Johnson said it was the triumph of hope over experience."); H.L. Mencken & George Jean Nathan, Heliogabalus 131 (Knopf 1920) ("She was complaining that love was beyond her comprehension – that it was ineffable, indescribable, transcendental. 'Love,' I replied, with droll perspicacity, 'Love,' I replied, 'is the triumph of imagination over intelligence.'").

106 It is possible, that is, that little should change other than who can participate, though I do not present the case for that position here.

107 Alexander Pope, Essay on Man (1734) (ll. 293–94).

108 See, e.g., Edmund Burke, Reflections on the Revolution in France, in The Portable Edmund Burke 456 (Isaac Kramnick ed., 1999).

109 See Laughter Soothes the Wounded Heart, No Joke: Animals Laugh, Too, http://www.flatrock.org.nz/topics/humour/no_Joke.htm (offering slightly different wording).

110 See also Aha Jokes, Economist Jokes, http://www.aha-jokes.com/econ002.html ("Q: How many Chicago School economists does it take to change a light bulb? A: None. If the light bulb needed changing the market would have already done it.").

111 On the former, see Gary Blasi & John T. Jost, System Justification Theory and Research: Implications for Law, Legal Advocacy, and Social Justice, 94 Calif. L. Rev. 1119, 1119 (2006) (discussing, as the focus of System Justification Theory, "the motive to defend and justify the social status quo, even among those who are seemingly most disadvantaged by it"); Russell Korobkin, The Endowment Effect and Legal Analysis. 97 Nw. U. L. Rev. 1227, 1228–29 (2003) (explaining "status quo bias" as the tendency of "individuals . . . to prefer the present state of the world to alternative states, all other things being equal"); see also Martha Minow, Making All the Difference (1991). On the latter, see Diane Vaughan, The Dark Side of Organizations: Mistake, Misconduct, and Disaster, 25 Ann. Rev. Soc. 271 (1999); see also Kenneth A. Bamberger, Regulation as Delegation: Private Firms. Decisionmaking, and Accountability in the Administrative State, 56 Duke L.J. 377, 417–20 (2006).

112 See, e.g., Martha Nussbaum, Narratives of Hierarchy: Loving v. Virginia and the Literary Imagination. 17 Ouinnipiac L. Rev. 337 (1997).

113 Oliver Wendell Holmes, The Path of Law, 10 Harv. L. Rev. 457, 469 (1897). Holmes continued, "[i]t is still more revolting if the grounds upon which it was laid down have vanished long since, and the rule simply persists from blind imitation of the past." Id.

13

A Traditionalist Case for Gay Marriage

Dale Carpenter

Summary

Argues that contrary to popular assumption, a certain form of conservatism actually supports the legalization of same-sex marriage. Traditionalist or Burkean conservatism promotes the idea that we should generally prefer stability to change, the tried to the untried, and continuity to experiment. Given new knowledge about the existence of gay people, the numbers of gay people raising children, and desire of gay people to have access to the venerable institution of marriage, conservatives should consider the advantages of legalizing gay marriage. Advantages include personal and social benefits, increased relationship stability, the social responsibility reinforced by a public commitment, practical benefits to children, reduced demands on state welfare services, and reforming gay culture. Conservative worries that gay marriage will harm heterosexual marriage and is too radical a change are highly overstated and ignore the incremental changes in perceptions of homosexuality that have been occurring for some time. Conservatives should recognize that the push for gay marriage implies many gay people are essentially conservative – seeking entry into a traditional social institution over the more radical goals of anti-marriage sexual liberationists.

Original publication details: Dale Carpenter, "A Traditionalist Case for Gay Marriage," pp. 93–104 from *South Texas Law Review* 50 (2008). Reproduced with permission of Dale Carpenter.

Sexual Ethics: An Anthology, First Edition. Edited by Patrick D. Hopkins.

I will present here the outline of an argument for same-sex marriage within a particular school of conservatism. Let's call it traditionalism or Burkeanism, after the eighteenth century British statesman and writer Edmund Burke. It is important, I think, to note at the outset what I am not talking about. I am not talking about libertarianism. It is not economic conservatism. It is not neo-conservatism. It is not religious conservatism. And it is not compassionate conservatism.

My aim is not to argue normatively for Burkean conservatism as an approach to all social change and public policy. My own view is that while it is generally preferable, there are times when it is not appropriate. Emergency circumstances, for example, would not be a time for Burkean incrementalism. It is also not my aim to make constitutional arguments for a right to same-sex marriage. I could not improve on the presentation by Dean Choper on that score,[1] and I will not even try to do so. Instead, I am basically attempting to do five things.

First of all, I will describe briefly what I mean by Burkean conservatism. Second, I will sketch, based on that description, a case against the recognition of gay marriages. Third, I will outline an affirmative argument for same-sex marriage. Fourth, I will reconsider, in the light of those arguments, the Burkean case against same-sex marriage. Finally, I will discuss what a Burkean conservative ought to say about the pace and the process for achieving same-sex marriage.

First, what do I mean by Burkean conservatism? The basic idea of Burkean thought is that we should respect tradition and history. We should, in general, prefer stability to change, the tried to the untried, and continuity to experiment.

I think the best quotation from Burke's writing that captures this basic idea comes from his most famous work, Reflections on the Revolution in France. He wrote:

[I]nstead of casting away all our old prejudices, we cherish them to a very considerable degree, and, to take more shame to ourselves, we cherish them because they are prejudices; and the longer they have lasted, and the more generally they have prevailed, the more we cherish them. We are afraid to put men to live and trade each on his own private stock of reason; because we suspect that this stock in each man is small, and that the individuals would do better to avail themselves of the general bank and capital of nations, and of ages.

Russell Kirk was a modern American disciple of Edmund Burke. Reflecting on Burke's approach to the past and to change, Kirk wrote that Burke did not believe we are condemned to a perpetual retreading in the footsteps of our ancestors. Burke was obviously not opposed to all evolution in a society that honors traditions and values. That would be, as Burke once said, like trying to rock "a grown man in the cradle of an infant." Instead, Burke counseled deliberation and patience in reform. He said that we should base change on experience, not on abstraction and not on philosophical principles divorced from lived reality. Burke wanted a slow but well-sustained progress, and for that reason, he supported incremental change rather than the kind of convulsive upheaval he saw in events of his own time like the French Revolution. Notably for Burke, even what we presently regard as fundamental principles are not immune to critique and revision based on the lessons derived from experience.

With that very brief primer on Burkean conservatism, how would we sketch a case against the recognition of gay marriage? The case would have four basic elements. First, gay marriage is, of course, a change. Because of that alone, we should be resistant to it and suspicious of it. Second, marriage is a long-standing cherished and important institution that has never before in its history included the union of a man and a man or a woman and a woman. This historic practice of uniting men and women and not same-sex partners may have a reason that our current logic cannot fully understand. Third, gay marriage is being brought to us in the service of non-marital and abstract causes, such as equality, inclusion, and tolerance. Fourth, and worst of all perhaps, it is a radical change being thrust upon us suddenly by impatient activists and courts. These activists and courts have tended to be hostile, both to marriage itself and to tradition as a basis for law. That, I think, is the strongest case that one can make against same-sex marriage using Burkean premises.

Against that Burkean critique, how might we construct a response? We must begin with an observation that much of the public policy toward homosexuals in this country was developed in a time when, quite frankly, we did not know much about homosexuals, how they lived, what they were like, how many there were, and so on. We filled in the gaps in our knowledge with myths about homosexuals: that they were dangerous, that they were predatory, especially toward children, psychopathic, and maladjusted.

In the twentieth century, a process of medicalization of the homosexual and of homosexuality occurred, in which homosexuality was viewed as a kind of disease to be cured – not a physical one, but a psychological one.

This basic perspective has changed in the past century, especially in the last fifty to sixty years as homosexuals came out of the closet in large numbers and as homosexuality has become a subject of systematic study and experience. From that study, a strong consensus has developed in the scientific, medical, sociological, and psychological communities about homosexuals. They are not mentally ill or dangerous. They are much the same as heterosexuals in all measures of adjustment and in terms of need for love and companionship.

While we don't know with certainty what causes a person to have a homosexual orientation, or a heterosexual orientation for that matter, we do know that homosexuality as an orientation is not consciously chosen and cannot easily be changed, if at all. It is not contagious. As Judge Richard Posner pointed out in his book, Sex and Reason, homosexuals are not created by recruitment or persuasion or seduction.

There are people, of course, who dissent from one or more of these propositions. It would be surprising in a country of some three hundred million people not to find someone dissenting from these views. But in contrast to the past, they now hold a distinctly minority view that has, frankly, no good empirical or experiential support.

All of these are things that we did not know until the last fifty or so years. Also, consider the dimensions of the issue. Conservatively speaking, there are about nine million gay people in the United States using a three percent baseline to estimate the number. According to a 2005 federal government estimate, there are about 770,000 same-sex couple households in the United States. And that is almost certainly an undercount. That is, as Charles Murray has pointed out,[2] a small percentage of the whole population of the United States. If sacrificing the interest of that larger group is required in order to recognize the interests of this small minority, then that sacrifice is probably not worthwhile.

The numbers of gay people and same-sex couple households in the country are things that we did not count, and that the government certainly did not count, until about two decades ago. When you think about it, that is a considerable number of people who will never have a reasonable prospect of marriage in their lives. It denies to them the most powerful social and legal institution we have for encouraging values that traditionalists hold dear such as commitment, fidelity, and monogamy. Perhaps that denial is justified and we are right to withhold these encouragements and incentives from homosexuals, but at the very least, we have to recognize that a trade-off is involved.

According to the 2000 Census, about twenty percent of all of the male couple households in the United States and thirty-three percent of all the female couple households in the United States are raising children. That might somewhat overestimate the percentages, but it is not too far off. What we do know, using the most conservative numbers available, is that there are at least one million children in this country right now being raised either by single gay people or by gay couples. None of these children have the protection and benefits that marriage would provide to their families. We were unaware of the dimensions of this phenomenon until recently, so we could easily ignore or dismiss its growth and development. We no longer have that excuse. The question now is, "Now that we know, what do we do?" How might marriage help?

There are certainly possible benefits, both to individuals and to communities, in the recognition of same-sex marriages. Let me first discuss the possible individualistic benefits, some of which have already been alluded to. Certainly for the couples who would participate in same-sex marriages, there is little doubt, I think, that marriage would improve their prospects as couples in the long-term and enhance their lives in a number of ways. The only question really on the table is what the magnitude of that benefit would be and whether it would be as great as it is for heterosexual couples.

Certainly legal benefits are involved – more than a thousand of them at the federal level and more importantly, even more at the state level. Same-sex marriage advocates usually treat these legal benefits as the most important benefits provided by the right to marry. I doubt that is the case.

More important than the legal benefits are the caregiving benefits. Marriage makes one other person responsible for your well-being. Someone watches you when you are ill, helps you when you lose your job or suffer an injury, and promises to be there for the long term.

After legal and caregiving benefits, the third class of benefits may be the most important of all. These are the social benefits of marriage. As Jonathan Rauch has pointed out, marriage is the way a couple signals the depth of its commitment to each other and signals that commitment to families, to friends, to workers, and to communities. That commitment is then reinforced by social expectations.

Professor Nagel[3] made an excellent point in noting that at least some of that social expectation may not apply initially to same-sex couples because of resistance to the idea of gay marriage. However, the most important socially-reinforced expectations come from families and friends, people who are likely to be most supportive, even initially, of the relationship that has just been entered. Perhaps the whole social benefit will not be immediately captured, but it is reasonable to expect that a large amount of it will.

In addition, there are the benefits to children. The children being raised by gay couples would surely be better off if their parents could be married, both for legal reasons and because of the enhanced stability that their families would enjoy.

Any time you talk about gay marriage and children, you always hear something like the following objection: A married mother and father is the best environment for raising children. This is what Professor Bradley calls the optimality view.[4] It's essentially a reasonable view – and it might be the correct view – but I think Professor Bradley was correct to dismiss it, though perhaps not for the reason that he gives.

The reason I would give for dismissing the optimality argument is that it is largely irrelevant to the debate over same-sex marriage. Here's why: No serious opponent of same-sex marriage advocates removing children from their gay parents. No opponent in this symposium proposes that.

Whether or not gay marriage is allowed, children will continue to be raised by gay parents in this country, and it will happen in increasing numbers, as it has over the past several decades.

The real question on the table when it comes to the welfare of children is this: Will these children be raised in homes that enjoy the protections and benefits of marriage or will they not?

There are also communitarian benefits, that is, benefits for the entire community, in the recognition of gay marriage. I go back to Professor Bradley again because he asked exactly the right questions: What would be the state's interest in recognizing same-sex marriage? What would be the public purpose or interest in recognizing these marriages? I can think of four.

First a possible communitarian benefit, or State interest, would be that marriage by some measure, would better the lot of millions of our fellow citizens who are living in gay families today. That is a material and moral interest that we all have, and it cannot be easily dismissed.

Second, there might be an advantage to limited government, or the concept of limited government. Consider this: Married people make relatively fewer demands on state welfare services and on the healthcare system. The Congressional Budget Office in 2004 estimated that nationwide same-sex marriage would save the federal government almost a billion dollars a year in healthcare and other costs. More savings will occur at the state level. I am not proposing same-sex marriage as a way to balance the federal budget, but a billion here and a billion there adds up to real money. This savings should serve the goal of limited government, something that conservatives believe in, or used to believe in.

Third, gay life and culture in general could benefit from the recognition of same-sex marriages. One concern often heard from traditionalist conservatives is that gay culture is characterized by a series of cultural pathologies: too much promiscuity, too much drug use, too much alcohol abuse, too little personal responsibility, and too little connection. One fear is that this culture will infect marriage and somehow change it. I believe that particular fear is overblown as it assumes a large effect from what will, after all, be a very small cause because gay marriages will be a tiny proportion of all marriages. We have been reminded repeatedly that gay people comprise such a small portion of the population that they are irrelevant to the discussion about marriage in the country. One has to turn around and ask: If homosexuals are such a tiny minority, how is it that they will bring about the destruction of marriage?

However, if the concern is with gay culture itself, the question then is this: What should the policy on marriage be? Should we allow it or prohibit it for these couples? Could marriage have the sort of traditionalizing effect on gay culture and individuals that conservatives, and especially traditionalist conservatives, would cheer?

Law has only a limited role in changing culture. Up to now the law's role and the law's message to gay people has been entirely perverse from a traditionalist perspective. Here's one way to think about it: American law embodies a kind of asymmetry. On the one hand, the law says to gay people, "Go out and have as much sex as you like. You have a constitutional right to it." On the other hand, the law says to these same people, "There will be nothing available to you to channel all of that sexual activity into a productive, healthy, and stable family life." I cannot think of another demographic group in our society to which that double message is being sent. Because we are not returning to the criminalization of sodomy – the question really is: What do we do about the second half of that message? When same-sex marriage is permitted, gay couples – to borrow the words of Martin Luther King – will not be free at last. In a sense, they will be bound at last – bound to traditions, to other people, to communities, and to a culture.

These possible traditionalizing effects of same-sex marriage on gay culture and life have led to a great deal of concern and anxiety on the part of some activists on the left. Paula Ettelbrick, a well-known lesbian writer and early critic of same-sex marriage, worries about this effect:

Ironically, gay marriage, instead of liberating gay sex and sexuality, would further outlaw all gay and lesbian sex which is not performed in a marital context. Just as sexually active non-married women face stigma and double standards around sex and sexual activity, so too would non-married gay people. The only legitimate gay sex would be that which is cloaked and regulated by marriage. . . . Lesbians and gay men who did not seek the state's stamp of approval would clearly face increased sexual oppression.[5]

I believe that reaction is exaggerated, but there's enough truth in it that I believe it should warm a traditionalist's heart.

Fourth, there might be a possible communitarian benefit to marriage as an institution. Conservatives, I think, rightly worry that there are a lot of problems with marriage today: high divorce rates, lots of births out of wedlock, and very little respect for marriage. But none of these threats to marriage were created by gay people.

Conservatives nevertheless say that this is a time of instability and that it is risky to add to the pressures and strains on marriage by making such an important change now. I have some sympathy with that concern. There are possible unintended consequences of any change, and we have to pay attention to them. But instead of being a threat to marriage, consider that gay marriage might be a very small part of its revival. Gay couples are now living together and are raising more than a million children in this country, entirely outside of marriage. As Jonathan Rauch has argued, their very existence is a message to the culture that it is okay not to be married, that you can raise your children, you can have a happy life, you can live a long time, and you can do very well entirely outside of this institution.

Now, there are a lot of people who think that the message being sent by all of these unmarried gay couples raising children outside of marriage is a wonderful message. We need a multiplicity of family structures and forms. These are terrific developments, they believe. But I would not think that is the kind of message a traditionalist would like very much. Gay marriage could reinforce the idea that marriage is the normative status for people who are willing to make the legal and social commitment that it entails.

This is exactly what sexual liberationists fear so much about same-sex marriage. Consider, for example, what Michael Warner, a professor at Rutgers, had to say about the possible effects of gay marriage in a book he wrote a few years ago. The effect of gay marriage "would be to reinforce the material privileges and cultural normativity of marriage. . . . Buying commodities sustains the culture of commodities whether the buyers like it or not. That is the power of a system. Just so, marrying consolidates and sustains the normativity of marriage."[6] My reaction to that is, "Well, just so." What Warner fears, traditionalists should, at least in principle, cheer.

With all of that in mind, let us revisit the Burkean case against the recognition of same-sex marriages, and look at the four points that I raised earlier.

First, of course, gay marriage is a change; however, it is obvious that not all change should be resisted. Burke himself recognized that change is a means of society's preservation. I believe what the Burkean approach would counsel is that gay marriage advocates, in this debate, have the burden of proof. But it cannot be and should not be an impossible burden.

Second, it is also true that the man-woman traditional definition and understanding of marriage may embody a logic of its own that we cannot fully appreciate or that we have somehow lost over time. That urges a special caution on the part of reformers, but it does not entirely defeat the argument in favor of same-sex marriage. The same type of argument could be made any time a traditional practice has been changed, from ending slavery to granting women the right to vote. Also, it could be argued that while there have been a lot of changes in marriage, nothing but man-woman marriages have existed because we have never had man–man or woman–woman marriages.

Yet the same sort of thing could be said about any change in marriage. Prior to the change we never practiced the thing that changed. Every time we confront this question of whether we should change, we could always confront the objection that we have never done that before. Burke's insight about tradition is a warning to base change on actual lived experience and not simply on reason. It is not a command to resist all change.

Third, while some same-sex marriage advocates do in fact speak in very abstract terms about their cause, gay couples and families are not an abstraction. Their existence is not theoretical. They are not people who happen to live under the same roof, who are joined together only by a shared commitment to the philosophy of Michel Foucault. Gay families are part of the lived experience of this country.

Fourth, is gay marriage really such a radical change that is suddenly being forced upon us?

As for whether it is really radical, other marriage reforms in the past hundred years certainly seem to have affected marriage much more comprehensively. Consider no-fault divorce for example, which affects every marriage in a jurisdiction that accepts that idea, or women's equality, which has grown up over the past one hundred and fifty years. Both affect every marriage involving a man and a woman. In comparison to that, gay marriages will represent an incremental addition of perhaps three percent in the number of married couples. If David Frum is correct in asserting that the take-up rate by same-sex couples has been very small,[7] then the numbers should be even smaller than that.

As for the suddenness of this change, gay families have in fact been growing up around us organically for a century. They are not the top-down creations of government bureaucrats or radical visionaries. They are bottom-up facts of life.

Let me say a few things about pace and process. As I mentioned earlier, Burke believed in a slow but well-sustained progress. Is that what we have been witnessing? The truth is for some time in this country that we have already been on an incremental path to the full recognition of same-sex relationships.

First, I would include as part of this path the decriminalization of sexual relations between people of the same sex which has occurred since the drafting of the Model Penal Code and has occurred legislatively and judicially over a period of about fifty years. I mentioned earlier medicalization. A de-medicalization of homosexuality has occurred in our society, particularly when the American Psychiatric Association removed homosexuality from its list of mental disorders in 1973.

[. . .]

Now for the Burkean, what would be the steps ahead? First, there should not be an immediate nationwide resolution of this issue either in favor of gay marriage or against it. There should be no Supreme Court decision telling the states they must recognize same-sex marriages. There should also, however, be no federal marriage amendment foreclosing state experimentation in this area.

Second, the reform toward gay marriage should continue to move incrementally and with a strong preference that it move legislatively. One of the advantages of this approach is that it is having a profound effect on the

debate over gay marriage. The debate about gay marriage is moving from the realm of the theoretical and the abstract into the realm of the experiential and the empirical. Increasingly, the debate about gay marriage is not going to be about highfalutin principles, but about issues such as divorce rates, marriage rates, and illegitimacy. I think that is a Burkean development.

Consider one minor point in this regard. Eighteen years after recognizing same-sex relationships in Scandinavia, there are higher marriage rates for heterosexuals, lower divorce rates, lower rates for out-of-wedlock births, lower STD rates, more stable and durable gay relationships, more monogamy, and more respect for monogamy. So far there is no slippery slope to polygamy, incestuous marriages, or as Senator Rick Santorum once said, to man-on-dog unions.

Did same-sex marriage contribute to these retraditionalizing trends? The answer is that we do not know. We have only a correlation. But the evidence so far, I think, at least makes any claim about doomsday scenarios very hard to credit.

Finally, given that gay people exist and are not going to be eliminated or converted by any means acceptable to the American people, the question for conservatives is now, "What is to be done with them?" Is it better for our society and for traditional values that they be pushed aside, marginalized and ostracized, and made to feel alien to traditional values and institutions? Or is it better for society and for traditionalists that they be included in the fabric of American life, including in the most important social institution we have for encouraging, recognizing, and reinforcing loving relationships?

I can understand why a feminist critic of marriage like Paula Ettelbrick, or a libertarian, might want government out of all of this and might therefore oppose same-sex marriage. Same-sex marriage might be a threat to their values. I have a harder time now understanding why a traditionalist would.

Sometimes it seems that gay people are practically the last people in the country who still believe in marriage, who are reaffirming its importance in their lives with their very existence and their families, and who actually believe it can make their lives better. They are saying "yes" to a traditionalizing institution. So the question for conservatives at the end of the day is, why can't they take "yes" for an answer?

[. . .]

Notes

1   See Jesse H. Choper & John C. Yoo, Can the Government Prohibit Gay Marriage?, 50 S. Tex. L. Rev. 15 (2008).
2   See Charles Murray, Love Has Nothing to Do with It, 50 S. Tex. L. Rev. 77 (2008).
3   See Robert F. Nagel, Marriage and Practical Knowledge. 50 S. Tex. L. Rev. 37 (2008).
4   See Gerard V. Bradley, Three Liberal – but Mistaken – Arguments for Same-Sex Marriage. 50 S. Tex. L. Rev. 45 (2008).
5   Paula Ettelbrick, Since When is Marriage a Path to Liberation?, Out/look: National Gay and Lesbian Quarterly, Fall 1989, at 9, reprinted in Lesbians, Gay Men, and the Law 401, 403 (William B. Rubenstein ed., 1993).
6   Michael Warner, The Trouble with Normal: Sex, Politics, and the Ethics of Queer Life 109 (1999).
7   See David Frum, Same-Sex Marriage: Unconservative in Purpose, in Application, and in Result, 50 S. Tex. L. Rev. 85 (2008).

14

A Response to the 'Conservative Case' for Same-Sex Marriage: Same-Sex Marriage and the 'Tragedy of the Commons'

Lynn D. Wardles

Summary

Argues that the conservative arguments in support of same–sex marriage fail because they are lacking factually, logically, and are in conflict with conservative principles. Seven basic principles of conservatism are explicated and five conservative arguments for legalizing gay marriage are analyzed. Each of the five arguments contain faulty psychological and sociological claims, makes radical changes in established social institutions, discards historical wisdom, relies too much on government, promotes too much individual autonomy over individual responsibility, and promotes too much change too quickly. Conservative principles not only cannot be used to defend gay marriage, but actually compel opposing it. All marriage is threatened by gay marriage because gay relationship and sexual lifestyles will set a dangerous new minimum standard, as they are notoriously unstable, encourage infidelity, and promote purely individualistic goals over the common good promoted by traditional marriage.

Original publication details: Lynn D. Wardles, "A Response to the 'Conservative Case' for Same-Sex Marriage: Same-Sex Marriage and the 'Tragedy of the Commons'," pp. 441–473 from *Brigham Young University Law Review* 22 (2008). Reproduced with permission of Brigham Young University.

Ruin is the destination toward which all men rush, each pursuing his own best interest in . . . the commons.

– Garrett Hardin, The Tragedy of the Commons.

I. Introduction: Considering the Conservative Case for Same-Sex Marriage

A. Conservatism, Same-Sex Marriage, and the "Tragedy of the Commons"

A number of thoughtful, conservative commentators have made arguments for legalizing same-sex marriage that draw upon principles such as tradition, institutionalism, values, communitarianism, and the social good.[1] These arguments are sometimes called "the conservative case" for legalizing same-sex marriage. These arguments are not only quite interesting and appealing, but they are certainly among the most coherent and persuasive arguments for same-sex marriage.

[. . .]

This paper considers and refutes some of the common conservative arguments for legalizing same-sex marriage and shows that the position most clearly consistent with the conservative political philosophy opposes legalization of same-sex marriage.[2] The basic principles of conservative political philosophy are reviewed in Part II of this paper. In Part III, popular "conservative" claims for same-sex marriage are reviewed and challenged; they are found wanting factually, logically, and as measured against the principles of conservatism. In Part IV, a conservative case against same-sex marriage is suggested. First, the principles of conservatism, when systematically applied to the proposal to legalize same-sex marriage, show that the most valid conservative position mandates opposition to legalization of same-sex marriage (in Part IV.A.). Some of the most seriously harmful consequences of legalizing same-sex marriage are reviewed to underscore the solid factual basis for conservative opposition to same-sex marriage (Part IV.B.). [. . .] Part V concludes by emphasizing the "day of reckoning" is the inexorable and tragic conclusion of such practices as the overgrazing of the commons and the legalization of same-sex marriage. Same-sex marriage must be rejected upon conservative principles to avoid a tragedy of the commons.

[. . .]

II. Basic Principles of Conservatism?

To determine systematically whether a credible case for same-sex marriage can be called "conservative," one must first describe the elements that make an argument "conservative." Conservatism is a well-established political philosophy that falls midway between revolutionary ideologies, on the one side, and reactionary philosophies on the other side.[3] With roots deeply imbedded in the writings of ancient political philosophers and leaders, conservatism has existed as a discrete and disciplined modern political philosophy for over two centuries since it was systematically applied in and popularized by Edmund Burke's Reflections on the French Revolution.[4] Burke catapulted to fame as a political thinker, and conservatism emerged as a highly respected, rediscovered political philosophy because his Reflections on the Revolution in France, published in 1790, was so prophetically accurate. He predicted correctly that the radical and abrupt destruction of the ancient institutions, customs, and habits of the French nation, society, and government would produce chaos and bloodshed that could only be quenched by force,[5] and he forecasted, with perfect vision, that the resulting social disruption would require the ascension of a powerful dictator-led military to control the nation.[6] Burke was proven right by the ensuing bloody history of Post-Revolutionary France, and by the emergence of the aggressive military dictatorship of Napoleon Bonaparte who ultimately imposed order.

Today, conservatism consists of a complex mix (and daunting range and variety) of philosophical and political principles.[7] Seven keywords identify the core concepts of contemporary conservatism: (1) preservation, (2) institutions, (3) caution, (4) experience, (5) distrust, (6) individualism, and (7) morality.

First, conservatism seeks to preserve things from the past that are of value.[8] Abraham Lincoln defined preservation as the core belief of conservatism when he asked, "Is it not adherence to the old and tried, against the new and untried?"[9] "Conservatism by its name announces that it conserves. . . ."[10] A contemporary college primer on modern political philosophies identifies "reverence for tradition" as one of the key precepts of modern conservatism.[11]

Second, conservatism values and seeks to protect important, time-proven social (and political, and other) institutions.[12] Conservatives value order, stability, and tradition, which established institutions foster, preserve, and uphold.[13] Third, the conservative political and judicial approach is cautious of major innovations, preferring gradual organic evolution instead of revolution.[14] They distrust revolutionary proposals and radical innovations. Russell Kirk noted conservatism's distrust of "innovation . . . [as] a devouring conflagration more often than it is a torch of progress. . . . [S]low change is the means of [social] conservation."[15] Conservatives are not opposed to change qua change, but to sudden, radical change. As F. A. Hayek wrote, "The conservative does not oppose change, but he does resist it."[16] As another political scientist put it, "[Conservatism from Burke on, . . . has advocated what it will be a good idea to call alterations. It has made a lot of them."[17] The conservatives accept "a little alteration or indeed a little transformation."[18]

Fourth, conservatism relies primarily upon experience, common-sense, habit, and tradition to guide both individual conduct and public policy.[19] "[T]he essence of conservatism is preservation of the ancient moral traditions of humanity. Conservatives respect the wisdom of their ancestors. . . ."[20] They believe that "tradition . . . c hecks . . . man's anarchic impulse."[21] "Reverence for tradition" is still a fundamental principle of conservatism.[22] The conservative is familiar "with the accumulated wisdom and experience of history, and he is not too proud to learn from the great minds of the past."[23] Conservatives prefer to trust tradition over mere intellectualism or reason because, as Burke put it, "[e]ven the best minds are too weak to comprehend the problems of society as a whole. . . ."[24]

Fifth, conservatism distrusts concentrated power and government generally. Modern conservatives especially oppose judicial invention of constitutional rights that are not clearly grounded in the constitutional text, history, or tradition.[25] They distrust government in general,[26] judicial elites and manipulable majorities in particular.[27] "The conservative constitutional position [is]: Governmental powers (especially those of the federal government) may be construed very strictly; limitations upon those powers . . . should be interpreted very broadly in order to protect individual (and corporate) liberties against government encroachment. . . ."[28]

Sixth, conservatism staunchly defends individualism and individual liberty against pressures for mass conformity and stifling, egalitarianism.[29] Thus, Russell Kirk saw collectivism and egalitarianism as the radical beliefs most dominant and threatening in the last half of the twentieth century.[30] Sargent identified both "anti-egalitarianism" and "preference for individual freedom"

as core principles of contemporary conservatism.[31] Goldwater wrote that the conservative believes that each man is unique, not just a part of the mass.[32]

Finally, conservatism sees that mankind and life have non-material, moral-spiritual dimensions; it recognizes, respects, and supports morality and virtue.[33] As Barry Goldwater put it, "[t]he root difference between the Conservatives and the Liberals of today is the Conservatives take account of the whole man, while the Liberals tend to look only at the material side of man."[34] [. . .]

These seven principles embody the basic philosophical foundations of modern conservatism. Both opponents and supporters of the legalization of same-sex marriage have claimed that conservative principles support their positions. While arguments on both sides can reflect some conservative principles, conservatism cannot ultimately support both positions.

III.   A Critique of the Conservative Case for Legalizing Same-Sex Marriage

Several prominent conservative legal and social commentators, including Professor Dale Carpenter, a distinguished participant in this symposium, have asserted what has become known as the "conservative case" for same-sex marriage.[35] Five specific claims that are at the core of [. . .] the conservative case for same-sex marriage can be summarized as (1) "we exist," (2) stabilization, (3) sexual taming, (4) society gains, and (5) no harm. These arguments will be examined, and they will be compared against the seven principles of conservatism. The following analysis shows that all the so-called "conservative" arguments for same-sex marriage are flawed as a matter of logic, as a matter of fact, and, most importantly for this paper, as a matter of conservative principle as well.

First, one common argument in the conservative case for same-sex marriage is the "we exist" argument – that gay and lesbian couples exist in large numbers in society, love each other, and need the benefits of marriage for themselves and for their children.[36] Factually, it is undeniable that hundreds of thousands of gay and lesbian couples live in America (the 2000 census found 594,392 same-sex couples living together that year – not all of whom necessarily were homosexual couples),[37] and many of them are raising children.[38] A November 2007 report by the respected gay demographer Gary Gates of the UCLA Law School's Williams Institute indicates that by

2006, Census Bureau American Community Surveys identified 780,000 same-sex couples,[39] while another report by Gates and others in September 2005 confirmed that as of 2000, "more than 39% of same-sex couples in the United States aged 22–55 [we]re raising . . . more than 250,000 children under age 18."[40] Clearly, these couples and families exist, and it is equally clear that the children being raised by gay and lesbian couples would benefit from being raised in marital homes. But those facts do not necessarily support the claim for radically redefining the institution of marriage, nor does the existence of these facts amount to a solid conservative argument.

Comparing this argument with the seven principles of conservatism reveals that it is not really a conservative argument. The proposal is (1) to radically redefine, not preserve, (2) the crucial social institution of conjugal marriage, (3) by sudden, dramatic change. Since it is the absence of marriage as we now know and understand it that is the cause of the deprivation of those couples and children, it hardly seems cautious or prudent or conservative to radically change the very institution – conjugal marriage – which we agree generally provides the very benefits which unmarried, cohabiting couples and their children do not enjoy. (4) It deviates from the historical form of family that has proven most beneficial to individuals, especially to children. (5) It would be imposed by government action. (6) While it may enhance the relational autonomy of gay and lesbian adults, it jeopardizes the future independence of some children by subjecting them to a grand social experiment. (7) It would radically alter the moral understanding of marriage. Thus, the "we exist" argument for legalizing same-sex marriage is not really a conservative argument.

The second conservative argument for legalizing same-sex marriage is that allowing same-sex couples to marry will bring stability to those gay and lesbian couples and will alleviate much of suffering and disadvantage of the children they are raising.[41] The first, factual problem with this argument is that the hard evidence to support the claim is almost non-existent; it is a speculative, theoretical argument. In fairness, it must be noted that the legalization of same-sex marriage is such a recent innovation that it is not surprising that the evidence is sparse. On the other hand, there already is evidence that allowing gays and lesbians to marry or enter into marriage-equivalent "civil unions" has little effect upon the stability of those relationships. For example, a 2003 report on a Dutch study of gay men in the most

gay-friendly city on earth (Amsterdam) found that the average duration of gay "steady partner" relations was only 1.5 years – in the most gay-affirming, gay-supportive nation on earth, when marriage-equivalent same-sex domestic partnerships were legal, and the full status of same-sex marriage was being implemented.[42]

In 2006, a Scandinavian study of the demographics of marriage-equivalent same-sex registered partnerships in Norway and Sweden noted significant problems with the stability of such relationships, and showed significantly higher rates of breakup.[43] Despite the fact that same-sex couples were considerably older than male-female couples (a factor that generally correlates with greater stability in marriage),[44] and the ratio of partners from higher socio-economic status was up to 50% higher for gay and lesbian couples (another factor that may be associated with greater stability),[45] the divorce-risk levels for registered gay men partnerships were about 50% higher than for comparable heterosexual couples; and controlling for variables, the risk of divorce was twice as high for lesbian couples as it was for gay men couples.[46]

Another study of Swedish registered partnerships found that gay male couples were 50% more likely to divorce than married heterosexual couples, while lesbian couples were over 150% more likely to divorce than heterosexual couples.[47] Controlling for variables, gay couples were 35% and lesbian couples 200% more likely to divorce than heterosexual couples in that very gay-supportive nation.[48]

These studies are from countries where same-sex formal unions have been legalized, destigmatized, dignified, encouraged, socially supported, and given full legal equality for a decade longer than anywhere in this country. The studies raise serious challenges to the claim that legalizing same-sex marriage will produce significant stability for same-sex couples.

As a matter of conservative principles, this argument is very dubious. Again, (1) it's purpose is not to preserve, nor to support (2) the basic social institution of conjugal marriage. (3) It proposes radical, not incremental social change. (4) It ignores the experience of the most experienced countries and relies upon fantastic, rose-colored speculations. (5) It relies upon the use of government manipulation to redefine a basic social institution. (6) In one sense, it promotes adult gay/lesbian individual autonomy, but does so by using a social tool (not individualism), and it promotes individualism for the purpose of achieving a new egalitarianism. (7) While it acknowledges the existing morality of marital

Lynn D. Wardles

stability and the social benefits of the institution of marriage, it endangers those very qualities of marriage in hopes that by including same-sex relations, those marital qualities might rub off on unstable and immoral homosexual relations. Yet it fails to consider that the "rub-off" may go the other way, undermining the stability and integrity of marriage. Moreover, this argument equates the stable morality of marriage with the dubious morality of same-sex sexual relationships.

Third, conservative supporters of same-sex marriage argue that legalizing same-sex marriage will tame and civilize the irresponsible sexual behaviors of same-sex (especially gay male) couples.[49] This claim, however, is counter-factual. It does not appear that giving marital or marriage-like status to same-sex couples significantly alters their troubling behaviors. For example, a Vermont study published in 2005 examined characteristics, including sexual practices, of same-sex couples in civil unions with those not in civil unions and with heterosexual married couples.[50] The difference in infidelity rates between gay men in a civil union and those not in a civil union was less than 3% (2.8%).[51] The authors concluded that "same-sex couples [registered and unregistered] were similar to each other on demographic and relationship factors when compared with married heterosexual couples."[52] In other words, formalizing gay relationships with full, formal, registered marriage-equivalent legal status has virtually no impact on the high infidelity rates of gay men.

Moreover, this taming argument for same-sex marriage fails the test of conservative principles. While (2) it recognizes the institution of conjugal marriage as the gold standard of sexual responsibility, (1) it would not conserve nor uphold the core understanding of marriage as a conjugal institution. (3) As for caution, one might question whether it is prudent to risk the moral meaning of an institution already buffeted by massive social changes (cohabitation, child-bearing out of wedlock, unilateral no-fault divorce, and very high divorce rates) in a social experiment designed to radically overhaul the institution of marriage to include same-sex couples. (4) This argument is built on theoretical speculation, not upon (but in blind neglect of) experience and common sense. (5) Unconservatively, it calls upon government to reshape a basic social institution. (6) While it supports sexual individualism to an extent, it does by a means that jeopardizes the independence of those who might become caught in the addicting homosexual lifestyle, and it endangers the nursery of individualism – the marital family. (7) It also disregards and endangers the

morality of marriage by ignoring the transformative effect upon marriage of gay and lesbian couples who have dramatically different sexual standards regarding fidelity and promiscuity.

Fourth, some conservative advocates of same-sex marriage make a "social benefit" claim – that society as a whole will benefit from gay and lesbian couples entering into same-sex marriages.[53] Again, this is a claim built on rhetoric and pure optimism. The supporting evidence is wanting. The contrary evidence is overwhelming.

For example, gay and (to a lesser degree) lesbian sexual relations are disproportionately "unsafe" in terms of social responsibility and public health. Gay male homosexual sex still remains the primary means of transmission of AIDS disease in the United States. Overall, 55% of cumulative AIDS cases reported through 2004 (402,722 cases) involved the single mode of exposure of men who have sex with men; and the numbers continue to rise.[54] If the multiple modes of exposure that include male homosexual behavior are included, male homosexual behavior is the sole or a potential cause of more than 70% of all AIDS cases that have been reported in the United States from the first case through 2005.[55] A summary of HIV seroprevalence data from STD clinics revealed that, nationally, the median percentage of men who, since 1978, have had sex with other men who were positive for HIV was 25.5%, compared with only 7.1% of male heterosexual drug injectors.[56]

Internationally, the transmission pattern is the same in most of the world (except in sub-Saharan Africa). In December 2007, UNAIDS and the World Health Organization (WHO) reported that 33.2 million persons were living with HIV, including 2.5 million children aged fourteen or younger; in 2007 2.1 million people died from AIDS, and 2.5 million people were newly infected with HIV.[57] The "global prevalence of HIV infection (percentage of persons infected with HIV) is remaining at the same level. . . ."[58] Moreover, "[t]he United States of America is one of the countries with the largest number of HIV infections in the world."[59] In most of the world, the AIDS epidemic is "primarily concentrated among populations most at risk, such as men who have sex with men, injecting drug users, sex workers and their sexual partners."[60]

[. . .]

Mental health reports are no more encouraging. Both lesbians and gay men exhibit much higher levels of "psychiatric illness, including depression, drug abuse and suicide attempts," as many studies have confirmed.[61]

158

It might be argued that this is due to the lack of legal marriage or marriage-like status, but research shows otherwise. Dutch researchers found that eighty-six percent of new HIV/AIDS infections in gay men were in men who had steady partners, and that gay men with steady partners engage in more risky sexual behaviors than gays without steady partners.[62]

In terms of conservative principles, this "social benefit" claim also fails to measure up. (2) It devalues and endangers the existing institution of marriage, (3) seeks its abrupt metamorphosis, (1) not its preservation. (4) It is not grounded in history or experience, but in self-interested speculations. (5) It is manipulative and positivist, seeking by means of government to artificially create a new order of marriage. (6) It is individualistic in one sense; but (7) it falsely tries to equate the virtues of conjugal marriage with those of same-sex relations.

Fifth, some presenters of the conservative case for same-sex marriage claim that no harm to the institution of marriage or to conjugal marriage will result from legalizing same-sex marriage.[63] That simply defies the reality of what is happening in Scandinavia, the Netherlands, Canada, and Massachusetts. That claim is so critical, and the factual evidence to the contrary so great, that it is examined in greater detail below in part IV.B.

This no harm argument also fails the test of conservative principles. (1) It claims to be preservationist, but that is simply not factual. (2) It is anti-institutional, embracing a form of deinstitutionalizing "let-each-define-marriage-as-his/her-heart-chooses." (3) It changes marriage by revolution, not evolution. (4) It discards and disregards the learning of history and human experience about the uniqueness of conjugal marriage. (5) It relies upon government to prevent or conceal the harmful consequences of its new order of marriage. (6) It promotes individual autonomy rather than the integrity of individual responsibility. (7) It devalues and disregards the moral significance of conjugal marriage.

The overall flaws of all of these ostensibly "conservative" arguments for same-sex marriage are three. First, they plead on the basis of highly speculative, imagined, theoretical benefits. The empirical evidence that giving formal marital or equivalent legal status to same-sex couples will make gay and lesbian couples more responsible sexually or more stable, or will benefit their children or will benefit society is lacking The evidence supports exactly the opposite position – against same-sex marriage.[64]

Second, these arguments ignore or cannot see the other side of the ledger, the harmful effects upon the institution of marriage itself from redefining it to include same-sex couples. The transformative power of inclusion cannot be ignored. The negative characteristics of same-sex couples will and already are beginning to transform the social expectations of marriage, and of the people who enter into marriage in ways that will make that institution less responsible, less stable, less monogamous, less faithful, and less committed to responsible child-rearing.[65] The evidence of immediate harm, admittedly, is in its infancy, as same-sex marriage is so new and exists in so few countries. Measuring these detrimental effects is also difficult for at least three reasons. First, marriages have been deteriorating and disintegrating for some time (decades) already due to other powerful social forces (including social approval for and rising incidence of cohabitation, child-bearing out of wedlock, and divorce), so separating out the impact of same-sex marriage from the impact of those other influences will be challenging.[66] Second, the gay-and-lesbian community is very self-protective, and obtaining information and cooperation from members of that community that might document problems and troubles and failings in that community, has in the past and will in the future not be easily or simply accomplished. Third, the most important consequences are not immediate or short-term, but most of them are expected to take a full generation to develop and to be discerned and documented clearly.

Finally, these popular conservative arguments for same-sex marriage are not really conservative at all because they contradict most of the basic conservative principles.[67] They do not conserve or preserve the institution of marriage that has existed for thousands of years as the basic social unit of all cultures. They are not cautious or prudent but seek a revolutionary redefinition (not modes, evolutionary, incremental modifications) of that essential social institution. They are not supported by experience or history, but primarily by abstract theorizing, pure speculation, and mere rhetoric. They are positivist and statist, and trust government decrees and coercion to reshape a pre-governmental social institution. They do support individualism in the sense of individual autonomy, but at the expense of the institution that throughout history has best fostered and protected and inculcated individualism. They seek to create an artificial and unstable government-mandated equality of relations that, in truth, are not the same or equivalent. They endanger the morality of marriage by inviting the transformation of the moral meaning of marriage by including couples with very different moral qualities, standards and behaviors.

Lynn D. Wardles

IV. A Conservative Case Against Same-Sex Marriage

A. Conservative Principles Require Rejection of Same-Sex Marriage

Not only do the "conservative" arguments for legalizing same-sex marriage fail the test of conservative principles, but all of the basic principles of conservatism compel opposition to the legalization of same-sex marriage. The preservation principle opposes legalizing same-sex marriage. Marriage has always been (until just six years ago) an exclusively conjugal institution, in all the nations and societies in all the history of the world. Throughout recorded history, marriage of persons of the same sex never existed and was never known or allowed, until The Netherlands legalized same-sex marriage in 2001. Conjugal marriage still is the overwhelmingly dominant and exclusive understanding of marriage in contemporary nations and cultures. The conservative argument for preservation and conservation does not support legalizing same-sex marriage, but favors preservation and protection of the long-recognized (if now embattled) and exclusive relationship of conjugal marriage.

The institutional argument also opposes legalizing same-sex marriage. The social institution of conjugal marriage is one of the most ancient, long-established, institutions, and is the basic social unit in all societies. Protecting that institution is critical, for it is the foundation of government and society. Protection of so fundamental an institution manifests the very core and very best of conservatism. Because of the importance of protecting critical social institutions for conservatives, many American conservatives "define issues centering on the family . . . and religion as their issues."[68] Deconstructing so basic an institution is contrary to this essential principle of conservatism. Russell Kirk, in The Conservative Mind, wrote that one of the greatest problems facing conservatives today is that "men must find status and hope within society: true family, respect for the past, responsibility for the future, private property, duty as well as right, inner resources. . . . The degeneration of the family to mere common house-tenancy menaces the very essence of recognizable human character. . . ."[69]

The cautious innovation principle also opposes revolutionary same-sex marriage legalization. To jettison the conjugal, male-female uniting, gender-integrating, procreative-linking element of marriage is a radical change. It is not a mere, prudential alteration or cautious transformation. It is revolutionary, not evolutionary. Its potential ramification for unloosening the connections, expectations, and responsibilities of marriage, parenting, and families in general is hard to overstate. To support the legalization of same-sex marriage is contrary to this core principle of conservatism, while to oppose same-sex marriage is consistent with this mode-and-pace-of-change precept of conservatism.

[. . .]

It might be argued that resolving the issue by majority vote is consistent with a conservative position. Structurally, that has some plausibility. However, in the long-run it would undermine core moral-normative conservatism. Just as Stephen Douglas' position of popular sovereignty (letting the people in the territories decide for themselves whether to allow slavery) was conservative in a procedural sense, in the larger sense it defied and (fortunately) was overwhelmed by the normative conservatism of Abraham Lincoln's national abolition of slavery because it was inconsistent with the basic moral principles of the Declaration of Independence. Lincoln's substantive (moral) conservatism saved not only the conservative political philosophy in America, but saved America.[70] Likewise, the structural popular sovereignty position on same-sex marriage has some credibility, and insofar as it is a step towards and not away from the normative conservative position of protecting the institution of conjugal marriage, it is valid. However, it is subordinate to the normative principle that values and preserves the institution of conjugal marriage. Just as the nation ultimately could not endure part-slave and part-free, so the institution of marriage, and our constitutional society based it, cannot long survive part conjugal and part same-sex in nature. Conservatism stands in support of preserving the traditional, moral institution of conjugal marriage for the sake of preserving a society that fosters individual rights.

The protect individualism principle also largely opposes same-sex marriage, especially if one takes a long view. Conservatives respect the complete integrity of responsible individual choice, not the hollow substitute of "do-whatever-I-want" autonomy. To protect individual liberties, one must protect the institutions that foster, nurture, and develop both individualism and liberty – and the seedbed of both is conjugal marriage. There is no doubt that most contemporary conservatives see the effort to protect the institution of marriage as critical to preserve individual freedom. The disintegration of marriage only produces greater government control over the lives of the people, because as more marriages are avoided (by cohabitation and child-bearing out of wedlock) and break up (by separation and divorce) many social control functions non-coercively resolved within the family must instead be resolved by judges, policemen, and state child protection officials, requiring more intrusion by state educational and health agencies. Conservatives see the legalization of same-sex marriage as undermining the meaning of marriage and further loosening the ties that make marriages inviting, stable, and responsible.

A plausible argument might be put forward that letting the people decide is consistent with conservative structural principles in two ways – letting private individuals define marriage for themselves and letting legislative majorities legalize same-sex marriage. But this argument would have to overcome the conservative fear of government, especially when it seeks to break with tradition and radically redefine a basic social institution. It would entail allowing the government to redefine a pre-governmental social institution – a prime example of non-conservative social engineering. It would have to answer concerns about the impact of such redefinition of marriage upon the critical institution of marriage and the resultant limiting effect of individual rights accompanying the growth of government to cope with failed marriages.

Finally, the morality principle resonates in the position of those who oppose legalizing same-sex marriage. Their cause is that of the moral regeneration of society by protecting and revitalizing the key morality-generating institution of society – the institution of marriage and the marital family. [. . .] Conservatives oppose legalization of same-sex marriage because they see same-sex relations as immoral, and as having a de-moralizing influence upon the institution of marriage if same-sex relations are deemed marriages. They warn of this transformative effect of inclusion of same-sex relations upon the social institution of marriage. They agree with Kirk that "[c]onservativism must teach humanity once more that the germ of public affections (in Burke's words) is 'to love the little platoon we belong to in society.'"[71] That "little platoon" of which Burke wrote is marriage and the marital family that grows out of it.

B. The Detrimental Consequences of Legalizing Same-Sex Marriage

Including same-sex couples within the institution of marriage will transform the institution of marriage to the detriment of all. The characteristics of same-sex relationships will set a new and devastating minimum standard for marital relations. The moral and behavioral norms of marriage will be distorted by inclusion of the behavioral and moral norms of gay and lesbian lifestyles within the institution of marriage.

For example, same-sex relationships are notoriously unstable. Edward O. Laumann and his colleagues at the University of Chicago reported, "typical gay urban men spend most of their adults lives in 'transactional' relationships or short-term commitments of less than six months."[72] Judith Stacey's recent report on gay lifestyles in the Los Angeles area confirms that temporary relationships are the norm in that community.[73] One might expect gays in committed relationships to have more stability in the Netherlands, the most gay-affirming nation on earth. The 2003 Dutch study noted above found that the average duration of gay "steady partner" relations was only 1.5 years – in the most gay-affirming, gay-supportive nation on earth, when marriage-equivalent same-sex domestic partnerships were legal, and the full status of same-sex marriage was being implemented.[74]

Expectations among gay couples is dramatically different from the expectations of married conjugal couples. Thus, Kirk and Madison in 1989 wrote that "[m]any gay lovers, bowing to the inevitable, agree to an 'open relationship,' for which there are as many sets of ground rules as there are couples."[75] Thus, it should come as no surprise that a more recent study found that nearly half of all gay men in relationships have agreements with their partners that sex outside the relationship is acceptable.[76] The 2005 Vermont study noted that there was a dramatic difference in the percentage of couples who had decided that extra-relationship sex was acceptable; for lesbians both in and not in civil unions it was about 50% higher than for conjugally married women, and for gay men both in civil unions and not in registered unions it was from 1250% to 1400% higher than for men in conjugal marriages.[77] The expectation of fidelity that came with the relationship commitment was drastically different for conjugally married men and women than for gays and lesbians in formal and non-registered same-sex relationships.

Sexual infidelity characterizes same-sex relationships. Kirk and Madsen acknowledged that "the cheating ratio of 'married' gay males, given enough time, approaches 100%. . . ."[78] The 2005 report on same-sex couples in Vermont reported that "over one-half of gay men in both types of couples [formal civil unions and informal relationships] had had sex outside their primary relationship, whereas only 15.2% of married heterosexual men had done so."[79] Gay men both in and not in civil unions had nearly four times the rate of infidelity (approximately 60%) as married heterosexual men (15.2%), even though married relationships which have long existed logically could have been on average much longer-lasting (and with more time for infidelity) than the recent civil unions.[80] The 2003 AIDS journal report from the Netherlands reported that gay men with steady partners had eight other sex partners ("casual partners") per year, on average.[81]

While monogamy is the standard and expectation in conjugal marriage, promiscuity and polyamory are the standard in gay and lesbian relationships. In their groundbreaking, sympathetic 1978 study of homosexual behaviors, Bell and Weinberg reported that 43% of white male homosexuals had sex with five hundred or more partners, with 28% having one thousand or more sex partners.[82] Twenty-years later, researchers studying the sexual behaviors of 2,583 older sexually active gay men reported that most gay men still have huge numbers of sex partners; "the modal range for number of sexual partners ever . . . was 101–500," while 10.2% to 15.7% had between 501 and 1,000 partners, and another 10.2% to 15.7% reported having had more than 1,000 sexual partners in their lifetime.[83]

Thus, in terms of expectations of marital loyalty, stability, relational monogamy, actual infidelity, and promiscuity, the introduction of gay and lesbian relationships into the institution of marriage entails a serious risk of lowering the standards, understanding,

expectations and behaviors of marriage for all members of society.

[. . .]

V. Conclusion: A Day of Reckoning

Expanding the definition of marriage so that more special interest groups like same-sex couples may enjoy the label of "marriage," is dangerously short-sighted. In the short-term, like unregulated grazing on the commons, other factors may protect the community from having to face the consequences. In the long run (and perhaps in the not-so-distant future), the community will have to pay the piper and cope with the devastating social consequences.

[. . .]

By redefining marriage to include same-sex couples, the meaning of marriage will be changed in ways that will loosen the already-impaired link between marriage and parenting; the intergenerational connections of marriage will become attenuated. The notion that marriage is merely a private matter – a "common" that should be open to all – will grow, as the public commitments and expectations of marriage erode. The chaos of sexual irresponsibility (especially infidelity and promiscuity within marriage) will grow, and the moral expectations of the basic institution of society will fade as the sexual ethic of gay and lesbian lifestyles is embraced as marriage. Instability in marriages will increase as the pattern of transitory relationships of same-sex couples is included in the social understanding of what is marriage.

[. . .]

Notes

1 See infra note 35. Among the most articulate and respected of these advocates of same-sex marriage is Professor Dale Carpenter of the University of Minnesota, who participated in this symposium.

2 I plan to prepare later a companion article to this one that presents a "liberal" case against same-sex marriage based on the principles that underlie that liberal political philosophy.

3 See generally Encyclopedia Americana, s.v. "Conservatism," (1999 ed.) (by Frederick M. Watkins) [hereinafter Watkins].

4 Id.; Russell Kirk, The Conservative Mind 4 (3d ed. 1960).

5 Edmund Burke, Reflections on the Revolution in France 53 (1790), available at http://www.constitution.org/eb/rev_fran.htm.

The military conspiracies, which are to be remedied by civic confederacies; the rebellious municipalities, which are to be

rendered obedient by furnishing them with the means of seducing the very armies of the state that are to keep them in order; all these chimeras of a monstrous and portentous policy must aggravate the confusion from which they have arisen. There must be blood. The want of common judgment manifested in the construction of all their descriptions of forces and in all their kinds of civil and judicial authorities will make it flow. Disorders may be quieted in one time and in one part. They will break out in others, because the evil is radical and intrinsic. All these schemes of mixing mutinous soldiers with seditious citizens must weaken still more and more the military connection of soldiers with their officers, as well as add military and mutinous audacity to turbulent artificers and peasants.

Id.

6　Id.

EVERYTHING depends upon the army in such a government as yours, for you have industriously destroyed all the opinions and prejudices and, as far as in you lay, all the instincts which support government. Therefore, the moment any difference arises between your National Assembly and any part of the nation, you must have recourse to force. Nothing else is left to you, or rather you have left nothing else to yourselves. . . . You must rule by an army; and you have infused into that army by which you rule, as well as into the whole body of the nation, principles which after a time must disable you in the use you resolve to make of it.
Id.

7　Watkins, supra note 3, at 639 (noting that the "range and variety of contemporary conservative parties is too great to be described").

8　See Oxford English Dictionary Online, s.v. "conservative," http://dictionary.oed.com/cgi/entry/50047828?single=1&query_type=word&queryword=conservative&first=1&max_to_show=10 (last visited Feb.7, 2008) [hereinafter Oxford English Dictionary] ("1. . . . preservative."); Merriam-Webster Online Dictionary, s.v. "conservative," http://m-w.com/dictionary/conservative (last visited Feb. 7, 2008) ("1: preservative"); Watkins, supra note 3, at 638 (conservatism seeks to "maintain things as they are").

9　Kirk, supra note 4, at 6–7.

10　Ted Honderich, Conservatism 1 (Pluto Press 2005) (1989).

11　Lynn Tower Sargent, Contemporary Political Ideologies, 92 (rev. ed. 1972).

12　Routledge Encyclopedia of Philosophy, s.v. "conservatism," available at http://www.rep.routledge.com/article/S012 (last visited Oct 18, 2007) [hereinafter Routledge Encyclopedia] ("For Burke, a good constitution . . . dissipates power in society through autonomous institutions independent of the state." Furthermore, "[t]he market needs to be supplemented by the morality, the institutions and . . . authority."); Watkins, supra note 3, at 638 (conservatives are generally committed to established institutions, procedures, and authorities).

13　Kirk, supra note 3, at 7 ("civilized society requires orders and classes").

14　See Oxford English Dictionary, supra note 8 ("3.b. Characterized by caution or moderation. . . ."); Routledge Encyclopedia, supra note 12 (Conservatism's perceived complacency or caution "may be said to be more realistic than its opponents." Conservatism "mistrusts both a priori reasoning an revolution, preferring to put its trust in experience and in the gradual improvement of tried and tested arrangements."); Watkins, supra note 3, at 639 ("Their starting point always has been to protest dangers of excessive innovation." Conservatives are "wary" of innovations and conservatism stresses "the organic and gradual character of social evolution.").

15　Kirk, supra note 4, at 8.

16　Sargent, supra note 11, at 98 (quoting Jay A. Sigler, Introduction to The Conservative Tradition in American Thought 13 (Jay A. Sigler, ed. 1969)).

17　Honderich, supra note 10, at 8.

18　Id. at 9 (emphasis added).

19　Watkins, supra note 3, at 638–39 (Conservatives stress "common sense and experience" and conservatives prefer to rely on collective experience rather than reason. Conservatives distrust reason believing as Burke put it, that "Even the best minds are too weak to comprehend the problems of society as a whole. . . ." Habit, not reason, is the true basis of social order according to Burke.).

20　Kirk, supra note 4, at 6.

21　Id. at 8.

22　Sargent, supra note 11, at 92.

23　Barry M. Goldwater, The Conscience of a Conservative 11 (1960).

24　Watkins, supra note 3, at 638.

25　Goldwater, supra note 23, at 15–24 (1960) (conservatives today recognize the perils of power and seek to limit government power).

26　Sargent, supra note 11, at 98 (rejecting the use of government to improve the human condition).

27　Carlton C. Rodee, Defenders and Critics of American Capitalism and Constitutionalism: Conservatism and Liberalism, in Twentieth Century Political Thought 388 (Joseph S. Roucek ed., 1946).

28　Id. at 389.

29　Goldwater, supra note 23, at 13 (The goal of conservatives is "achieving the maximum amount of freedom for individuals that is consistent with the . . . social order.").

30　Kirk, supra note 4, at 525.

31　Sargent, supra note 11, at 92.

32　Goldwater, supra note 23, at 12.

33　Routledge Encyclopedia, supra note 12 (social structures such as "the market needs to be supplemented by . . . morality"); see also Harry Jaffa, The False Prophets of American Conservatism Claremont Inst. (1998) Writings, http://www.claremont.org/publications/pubid.670/pub_detail.asp (last visited Feb. 27, 2008); The Federalist No. 57, at 350 (James Madison) (Clinton Rossiter ed., 1961) ("The aim of every political constitution is, or ought to be, first to obtain for rulers men who possess most wisdom to discern, and most virtue to pursue, the common good of the society; and in the next place, to take the most effectual precautions for keeping them virtuous whilst they continue to hold their public trust."); The Federalist No. 55 (James Madison) (Clinton Rossiter ed., 1961) ("Were the pictures which have been drawn by the political jealousy of some among us faithful likenesses of the human character, the inference would be, that there is not sufficient virtue among men for self-government; and that nothing less than the chains of despotism can restrain them from destroying and devouring one another.").

34   Goldwater, supra note 23, at 10.

35   See, e.g., Andrew Sullivan, The Conservative Soul 70 (2006) ("And you have the fact that the least fundamentalist and most tolerant of states, Massachusetts, has both civil marriage rights for gay couples and the lowest divorce rates in the country."); Andrew Sullivan, Same–Sex Marriage Pro & Con: A Reader 69 (2004) ("The heterosexual community needs to see and experience homosexual unions that are marked by integrity and caring and are filled with grace and beauty."); Andrew Sullivan, Virtually Normal 111, 185 (1995) ("Why would accepting that such people [homosexuals] exist, encouraging them to live virtuous lives, incorporating their difference into society as a whole, necessarily devalue the traditional family? It is not a zero-sum game. Because they have no choice but to be homosexual, they are not choosing that option over heterosexual marriage; and so they are not sending any social signals that heterosexual life should be denigrated. . . . Gay marriage is not a radical step; it is a profoundly humanizing, traditionalizing step."); see also Jonathan Rauch, Gay Marriage, Why It is Good for Gays, Good for Straights, and Good for America 85, 105 (2004) [hereinafter Rauch, Good for America] ("To the skeptics I would say: I can't prove you wrong. But do you really want to bet against marriage? Do you want to put your money on quasi-marriage or semi-marriage or nonmarriage? That would not be particularly conservative bet. Indeed, it would be a radical one. . . . America has a problem with too few marriages, not too many. One would think that encouraging a whole new population of cohabitants to tie the knot would be a step in the right direction."); Dale Carpenter, The Traditionalist Case for Gay Marriage, in State of the Family 2007 at III-B-1 (National Center for Family Law at the University of Richmond School of Law September 16–18, 2007) [hereinafter Carpenter, The Traditionalist Case] (CLE materials) (marriage will help stabilize gay families, will promote commitment, monogamy, will make available the most moral life, will not hurt conjugal marriages, and may revive marriage); Dale Carpenter, Bad Arguments Against Gay Marriage, 7 Fla. Coastal L. Rev. 181 (2005) (rejecting definitional, procreational, and polygamy-slippery slope arguments); Dale Carpenter, A Conservative Defense of Romer v. Evans, 76 Ind. L.J. 403, 404, 441 (2001) ("this Article places the [Romer v. Evans] decision within the foundational strain of modern conservatism. This conservatism prefers an incremental method and pace of change. . . ." Romer is "consistent with conservatives preference for slow, incremental change in society"); Dale Carpenter, Four Arguments Against the Federal Marriage Amendment That Even an Opponent of Gay Marriage Should Accept, 2 St. Thomas L. Rev. 71 (2004) (opposing Federal Marriage Amendment because it alters the constitutional structure of federalism, cuts short an ongoing national debate, and is overkill); Jonathan Rauch, Dire Straights, Washington Monthly, April 2004, available at http://www.washingtonmonthly.com/features/2004/0404.rauch.html

("Why outlawing marriage for gays will undermine marriage for all." The "social expectations" of marriage will produce benefits in the lives of gays; civil unions do not provide the same social expectations or produce the same benefits.); Jonathan Rauch, The Marrying Kind, Atlantic Monthly, May 2002, available at http://www.theatlantic.com/doc/prem/200205/rauch ("Why social conservatives should support same-sex marriage. . . . [M]arriage itself brings something beneficial to the table."); Press Release, Denison Hosts Andrew Sullivan to Discuss "Conservative Case for Gay Marriage," (Jan. 24,2005), http://www.denison.edu/offices/publicaffairs/pressreleases/sidlivan_2-05.html; Jonathan Rauch, Marriage for All, National Review Online, Aug. 10, 2001, http://www.nationalreview.com/comment/comment-rauch081001.shtml (the "social regularity" of marriage, i.e., "commitment to care for another person for life – has good effects on human populations."); Reference – Interview with Dale Carpenter on Same-Sex Marriage, in Craig Westover (Jan. 1,2005), available at http://craigwestover.blogspot.com/2005/01/reference-interview-with-dale.html ("My own conservatism is rooted in Edmund Burke. For Edmunt Burke, 'conservatism' did not mean we never change anything. It meant. . . . [w]e change [] things incrementally. . . . We change things in light of our actual lived experience." Gay marriage is conservative if brought "incrementally and democratically." Gay couples raising children exist, so we should not deny them the family benefits of marital status; gay marriage (not civil unions) carries deeply-rooted social expectations that would benefit gay couples.).

36   See, e.g., Carpenter, The Traditionalist Case, supra note 35, at III-B-1-4 ("[Same-sex] Marriage will help support and stabilize gay families, including the many such families raising children. . . ."); Rauch, Good for America, supra note 35, at 75 ("Given the reality of children in gay households, and given the many ways in which marriage supports and sustain unions, the relevant point is that children will be more secure and happy with married gay couples than with unmarried gay couples.").

37   2002 Statistical Abstract of the United States 48, tbl. 49 (2002).

38   Jason Fields, Children's Living Arrangements and Characteristics: March 2002 2 (2003) (Table 1, Children by Age and Family Structure, March 2002), http://www.census.gov/prod/2003pubs/p20-547.pdf (Applying the 11% same-sex ratio of all cohabiting couples to the number of children living in a home with unmarried parents or parent-and-partners (2,888,000 children) yields approximately 317,000 children being raised by same-sex couples.). See generally Lynn D. Wardle, The Curious Case of the Missing Legal Analysis. 18 BYU J. Pub. L. 309, 336–38 (2004)

39   Gary J. Gates, Geographic Trends Among Same-Sex Couples in the U.S. Census and the American Community Survey, 2007 Williams Inst. 1–2.

40 R. Bradley Sears, Gary Gates & William B. Rubenstein, Same-Sex Couples and Same-Sex Couples Raising Children in the United States, Data from Census 2000 (2005), available at http://www.law.ucla.edu/williamsinstitute/publications/USReport.pdf.

41 See, e.g., Carpenter, The Traditionalist Case, supra note 35, at III-B-1, B-4-B-10.

42 Maria Xiridou et al., The Contribution of Steady and Casual Partnerships to Incidence of HIV Infection Among Homosexual Men in Amsterdam, 17 AIDS 1029 (2003), available at http://www.aidsonline.com/pt/re/aids/pdfhandler.00002030-200305020-00012.pdf; jsessionid=FrMF7bsJNJx6Znq8QlqzTFXPQSShnmnLTy4TG4pm!1057067369!-949856144!8091!-1 (The purpose of the study was to assess whether provision of certain AIDS drugs had resulted in an increase of unsafe sexual practices in the gay community in The Netherlands.)

43 Gunnar Andersson et al., The Demographics of Same-Sex Marriages in Norway and Sweden, 43 Demography 79 (2006), available at http://muse.jhu.edu/journals/demography/v043/43.landersson.html#tab02.

44 Id. at 85. (On the other hand, 43–45% of gay men partnerships involved a partner from a foreign country, a factor likely to be associated with less harmony in the marriage.).

45 Id. at 87–88.

46 Id. at 89–90.

47 Maggie Gallagher & Joshua K. Baker, Same-Sex Unions and Divorce Risk: Data from Sweden, 2004 iMAPP Policy Brief 1 (copy in author's possession).

48 Id.

49 See, e.g., Carpenter, The Traditionalist Case, supra note 35, at III-B-1, B-6, B-12-13 (advocating stabilizing effect of same-sex marriage); William N. Eskridge, Jr., The Case for Same-Sex Marriage: From Sexual Liberty to Civilized Commitment 8, 104 (1996) ("My further thesis is that same-sex marriage . . . civilizes gays and it civilizes America." Furthermore, "[s]ame-sex marriage will civilize both gays and straights, teaching each something about the unitive features of marriage."); Rauch, Good for America, supra note 35, at 18 (same-sex marriage will "settl[e] the young, particularly young men; and provid[e] reliable caregivers."); see also Justin T. Wilson, Note, Preservationism. or The Elephant in the Room: How Opponents of Same-Sex Marriage Deceive Us Into Establishing Religion, 14 Duke J. Gender L. & Pol'y 561, 662–63 (2007) ("According to the argument's premise, same-sex couples are more prone to contracting STIs; as such, marriage would civilize them for the betterment of all society: their relationships would stabilize, they would be less likely to engage in extra-relationship sexual activities, and they would benefit from increased commitment to one another. . . . If the government's public-health interest is in slowing the spread of STIs, it is irrational to prevent same-sex couples from marrying.").

50 Sondra E. Solomon et al., Money, Housework, Sex, and Conflict: Same-Sex Couples in Civil Unions, Those Not In Civil Unions, and Heterosexual Married Siblings, 52 Sex Roles 561 (2005).

51 Id.

52 Id. at 562.

53 See, e.g., Carpenter, The Traditionalist Case, supra note 35, at III-B-1, B-10-12 (universal benefits of same-sex marriage espoused); Eskridge, supra note 49, at 116 (asserting "the substantial benefits that same-sex marriage offers to society as a whole. . . ."); Rauch, Good for America, supra note 35, at 5 (asserting that same-sex marriage is a "win-win-win" proposition, "good for homosexuals, good for heterosexuals, and good for the institution of marriage: good, in other words, for American society.").

54 Centers for Disease Control and Prevention, U.S. Dep't of Health and Human Serv., 16 HIV/AIDS Surveillance Report 32, tbl. 17 (2005). The second most common method of transmission was injection drug use, which accounted for 21% of the AIDS cases. Id; see also Centers for Disease Control and Prevention, U.S. Department of Health and Human Services, A Glance at the HIV/AIDS Epidemic 2 (2007), available at http://www.cdc.gov/hiv/resources/factsheets/At-A-Glance.htm ("From 2001 through 2005, the estimated number of persons in the 50 states and D.C. living with AIDS increased from 331,482 to 421,873 – an increase of 27%." Furthermore, the number of persons with AIDS diagnoses in the USA in 2005 was 40,608; the number of such diagnoses from 1981–2005 was 952,629, of whom 530,756 have died.)

55 Id. at 1 ("In 2005, the largest estimated proportion of the HIV/AIDS diagnoses were for men who have sex with men (MSM). . . .").

56 Center For Disease Control and Prevention, U.S. Dep't of Health and Human Servs., National HIV Serosurveillance Summary: Results Through 1992, 26 tbl. 5 (1994).

57 UNAIDS and World Health Organization, AIDS Epidemic Update, December 2007 1 (2007), available at http://data.unaids.org/pub/EPISlides/2007/2007_epi-update_en.pdf.

58 Id. at 4 (The total estimates are down 16% from 2006 due to revision of estimates in India and five African nations, but the total rate globally is unchanged.)

59 Id. at 33 (Good treatment prolonging life may contribute to the rising cumulative number of infections in the United States.)

60 Id. at 4.

61 Id. at 6–7.

62 Xiridou et al., supra note 42, at 1033.

63 See, e.g., Carpenter, The Traditionalist Case, supra note 35, at III-B-1, 19–25 (no harm to heterosexual marriages); Monte Neil Stewart, Eliding in Washington and California, 42 Gonz. L. Rev. 501, 519 (2006/07) (citing judicial opinions in same-sex marriage cases in Washington and

California asserting that "allowing same-sex couples to marry will not only result in no harm to but will actually benefit marriage in our society. . . ."); see also Wilson, supra note 35, at 655 ("Same-sex marriage does no harm to [specific social interests in marriage]."); Lisa M. Polk, Comment, Montana's Marriage Amendment: Unconstitutionally Denying a Fundamental Right 66 Mont. L. Rev. 405, 442 (2005) ("Montanans face no harm whatsoever if lesbians and gays obtain marriage licenses.").

64 See supra notes 42–46, and accompanying text.

65 See infra notes 73–83, and accompanying text.

66 Compare Allan Carlson, Deconstruction of Marriage: The Swedish Case, 44 San Diego L. Rev. 153 (2007) (discussing relationships between same-sex marriage and disintegration of marriage in Sweden), with William N. Eskridge, Jr., & Darren R. Spedale, Gay Marriage: For Better or for Worse? passim (2006) (arguing that same-sex marriage has not weakened marriage in Scandinavia or The Netherlands).

67 See supra Part II; see also infra, Part IV.

68 Sargent, supra note 11, at 98. They also "strongly oppose the movement for gay rights. . . . The prolife movement, which they support, includes their concerns with both family and religion." Id. The same could be said for their support of the marriage protection movement in the first decade of the twenty-first century.

69 Kirk, supra note 4, at 540 (describing what Kirk calls "the problem of the proletariat") (emphasis added).

70 Jaffa, supra note 33. (Jaffa is not only a renowned Lincoln scholar but also a renowned conservative political scientist.).

71 Id. at 525.

72 Edward O. Laumann et al., The Sexual Organization of the City 216 (2005); see also id. at 96 (gay cultures "sanction and celebrate a transactional orientation toward sexual partnering."); id. at Chapter 1, The Theory of Sex Markets, available at http://www.press.uchicago.edu/ Misc/Chicago/470318.html (last visited March 13, 2008) ("The male same-sex markets for both whites and racial/ ethnic minorities are predominantly transactional. . . .").

73 Judith Stacey, The Families of Man: Gay Male Intimacy and Kinship in a Global Metropolis, 30 Signs 1911 (Spring 2005).

74 Xiridou et al., supra note 42, at 1031 tbl. 1.

75 Marshall Kirk & Hunter Madsen, After the Ball 330 (1989). Likewise, Andrew Sullivan contrasts male-female marriages with same sex relationships and explains, "there is more likely to be a greater understanding of the need for extramarital outlets between two men than between a man and a woman." Sullivan, supra note 35, at 202 (1996).

76 Solomon et al., supra note 50, at 569 (40.3% of gay men in Vermont civil unions and 49.3% of coupled gay men not in civil unions have agreements with their partners that sex outside of the relationship is alright, compared to 3.5% of heterosexual married men.).

77 Id. at 566 (For women the results agreeing that extrarelational relations were okay was 5.3% and 5.0 for lesbians compared to 3.5% of married women, and for gay couples it was 40.3% and 49.5% compared to 3.5% for married men.).

78 Kirk & Madsen, supra note 75, at 330. Likewise, Andrew Sullivan contrasts male-female marriages with same sex relationships and explains, "there is more likely to be a greater understanding of the need for extramarital outlets between two men than between a man and a woman." Sullivan, supra note 35, at 202 (1996).

79 Solomon et al., supra note 50, at 571.

80 Id.

81 Id.

82 Martin S. Bell & Alan P. Weinberg, *Homosexualities* 308–09 (1978).

83 Paul Van de Ven et al., A Comparative Demographic and Sexual Profile of Older Homosexually Active Men, 34 *Journal of Sex Research* 354 (1997).

15

United States v. Windsor, Executor of the Estate of Spyer

Supreme Court of the United States

CERTIORARI TO THE UNITED STATES COURT OF APPEALS FOR THE SECOND CIRCUIT
Argued March 27, 2013 – Decided June 26, 2013

Summary

The US Supreme Court ruled that the 1996 Defense of Marriage Act, which defined marriage for federal purposes as limited to the legal union of one man and one woman, was unconstitutional because it rejects the long–established precept that individual states have sovereign authority to define marriage and other elements of domestic relations, deprives certain people of the equal liberty protections of the Fifth Amendment, seeks to injure the very class of people that New York state law sought to protect, deliberately imposes a disadvantage and separate status upon same-sex spouses, and creates two contradictory marriage regimes within the same state.

Original publication details: *United States v. Windsor, Executor of the Estate of Spyer* (Syllabus) 570 U.S. No. 12-307 (2013). Public Domain.

Sexual Ethics: An Anthology, First Edition. Edited by Patrick D. Hopkins.
© 2023 John Wiley & Sons, Inc. Published 2023 by John Wiley & Sons, Inc.

The State of New York recognizes the marriage of New York residents Edith Windsor and Thea Spyer, who wed in Ontario, Canada, in 2007. When Spyer died in 2009, she left her entire estate to Windsor. Windsor sought to claim the federal estate tax exemption for surviving spouses, but was barred from doing so by §3 of the federal Defense of Marriage Act (DOMA), which amended the Dictionary Act – a law providing rules of construction for over 1,000 federal laws and the whole realm of federal regulations – to define "marriage" and "spouse" as excluding same-sex partners. Windsor paid $363,053 in estate taxes and sought a refund, which the Internal Revenue Service denied. Windsor brought this refund suit, contending that DOMA violates the principles of equal protection incorporated in the Fifth Amendment. While the suit was pending, the Attorney General notified the Speaker of the House of Representatives that the Department of Justice would no longer defend §3's constitutionality. In response, the Bipartisan Legal Advisory Group (BLAG) of the House of Representatives voted to intervene in the litigation to defend §3's constitutionality. The District Court permitted the intervention. On the merits, the court ruled against the United States, finding §3 unconstitutional and ordering the Treasury to refund Windsor's tax with interest. The Second Circuit affirmed. The United States has not complied with the judgment.

Held:

1. This Court has jurisdiction to consider the merits of the case. This case clearly presented a concrete disagreement between opposing parties that was suitable for judicial resolution in the District Court, but the Executive's decision not to defend §3's constitutionality in court while continuing to deny refunds and assess deficiencies introduces a complication. Given the Government's concession, *amicus* contends, once the District Court ordered the refund, the case should have ended and the appeal been dismissed. But this argument elides the distinction between Article III's jurisdictional requirements and the prudential limits on its exercise, which are "essentially matters of judicial self-governance." *Warth* v. *Seldin*, 422 U. S, 490, 500. Here, the United States retains a stake sufficient to support Article III jurisdiction on appeal and in this Court. The refund it was ordered to pay Windsor is "a real and immediate economic injury," *Hein* v. *Freedom From Religion Foundation, Inc.*, 551 U. S. 587, 599, even if the Executive disagrees with §3 of DOMA. Windsor's ongoing claim for funds that the United States refuses to

pay thus establishes a controversy sufficient for Article III jurisdiction. Cf. *INS* v. *Chadha*, 462 U. S. 919.

[. . .]

2. DOMA is unconstitutional as a deprivation of the equal liberty of persons that is protected by the Fifth Amendment. Pp. 13–26.

a. By history and tradition the definition and regulation of marriage has been treated as being within the authority and realm of the separate States. Congress has enacted discrete statutes to regulate the meaning of marriage in order to further federal policy, but DOMA, with a directive applicable to over 1,000 federal statues and the whole realm of federal regulations, has a far greater reach. Its operation is also directed to a class of persons that the laws of New York, and of 11 other States, have sought to protect. Assessing the validity of that intervention requires discussing the historical and traditional extent of state power and authority over marriage.

Subject to certain constitutional guarantees, see, *e.g.*, *Loving* v. *Virginia*, 388 U. S. 1, "regulation of domestic relations" is "an area that has long been regarded as a virtually exclusive province of the States," *Sosna* v. *Iowa*, 419 U. S. 393, 404. The significance of state responsibilities for the definition and regulation of marriage dates to the Nation's beginning; for "when the Constitution was adopted the common understanding was that the domestic relations of husband and wife and parent and child were matters reserved to the States," *Ohio ex rel. Popovici* v. *Agler*, 280 U. S. 379, 383–384. Marriage laws may vary from State to State, but they are consistent within each State.

DOMA rejects this long-established precept. The State's decision to give this class of persons the right to marry conferred upon them a dignity and status of immense import. But the Federal Government uses the state-defined class for the opposite purpose – to impose restrictions and disabilities. The question is whether the resulting injury and indignity is a deprivation of an essential part of the liberty protected by the Fifth Amendment, since what New York treats as alike the federal law deems unlike by a law designed to injure the same class the State seeks to protect. New York's actions were a proper exercise of its sovereign authority. They reflect both the community's considered perspective on the historical roots of the institution of marriage and its evolving understanding of the meaning of equality. Pp. 13–20.

b. By seeking to injure the very class New York seeks to protect, DOMA violates basic due process and equal protection principles applicable to the Federal Government. The Constitution's guarantee of equality "must at the very least mean that a bare congressional desire to harm a politically unpopular group cannot" justify disparate treatment of that group. *Department of Agriculture* v. *Moreno*, 413 U. S. 528, 534–535. DOMA cannot survive under these principles. Its unusual deviation from the tradition of recognizing and accepting state definitions of marriage operates to deprive same-sex couples of the benefits and responsibilities that come with federal recognition of their marriages. This is strong evidence of a law having the purpose and effect of disapproval of a class recognized and protected by state law. DOMA's avowed purpose and practical effect are to impose a disadvantage, a separate status, and so a stigma upon all who enter into same-sex marriages made lawful by the unquestioned authority of the States.

DOMA's history of enactment and its own text demonstrate that interference with the equal dignity of same-sex marriages, conferred by the States in the exercise of their sovereign power, was more than an incidental effect of the federal statute. It was its essence. BLAG's arguments are just as candid about the congressional purpose. DOMA's operation in practice confirms this purpose. It frustrates New York's objective of eliminating inequality by writing inequality into the entire United States Code.

DOMA's principal effect is to identify and make unequal a subset of state-sanctioned marriages. It contrives to deprive some couples married under the laws of their State, but not others, of both rights and responsibilities, creating two contradictory marriage regimes within the same State. It also forces same-sex couples to live as married for the purpose of state law but unmarried for the purpose of federal law, thus diminishing the stability and predictability of basic personal relations the State has found it proper to acknowledge and protect. Pp. 20–26.

699 F. 3d 169, affirmed.

KENNEDY, J., delivered the opinion of the Court, in which GINSBURG, BREYER, SOTOMAYOR, and KAGAN, JJ., joined. ROBERTS, C. J., filed a dissenting opinion. SCALIA, J., filed a dissenting opinion, in which THOMAS, J., joined, and in which ROBERTS, C. J., joined as to Part I. ALITO, J., filed a dissenting opinion, in which THOMAS, J., joined as to Parts II and III.

16

Marriage

Marci Hamilton

Summary

Argues that polygamy should not be accommodated under the law or social custom because it is contrary to public reason, harms the public good, and exploits women and children. Most arguments for polygamy are based on religious freedom (although very few religious groups support polygamy), but these arguments fail to distinguish constitutional protections of belief from protections of conduct. While religious belief may be protected absolutely under the Constitution, conduct is not. Conduct should only be protected after a consideration of the public good and potential harms to individuals. Polygamy has largely been practiced in a way that treats women and children as property, forces underage girls into marrying, limits women's education, and promotes serious inequality. As such, it does not pass the public good test.

Original publication details: Marci A. Hamilton, "Marriage," pp. 50–77 from *God vs. the Gavel: Religion and the Rule of Law*. Cambridge University Press, 2007. Reproduced with permission of Cambridge University Press.

Sexual Ethics: An Anthology, First Edition. Edited by Patrick D. Hopkins.
© 2023 John Wiley & Sons, Inc. Published 2023 by John Wiley & Sons, Inc.

Recent wars of religious power have been intense on the subject of marriage – whether the issue is gay marriage or polygamy. Both topics have earned headlines in the early part of the 21st century, with religious entities intent on imposing their religious viewpoint on public policy. The religious have every right to contribute their religious viewpoints to the public debate and to try to persuade leaders and fellow citizens that their ideas about social problems have merit; wisdom can be found in many corners. But they do not have a right in the United States to mold public policy to their beliefs, and their beliefs alone. The hard choices depend on a more broad-ranging inquiry than any one religious worldview encompasses (even when that perspective is shared by a significant number of individuals and institutions).

The complication in the debates over marriage in 21st century America is that few in government seem to understand or be willing to shoulder their role, which demands significantly more than deference to religious entities. Citizens may speak to them from the heart and soul, but it is up to our elected officials to contextualize the debate by adding the scope of the public good to all public consideration. That is not secularization, as those who would employ religious rhetoric to drown out all discourse might insist, but rather the hallmark of a successful representative democracy. If government officials do not move the conversation off of its solely religious bottom, they have shortchanged everyone, because they have abdicated their responsibilities. To be sure, it is easier to react to religious voices and to give them what they demand. They are, after all, typically quite passionate. But that is no excuse for elected representatives to abandon the public good.

The controversy over marriage has stretched from coast to coast. On the eastern side of the United States, the Supreme Judicial Court of Massachusetts in February 2004 held that the state was required to permit same-sex couples to get married. Fourteen homosexual couples in long-term relationships had challenged Massachusetts's heterosexual-only marriage law.[1] Their argument, which was reflected in the court's opinion, was in a nutshell that their unions were not distinguishable from heterosexual unions. They were monogamous and dedicated, and they nurtured their children. The purposes of Massachusetts's marriage laws were served by their unions, and therefore, Massachusetts's distinction between gay and traditional marriages rested on invidious discrimination on the basis of sexual orientation.[2]

[. . .]

Once the presumed invincibility of heterosexual marriage was pierced by the Massachusetts decision, and it became necessary to articulate why one man/one woman marriage is important (or not), the subject of polygamy was reintroduced into the public square as well. Some have tried to link the two issues by saying that opening the door to one opens the door to the other, but they have fundamentally missed the point of the legislative role. Constitutional principles can be subject to what is called a "slippery slope" effect, where the granting of one right logically entails the granting of another; those who have argued that judicial recognition of gay marriage demands recognition of polygamy are employing slippery-slope reasoning. For example, the Liberty Counsel in a letter in support of the Federal Marriage Amendment asserted as fact that "[i]f same-sex marriage were sanctioned it would be virtually impossible to ban polygamy."[3] They are speaking to the wrong branch of government, though. In most states, this is a policy and not a constitutional issue. There is no such slippery slope when it comes to crafting public policy on marriage. The legislature is required to determine what elements of marriage best serve the common good, and they must take into account how the arrangement affects children, inheritance, and the culture at large, just for starters. From that perspective, the two challenges to traditional marriage, which are factually quite distinct, are also, for public policy purposes, separate topics for legislative consideration.

In the Western United States, fundamentalist Mormons are actively challenging the laws that ban polygamy.[4] Polygamist Tom Green, who was convicted of bigamy,[5] asked the Supreme Court to hear his constitutional defense of polygamy. The Utah Civil Rights and Liberties Foundation[6] defended the right to polygamous marriage when a couple that sought to add an additional wife were denied a license. They claimed that the three adults had a right to the free exercise of religion to be exempt from the federal and state antipolygamy laws. Their arguments have fallen on deaf judicial ears, as they should, but they provide an excellent example of religious conduct that cannot be vouchsafed by the First Amendment – which incorporates the need to deter and punish conduct that harms individuals and society.

[. . .]

In the gay marriage context, fundamentalist religions have been insisting quite loudly in the public square that their biblical values mandate a particular form of marriage and that their belief should in fact be the law. They are intent on using what political power they have to ensure the law matches their religious worldview.

The polygamy debate is quite different, at least from a constitutional perspective. The polygamists are not trying to impose their beliefs on everyone else. Rather, they are asking for relief from the law that governs everyone else. It is typical, therefore, to hear polygamists talk in libertarian terms and to dwell on the right to be left alone by the government. In contrast, those trying to forestall gay marriage talk in terms of the "Christian tradition" and the necessity of maintaining social order. Despite the differences, though, in the end, both religious entities are trying to shape the law to their religious conduct, and it is the government's obligation to persistently reframe the issues in light of public interest.

[. . .]

In the case of polygamous marriage, there are very few religious sects that advocate the practice. They are small in number and even smaller in political power; they lack the close relationships with those in power that the same-sex marriage opponents enjoy. Nor do they argue that the law should reflect their religious teaching. They do not suggest, as do the opponents to gay marriage, that every marriage should reflect their particular beliefs. Rather, they argue that the First Amendment gives them the right to practice polygamy, despite the laws against it.

In the end though, the two sets of arguments by religious entities are quite similar. Both expect religious belief to direct public policy, and neither has a sufficient appreciation for the role of the legislature in achieving the public good, or in the content of the public good, for that matter. Their horizons are defined by their religious belief, and they transport those horizons into the public square as though they should delineate good and bad public policy by themselves. Yet, religious belief, no matter who holds it, or even how many hold it, cannot be the sole measuring rod for U.S. policy. [. . .]

The Polygamy Question: Demands for Accommodation vs. The Public Good

Well over a hundred years ago, when the Church of Jesus Christ of Latter-day Saints believed that polygamy on earth paved the way to heaven, the federal government outlawed the practice.[7] Polygamy is "[t]he condition or practice of having more than one spouse at one time."[8] The most common form of polygamy is polygyny, which is "the condition or practice of having more than one

wife at one time."[9] The laws, however, outlawed multiple spouses of either gender. For purposes of this discussion, I will use "polygamy" to mean just that. It does not mean, by the way, "polyamory," the practice of having multiple sexual partners. When the Supreme Court decided *Lawrence v. Texas*, it made it rather clear that personal sexual relations between consenting adults were protected by the right of privacy.[10] Thus, polyamory has been left to private choice. That does not mean it is the right choice from a moral perspective, but it does mean it is beyond the government's purview. "Polygamy," by contrast, implicates the larger social construct of marriage, not the sexual relations between adults. For these purposes, the two universes need to be kept distinct.

George Reynolds, a polygamist Mormon, challenged the federal law outlawing polygamy in the 1870s, arguing that because his actions in taking two wives were the result of religious belief, they were outside the force of the law. In other words, the antipolygamy law might be okay as applied to someone who took two wives simply because he liked two women equally, but where a man's religious beliefs required taking multiple wives, then the government was powerless.

Essentially, Reynolds asked the Court to interpret the First Amendment to mean that belief and conduct are the same thing. That religious belief should be protected was not contested. The Court certainly had no problem in protecting the absolute freedom of conscience, but it refused to extend that unassailable protection to conduct.[11] In *Reynolds v. United States*, it uttered one of the most famous lines in free exercise cases: "Can a man excuse his practices to the contrary because of his religious belief? [To] permit this would be to make the professed doctrines of religious belief superior to the law of the land, and in effect to permit every citizen to become a law unto himself."[12] And common sense requires this reasoning. Religious individuals harm the public good by violating the law no less (and no more) than any other entity breaking the law. As I will explain in Chapter 10, the touchstone in conduct cases must be harm or damage, not the perspective of the religious entity. No proper democracy exists that permits individuals to harm others at will simply because of their beliefs. The principle is often repeated in federal and state cases. One particular case comes to mind: a 1944 Utah decision upholding a conviction for cohabitation with more than one member of the opposite sex avowed, "when the offense consists of a positive act which is knowingly done, it would be dangerous to hold that the offender might escape punishment because he religiously believed the law which he had broken ought never to have been made."[13]

[. . .]

Reynolds initiated a series of cases implementing a remarkably consistent and persistent principle: one's actions are measured by their effects and the law, not by their motivation. No one's conduct, with its capacity to harm others, is immune. In 1971, the U.S. Supreme Court in *Gillette v. United States*,[14] stated it as clearly as it has ever been stated: "Our cases do not at their farthest reach support the proposition that a stance of conscientious opposition relieves an objector from any colliding duty fixed by a democratic government."[15] Mr. Reynolds's actions directly collided with the law, and the resultant crash was not averted simply because of his beliefs.

There is no question in the United States that polygamy is not constitutionally mandated, and the current challenges coming out of Utah, where the most polygamists reside, do not change that fact.[16] The arguments were rejected first in 1879 and that rejection has been cemented in multiple federal and state decisions, including in Utah, ever since.[17] One 1955 Utah decision put it as plainly as possible:

> It was never intended or supposed that the amendment could be invoked as a *protection against legislation for the punishment of acts inimical to the peace, good order, and morals of society*. . . . However free the exercise of religion may be, it must be subordinate to the criminal laws of the country, passed *with reference to actions regarded by general consent as properly the subjects of punitive legislation*.[18]

But to say there is no constitutional right to polygamy is not to say that the religious accommodation discussion is necessarily over. The Constitution does not force the government to abandon its policy goals in the face of individuals' religious beliefs. It equally does not require that polygamy (or same-sex marriage) be banned. The question is not whether polygamists may trump the law, but rather whether polygamy can coincide with the public good.

To date, in the United States, the answer has been a rather resounding "no." There is never any harm, though, in a free society reexamining the bases of public policy, even when that which is being examined has been entrenched since the beginning of the country. Tradition by itself cannot and should not determine whether the

common good has been adequately served. When polygamy was first outlawed in the United States, it was considered, along with slavery, to be one of the "twin relics of barbarism,"[19] and there is some modern evidence that at least in religious polygamous households, wives are servants of the husband. There was a strong sense in that era that humankind had moved beyond it, to a better social order,[20] and that may be true. But the debate is not off limits.

[. . .]

In the last decade in the United States, there has been a growing rumble from formerly polygamous wives, who criticize the notion that polygamy is a victimless crime. Tapestry Against Polygamy was founded by a group of formerly polygamous wives who decided to fight polygamy. It describes its mission as advocating "against the human right violations inherent in polygamy and provides assistance to individuals leaving polygamous cults."[21] Journalist Andrea Moore-Emmett has taken an in-depth look at the problems expressed by formerly polygamous wives across a range of polygamous religious communities, and concluded that religiously based marriages involving one man and multiple women frequently entail spousal and child abuse.[22] Canadian Nancy Mereska formed an email network campaign dubbed "Stop Polygamy in Canada" after learning of the abuses that seem to be endemic in many of the known polygamous communities.[23]

Former polygamous wives argue that the typical religious polygamy community elevates certain men over all others, and that women and children are nothing more than property to accumulate. In chapter 2, I described polygamy's impact on children; it has also harmed women. When underage girls are forced into marrying much older men in these communities, they are taken out of school, deprived of any means of future earning or self-support, and burdened with the expectation of bearing as many children as possible. The cost of such enormous families can prove to be too much for any one man, leading some polygamist men to support only their first wives, leaving all later wives (and their children) no option but state support.[24] Moreover, home schooling is favored in order to avoid the public school system, which could lead to discovery of their criminal acts. So mothers who have marginal educations themselves are teaching their children. These children would appear to be destined to be as undereducated as their mothers, despite federal legislation that purports to leave no child behind. When government refuses to prosecute the legal violations within these polygamous enclaves, it further isolates the women and leaves their children far behind the standardized goals set by the federal legislation.[25]

There is some debate whether this describes the natural propensities of polygamy, or whether only the bad polygamous actors get the attention of the public. Some of the wives from the FLDS Bountiful commune have defended their lifestyle, saying that they enter the marriages freely, that the women are educated, and that there is no abuse.[26] There is also a Utah organization of polygamous women in Utah, Principle Voices of Polygamy, which defends the practice.[27]

Polygamy's defenders are not only Mormon fundamentalists. Mark Henkel is a self-proclaimed spokesman for a Christian polygamy advocacy group in Maine, who "cites biblical scripture and the polygamists' lifestyle of such Old Testament biblical figures as Abraham and King David as justification." He asserts he does not, however, support forced marriages and believes in the free choice of women to enter the arrangement.[28]

Legislators who take up the issue, though, must consider whether the unbalanced numbers in a polygamous marriage institute an inherently unequal situation. While there are a certain number in the United States who argue that the above abuses are simply perversions of what can be a productive and happy relationship, others have seen in polygamy an internal contradiction with the rule of law and democracy. At the very least, polygamy sends the message that only one man need satisfy multiple women, so that the women are not equal to the man. Naomi Schaefer Riley, who is a Fellow at the Ethics and Public Policy Center, in Washington, D.C., believes the latter, saying that it "corrupt(s) civil society as a whole, destroying education, individual rights and the rule of law – in other words the foundations of democratic governance."[29] Others, like political science professor Thomas Flanagan at the University of Calgary, Canada, are more blunt, arguing that polygamous societies are highly unequal and a deadly foe of constitutional government. He offers as proof that constitutional democracies have arisen only from monogamous societies.[30]

The facts of religious polygamy are the proper focus of any social and legislative reconsideration of marriage. The victims of polygamy should be heard, as should the continuing practitioners who would defend the practice. The typical defense by the men is that their religion demands it, and the government should have no power to regulate their religion. "[M]embers of the Fundamentalist Church of Jesus Christ of Latter-day Saints . . . believe that men must have at least three wives

to reach heaven's highest echelon."[31] One leader elaborated by pointing out that it was a blessing for the women, because "the only way she could ever be happy was – that she would let her husband, a faithful man, rule over her. That was the only way back to Heavenly Father for the woman."[32] He was not quite as subtle when dealing with recalcitrant wives: "You can either live here and live in hell, and then when you die have eternal happiness. Or else, you can go out into the world and live in hell and die and even have more eternal hell."[33]

It is not as though the United States is the first culture to deal with polygamy. Although, to be quite frank, the United States is always sorely tempted to assume it stands alone and ahead of others on issues addressing religious practice. Many countries in the world permit it, and it does have some political clout. For example, in Afghanistan's 2004 elections, the Afghanistan Supreme Court demanded one candidate be prohibited from the election, because he had publicly criticized polygamy.[34] Even so, its legality has not meant that it is widely followed. In East Malaysia, for example, where the practice is legal, there were only 168 polygamous marriages recorded between 1999 and 2003, amounting to only .6 percent of marriages recorded.[35]

In other underdeveloped regions of the world where polygamy is still widely practiced the issues are more complex. Florence Butegwa, former regional director of Women in Law & Development in Africa (WiLDAF) has commented on the contradicting views of polygamy in Uganda, where women have organized "to demand the abolition of polygamy as a necessary step for protecting women's rights in marriage." At the same time, Muslim women, "either on their own volition or on the demands of their Islamic leaders," opposed the movement. "They liked polygamy, they [didn't] want it to go away." Their claims "provided the government with an escape route."[36] Similar campaigns against polygamy have been started in other African nations, especially Nigeria, where The Campaign Against Polygamy & Women Oppression In Nigeria and Africa (CAPWONA), and the Total World Women Freedom Alliance (TOWWFA), believe that polygamous marriages are inherently unequal and lead to unhappiness for the women, but they also see a larger issue involving the building blocks of the society.[37] Given the multitude of issues surrounding women's rights in Africa, including access to healthcare, child custody issues and basic property laws, Professor Mojubaolu Olufunke Okome of Brooklyn College, CUNY, put it this way: "I don't think that many women in Nigeria think polygamy is a problem in and of itself. . . . [it is the] the unjust treatment of a woman under the polygamous system may be a problem."[38]

However, without addressing polygamy, it will be virtually impossible to address the other concerns of these women. If the family is a group unit, how can courts decide custodial issues? If a man has more than one wife, which wife should inherit his property when he dies without a will? If a man can marry as many women as he wants, will there ever be a solution to the endemic problem of AIDS in Africa? Indeed, some believe the culture of polygamy has contributed to the spread of AIDS in Africa.[39]

While United States officials have been apt to turn the other way, international treaties have labeled polygamy as an inherently unequal relationship that violates fundamental principles of equality. For example, following the creation of the Convention for the Elimination of All Forms of Discrimination Against Women (CEDAW), the United Nations offered the following analysis: "Polygamous marriage contravenes a woman's right to equality with men, and can have such serious emotional and financial consequences for her and her dependents that such marriages ought to be discouraged and prohibited."[40]

All of this is proper fodder for legislative consideration, including the experiences of those in the United States who have lived within the institution, the views of those who have left it, and the knowledge of the international community. And the focus needs to be on polygamy, religious and secular, not just religious. There may be those polygamous situations that do not entail the severe civil rights abuses apparent in the religiously motivated polygamy that has been at the forefront of the debate. Those individuals should be encouraged to make their case to their legislators. But in the end, it is the obligation of the legislators to determine what is in the best interests of all the people – men, women, children, and society as a whole. And the debate belongs in the legislature, not the courts.

[. . .]

To the extent the religious polygamists insist that the Constitution mandates permission for their practices, they are on quicksand. The argument has no foundation. If they are arguing instead that polygamy is a socially beneficial practice that is capable of serving the public good, then they should make the case.

Here, as elsewhere, legislators need to be reminded that they are not in their positions of power to roll over for religious organizations that demand rights to do whatever their beliefs dictate. It is never enough for representatives to assert they are furthering religious liberty. They must also always ask whether the conduct in question comports with the public good, and that means they must examine with some care how the conduct impacts others. [. . .]

Notes

1 Goodridge v. Dep't of Pub. Health, 440 Mass. 309, 313–14 (2003).

2 *Id*. at 320–21.

3 Matthew D. Staver, *Why Do We Need a Federal Marriage Amendment?, in* SAME-SEX MARRIAGE: PUTTING EVERY HOUSEHOLD AT RISK (2004), *available at* http://www. lc.org/ProFamily/FMA_why_weneed04.htm (last visited Oct. 15, 2004).

4 *See National Briefs: Polygamist's Appeal Based on Gay Sex Ruling,* HOUSTON CHRON., Dec. 2, 2003, at A17; Complaint, Bronson v. Swenson, No. 04-CV-0021 (D. Utah filed Jan 12, 2004), *also available at* http://marriagelaw.cua.edu/ Law/cases/ut/Complaint.pdf (last visited Oct. 12, 2004).

5 See Angie Welling, *Green's Conviction Is Upheld by Ruling,* DESERET MORNING NEWS (Salt Lake City), Sept. 4, 2004, *also available at* http://deseretnews.com/dn/view/0,1249, 595089043,00.html (last visited Oct. 12, 2004).

6 *See* Complaint, Bronson v. Swenson, No. 04-CV-0021 (D. Utah filed Jan 12, 2004), *also available at* http:// marriagelaw.cua.edu/Law/cases/ut/Complaint.pdf (last visited Oct. 12, 2004).

7 Anti-Polygamy Acts (the Morrill Act), ch. 126, 12 Stat. 501 (1862) (repealed 1910). The only reference to polygamy in the current U.S. Code deals with immigration law (Inadmissible aliens include "Practicing polygamists. Any immigrant who is coming to the United States to practice polygamy is inadmissible." 8 U.S.C.S. § 1182 (a)(10)(A) (2004)).

8 AMERICAN HERITAGE DICTIONARY OF THE ENGLISH LANGUAGE (4th ed. 2000), *also available at* http://www. bartleby.com/61/41/P0424100.html (last visited Oct. 17, 2004).

9 AMERICAN HERITAGE DICTIONARY OF THE ENGLISH LANGUAGE (4th ed. 2000), *also available at* http://www. bartleby.com/61/48/P0424800.html (last visited Oct. 17, 2004).

10 *Lawrence*, 539 U.S. at 578.

11 Reynolds v. United States, 98 U.S. 145,166 (1879) ("Laws are made for the government of actions, and while they cannot interfere with mere religious belief and opinions, they may with practices.").

12 *Id*. at 166–76.

13 State v. Barlow, 153 P.2d 647, 653 (Utah 1944).

14 401 U.S. 437 (1971).

15 *Id.* at 461.

16 *See* Angie Welling, *Green's Conviction Is Upheld by Ruling,* DESERET MORNING NEWS (Salt Lake City), Sept. 4, 2004 (quoting Green's attorney John Bucher on his plans to appeal to the Supreme Court because "It's got to be appealed. It can't stand. . . ."); *see also* Complaint, Bronson v. Swenson, No. 04–CV–0021 (D. Utah filed Jan 12, 2004).

17 *See, e.g.,* Davis v. Beason, 133 U.S. 333, 348 (1890); *Reynolds,* 98 U.S. at 166; White v. United States, No. 01–4225, 41 Fed. Appx. 325, 326 (10th Cir. May 23, 2002); Potter v. Murray City, 760 F.2d 1065, 1070 (10th Cir 1985); *In re* State in Interest of Black, 283 P.2d 887, 903–904 (Utah 1955); State v. Barlow, 153 P.2d 647, 653 (Utah 1944); United States v. Snow, 9 P. 697, 700–701 (Utah 1886).

18 *In re* State in Interest of Black, 283 P.2d at 904 (emphasis in original).

19 Republican Platform of 1856, *in* 1 NATIONAL PARTY PLATFORMS 1840–1972, at 27, 27 (Donald B. Johnson & Kirk H. Porter eds., 5th ed. 1975).

20 *See* Sarah Barringer Gordon, Symposium, *A War of Words: Revelation and Storytelling in the Campaign Against Mormon Polygamy,* 78 CHI.-KENT. L. REV. 739, 747–57 (2003).

21 Press Release, Tapestry Against Polygamy, June 18, 2004, (on file with author), *also available at* http://www.polygamy.org/releases.shtml (last visited Oct. 14, 2004).

22 ANDREA MOORE-EMMETT, GOD'S BROTHEL: THE EXTORTION OF SEX FOR SALVATION IN CONTEMPORARY MORMON AND CHRISTIAN FUNDAMENTALIST POLYGAMY AND THE STORIES OF 18 WOMEN WHO ESCAPED (2004) [hereinafter GOD'S BROTHEL].

23 Email from Nancy Mereska, Coordinator, Stop Polygamy in Canada, to Marci A. Hamilton, Oct. 18, 2004 (on file with author).

24 *See, e.g.,* GOD'S BROTHEL, *supra* note 101, at 38; TODD COMPTON, IN SACRED LONELINESS: THE PLURAL WIVES OF JOSEPH SMITH 199 (1997).

25 No Child Left Behind Act of 2001, 20 U.S.C. §§ 6301 et seq. (2004). "The purpose of this title is to ensure that all children have a fair, equal, and significant opportunity to obtain a high-quality education and reach, at a minimum, proficiency on challenging State academic achievement standards and state academic assessments." 20 U.S.C. § 6301.

26 Mike D'Amour, *Sect Wives Defend Lives: Women Say Polygamy Choice Is Theirs,* CALGARY SUN (Alta.), July 29, 2004, at 4.

27 *See* Brooke Adams, *Plural Wives Defend Lifestyle,* SALT LAKE TRIB., Feb. 13, 2004, at C1. *See also* MARY BATCHELOR, ET AL., VOICES IN HARMONY: CONTEMPORARY WOMEN CELEBRATE PLURAL MARRIAGE (2000) (a collection of essays by women who are living in polygamous marriages supporting their lifestyle); *see also* Catherine Elsworth, *Investigation Launched into Polygamous Sect Dubbed "Canada's Dirty Little Secret,"* DAILY TELEGRAPH (London), Aug. 5, 2004, at 14.

28 Rasheed Oluwa, *In Marriage, Three's a Crowd – And a Crime,* POUGHKEEPSIE JOURNAL (N.Y.), Apr. 28, 2003, at 1A.

29 Naomi Schaefer Riley, *Yes, Polygamy Is Everybody's Business,* LA TIMES, Feb. 9, 2004, at 11.

30 *See* Nicholas Bala and Rebecca Jaremko Bromwich, *Context and Inclusivity in Canada's Evolving Definition of the Family,* 16 INT'L J. L. POL'Y & FAM. 145, 169 (2002) (quoting Flanagan: "'the historical record shows that monogamy, like private property, is indispensable to constitutional democracy . . . Constitutional government has emerged only in societies where monogamy was the legally enforced, or at least the commonly observed, social norm . . . The modern adoption of constitutional democracy in non-Western societies such as Japan and India has been accompanied by the parallel acceptance of monogamy. Those regions of die world where polygamy is still practiced . . . are precisely the areas where constitutional democracy has made die least progress.'").

31 *See* John Dougherty, *Double Exposure: Arizona's Finally Followed Utah's Lead and Launched Serious Action to Stop Abuses by Polygamists,* PHOENIX NEW TIMES (Ariz.), Dec. 25, 2003; *see also* Mark Havnes, *Hildale Polygamist Guilty of Unlawful Sex, Bigamy,* SALT LAKE TRIB., Aug. 15, 2003, at A1 ("FLDS members believe taking plural wives is a direct commandment from God, to be followed even if it means violating civil law.").

32 John Dougherty, *Blasphemous Backlash,* PHOENIX NEW TIMES (Ariz.), Jan. 29, 2004.

33 John Dougherty, *Bound by Fear: Polygamy in Arizona,* PHOENIX NEW TIMES (Ariz.), Mar. 13, 2003 (reporting what Ruth Stubbs says Jeffs told her when she considered leaving the sect).

34 Reuters, *Taliban Ally Urges Afghans to Boycott Elections,* NAVHIND TIMES (India), Sep. 3, 2004, *available at* http://www.navhindtimes.com/stories.php?part=news&Story_ID=090362 (last visited Oct. 16, 2004).

35 *Polygamy Law Streamlined,* DAILY EXPRESS (East Malaysia), Aug. 12, 2004.

36 Dorothy L. Hodgson, *Women's Rights as Human Rights: Women in Law and Development in Africa (WiLDAF),* 49 AFRICA TODAY 3 (2002), *also available at* http://iupjournals.org/africatoday/aft49-2.html (last visited Oct 26, 2004).

37 Campaign Against Polygamy & Women Oppression In Nigeria and Africa, *available at* http://www.tk-one.com/ (last visited Oct. 24, 2004) (explaining the beliefs of the organization).

38 Traci Mayette, Interview, A *Conversation with Dr. Mojubaolu Olufunke Okome, reprinted in* 10:2 AFRICA UPDATE NEWSLETTER (2003), *also available at* http://www.ccsu.edu/Afstudy/upd10-2.html (last visited Oct. 26, 2004).

39 Phillip Bobbitt, *Africa's Plight – The* 2050 *Scenario,* 'THE GLOBALIST (Online Magazine), Jan. 10, 2004, *available at* http://www.theglobalist.com/DBWeb/StoryId.aspx?StoryId=3681 (last visited Oct. 26, 2004).

40 *General Recommendation 21 on Equality in Marriage and Family Relations,* Comm. on the Elimination of Discrimination Against Women, 13th Sess., at 14, U.N. Doc. A/49/38 (1994). President Jimmy Carter signed it on July 17, 1980, but the Senate never ratified it. "Both last fell and for years beforehand, the vigilance of Sen. Jesse Helms (R–NC), a longtime opponent of measures that compromise U.S. sovereignty, was the dominant reason why CEDAW never came up for ratification." Melana Zyla Vickers, *The Convention on the Elimination of All Forms of Discrimination Against Women: A Leading Example of What's Wrong With International Law* 2, FEDERALIST SOCIETY FOR LAW AND PUBLIC POLICY STUDIES, *available at* www.fed-soc.org/Intllaw&AmerSov/CEDAWvic.pdf (last visited Oct. 17, 2004).

17

Liberalism and the Polygamy Question

Jon Mahoney

Summary

Argues that the polygamy issue is not settled by resolutions on religious freedoms or religious restrictions. Polygamy is conceptually independent of religion and a liberal society's toleration of it should center on whether it can be accommodated under general liberal principles of equality, public reason, and distributive justice. Mahoney criticizes and rejects Hamilton's arguments against legalizing polygamy because her concept of public reason is too restrictive, her concept of democracy presupposes a flawed concept of rights in which rights are balanced against the public good, and her argument concerning exploitation could be met provided one could design a form of polygamous marriage that did not include exploitation.

Original publication details: Jon Mahoney, "Liberalism and the Polygamy Question," pp. 161–174 from *Social Philosophy Today* 23 (2008). Reproduced with permission of Philosophy Documentation Center.

Sexual Ethics: An Anthology, First Edition. Edited by Patrick D. Hopkins.
© 2023 John Wiley & Sons, Inc. Published 2023 by John Wiley & Sons, Inc.

I. Introduction

In *God* vs. *the Gavel: Religion and the Role of Law*[1] Marci Hamilton claims that were a liberal state to accommodate same-sex marriage, marriage law would be consistent with liberal equality and no citizens' rights would be undermined. By contrast, were a liberal state to accommodate polygamous marriage, marriage law would bend to religious convictions and expose some to a high risk of exploitation. I suspect that many liberals, though likely to quibble with some of the reasons Hamilton offers, will agree with her positions on same-sex marriage and polygamy. But liberals should not agree with Hamilton's position on polygamy.

This paper has two main parts. Part II examines liberal toleration and its relevance to the debate on polygamy. Part III considers Hamilton's claim that polygamy should not be accommodated. Hamilton's position rests on three kinds of arguments which I call: 1) *the argument from public reason*; 2) *the argument from democracy*; and 3) *the argument from exploitation*. Each of these fails: 1) fails because Hamilton's conception of public reason is too restrictive; 2) fails because it rests on a procedural test which attempts to balance claims about rights against claims about the public good – and thus presupposes a flawed conception of rights; 3) is the most compelling of Hamilton's arguments but could be met in principle if one can show that the right design of background institutions can accommodate polygamy without sponsoring an exploitative form of marriage.

II. Liberalism and Polygamy

Although the debate on polygamy implicates religious freedom there are at least two reasons for claiming the issue cannot be settled by one's convictions about religious toleration. One is that there may be those who wish to practice polygamy for exclusively secular reasons. An analysis of polygamy which focuses exclusively on those who favor it for religious reasons will thus be incomplete.[2] Secondly, in a liberal state which promotes marriage by coercively distributing resources in ways which affect how benefits and burdens are shared, prohibitions against polygamy implicate foundational liberal principles which extend beyond the issue of religious toleration. For instance, questions about equal access to goods coercively distributed by the state are relevant to the debate on polygamy.

Polygamy implicates a more expansive set of liberal ideals than is suggested by those who construe the debate on polygamy as one that centers on the topic of religious freedom. This point is especially important in the U.S. where the debate on polygamy has been framed in terms of whether Mormon polygamy ought to be accommodated on First Amendment grounds.[3] In *Reynolds v. United States*, the Supreme Court established the precedent for denying that polygamy should be accommodated on grounds of religious freedom. The Court reasoned as follows:

> Can a man excuse his practices to the contrary [of prevailing norms] because of his religious belief? [To] permit this would be to make the professed doctrines of religious belief superior to the law of the land, and in effect to permit every citizen to become a law unto himself.[4]

This claim is true but only because liberal toleration circumscribes the kinds of religious practices that are permissible within a liberal political society. However, the Court's reasoning is disingenuous; *no practice should be permitted on the sole grounds that its practitioners have a religious reason to engage in it*; all practices, religious or otherwise, should be subject to regulation and prohibition when they cannot be exercised in a manner compatible with a scheme of rights consistent with the liberty and equal standing of all. Any practice that is permitted by a liberal conception of toleration is permitted because it is compatible with liberal ideals; the reasons that motivate those who support the practice are relevant only because these reasons are evaluated in terms of their compatibility with liberal ideals; the religious or non-religious nature of the reasons advanced by defenders of a policy is beside the point.

In *Reynolds* the Court invokes a sound principle, namely, that having a religious reason does not exempt one from a law or policy, yet errs in applying this principle because it misconstrues the issues polygamous marriage raises for a liberal state. The real legal question in *Reynolds* isn't, 'Do personal religious convictions trump the Constitution?' – the answer to this question is, 'Of course they don't!' – but rather, 'Can a liberal state which sponsors monogamous marriage prohibit polygamous marriage?' The Court likely would have reached the same decision had it asked the right question – although arguably only because of animus towards a despised religious minority – but framing the issue in the correct way has a significant implication; it shows that liberals should examine polygamy in light of their positions on liberal values such as equality, public reason, and distributive justice; these principles are what justify the liberal conception of forms of marriage which may be sponsored by the state. The liberal position on which forms of marriage ought to be promoted isn't settled by the liberal conception of religious toleration; rather, it's settled by principles from which the liberal conception of religious toleration is derived.[5] Debates about polygamy tend to frame the issue in terms of accommodating a conception of marriage advocated by a religious minority, and this is a mistake.[6]

There is also good reason for construing the issue of polygamy as one that cannot be resolved by appealing to the liberal conception of freedom of expression. Liberals should insist that there is an important difference between, 'should polygamous cohabitation be tolerated?' and 'should polygamous marriage be included among the forms of marriage promoted as a good by the state?' Many liberals will oppose the prosecution of polygamous cohabitation engaged as a species of experimental living. Of course, prosecution of polygamous cohabitation may be supported on grounds other than that the cohabitation is polygamous (e.g., to protect the rights of children, to protect victims of abusive relationships, etc.).[7]

In liberal states which do sponsor marriage, toleration and freedom of expression should not serve as the sole basis for framing the issue of polygamy. Rather, the issue is really about whether the liberal state should be in the business of promoting the good of polygamous marriage along with the good of monogamous marriage. Liberals should ask, 'is polygamy an arrangement among persons and families which entitles members to state-sponsored benefits the non-married do not enjoy?'

III. The Argument from Public Reason

Hamilton claims that those who favor law and policies designed to prohibit same sex-marriage, at least in the United States, are typically motivated by religious convictions. On her view, this is problematic because a constitutional democracy founded upon liberal principles should prohibit any law or policy which rests solely upon religious convictions. For example, even if one's personal religious convictions favor prohibiting same-sex marriage this does not suffice as a justification for law and public policy measures designed to deny same-sex

couples benefits that heterosexual couples can secure by means of marriage:

> The religious have every right to contribute their religious viewpoints to the public debate and to try to persuade leaders and fellow citizens that their ideas about social problems have merit. . . . But they do not have the right . . . to mold public policy to their beliefs and their beliefs alone.[8]

In another passage, Hamilton notes the similarities and differences between those who support prohibitions against same-sex marriage and those who favor accommodating polygamy:

> The issue of polygamous marriage presents both a different and a similar issue. In the case of polygamous marriage, there are very few religious sects that advocate the practice. They are small in number and even smaller in political power; they lack the close relationships with those in power that the same-sex marriage opponents enjoy. Nor do they argue that the law should reflect their religious teaching. . . . Rather, they argue that the First Amendment gives them the right to practice polygamy, despite the laws against it. In the end though, the two sets of arguments by religious entities are quite similar. Both expect religious belief to direct public policy.[9]

Hamilton claims that one can reject the claim that a liberal state must accommodate polygamy for the same reason that one can reject the claim that a liberal state must prohibit same-sex marriage.

Hamilton is right to claim that religious belief cannot be the basis for law in a liberal state. Norms of public reason require of citizens that when they support policies that call upon the powers of government they should present a justification that can be shared by other citizens many of whom will not share religious convictions. Public reason is in this sense strictly secular and nonsectarian. However, there is something very misleading about Hamilton's characterization of why those who argue in favor of accommodating polygamy violate norms of public reason. Hamilton seems to imply that were a citizen to advocate polygamy for religious reasons alone it follows that this is sufficient to disqualify polygamy as a candidate for inclusion in the liberal conception of permissible marriage arrangements. This can't be right. The liberal conception of public reason is restrictive, but not this restrictive. To see why, consider the religious convictions invoked by abolitionists and civil rights activists. Arguably, these are the best counter examples to a conception of public reason that rules out polities simply because those who support them have religious reasons for doing so.[10] Since abolitionists and civil rights activists advocated polities that in principle satisfy the norms of public reason, the mere fact that some abolitionists and some civil rights activists were motivated by religious conviction is beside the point. In fact, the liberal conception of public reason should be construed in a way that shows that even if every abolitionist and every civil rights activist was motivated by religious conviction, the policies they defended satisfy public reason.

Norms of public reason require only that reasons for law and public policy can be advanced on secular grounds; it does not require that citizens' actual reasons cannot be religiously motivated.[11] There are familiar reasons for qualifying the liberal conception of public reason in this manner. The example just mentioned regarding abolitionists and civil rights activists illustrates that the liberal conception of public reason does not reject policies simply because they are supported by citizens with religious convictions. The principled test for whether a policy is compatible with public reason is *counterfactual: we ask, can the policy be supported by non-sectarian reasons that all reasonable persons can accept?* In practice this entails that norms of public reason have both lateral and vertical reach; they impose demands on the kinds of reasons that citizens can reasonably expect other citizens to endorse; and they impose demands on the kinds of reasons that government can invoke in the name of its coercive authority. Norms of public reason bind both citizens and public officials.

If my formulation of the liberal conception of public reason is sound, then it follows that Hamilton's claim that polygamous marriage ought not to be accommodated because its proponents invoke religious convictions is false. Of course, it doesn't follow from this that polygamy should be accommodated, but at this point I am claiming only that, from the standpoint of the liberal conception of public reason, Hamilton misconstrues the perspective from which liberals should evaluate polygamous marriage. The argument from public reason would support the conclusion that a liberal state should prohibit polygamy if the following two claims could be established. First, only religious reasons can be invoked in support of accommodating polygamy. Second, non-sectarian reasons can be invoked to prohibit accommodating

polygamy. Since it is false, the first does not support the conclusion that polygamy is a practice which violates norms of public reason; and establishing the second requires showing that polygamy is in principle incompatible with a liberal conception of justice.

IV. The Argument from Democracy

Hamilton proposes a procedural test which she claims is a fair measure for deciding which practices to accommodate and which to prohibit;

> [there are] three necessary conditions for legitimate religious accommodation, [policies must be] (1) duly enacted by a legislature, not decreed by a court; (2) debated under the harsh glare of public scrutiny; and (3) consistent with the public good.[12]

Since this procedural test rests upon a conception of democracy, I will term the anti-polygamy argument which rests upon it *the argument from democracy*. Hamilton's proposal is that a majoritarian procedural test should be the means by which a democratic society seeks to adjudicate claims by religious and cultural minorities which demand that public policy accommodate distinct ways of life. This proposal does not necessarily qualify as a conception of pure procedural justice because principle 3) implies that the public good is a constraint on both legislators and citizens. Nevertheless, it is dear that in Hamilton's view, the public good is a matter to be defined by the legislature, not the courts.

To support her argument, Hamilton focuses on recent developments in U.S. law relevant to the issue of cultural and religious pluralism. *Wisconsin V. Yoder* is a well-known example.[13] In this decision the Supreme Court granted a religious exemption to what Hamilton regards as a legitimate and democratically enacted state education statute. The Court treated an argument motivated by religious conviction as sufficient to exempt parents of the Old Order Amish community from a state education law that required parents to provide an education for their children at least up to the age of sixteen. According to Hamilton, by granting the Old Order Amish an exemption that permits parents to end their children's education at fourteen, the will of the people, expressed through the Wisconsin state legislature, was annulled by the Supreme Court in an undemocratic act of judicial review.

The relevance of *Yoder* for polygamy is clear. Were one to advocate Hamilton's procedural test, then state laws prohibiting polygamy are sound polity just so long as such laws are a product of the legislative process. At the same time, as Hamilton herself concedes, the pro-polygamy argument might persuade enough legislators to rethink state anti-polygamy statutes. In her words,

> All of this is proper fodder for legislative considera-
> tion, including the experiences of those in the United
> States who have lived within the institution [of
> polygamy and], the views of those who have left
> it. . . . There may be those polygamous situations
> which do not entail the severe civil rights abuses
> apparent in the religiously motivated polygamy that
> has been at the forefront of the debate. Those indi-
> viduals should be encouraged to make their case to
> their legislators. But in the end, it is the obligation of
> the legislators to determine what is in the best inter-
> ests of all people – men, women, children, and soci-
> ety as a whole. And that debate belongs in the
> legislature, not the courts.[14]

Were one to accept Hamilton's procedural test, there is every reason to believe that anti-polygamy statues will not be challenged by legislators anytime soon. Yet liberals should reject this procedural test for reasons that are independent of the debate on *Yoder* and polygamy.

The main problem with Hamilton's test is that it leaves the status of claims on behalf of rights *that are not already recognized* subject to their popularity. This imposes a significant burden on minority groups that claim their equal standing is not affirmed. This is among the reasons many liberals reject majoritarian concep-tions of democracy. Anytime the state coercively distrib-utes resources to some but not others, the burden of justification should be on the state and on those who enjoy access to such resources; the state and its benefi-ciaries must show why those denied access have no grounds for complaint. Liberalism is not a doctrine of the status quo; instead, it is a doctrine for the unjustly denied and excluded.[15] Hamilton's procedural test puts liberal ideals into the hands of the powers and thus where they don't belong.

To highlight this problem with Hamilton's argument from democracy we can consider two ways of construing the debate on same-sex marriage. Were the issue of same-sex marriage left to the legislature or to popular referenda, demands for equal access to resources on the grounds of equal treatment will succeed only so far as a minority group can persuade the majority to favor a more inclusive conception of marriage. By contrast, were the issue of same sex marriage construed as an issue of equal treatment understood as a constraint on legisla-tion, then defenders of same-sex marriage are required only to show that as a matter of principle current mar-riage law is in violation of due process and other funda-mental principles of political morality which animate constitutional law in the U.S.

One thing to note is that the difference between these ways of construing the same sex marriage debate does not reflect a choice between democratic and non-democratic forms of governance. Rather, each reflects differing conceptions of democracy: the first is majori-tarian, and the second is egalitarian. To be sure, some critics of judicial review claim that a majoritarian proce-dure for deciding disputes about religious and cultural toleration is the only option compatible with democracy. Yet anyone who holds this view has to reject the thesis that justice – understood to be inclusive of liberty and equality – is the first virtue of political institutions.[16] In Dworkin's words, "the institution of rights . . . repre-sents the majority's promise to minorities that their dig-nity and equality will be respected."[17] There are well-known and compelling arguments which show that a majoritarian conception of democracy fails to take rights and moral equality seriously and Hamilton's argu-ment from democracy all but ignores them.

[. . .]

The policy implications of the egalitarian conception of democracy differ from Hamilton's position in the fol-lowing ways. On the topic of same-sex marriage and polygamy, the debate should not be left to the legislature and popular referenda. Rather, insofar as the state already sponsors and subsidizes heterosexual monoga-mous marriage, equality before the law and equal access to resources that are coercively allotted by the state should be understood as substantive constraints on the legislature and popular referenda; and it is the judici-ary's job to enforce these substantive constraints. [. . .]

It does not follow from the egalitarian conception of democracy that polygamy should be accommodated. One could argue, as some have, that only monogamous marriage can be realized in a non-exploitative form. If true, this would show that the egalitarian conception of democracy favored by egalitarian liberalism can rebut the claim that polygamy should be accommodated on the grounds that polygamy is not compatible with equal treatment and fair equality of opportunity. To show that an egalitarian liberal should favor the accommodation of polygamy one must offer more than an argument which purports to show that polygamy can be accommodated without compromising values such as 'equal treatment before the law.' One must also show that polygamy is a form of marriage which can be realized in a non-exploitative form. I now consider Hamilton's argument that the exploitative nature of polygamy is a sufficient reason for a liberal state to prohibit polygamous marriage.

V. The Argument from Exploitation

Hamilton's strongest argument against polygamous marriage appeals to empirical facts that support the claim that polygamy is exploitative. Much of this evidence is drawn from recent cases studies of polygamy in the U.S. and Canada. For example,

> In the last decade in the United States there has been a growing rumble from formerly polygamous wives, who criticize the notion that polygamy is a victimless crime. Tapestry Against Polygamy was founded by a group of formerly polygamous wives who decided to fight polygamy. . . . Former polygamous wives argue that the typical religious polygamy community elevates certain men over all others, and that women and children are nothing more than property.[18]

These facts must be taken seriously; they provide a compelling reason to reject proposals to accommodate some forms of polygamy. Additional support for Hamilton's claim comes from an examination of nineteenth-century polygamy as practiced by the Mormon Church, which under the leadership of Joseph Smith was especially exploitative. The disingenuous appeals to specious concepts such as "spiritual wifery"[19] were no doubt a ruse to justify the sexual and personal domination of women by men.

It is beyond dispute that there is a lot of empirical evidence showing that polygamy in contemporary North America is morally problematic and often exploitative. However, it does not follow that polygamy is necessarily exploitative; nor does it follow that polygamy cannot in principle be realized in a manner compatible with liberal principles of justice. None of the examples cited by Hamilton support an inference to the claim that polygamy is necessarily exploitative wherever it is practiced and whoever practices it. Of course, the burden remains on defenders of polygamous marriage to show that polygamy can be realized in a non-exploitative form.

In order to address these considerations, an assessment of polygamy must evaluate social, economic, and anthropological facts about marriage. Such an empirical investigation could establish one of three claims: 1) polygamy is necessarily exploitative; 2) polygamy is exploitative because of background conditions extrinsic to polygamous arrangements; or 3) polygamy is not exploitative. In spite of claims by those currently in polygamous relationships,[20] 3) is unlikely to withstand even a superficial investigation of polygamy as practiced today – at least in the U.S. – and I will proceed on the assumption that it is false. My own view is that liberals must be open to the possibility that either 1) or 2) might turn out to be true in light of economic, anthropological and social facts about polygamy. From the standpoint of political theory, unless there is an anti-polygamy argument establishing that even in a society that has realized just background conditions polygamy cannot be realized in a non-exploitative form, then 2) is a live option.

Hamilton focuses on those instances of polygamy which are involuntary or in some other way constituted by terms that are incompatible with the liberal conception of justice. This is evidence in favor of the claim that in some cases polygamy is exploitative and ought to be prohibited. Moreover, it also illustrates that empirical facts about marriage are essential to any attempt to assess claims about the forms of marriage which ought to be accommodated. For example, the facts assembled by Mary Wollstonecraft in *Vindication of the Rights of Women* provide empirical evidence for the claim that monogamous marriage in eighteenth-century Europe was unjust and made to be unjust by law and public policy.[21] However, granted that there is indisputable evidence that polygamy in some contexts is exploitative, does this evidence entail that liberals should as a matter of principle be opposed to accommodating polygamy? Or does it establish something analogous to what Wollstonecraft thought she was able to establish about monogamous marriage in the eighteenth century (i.e., that the institution of marriage must be transformed in order to enable egalitarian relations among men, women, and children)?

The empirical evidence marshaled by Hamilton shows that polygamy as it is illegally practiced in certain pans of the U.S. and Canada is morally problematic and ought to be both outlawed and proactively eliminated. But suppose questions about whether polygamy is intrinsically exploitative are put more abstractly, as they ought to be from the standpoint of political theory. Is polygamous marriage inevitably exploitative? Or might current forms of polygamy be exploitative as a result of factors extrinsic to the nature of polygamous relations? Answers to these questions require careful examination of both empirical evidence and principles of justice. Moreover, answers to empirical questions about human relations might not track universal features but instead may track culture-specific and historically contingent features of human relations.

[. . .]

My suggestion here is that, lacking a justification for the prohibition against polygamy in all contexts, liberals should be open to accommodating it provided other facts about society do not conspire to undermine the possibility that polygamous marriage can be realized in ways compatible with principles of justice.

[. . .]

Notes

1 Marci Hamilton, *God vs. the Gavel: Religion and the Rule of Law* (New York: Cambridge University Press, 2005), 6.
2 As Deborah Satz notes, some contractarian feminists favor the abolition of state-defined marriage and support the claim that various kinds of contract-based marriage ought to be permitted, including plural marriage. "Feminist Perspectives on Reproduction and the Family," *Stanford Encyclopedia of Philosophy* (2004), 6–7. For good accounts of some classical liberal positions on polygamy and marriage, see Bruce Baum, "Feminism, Liberalism and Cultural Pluralism: J. S. Mill on Mormon Polygyny," *The Journal of Political Philosophy* 5:3, (1997): 230–253; and Donald 'Wilson, "Kant and the Marriage Sight," Pacific *Philosophical Quarterly* 85 (2004): 102–123.
3 See Richard S. Van Wagoner, *Mormon Polygamy: A History*. 2nd edn. (Salt Lake City: UT, Signature Books, 1989).
4 *Reynolds* v. *United States* (1879), quoted in Hamilton, 67.
5 See for instance John Rawls, *Justice as Fairness: A Restatement* (Cambridge, MA: Harvard University Press, 2001), 163.
6 In this paper 1 endorse Rawls's conception of the *ideal of public reason*. See, John Rawls, "The Idea of Public Reason Revisted" in *The Law of Peoples* (Cambridge. MA: Harvard University Press, 1999), 131–180.
7 Utah's anti-polygamy statute prohibits polygamous cohabitation and thus is something many liberals will oppose. Moreover, in Lawrence v. *Texas* (U.S. 558: 2003) the Court recently struck down an anti-sodomy law in part on grounds that the government has no compelling interest in regulating the consensual intimate relations among adults. Arguably, should Utah's anti-polygamy statute be challenged, *Lawrence* could be invoked to support overturning it.
8 Hamilton, 50.
9 Ibid., 65.
10 These examples are considered by Rawls in "The Idea of Public Reason Revisited."
11 Of course when citizens fail to recognize that religiously motivated reasons can't serve as the basis for law and public policy they may be more likely to affirm policies which do run afoul of public reason.
12 Hamilton, 275.
13 *Wisconsin v. Yoder* (U.S. 205: 1972).
14 Hamilton, 76.
15 For more on this see Ronald Dworkin's critique of the majoritarian conception of democracy in *Freedom's Law: The Moral Reading of the American Constitution* (Cambridge, MA: Harvard University Press, 1996), 1–38.
16 John Rawls, *A Theory of Justice*, revised edn. (Cambridge, MA: Harvard University Press, 1999).
17 Ronald Dworkin, "Taking Rights Seriously," in his *Taking Rights Seriously* (Cambridge, MA: Harvard University Press, 1977), 205.
18 Hamilton, 73.
19 Van Wagoner.
20 See for example Elizabeth Joseph's op-ed piece "Polygamy is Good Feminism," *The New York Times*, May 1991, A31.
21 Mary Wollsonecraft, *Vindication of the Rights of Women* (Penguin Classics: Reissue Edition, 1993).

18

Multi-Player Option

Michelle Chihara

Summary

Argues that the conservative fear that gay marriage will start a slippery slope to polygamy and polyamory may have some substance to them, even if the fear is primarily used to oppose same-sex marriage. Polyamory is becoming more of an option for people who question monogamy, are disillusioned with traditional marriage, dislike the conventional dating model, are sexually experimental, and tend to believe no one person can meet all emotional needs. Polyamorous relationships (romantic and sexual arrangements with more than one person at a time) include a variety of forms, including gay triads, straight quads, open marriages, group households, and cohabiting platonic friends. Although often raised as a potential negative outcome of legalizing gay marriage, much of the criticism of polyamory has come from the gay community, which sometimes worries that polyamorists are interfering with the perception of gay people as normal.

Original publication details: Michelle Chihara, "Multi-Player Option," from Nerve.com (June 8, 2004). Reproduced with permission of Nerve.com.

Sexual Ethics: An Anthology, First Edition. Edited by Patrick D. Hopkins.
© 2023 John Wiley & Sons, Inc. Published 2023 by John Wiley & Sons, Inc.

Among the likeliest effects of gay marriage is to take us down a slippery slope to legalized polygamy and "polyamory" (group marriage). Marriage will be transformed into a variety of relationship contracts, linking two, three or more individuals (however weakly and temporarily) in every conceivable combination of male and female. A scare scenario? Hardly.

— *Stanley Kurtz, writing in the* Weekly Standard

To conservatives like Kurtz, the slippery slope might look something like this: Joshua is a twenty-four-year-old recent college grad from Philadelphia. After graduation, he started an internship at an organic farm in Massachusetts. Then he started dating Raven, the farm's owner, and moved in. Raven, a female-to-male transsexual, bought the homestead with his lover, Bella, seven years ago. In 1999, Raven and Bella got married there. Raven's daughter was raised there; she only moved out recently when she turned eighteen. Today, Joshua, Raven and Bella share a bed, with Raven in the middle. They are neither encouraged nor discouraged by the binary nature of legal marriage.

Or it might look like this: James is an Internet executive for a well-known company in San Francisco. He lives with his wife, his younger girlfriend and their best friend. Successful professionals, the four of them share responsibility for James's five-year-old son. They own their house together. The two women "time share" James. All four are committed for life. Their son gets a lot of bedtime stories.

Kate, a twenty-one-year-old physics major at Hampshire College, says this non-binary approach to commitment has become "very common" among her friends. She has a boyfriend (a twenty-one-year-old grad who lives in Amherst, Massachusetts, and is selling Macs until he gets his career in independent TV going) and a close friend who is also sometimes a girlfriend. Her boyfriend still dates two other women. Kate gets along with one of them ("nothing has happened between us, yet"), but the other girlfriend wants him to be monogamous, and that's causing problems. Still, Kate sees traditional dating as more combustible. "This just feels much more sincere," she says. "1 see people who don't talk, then they cheat on each other, and that just seems like the worst thing in the world."

Polyamory – the practice of loving more than one person at a time – is a practice often associated with aging hippies. For social conservatives, it is evidence that the '60s sowed the seeds for the decline of our civilization. Maybe so. But a new breed of polyamorist is springing up. They're young, In their teens or twenties. Some fold polyamory into another "alternative lifestyle:" bisexuality, BDSM, paganism. Others, like Kate, could be the discreetly tattooed girl next door. What they all have in common is that they've looked at the traditional cycle of dating-cheating-marrying-and-divorcing and thought, *that just makes no sense to me at all.*

Given that monogamous love has been reduced to something between a game show and a bloodsport by pop-cultural bellwethers like *The Bachelor* and *Cheaters*, it's hard to argue that the mainstream idea of marriage and fidelity isn't in need of an overhaul. Polyamorists have traditionally believed that the impulse to "cheat" is natural, and can be dealt with, even embraced. But young polyamorists often seem most committed to writing their own rules. They're not subscribing to "polyamory" per se. Among a pantheon of failed traditional institutions – public schools, the corporation – marriage is just one more area of life where they don't trust received wisdom.

"I just always wanted to have a big household, with a lot of people," says Joshua, who was raised by a single mother, his grandmother and various uncles under one roof. His first partner tried to convince him of the benefits of monogamy, but Joshua found the idea unworkable. "He was very into the romantic image, where you fail in love forever and ever, and you wouldn't even think about anyone else, or if you did, then something was wrong," he says. "But I was pretty arrogant when I was a teenager. I just thought I could convince any partner that this was the way things ought to go. And I thought heterosexual dating was strange."

Arrangements like Joshua's and James's are sometimes called a "V" in polyamorous circles. Raven is a "pivot" with his wife and lover, who are close but not romantic; all are free to pursue romantic and sexual relationships outside the house. Many polyamorists have a basic understanding that they can see other people, but there are different sets of rules. Some people allow only for sexual liaisons outside the house. Some demand that new partners be brought home. Polyfidelity, where a group of people are committed and sexually faithful to each other (with or without the understanding that you can always add to the group), is a sub-category of polyamory. Triads are committed threesomes. Open relationships – even ones where young members of a couple move to different cities and agree to see other people – count as polyamory There are certainly sex parties, and polyamorous parties, and there's even a polyamorous matchmaking site. But the term is primarily an umbrella that applies to any relationship that isn't one on one.

Outspoken queer and kinky polyamorists are sometimes easier to find, but if you can imagine the configuration – a triad of three gay lovers? a straight quad? a big houseful of lovers in some hip urban neighborhood? – you can be sure that somewhere, out there, it exists. Mike, a twenty-eight-year-old gay personal trainer in San Francisco, has other lovers but is committed for life to his boyfriend. "Make no decision based on fear," he says. "I cheated on every boyfriend I had, before. We both came from closed relationships that had led to cheating and distrust. So we decided to be open, in all aspects." Jen, a political writer in Austin, is twenty-nine and has an arrangement with her girlfriend where she can sleep with other people as long as she doesn't get emotionally involved. For her, polyamory is mostly the agreement that the occasional hook-up with someone else is okay. "We're not very traditional people," Jen says, "I saw a guy on *60 Minutes* who had something like fifteen wives, somewhere in New Mexico, and for the first time I realized that wasn't a big deal. They're all happy. People just get freaked out, but it's just another way of being with someone."

And people do get freaked out. Joshua's grandfather remains convinced that Joshua has joined a cult which recruits teenagers off the Internet. In fact, however, the V has actually become quite domestic. And besides, "the quality of teenagers you can recruit over the Internet is pretty low," says Joshua with a laugh.

It might not be a recruitment tool per so, but the Internet has been instrumental in spreading the polyamorous word among younger people. Polyamory.org, now the most established center for all things poly, has a private "Under 30" mailing list with more than 150 members, from teenagers up. According to one young polyamorist, however, that list is mostly "newbies." Once they've figured out their own way of thinking, people create their own Web spaces. Like thirty-three-year-old Leila, who runs a sex Web site with her (male) partner, where they've posted black-and-white photos of themselves alongside their polygamous creed. And in one LiveJournal polyamorist community, a recent college grad in the D.C, area named Colin posted lyrics to a song he wrote:

> *The radio blares*
> *song after song*
> *of 'baby I'll never leave you*
> *you know I'd never deceive you*
> *and it seems no one cares*
> *that the tunes they play right after*

> *are all 'Dammit, you cheating bastard*
> *how could you do me so wrong'*
> *Do I still have to sing along?*

As in the pop lyrics, honesty is a running theme with polyamorists. In their conversation, on their Web sites and newsgroups, the words "healthy," "consensual" and "communication" crop up often (especially "communication"). People under thirty have grown up under the shadow of AIDS; as adults, they've had to contend with rising rates of herpes and HPV. While in practice, there is some overlap with sex parties (or swinging), the most outspoken polyamorists are interested in experimenting with commitment as much as – if not more than – sex.

Brendan Coffey, a twenty-nine-year-old software engineer in San Francisco, is talking marriage with his live-in girlfriend of three years. She's currently dating another man. So is Brendan. When he first started acting polyamorous, Brendan didn't know the word existed. "When I got into a new relationship, with sexual and romantic components, I didn't want to give up the old one just because there was a new one," he says. Monogamy, to Brendan, always seemed doomed to fail, "The man says, 'I have sexual feelings for another woman, what should I do?' and the woman is like, 'I can't deal with this, I'm leaving you.' If you don't have a space where you can at least talk to one another about this – whether or not you can entertain the ideas or act on them – that just seems inherently dangerous."

Polyamorists aim for greater emotional intimacy by removing the spectre of cheating, by opening the boundaries of relationships and encouraging communication. No one pretends that it's easy. Polyamorists are doing their best to live out a new definition of commitment as something emotional, and highly verbal, rather than physical. They try to break jealousy down into its components: What does it mean if you're jealous of your wife's live-in boyfriend's date? Something new and different. But jealousy doesn't disappear. A formula that delivers triple the sex and twice the intimacy can also go exponential on the heartbreak. "It doesn't make you a superhero," says Brendan. "It's not an enlightenment contest, it's not about who can not be jealous, ever. Some people think polyamory is 'I don't care who my partner fucks,' but I haven't met anyone like that."

Along with the changing definitions of relationships and commitments come changing definitions of gender itself. For M'issa, a cute, punky twenty-two-year-old who's getting her master's degree in library science in San Jose, California, not only is marriage a bankrupt

Institution that "keeps a lot of binary sex-power dynamics in place," but also, gender roles have lost their meaning. "I don't see gender as a binary," she says. "I don't see an opposite sex." M'issa now has a girlfriend, and a list of "entanglements" it takes her twenty minute to describe. "No one person will be anybody else's everything," she says. She recently transitioned out of a five-person relationship with "Kelly, who sees herself as a little boy," Todd, "who transitioned," Andrew, who was a she and is now a he "who's getting married, and they're going to have an orgy at the festivities for their wedding," and one other girl. So it is perhaps understandable that she calls herself "queer" but can't be pinned down by any other labels.

In fact, the most resistance to polyamory that M'issa has seen or heard has come from the gay community. She remembers a lesbian psychology class she took at her liberal arts college, where the professor put M'issa in a discussion group with some self-identified dykes. "Polyamory came up in a conversation about 'myths about bisexual women,'" M'issa says, "It was like the worst kind of woman is one who would date a man and a woman at the same time! That kind of woman was supposed to be a myth!" She tried to explain that her girlfriend had had a boyfriend for five years. "But it was like, "why would any self-respecting person date more than one person at the same time?' I think it's this feeling they have, like, 'you're setting us back, you're being weird and we're trying to be normal.'"

And of course, the conservative right is trying to use the specter of legally recognized polyamory to set back the cause of gay marriage. But in reality, the law and most of society are a long way from recognizing any of these experiments. Most polyamorous people believe that all consenting adults should be able to bind themselves to any other consenting adults of their choosing. Were gay marriage to become fully legal, polyamorous activists would certainly try to use that to their advantage. But there is no obvious legal equation between allowing gay marriage and allowing polyamorous marriages (for better or for worse, depending on your take).

Nan Wise, a relationship counselor who's about to move in with her husband's lover and her own lover in a house in the Jersey suburbs, thinks there is increased fuss around polyamory partly as a "backlash to what's going on with the gays." She cites a "great" recent Discovery Channel documentary and an invitation to appear on The *O'Reilly Factor* as evidence of heat (she declined the Fox News gig). She has been interviewed by *Esquire* and was contacted by a filmmaker from HBO who's doing a movie on fidelity. Overall, she sees polyamory growing, and soon. "There are more conferences," she says, "And there used to be just one. Obviously, there's interest." As a counselor, she is anxious for new polyamorists to understand that the decision to love more than one must come "from a position of strength" in a relationship, "not as a measure to fix things." She is aware of the "paradigm shift" that polyamory requires and recognizes the backlash. But she predicts it will only see increased acceptance. "Poly," she says with satisfaction, "is the new gay."

Whether or not it will prove to be the next organized movement, polyamory is certainly an "interesting life," as M'issa says. She doesn't have a lot of role models, but of the ones she has, she says, "they're blurring gender roles at the same time they're redefining relationships. And maybe they're into leather too. If you can be all of those things, and at the same time be open and honest with your children, . . . well, that's pretty fucking awesome."

19

Is Adultery Immoral?

Richard Wasserstrom

Summary

Argues that adultery is typically seen as morally wrong because it is interpreted as a case of promise-breaking or as a case of deception about an act of great moral significance. This perception is inaccurate because in open marriage neither promise-breaking nor deception would apply, sexual exclusivity is not a necessary condition for marriage, and sex does not necessarily have to be seen as act of great intimacy and moral significance in the first place. Adultery is therefore sometimes morally permissible.

Original publication details: Richard Wasserstrom, "Is Adultery Immoral?" pp. 513–528 from *The Philosophical Forum: A Quarterly* 5 (1974). Reproduced with permission of John Wiley & Sons.

Sexual Ethics: An Anthology, First Edition. Edited by Patrick D. Hopkins.

Many discussions of the enforcement of morality by the law take as illustrative of the problem under consideration the regulation of various types of sexual behavior by the criminal law. It was, for example, the Wolfenden Report's recommendations concerning homosexuality and prostitution that led Lord Devlin to compose his now famous lecture, "The Enforcement of Morals." And that lecture in turn provoked important philosophical responses from H. L. A. Hart, Ronald Dworkin and others.

Much, if not all, of the recent philosophical literature on the enforcement of morals appears to take for granted the immorality of the sexual behavior in question. The focus of discussion, at least, is whether such things as homosexuality, prostitution and adultery ought to be made illegal even if they are immoral, and not whether they are immoral.

I propose in this paper to think about the latter, more neglected topic, that of sexual morality, and to do so in the following fashion. I shall consider just one kind of behavior that is often taken to be a case of sexual immorality – adultery. I am interested in pursuing at least two questions. First, I want to explore the question of in what respects adulterous behavior falls within the domain of morality at all. For this surely is one of the puzzles one encounters when considering the topic of sexual morality. It is often hard to see on what grounds much of the behavior is deemed to be either moral or immoral, e.g. private homosexual behavior between consenting adults. I have purposely selected adultery because it seems a more plausible candidate for moral assessment then many other kinds of sexual behavior.

The second question I want to examine is that of what is to be said about adultery, without being especially concerned to stay within the area of morality. I shall endeavor, in other words, to identify and to assess a number of the major arguments that might be advanced against adultery. I believe that they are the chief arguments that would be given in support of the view that adultery is immoral, but I think they are worth considering even if some of them turn out to be nonmoral arguments and considerations.

[. . .]

Before I turn to the arguments themselves there are two preliminary points that require some clarification. Throughout the paper I shall refer to the immorality of such things as breaking a promise, deceiving someone, etc. In a very rough way, I mean by this that there is something morally wrong that is done in doing the action in question. I mean that the action is, in a strong sense of "*prima facie*" *prima facie* wrong or unjustified. I do not mean that it may never be right or justifiable to do the action; just that the fact that it is an action of this description always does count against the rightness of the action. I leave entirely open the question of what it is that makes actions of this kind immoral in this sense of "immoral".

The second preliminary point concerns what is meant or implied by the concept of adultery. I mean by "adultery" any case of extramarital sex, and I want to explore the arguments for and against extramarital sex, undertaken in a variety of morally relevant situations. [. . .]

One argument for the immorality of adultery might go something like this: what makes adultery immoral is that it involves the breaking of a promise, and what makes adultery seriously wrong is that it involves the breaking of an important promise. For, so the argument might continue, one of the things the two parties promise each other what they get married is that they will abstain from sexual relationships with third persons. Because of this promise both spouses quite reasonably entertain the expectation that the other will behave in conformity with it. Hence, when one of the parties has sexual intercourse with a third person he or she breaks that promise about sexual relationships which was made when the marriage was entered into, and defeats the reasonable expectations of exclusively entertained by the spouse.

In many cases the immorality involved in breaching the promise relating to extramarital sex may be a good deal more serious than that involved in the breach of other promises. This is so because adherence to this promise may be of much greater importance to the parties than is adherence to many of the other promises given or received by them in their lifetime. The breaking of this promise may be much more hurtful and painful than is typically the case.

Why is this so? To begin with, it may have been difficult for the nonadulterous spouse to have kept the promise. Hence that spouse may feel the unfairness of having restrained himself or herself in the absence of reciprocal restraint having been exercised by the adulterous spouse. In addition, the spouse may perceive the breaking of the promise as an indication of a kind of indifference on the part of the adulterous spouse. If you really cared about me and my feelings – the spouse might say – you would not have done this to me. And third, and related to the above, the spouse may see the act of sexual intercourse with another as a sign of affection for the other person and as an additional rejection of the nonadulterous spouse as the one who is loved by the adulterous spouse. It is not just that the adulterous spouse does not take the feelings of the spouse sufficiently into account, the adulterous spouse also indicates through the act of adultery affection for someone other than the spouse. I will return to these points later. For the present, it is sufficient to note that a set of arguments can be developed in support of the proposition that certain kinds of adultery are wrong just because they involve the breach of a serious promise which, among other things, leads to the intentional infliction of substantial pain by one spouse upon the other.

Another argument for the immorality of adultery focuses not on the existence of a promise of sexual exclusivity but upon the connection between adultery and deception. According to this argument, adultery involves deception. And because deception is wrong, so is adultery.

Although it is certainly not obviously so, I shall simply assume in this paper that deception is always immoral. Thus, the crucial issue for my purposes is the asserted connection between extramarital sex and deception. Is it plausible to maintain, as this argument does, that adultery always does involve deception and is on that basis to be condemned?

The most obvious person upon whom deceptions might be practiced is the nonparticipating spouse; and the most obvious thing about which the nonparticipating spouse can be deceived is the existence of the adulterous act. One clear case of deception is that of lying. Instead of saying that the afternoon was spent in bed with A, the adulterous spouse asserts that it was spent in the library with B, or on the golf course with C.

There can also be deception even when no lies are told. Suppose, for instance, that a person has sexual intercourse with someone other than his or her spouse and just does not tell the spouse about it. Is that deception? It may not be a case of lying if, for example, the spouse is never asked by the other about the situation. Still, we might say, it is surely deceptive because of the promises that were exchanged at marriage. As we saw earlier, these promises provide a foundation for the reasonable belief that neither spouse will engage in sexual relationships with any other persons. Hence the failure to bring the fact of extramarital sex to the attention of the other spouse deceives that spouse about the present state of the marital relationship.

Adultery, in other words, can involve both active and passive deception. An adulterous spouse may just keep silent or, as is often the fact, the spouse may engage in an increasingly complex way of life devoted to the concealment of the facts from the nonparticipating spouse. Lies, half-truths, clandestine meetings and the like may become a central feature of the adulterous spouse's existence. These are things that can and do happen, and when they do they make the case against adultery an easy one. Still, neither active nor passive deception is inevitably a feature of an extramarital relationship.

It is possible, though, that a more subtle but pervasive kind of deceptiveness is a feature of adultery. It comes about because of the connection in our culture between sexual intimacy and certain feelings of love and affection. The point can be made indirectly at first by seeing that one way in which we can, in our culture, mark off our close friends from our mere acquaintances is through the kinds of intimacies that we are prepared to share with them. I may, for instance, be willing to reveal my very private thoughts and emotions to my closest friends or to my wife, but to no one else. My sharing of these intimate facts about myself is from one perspective a way of making a gift to those who mean the most to me. Revealing these things and sharing them with those who mean the most to me is one means by which I create, maintain and confirm those interpersonal relationships which are of most importance to me.

Now in our culture, it might be claimed, sexual intimacy is one of the chief currencies through which gifts of this sort are exchanged. One way to tell someone – particularly someone of the opposite sex – that you have feelings of affection and love for them is by allowing to them or sharing with them sexual behaviors that one doesn't share with the rest of the world. This way of measuring affection was certainly very much a part of the culture in which I matured. [. . .]

The scale of possible sexual behavior ran from brief, passionless kissing or hand-holding at the one end to sexual intercourse at the other. And the correlation between the two scales was quite precise. As a result, any act of sexual intimacy carried substantial meaning with it, and no act of sexual intimacy was simply a pleasurable set of bodily sensations. Many such acts were, of course, more pleasurable to the participants because they were a way of saying what the participants' feelings were. And sometimes they were less pleasurable for the same reason. The point is, however, that in any event sexual activity was much more than mere bodily enjoyment. It was not like eating a good meal, listening to good music, lying in the sun, or getting a pleasant back rub. It was behavior that meant a great deal concerning one's feelings for persons of the opposite sex in whom one was most interested and with whom one was most involved. It was among the most authoritative ways in which one could communicate to another the nature and degree of one's affection.

If this sketch is even roughly right, then several things become somewhat clearer. To begin with, a possible rationale for many of the rules of conventional sexual morality can be developed. If, for example, sexual intercourse is associated with the kind of affection for and commitment to another that is regarded as characteristic of the marriage relationship, then it is natural that sexual intercourse should be thought properly to take place between persons who are married to each other. And if it is thought that this kind of affection and commitment is only to be found within the marriage relationship, then it is not surprising that sexual intercourse should only be thought to be proper within marriage.

Related to what has just been said, is the idea that sexual intercourse ought to be restricted to those who are married to each other as a means by which to confirm the very special feelings that the spouses have for each other. Because the culture teaches that sexual intercourse means that the strongest of all feelings for each other are shared by the lovers, it is natural that persons who are married to each other should be able to say this to each other in this way. Revealing and confirming verbally that these feelings are present is one thing that helps to sustain the relationship; engaging in sexual intercourse is another.

[. . .]

[G]iven this way of viewing the sexual world, extramarital sex will almost always involve deception of a deeper sort. If the adulterous spouse does not in fact have the appropriate feelings of affection for the extramarital partner, then the adulterous spouse is deceiving that person about the presence of such feelings. If, on the other hand, the adulterous spouse does have the corresponding feelings for the extramarital partner but not toward the nonparticipating spouse, the adulterous spouse is very probably deceiving the nonparticipating spouse about the presence of such feelings toward that spouse. Indeed, it might be argued, whenever there is no longer love between the two persons who are married to each other, there is deception just because being married implies both to the participants and to the world that such a bond exists. Deception is inevitable, the argument might conclude, because the feelings of affection that ought to accompany any act of sexual intercourse can only be held toward one other person at any given time in one's life. And if this is so, then the adulterous spouse always deceives either the partner in adultery or the nonparticipating spouse about the existence of such feelings. Thus extramarital sex involves deception of this sort and is for this reason immoral even if no deception vis-a-vis the occurrence of the act of adultery takes place.

What might be said in response to the foregoing arguments? The first thing that might be said is that the account of the connection between sexual intimacy and feelings of affection is inaccurate. Not inaccurate in the sense that no one thinks of things that way, but in the sense that there is substantially more divergence of opinion than that account suggests. For example, the view I have delineated may describe reasonably accurately the concepts of the sexual world in which I grew up, but it does not capture the sexual Weltanschauung of today's youth at all. Thus, whether or not adultery implies deception in respect to feelings depends very much on the persons who are involved and the way they look at the "meaning" of sexual intimacy.

Secondly, the argument leaves to be answered the question of whether it is desirable for sexual intimacy to carry the sorts of messages described above. For those persons for whom sex does have these implications, there are special feelings and sensibilities that must be taken into account. But it is another question entirely whether any valuable end – moral or otherwise – is served by investing sexual behavior with such significance. That is something that must be shown and not just assumed. It might, for instance, be the case that substantially more good than harm would come from a kind of demystification of sexual behavior; one that would encourage the enjoyment of sex more for its own sake and one that would reject the centrality both of the association of sex with love and of love with only one other person.

I regard these as two of the more difficult, unresolved issues that our culture faces today in respect to thinking sensibly about the attitudes toward sex and love that we should try to develop in ourselves and in our children. Much of the contemporary literature which advocates sexual liberation of one sort or another embraces one or the other of two different views about the relationship between sex and love.

One view holds that sex should be separated from love and affection. To be sure sex is probably better when the partners genuinely like and enjoy each other. But sex is basically an intensive, exciting sensuous activity which can be enjoyed in a variety of suitable settings with a variety of suitable partners. The situation in respect to sexual pleasure is no different from that of the person who knows and appreciates fine food and who can have a very satisfying meal in any number of good restaurants with any number of congenial companions. One question that must be settled here is whether sex can be so demystified; another, more important question is whether it would be desirable to do so. What would we gain and what might we lose if we all lived in a world in which an act of sexual intercourse was no more or less significant or enjoyable than having a delicious meal in a nice setting with a good friend? The answer to this question lies beyond the scope of this paper.

The second view seeks to drive the wedge in a different place. It is not the link between sex and love that needs to be broken, rather, on this view, it is the connection between love and exclusivity that ought to be severed. For a number of the reasons already given, it is desirable, so this argument goes, that sexual intimacy continue to be reserved to and shared with only those for whom one has very great affection. The mistake lies in thinking that any "normal" adult will only have those feelings toward one other adult during his or her lifetime – or even at any time in his or her life. It is the concept of adult love, not ideas about sex, that, on this view, needs demystification. What are thought to be both unrealistic and unfortunate are the notions of exclusivity and possessiveness that attach to the dominant conception of love between adults in our and other cultures. Parents of four, five, six or even ten children can certainly claim and sometimes claim correctly that they love all of their children, that they love them all equally, and that it is simply untrue to their feelings to insist that the numbers involved diminish either the quantity or the quality of their love. If this is an idea that is readily understandable in the case of parents and children, there is no necessary reason why it is an impossible or undesirable ideal in the case of adults. To be sure, there is probably a limit to the number of intimate, "primary" relationships which any person can maintain at any given time without the quality of the relationship being affected. But one adult ought surely be able to love two, three, or even six other adults at any one time without that love being different in kind or degree from that of the traditional, monogamous, lifetime marriage. And as between the individuals in these relationships, whether within a marriage or without, sexual intimacy is fitting and good.

The issues raised by a position such as this one are also surely worth exploring in detail and with care. Is there something to be called "sexual love" which is different from parental love or the nonsexual love of close friends? Is there something about love in general that links it naturally and appropriately with feelings of exclusivity and possession? Or is there something about sexual love, whatever that may be, that makes these feelings especially fitting here? Once again the issues are conceptual, empirical, and normative all at once: What is love? How could it be different? Would it be a good thing or a bad thing if it were different?

Suppose, though, that having delineated these problems we were now to pass them by. Suppose, moreover, we were to be persuaded of the possibility and the desirability of weakening substantially either the links between sex and love or the links between sexual love and exclusivity. Would it not then be the case that adultery could be free from all of the morally objectionable features described so far? To be more specific, let us imagine that a husband and wife have what is today sometimes characterized as an "open marriage." Suppose, that is, that they have agreed in advance that extramarital sex is – under certain circumstances – acceptable behavior for each to engage in. Suppose, that as a result there is no impulse to deceive each other about the occurrence or nature of any such relationships, and that no deception in fact occurs. Suppose, too, that there is no deception in respect to the feelings involved between the adulterous spouse and the extramarital partner. And suppose, finally, that one or the other or both of the spouses then has sexual intercourse in circumstances consistent with these understandings. Under this description, so the agreement might conclude, adultery is simply not immoral. At a minimum, adultery cannot very plausibly be condemned either on the ground that it involves deception or upon the ground that is requires the breaking of a promise.

At least two responses are worth considering. One calls attention to the connection between marriage and adultery; the other looks to more instrumental arguments for the immorality of adultery. Both issues deserve further exploration.

One way to deal with the case of the "open marriage" is to question whether the two persons involved are still properly to be described as being married to each other. Part of the meaning of what it is for two persons to be married to each other, so this argument would go, is to have committed oneself to have sexual relationships only with one's spouse. Of course, it would be added, we know that that commitment is not always honored. We know that persons who are married to each other often do commit adultery. But there is a difference between being willing to make a commitment to marital fidelity, even though one may fail to honor that commitment, and not making the commitment at all. Whatever the relationship may be between the two individuals in the case described above, the absence of any commitment to sexual exclusivity requires the conclusion that their relationship is not a marital one. For a commitment to sexual exclusivity is a necessary although not a sufficient condition for the existence of a marriage.

Although there may be something to this suggestion, as it is stated it is too strong to be acceptable. To begin with, I think it is very doubtful that there are many, if any, *necessary* conditions for marriage; but even if there are, a commitment to sexual exclusivity is not such a condition.

To see that this is so, consider what might be taken to be some of the essential characteristics of a marriage. We might be tempted to propose that the concept of marriage requires the following: a formal ceremony of some sort in which mutual obligations are undertaken between two persons of the opposite sex; the capacity on the part of the persons involved to have sexual intercourse with each other; the willingness to have sexual intercourse only with each other; and feelings of love and affection between the two persons. The problem is that we can imagine relationships that are clearly marital and yet lack one or more of these features. For example, in our own society, it is possible for two persons to be married without going through a formal ceremony, as in the common law marriages recognized in some jurisdictions. It is also possible for two persons to get married even though one or both lacks the capacity to engage in sexual intercourse. Thus, two very elderly persons who have neither the desire nor the ability to have intercourse can, nonetheless, get married, as can persons whose sexual organs have been injured so that intercourse is not possible. And we certainly know of marriages in which love was not present at the time of the marriage, as, for instance, in marriage of state and marriages of convenience.

Counterexamples not satisfying the condition relating to the abstention from extramarital sex are even more easily produced We certainly know of societies and cultures in which polygamy and polyandry are practiced, and we have no difficulty in recognizing these relationships as cases of marriage. It might be objected, though, that these are not counterexamples because they are plural marriages rather than marriages in which sex is permitted with someone other than with one of the persons to whom one is married. But we also know of societies in which it is permissible for married persons to have sexual relationships with persons to whom they were not married, e.g., temple prostitutes, concubines, and homosexual lovers. And even if we knew of no such societies, the conceptual claim would still, I submit, not be well taken. For suppose all of the other indicia of marriage were present: Suppose the two persons were of the opposite sex. Suppose they had the capacity and desire to have intercourse with each other, suppose they participated in a formal ceremony in which they understood themselves voluntarily to be entering into a relationship with each other in which substantial mutual commitments were assumed. If these conditions all were satisfied, we would not be in any doubt as to whether or not the two persons were married even though they had not taken on a commitment of sexual exclusivity and even though they had expressly agreed that extramarital sexual intercourse was a permissible behavior for each to engage in.

A commitment to sexual exclusivity is neither a necessary nor a sufficient condition for the existence of a marriage. It does nonetheless, have this much to do with the nature of marriage: like the other indicia enumerated above, its presence tends to establish the existence of a marriage. Thus, in the absence of a formal ceremony of any sort, an explicit commitment to sexual exclusivity would count in favor of regarding the two persons as married. The conceptual role of the commitment to sexual exclusivity can, perhaps, be brought out through the following example. Suppose we found a tribe which had a practice in which all the other indicia of marriage were present but in which the two parties were *prohibited* ever from having sexual intercourse with each other. Moreover, suppose that sexual intercourse with others was clearly permitted. In such a case we would, I think, reject the idea that the two were married to each other and we would describe their relationship in other terms, e.g. as some kind of formalized, special friendship relation – a kind of heterosexual "blood-brother" bond.

Compare that case with the following. Suppose again that the tribe had a practice in which all of the other indicia of marriage were present, but instead of a prohibition upon sexual intercourse between the persons in the relationship there was no rule at all. Sexual intercourse was permissible with the person with whom one had this ceremonial relationship, but it was no more or less permissible than with a number of other persons to whom one was not so related (for instance all consenting adults of the opposite sex). While we might be in doubt as to whether we ought to describe the persons as married to each other, we would probably conclude that they were married and that they simply were members of a tribe whose views about sex were quite different from our own.

What all of this shows is that a *prohibition* on sexual intercourse between the two persons involved in a relationship is conceptually incompatible with the claim that the two of them are married. The *permissibility* of intramarital sex is a necessary part of the idea of marriage. But no such incompatibility follows simply from the added permissibility of extramarital sex.

These arguments do not, of course, exhaust the arguments for the prohibition upon extramarital sexual relations. The remaining argument that I wish to consider – as I indicated earlier – is a more instrumental one. It seeks to justify the prohibition by virtue of the role that it plays in the development and maintenance of nuclear families. The argument, or set of arguments, might, I believe, go something like this.

Consider first a far-fetched nonsexual example. Suppose a society were organized so that after some suitable age – say 18, 19, or 20 – persons were forbidden to eat anything but bread and water with anyone but their spouse. Persons might still choose in such a society not to get married. Good food just might not be very important to them because they have underdeveloped taste buds. Or good food might be bad for them because there is something wrong with their digestive system. Or good food might be important to them but they might decide that the enjoyment of good food would get in the way of the attainment of other things that were more important. But most persons would, I think, be led to favor marriage in part because they preferred a richer, more varied, diet to one of bread and water. And they might remain married because the family was the only legitimate setting within which good food was obtainable. If it is important to have society organized so that persons will both get married and stay married, such an arrangement would be well-suited to the preservation of the family, and the prohibitions relating to food consumption could be understood as fulfilling that function.

It is obvious that one of the more powerful human desires is the desire for sexual gratification. The desire is a natural one, like hunger and thirst, in the sense that it need not be learned in order to be present within us and operative upon us. But there is in addition much that we do learn about what the act of sexual intercourse is like. Once we experience sexual intercourse ourselves – and in particular once we experience orgasm – we discover that it is among the most intensive, short-term pleasures of the body.

Because this is so, it is easy to see how the prohibition upon extra-marital sex helps to hold marriage together. At least during that period of life when the enjoyment of sexual intercourse is one of the desirable bodily pleasures, persons will wish to enjoy those pleasures. If one consequence of being married is that one is prohibited from having sexual intercourse with anyone but one's spouse, then the spouses in a marriage are in a position to provide an important source of pleasure for each other that is unavailable to them elsewhere in the society.

The point emerges still more clearly if this rule of sexual morality is seen as of a piece with the other rules of sexual morality. When this prohibition is coupled, for example, with the prohibition upon nonmarital sexual intercourse, we are presented with the inducement both to get married and to stay married. For if sexual intercourse is only legitimate within marriage, then persons seeking that gratification which is a feature of sexual intercourse, are furnished explicit social directions for its attainment; namely, marriage.

Nor, to continue the argument, is it necessary to focus exclusively on the bodily enjoyment that is involved. Orgasm may be a significant part of what there is to sexual intercourse, but it is not the whole of it. We need only recall the earlier discussion of the meaning that sexual intimacy has in our own culture to begin to see some of the more intricate ways in which sexual exclusivity may be connected with the establishment and maintenance of marriage as the primary heterosexual, love relationship. Adultery is wrong, in other words, because a prohibition upon extramarital sex is a way to help maintain the institutions of marriage and the nuclear family.

Now I am frankly not sure what we are to say about an argument such as this one. What I am convinced of is that, like the arguments discussed earlier, this one also reveals something of the difficulty and complexity of the issues that are involved. So, what I want now to do – in the brief and final portion of this paper – is to try to delineate with reasonable precision what I take several of the fundamental, unresolved issues to be.

The first is whether this last argument is an argument for the *immorality* of extramarital sexual intercourse. What does seem clear is that there are differences between this argument and the ones considered earlier. The earlier arguments condemned adulterous behavior because it was behavior that involved breaking of a promise, taking unfair advantage, or deceiving another. [. . .]

The argument which connects the prohibition upon extramarital sex with the maintenance and preservation of the institution of marriage is an argument for the instrumental value of the prohibition. To some degree this counts, I think, against regarding all violations of the prohibition as obvious cases of immorality. This is so partly because hypothetical imperatives are less clearly within the domain of morality than are categorical ones, and even more because instrumental prohibitions are within the domain of morality only if the end that they serve or the way that they serve it is itself within the domain of morality.

What this should help us see, I think, is the fact that the argument which connects the prohibition upon adultery with the preservation of marriage is at best seriously incomplete. Before we ought to be convinced by it, we ought to have reasons for believing that marriage is a morally desirable and just social institution. And this is not quite as easy or obvious a task as it may *seem* to be. For the concept of marriage is, as we have seen, both a loosely structured and a complicated one. There may be all sorts of intimate, interpersonal relationships which will resemble but not be identical with the typical marriage relationship presupposed by the traditional sexual morality. There may be a number of distinguishable sexual and loving arrangements which can all legitimately claim to be called *marriages*. The prohibitions of the traditional sexual morality may be effective ways to maintain some marriages and ineffective ways to promote and preserve others. The prohibitions of the traditional sexual morality may make good psychological sense if certain psychological theories are true, and they may be purveyors of immense psychological mischief, if other psychological theories are true. The prohibitions of the traditional sexual morality may seem obviously correct if sexual intimacy carries the meaning that the dominant culture has often ascribed to it, and they may seem equally bizarre when sex is viewed through the perspective of the counter-culture. Irrespective of whether instrumental arguments of this sort are properly deemed moral arguments, they ought not fully convince anyone until questions like these are answered.

20

What's Really Wrong with Adultery?

Michael J. Wreen

Summary

Argues against Wasserstrom that adultery is always at least prima facie immoral, because the very concept of marriage is centrally about commitment and includes the commitment of sexual exclusivity. Any violation of exclusivity counts as a violation of the terms of the concept. In fact, the very concept of adultery itself makes no sense without the prior concept of sexually exclusive marriage. Counterexamples of polygamy, accepted mistresses, and open marriage do not negate this. Polygamy is a type of marriage and still requires sexual exclusivity with spouses. Accepted mistresses may be expected but not publicly applauded and promoted. Open marriages violate the definition of marriage in the first place.

Original publication details: Michael J. Wreen, "What's Really Wrong with Adultery?" pp. 45–49 from *International Journal of Applied Philosophy* 3:2 (1986). Reproduced with permission of Philosophy Documentation Center.

Sexual Ethics: An Anthology, First Edition. Edited by Patrick D. Hopkins.
© 2023 John Wiley & Sons, Inc. Published 2023 by John Wiley & Sons, Inc.

Michael J. Wreen

While philosophers are probably as interested in adultery as everyone else is – and that's pretty interested – philosophical literature on the topic is somewhat scarcer than that on golden mountains or unicorns. To my knowledge, only one paper devoted exclusively to the topic, Richard Wasserstrom's "Is Adultery Immoral?"[1] has appeared in print thus far. In this paper I will argue that, contrary to Wasserstrom's admittedly well-considered views, we do in fact have good grounds for thinking that adultery is *prima facie* wrong.

[. . .]

Wasserstrom argues that although many, many cases of adultery involve promise breaking, deception, or hurting others, not all do, and so none can serve as a reason for thinking that adultery *per se* is immoral. He is undoubtedly correct about this. Indeed, other reasons for thinking that adultery as such is immoral – that it involves a breach in the relations between two individuals respecting sex and feelings of deep affection (love), or love and exclusivity, or that it threatens the development and maintenance of the nuclear family – all fare little better, according to Wasserstrom, since in each case the argument is incomplete. Sex without love may be not only possible but desirable, and so adultery not immoral (the proper place for love being assumed here, for the sake of argument, to be within, and only within, the confines of marriage). Or, sex without love not being possible or desirable, love with more than one person, or more than the permissible number of marital partners, may be both possible and desirable, and so adultery not immoral. And, as for the preservation of the nuclear family: this argument is predicated on the nuclear family's being desirable, but whether it really is such is far from clear.

The reason that I think that adultery is wrong, however, focuses on what adultery itself is. The key concept is *marriage*. Marriage, on my view, is living together (or at least a commitment to do so), plus a commitment to at least occasional sexual intercourse if possible – and if not possible, the fact known to both (or however many) marital partners – plus a commitment to exclusivity as far as sexual intercourse is concerned. This definition allows the newly wedded, elderly couples incapable of sexual intercourse, and those married for convenience's sake all to be married. It captures the common view that marriage is commitment, specifically the commitment to be and love as one, and explains why non-consummation is a legally sufficient ground for annulment. But it is the commitment to sexual exclusivity that is important here.[2]

Let us assume for the present, then, that marriage involves a commitment to exclusivity as far as sexual intercourse is concerned. If so, then there does seem to be something wrong with adultery. For, first, such a commitment is, or at least entails, the adoption of a policy, namely the policy to have sexual congress only with a single, particular person of the opposite sex (the example of standard monogamy being used here for simplicity's sake). And secondly, the concept of adultery is logically parasitic on that of marriage; it is defined in terms of marriage, and adulterous behavior logically impossible in the absence of marriage. Given these facts, and given what adultery is, adultery necessarily involves a contradiction in the will – or, to be more accurate (and Kantian), a contradiction in conception. For marriage involves the adoption of a policy of sexual exclusivity; and adultery, by definition, is a violation of that policy, an attack on one of the conceptual cornerstones of marriage itself. The contradiction consists in adopting policies which cannot be consistently acted upon, or universalized. It is inconsistent to adopt both a policy of sexual exclusivity and a policy of engaging in sexual intercourse with a person not specified in the original policy when, for whatever reason, that seems to be a good idea. [. . .]

It will be noticed that this is a formalistic, Kantian objection to adultery. If a good objection, it holds even if the spouse of an adulterer knows of and condones his/her spouse's adulterous behavior. The fact that they are married is sufficient for such behavior to be wrong. [. . .]

The above argument, however, would seem to apply only to married adulterers; and, us I've noted, not all adulterers are married. What of the non-married person who engages in adultery? Does he/she do anything wrong? I think so; I think the above argument applies at one remove to non-married adulterers, at least in most cases. For *if* such a person accepts the institution of marriage at all, then his/her act of adultery involves a similar contradiction in conception, one between a policy which accepts marriage, and so is committed to honoring the marital commitments of others, and a policy which permits him/her to engage in sexual intercourse whenever such-and-such or so-and-so reasons obtain, regardless of the sexual commitments of his/her partner. The first policy here commits one to respecting marriage commitments; the second allows one to disregard them; and the result is a contradiction in conception similar to that of a married adulterer. But, of course, a non-married adulterer may not accept the institution of marriage at all; it is possible to reject the institution altogether. In that case, then, there would seem to be nothing wrong with adultery as such. Rebels of the above sort, though, are, like Cartesian madmen, more the product of the philosopher's imagination than the stuff of flesh and blood people.

One objection to the above argument is that it depends on a false premise; viz., that a commitment to sexual exclusivity is a necessary condition of marriage. Wasserstrom, for instance, holds that "it is doubtful that there are many, if any, *necessary* conditions for marriage; but even if there are, a commitment to sexual exclusivity is not such a condition" (p. 217). Why? Because "counterexamples not satisfying [such a] condition are . . . easily produced." Societies in which "polygamy and polyandry are practiced" are no such counterexamples, as Wasserstrom himself recognizes, because these are not societies in which "sex is permitted with someone other than one of the persons to whom one is married." Genuine counterexamples do exist, though, according to Wasserstrom: there are societies "in which it is permissible for married persons to have sexual relations with persons to whom they are not married, for example, temple prostitutes, concubines, and homosexual lovers" (p. 217). And secondly, if "all of the other indicia of marriage were present [– if] the two persons were of the opposite sex . . . and had the capacity and desire to have intercourse with each other. . . and participated in a formal ceremony in which they understood themselves to be entering into a relationship with each other in which substantial mutual commitments were assumed [– *then*] we would not be in any doubt as to whether the two person were married, even though they had not taken on a commitment to sexual exclusivity and even though they had agreed that extramarital sexual intercourse was permissible behavior for each to engage in" (pp. 217–218).[3]

Neither of these counterarguments convinces me, however. To take the second one first: I *do* doubt that such a couple is married. From Wasserstrom's description, what I would conclude is that the two people have entered in a public, formalized contractual agreement, one *apparently* regarding sexual intercourse, i.e., that they had agreed to have sexual intercourse with each other, and, apparently, regarding important business matters as well – at least "business matters" is what comes to mind most readily, given that the "substantial mutual commitments" assumed don't include a commitment to sexual exclusivity. Wasserstrom's description, in short, is one of contractual sex plus other mutual services. A formalized, extended prostitute/"John" relationship, one which also included, say, health care in

exchange for extensive home repair, as well as sex for money, satisfies his description, as does any other formalized, sex-plus contractual relationship.

As for societies "in which it is permissible for married persons to have sexual relations with persons to whom they are not married. . .temple prostitutes, concubines, and homosexual lovers" – and, perhaps, geisha girls: in and of itself this does not show that marriage does not involve a commitment to sexual exclusivity in such societies. What it does show is that even if marriage does involve a commitment to sexual exclusivity, such societies permit, and may even promote, to some extent, extramarital sex. In point of fact, in the United States, there exist states in which prostitution is legal – and legal not just for the unmarried. There might be any number of reasons why a society condones or even encourages extramarital sex. Legal moralism might be thought objectionable; there might be laws against adultery, but society might, for whatever reason, "look the other way" whenever violations occur, e.g., violations might be pervasive but not harm the society to any appreciable extent (as Is the case with widespread violations of anti-jay-walking laws in the United States); tax revenues might be needed (as is the case with legalized, state regulated prostitution in Mexico and Nevada); the general populace might be indifferent to the practice of adultery; and so on.

As a matter of fact, there are even sub-sectors of societies in which, for cultural reasons, the practice of "the big house" and "the little house" obtains and is enthusiastically supported by members of those sub-sectors.[4] In some Latin American countries – or at least parts of those countries – a man is not only expected to marry and maintain a "big house" for his wife and legitimate offspring; he is also expected – and virtually socially required – to have at least one mistress and to maintain a "little house," which may include supporting illegitimate offspring. The practice may not be publicly proclaimed and applauded, but it is as obvious to, and as accepted by, everyone in such subsectors as the sky. Indeed, the practice is so deeply entrenched that if a husband does not have a mistress, his wife is likely to badger and insult him until he acquires one – *machismo* is *that* important, and that accepted, a cultural concept in such subsectors. Societies, like people, are complex – far too complex to infer, as Wasserstrom apparently does, that because extramarital sexual intercourse is permitted in some societies, marriage does not involve a commitment to sexual exclusivity in those societies.

[. . .]

Michael J. Wreen

Two other objections to my argument can be more briefly stated and answered. First, it might be objected that there is nothing particularly immoral about conduct which entails a contradiction in conception. Contradictions in conception can arise in relation to purely prudential behavior; hence, the question of whether adultery is immoral remains unanswered. Second, it could be argued that there are many imaginable circumstances in which adultery would seem to be morally permissible or even obligatory (or at least an "ought to engage in adultery" judgment would seem to be true). For example, a married man or woman might be experiencing sexual dysfunction, and the couple might realize that the dysfunctional partner's engaging in sexual intercourse with another would help remedy the dysfunction and, in the long run, strengthen the marriage and make them both happier. Adultery would seem to be at least permissible in such circumstances, if the husband, wife, and third party knowingly and voluntarily agree to its occurrence.

The proper answer to the first of these objections, I think, is that adultery is immoral not just because a contradiction in conception is involved, but because the contradiction essentially includes a social, as well as personal, commitment to a second party. Such relationships are, or at least are close to, the paradigm of moral relationships.

The second objection is adequately answered by noting that if my argument is successful, all that it establishes is the *prima facie* wrongness of adultery. Failure of universalizability seems to me, and to most moral philosophers (but not to Kant, of course), to establish no more than the *prima facie* wrongness of a course of behavior. And *prima facie* wrongness can be overridden in some circumstances, such as, in the case of adultery, those indicated above.

So, as I can think of no other objections to my argument, I conclude that adultery is indeed *prima facie* immoral.

Notes

1 Originally published in Richard Wasserstrom, ed., *Today's Moral Problems* (New York: Macmillan Co., 1975); reprinted in Robert Baker and Frederick Elliston, eds., *Philosophy and Sex* (Buffalo, NY: Prometheus Books. 1975), pp. 207–221. Subsequent references are to *Philosophy and Sex* and are indicated in parentheses.

2 And which I need to, and will, defend below.
3 Virtually the same-argument is offered for a second time on p. 218.
4 I am grateful to David Decker for bringing the facts noted in this paragraph to my attention.

21

Sex Online: Is This Adultery?

Christine Tavella Hall

Summary

Argues that the proliferation of online opportunities to pursue emotional and romantic relationships has led to people suing for divorce on the grounds that romantic and sexually explicit online relationships with non-spouses are a type of adultery. This requires that we reconsider what the law should define as adultery. Prior to "no-fault" divorce laws that appeared after the 1960s, most divorce requests required a specific reason justifying a court's dissolution of the marriage, such as adultery. Even in no-fault states today, however, adultery can be considered in divorce proceedings relating to custody and alimony decisions. Historically, adultery has been characterized as theft, betrayal, and interfering with procreative legitimacy and most legal definitions required that adultery include physical sexual intercourse. The new option of virtual adultery should not lead to our redefining this requirement because virtual adultery does not raise questions of paternity, does not lead to sexually transmitted diseases, is consistent with older rulings that love letters do not constitute adultery, and does not generate the real-world-adultery consequences that would justify the state's involvement.

Original publication details: Christine Tavella Hall, "Sex Online: Is This Adultery?" pp. 201–221 from *Hastings Communications and Entertainment Law Journal* 20 (1997). Reproduced with permission of UC Hastings Law.

Sexual Ethics: An Anthology, First Edition. Edited by Patrick D. Hopkins.

Introduction

With the proliferation of computers during the last decade, a majority of the population has become comfortable with high-technology.[1] Many people use the Internet[2] as a research tool, meeting place, and primary mode of communication.[3] Sending memos, letters, and even personal notes via e-mail has become the norm for many, both in Silicon Valley and beyond.[4] For some, e-mail has even become an avenue for meeting people and pursuing romance. In January of 1996, the cyber-savvy world received a shock, as e-mail romance reached a new plateau in mainstream acceptance: An online affair became the subject of a divorce suit.

What began as an innocent flirtation between Diane Goydan of New Jersey, and a married man from North Carolina,[5] became a passionate online affair conducted in private "chat rooms."[6] Steamy e-mails[7] flew fast and furious between Ray,[8] whose online moniker was "The Weasel," and Mrs. Goydan, a suburban mother of two. Though the two lovebirds never met in person and never had any actual physical contact,[9] the relationship began to permeate their lives. Mrs. Goydan spent hours online and began neglecting her job, family, and marriage. She knew the affair had to end, but her husband caught on to her virtual trysts. John Goydan noticed his wife's increased fascination with America Online ("AOL")[10] and watched their monthly charges steadily increase.[11] Finally, after seeing scraps of messages in the garbage,[12] he took matters into his own hands. Mr. Goydan began monitoring his wife's online conversations with "The Weasel" and starting saving them on his hard drive.[13] After eight months, Mr. Goydan confronted his wife with divorce papers.[14] His grounds for divorce? Adultery.[15]

Did Mr. Goydan have a valid claim? The trial court was not forced to decide this issue.[16] However, his situation grows increasingly pertinent as our society becomes more infatuated with romance online.[17] This technological phenomenon begs the question: How far should the law extend into cyberspace? Examining online infidelity and evaluating its place in the law requires an examination of the legal roots of divorce and, more specifically, adultery.

Looking back to the roots of common law, the advent of the concept of divorce was based in part on the problems which arose when one spouse had sexual relations with someone other than his or her lawful mate.[18] Adultery remained a viable reason for divorce throughout the evolution of the American legal system.[19] Then, with the advent of no-fault divorce in the 1970s and 1980s, many courts abolished the necessity of proving adultery (or any other fault-based grounds) as justification for divorce.[20] However, in recent years, fault-based grounds have had a revival of sorts.[21] In states that never fully codified no-fault divorce,[22] and in other states where legislators are contemplating a return to "family values," fault-based grounds are again gaining popularity.

Should e-mail infidelity be included in modern adultery statutes? Or, in states which continue to employ fault-based divorce, should affairs via e-mail constitute adultery for legal purposes? This note explores the historical roots of these dilemmas in order to analyze this new intersection of technology and marriage. Based on historical criteria, this note concludes that courts are an improper venue for addressing online affairs. Instead, it recommends that this "evolution" in the use of technology remain an issue better left to individuals, their spouses, and perhaps, their online service providers.

Part I of this note explores the history of divorce in the law in order to evaluate online adultery as a valid ground for divorce. This section examines traditional fault-based grounds, their gradual evolution, and partial extinction in divorce law. The recent resurgence in fault-based divorce will be critiqued in light of the support this movement might offer complainants like Mr. Goydan. Part II focuses specifically on adultery as a fault-based justification for divorce. This section will look at the different definitions attached to adultery and the policy reasoning for these distinctions in order to place the Goydans' situation in the proper legal context. This section also examines the increasing importance of emotional connections in modern-day marriages and how this characteristic might lead to changing ideas about adultery. Part III scrutinizes how these age-old doctrines work in conjunction with the tools and toys of cyberspace. By looking at the technologies available and their potential impact on marriages, the temptations which technology provides for the over-worked[23] and under-sexed[24] marital partner can be evaluated. Part IV highlights older divorce cases analogous to the Goydan case. By examining how courts addressed these non-traditional adultery cases, parallels can be drawn to courts' possible treatment of virtual affairs in the future. In conclusion, the careful evaluation of these elements will determine that online affairs, though harmful, and perhaps, even fatal to marriage, are not "adultery" for legal purposes and should not be considered adequate grounds for divorce in a fault-based proceeding.

I. Divorce

Mr. Goydan's complaint sought to take advantage of a highly evolved legal institution: divorce. The basis of this institution predates printing, not to mention computers.[25] The first divorces were granted by the English ecclesiastical courts in the Middle Ages.[26] At that time the two main types of divorce were "absolute divorce" and divorce *a mensa et thoro*.[27] The former allowed parties to remarry, and was granted only in the most extreme circumstances. The latter allowed spouses to live apart, but not to marry again. These types of separations paved the way for modern divorce, but bore little resemblance to its current incarnation.

In the nineteenth century, divorce began to evolve into something similar to current-day divorce.[28] However, a distinction remained between marriages which were void *(void ab initio)* and voidable. Parties to a marriage which was declared void would be allowed an annulment. Thus, they were considered by the church never to have married and were allowed to seek another spouse. Grounds for declaring a marriage void included impotence, bigamy and incest.[29] A voidable marriage afforded the parties less freedom. Parties were not allowed to re-marry and were stigmatized by society.

As the United States began to expand outside the colonies and society became increasingly secularized, divorce began to take a more recognizable form. Though divorce was generally still considered morally questionable by the 1800s, most states had divorce laws which roughly parallel the modern procedure.[30] New Jersey, the Goydans' home state, enacted its first modern divorce law before the turn of the century.[31] The principal distinguishing feature of divorce from this period until the late 1960s was the importance of the proper "grounds" for divorce. In order to be granted a divorce, one spouse had to present a specified reason why the court should dissolve the marriage in question. Appropriate grounds included adultery, cruelty, desertion, willful non-support, criminal conviction, drunkenness, drug-addiction, and insanity.[32] In order for a divorce claim to succeed on any of these arguments, the plaintiff had to provide proof of the alleged fault.[33] The other spouse could then rebut these claims with specified defenses. These defenses included recrimination,

condonation, connivance, and collusion.[34] Without proving one of these grounds and overcoming any defenses presented, a person could not be granted a divorce. However, if one spouse was found to be "at fault," the rights regarding custody, property settlements, and alimony were heavily impacted.[35] These same considerations shaped Mr. Goydan's cause of action.[36]

This resulted in harsh consequences for many women found "at fault," some of whom were ill-equipped to support themselves, and were often shunned by society. Additionally, couples' reticence to air their "dirty laundry" in a trial left many stuck in horrible marriages. For these reasons, and many others, a movement arose in the 1970s and 1980s towards a "no-fault" divorce.[37] This procedure cast aside the traditional requirement of proving some "sin" by a marital partner.[38] Instead, parties made a pleading of "irreconcilable differences"[39] or "irretrievable breakdown."[40] When California first adopted the irreconcilable differences standard in 1969,[41] the initial public outcry was deafening. Politicians, religious and community leaders saw this standard as the beginning of the collapse of the institution of marriage.[42] However, in a slow and painstaking process, other states began to adopt this standard. Today, most states have some form of no-fault divorce.[43]

Mr. Goydan could have based his suit on a no-fault standard;[44] however, he chose fault-based grounds for many of the reasons that still exist in several states.[45] States generally fall into one of three categories in terms of their approach to divorce. The first approach, as seen in states including California, employs a completely fault-free standard. A second approach, as seen in many states,[46] including New Jersey,[47] uses no-fault divorce as one of the grounds for divorce. In these jurisdictions, traditional fault-based grounds of divorce which include adultery, cruelty and desertion can still be alleged.[48] Finally, Missouri takes a distinctive approach to divorce by allowing no-fault divorce only upon mutual agreement of the parties.[49] If no agreement is reached, the fault-based grounds can be used as a basis for divorce.[50] This patchwork of legal theories shows the divergence of thought on the subject of divorce and the grip which fault-based grounds still has in the legal community. For the purposes of this, note, the latter two jurisdictions are of primary interest.

Regardless of the so-called "no-fault revolution,"[51] fault still plays a crucial role in almost all divorce cases in determining custody, property, and maintenance.[52] A spouse found guilty of adultery, cruelty or some other fault, even in a no-fault state, is more likely to pay a higher amount of support and less likely to gain sole custody of any children.[53] These were all considerations cited by Mr. Goydan's attorney as justification for his claim.[54] Critics also argue that the perception that no one party is "at fault" in a divorce may do a disservice to many.[55] Specifically, battered women and parties who have diminished funds[56] due to the other spouse's support of an illicit affair, have been portrayed as deserving a greater share of property.[57] Additionally, many observers feel that the wayward spouse deserves a greater degree of blame. For these reasons, many legal commentators and legislators have argued for the re-enactment of fault-based grounds in divorce cases.[58]

[. . .]

II. Adultery

"Thou shalt not covet thy neighbors' wife."[59] The seventh commandment is viewed by many as the first adultery law.[60] In fact, this biblical decree's emphasis on emotional sin, rather than the physical, could be viewed as support for more esoteric standards for adultery. Mr. Goydan argued that the law should condemn the spirit of adultery, whether via e-mail or hard copy, because of the effect this infidelity had on him emotionally, not because of the physical betrayal.[61] However, this 90s twist on sin does not correspond to any codified secular law since Moses left the Mount.[62]

Early on, adultery was characterized as theft. Prior to the passage of the Married Women's Property Acts during the late nineteenth century,[63] women were considered the "property" of their husbands. Thus, a man who committed adultery was convicted of theft.[64] He was considered to have stolen from the woman's husband.[65] Historically, the law harshly punished the wayward spouse for "lying"[66] with another man's wife.[67] The offender might suffer social ostracism, and in some situations, death.[68]

As divorce became more widespread, adultery had to be defined in more concrete terms. In New York, where adultery was the only grounds for divorce until 1967, the elements of this crime were set-out succinctly as voluntary sexual intercourse of a married person with someone other than their spouse.[69] In most states, in order to prove adultery in a divorce proceeding, the wronged spouse had to show both the opportunity and the disposition to commit this offense. These elements were often proven by "circumstance, implication, or espionage."[70]

Unlike Mr. Goydan's indisputable computer disks, evidence prior to the computer age took murkier forms: hotel registers,[71] testimony of household help, venereal disease,[72] or, in some cases, children who did not resemble their legal father.[73]

In more recent times, divorce statutes commonly specify that adultery required "intercourse." A 1967 legal textbook on the subject specified that adultery must include sexual intercourse:

> 'Sexual intercourse' involves the full and complete meaning of that term. Mere intimacies or 'making out' (as it is currently phrased), 'necking,' or 'petting' (so called in the author's generation) are quite insufficient. There must be physical penetration by the male organ into the female to constitute adultery, even though emission is not necessary.[74]

There are many critics of this literal standard.[75] Christian fundamentalists and legal scholars argue that definitions of adultery should be expanded beyond traditional definitions.[76] Despite these advocates, courts have been slow in extending the legal meaning of adultery. Cases have been spilt as to whether same-sex acts constitute adultery,[77] although the modern trend seems to lean towards abolishment of gender distinctions.

Over the past twenty years, case law has remained divided on whether a coital act is required for a finding of adultery.[78] Some courts follow the British practice of considering non-coital acts adultery.[79] For example, in *Bonura* v. *Bonura,* a Louisiana appellate court found Mrs. Bonura guilty of adultery despite the lack of sexual intercourse.[80] Basing their holding on a broad interpretation of the state's adultery law, the court determined that Mrs. Bonura's kissing, hugging and foreplay constituted adultery, despite the absence of penetration.[81] Despite Mrs. Bonura's contention that sexual intercourse was needed in order to find adultery, the court held, "Louisana law and jurisprudence does not define adultery per se . . . . [Thus] we conclude that adultery, as grounds for divorce . . . is not limited to actual sexual intercourse."[82]

Similarly in *Commonwealth v. Bucaulis,* the term "sexual intercourse" was found to encompass acts of "a variety of sexual conduct," including oral sex.[83] Though *Bucaulis* was not a divorce case, the court's reasoning is applicable to this family law context. Holdings of this sort are seminal to the analysis of online affairs, where traditional sexual intercourse never occurs. However, in the aforementioned cases, there was physical contact of some sort, a fact which distinguishes the purely electronic caresses which Mrs. Goydan exchanged with "The Weasel."

Mr. Goydan and his counsel argued that adultery should not be confined to the physical act, but that infidelity should encompass emotional and technological dalliances as well.[84] This extension of traditional law may reflect the attitudes of many spouses, especially wives.[85] Increased concern with emotional fidelity may be due to the waning of factors which historically stigmatized physical adultery: religious condemnation,[86] and dilution of the inheritance due to "spurious offspring."[87] With the general relaxation of the church's role in society,[88] and the advent of cheap and effective birth control,[89] these factors lack pertinence for many couples.[90]

Conversely, the emotional aspects of marriage have endured throughout time. Some sociologists argue that this aspect of marriage has gained increasing importance in the last few decades.[91] Thus, perhaps, the time has come for the law to prohibit more cerebral violations of the marital relationship. Would this, as Mr. Goydan seems to suggest, include only e-mail liaisons which progressed into physical meetings?[92] Or could a rating system be created to address the level of intimacy in an online chat? How would video, audio, and other types of transmissions affect cases of this sort? In order to consider the implications of expanding divorce law in this way, the technology involved must be understood.

III. Technology

Technology has become such a pervasive force in our society,[93] it is little wonder that spouses who are bored, dissatisfied, or just plain curious about the Internet have turned to their computers as a social outlet.[94] The computer provides a fast, easy, and safe[95] method by which relationships can be built. There are a myriad of options online for people to communicate and interact, some of which might lead to romance, as was the case with Mrs. Goydan.[96] [. . .]

Video conferencing allows people to see and talk with their correspondents whether they are in the next room or the next time zone. Developments in virtual reality allow computers to stimulate physical sensations in surreal environments.[97] High cost and limited availability of technology are probably the biggest reasons why we have not yet seen all these products cited in divorce cases.

All technologies could be used in one way or another to experience a unique relationship. In many ways online relationships mimic "real" affairs. Online interactions can be much more exciting than casual acquaintances.

Users of online technologies cite a lack of inhibition and a feeling of intimacy[98] with their online companions.[99]

Many users feel comfortable discussing topics and feelings which they would be shy about mentioning face-to-face. The lack of physical proximity also makes deceptions easier to conceal.[100] Gender, age and appearance are all fluid variables on the Internet.[101]

Online interactions may also result in some of the same problems brought about by less virtual affairs. Users spend large amounts of time online rather than with their real life spouses.[102] They may spend money on online charges,[103] faster modems and advanced software, which could be spent on their spouse or household. Most importantly, real life spouses may feel ignored or shunned due to their partner's interest in a virtual affair.[104] However, an online affair never raises questions of paternity or causes innocent spouses to be infected with sexually transmitted diseases.

Due to these distinctions, online affairs may not merit legal intervention. Though computer relationships inhabit a gray area of morality and family law, courts do not have a legitimate reason to get involved in this area. Exchanging e-mail does not result in consequences which raise a substantial government interest, despite the hurt feelings of spurned spouses.

IV. Case Studies

Mr. Goydan's charges broke new ground in the area of family law and in the area of technology. Existing case law does not provide a quick or easy answer for any court. In fact, New Jersey's adultery statute has never been used in a case where there was no physical contact.[105] This leads us to examine adultery cases in which the defendant spouse's actions were not "adultery" in the traditional sense. Based on these cases, it seems unlikely that courts would expand the definition of adultery to Mrs. Goydan's affair.

In *Maddox* v. *Maddox*, Alabama's appellate court held that love letters alone do not constitute adultery.[106] In this divorce suit, Mrs. Maddox accused her husband of adultery based on love letters which she found in his briefcase.[107] The husband argued that the trial court's finding of adultery based on the letters was an abuse of discretion.[108] The appellate court held that "[t]he letters do not show any adultery on the part of the husband, or even rise to the level of supplying evidence supporting a finding of adultery."[109] Though the court did not define what might constitute the type of letter that could supply evidence, the opinion is unequivocal. In order to find adultery, the court required something more than love letters to prove the charge.[110]

[. . .]

However, in a recent New Jersey case, the dicta seems to open the door to the possibility for adultery convictions not based on a physical act.[111] In *S.B.* v. *S.J.B.*, the court evaluated the importance of the effects of adultery on the other spouse, regardless of the physical acts undertaken:

> All laws dealing with the termination of a marriage must first be looked at through the eyes of the injured spouse. . . An extramarital relationship viewed from this perspective is just as devastating to the spouse irrespective of the specific sexual act performed by foe promiscuous spouse or foe sex of foe new paramour.[112]

This reasoning begins to open the doors for Mr. Goydan and other unfortunate spouses like him. However, since the case was decided based on the extramarital actual sexual act of the wife coupled with the rejection of the spouse, not her husband's hurt feelings or emotional pain, it does not set a clear precedent.[113]

V. Conclusion

Despite the very real side-effects of online affairs, traditionally the American legal system has based a finding of guilt on actions, not thoughts.[114] A computer user flirting online may be thinking about committing adultery, but that does not meet the legal standard. However, other types of online crimes have been treated as if the same illegal action had been completed outside the virtual realm. Courts have held liable persons found guilty of hacking, defamation, plagiarism, and various other types of fraud perpetrated on the computer. What makes adultery any different? The difference is that with these crimes, courts are not delving into the emotional and sacrosanct realm of family law.

The historical roots of family law do not support "virtual" adultery as grounds for divorce. Though it is important that the law not stagnate, modernizing the law to encompass this type of infidelity would be extending the long arm of the law too far into citizen's private lives.[115] The legislation of morality, though it has been undertaken by courts in the past, is something which should be avoided. The court's intervention in the areas of sexual activity and marriage should be limited only to the most egregious situations. Anything more would contradict our most fundamental notions of liberty.[116]

Online affairs, to a reasonable extent, bear only a fraction of the consequences which accompany actual adultery. Without physical contact, the possibility of an unwanted pregnancy or sexually transmitted disease is impossible. Additionally, the limitations of the computer screen, despite cutting-edge technology, keep online affairs from threatening families and marriages to the extent which a real affair might.[117] Thus, the state does not have a valid interest in condemning this activity.

[. . .]

Notes

1 See Sue Shellenbarger, Work & Family: Growing Web Use Alters the Dynamics of Life at Home, *Wall. St. J.*, Nov. 20, 1996, at B1 [hereinafter Growing Web Use]:
While most adults used home computers primarily as work tools, the rich menu of opportunities the Internet brings into the home is changing all that. Now, many adults tap computers as an avenue to both work and play, spending a growing portion . . . on personal e-mail or just surfing the Web. *Id.*

2 The Internet is a world-wide network of computers and information. "The Internet is not a physical or tangible entity, but rather a giant network which connects innumerable smaller groups of linked computer networks." ACLU v. Reno, 929 F. Supp. 824, 830 (E.D. Pa. 1996).

3 See Pat Craig, A Web of Seduction: Virtual Come-Hithers Can Lead to In-the-flesh Affairs, *Pittsburgh Post-Gazette*, Mar. 12, 1996, at D1 (discussing the 93 million people currently holding e-mail addresses in the United States).

4 "Email is a computer-to-computer version of the postal service that enables users to send and receive messages." SSI Medical Services v. State, 685 A.2d 1, 6 n.1 (N.J. 1995).

5 James Langton, *'We Just Clicked,'* *Sunday Telegraph* (London), Mar. 3, 1996, at 5.

6 Jeffrey Gold, *Explicit E-mail Isn't Adultery Lawyers Say*, Record, Feb. 8, 1996, at A5. For a more detailed description of how "chat rooms" work, see *infra* Part III.

7 The parties exchanged "proxy kisses and erotic fantasies." Craig, *supra* note 3, at D1. One message sent on Christmas Eve described a racy scene, "her stockings were hung/By the chimney with care/ Her bra and his shirt/ were draped from a chair." Andrew Billen, Kiss of the Cyber Woman, *Observer*, Feb. 11, 1996, at 8.

8 Mrs. Goydan's alleged lover's last name was not released to the popular press and Mr. Goydan's complaint referred only to "the Weasel's" online moniker.

9 Brian Sullivan et al., *Digital Dalliance: Online Affair Irks Hubby*, 82 A.B.A.J. 14 (1996) (noting that Ms. Goydan had never met "her alleged paramour," and they had not consummated their "virtual affair"). However, the two did make plans to meet. *See* Donald Munro, It's Adultery; Readers: Cheating is Cheating, Even Online, *Fresno Bee*, Apr. 9, 1996, at E1.

10 Gold, *supra* note 6, at A5. Interestingly, AOL's posted "Rules of the Road" warn members not to "harass, threaten, *embarrass or cause distress*. . . to another member or user of AOL or another person or entity." Margaret Mannix, It's a Jungle Out There, *U.S. News & World Rep.*, Apr. 29,1996, at 73 (emphasis added). However, AOL does not closely regulate what is said in chat rooms. *See* Rebecca Quick, Advertising: AOL Sponsors May Take Hits in Chat Rooms, *Wall St. J.*, Mar. 5,1997, at B6.

11 The two spouses shared a single e-mail account, but had separate passwords. The scenario which led to Mr. Goydan's finding of his wife's "affair," and the evidence which resulted, raises many complex evidentiary issues which will not be addressed in this note.

12 See CNN & Company (CNN television broadcast, Feb. 9, 1996) (Mary Tillson questioning Mr. Goydan's attorney, Richard Hurley).

13 Sullivan, *supra* note 9, at 14 (describing how Mr. Goydan had retrieved several "incriminating" e-mail messages from the hard drive of the couple's computer).

14 Gold, *supra* note 6, at A5.

15 In addition, Mr. Goydan's divorce claim included extreme cruelty. Craig, *supra* note 3, at D1. Mrs. Goydan promptly filed counterclaims of invasion of privacy, breach of New Jersey's wire-tapping laws, defamation of character and extreme cruelty. Gold, *supra* note 6, at A5. Based on a 1991 opinion by the New Jersey Supreme Court, it seems likely that Mrs. Goydan would have prevailed on the wiretapping claim. M.G. v. J.C., 603 A.2d 990, 994–95 (N.J. Super. Ct. 1991) (opening that in an adultery suit where spouses live together," a secretive taping of a spouse's calls . . . is an invasion in the most egregious fashion."). For a more detailed analysis of Mrs. Goydan's privacy interests, see Andru E. Wall, Prying Eyes: The Legal Consequences of Reading Your Spouse's Electronic Mail, 30 *Fam. L.Q.* 743, 744–52 (1996).

16 Eventually, Mr. and Mrs. Goydan reconciled and dropped all charges against one another. *See* Henry Gottlieb, *High Drama, Low Expectations in 1996*, 146 N.J.L.J. 1209,

17 See *Growing Web Use, supra* note 1, at B1 (noting "an Internet poll by Self-Help and Psychology, an online magazine, has drawn more than 100 responses by participants who said they had e-mail affairs").

18 *See* Lawrence Stone, *The Family, Sex and Marriage In England 1500–1800* 33–34 (abr. edn. 1979) (discussing how

divorce came about because of marital break-downs. usually caused by adultery and evolved into a tool used by wealthy men to disentangle themselves from marriages which did not produce a male heir).

19 *See* Lawrence M. Freidman, *A History of American Law* 181–84 (1973).

20 *See* Lynne Carol Halem, *Divorce Reform: Changing Legal and Social Perspectives* 238–39 (1980).

21 *See* Nancy Cleeland, No Fault Divorce on Horizon Again, *Sacrametro*, Jan. 1997, at 13 (discussing how legislative efforts to curb family break-ups is resulting in a trend towards fault-based divorce).

22 *See* Barbara Bennett Woodhouse, Sex, Lies and Dissipation; The Discourse of Fault in a No-Fault Era, 82 *Geo. L.J.* 2525, 2531 (1994) ("Fault is neither as outdated nor as invisible as we have made it seem.").

23 *See* Sue Shellenbarger, Work and Family People Are Working Harder – And Taking More Heat For It, *Wall St. J.*, Feb. 26,1997, at B1.

24 Jerry Adler et al., Sex in the Snoring 90's, *Newsweek*, Apr. 26, 1993, at 54 (discussing the results of recent sex surveys, sociologist Pepper Schwartz is quoted as saying, "[Married] people don't have sex every week; they have good weeks and bad weeks. But they think, '[I] should be having sex more.'").

25 *See* Jeremy D. Weinstein, Adultery, Law, and the State: A History, 38 *Hastings L.J.* 195, 202 (1986) (noting that with the advent of monogamy in modern-day England occurring sometime around 55 B.C. primitive forms of divorce followed soon thereafter).

26 This type of suit was created within the system of Canon Law, a legal system setup in the twelfth, thirteenth and fourteenth centuries by the Romans. This system was centered around courts which based their laws and holding on religious beliefs. These type of courts were separate from English civil courts which handled financial matters. *See generally* Sir Frederic pollack & Frederic William Maitland, *The History of English Law Before the Time of Edward I* (S.F.C. Milsom, ed., reprinted London, 1968) (1898).

27 John C. Sheldon, The Sleepwalker's Tour of Divorce Law, 48 *Me. L. Rev.* 7,22 (1996) (explaining that divorce *a et thoro*, literally "from bed and board," was the preferred form of divorce at the time).

28 The Matrimonial Causes Act, which was passed in Great Britain in 1857, allowed judicial divorce. This Act followed in the footsteps of legislation previously enacted in the United States. *See* Friedman, *supra* note 19, at 181.

29 Weisberg, D. K. and Appleton, S. F. (1998). Modern Family Law: Cases and Materials. Aspen Publishing, Los Angeles CA. (manuscript at ch. 5, p. 25, on file with author).

30 Freidman, *supra* note 19, at 181.

31 All the New England states, New York and Tennessee also had divorce laws on the books. *Id.*

32 Homer H. Clark, Jr., *Law of Domestic Relations* 327–58 (1968).

33 Proof of adultery in fault-based divorce included showing of opportunity and dis-position to commit the offense. This standard will be discussed in more detail in Part II, *infra*. This note will not address adultery as a criminal act

34 Courts found recrimination when both spouses were determined to be at fault. Courts found condonation when one spouse was determined to have forgiven the other for any actions in question. Connivance is defined as the willful participation of one spouse in the other spouse's wrongful conduct Collusion barred a divorce if an agreement was found between spouses who were seeking a divorce. Weisbbrg, *supra* note 29, at ch. 5, pp. 25–34.

35 *See* Fla. Stat. Ann. § 61.08 (West 1985); N.H. Rev. Stat. Ann. § 458:19 (1992).

36 Mr. Goydan sought custody of the couple's two small children and a property settlement.

37 Ira Mark Ellman, The Place of Fault in a Modern Divorce Law, 28 *Ariz. St. L.J.* 773, 774(1996).

38 Barbara Bennett Woodhouse, Property and Alimony in No-Fault Divorce (II), 42 *Am. J. Comp. L.* 175, 175 (1994) (noting that almost all states allow couples to divorce in certain circumstances without a showing of fault).

39 Cal. Fam. Code § 2310 (1996).

40 Unif. Marr. & Div. Act § 305(b)(1), 9A U.L.A. 181 (1987).

41 J. Thomas Oldham, Review Essay, Putting Asunder in the 1990s, 80 *Cal. L. Rev.* 1091 (1992). The next important step for the adoption of no-fault occurred in 1970, with the approval of sections 307 and 308 of the Uniform Marriage and Divorce Act. *See* Unif. Marr. & Div. Act §§ 307, 308, 9A U.L.A. 147 (1987). These sections specify that divorce shall be granted, and property divided, without a finding of fault.

42 Weisberg, *supra* note 29, at ch. 5, pp. 35–36.

43 Sheldon, *supra* note 27, at 13 (noting Maine's adoption of no-fault divorce, in 1973). *See also* Me. Rev. Stat. Ann. tit 19, § 691 (West 1996)

44 N.J. Stat. Ann. § 2A:34-2 (West 1996).

45 *See* Woodhouse, *supra* note 38, at 175.

46 *See, e.g.,* N.Y. Dom. Rel. Law § 170 (McKinney 1988); N.H. Rev. Stat. Ann. § 458:7 (1996).

47 N.J. Stat. Ann. § 2A;34-2 (West 1996). The statute does not define the term "adultery."

48 Woodhouse, *supra* note 22, at 2532 (labeling these jurisdictions as "hedged no-fault" systems).

49 Mo. Rev. Stat. § 452.320 (1996)

50 *Id.*

51 *See generally* Herbert Jacob, *Silent Revolution: The Transformation of Divorce Law in the United States* (1988).

52 *See* Jana B. Singer, Alimony and Efficiency: The Gendered Costs and Benefits of the Economic Justification for Alimony, 82 *Geo. L. J.* 2423,2425 (1994) (Asserting that maintenance, also known as "spousal support" or more traditionally as "alimony," became more problematic with the advent of no-fault divorce). See *also* Woodhouse, *supra* note 22, at 2528 ("Although fault plays a diminishing role

in the right to exit an unhappy marriage, it still figures significantly in the economics of marriage dissolution.").

53 *See generally* Woodhouse, *supra* note 22.

54 Craig, *supra* note 3, at D1.

55 Lenore J. Weitzman, The Economics of Divorce: Social and Economic Consequences of Property, Alimony and Child Support Awards, 28 *UCLA L. Rev.* 1181, 1249–50 (1981) (documenting the economic effects of no-fault divorce on women and children).

56 Woodhouse, *supra* note 22, at 2529–30.

57 Weisberg, *supra* note 29, at ch. 5, pp. 52–60.

58 *Cf.* Oldham, *supra* note 41, at 1096.

59 *Exodus* 20:17. A biblical definition of "Adultery" is "the lying with the wife of another man." *Deuteronomy* 22:22. Support for the premise that the Bible condemns emotional as well as physical adultery is seen in *Matthew* 5:28, "everyone who looks at a woman lustfully has already committed adultery. …." Craig, *supra* note 3, at Dl.

60 This premise may be incorrect, since evidence exists that early adultery laws were based on Ancient Roman laws of theft, which may have been meant to encompass this act Weinstein, *supra* note 25, at 199–200.

61 Mr. Goydan also made a claim of extreme cruelty based upon his wife's "affair." Gold, *supra* note 6, at A5.

62 Referring to the biblical story of Moses's presentation of the Ten Commandments. Weinstein, *supra* note 25, at 207 (discussing how prior to the spread of Christianity in England, during the eighth and ninth centuries, adultery was considered a "wrong against the husband.").

63 Weisberg, *supra* note 29, at ch. 3, p. 20.

64 This concept has its roots in Roman Law. Weinstein, *supra* note 25, at 238. It has since been completely abolished because of the modern idea articulated by one court in the following manner, "spousal love is not property subject to theft," Fundermann v. Mickelson, 304 N.W.2d 790, 794 (Iowa 1981).

65 This might also help to explain why early divorce laws in England specified that the third party also be married, in order for adultery to have been committed. Michael E. Mayer, *Divorce and Annulment in the Fifty States* 4 (1967).

66 *See* Linda E. Speth & Alison Duncan Hirsch, *Women, Family, And Community In Colonial America: Two Perspectives* 57 (1983) (describing the proceedings in an adultery-based divorce case in Connecticut in 1735).

67 The double-standard which pervaded much of the law surrounding adultery from Roman times on will not be addressed in detail. For more on this subject, see Annette Lawson, *An Analysis of Love and Betrayal* 41–43 (1988) (tracing bias against women in adultery laws from ancient times).

68 *See* Stone, *supra* note 18, at 396 (explaining the Puritan's cruel treatment of adulteresses).

69 N.Y. Dom. Rel. Law §170 (McKinney 1967).

70 MAYER, *supra* note 65, at 6.

71 *See* Lickle v. Lickle, 52 A.2d 910, 911–12 (Md. 1947) (holding maid's testimony and hotel registration on trips as providing clear and convincing evidence of adultery).

72   *See* Joel Prentiss Bishop, *Commentaries on the Law of Divorce* § 632 (Vol. 11) (6th edn. 1881).

73   *See* Richard H. Chused, *Private Acts in Public Places: A Social History of Divorce in the Formative Era of American Family Law* 29 (1994) (noting cases of the birth of mixed-race children to white women as prompting divorce in slave-owning households).

74   Mayer, *supra* note 65, at 5.

75   *See* Michael J. Wreen, What's Really Wrong with Adultery, in *The Philosophy of Sex* 59 (Alan Soble, ed., 2d edn. 1991).

76   *See* Munro, *supra* note 9, at El (discussing opinions of religious personnel and other community members).

77   *Compare* Owens v. Owens, 274 S.E.2d 484 (Ga. 1981), *with* Cohen v. Cohen, 103 N.Y.S.2d 426 (Sup. Ct. 1951).

78   Weisberg, *supra* note 29, at ch. 5, p. 11.

79   *Id. See Rayden On Divorce* 182, 23, n.(b) (6th edn. 1953). *Cf.* Cundy v. Cundy, 1 W.L.R. 207 (1956) (holding that a flirtation and kissing was not sufficient to revive case of adultery).

80   505 So.2d 143,144 (La. Ct. App. 1987).

81   *Id.*

82   *Id.*

83   373 N.E.2d 221,226 (Mass. App. a 1978).

84   Langton, *supra* note 5, at 5 (quoting Richard Hurley, Mr. Goydan's lawyer, "I know how the dictionary defines adultery, but technology has a way of changing definitions.").

85   In a study by psychologist David Buss, 45% of women surveyed said that emotional betrayal was more upsetting than sexual betrayal, as opposed to 30% of men. Sharon Begley, Infidelity and the Science of Cheating, *Newsweek*, Dec. 30,1996, at 56.

86   See Weinstein, *supra* note 25, at 218.

87   *See* Lawson, *supra* note 67, at 41–49 (discussing the Western European custom of patrilineal inheritance as contributing to legal concerns that any children born were the biological offspring of their mother's husband, and thus, were deserving of property).

88   *Cf.* Richard Grenier, The America You Don't Know, *Wash. Times*, Oct. 31, 1995, at A19.

89   Diane Greigo Erwin, Isn't Cost of Birth Control Cheaper than Alternative, *Sacramento Bee*, June 1,1995, at A2.

90   Despite the diminished role of the church in American society in general, many religious advocates are vocal in their disapproval of adultery, both physical and emotional. *See, e.g.,* Munro, *supra* note 9, at El (quoting Russell Willingham of New Christian Ministries).

91   *See* Ernest Watson Burgess & Harvey James Locke, *The Family: From Institution to Companionship* (1953) (arguing that marriages have grown more "companionate" over time). *See also* Theodore Caplow et al., *The Quality of Marriage in Middletown: 1924–1976, The Family in Transition: Rethinking Marriage, Sexuality, Child Rearing and Family Reorganization* 330–345 (Arlene Skolnick & Jerome Skolnick, eds., 4th edn. 1983).

92   Langton, *supra* note 5, at 3 (Mr. Goydan's lawyer explains, "we know that in the course of transmissions, they would go into private rooms; we can only assume the next step.").

93   Edward Wenk, Jr., Techno-sin – With Every Scientific Advance Comes the Temptation of Sin, *Seattle Times*, Mar. 10,1996, at B5 (arguing that with the development and increased use of technology there are negative effects, like child pornography on the Internet or hacker sabotage, which if left unchecked will supersede technology's positive impacts).

94   Sherry Turkle, *Life on the Screen: Identity in the Age of the Internet* 9 (1995) ("the computer offers us. . . . a new medium on which to project our ideas and fantasies.").

95   *Id.* AT 240, 244 (noting that virtual sex is a safe alternative to the real thing, and may provide a sexual alternative in an era plagued by sexually-transmitted diseases).

96   *Id.* AT 21 (a variety of virtual worlds "from MUDs to computer bulletin boards allow people to generate experiences, relationships. . . that arise only through interaction with technology.").

97   In 1994, a San Francisco couple used this technology in the world's first "virtual reality wedding." Bob Macintyre, *Couple Transported to Virtual Matrimony*, THE TIMES (London), Aug. 22, 1994. This event seems to suggest that virtual reality affairs can't be far behind; however, the difference being that the marriage was legal because it was supplemented by a traditional marriage license and solemnization.

98   Mr. Goydan's lawyer stated that, "computer networks like AOL and the Internet allow people to communicate so intimately that they can develop passionate relationships with people they've never met face to face." *All Things Considered* (NPR radio broadcast, Feb. 12,1996).

99   Samantha Miller & Sherry Turkle, *Net Worth: MIT's Sherry Turkle Says the Virtual World Can Improve Real Life*, People, Apr. 1,1996, at 95.

100 Turkle, *supra* note 94, at 210–11.

101 *See* Richard Barry, High Cost of Loving: Star-crossed or Wires-crossed? Richard Barry On Love in Cyberspace, *The Guardian* (London), Nov. 21,1996, at 12 ("a spotty 18-year-old schoolboy can become a musclebound hunk from Baywatch.").

102 *See* Dan Parks, *Growing Obsession: Internet Has Hold on Many, One Woman Left Spouse Over On-line Romance*, Milwaukee J. Sentinel, Apr. 22,1996 at 1 (describing "Internet Addiction" as a documented sickness which is characterized by spending excessive amounts of time on the Internet and often leads to divorce).

103 Monthly charges for obsessive users can run into hundreds of dollars.

104 Shellenbarger, *supra* note 1, at Bl.

105 *All Things Considered, supra* note 98.

Christine Tavella Hall

106 553 So. 2d 611 (Ala. Civ. App. 1989).

107 *Id.* at 612.

108 *Id.*

109 *Id.*

110 *Id.* ("Proof to support the charge of adultery must be such as to create more than a suspicion. It must be sufficiently strong to lead the guarded discretion of a reasonable and just mind to the conclusion of adultery as a necessary inference.") *See also* Boldon v. Boldon, 354 So. 2d 275, 276 (Ala. Civ. App. 1978).

111 S3, v. S.J.B., 609 A.2d 124, 126 (N.J. Super. 1992).

112 *Id.*

113 In *S.B.* v. *S.J.B.*, the court held that the crux of adultery under the law was the physical act. The court decided that the homosexual affair of the wife was adultery within the meaning of New Jersey's divorce statute. After tracing the roots of the meaning of adultery from biblical times, the court determined that homosexual activity constituted "carnal knowledge" and thus, adultery. In citing to both the criminal definition of "sexual penetration" and divorce cases where oral sex constituted adultery, the court based its holding on the existence of physical sexual contact between the accused spouse and her lover. *Id.* at 125–27.

114 *See generally* Jon R. Waltz & Roger C. Park, Evidence: Cases & Materials (8th edn. 1995). Cf. Susan Weiner, On-line Love Affair is Virtual Unreality, *Chi. Trib.*, Mar. 10, 1996, at 8 (Womannews) ("law in general holds us responsible for intent.").

115 *See* Griswold v. Connecticut, 381 U.S. 479, 486 (1965) (highlighting the "privacy surrounding the marriage relationship.").

116 *See* Palko v. Connecticut, 302 U.S. 319, 325–26 (noting rights "Implicit in the concept of ordered liberty," which if sacrificed "neither liberty nor justice would exist").

117 In a few bizarre cases; however, e-mail affairs have inflamed spouses to the point of violence. *See* Dan Parks, Growing Obsession, *Milwaukee J. Sentinel*, Apr. 22, 1996, at 1 (reporting battery charge against husband who attacked wife due to online affair); Tim Standage, Connected: Putting Your Life Online – It's the Same Old Love Story, *Daily Telegraph*, Feb. 11, 1997, at 4 (reporting woman stabbed to death by husband because she exchanged e-mails with a radio talk show host).

22

Virtual Adultery: No Physical Harm, No Foul?

Kathryn Pfeiffer

Summary

Argues that virtual infidelity is increasingly cited as a cause for ending marriage although most states only recognize physical infidelity as a fault-based ground for divorce. However, virtual affairs should count as real adultery because they enact the most important aspect of adultery – a destabilizing emotional intimacy with a person outside the marriage. As such, virtual adultery should be included in the legally actionable conduct relevant for fault-based divorce. The best way to do this would be to grant courts discretionary oversight for case-by-case analysis rather than trying to develop bright-line legal definitions.

Original publication details: Kathryn Pfeiffer, "Virtual Adultery: No Physical Harm, No Foul?" pp. 667–690 from *University of Richmond Law Review* 46 (2012). Reproduced with permission of University of Richmond.

[...]

I. Introduction

In 2007, Ric Hoogestraat's picture-perfect marriage to his partner, Tenaj – which included a house with a mortgage, pets, and pastimes such as riding together on his motorcycle – earned notoriety precisely for the normalcy it exemplified.[1] Their relationship, in fact, was anything but normal – because Tenaj was Ric's virtual wife whom he met and interacted with daily through a computer game – and Ric's *real* marriage was suffering.[2] His actual wife, Sue Hoogestraat, felt "widowed" by her husband's virtual life and did not expect him to return to her soon: "This other life is so wonderful; it's better than real life. Nobody gets fat, nobody gets gray. The person that's left can't compete with that."[3] Although this type of behavior affects the marital relationship, the law does not consider it actionable conduct. With so much socially driven media available, however, it is difficult to draw a bright line between reality and fantasy. For example, an ABC News survey conducted in 2004 found that forty-two percent of women and twenty-five percent of men considered visiting websites with sexual content to be cheating.[4] These findings covered only passive Internet sites – they did not include interactive sites in which a spouse engaged with a third person, like Ric and Tenaj.[5]

While the traditional definition of adultery describes the physical infidelity of a spouse,[6] new forms of social media and virtual communication are shaping the way relationships (including extramarital physical and non-physical relationships) are conducted. More communication takes place outside the confines of the marriage – even if still within the home.[7] New norms of interaction, such as the workplace relationship, are also becoming a source of significant extramarital communication.[8] These trends raise new questions about the meaning of adultery.

There is a long tradition of protecting marriage by deterring behavior that could impair the marital relationship. Adultery constitutes the classic erosion of trust in a marriage – it "entails lying, the breaking of promises, and the infliction of emotional pain."[9] "Virtual affairs" are emerging as a recognizable subset of infidelity, grounded in the idea that a nonphysical extramarital relationship can produce the same emotional intimacy of a sexual affair and cause the same type of harm to a marriage.[10] Commentators use the term "virtual infidelity" to describe nonphysical behavior that adopts one or more aspects of a romantic relationship and consequently creates a disconnect in the marriage.[11] Although virtual infidelity is a fairly new topic of legal discourse and has thus far earned more recognition as a cultural phenomenon than a legal claim,[12] it raises familiar policy questions about protecting the intimacy of the marital unit and insulating it from impairment.[13]

This comment considers whether virtual adultery should constitute actionable conduct in civil divorce litigation and proceeds in three parts. Following this introduction, Part II discusses the historical roots of adultery as a fault ground for divorce and its perpetuation of gender disparities. It then analyzes the application of adultery in the wake of no-fault divorce, including its emerging influence on civil divorce judgments. Part III discusses the intersection of social media and infidelity, evaluating the rise of emotional intimacy as an alternative to the traditional requirement of physical intimacy in the context of adultery. Part IV considers how the law should approach virtual infidelity as a potential subset of adultery.

Ultimately, Part IV seeks to contribute to the discussion of whether the definition of adultery should extend to virtual infidelity, and if so, what approaches might be used to identify virtual adultery. It evaluates the harms caused by traditional adultery in comparison to the emergence of virtual infidelity, and asks whether their mutual roots in emotional intimacy merit similar remedial schemes. Ultimately, it suggests incorporating virtual infidelity into existing statutory fault considerations and deferring to judicial discretion to determine its weight on a case-by-case basis.

II. Application of Adultery as a Fault Ground

A. Evolution of Fault-Based Divorce

Divorce law in the United States largely derives from evolving models of marital dissolution in Europe.[14] The advent of Christianity, particularly Roman Catholicism, began to shape divorce legislation in third-century Europe.[15] The underpinnings of fault were evident in Emperor Constantine's constitution, which created gender-specific standards for dissolution: "The husband had the right to divorce his wife if she were an adulteress, a poisoner or a conspirator. The wife could divorce her husband if he were a murderer, a prisoner or a violator of graves."[16] This legislation sought a middle ground between the absolute prohibition of divorce desired by emerging Christian sects and the policy interest in providing at least some avenue for dissolution, no matter how narrow.[17]

The United States looked to models of fault-based divorce in establishing its own approach to marital dissolution.[18] From the seventeenth through the nineteenth centuries, the states uniformly prohibited a spouse from obtaining a divorce in the absence of a legally recognized fault ground.[19] Available fault grounds generally included adultery, desertion, impotence, fraudulent contract, consanguinity, and bigamy.[20] Some jurisdictions also recognized cruelty, insanity, criminal behavior, and repeated substance abuse.[21] Although fault is no longer a prerequisite to divorce, many states still allow spouses to pursue a fault-based alternative and weigh fault as an important factor in allocating property and spousal support.[22]

B. Historical Application of Adultery as a Fault Ground

[. . .]

States' efforts to deter adultery historically involved assigning varying degrees of criminality to adulterous acts.[23] Although criminal statutes did little to discourage the actual practice of adultery, they have not only endured but also encountered little resistance.[24] Legislators have resisted dismantling statutes that regulate consensual intimacy because the principles driving them have persevered despite the behavior having flourished.[25] States have also identified policy interests for retaining criminal adultery statutes, namely preserving social morality and providing faithful spouses with legal recourse.[26] However, few modern courts prosecute adultery in a criminal context, preferring instead to address it in the realm of civil law disputes.[27]

Though criminal adultery bans were rooted in protecting a husband's property interest in his wife – and enforcement of criminal bans has largely disappeared – contemporary rationales exist for punishing adultery in civil divorce actions.[28] Courts have identified an important policy interest in protecting the marital unit from infidelity.[29] According to one commentator, "extramarital intercourse often violates important promises, results in lies and deception, inflicts emotional pain, and can terminate or severely disrupt a marriage."[30] One such disruption is the risk posed by physical infidelity of sexually transmitted disease or procreation.[31] Courts have also suggested that adulterous behavior can affect the welfare of children produced by the marriage because it endangers their "development and ability to experience a healthy, happy life."[32] To the extent that a court believes a child's best interests have been threatened, it may

factor adultery into its consideration of child custody as well as property and support awards.[33]

C. Modern Application of Adultery

Although adultery often represents the classic fault ground for divorce, the burden of proving it may have impaired its effectiveness as a remedy for the harm it causes. As a baseline requirement, states define adultery as sexual intercourse taking place between a married person and an unmarried or married third party, with some states recognizing lesser degrees of sexual contact described in their respective statutes.[34] Most courts require proof of adultery by clear and convincing evidence,[35] and though parties may bring in circumstantial evidence,[36] many litigants are deterred from initiating adultery claims by the level of intrusion necessary to gather evidence against their spouses.[37]

With the emergence of no-fault divorce, the role of adultery in civil divorce litigation has arguably been displaced, but not replaced. Even in no-fault divorce proceedings, many state statutes allow courts to factor adultery into determinations of property distributions and spousal support, and some states even require courts to do so.[38] Thus, while evidence of adultery – or a comparable statutory fault ground – is not required in order to obtain no-fault divorce, it may influence the allocation of assets to the divorcing parties and child custody.[39] Although courts have declined to penalize a spouse's adultery by denying custody, they have acknowledged that adulterous conduct may raise "moral fitness" concerns, which are important in determining whether a spouse can effectively parent his or her child.[40] As such, adultery may serve an indirect punitive function in custody rulings.

III. Intersection of Social Media and Infidelity

A. The Expanding Scope of Infidelity

The degree of physical infidelity required to constitute adultery has proved to be malleable depending on the court and the applicable statute. Some jurisdictions recognize that extramarital sexual acts other than intercourse may qualify as adultery.[41] Others have determined that same-sex affairs constitute adultery sufficient to bar the award of alimony.[42] One court has even held that for the purpose of adultery determinations, the appearance of infidelity outweighs any likelihood that no physical act occurred.[43] That court gave equal consideration to the manifestation of infidelity and the physical consummation of the affair, essentially giving weight to the effect of the wife's infidelity on the faithful husband rather than simply to the adulterous act itself.[44]

The notion of "virtual adultery," which also lacks a physical consummation, emerged in large part because of its ability to cause similar harms to the emotional component of the marriage. Professor Brenda Cossman suggests that the "violation of the promise of emotional and sexual exclusivity" resulting from the physical infidelity is the true harm to marriage, not the infidelity itself.[45] If the main harm is the broken verbal promise of monogamy – not the physical act – then adultery might describe any situation wherein a spouse contravenes the "emotional exclusivity" of the marriage.[46] The underpinnings of virtual adultery lie in what Cossman labels the "new infidelity," whereby increasing social outlets have created the opportunity to change how relationships are conducted.[47] The primary feature of this new infidelity, according to Cossman, is that it lacks any static definition.[48] It is used to describe extramarital relationships both in terms of *where* cheating occurs – in the workplace and online, for instance – and *what* behavior constitutes cheating.[49] For instance, this new infidelity can describe both a sexual romance in the office and an "emotional affair" with a colleague.[50] Rather than pinpoint a single way to cheat, the new infidelity describes how emerging social media have enabled spouses to intimately interact with others without straying physically.

Commentators point to the advantages of an intimacy that satisfies the same emotional cravings of an affair but without the same risks traditionally posed by adultery. Because health and reproductive issues are not at stake in the context of nonphysical affairs, Cossman suggests that the new focus becomes the emotional aspect of these relationships.[51] A 2004 ABC News survey showed that of the sixteen percent of adults polled who admitted to infidelity, thirty-three percent primarily wanted to satisfy an emotional void whereas forty-five percent did so purely for the physical affair.[52] Particularly in cases of online relationships, spouses can fashion the emotional affair they want without worrying about the risks of a physical affair.

Nonphysical affairs may also seem less harmful to the emotional stability of the marriage. According to psychiatrist Gail Saltz, "[w]e've all grown so used to watching, reading, and hearing sexually suggestive material that there's no longer an obvious verbal or physical line we think we're crossing."[53] Saltz posits that emotional

infidelity has flourished because "[p]eople enmeshed in nonsexual affairs preserve their deniability" and therefore suffer fewer feelings of culpability.[54] However, a variety of social commentary suggests that spouses often consider emotional affairs just as damaging – if not more so – than sexual infidelity.[55] Perhaps this is because the emotional affair intrudes most heavily on the communication aspect of marriage. Peggy Vaughan reasons that "[m]ost people . . . can recover from sexual infidelity more readily than from the fact that they were lied to."[56] *Psychology Today's* Michael J. Formica describes emotional infidelity as "any situation that creates or causes some degree of emotional unavailability on the part of one partner that interferes with one particular aspect of the relationship, along with the quality of the relationship as a whole."[57] Despite "harmless" shared commonalities, emotional infidelity can develop when the majority of personal communication occurs with someone outside of the marriage, especially if the tenor of the communication tends to be aspirational rather than practical.[58]

Ironically, one of the consequences of the expanding scope of infidelity – beyond increased opportunities to cheat – may be that spouses are unintentionally unfaithful. For a spouse who subscribes to the traditional definition of adultery, an extramarital relationship that lacks a physical component is not an affair all. [. . .]

B. The Role of Social Media in Facilitating Virtual Infidelity

The prevalence of existing social media, such as workplace relationships and newer Internet-based vehicles of communication, has facilitated interactions outside of the marriage and provided additional fora for virtual infidelity.[59] Infidelity in both types of social environments struggles to gain legitimacy as a legal claim because, while spouses treat the intimacy in their interactions as authentic, they simultaneously downplay their extramarital relationships as either fictional or merely collegial.[60] However, a CBS News survey found that, as early as 2009, virtual infidelity was the catalyst for one-third of divorces.[61] This suggests that emotionally faithful spouses hardly view online dalliances and office intimacy as harmless interactions.

The breadth of available social media – e-mail, the workplace, and virtual worlds to name a few – has given spouses the autonomy to build extramarital relationships on their own terms. Internet users' ability to dictate the tone, subject matter, and privacy level of their online conversations allows them to also control what features they reveal about themselves and to divulge information relatively free of consequences.[62] Christina Tavella Hall suggests that "[t]echnologies abound which make interacting with others online as enticing as meeting them in real life, or more so . . .. All these technologies could be used in one way or another to experience a unique relationship."[63] Some Internet games, for example, fabricate entire worlds wherein users create avatars of themselves and intermingle with other avatars.[64] In effect, these manufactured figures add an extra layer of separation between the computer user and his or her online actions. Yet from the nonparticipating spouse's perspective, virtual characters can seem less like a separate entity and more like an extension of the computer user. According to one spouse who met her husband in a virtual game world and subsequently found him "cuddling" with another avatar, the online persona's actions manifested the husband's impulse to cheat.[65] Psychologist David Greenfield suggests that more than simply enabling cheaters to cheat, the myriad opportunities for online infidelity have actually *induced* spouses to cheat.[66] For example, a Fox News survey suggested Facebook has made it possible for spouses to reunite with acquaintances – even former partners – in a casual setting.[67] Greenfield cites the opportunity to put oneself in a dating situation without the same risks as a face-to-face encounter as an attractive scenario, and suggests that spouses who would never attempt a physical affair might more comfortably try out an online affair.[68]

[. . .]

C. *Crossing Over to Realism: Effects of an Online Affair on Two Marriages*

This section compares two marriages that suffered the effects of an online affair. In both circumstances, the husband initiated a virtual relationship via a computer game and never met the woman on the other end of the computer. Their wives' reactions to the affair differed drastically, however. These comparisons illustrate how the meaning of a virtual relationship can vary considerably between spouses.

In 2007, the *Wall Street Journal* observed Sue and Ric Hoogestraat's marriage through the lens of Ric's attachment to a virtual-world computer game.[69] The game, aptly named Second Life, provides users with their own avatars as well as various accessories and real estate available for purchase with U.S. dollars.[70] Married less than one year, Ric began spending anywhere from six to

fourteen hours a day on Second Life, depending on his work schedule.[71] Sue, who declined to join him in the computerized world, was shocked to discover one day that he had acquired not only a virtual business and three-story house, but also a virtual wife.[72] Although neither avatar's human incarnation expressed a desire to the other to rendezvous in real life, Sue nonetheless felt betrayed.[73] Rather than eat meals or leave the house, Ric would log on to Second Life, where he would meet up with his avatar wife almost immediately.[74] The two avatars would then greet friends (avatars controlled by other users) and engage in virtual-world daily activities.[75] Back in the couple's home, Sue projected that her husband might spend years reenacting his youth on the computer while his actual life – and marriage – slipped away.[76]

In 2009, Second Life had an even more drastic effect on the marriage of a couple in England. According to Amy Taylor her husband's feelings for his avatar companion replaced those he felt for her.[77] Taylor had also joined Second Life, where the two held themselves out as a couple, and she "caught" her husband's avatar being unfaithful on at least two occasions.[78] Although Taylor considered leaving her husband for his virtual infidelity she suggested it was he who eventually ended the marriage by confessing that he was in love with another avatar.[79] Eventually, his profile indicated he had become engaged once more through the online game.[80]

These two scenes demonstrate important contrasts in the meaning of an online affair to the Internet user, the appearance of the relationship to the Internet user's spouse, and the potential for the new relationship to erode the marriage. In the first scenario, Ric insisted his online affair was simply a game and refused to accept that it had become an intrusion on his marriage, both to his physical relationship and to the emotional intimacy that he and his wife formerly shared.[81] The notion that he was committing infidelity was demonstrated more by the time he committed to his virtual partner – and diverted from his actual partner – than by an emotional connection with the woman controlling the avatar. Taylor's husband, on the other hand, seemed to merge his virtual identity with his existing social relationships, making it possible for a new virtual partner to displace a concrete marriage. His example illustrates that the meaning a spouse attributes to an online relationship may be an important gauge of its impact on the marriage.

As indicated by Sue and Taylor, a spouse's reaction to the other's online affair might vary depending on the depth of the virtual relationship.[82] Even though Ric's online gaming created a barrier to his marital relationship, he viewed the game almost as a building project.[83] Taylor's husband, on the other hand, allegedly treated the game as an alternate life. Because Taylor had joined Second Life as well, she interacted with her husband's dual personas and was therefore able to experience his virtual infidelity firsthand.[84] Although Ric did not cultivate new emotional connections, his absence from the marriage nevertheless deprived his wife of the emotional intimacy they formerly shared.

[. . .]

IV. Approaches to Recognizing Virtual Adultery

The contemporary policy justifications for adultery statutes – namely of insulating the marital unit and protecting family life – support the continued application of adultery to civil divorce judgments. Courts grant fault-based divorces, and/or make unfavorable spousal support and property awards on the basis of adultery in order to discourage this type of conduct and uphold established policy goals. Because virtual infidelity has begun to create similar harm to marriage – and trigger the same policy concerns – the current definition of adultery may not serve the interests it was designed to protect. Having discussed the similarity of harms virtual infidelity can produce in comparison to traditional adultery, the question becomes whether courts should recognize virtual adultery for remedial purposes in divorce proceedings. Deciding to recognize virtual adultery would raise an equally important question – how to gauge when harmful virtual behavior constitutes actionable virtual adultery.

There are at least two possible approaches to recognizing virtual adultery for remedial purposes. In the first approach, individual state legislatures may decide to establish bright-line rules regarding what types of virtual infidelity rise to the level of adultery for fault and other civil divorce purposes. A second approach acknowledges that virtual adultery deserves consideration in determining fault and other incidents of divorce, but rejects the use of bright-line rules to determine what specific behavior constitutes adultery – as opposed to traditional adultery statutes that impose baseline requirements such as sexual intercourse or other physical acts. Instead of defining virtual adultery in terms of specific conduct, the second approach would defer to judicial discretion to evaluate what constitutes adultery on a case-by-case basis. Conversely, in a status quo approach, state

legislatures may decline to extend the legal definition of adultery to virtual infidelity on the basis that virtual infidelity is either too amorphous to merit a judicial remedy or sufficiently distinguishable from traditional adultery to deny the same remedies that are available for the latter. This section rejects the status quo approach and addresses the two approaches that would introduce virtual adultery into remedial schemes, ultimately advocating adoption of the discretionary approach.

A. Rejecting the Status Quo Approach

The advantage to adopting approaches that penalize nonphysical extramarital intimacy is that they recognize that emotional intimacy with someone other than a spouse can produce the same damage to the marriage as physical infidelity. Cossman posits that "emotional infidelity has become as much a violation of marriage as is sexual infidelity. Sex has become an *expression* of the underlying emotional intimacy."[85] Another commentator suggests that "[a]dultery matters . . . because it erodes the intimacy between spouses. And if *this* is why adultery matters, then other erosions of spousal intimacy, other factors that similarly contribute to disconnection, should also justify divorce."[86] Despite changes in the type of conduct that adultery encompasses, the policy interests in preventing it remain largely the same – namely, protecting the strength of marriage and the family. To continue to achieve these policy goals, judicial remedies must capture the new harms that cause the same damage. [. . .]

Commentators who do not support legal recognition of virtual adultery as a fault ground suggest that the most substantial potential harms to the marriage caused by adultery are irrelevant to virtual affairs.[87] Hall posits that nonphysical affairs "bear only a fraction of the consequences which accompany actual adultery. Without physical contact, the possibility of an unwanted pregnancy or sexually transmitted disease is impossible."[88] Sue Hoogestraat and Amy Taylor might disagree with this comparison of potential harm. Even though the physical risks associated with traditional adultery do not translate to virtual adultery, this comment suggests that emotional affairs can inflict a comparable amount of harm on a marriage. Cossman adds that "[p]regnancy is no longer the central harm of adultery. Rather, adultery is now framed as a violation of the promise of emotional and sexual exclusivity."[89] Decreased physical risks of adulterous conduct do not lessen the breach of "exclusivity" that defines virtual infidelity.[90] [. . .]

B. Bright-Line Rule Approach

A bright-line rule approach to virtual adultery identifies specific nonphysical behavior that constitutes adultery in the context of divorce. This approach identifies virtual adultery when the nonphysical infidelity triggers the same policy goal of insulating the marriage. Since the physical component would not apply here, courts instead would look to whether the nonphysical infidelity impedes on the emotional component of the marriage. Regardless of the level of emotional intimacy achieved by the extramarital relationship, the key consideration is the extent to which it detracts from the emotional intimacy of the marriage. This determination pinpoints the types of nonphysical conduct that create the same emotional consequences as physical adultery, such as distrust of the unfaithful spouse. Rather than expanding the definition of adultery, this determination would fill a gap left by traditional adultery statutes that do not provide a remedy for the transfer of intimacy in the absence of a physical affair.[91]

The most apparent disadvantage to a bright-line rule approach is its potential to be over- or under-inclusive in defining adulterous virtual conduct. The difficulty in making rules for what degree of nonphysical conduct should be punished is foreshadowed even in current debates about the standards that should apply in determining traditional adultery. For example, in evaluating circumstantial evidence of adultery, courts have split on whether manifestations of adultery are sufficient for a faithful spouse to succeed on a fault-based divorce action. An Alabama court found that evidence of love letters did not provide sufficient proof of a husband's adultery.[92] Courts in both South Carolina and Louisiana found that a wife *had* committed adultery by sharing a bedroom with another man – even without proof that sexual intercourse had occurred.[93] Although the courts conducted their analyses to determine whether the circumstantial evidence against the spouse was sufficient to prove adultery, in doing so they evaluated whether certain conduct on the part of the accused spouse was inherently improper and suggestive of extramarital conduct – the same type of conduct that might harm the emotional trust in a marriage regardless of whether physical infidelity occurred.

The Louisiana court's standard for finding adultery was "the rejection of the spouse coupled with out-of-marriage intimacy."[94] "Rejection," which traditionally might have required an affirmative manifestation of intent to end the marriage, might today reflect Ric Hoogestraat's excessive gaming.[95] "Out-of-marriage intimacy," which traditionally required an extramarital

sexual act, might today include Ric's virtual wife.[96] The established rule punishing *only* physical sexual acts is easiest to enforce, but may potentially overlook behaviors that nonetheless harm the faithful spouse.

Legal recognition of virtual adultery does carry a risk of engendering a windfall of actionable nonphysical behavior. Because emotional infidelity is inherently more subjective than physical infidelity, it is difficult to draw boundaries for improper conduct. This is both because "faithful" spouses may subscribe to different ideas of what constitutes infidelity and because "unfaithful" spouses may not be aware that they have crossed the line beyond acceptable extramarital conduct. This risk must be weighed against the policy interest in strengthening marriage and the judicial interest in compensating innocent spouses via property and spousal support allocations.[97]

[. . .]

C. Discretionary Approach

A discretionary approach to virtual adultery acknowledges that certain nonphysical, intimate conduct can constitute adultery and implicate the same policy concerns, while simultaneously recognizing that it is difficult to identify that conduct in a vacuum. Instead, its advocates suggest writing virtual adultery into statutory fault ground considerations for divorce and deferring to judicial discretion to evaluate the totality of the circumstances in determining fault. Virginia law, for instance, states that a court "shall consider the circumstances and factors which contributed to the dissolution of the marriage, specifically including adultery."[98] A discretionary approach suggests placing virtual adultery within the totality of factors a state court applies in determining the cause of divorce, thereby allowing individual courts to recognize egregious instances of emotional infidelity while filtering out interactions that do not rise to the intimacy level of an inappropriate relationship.

The primary advantage in placing virtual adultery determinations within judicial discretion is that it recognizes the complexities of proving emotional intimacy under the traditional standard of clear and convincing evidence.[99] Although courts may consider reducing the standard of proof to a preponderance of the evidence, a lesser standard may not adequately address virtual infidelity either. The "ephemeral sphere of emotional or virtual infidelity" – which could involve such conduct as an online "proxy kiss" – would likely fail to satisfy any existing standard of proof for adultery.[100] Whereas an extramarital physical act may instantly trigger an adultery statute, courts cannot feasibly deter the series of small behaviors that may lead up to an emotional affair. An emotional affair, rather than initiating with a single physical catalyst, can build upon a continuing thread of ostensibly harmless communication.[127] A discretionary approach would identify on a case-by-case basis the point at which emotional intimacy becomes sufficiently integrated into the extramarital relationship to impose on the marital unit.

Considering the relevant costs and benefits, a discretionary approach is ultimately a better solution than the alternative bright-line rule approach to address virtual adultery in the fault system. A discretionary approach best supports the policy rationale for punishing virtual adultery – that courts should deter extramarital emotional intimacy for the effects it can produce on the marital unit. Although it may incidentally accomplish this goal, a bright-line rule approach – like its statutory predecessors – seeks to punish particular acts without giving thought to how that conduct affects the marriage. This might leave the exact same statutory gaps currently

in place, which compensate certain adulterous acts while failing to recognize others. Rather than deter spouses from seeking intimacy outside the marriage, bright-line rules merely add more behaviors to the list of actionable conduct – leaving the would-be unfaithful spouse free to engage in any type of emotional relationship not captured by the applicable fault scheme. A discretionary approach, on the other hand, looks to the compilation of behaviors that comprised the marital break-down. It might also look to the faithful spouse as a barometer for determining the severity of the other spouse's conduct, recognizing the faithful spouse's contribution to sustaining the marriage after the affair. A discretionary approach considers the entirety of an emotional affair – as opposed to a single nonphysical act – in deciding fault. Although less consistent with current statutory schemes that require specific adulterous acts, a discretionary method more closely conforms to policy goals of containing intimacy within the marriage and deterring harmful extramarital interactions.

[. . .]

Notes

1 *See* Alexandra Alter, Is This Man Cheating on His Wife?, *Wall St. J.*, Aug. 10, 2007, at W1.
2 *See id.*
3 *Id.*
4 4. Gaby Langer et al., ABC NEWS PRIMETIME LIVE POLL, THE AMERICAN SEX SURVEY: A PEEK BENEATH THE SHEETS 23 (2004).
5 *See id.; see also* Alter, *supra* note 1.
6 *See* Christina Tavella Hall, Sex Online: Is This Adultery?, 20 *Hastings Comm. & Ent. L.J.* 201, 210–11 (1997).
7 *See* Karen S. Peterson, Infidelity Reaches Beyond Having Sex, *USA Today*, Jan. 9, 2003, at 8D (noting that cybersex and virtual affairs on the Internet are popular areas of interest among professionals who study spousal infidelity).
8 *Id.*
9 Note, Constitutional Barriers to Civil and Criminal Restrictions on Pre- and Extramarital Sex, 104 *Harv. L. Rev.* 1660, 1674 (1991) [hereinafter *Constitutional Barriers*].
10 Brenda Cossman, The New Politics of Adultery, 15 *Colum. J. Gender & L.* 274, 280 (2006).
11 *See id.* at 277. This comment uses the term "virtual infidelity" to describe spousal infidelity more generally and the term "virtual adultery" to describe virtual infidelity that may rise to the level of legally actionable conduct.
12 *See* Hall, *supra* note 6, at 203–04, 212.
13 *See* Lynn D. Wardle, No-Fault Divorce and the Divorce Conundrum, 1991 *BYU L. Rev.* 79, 120 (1991).

14 *See* Shaakirrah R. Sanders, The Cyclical Nature of Divorce in the Western Legal Tradition, 50 *Loy. L. Rev.* 407, 421 (2004).
15 *Id.* at 409.
16 *Id.*
17 *See id.*
18 See id. at 421.
19 *See id.*
20 *Id.* at 416, 421.
21 Adriaen M. Morse, Jr., Fault; A Viable Means of Re-Injecting Responsibility in Marital Relations, 30 *U. Rich. L. Rev.* 605, 608–09 (1996).
22 Peter Nash Swisher, Marriage and Some Troubling Issues with No-Fault Divorce, 17 *Regent U. L. Rev.* 243, 259 (2004–2005); see Morse, *supra* note 21, at 614 (noting that thirty states have statutes that recognize both fault and no-fault grounds for divorce); *see also* Lenore J. Weitzman, *The Divorce Revolution: The Unexpected Social and Economic Consequences for Women and Children in America* 20 (1985) (explaining that California's new no-fault scheme created a ground for dissolution based on "marital break-down" or a semantic variation of the term generally labeled "irreconcilable differences").
23 *See* Martin J. Siegel, For Better or for Worse; Adultery, Crime & the Constitution, 30 *J. Fam. L.* 45, 50–52 (1991–1992). Twenty states have criminalized a singular adulterous act, regardless of whether the infidelity continued after

the first act; three states have criminalized cohabitation between a spouse and a third party but not the adulterous act itself; and one state has only criminalized repeated adultery. *Id.* at 50–51; *see also* Lawrence M. Friedman, The Eye That Never Sleeps: Privacy and Law in the Internet Era, 40 *Tulsa L. Rev.* 561, 568 (2005) (noting that some states have articulated statutory thresholds on the manifestation of adultery, criminalizing "open and notorious" adultery rather than "simple [discreet] adultery") (internal quotation marks omitted).

24 Hillary Greene, Note, Undead Laws: The Use of Historically Unenforced Criminal Statutes in Non-Criminal Litigation, 16 *Yale L. & Pol'y Rev.* 169, 173–74 (1997).

25 *Id,* at 173–74 & n.24; *see* Siegel, *supra* note 23, at 87 (explaining that states have identified certain continuing interests in curbing adulterous behavior, such as reducing illness and bolstering marriage). Although Siegel criticizes the validity of these rationales, he concedes there is a social impetus for maintaining them. *Id.* at 87–89; *see* Erik Encarnación, Note, Desuetude-Based Severability: A New Approach to Old Morals Legislation, 39 *Colum. J.L. & Soc. Probs.* 149, 167 (2005) ("[O]nce morals legislation is understood as serving a largely symbolic function, the judiciary may then preserve its symbolic elements while disarming its potentially harmful aspects.").

26 Phyllis Coleman, Who's Been Sleeping in My Bed? You and Me, and the State Makes Three, 24 *Ind. L. Rev.* 399, 400–01 (1991); *see* Dan Markel et al., *Privilege or Punish: Criminal Justice and the Challenge of Family Ties* 136 (2009).

27 *See generally* Encarnación, *supra* note 25, at 152–63 (providing a detailed description of the principle of desuetude, which addresses "dead letter" laws).

28 *See Constitutional Barriers, supra* note 9, at 1679–80.

29 *See id.* at 1680.

30 *Id.* at 1677.

31 *See* Cossman, *supra* note 10, at 277.

32 Lynn D. Wardle, Parental Infidelity and the "No-Harm" Rule in Custody Litigation, 52 *Cath. U. L. Rev.* 81, 83 (2002) [hereinafter *Parental Infidelity*]; *see Constitutional Barriers, supra* note 9, at 1679–80.

33 *See Parental Infidelity, supra* note 32, at 83; *see also Constitutional Barriers, supra* note 9, at 1679–80 (stating that for purposes of determining child custody, adultery should be a relevant factor only to the extent that the adulterous activity threatened the child's best interests).

34 *See* Douglas E. Abrams et al., *Contemporary Family Law* 420–29 (2d edn. 2009) (citing N.Y. DOM. REL. L. § 170(4) (Consol. 2008)); *see also* 49 AM. JUR. 3D *Proof of Facts* § 3 (1998).

35 Abrams et al., *supra* note 34, at 433; *see* Morse, *supra* note 21, at 609–10 (noting that some states require that a party satisfy only the least stringent preponderance of the evidence standard to prove adultery).

36 *See* 27A C.J.S. *Divorce* § 294 (2010). Although facts and circumstances sufficient to prove adultery need not be such that an inference of guilt is the only possible conclusion that can be drawn from them, they must be such as to lead to the fact of adulterous intercourse, not only by fair inference, but as a necessary conclusion. *Id.*

37 *See* Abrams et al., *supra* note 34, at 429 ("[S]pouses wishing to rely on adultery as a ground for divorce more often encounter evidentiary issues . . ..").

38 [See Barbara Bennett Woodhouse, *Sex, Lies, and Dissipation: The Discourse of Fault in a No-Fault Era*, 82 Geo L.J. 2525, 2532-2533), at 2536 ("[P]erhaps because of history, fault plays a more complex set of roles in alimony than in property distribution. It may determine eligibility to receive alimony, liability to pay alimony, and the amount of the award.").

39 *Id.* at 2528. In Virginia, for example, one spouse's adultery eliminates the innocent spouse's obligation of support unless "manifest injustice" would result from a bar to support. VA. CODE ANN. § 20-107.1(B) (Repl. Vol. 2008); *see id.* § 20-91; *see also* Morse, *supra* note 21, at 644. Vermont, on the other hand, defers to judicial discretion in weighing the effect of adultery on support allocations. VT. STAT. ANN. tit. 15, § 634 (1987).

40 *See* Bower v. Bower, 758 So. 2d 405, 409–10 (Miss. 2000).

41 *See, e.g.,* Rosser v. Rosser, 355 So. 2d 717, 719 (Ala. Civ. App. 1977); Menge v. Menge, 491 So. 2d 700, 701 (La. Ct. App. 1986).

42 RGM v. DEM, 410 S.E.2d 564, 567 (S.C. 1991). The court applied the reasoning of a Florida court that had found "no substantial distinction [between heterosexual and same-sex adultery], because both involve extra-marital sex and therefore marital misconduct" *Id.* (quoting Patin v. Patin, 371 So. 2d 682, 683 (Fla. Dish Ct. App. 1979)) (internal quotation marks omitted).

43 Nemeth v. Nemeth, 481 S.E.2d 181, 184 (S.C. Ct. App. 1997) (determining that a "[w]ife's opportunity and inclination to commit adultery" by sharing sleeping quarters with a man who was not her husband satisfied the husband's burden of proof even though a pre-existing medical condition may have prevented the wife from carrying out a physical affair).

44 *See id.*

45 Cossman, *supra* note 10, at 279.

46 *See id.* at 279–80.

47 *See id.* at 280.

48 *Id.* at 277.

49 *See id.* at 276–77.

50 When Friendship Becomes an Emotional Affair, *TODAY Weekend Edition* (Aug. 11, 2006, 1:11 PM), http://today.msnbc.msn.com/id/14287231/ns/today-today_weekend_edition/twhenfriendship-becomes-emotional-affair/#.TvA0xXP4H64. An "emotional affair," according

to Dr. Dale Atkins, "is about forming meaningful attachments with people other than your partner in ways that prevent your partner from having . . . deep emotional intimacy with you." *Id.*

51 *See* Cossman, *supra* note 10, at 279.

52 Langer et al., *supra* note 4, at 24.

53 Gail Saltz, Could You Be Having an Emotional Affair?, *CNN Living* (May 21, 2009), http://articles.cnn.com/2009-05-21/living/o.having.emotional.affair_1_sharon-affair-marriage?_s=PM:LIVING.

54 *Id.*

55 *See* Aaron Ben-Zeév, Does Being True to Your Heart Imply Emotional Infidelity?, *Psychol. Today Blog* (Sept. 8, 2008), http://www.psychologytoday.com/blog/in-the-name-love/200809/does-being-true-your-heart-imply-emotional-infidelity.

56 Denise Schipani, *Are You Emotionally Cheating?*, Woman's Day (Dec. 23, 2009), http://www.womansday.com/sex-relationships/dating-marriage/are-you-emotionally-cheating-101955.

57 Michael J. Formica, Emotional Infidelity: When Is Cheating Really Cheating?, *Psychol. Today Blog* (Sept. 7, 2008), http://www.psychologytoday.com/blog/enlightened-living/200809/emotional-infidelity.

58 *See* Heather Johnson Durocher, The Affair You Don't Know You're Having, *Redbook*, Aug. 1, 2007, at 97.

59 Schipani, *supra* note 56.

60 *See* Aaron Ben-Zeév, Is Chatting Cheating?, *Psychol. Today Blog* (Sept. 5, 2008), http://www.psychologytoday.com/blog/in-the-name-love/200809/is-chatting-cheating.

61 Tatiana Morales, A Look at Internet Infidelity, *CBS NEWS* (Aug. 4, 2003), www.cbsnews.com/stories/2003/08/04/earlyshow/living/caught/main566488.shtml.

62 *See* Hall, *supra* note 6, at 214–17.

63 *Id.* at 216.

64 *See* Alter, *supra* note 1.

65 *See* Cyndy Aleo-Carreira, Is It Adultery if It Was in a Virtual World?, *PC World Australia* (Nov. 18, 2008, 9:54 AM), http://www.pcworld.idg.com.au/article/267757/it_adultery_it_virtual_world_/.

66 *A* Private Eye for Online Affairs, *CBS NEWS* (Feb. 11, 2009, 8:34 PM) www.cbsnews.com/stories/2003/07/30/tech/main565915.shtml [hereinafter *A Private Eye*] (explaining that the low cost, ease of use, and "anonymity of the Internet" has lowered the "threshold" for initiating affairs).

67 *See Facebook Is Driving the Divorce Rate Up, Says One Survey*, FOXNews.com (June 2, 2010), http://www.foxnews.com/scitech/2010/06/02/survey-shows-facebook-driving-divorce-rate/.

68 *See A Private Eye, supra* note 66.

69 Alter, *supra* note 1.

70 *See id.*

71 *See id.*

72 *Id.*

73 *Id.*

74 *Id.*

75 *Id.*

76 *See id.*

77 After Virtual Affair, Real Divorce, *CBS NEWS* (Feb. 11, 2009, 2:01 PM), www.cbsnews.com/stories/2008/11/14/tech/main4606394.shtml. Taylor's story correlates to a 2008 survey conducted by the Oxford Internet Institute analyzing the effect of Internet behavior on intimate relationships both before and after partners had met. *The Role of the Internet in UK Married Life; Survey Results from the Oxford Internet Institute,* Univ. of Oxford (Apr. 7, 2008), http://www.oii.ox.ac.uk/newe/?id=258. "Survey respondents said they would be 'unhappy' about their partner doing the following online with somebody else: falling in love (97%); having cyber-sex (94%); disclosing intimate details (92%); communicating relationship troubles to others (89%); sharing personal information about the other partner (88%); flirting (85%)." *Id.*

78 *After Virtual Affair, Real Divorce, supra* note 77.

79 *See id.*

80 *Id.*

81 *See* Alter, *supra* note 1.

82 *Compare id., with After Virtual Affair, Real Divorce, supra* note 77.

83 *See* Alter, *supra* note 1.

84 *See After Virtual Affair, Real Divorce, supra* note 77.

85 Cossman, *supra* note 10, at 280 (emphasis added).

86 Gary Chartier, Divorce: A Normative Analysis, 10 *Fla. Coastal L. Rev.* 1, 9 (2008).

87 *See* Hall, *supra* note 6, at 204–05.

88 *Id.* at 220.

89 Cossman, *supra* note 10, at 279.

90 *See id.*

91 *See* Va. Code Ann. § 18.2-365 (Repl. Vol. 2009) (stating that adultery involves "[a]ny person, being married, who voluntarily [has] sexual intercourse with any person who is not his or her spouse").

92 Maddox v. Maddox, 553 So. 2d 611, 612 (Ala. Civ. App. 1989).

93 *See* Bonura v. Bonura, 505 So. 2d 143, 145 (La. Ct. App. 1987); Nemeth v. Nemeth, 481 S.E.2d 181, 184 (S.C. Ct. App. 1997).

94 S.B. v. S.J.B., 609 A.2d 124, 127 (N.J. 1992); *see also Bonura*, 505 So. 2d at 145 (limiting the court's holding to the facts of the case and suggesting an analysis of individual facts and circumstances in future cases).

95 *See* Alter, *supra* note 1.

96 *See id.*

97 *See* Swisher, *supra* note 22, at 258–59.

98 Va. Code Ann. § 20-107.1(E) (Repl. Vol. 2008 & Cum. Supp. 2011).

99 *See* Abrams et al., *supra* note 34, at 433.

100 *See* Hall, *supra* note 6, at 221.

PART IV

Homosexuality and Policy

Introduction

The nature of sexual attraction and the objects of sexual attraction are clearly central elements of any study of sex. Where sexual desire comes from and what it is directed toward are questions that intrigue anyone trying to understand human behavior, human experience, and the terrain of human relationships.

But these questions also intrigue anyone who might be trying to determine what sort of social and legal arrangements are best fitted for individuals and for society at large. Whether or not the source of sexual desire is relevant to moral and legal issues is itself a question, however. Does it matter where sexual desire comes from? Should we treat sexual desires differently depending on how they came about? And why worry about how sexual desire is directed? Does it make a difference what a person finds appealing? Homosexuality is a case in which these questions have historically been prominent. Though certainly a minority sexual orientation and a minority sexual behavior in the global historical context, homosexuality has long been a flashpoint for thinking about the complicated moral relationship between sexual desire, sexual behavior, procreation, and the role of sex and gender in

religion, biology, and culture. Conceptualized variously as expected, sinful, pathological, perverse, normal variation, mysterious, decadently Western, political, personal, defective, enlightened, and immature, homosexuality seems to be different enough to encapsulate debates on sexual variation, familiar enough to be taken seriously, infrequent enough to be seen as exceptional, and yet important enough to be treated as a major moral issue of our day.

Part IV examines issues of homosexuality and policy. Though such issues involve a variety of concepts and values that can be applied to other cases, they are explored here by focusing on concerns about the biological and psychological positioning of homosexuality, the legal treatment of homosexuality, and the attempt to eliminate it.

Framing Questions

- *How should homosexuality be understood?*
- *What should the law be about homosexuality?*
- *How should we assess attempts to change sexual orientation?*

23

Why Homosexuality Is Abnormal

Michael Levin

Summary

Argues from an evolutionary perspective that homosexuality is abnormal because it is a misuse of the body for the purposes developed through evolutionary means. As such, it is maladaptive, harmful to society, and inevitably leads to relatively greater levels of unhappiness for those affected. As such, public policy should attempt to minimize the frequency of homosexuality if possible and foster an environment in which as many children as possible grow up to be heterosexual. This position is entirely non-religious, making no claim that homosexuality is sinful or immoral.

Original publication details: Michael Levin, "Why Homosexuality Is Abnormal," pp. 251–283 from *The Monist* 67 (1984). Reproduced with permission of Oxford University Press.

Sexual Ethics: An Anthology, First Edition. Edited by Patrick D. Hopkins.

Michael Levin

1 Introduction

This paper defends the view that homosexuality is abnormal and hence undesirable – not because it is immoral or sinful, or because it weakens society or hampers evolutionary development, but for a purely mechanical reason. It is a misuse of bodily parts. Clear empirical sense attaches to the idea of *the use* of such bodily parts as genitals, the idea that they are *for* something, and consequently to the idea of their misuse. I argue on grounds involving natural selection that misuse of bodily parts can with high probability be connected to unhappiness. I regard these matters as prolegomena to such policy issues as the rights of homosexuals, the rights of those desiring not to associate with homosexuals, and legislation concerning homosexuality, issues which I shall not discuss systematically here. However, I do in the last section draw a seemingly evident corollary from my view that homosexuality is abnormal and likely to lead to unhappiness.

[. . .]

Despite the publicity currently enjoyed by the claim that one's "sexual preference" is nobody's business but one's own, the intuition that there is something unnatural about homosexuality remains vital. The erect penis fits the vagina, and fits it better than any other natural orifice; penis and vagina seem made for each other. This intuition ultimately derives from, or is another way of capturing, the idea that the penis is not *for* inserting into the anus of another man – that so using the penis is not the way it is *supposed,* even *intended,* to be used. Such intuitions may appear to rest on an outmoded teleological view of nature, but recent work in the logic of functional ascription shows how they may be explicated, and justified, in suitably naturalistic terms. Such is the burden of Section 2, the particular application to homosexuality coming in Section 3. Furthermore, when we understand the sense in which homosexual acts involve a misuse of genitalia, we will see why such misuse is bad and not to be encouraged. (The case for this constitutes the balance of Section 3.) Clearly, the general idea that homosexuality is a pathological violation of nature's intent is not shunned by scientists. Here is Gadpille:

> The view of cultural relativity seems to be without justification. Cultural judgment is collective human caprice, and whether it accepts or rejects homosexuality is irrelevant. Biological intent . . . is to differentiate male and female both physiologically and psychologically in such a manner as to insure species

survival, which can be served only through heterosexual union ([10], 193).

Gadpille refers to homosexuality as "an abiological maladaptation." The novelty of the present paper is to link adaptiveness and normality via the notion of happiness.

[. . .]

2 On "Function" and Its Cognates

To bring into relief the point of the idea that homosexuality involves a misuse of bodily parts, I will begin with an uncontroversial case of misuse, a case in which the clarity of our intuitions is not obscured by the conviction that they are untrustworthy, Mr. Jones pulls all his teeth and strings then around his neck because he thinks his teeth look nice as a necklace. He takes pureéd liquids supplemented by intravenous solutions for nourishment. It is surely natural to say that Jones is misusing his teeth, that he is not using them for what they are for, that indeed the way he is using them is incompatible with what they are for. Pedants might argue that Jones's teeth are no longer part of him and hence that he is not misusing any bodily parts. To them I offer Mr. Smith, who likes to play "Old MacDonald" on his teeth. So devoted is he to this amusement, in fact, that he never uses his teeth for chewing – like Jones, he takes nourishment intravenously. Now, not only do we find it perfectly plain that Smith and Jones are misusing their teeth, we predict a dim future for them on purely physiological grounds; we expect the muscle of Jones's jaw that are used for – that *are* for – chewing to lose their tone, and we expect this to affect Jones's gums. Those parts of Jones's digestive tract that are for processing solids will also suffer from disuse. The net result will be deteriorating health and perhaps a shortened life. Nor is this all. Human beings enjoy chewing. Not only has natural selection selected in muscles for chewing and favored creatures with such muscles, it has selected in a tendency to find the use of those muscles reinforcing. Creatures who do not enjoy using such parts of their bodies as deteriorate with disuse, will tend to be selected out. Jones, product of natural selection that he is, descended from creatures who at least tended to enjoy the use of such parts. Competitors who didn't simply had fewer descendants. So we expect Jones sooner or later to experience vague yearnings to chew something, just as we find people who take no exercise to experience a general listlessness. Even waiving for now my apparent reification of the evolutionary process, let me emphasize how little anyone is tempted to say "each to his own" about Jones or to regard Jones's disposition of his teeth as simply a deviation from a statistical norm. This sort of case is my paradigm when discussing homosexuality.

The main obstacle to talk of what a process or organic structure is for is that, literally understood, such talk presupposes an agent who intends that structure or process to be used in a certain way. Talk of function derives its primitive meaning from the human use of artifacts, artifacts being for what purposive agents intend them for. Indeed, there is in this primitive context a natural reason for using something for what it is for: to use it otherwise would frustrate the intention of some purposeful agent. Since it now seems clear that our bodily parts were not emplaced by purposeful agency, it is easy to dismiss talk of what they are for as "theologically" based on a faulty theory of how we came to be built as we are:

The idea that sex was designed for propagation is a theological argument, but not a scientific one. . . . . To speak of the "fit" of penis and vagina as proof of nature's intention for their exclusive union is pure theological reasoning – imposing a meaning or purpose upon a simple, natural phenomenon (Gould 1974, 63).

Barash – who elsewhere uses its cognates freely – dismisses "unnatural" as a mere term of abuse: "people with a social or political axe to grind will call what they don't like 'unnatural' and what they do, 'natural' (1979, 237). Hume long ago put the philosopher's case against the term 'natural' with characteristic succinctness: "'Tis founded on final Causes; which is a consideration, that appears to me pretty uncertain & unphilosophical. For pray, what is the End of Man? Is he created for Happiness or for Virtue? For this Life or the next? For himself or for his Maker?" (Mossner 1954, 134).

Until recently, philosophers of science half-countered, half-conceded such doubts by "rationally reconstructing" the locution "structure S is for function F in organism O" as – omitting inessential refinements – "S's doing F in O is necessary for the integrity or prosperity of O" (Nagel 1961). This, the classical analysis, suffers from two weaknesses. First, it quite severs the link stressed earlier between a structure's having a function and the inadvisability of using that structure in a way inconsistent with its function. An organism may not be interested in survival, or prosperity, or the prosperity of some genetically defined group that contains the organism. The classical analysis provides no clue as to why Jones should desist from stringing his teeth on a necklace. It must be supplemented with the premise that survival or fitness are desirable, and however strong the desire to survive may be as a *de facto* motive, there are too many cogent arguments against survival as a basic norm for this supplement to be plausible.

None of this will disturb proponents of the classical analysis, since their very aim was, in part, to remove the teleological and normative connotations of "function" as unscientific ideas. So what if the classical analysis obstructs the inference from "Jones is not using his teeth for what they are for" to "Jones is misusing his teeth"? That is one of its virtues. However, the more decisive second objection to the classical analysis is the existence of clear counter-examples – counter-examples that turn out, on reflection, to be connected to the first objection. An accidentally incurred heart lesion might be necessary for the heart's pumping blood if it is otherwise diseased; but the lesion is not *for* pumping blood. A patient's heartbeat might be the only way his doctor can diagnose a disease that would be fatal if undiagnosed; but the beat of his heart is not *for* diagnosis. Such cases suggest that the classical analysis pays insufficient attention to how structures come to be in organisms and why they persist in reproductive cohorts. In light of this, a more adequate explication of "S is for F in O" runs:

(i) S conduces to F in O,
(ii) O's being F is necessary for the maintenance of O or O's genetic cohort, and
(iii) (i) and (ii) are part of the causal explanation of the existence or persistence of S in O and member's of O's genetic cohort (Bennet 1976, Levin 1976, Wright 1973).

In rougher and plainer English: an organ is for a given activity if the organ's performing that activity helps its host or organisms suitably related to its host, *and* if this contribution is how the organ got and stays where it is. This disqualifies the fortuitous heart lesion and the symptomatic heartbeat, which did not arise or persist by increasing (inclusive) fitness. This definition also distinguishes what something is for from what it may be *used* for on some occasion. Teeth are for chewing – we have teeth because their use in chewing favored the survival of organisms with teeth – whereas Jones is using his teeth for ornamentation.

[. . .]

Notice that my definition refers to an organism's "genetic cohort" rather than its species. Dawkins (1976) and others have argued that species-selection does not actually occur in nature. Taking the natural unit of replication, the "gene," as whatever bit of chromosome can retain its identity through enough generations to matter, a gene will most fecundly copy itself if either the organism that contains it, or organisms with a good chance of containing it – relatives of the gene's organism – reproduce prolifically. A gene is not helping itself reproduce if it instructs the body housing it to assist unrelated members of that body's species; it helps itself reproduce by instructing the body housing it to assist the organisms that might have reproducible copies of itself. So natural selection selects for "inclusive fitness": for traits that benefit an organism taken together with some group of relatives (Will 1977, 343). How wide the group should be is a matter of some debate, and will indeed be different for different kinds of organisms. Nor has species-selection lost all its defenders. For this reason, I am using "genetic cohort" to name whatever degree of relatedness turns out to be most appropriate for evolutionary theory.

One might well ask how my analysis of "function" can be what people meant before Darwin was ever heard of, even if people did have some inchoate notion of "minimum chain of emplacement" in mind. Doesn't "function" inherently refer to someone with a purpose – or, if not. what is simply *de facto* beneficial to organisms? No. What happened, I believe, was that before Darwin people thought that the only way S's aptness for F could cause S's existence was for someone, namely God, to notice that S is apt for F and for this reason choose to put S in O. We now know this is false; we now know of another way S's aptness for F can result in S's implantation – mutations emergence and subsequent natural selection. The core meaning of "function' was always (i)–(iii), the idea that God put organs in organisms being merely a theory about how (iii) was or had to be realized. This theory was so "obvious," however, that it appeared to be part of the meaning of "function" itself. Perhaps in concession to our ancestor's ignorance of causes "reproductive" ought to replace "genetic" in (iii); beyond that, the present definition does capture what people meant by "function" even before Darwin was ever heard of.

Within a Darwinian setting, the function of bodily parts can be linked to normative notions in a way that imputes no extrinsic direction to evolution. The empirical sense coaxed from "S is for F in O" explains our intuition that, since their efficacy in chewing got them selected in, teeth are for masticating and Jones is preventing his teeth from doing their proper job. To begin, it is clear that "Man has teeth because teeth grind food" cannot mean that the power of teeth to grind food is literally what provided Jones or anyone else with teeth. Causal powers aren't causes, and anyway the causal powers an object would have can hardly be what brings the object into existence. Rather, the presence or persistence of S in O's cohort is better understood in more general evolutionary terms. Genetic mutation brought forth the first S in one of our ancestors. There is a mechanism, the coding of the DNA, that transmits S. Here is where S's causal powers come in. Possession of S aided its first possessor and his cohorts in the struggle for survival, and since S is transmissible, this initial possessor survived to transmit S to his descendants who, in turn, were better fitted than their S-less competitors to reproduce and transmit S . . . We, the descendants of S's original possessors, possess S as a result of this filtration. And it is just here that a eudaimonistic normative link begins to appear.

Consider this first-approximation guess about one of the mechanisms of natural selection. Imagine for a moment that S is for F in the sense explained, and that exercise of S does not lie wholly within the province of O's autonomic nervous system. It is, loosely speaking, up to O whether to use S, or use S for F. Imagine as well two subpopulations O_1 and O_2. Members of O_1 *enjoy* using S to F, while members of O_2 do not. Since O_2's do not enjoy using S to F, they will use S to F less frequently than do O_1's. Since S favors the survival of possessors of S precisely because S conduces to F, it is the members of O_1 who are more likely to reproduce themselves and transmit, in addition to S, a desire to use S to F. It is thus likely that present-day O's will enjoy using S to F, because they are more probably descendants of the O_1 than of the O_2. Nature is interested in making its creatures like what is (inclusively) good for them. A creature that does not enjoy using its teeth for chewing uses them less than does a toothed competitor who enjoys chewing. Since the use of teeth for chewing favors the survival of an individual with teeth, and, other things being equal, traits favorable to the survival of individuals favor survival of the relevant cohort, toothed creatures who do not enjoy chewing tend to get selected out. We today are the filtrate of this process, descendants of creatures who liked to chew.

To be sure, the best evolutionary strategy might be a mix of O_1-ness and O_2-ness, so that the filtrate of evolution will be creatures with alleles for enjoying, and alleles for not enjoying, the use of S. Constant use of S might be too much of a good thing. The filtrate would be a population mixing O_1's and O_2's. We will consider in due course whether this model is applicable to homosexuality. But even in its simplified form, the present analysis does suggest that a gene for enjoying the use of S to F would at least tend to spread rapidly through O. It is hard to imagine how the enjoyment of the use of such things as human teeth could not take over, and there seems to be no current benefit associated with the absence of this enjoyment. And here – to return to the main strand of the argument – is why it is advisable to use your organs for what they are for: you will enjoy it. [. . .]

My loose talk of "enjoyment" can be tightened by appeal to the notion of reinforcement. Psychologists define "R is a reinforcer or reward" as: "R makes more probable the repetition of any behavior R follows." Contrary to a surprisingly wide misconception, this definition allows internal states to be rewards, even unconditioned rewards. We can say that organism O enjoys emitting behavior B without explicitly appealing to O's feeling-tone by saying that O's emission of B puts O in a rewarding internal state. In these terms, my general evolutionary hypothesis holds that nature tends to make rewarding behavior that favors cohort survival, and to make unrewarding behavior that does not. More specifically, it holds that if S is for F, using S to F will be rewarding, white using S for something incompatible with F will be unrewarding. [. . .]

3 Applications to Homosexuality

The application of this general picture to homosexuality should be obvious. There can be no reasonable doubt that one of the functions of the penis is to introduce semen into the vagina. It does this, and it has been selected in because it does this. (Sexual intercourse itself can probably be explained by the evolutionary value of bisexual reproduction. For $n > 2$, n-sexual reproduction would increase genetic variety at the cost of hardly ever occurring (Beadle and Beadle 1967). The advantages accruing to relatively motile gametes seems to account for the emergence of bisexual reproduction itself. Nature has consequently made this use of the penis rewarding. It is clear enough that any proto-human males who found unrewarding the insertion of penis into vagina have left no descendants. In particular, proto-human males who enjoyed inserting their penises into each

other's anuses have left no descendants. This is why homosexuality is abnormal, and why its abnormality counts prudentially against it. Homosexuality is likely to cause unhappiness because it leaves unfulfilled an innate and innately rewarding desire. And should the reader's environmentalism threaten to get the upper hand, let me remind him again of an unproblematic case. Lack of exercise is bad and even abnormal not only because it is unhealthy but also because one feels poorly without regular exercise. Nature made exercise rewarding because, until recently, we had to exercise to survive. Creatures who found running after game unrewarding were eliminated. Laziness leaves unreaped the rewards nature has planted in exercise, even if the lazy man cannot tell this introspectively. If this is a correct description of the place of exercise in human life, it is by the same token a correct description of the place of heterosexuality.

It hardly needs saying, but perhaps I should say it anyway, that this argument concerns tendencies and probabilities. Generalizations about human affairs being notoriously "true by and large and for the most part" only, saying that homosexuals are bound to be less happy than heterosexuals must be understood as short for "Not coincidentally, a larger proportion of homosexuals will be unhappy than a corresponding selection of the heterosexual population." There are, after all, genuinely jolly fat men. To say that laziness leads to adverse affective consequences means that, because of our evolutionary history, the odds are relatively good that a man who takes no exercise will suffer adverse affective consequences. Obviously, some people will get away with misusing their bodily parts. Thus, when evaluating the empirical evidence that bears on this account, it will be pointless to cite cases of well-adjusted homosexuals. I do not say they are non-existent; my claim is that, of biological necessity, they are rare.

My argument might seem to show at most that heterosexual behavior is (self-) reinforcing, not that homosexuality is self-extinguishing – that homosexuals go without the built-in rewards of heterosexuality, but not that homosexuality has a built-in punishment. This distinction, however, is merely verbal. They are two different ways of saying that homosexuals will find their lives less rewarding than will heterosexuals. Even if some line demarcated happiness from unhappiness absolutely, it would be irrelevant if homosexuals were all happily above the line. It is the comparison with the heterosexual life that is at issue. A lazy man might count as happy by some mythic absolute standard, but he is likely to be less happy than someone otherwise like him who exercises.

Another objection to my argument, or conjectural evolutionary scenario, is that heterosexuality might have been selected in not because it favors survival, but as a by-product of some other inclusively fit structure or behavior. A related suggestion is that what really has been selected in is some blend of dominant heterosexual and recessive homosexual genes. As for the former, it seems extraordinarily unlikely, given how long life has reproduced itself by sexual intercourse, that the apparently self-reinforcing character of heterosexuality is a by-product of some other fitness-enhancing trait. If heterosexual intercourse is not *directly* connected to propagation, what is? Biologists have no trouble determining when bird plumage is there to attract mates, and hence favors survival. It would be astounding if the same could not be said for heterosexual intercourse.

The sophisticate might complain that I am not giving "by-product" hypotheses their due. And indeed at this point sociobiological hypotheses come thick and fast. I will be discussing some others later in this paper, and making some overall observations about sociobiology and homosexuality. Here it is appropriate to examine one hypothesis of the "by-product" school, that of Hutchinson (1959). Fact: there can be recessive genes for a trait that inhibits the reproduction of and even kills organisms which exhibit it, but which, when co-occurring with the dominant trait-suppressing allele, give rise to an organism or phenotype more inclusively fit than a comparable organism with two of the dominant alleles. In such cases, the "bad" allele will be passed along in fit heterozygous organisms and its associated trait will occasionally surface. For example, sickle-cell anemia persists because the heterozygote Cc (Non-sickle-cell C, sickle-cell c) confers resistance to malaria. Perhaps a recessive gene predisposing to homosexuality persists in this way. Organisms of genotype Hh – a dominant allele H for heterosexuality, a recessive allele h for homosexuality – might be most fit, and then of course organisms with hh genotype will surface with some regularity.

Without even considering the empirical likelihood of this elegant hypothesis, it is clearly consistent with my chief claim. For as it stands it represents sickle-cell anemia and the perpetuation of the c allele as *unfortunate by-products* of a process that selects in resistance to malaria; and, presumably, the same would go for homosexuality. For what does it mean to say that sickle-cell anemia is a by-product? Precisely this: had immunity to malaria not been associated with the Cc genotype, the "gene" for malarial immunity would have been selected

in anyway; however, had the Cc genotype and hence sickle-cell anemia not been associated with malarial immunity or some other inclusive-fitness-enhancing trait, the c allele would have disappeared. Recurring to our definition of "function," the cause of the persistence of the c allele and the Cc genotype, what that genotype is for, is fending off malaria. Sickle-cell anemia is a maladaptive by-product of the Cc genotype since, had it not been associated with what is in fact the function of the Cc genotype, sickle-cell anemia would have caused the disappearance of the Cc genotype. Nothing, not even the c allele, has sickle-cell anemia as its function. The key question, of course, is whether a maladaptive by-product, so understood, is reinforcing. On the present model, it is not. For suppose sickle-cell anemia could be contracted voluntarily, and there were a gene which (a) made contracting or becoming vulnerable to it reinforcing, but (b) was not connected with malarial immunity. A strain with the tastes this gene confers would soon be selected out. Therefore, surviving humans who get sickle-cell anemia do not find it in any way reinforcing. So the "heterozygote fitness" hypothesis (and the kin-selection hypothesis: see below) predict, consistently with my view, that homosexuality is associated with unhappiness; and, conversely, widespread homosexual unhappiness would confirm that homosexuality is a maladaptive by-product.

An important methodological corollary of this discussion is that a trait or tendency may be "in the genes" but still be abnormal. It is normal only if it is in the genes because it itself enhances fitness, not because it is associated with something else that enhances fitness on independent grounds. Sickle-cell anemia is a malfunction of its victims' blood, which was selected in to oxygenate the muscles. A comparable story for homosexuality would involve a gene that instructed its organism to make just a little testosterone. This might have survival value by raising phenotypic verbal sensitivity, and perhaps low testosterone is the only way nature has figured out to secure this inclusively fit trait. Suppose, too, that a disposition to homosexuality was a causal consequence, a by-product, of low testosterone – but not so disadvantageous a by-product that the gene was selected out. Homosexuality would then be a necessary condition for advantageous verbal ability, but it would not follow that homosexuality was selected in because it conduced to verbal ability, or for any other reason. It would not follow that homosexuality is the least reinforcing. Unhappy homosexuals might be the price nature pays for verbal ability, homosexuality being no more a cause of verbal ability than sickle-cell anemia is a cause of malarial resistance.

Talk of what is "in the genes" inevitably provokes the observation that we should not blame homosexuals for their homosexuality if it is "in their genes." True enough. Indeed, since nobody decides what he is going to find sexually arousing, the moral appraisal of sexual object "choice" is entirely absurd. However, so saying is quite consistent with regarding homosexuality as a misfortune, and taking steps – this being within the realm of the will – to minimize its incidence, especially among children. Calling homosexuality involuntary does not place it outside the scope of evaluation. Victims of sickle cell anemia are not blameworthy, but it is absurd to pretend that there is nothing wrong with them. Homosexual activists are partial to genetic explanations and hostile to Freudian environmentalism in part because they see a genetic cause as exempting homosexuals from blame. But surely people are equally blameless for indelible traits acquired in early childhood. And anyway, a blameless condition may still be worth trying to prevent. (Defenders of homosexuality fear Freud at another level, because his account removes homosexuality from the biological realm altogether and deprives it of whatever legitimacy adheres to what is "in the genes.")

My sociobiological scenario also finds no place for the fashionable remark that homosexuality has become fitness-enhancing in our supposedly overpopulated world. Homosexuality is said to increase our species' chances by casing the population pressure. This observation, however correct, is irrelevant. Even if homosexuality has lately come to favor species survival, this is no part of how homosexuality is created. Salvation of the human species would be at best a fortuitous by-product of behavior having other causes. It is not easy, moreover, to see how this feature of homosexuality could get it selected in. If homosexuality enhances inclusive fitness precisely because homosexuals don't reproduce, the tendency to homosexuality cannot get selected for by a filtering process when it is passed to the next generation – it doesn't get passed to the next generation at all. The same applies, of course, to any tendency to find homosexuality rewarding.

The whole matter of the survival advantage of homosexuality is in any case beside the point. Our organs have the functions and rewards they do because of the way the world was, and what favored survival, many millions of years ago. *Then*, homosexuality decreased fitness and heterosexuality increased it; an innate tendency to homosexuality would have gotten selected out if

anything did. We today have the tendencies transmitted to us by those other ancestors, whether or not the race is going to pay a price for this. That 50 years ago certain self-reinforcing behavior began to threaten the race's future is quite consistent with the behavior remaining self-reinforcing. Similarly, widespread obesity and the patent enjoyment many people experience in gorging themselves just show that our appetites were shaped in conditions of food scarcity under which gorging oneself when one had the chance was good policy. Anyway, the instability created by abundance is, presumably, temporary. If the current abundance continues for 5000 generations, natural gluttons will almost certainly disappear through early heart disease and unattractiveness to the opposite sex. The ways in which the populous human herd will be trimmed is best left to speculation.

I should also note that nothing I have said shows bisexuality or sheer polymorphous sexuality to be unnatural or self-punishing. One might cite the Greeks to show that only exclusive homosexuality conflicts with our evolved reinforcement mechanism. But in point of fact bisexuality seems to be a quite rare phenomenon – and animals, who receive no cultural conditioning, seem instinctively heterosexual in the vast majority of cases. [. . .]

[. . .]

4 Evidence and Further Clarification

I have argued that homosexuality is "abnormal" in both a descriptive and a normative sense because – for evolutionary reasons – homosexuals are bound to be unhappy. In Kantian terms, I have explained how it is possible for homosexuality to be unnatural even if it violates no cosmic purpose or such purposes as we retrospectively impose on nature, What is the evidence for my view? For one thing, by emphasizing homosexual unhappiness, my view explains a ubiquitous fact in a simple way. The fact is the universally acknowledged unhappiness of homosexuals. Even the staunchest defenders of homosexuality admit that, as of now, homosexuals are not happy. (Writers even in the very recent past, like Lord Devlin, could not really believe that anyone could publicly advocate homosexuality as intrinsically good (Devlin 1965). A conspicuous exception to this is Bell and Weinberg (1978), which has been widely taken to show that homosexuals can be just as happy as heterosexuals. A look at their statistics tells a different story – an important matter I have dealt with in some detail in the Appendix.

Michael Levin

The usual environmentalist explanation for homosexuals' unhappiness is the misunderstanding, contempt and abuse that society heaps on them. But this not only leaves unexplained why society has this attitude, it sins against parsimony by explaining a nearly universal phenomenon in terms of variable circumstances that have, by coincidence, the same upshot. Parsimony urges that we seek the explanation of homosexual unhappiness in the nature of homosexuality itself, as my explanation does. Having to "stay in the closet" may be a great strain, but it does not account for all the miseries that writers on homosexuality say is the homosexual's lot.

[. . .]

One crucial test of my account is its prediction that homosexuals will continue to be unhappy even if people altogether abandon their "prejudice" against homosexuality. This prediction, that homosexuality being unnatural homosexuals will still find their behavior self-punishing, coheres with available evidence. It is consistent with the failure of other oppressed groups such as American Negroes and European Jews, to become warped in the direction of "cruising," sado-masochism and other practices common in homosexual life (McCracken 1979). It is consistent as well with the admission by even so sympathetic an observer of homosexuality as Rechy (1977) that the immediate cause of homosexual unhappiness is a taste for promiscuity, anonymous encounters, and humiliation. It is hard to see how such tastes are related to the dim view society takes of them. Such a relation would be plausible only if homosexuals courted multiple anonymous encounters *faute de mieux*, longing all the while to settle down to some sort of domesticity. But, again, Europeans abhorred Jews for centuries, but this did not create in Jews a special weakness for anonymous, promiscuous sex. Whatever drives a man away from women, to be fellated by as many different men as possible, seems independent of what society thinks of such behavior. It is this behavior that occasions misery, and we may expect the misery of homosexuals to continue.

In a 1974 study, Weinberg and Williams found no difference in the distress experienced by homosexuals in Denmark and the Netherlands, and in the U.S., where they found public tolerance of homosexuality to be lower. This would confirm rather strikingly that homosexual unhappiness is endogenous [. . .]

But does not my position also predict – contrary to fact – that any sexual activity not aimed at procreation or at least sexual intercourse leads to unhappiness? First, I am not sure this conclusion is contrary to the facts properly understood. It is universally recognized that, for humans and the higher animals, sex is more than the insertion of the penis into the vagina. Foreplay is necessary to prepare the female and, to a lesser extent, the male. Ethologists have studied the elaborate mating rituals of even relatively simple animals. Sexual intercourse must therefore be understood to include the kisses and caresses that necessarily precede copulation, behaviors that nature has made rewarding. What my view does predict is that exclusive preoccupation with behaviors normally preparatory for Intercourse is highly correlated with unhappiness. [. . .]

It should also be clear that my argument permits gradations in abnormality. Behavior is the more abnormal, and the less likely to be rewarding, the more its emission tends to extinguish a genetic cohort that practices it. The less likely a behavior is to get selected out, the less abnormal it is. Those of our ancestors who found certain aspects of foreplay reinforcing might have managed to reproduce themselves sufficiently to implant this strain in us. There might be an equilibrium between intercourse and such not directly reproductive behavior. It is not required that any behavior not directly linked to heterosexual intercourse lead to maximum dissatisfaction. But the existence of these gradations provides no entering wedge for homosexuality. As no behavior is more likely to get selected out than rewarding homosexuality – except perhaps an innate tendency to suicide at the onset of puberty – it is extremely unlikely that homosexuality can now be unconditionally reinforcing in humans to any extent.

Nor does my position predict, again contrary to fact, that celibate priests will be unhappy. My view is compatible with the existence of happy celibates who deny themselves as part of a higher calling which yields compensating satisfactions. Indeed, the very fact that one needs to explain how the priesthood can compensate for the lack of family means that people do regard heterosexual mating as the natural or "inertial" state of human relations. The comparison between priests and homosexuals is in any case inapt. Priests do not simply give up sexual activity without ill-effect; they give it up for a reason. Homosexuals have hardly given up the use of their sexual organs, for a higher calling or anything else. Homosexuals continue to use them, but, unlike priests, they use them for what they are not for.

[. . .]

6   On Policy Issues

Homosexuality is intrinsically bad only in a prudential sense. It makes for unhappiness. However, this does not exempt homosexuality from the larger categories of ethics – rights, duties, liabilities. Deontic categories apply to acts which increase or decrease happiness or expose the helpless to the risk of unhappiness.

If homosexuality is unnatural, legislation which raises the odds that given child will become homosexual raises the odds that he will be unhappy. The only gap in the syllogism is whether legislation which legitimates, endorses or protects homosexuality does increase the chances that a child will become homosexual. If so, such legislation *is prima facie* objectionable. The question is not whether homosexual elementary school teachers will molest their charges. Pro-homosexual legislation might increase the incidence of homosexuality in subtler ways. If it does, and if the protection of children is fundamental obligation of society, legislation which legitimates homosexuality is a dereliction of duty. I am reluctant to deploy the language of "children's rights," which usually serves as one more excuse to interfere with the prerogatives of parents. But we do have obligations to our children, and one of them is to protect them from harm. If, as some have suggested, children have a right to protection from a religious education, they surely have a right to protection from homosexuality. So protecting them limits somebody else's freedom, but we are often willing to protect quite obscure children's rights at the expense of the freedom of others. There is a movement to ban TV commercials for sugar-coated cereals, to protect children from the relatively trivial harm of tooth decay. Such a ban would restrict the freedom of advertisers, and restrict it even though the last clear chance of avoiding the harm, and thus the responsibility, lies with the parents who control the TV set. I cannot see how one can consistently support such legislation and also urge homosexual rights, which risk much graver damage to children in exchange for increased freedom for homosexuals. [. . .]

It is commonly asserted that legislation granting homosexuals the privilege or right to be firemen endorses not homosexuality, but an expanded conception of human liberation. It is conjectural how sincerely this can be said in a legal order that forbids employers to hire whom they please and demands hours of paperwork for an interstate shipment of hamburger. But in any case legislation "legalizing homosexuality" cannot be neutral because passing it would have an inexpungeable speech-act dimension. Society cannot grant unaccustomed rights and privileges to homosexuals while remaining neutral about the value of homosexuality. [. . .] A society that grants privileges to homosexuals while recognizing that, in the light of generally known history, this act can be interpreted as a positive re-evaluation of homosexuality, is signalling that it now thinks homosexuality is all right. Many commentators in the popular press have observed that homosexuals, unlike members of racial minorities, can always "stay in the closet" when applying for jobs. What homosexual rights activists really want, therefore, is not access to jobs but legitimation of their homosexuality. Since this is known, giving them what they want will be seen as conceding their claim to legitimacy. And since legislators know their actions will support this interpretation, and know that their constituencies know they know this, the Gricean effect or symbolic meaning of passing anti-discrimination ordinances is to declare homosexuality legitimate (Will 1977).

[. . .]

Notes

1   Nagel attempts to meet these counterexamples in (1977) in effect by accepting such consequences of the classical analysis as that the beat of the heart is sometimes for diagnosis. The only reply to this sort of defense is that this is *not* what people mean. Met with such a reply, many philosophers feel impelled to say, "Well, it ought to be what you mean." This invitation to change the subject is attractive or relevant only if we haven't meant anything the first time around. If a coherent thought can be found behind our initial words which maximizes coherence with all hypothetical usages, it is *that thought we* were expressing and whose articulation was the aim of the analytic exercise.
[. . .]

2   A number of authors trace the present culture's taboo against "hemophilia" (Wilson's term) to the Old Testament proscription against nonproductive practices, and summarily dismiss it as "simplistic" and "archaic" nonsense (Wilson 1978, 142–143). While I have no sympathy for theological teleology, it should be recalled that the ban on homosexuality in Leviticus is one of just three rules set down as absolutely binding. Another one prohibits the shedding of innocent blood. This prohibition against using convenient victims for ulterior purposes is the basis for Western law and morality, and I trust Wilson does not find it simplistic or archaic.
[. . .]

Michael Levin

References

Barash, D. *The Whispering Within*. New York: Harper & Row, 1979.

Beach, F. "Cross-Species Comparisons and the Human Heritage." *Archives of Sexual Behavior* 5 (1976): 469–85.

Beadle, Q. and M. The Language of Life. New York: Anchor, 1967.

Beigl, H. Review of [34]. *Journal of Sex Research* 10: 339–40.

Bell, A. and M. Weinberg. *Homosexualities*. New York: Simon and Schuster, 1978.

Bennett, J. *Linguistic Behavior*. Cambridge: Cambridge University Press, 1976.

Dawkins, R. *The Selfish Gene*. Oxford: Oxford University Press, 1976.

Devlin, P. *The Enforcement of Morals*. Oxford: Oxford University Press, 1965.

Dworkin, G. Review of [36]. *Philosophical Review* 88: 660–63.

Gadpille, W. "Research into the Physiology of Maleness and Femaleness: Its Contribution to the Etiology and Psychodynamics of Homosexuality." *Archives of General Psychiatry* (1972): 193–206.

Goldberg, S. "What is 'Normal'? Logical Aspects of the Question of Homosexual Behavior." *Psychiatry* (1975):

Gould, R. "What We Don't Know about Homosexuality." *New York Times Magazine*, Feb. 24, 1974.

Gary, R. "Sex and Sexual Perversion." *Journal of Philosophy* 74 (1978): 189–99.

Greer, G. *The Obstacle Race*. New York: Farrar, Strauss & Giroux, 1979.

Grice, H. "Utterer's Meaning, Sentence-Meaning, and Word-Meaning." *Foundations of Language* 4 (1968): 1–18.

Hutchinson, G. "A Speculative Consideration of Certain Possible Forms of Sexual Selection in Man." *American Naturalist* 93 (1959): 81–91.

Karlen, A. *Sexuality and Homosexuality: A New View*. New York: Norton, 1967.

Levin, M. "On the Ascription of Functions to Objects." *Philosophy of the Social Sciences* 6 (1976): 227–34.

Levin, M. *Metaphysics and the Mind-Body Problem*. Oxford: Oxford University Press, 1979.

Levin, M. "'Sexism' is Meaningless." *St. John's Review* XXXIII (1981): 35–40.

Lewis, D. *Convention*. Cambridge, MA: Harvard University Press, 1970.

Masters, W. and V. Johnson. *Homosexuality in Perspective*. Boston, MA: Little, Brown and Company, 1979.

McCracken, S. "Replies to Correspondents." *Commentary*, April 1979.

Mossner, E. *The Life of David Hume*, 1st edn. New York: Nelson & Sons, 1954.

Nagel, E. *The Structure of Science*. New York: Harcourt & Brace, 1961.

Nagel, E. "Teleology Revisited." *Journal of Philosophy* 74 (1977): 261–301.

Nagel, T. "Sexual Perversion." *Journal of Philosophy* 66 (1969): 5–17.

Rechy, J. *The Sexual Outlaw*. New York: Grove Press, 1977.

Sagarin, E. "The Good Guys, the Bad Guys, and the Gay Guys." *Contemporary Sociology* (1973): 3–13.

Sagarin, E. and R. Kelley. "The Labelling of Deviance," in W. Grove, ed., *The Labelling of Deviance*. New York: Wiley & Sons, 1975.

Sayre, K. *Cybernetics and the Philosophy of Mind*. Atlantic Highlands, NJ: Humanities Press, 1976.

Schiffer, S. *Meaning*. Oxford: Oxford University Press, 1972.

Singer, P. *Democracy and Disobedience*, Oxford: Oxford University Press, 1968.

Weinberg, M. and C. Williams. *Male Homosexuals: Their Problems and Adaptations*. Oxford: Oxford University Press, 1974.

Will, G. "How Far Out of the Closet?" *Newsweek* 30 May 1977, p. 92.

Wilson, E. *Sociobiology: The New Synthesis*. Cambridge, MA: Harvard University Press, 1975.

Wilson, E. *On Human Nature*. Cambridge, MA: Harvard University Press, 1978.

Wright, L. "Functions." *Philosophical Review* 82 (1973): 139–68.

24

Homosexuality and Nature: Happiness and the Law at Stake

Timothy F. Murphy

Summary

Argues that Levin's and all similarly constructed arguments based on the notion of evolutionary aberration fail to show that evolutionary origins of sexual behavior have any normative force, that there are alternative evolutionary adaptation explanations of homosexuality, and that attributing the unhappiness of homosexuals to unsatisfied intrinsic biological drives is unjustified when homosexuals exist in a cultural context of discrimination and oppression. As such, public policy should not discriminate against homosexuals or attempt to minimize homosexuality.

Original publication details: Timothy Murphy, "Homosexuality and Nature: Happiness and the Law at Stake," pp. 195–204 from *Journal of Applied Philosophy* 4 (1987). Reproduced with permission of John Wiley & Sons.

Timothy F. Murphy

[. . .]

There are many ways used to argue against the moral legitimacy of homosexual behaviour, whether such behaviour is transient or exclusive. Some seek recourse to concepts of sinfulness, disease or crime in order to flesh out objections. Others appeal to the argument that homosexuality, its religious, medical, and criminal implications apart, is a kind of unnatural aberration which undermines its practitioners' prospects for happiness. I will consider this kind of argument here and contend that such an argument fails to establish that homosexuality is any significant abnormality and that neither its purported abnormality nor the unhappiness said to be associated with such behaviour can constitute a basis for criminalizing consensual homosexual behaviour or for failing to provide equal protections under the law for homosexuals in the area of public housing, service, jobs, and so on. I consider Michael Levin's 'Why homosexuality is abnormal' as paradigmatic of the kind of argument I wish to investigate[1]. Although I confine myself to his specific argument and frequently use its language, my position is applicable *a fortiori* to all similar kinds of positions.

The Argument from Nature

Levin says homosexuality is abnormal because it involves a misuse of body parts, that there is 'clear empirical sense' of that misuse, and that homosexual behaviour is contrary to the evolutionary adaptive order. Homosexual behaviour is abnormal, he says, because it is not the kind of behaviour which brought us to be the kind of physically constituted persons that we are today. Persons who used their penises for *coitus per anum* presumably left no ancestors. (Levin does not accept sociobiological contentions that homosexuality plays a supporting role in adaptive success.) That there are penises and vaginas today is due to the fact that they *were* used for heterosexual coitus, and hence we can infer that heterosexual coitus is indeed what such organs are for. Levin says: "an organ is for a given activity if the organ's performing that activity helps its host or organisms suitably related to its host, *and* if this contribution is how the organ got and stays where it is"[2]. Homosexual behaviour constitutes, according to this line of thought, an abandonment of certain functions on which species survival depended, and that abandonment is said to imply the loss of naturally occurring rewards selected for by adaptive success. This latter point does not mean that there are *no* compensatory pleasures, for just as the obese person will find gustatory

rewards in his or her food, the homosexual who misuses his or her body parts can find *some* compensatory sexual rewards. It is just that the wilful overeater or homosexual cannot reap the deepest rewards that nature has provided for in heterosexual usages and achievements.

Despite the effort which Levin takes to show that homosexual behaviour falls outside the behaviour upon which human adaptive success depended, I cannot say that I think this argument is even remotely convincing. Indeed, I believe it to be subject to a damning criticism. Even if it were certainly established that homosexuality was not part of originally adaptive behaviour, I do not see how that conclusion alone could establish the abnormality of homosexuality because there is neither a premise that natural selection has any kind of ultimate normative force nor a premise that human beings are bound to continue to be the kind of things that cosmic accident brought them to be. There is nothing in Levin's argument to sustain a claim that departures from a blind, accidental force of nature, or whatever metaphor of randomness is chosen, must be resisted. Without a logically prior and controlling premise that patterns of adaptive success possess ultimate, normative force, then it seems that human beings are completely at liberty to dispose of their world, their behaviour, and even such things as their anatomy and physiology as they see fit. [. . .]

Levin's argument, and others like it, ignore the prospects of beneficial departures from the naturally adaptive order. His argument assumes that each departure from our adaptive heritage will be unhappy in result. The argument, too, assumes that *all* behaviour of *all* persons must serve the purpose of adaption. Clearly, it is possible that some departures from the adaptive order are possible which do not threaten a species survival as a whole. If a species can survive if only a majority of its members use their organs in a particular fashion, then it may enjoy a surplus of adaptive protection even for those who act in wholly non-procreative fashion. Homosexuality, then, might have served some beneficial advantage (as sociobiology asserts) or it may have been (and this is more important for my argument) no impediment to selective adaptation. If this is so, it is hard to see in what sense homosexuality would have to be reckoned as a natural aberration.

[. . .]

Prospects for Happiness

Levin makes a great deal of the supposed link between homosexuality and unhappiness. One may assume that he would reply *to my* foregoing remarks by admitting that even if it were true that humans are not bound by any ultimate metaphysical sexual directive, then it would still remain true that prudential cautions obtain against homosexuality and that these cautions are sufficient to ground legal measures designed to minimize the occurrence of homosexuality. "Homosexuality," Levin says, "is likely to cause unhappiness because it leaves unfulfilled an innate and innately rewarding desire"[3], a desire supposedly ingrained through millennia of evolutionary selection. One might find some happy homosexuals, but Levin believes that such exceptions are inconsequential and do not disable his argument. He does not say that happy homosexuals are non-existent, only that they are rare and that their lives will be inherently less rewarding than those of heterosexuals. Moreover, "Even if some line demarcated happiness from unhappiness absolutely, it would be irrelevant if homosexuals were all happily above that line. It is the comparison with the heterosexual life that is at issue"[4]. The happiest persons are practitioners of heterosexuality, therefore, even if, according to Levin, each and every homosexual was, by his or her own admission, happy. But homosexuals are not even proximately happy, Levin says. According to him, awash in the travails of their own self-punishing promiscuity, present-day homosexuals would like to believe that all their ills are the result of an ill-constructed society, that their unhappiness is merely artifactual and in principle eliminable by the appropriate cultural and political accommodations. Levin suggests that this belief is a self-serving rationalization. Happiness has not followed, he says, the Danish and Dutch abandonment of prejudice against homosexuals. Happiness has not followed the work of various American organs to provide a positive image of homosexuals, judges allowing homosexuals to adopt their lovers, the Hollywood production of "highly sanitized" movies about homosexuality, publishers urging their authors to show little boys using cosmetics, or advertisers appealing directly to the homosexual market. That there has not been a resultant rise in homosexual happiness is said to be evident from (a) the gay press not liking Hollywood's movies, (b) the appearance of especially virulent diseases in homosexual populations, and (c) gay men needing frivolous enticements to get them to support important political causes on their behalf[5].

By way of comment on all this, I would first note that Levin has formulated his position in terms that *in principle* do not admit of refutation. He said that in principle, however happy homosexuals may be, they still cannot be as happy as heterosexuals. Of course, it is possible that a

claim is unfalsifiable because the claim is indeed true. On the other hand, I think one would do better to see a definitional fiat being asserted here; human happiness, *true* human happiness is said to be coextensive with the happiness of heterosexual behaviour. By definition there is nothing which could falsify this proposition, *not even* the self-asserted happiness of each and every homosexual person. I believe that this claim is no argument, avoiding as it does any potentially falsifying statement, and that it ought to be rejected as untestable rather than accepted as true by definition. As I have urged above, moreover, I do not believe that the accidental contingency of the primacy of heterosexual sexuality requires that all human happiness be sought there or that, perhaps, other kinds of happiness cannot be engineered.

Secondly, the kind of evidence that Levin uses to establish the unhappiness of homosexuals is altogether anecdotal and trivial[6]. That Hollywood continues to make bad movies, even when their subjects are 'sanitized' gay men and lesbians, is no evidence that homosexuality *per se* leads to unhappiness. The existence of viral disease *is* a major concern of gay men, but it is not because they are gay that it is their concern; it is because these viral diseases happen by accident of fate to affect the gay population. Would one want to argue that heterosexuals qua heterosexuals are somehow intrinsically headed for unhappiness as AIDS expands into that population? Moreover, that homosexuals mix business with pleasure is no argument that they are any less serious about their political agenda (let alone unhappier) than others. There is a kind of unfair asymmetry being used here in adducing Levin's evidence. If one uses such issues as he conjures up as evidence of the continuing unhappiness of homosexuals, why couldn't one equally and legitimately use similar evidence against the supposed happiness of heterosexuals? Most wars, for example, are the doing of heterosexuals. Nuclear weapons are their products. Most bad movies are also theirs. Must one infer therefore the continuing unhappiness of heterosexuals and assert prudential cautions against heterosexuality? If Levin's use of anecdotal evidence is acceptable against homosexuals, then it ought to be equally acceptable as an indictment of heterosexuality. Ironically, the case against heterosexuality would probably have to be seen as more damaging.

As for Levin's claims that homosexuals ought to be happier these days than they were in the past, it is probably the case that this is true. Anecdotal evidence may be used here since Levin uses it. The increasing success of gay pride parades ought to be taken as an indicator of some measure of increased homosexual happiness. At the very least persons who participate in them have been freed of the fear of some of the unhappy consequences that could befall them following public identification of their being gay. It is not without significance that in Boston, for example, the 1986 gay pride parade attracted some 25,000–30,000 participants whereas the first parade of 1970 had but 50! Furthermore, the heady increase in the number of gay and lesbian organizations for social, business, and political and support services indicates that homosexuals are not much inclined to wallow in despair over them sexual fate. One could go on in this vein, but I think it is important to consider that a verdict about the happiness of homosexuals would be a one-sided verdict indeed if it were to follow only from the evidence Levin puts forward.

To put specific quarrels about evidence aside, it seems to me that Levin fails almost culpably to imagine what a society would have to be like in order to be free of the oppressive elements which contribute to the putative unhappiness of homosexuals. In order to see the extent to which homosexual unhappiness is caused by social repressions and to what extent it is intrinsic, society would have to be completely free at every significant level of bias against homosexuals. To begin with – let's call this Phase I of the agenda: there should be no gratuitous assumption of heterosexuality in education, politics, advertising, and so on, just as a gender-neutral society would not presume the priority, real and symbolic, of males. For example, in education, texts and films ought to incorporate the experiences of gay men and lesbians. Educational measures should attempt to reduce anti-homosexuality in the same ways and to the same extent they educate against racism. In a society reconstructed along these lines, moreover, there would also have to be no right of access or entitlement possessed by a heterosexual that could be denied to a homosexual. *Only* in such a radically restructured society would one be able to see if homosexual unhappiness were immune to social deconstruction. Even if it weren't, one could still argue that homosexuals are not necessarily unhappy but that their happiness requires social protections or accommodations unrequired by heterosexuals. That is, homosexuals might need, as Phase II of the agenda, entitlements which heterosexuals do not in the way, for example, that legally-mandated minority hiring quotas serve other specific populations. Of course, one might want to argue that such entitlements would be anti-democratic and therefore objectionable. This protestation however would not by itself diminish the point

being made: that homosexual unhappiness is perhaps adventitious and that the only way of discovering this is to protect homosexuals in their lives, jobs, and interests in ways that are not presently served.

It is unlikely, of course, that the above-described experiment in social reconstruction is in any important sense immediately forthcoming. Nevertheless, that the experiment may be clearly formulated and seen as the definitive test of the social-reaction theory of homosexual unhappiness is sufficient ground to show that Levin's account of the unhappiness of homosexuals is unproved, its adduced evidence merely anecdotal. Even if it were true, I will argue later, since not all human unhappiness is tractable to social interventions, any residual unhappiness that was to survive Phase I and II of our social reformation agenda would still be no evidence against homosexuality.

Issues at Law

Levin believes that the abnormality of homosexuality and its attendant unhappiness are warrant enough to ground legal enactments against homosexuality and this is a matter of protecting citizens from lives impoverished by the loss of heterosexual rewards. Any legislation therefore that raises the odds that a child will become homosexual ought to be rejected as prima facie objectionable, as a dereliction of the duty of protecting children from the unhappy homosexual selves they might become[7]. The US Supreme Court recently ruled in Bowers v. Hardwick that states may enact, if they choose, statutes proscribing private consensual homosexual behaviour since, according to the opinion, there is nothing in the Constitution making such behaviour a fundamental right[8]. Levin's argument would presumably extend further since private consensual homosexual behaviour is socially invisible and unlikely as such to influence persons to become homosexual. Although he does not specifically mention what kinds of laws ought to be called for, or what kinds of laws ought to be rejected, presumably he means denying homosexuals protections in jobs, housing, foster-parenting, and so on. In short, the law would presumably have to serve the function of rendering homosexuality entirely invisible else there would continue to exist subtle promptings to homosexuality by virtue of degree of acceptance extended to it. Levin says he does not believe that this legal scenario would put any undue burden on any actual homosexual since, unlike members of racial minorities, he or she can always stay in the closet while applying for jobs, housing and the like. Therefore to give homosexuals protections they don't really need would have to be interpreted as a de facto social legitimation of homosexuality. This implied approval might be causally involved in the production of more homosexuals and therefore ought to be rejected.

I do not believe that this argument is convincing. First of all, the 'cause' or 'causes' of homosexuality are a matter of continuing controversy. There are metaphysical arguments that homosexuality is the result of some cosmic principle of world ordering; Plato's *Symposium* depicts homosexuals (and heterosexuals) as the result of an angry god's punishment. Biological theories hold homosexuality to be the result of some developmental variance or organismal dysfunction. Genetic theories try to locate the origins of homosexuality at the lowest level of biological causality, the gene. The most numerous kinds of theories are psychosocial theories which see homoeroticism as the result of either original psychical constitution or some developmental influences. Even the briefest perusal of the literature of the 'cause' of homosexuality leaves one with the conclusion that the 'cause' is an essentially disputed concept. There is not even agreement that homosexuality is a reifiable trait (any more than, say, courage) that can be explained by reference to a universally pre-existing set of conditions[9]. This dispute is important to consider since Levin seems to hold, without justification (at least without explanation), a developmental theory of homosexuality, a theory that homosexuals are made not born. This may or may not be true, but it seems wrong-headed to establish legal policy on the basis of one particular speculative theory of the origins of homosexual behaviour. If homosexuality is primarily a function of biological variance, for example, such laws and forbearances that Levin would see as desirable would have no effect whatever on the production of more homosexuals. Even if the law diligently erased all evidence of homosexual behaviour and persons from public view, one could not automatically assume a reduced number of homosexuals or a decrease in homosexual behaviour. I suspect that most persons are homosexual and become homosexual in ways completely immune to the written or enforced statutes of the various states. Children who never hear a word about homosexuality in their youth nevertheless become homosexuals. Children who walk past homosexual clubs and persons in the streets of certain American cities do not thereby automatically become homosexuals. Would it really be the case that there are more homosexuals

spawned in West Virginia because there are no laws against private, consensual homosexual behaviour there than in Virginia where there are such laws?[10] The net result of efforts to criminalize and reduce the visibility of homosexuality then would be to impose burdens on those who are perhaps involuntarily homosexual. At the very least, Levin's theory gratuitously supposes a developmental theory of homosexuality, a theory which has its insistent critics. One should also point out that even if some developmental theory of homosexuality were true, it is not necessarily the case that changing statutes would halt the flow of homosexuals since there may be other pathways to homosexuality. It is also the suspicion of many psychologists that homosexual tendencies are established very early on in childhood, in which case one presumes fairly that statutes criminalizing sodomy and lacks of protection in housing on the basis of sexual orientation have little to do with either ingraining or stifling homosexual dispositions.

If the reason that Levin suggests anti-homosexual measures is to contain human unhappiness, then his argument may be turned on its head. If the reason, or part of the reason that homosexuals are unhappy is because of the existence of certain legally permissible discriminations (or what comes to the same thing: fear of such), then it can certainly be suggested that laws ought to be changed in order to protect and enlarge the happiness of homosexuals, whether their homosexuality is elective or involuntary. In the name of their happiness, they ought to be afforded protections under the law, freedom from fear of prosecution for their private consensual behaviour and freedom to occupy jobs as persons they are, not as the persons others would have them be. The law could further protect them by saving them from blackmailers who would expose their homosexuality to employers, landlords, and so on. It is eminently clear that the law could at least enlarge the happiness of gay men and lesbians in these respects even if it cannot vouchsafe them absolute satisfaction in their lives.

Interestingly enough, even if all the unhappiness said to be associated with being homosexual were not eliminated by a dogged social reconstruction that achieved full parity between homosexuality and heterosexuality, it would still not follow that the law ought to be put to the purpose of eliminating homosexuality (assuming it could). Life, sad to say, is in some of its aspects inherently tragic. For example, in some important ways, law or society could never fully compensate the atheist for the lost rewards of religion. Atheism can discover in the world no incentives to conduct, no promise of the eventual recompense for injustices borne, and no guarantee that the heart's desires will be met[11]. Society might provide such consolations as it can, but it is certainly the case that a certain tragedy antagonistic to human happiness is an irreducible element of atheistic thought. That atheism leads to this measure of unhappiness would certainly not be a reason for instituting social and legal barriers to atheism on the theory that children ought to be glowingly happy (if self-deceived) theists rather than unhappy atheists. Human dignity is not automatically overthrown by a position of atheism; the atheist accepts and honours those satisfactions that are within his or her power. That homosexuality too might lead to a certain amount of unhappiness does not thereby overthrow the dignity of homosexual persons. One realizes merely that the law is no unfailing conduit to human happiness.

Levin's conclusions that legal measures ought to be taken to minimize the possibility that children become themselves the sad new recruits of homosexuality therefore cannot stand. I believe, on the contrary, that the law ought to do what it can to protect homosexuals from socially inflicted unhappiness. Levin's point that to decriminalize homosexual behaviour and to provide legal protections for homosexual persons would be seen as social legitimization of homosexuality (and not just tolerance) is correct. But this is no point over which to despair, for this inference is precisely compatible with the underlying metaphysics of gay activism, that homosexuality is no degrading impoverishment of human life. On the contrary, it has an integrity of its own apart from invidious comparisons with heterosexuality. Therefore, lest society be a political enforcer of sexual ideology, homosexuals ought to be afforded equal standing and protections under the law, and this in the name of serving human happiness.

[. . .]

Notes

1 MICHAEL LEVIN (1985) Why homosexuality is abnormal, *Monist* (Spring) pp. 251–283.
2 Levin, p. 256.
3 Levin, p. 261.
4 Levin, p. 262.
5 Levin, pp. 268–269.
6 Levin's leading of the 'evidence' is also suspect. At one point he refers to the narrative (1977) *The Sexual Outlaw* (New York, Grove Press), saying that even such a sympathetic observer as John Rechy admits that the immediate cause of homosexual unhappiness is a taste for promiscuity, anonymous encounters, and humiliation. This, I submit, is an embarrassing misrepresentation of Rechy's book, for that book explicitly, insistently, and frequently criticizes the hypocritical, violent sociolegal ethic which Rechy identifies itself as a (the?) major cause of homosexual promiscuity and unhappiness. He says, for example: "Imagine the horror of living with that constant fear, those threats. Imagine being forbidden to seek out a sexual partner. Imagine that – and you begin to understand the promiscuous rage of the sexual outlaw" (p. 102).
7 Levin, p.274.
8 Bowers v. Hardwick, No. 85–140 (30 June, 1986).
9 DOUGLAS FUTUYMA & STEPHEN J. RISCH (1984) Sexual orientation, sociobiology and evolution, in: J.P. DeCecco & M.G. Shiveley (eds.) *Bisexual and Homosexual Identities: critical theoretical issues*, PP. 157–168 (New York, Haworth Press).
10 Sodomy laws in US (illus.), *New York Times*, 1 July 1986, p. A19.
11 ERNEST NAGEL (1965) A defense of atheism, in: P. Edwards & A. Pap *A Modern Introduction to Philosophy*, pp. 460–472, rev edn. (New York, Free Press).

25

Bowers v. Hardwick

United States Supreme Court

Summary

The U.S. Supreme Court ruled that a Georgia statute criminalizing sodomy was constitutional because the Constitution does not provide a fundamental right to homosexuals to engage in sodomy, no previous cases involving relationships or marriage are relevant to sodomy, history and tradition have long condemned homosexual conduct, and popular opinion that sodomy is immoral is an adequate rationale to support such laws. Dissenting opinion argued that the Court misinterpreted the case narrowly as a fundamental right to engage in sodomy, when in fact the case is about the much broader right to privacy from governmental intrusion and about the right of individuals to define and express themselves through their intimate relationships.

Original publication details: Bowers v. Hardwick 478 U.S. 186, No. 85–140 (1986). Public domain.

Sexual Ethics: An Anthology, First Edition. Edited by Patrick D. Hopkins.
© 2023 John Wiley & Sons, Inc. Published 2023 by John Wiley & Sons, Inc.

SUPREME COURT OF THE UNITED STATES
No. 85-140
Syllabus
Bowers v. Hardwick
CERTIORARI TO THE UNITED STATES COURT OF APPEALS FOR THE ELEVENTH CIRCUIT
Argued: March 31, 1986 – Decided: June 30, 1986

After being charged with violating the Georgia statute criminalizing sodomy by committing that act with another adult male in the bedroom of his home, respondent Hardwick (respondent) brought suit in Federal District Court, challenging the constitutionality of the statute insofar as it criminalized consensual sodomy. The court granted the defendants' motion to dismiss for failure to state a claim. The Court of Appeals reversed and remanded, holding that the Georgia statute violated respondent's fundamental rights.

Held: The Georgia statute is constitutional. . . .

(a) The Constitution does not confer a fundamental right upon homosexuals to engage in sodomy. None of the fundamental rights announced in this Court's prior cases involving family relationships, marriage, or procreation bear any resemblance to the right asserted in this case. And any claim that those cases stand for the proposition that any kind of private sexual conduct between consenting adults is constitutionally insulated from state proscription is unsupportable. . . .

(b) Against a background in which many States have criminalized sodomy and still do, to claim that a right to engage in such conduct is "deeply rooted in this Nation's history and tradition" or "implicit in the concept of ordered liberty" is, at best, facetious. . . .

(c) There should be great resistance to expand the reach of the Due Process Clauses to cover new fundamental rights. Otherwise, the Judiciary necessarily would take upon itself further authority to govern the country without constitutional authority. The claimed right in this case falls far short of overcoming this resistance. . . .

(d) The fact that homosexual conduct occurs in the privacy of the home does not affect the result. *Stanley v. Georgia*, 394 U.S. 557, distinguished. . . .

(e) Sodomy laws should not be invalidated on the asserted basis that *majority belief that* sodomy is immoral is an inadequate rationale to support the laws. . . .

[. . .]

OPINION
JUSTICE WHITE delivered the opinion of the Court.

In August, 1982, respondent Hardwick (hereafter respondent) was charged with violating the Georgia statute criminalizing . . . sodomy[1] by committing that act with another adult male in the bedroom of respondent's home. After a preliminary hearing, the District Attorney decided not to present the matter to the grand jury unless further evidence developed.

Respondent then brought suit in the Federal District Court, challenging the constitutionality of the statute insofar as it criminalized consensual sodomy.[2] He asserted that he was a practicing homosexual, that the Georgia sodomy statute, as administered by the defendants, placed him in imminent danger of arrest, and that the statute for several reasons violates the Federal Constitution. The District Court granted the defendants' motion to dismiss for failure to state a claim, relying on *Doe v. Commonwealth's Attorney for the City of Richmond*, 403 F.Supp. 1199 (ED Va.1975), which this Court summarily affirmed, 425 U.S. 901 (1976). . . .

A divided panel of the Court of Appeals for the Eleventh Circuit reversed. 760 F.2d 1202 (1985). The court first held that, because *Doe* was distinguishable and, in any event, had been undermined by later decisions, our summary affirmance in that case did not require affirmance of the District Court. Relying on our decisions in *Griswold v. Connecticut*, 381 U.S. 479 (1965); *Eisenstadt v. Baird*, 405 U.S. 438 (1972); *Stanley v. Georgia*, 394 U.S. 557 (1969); and *Roe v. Wade*, 410 U.S. 113 (1973), the court went on to hold that the Georgia statute violated respondent's fundamental rights because his homosexual activity is a private and intimate association that is beyond the reach of state regulation by reason of the Ninth Amendment and the Due Process Clause of the Fourteenth Amendment. The case was remanded for trial, at which, to prevail, the State would have to prove that the statute is supported by a compelling interest and is the most narrowly drawn means of achieving that end.

Because other Courts of Appeals have arrived at judgments contrary to that of the Eleventh Circuit in this case,[3] we granted the Attorney General's petition for certiorari questioning the holding that the sodomy statute violates the fundamental rights of homosexuals. We agree with petitioner that the Court of Appeals erred, and hence reverse its judgment.[4] . . .

This case does not require a judgment on whether laws against sodomy between consenting adults in general, or between homosexuals in particular, are wise or desirable. It raises no question about the right or propriety of state legislative decisions to repeal their laws that criminalize homosexual sodomy, or of state court decisions invalidating those laws on state constitutional grounds. The issue presented is whether the Federal Constitution confers a fundamental right upon homosexuals to engage in sodomy, and hence invalidates the laws of the many States that still make such conduct illegal, and have done so for a very long time. The case also calls for some judgment about the limits of the Court's role in carrying out its constitutional mandate.

We first register our disagreement with the Court of Appeals and with respondent that the Court's prior cases have construed the Constitution to confer a right of privacy that extends to homosexual sodomy and, for all intents and purposes, have decided this case. The reach of this line of cases was sketched in *Carey v. Population Services International*, 431 U.S. 678, 685 (1977). *Pierce v. Society of Sisters*, 268 U.S. 510 (1925), and *Meyer v. Nebraska*, 262 U.S. 390 (1923), were described as dealing with childrearing and education; *Prince v. Massachusetts*, 321 U.S. 158 (1944), with family relationships; *Skinner v. Oklahoma ex rel. Williamson*, 316 U.S. 535 (1942), with procreation; *Loving v. Virginia*, 388 U.S. 1 (1967), with marriage; *Griswold v. Connecticut, supra*, and *Eisenstadt v. Baird, supra*, with contraception; and *Roe v. Wade*, 410 U.S. 113 (1973), with abortion. The latter three cases were interpreted as construing the Due Process Clause of the Fourteenth Amendment to confer a fundamental individual right to decide whether or not to beget or bear a child. *Carey v. Population Services International, supra*, at 688–689.

Accepting the decisions in these cases and the above description of them, we think it evident that none of the rights announced in those cases bears any resemblance to the . . . claimed constitutional right of homosexuals to engage in acts of sodomy that is asserted in this case. No connection between family, marriage, or procreation, on the one hand, and homosexual activity, on the other, has been demonstrated, either by the Court of Appeals or by respondent. Moreover, any claim that these cases nevertheless stand for the proposition that any kind of private sexual conduct between consenting adults is constitutionally insulated from state proscription is unsupportable. Indeed, the Court's opinion in *Carey* twice asserted that the privacy right, which the *Griswold* line of cases found to be one of the protections provided by the Due

Process Clause, did not reach so far. 431 U.S. at 688, n. 5,694, n. 17.

Precedent aside, however, respondent would have us announce, as the Court of Appeals did, a fundamental right to engage in homosexual sodomy. This we are quite unwilling to do. It is true that, despite the language of the Due Process Clauses of the Fifth and Fourteenth Amendments, which appears to focus only on the processes by which life, liberty, or property is taken, the cases are legion in which those Clauses have been interpreted to have substantive content, subsuming rights that to a great extent are immune from federal or state regulation or proscription. Among such cases are those recognizing rights that have little or no textual support in the constitutional language. *Meyer, Prince,* and *Pierce* fall in this category, as do the privacy cases from *Griswold* to *Carey*.

Striving to assure itself and the public that announcing rights not readily identifiable in the Constitution's text involves much more than the imposition of the Justices' own choice of values on the States and the Federal Government, the Court has sought to identify the nature of the rights qualifying for heightened judicial protection. In *Palko v. Connecticut*, 302 U.S. 319, 325, 326 (1937), it was said that this category includes those fundamental liberties that are "implicit in the concept of ordered liberty," such that "neither . . . liberty nor justice would exist if [they] were sacrificed." A different description of fundamental liberties appeared in *Moore v. East Cleveland*, 431 U.S. 494, 503 (1977) (opinion of POWELL, J.), where they are characterized as those liberties that are "deeply rooted in this Nation's history and tradition." *Id.* at 503 (POWELL, J.). *See also Griswold v. Connecticut*, 381 U.S. at 506.

It is obvious to us that neither of these formulations would extend a fundamental right to homosexuals to engage in acts of consensual sodomy. Proscriptions against that conduct have ancient roots. *See generally* Survey on the Constitutional Right to Privacy in the Context of Homosexual Activity, 40 U.Miami L.Rev. 521, 525 (1986). Sodomy was a criminal offense at common law, and was forbidden by the laws of the original 13 States when they ratified the Bill of Rights.[5] In 1868, when the Fourteenth Amendment was . . . ratified, all but 5 of the 37 States in the Union had criminal sodomy laws.[6] In fact, until 1961,[7] all 50 States outlawed sodomy, and today, 24 States and the District of Columbia . . . continue to provide criminal penalties for sodomy performed in private and between consenting adults. *See* Survey, U.Miami L.Rev. *supra*, at 524, n. 9. Against this background, to claim that a right to engage in such conduct is "deeply rooted in this Nation's history and tradition" or "implicit in the concept of ordered liberty" is, at best, facetious.

Nor are we inclined to take a more expansive view of our authority to discover new fundamental rights imbedded in the Due Process Clause. The Court is most vulnerable and comes nearest to illegitimacy when it deals with judge-made constitutional law having little or no cognizable roots in the language or design of the Constitution. That this is so was painfully demonstrated by the face-off between the Executive and the Court in the 1930s, which resulted in the repudiation . . . of much of the substantive gloss that the Court had placed on the Due Process Clauses of the Fifth and Fourteenth Amendments. There should be, therefore, great resistance to expand the substantive reach of those Clauses, particularly if it requires redefining the category of rights deemed to be fundamental. Otherwise, the Judiciary necessarily takes to itself further authority to govern the country without express constitutional authority. The claimed right pressed on us today falls far short of overcoming this resistance.

Respondent, however, asserts that the result should be different where the homosexual conduct occurs in the privacy of the home. He relies on *Stanley v. Georgia*, 394 U.S. 557 (1969), where the Court held that the First Amendment prevents conviction for possessing and reading obscene material in the privacy of one's home:

If the First Amendment means anything, it means that a State has no business telling a man, sitting alone in his house, what books he may read or what films he may watch.

Id. at 565.

Stanley did protect conduct that would not have been protected outside the home, and it partially prevented the enforcement of state obscenity laws; but the decision was firmly grounded in the First Amendment. The right pressed upon us here has no similar support in the text of the Constitution, and it does not qualify for recognition under the prevailing principles for construing the Fourteenth Amendment. Its limits are also difficult to discern. Plainly enough, otherwise illegal conduct is not always immunized whenever it occurs in the home. Victimless crimes, such as the possession and use of illegal drugs, do not escape the law where they are committed at home. *Stanley* itself recognized that its holding offered no protection for the possession in the home of drugs, firearms, or stolen goods. *Id.* at 568, n. 11. And if respondent's submission is limited to the voluntary

sexual conduct between consenting adults, it would be difficult, except by fiat, to limit the claimed right to homosexual conduct . . . while leaving exposed to prosecution adultery, incest, and other sexual crimes even though they are committed in the home. We are unwilling to start down that road.

Even if the conduct at issue here is not a fundamental right, respondent asserts that there must be a rational basis for the law, and that there is none in this case other than the presumed belief of a majority of the electorate in Georgia that homosexual sodomy is immoral and unacceptable. This is said to be an inadequate rationale to support the law. The law, however, is constantly based on notions of morality, and if all laws representing essentially moral choices are to be invalidated under the Due Process Clause, the courts will be very busy indeed. Even respondent makes no such claim, but insists that majority sentiments about the morality of homosexuality should be declared inadequate. We do not agree, and are unpersuaded that the sodomy laws of some 25 States should be invalidated on this basis.[8]

Accordingly, the judgment of the Court of Appeals is

Reversed.

[. . .]

CONCURRING

CHIEF JUSTICE BURGER, concurring.

I join the Court's opinion, but I write separately to underscore my view that, in constitutional terms, there is no such thing as a fundamental right to commit homosexual sodomy.

As the Court notes, *ante* at 192, the proscriptions against sodomy have very "ancient roots." Decisions of individuals relating to homosexual conduct have been subject to state intervention throughout the history of Western civilization. Condemnation of those practices is firmly rooted in Judeo-Christian moral and ethical standards. Homosexual sodomy was a capital crime under Roman law. *See* Code Theod. 9.7.6; Code Just. 9.9.31. *See also* D. Bailey, Homosexuality . . . and the Western Christian Tradition 70–81 (1975). During the English Reformation, when powers of the ecclesiastical courts were transferred to the King's Courts, the first English statute criminalizing sodomy was passed. 25 Hen. VIII, ch. 6. Blackstone described "the infamous *crime against nature*" as an offense of "deeper malignity" than rape, a heinous act "the very mention of which is a disgrace to human nature," and "a crime not fit to be named." 4 W. Blackstone, Commentaries *215. The common law of England, including its prohibition of sodomy, became the received law of Georgia and the other Colonies. In 1816, the Georgia Legislature passed the statute at issue here, and that statute has been continuously in force in one form or another since that time. To hold that the act of homosexual sodomy is somehow protected as a fundamental right would be to cast aside millennia of moral teaching.

This is essentially not a question of personal "preferences," but rather of the legislative authority of the State. I find nothing in the Constitution depriving a State of the power to enact the statute challenged here.

[...]

DISSENTING

JUSTICE BLACKMUN, with whom JUSTICE BRENNAN, JUSTICE MARSHALL, and JUSTICE STEVENS join, dissenting.

This case is no more about "a fundamental right to engage in homosexual sodomy," as the Court purports to declare, *ante* at 191, than *Stanley v. Georgia*, 394 U.S. 557 (1969), was about a fundamental right to watch obscene movies, or *Katz v. United States*, 389 U.S. 347 (1967), was about a fundamental right to place interstate bets from a telephone booth. Rather, this case is about "the most comprehensive of rights and the right most valued by civilized men," namely, "the right to be let alone." *Olmstead v. United States*, 277 U.S. 438, 478 (1928) (Brandeis, J., dissenting).

The statute at issue, Ga.Code Ann. § 16-6-2 (1984), denies individuals the right to decide for themselves whether to engage in particular forms of private, consensual sexual activity. The Court concludes that § 16-6-2 is valid essentially because "the laws of . . . many States . . . still make such conduct illegal and have done so for a very long time." *Ante* at 190. But the fact that the moral judgments expressed by statutes like § 16-6-2 may be

"natural and familiar . . . ought not to conclude our judgment upon the question whether statutes embodying them conflict with the Constitution of the United States."

Roe v. Wade, 410 U.S. 113, 117 (1973), quoting *Lochner v. New York*, 198 U.S. 45, 76 (1905) (Holmes, J,, dissenting). Like Justice Holmes, I believe that

[i]t is revolting to have no better reason for a rule of law than that so it was laid down in the time of Henry IV. It is still more revolting if the grounds upon which it was laid down have vanished long since, and the rule simply persists from blind imitation of the past.

Holmes, The Path of the Law, 10 Harv.L.Rev. 457, 469 (1897). I believe we must analyze respondent Hardwick's claim in the light of the values that underlie the constitutional right to privacy. If that right means anything, it means that, before Georgia can prosecute its citizens for making choices about the most intimate . . . aspects of their lives, it must do more than assert that the choice they have made is an "'abominable crime not fit to be named among Christians.'" *Herring v. State*, 119 Ga. 709, 721, 46 S.E. 876, 882 (1904).

I

In its haste to reverse the Court of Appeals and hold that the Constitution does not "confe[r] a fundamental right upon homosexuals to engage in sodomy," *ante* at 190, the Court relegates the actual statute being challenged to a footnote, and ignores the procedural posture of the case before it. A fair reading of the statute and of the complaint clearly reveals that the majority has distorted the question this case presents.

First, the Court's almost obsessive focus on homosexual activity is particularly hard to justify in light of the broad language Georgia has used. Unlike the Court, the Georgia Legislature has not proceeded on the assumption that homosexuals are so different from other citizens that their lives may be controlled in a way that would not be tolerated if it limited the choices of those other citizens. *Cf. ante* at 188, n. 2. Rather, Georgia has provided that

[a] person commits the offense of sodomy when he performs or submits to any sexual act involving the sex organs of one person and the mouth or anus of another.

Ga.Code Ann. § 16-6-2(a) (1984). The sex or status of the persons who engage in the act is irrelevant as a matter of state law. In fact, to the extent I can discern a legislative purpose for Georgia's 1968 enactment of § 16-6-2, that purpose seems to have been to broaden the coverage of the law to reach heterosexual as well as homosexual activity.[9] I therefore see no basis for the . . . Court's decision to treat this case as an "as applied" challenge to § 16-6-2, *see ante* at 188, n. 2, or for Georgia's attempt, both in its brief and at oral argument, to defend § 16-6-2 solely on the grounds that it prohibits homosexual activity. Michael Hardwick's standing may rest in significant part on Georgia's apparent willingness to enforce against homosexuals a law it seems not to have any desire to enforce against heterosexuals. *See* Tr. of Oral Arg. 4–5; *cf.* 760 *F.2d* 1202, 1205–1206 (CA11 1985). But his claim that § 16-6-2 involves an unconstitutional intrusion into his privacy and his right of intimate association does not depend in any way on his sexual orientation.

Second, I disagree with the Court's refusal to consider whether § 16-6-2 runs afoul of the Eighth or Ninth Amendments or the Equal Protection Clause of the Fourteenth Amendment. *Ante* at 196, n. 8. Respondent's complaint expressly invoked the Ninth Amendment, *see* App. 6, and he relied heavily before this Court on *Griswold v. Connecticut*, 381 U.S. 479, 484 (1965), which identifies that Amendment as one of the specific constitutional provisions giving "life and substance" to our understanding of privacy. *See* Brief for Respondent Hardwick 10–12; Tr. of Oral Arg. 33. More importantly, the procedural posture of the case requires that we affirm the Court of Appeals' judgment if there is *any* ground on which respondent may be entitled to relief. This case is before us on petitioner's motion to dismiss for failure to state a claim, Fed.Rule Civ.Proc. 12(b)(6). *See* App. 17. It is a well-settled principle of law that

> a complaint should not be dismissed merely because a plaintiffs allegations do not support the particular legal theory he advances, for the court is under a duty to examine the complaint to determine if the allegations provide for relief on any possible theory. . . . *Bramlet v. Wilson*, 495 F.2d 714, 716 (CA8 1974); *see Parr v. Great Lakes Express Co.*, 484 F.2d 767,773 (CA7 1973); *Due v. Tallahassee Theatres, Inc.*, 333 F.2d 630, 631 (CA5 1964); *United States v. Howell*, 318 F.2d 162, 166 (CA9 1963); 5 C. Wright & A. Miller, Federal Practice and Procedure § 1357, pp. 601–602 (1969); *see also Conley v. Gibson*, 355 U.S. 41, 45–46 (1957). Thus, even if respondent did not advance claims based on the Eighth or Ninth Amendments, or on the Equal Protection Clause, his complaint should not be dismissed if any of those provisions could entitle him to relief. I need not reach either the Eighth Amendment or the Equal Protection Clause issues, because I believe that Hardwick has stated a cognizable claim that § 16-6-2 interferes with constitutionally protected interests in privacy and freedom of intimate association. But neither the Eighth Amendment nor the Equal Protection Clause is so clearly irrelevant that a claim resting on either provision should be peremptorily dismissed.[10] The Court's cramped reading of the . . . issue before it makes for a short opinion, but it does little to make for a persuasive one.

II

Our cases long have recognized that the Constitution embodies a promise that a certain private sphere of individual liberty will be kept largely beyond the reach of government.

Thornburgh v. American College of Obstetricians & Gynecologists, 476 U.S. 747, *772* (1986). In construing the right to privacy, the Court has proceeded along two somewhat distinct, . . . albeit complementary, lines. First, it has recognized a privacy interest with reference to certain decisions that are properly for the individual to make. *E.g.*, *Roe v. Wade*, 410 U.S. 113 (1973); *Pierce v. Society of Sisters*, 268 U.S. 510 (1925). Second, it has recognized a privacy interest with reference to certain places without regard for the particular activities in which the individuals who occupy them are engaged. *E.g.*, *United States v. Karo*, 468 U.S. 705 (1984); *Payton v. New York*, 445 U.S. 573 (1980); *Rios v. United States*, 364 U.S. 253 (1960). The case before us implicates both the decisional and the spatial aspects of the right to privacy.

A

The Court concludes today that none of our prior cases dealing with various decisions that individuals are entitled to make free of governmental interference "bears any resemblance to the claimed constitutional right of homosexuals to engage in acts of sodomy that is asserted in this case." *Ante* at 190–191. While it is true that these cases may be characterized by their connection to protection of the family, *see Roberts v. United States Jaycees*, 468 U.S. 609, 619 (1984), the Court's conclusion that they extend no further than this boundary ignores the warning in *Moore v. East Cleveland*, 431 U.S. 494, 501 (1977) (plurality opinion), against

> clos[ing] our eyes to the basic reasons why certain rights associated with the family have been accorded shelter under the Fourteenth Amendment's Due Process Clause.

We protect those rights not because they contribute, in some direct and material way, to the general public welfare, but because they form so central a part of an individual's life. "[T]he concept of privacy embodies the 'moral fact that a person belongs to himself, and not others nor to society as a whole.'" *Thornburgh v. American College of Obstetricians & Gynecologists*, 476 U.S. at 777,

n. 5 (STEVENS, J., concurring), quoting Fried, Correspondence, 6 Phil. & Pub.Affairs 288–289 (1977). And so we protect the decision whether to . . . marry precisely because marriage

is an association that promotes a way of life, not causes; a harmony in living, not political faiths; a bilateral loyalty, not commercial or social projects.

Griswold v. Connecticut, 381 U.S. at 486. We protect the decision whether to have a child because parenthood alters so dramatically an individual's self-definition, not because of demographic considerations or the Bible's command to be fruitful and multiply. *Cf. Thornburgh v. American College of Obstetricians & Gynecologists, supra*, at 777, n. 6 (STEVENS, J., concurring). And we protect the family because it contributes so powerfully to the happiness of individuals, not because of a preference for stereotypical households. *Cf. Moore v. East Cleveland*, 431 U.S. at 500–506 (plurality opinion). The Court recognized in *Roberts*, 468 U.S. at 619, that the "ability independently to define one's identity that is central to any concept of liberty" cannot truly be exercised in a vacuum; we all depend on the "emotional enrichment from close ties with others." *Ibid.*

Only the most willful blindness could obscure the fact that sexual intimacy is "a sensitive, key relationship of human existence, central to family life, community welfare, and the development of human personality," *Paris Adult Theatre I v. Slaton*, 413 U.S. 49, 63 (1973); *see also Carey v. Population Services International*, 431 U.S. 678, 685 (1977). The fact that individuals define themselves in a significant way through their intimate sexual relationships with others suggests, in a Nation as diverse as ours, that there may be many "right" ways of conducting those relationships, and that much of the richness of a relationship will come from the freedom an individual has to choose the form and nature of these intensely personal bonds. *See* Karst, The Freedom of Intimate Association, 89 Yale LJ. 624, 637 (1980); *cf. Eisenstadt v. Baird*, 405 U.S. 438, 453 (1972); *Roe v. Wade*, 410 U.S. at 153.

In a variety of circumstances we have recognized that a necessary corollary of giving individuals freedom to choose . . . how to conduct their lives is acceptance of the fact that different individuals will make different choices. For example, in holding that the clearly important state interest in public education should give way to a competing claim by the Amish to the effect that extended formal schooling threatened their way of life, the Court declared:

There can be no assumption that today's majority is "right" and the Amish and others like them are "wrong." A way of life that is odd or even erratic, but interferes with no rights or interests of others, is not to be condemned because it is different.

Wisconsin v. Yoder, 406 U.S. 205, 223–224 (1972). The Court claims that its decision today merely refuses to recognize a fundamental right to engage in homosexual sodomy; what the Court really has refused to recognize is the fundamental interest all individuals have in controlling the nature of their intimate associations with others.

B

The behavior for which Hardwick faces prosecution occurred in his own home, a place to which the Fourth Amendment attaches special significance. The Court's treatment of this aspect of the case is symptomatic of its overall refusal to consider the broad principles that have informed our treatment of privacy in specific cases. Just as the right to privacy is more than the mere aggregation of a number of entitlements to engage in specific behavior, so too protecting the physical integrity of the home is more than merely a means of protecting specific activities that often take place there. Even when our understanding of the contours of the right to privacy depends on "reference to a 'place,'" *Katz v. United States*, 389 U.S. at 361 (Harlan, J., concurring),

the essence of a Fourth Amendment violation is "not the breaking of [a person's] doors, and the rummaging of his drawers," but rather is "the invasion of his indefeasible right of personal security, personal liberty and private property."

California v. Ciraolo, 476 U.S. 207, 226 (1986) (POWELL, J., dissenting), . . . quoting *Boyd v. United States, 116* U.S. 616, 630 (1886).

The Court's interpretation of the pivotal case of *Stanley v. Georgia*, 394 U.S. 557 (1969), is entirely unconvincing. *Stanley* held that Georgia's undoubted power to punish the public distribution of constitutionally unprotected, obscene material did not permit the State to punish the private possession of such material. According to the majority here, *Stanley* relied entirely on the First Amendment, and thus, it is claimed, sheds no light on cases not involving printed materials. *Ante* at 195. But that is not what *Stanley* said. Rather, the *Stanley* Court anchored its holding in the Fourth

Amendment's special protection for the individual in his home:

> "The makers of our Constitution undertook to secure conditions favorable to the pursuit of happiness. They recognized the significance of man's spiritual nature, of his feelings and of his intellect. They knew that only a part of the pain, pleasure and satisfactions of life are to be found in material things. They sought to protect Americans in their beliefs, their thoughts, their emotions and their sensations."

* * * *

These are the rights that appellant is asserting in the case before us. He is asserting the right to read or observe what he pleases – the right to satisfy his intellectual and emotional needs in the privacy of his own home.

394 U.S. at 564–565, quoting *Olmstead v. United States*, 277 U.S. at 478 (Brandeis, J., dissenting).

The central place that *Stanley* gives Justice Brandeis' dissent in *Olmstead*, a case raising no First Amendment claim, shows that *Stanley* rested as much on the Court's understanding of the Fourth Amendment as it did on the First. Indeed, in *Paris Adult Theatre I v. Slaton*, 413 U.S. 49 (1973), the Court suggested that reliance on the Fourth . . . Amendment not only supported the Court's outcome in *Stanley* but actually was *necessary* to it:

If obscene material unprotected by the First Amendment, in itself, carried with it a "penumbra" of constitutionally protected privacy, this Court would not have found it necessary to decide *Stanley* on the narrow basis of the "privacy of the home," which was hardly more than a reaffirmation that "a man's home is his castle."

413 U.S. at 66. "The right of the people to be secure in their . . . houses," expressly guaranteed by the Fourth Amendment, is perhaps the most "textual" of the various constitutional provisions that inform our understanding of the right to privacy, and thus I cannot agree with the Court's statement that "[t]he right pressed upon us here has no . . . support in the text of the Constitution," *ante* at 195. Indeed, the right of an individual to conduct intimate relationships in the intimacy of his or her own home seems to me to be the heart of the Constitution's protection of privacy.

III

The Court's failure to comprehend the magnitude of the liberty interests at stake in this case leads it to slight the question whether petitioner, on behalf of the State, has justified Georgia's infringement on these interests. I believe that neither of the two general justifications for § 16-6-2 that petitioner has advanced warrants dismissing respondent's challenge for failure to state a claim.

First, petitioner asserts that the acts made criminal by the statute may have serious adverse consequences for "the general public health and welfare," such as spreading communicable diseases or fostering other criminal activity. Brief for Petitioner 37. Inasmuch as this case was dismissed by the District Court on the pleadings, it is not surprising that the record before us is barren of any evidence to support petitioner's claim.[11] In light of the state of the record, I see . . . no justification for the Court's attempt to equate the private, consensual sexual activity at issue here with the "possession in the home of drugs, firearms, or stolen goods," *ante* at 195, to which *Stanley* refused to extend its protection. 394 U.S. at 568, n. 11. None of the behavior so mentioned in *Stanley* can properly be viewed as "[v]ictimless," *ante* at 195: drugs and weapons are inherently dangerous, *see, e.g., McLaughlin v. United States*, 476 U.S. 16 (1986), and for property to be "stolen," someone must have been wrongfully deprived of it. Nothing in the record before the Court provides any justification for finding the activity forbidden by § 16-6-2 to be physically dangerous, either to the persons engaged in it or to others.[12] . . .

The core of petitioner's defense of § 16-6-2, however, is that respondent and others who engage in the conduct prohibited by § 16-6-2 interfere with Georgia's exercise of the "'right of the Nation and of the States to maintain a decent society,'" *Paris Adult Theatre I v. Slaton*, 413 U.S. at 59–60, quoting *Jacobellis v. Ohio*, 378 U.S. 184, 199 (1964) (Warren, C.J., dissenting). Essentially, petitioner argues, and the Court agrees, that the fact that the acts described in § 16-6-2 "for hundreds of years, if not thousands, have been uniformly condemned as immoral" is a sufficient reason to permit a State to ban them today. Brief for Petitioner 19; *see ante* at 190, 192–194, 196.

I cannot agree that either the length of time a majority has held its convictions or the passions with which it defends them can withdraw legislation from this Court's scrutiny. *See, e.g., Roe v. Wade*, 410 U.S. 113 (1973); *Loving v. Virginia*, 388 U.S. 1 (1967); *Brown v. Board of Education*, 347 U.S. 483 (1954).[13] As Justice Jackson wrote so eloquently . . . for the Court in *West Virginia Board of Education v. Barnette*, 319 U.S. 624, 641–642 (1943),

> we apply the limitations of the Constitution with no fear that freedom to be intellectually and spiritually

diverse, or even contrary, will disintegrate the social organization. . . . [F]reedom to differ is not limited to things that do not matter much. That would be a mere shadow of freedom. The test of its substance is the right to differ as to things that touch the heart of the existing order.

See also Karst, 89 Yale L.J. at 627. It is precisely because the issue raised by this case touches the heart of what makes individuals what they are that we should be especially sensitive to the rights of those whose choices upset the majority.

The assertion that "traditional Judeo-Christian values proscribe" the conduct involved, Brief for Petitioner 20, cannot provide an adequate justification for § 16-6-2. That certain, but by no means all, religious groups condemn the behavior at issue gives the State no license to impose their judgments on the entire citizenry. The legitimacy of secular legislation depends, instead, on whether the State can advance some justification for its law beyond its conformity to religious doctrine. *See, e.g., McGowan v. Maryland*, 366 U.S. 420, 429–453 (1961); *Stone v. Graham*, 449 U.S. 39 (1980). Thus, far from buttressing his case, petitioner's invocation of Leviticus, Romans, St. Thomas Aquinas, and sodomy's heretical status during the Middle Ages undermines his suggestion that § 16-6-2 represents a legitimate use of secular coercive power.[14] A State can no more punish private behavior because . . . of religious intolerance than it can punish such behavior because of racial animus.

The Constitution cannot control such prejudices, but neither can it tolerate them. Private biases may be outside the reach of the law, but the law cannot, directly or indirectly, give them effect.

Palmore v. Sidoti, 466 U.S. 429, 433 (1984). No matter how uncomfortable a certain group may make the majority of this Court, we have held that "[m]ere public intolerance or animosity cannot constitutionally justify the deprivation of a person's physical liberty." *O'Connor v. Donaldson*, 422 U.S. 563, 575 (1975). *See also Cleburne v. Cleburne Living Center, Inc.*, 473 U.S. 432 (1985); *United States Dept. of Agriculture v. Moreno*, 413 U.S. 528, 534 (1973).

Nor can § 16-6-2 be justified as a "morally neutral" exercise of Georgia's power to "protect the public environment," *Paris Adult Theatre I*, 413 U.S. at 68–69. Certainly, some private behavior can affect the fabric of society as a whole. Reasonable people may differ about whether particular sexual acts are moral or immoral, but

we have ample evidence for believing that people will not abandon morality, will not think any better of murder, cruelty and dishonesty, merely because some private sexual practice which they abominate is not punished by the law.

H. L. A. Hart, Immorality and Treason, *reprinted in* The Law as Literature 220, 225 (L. Blom-Cooper ed.1961). Petitioner and the Court fail to see the difference between laws that protect public sensibilities and those that enforce private morality. Statutes banning . . . public sexual activity are entirely consistent with protecting the individual's liberty interest in decisions concerning sexual relations: the same recognition that those decisions are intensely private which justifies protecting them from governmental interference can justify protecting individuals from unwilling exposure to the sexual activities of others. But the mere fact that intimate behavior may be punished when it takes place in public cannot dictate how States can regulate intimate behavior that occurs in intimate places. *See Paris Adult Theatre I*, 413 U.S. at 66, n. 13 ("marital intercourse on a street corner or a theater stage" can be forbidden despite the constitutional protection identified in *Griswold v. Connecticut*, 381 U.S. 479 (1965)).[15]

This case involves no real interference with the rights of others, for the mere knowledge that other individuals do not adhere to one's value system cannot be a legally cognizable interest, *cf. Diamond v. Charles*, 476 U.S. 54, 65–66 (1986), let alone an interest that can justify invading the houses, hearts, and minds of citizens who choose to live their lives differently.

IV

It took but three years for the Court to see the error in its analysis in *Minersville School District v. Gobitis*, 310 U.S. . . . 586 (1940), and to recognize that the threat to national cohesion posed by a refusal to salute the flag was vastly outweighed by the threat to those same values posed by compelling such a salute. *See West Virginia Board of Education v. Barnette*, 319 U.S. 624 (1943). I can only hope that here, too, the Court soon will reconsider its analysis and conclude that depriving individuals of the right to choose for themselves how to conduct their intimate relationships poses a far greater threat to the values most deeply rooted in our Nation's history than tolerance of nonconformity could ever do. Because I think the Court today betrays those values, I dissent.

[. . .]

JUSTICE STEVENS, with whom JUSTICE BRENNAN and JUSTICE MARSHALL join, dissenting.

Like the statute that is challenged in this case,[16] the rationale of the Court's opinion applies equally to the prohibited conduct regardless of whether the parties who engage in it are married or unmarried, or are of the same or different sexes.[17] Sodomy was condemned as an odious and sinful type of behavior during the formative period of the common law.[18] . . . That condemnation was equally damning for heterosexual and homosexual sodomy.[19] Moreover, it provided no special exemption for married couples.[20] The license to cohabit and to produce legitimate offspring simply did not include any permission to engage in sexual conduct that was considered a "crime against nature."

The history of the Georgia statute before us clearly reveals this traditional prohibition of heterosexual, as well as homosexual, sodomy.[21] Indeed, at one point in the 20th century, Georgia's law was construed to permit certain sexual conduct between homosexual women even though such conduct was prohibited between heterosexuals.[22] The history of the statutes cited by the majority as proof for the proposition that sodomy is not constitutionally protected, *ante* at 192–194, . . . and nn. 5 and 6, similarly reveals a prohibition on heterosexual, as well as homosexual, sodomy.[23]

Because the Georgia statute expresses the traditional view that sodomy is an immoral kind of conduct regardless of the identity of the persons who engage in it, I believe that a proper analysis of its constitutionality requires consideration of two questions: first, may a State totally prohibit the described conduct by means of a neutral law applying without exception to all persons subject to its jurisdiction? If not, may the State save the statute by announcing that it will only enforce the law against homosexuals? The two questions merit separate discussion.

I

Our prior cases make two propositions abundantly clear. First, the fact that the governing majority in a State has traditionally viewed a particular practice as immoral is not a sufficient reason for upholding a law prohibiting the practice; neither history nor tradition could save a law prohibiting miscegenation from constitutional attack.[24] Second, individual decisions by married persons, concerning the intimacies of their physical relationship, even when not intended to produce offspring, are a form of "liberty" protected by the Due Process Clause of the Fourteenth Amendment. *Griswold v. Connecticut*, 381 U.S. 479 (1965). Moreover, this protection extends to intimate choices by unmarried, as well as married, persons. *Carey v. Population Services International*, 431 U.S. 678 (1977); *Eisenstadt v. Baird*, 405 US. 438 (1972). . . .

In consideration of claims of this kind, the Court has emphasized the individual interest in privacy, but its decisions have actually been animated by an even more fundamental concern. As I wrote some years ago:

These cases do not deal with the individual's interest in protection from unwarranted public attention, comment, or exploitation. They deal, rather, with the individual's right to make certain unusually important decisions that will affect his own, or his family's, destiny. The Court has referred to such decisions as implicating "basic values," as being "fundamental," and as being dignified by history and tradition. The character of the Court's language in these cases brings to mind the origins of the American heritage of freedom – the abiding interest in individual liberty that makes certain state intrusions on the citizen's right to decide how he will live his own life intolerable. Guided by history, our tradition of respect for the dignity of individual choice in matters of conscience and the restraints implicit in the federal system, federal judges have accepted the responsibility for recognition and protection of these rights in appropriate cases.

Fitzgerald v. Porter Memorial Hospital, 523 F.2d 716, 719–720 (CA7 1975) (footnotes omitted), *cert, denied*, 425 U.S. 916 (1976).

Society has every right to encourage its individual members to follow particular traditions in expressing affection for one another and in gratifying their personal desires. It, of course, may prohibit an individual from imposing his will on another to satisfy his own selfish interests. It also may prevent an individual from interfering with, or violating, a legally sanctioned and protected relationship, such as marriage. And it may explain the relative advantages and disadvantages of different forms of intimate expression. But when individual married couples are isolated from observation by others, the way in which they voluntarily choose to conduct their intimate relations is a matter for them – not the . . . State – to decide.[25] The essential "liberty" that animated the development of the law in cases like *Griswold, Eisenstadt,* and *Carey* surely embraces the right to engage in nonreproductive sexual conduct that others may consider offensive or immoral.

Paradoxical as it may seem, our prior cases thus establish that a State may not prohibit sodomy within "the sacred precincts of marital bedrooms," *Griswold,* 381 U.S. at 485, or, indeed, between unmarried heterosexual adults. *Eisenstadt,* 405 U.S. at 453. In all events, it is perfectly clear that the State of Georgia may not totally prohibit the conduct proscribed by § 16-6-2 of the Georgia Criminal Code.

II

If the Georgia statute cannot be enforced as it is written – if the conduct it seeks to prohibit is a protected form of liberty for the vast majority of Georgia's citizens – the State must assume the burden of justifying a selective application of its law. Either the persons to whom Georgia seeks to apply its statute do not have the same interest in "liberty" that others have, or there must be a reason why the State may be permitted to apply a generally applicable law to certain persons that it does not apply to others.

The first possibility is plainly unacceptable. Although the meaning of the principle that "all men are created equal" is not always clear, it surely must mean that every free citizen has the same interest in "liberty" that the members of the majority share. From the standpoint of the individual, the homosexual and the heterosexual have the same interest in deciding how he will live his own life, and, more narrowly, how he will conduct himself in his personal and voluntary . . . associations with his companions. State intrusion into the private conduct of either is equally burdensome.

The second possibility is similarly unacceptable. A policy of selective application must be supported by a neutral and legitimate interest – something more substantial than a habitual dislike for, or ignorance about, the disfavored group. Neither the State nor the Court has identified any such interest in this case. The Court has posited as a justification for the Georgia statute "the presumed belief of a majority of the electorate in Georgia that homosexual sodomy is immoral and unacceptable." *Ante* at 196. But the Georgia electorate has expressed no such belief – instead, its representatives enacted a law that presumably reflects the belief that *all sodomy* is immoral and unacceptable. Unless the Court is prepared to conclude that such a law is constitutional, it may not rely on the work product of the Georgia Legislature to support its holding. For the Georgia statute does not single out homosexuals as a separate class meriting special disfavored treatment.

Nor, indeed, does the Georgia prosecutor even believe that all homosexuals who violate this statute should be punished. This conclusion is evident from the fact that the respondent in this very case has formally acknowledged in his complaint and in court that he has engaged, and intends to continue to engage, in the prohibited conduct, yet the State has elected not to process criminal charges against him. As JUSTICE POWELL points out, moreover, Georgia's prohibition on private, consensual sodomy has not been enforced for decades.[26] The record of nonenforcement, in this case and in the last several decades, belies the Attorney General's representations . . . about the importance of the State's selective application of its generally applicable law.[27]

Both the Georgia statute and the Georgia prosecutor thus completely fail to provide the Court with any support for the conclusion that homosexual sodomy, *simpliciter,* is considered unacceptable conduct in that State, and that the burden of justifying a selective application of the generally applicable law has been met.

III

The Court orders the dismissal of respondent's complaint even though the State's statute prohibits all sodomy; even though that prohibition is concededly unconstitutional with respect to heterosexuals; and even though the State's *post hoc* explanations for selective application are belied by the State's own actions. At the very least, I think it clear at this early stage of the litigation that respondent has alleged a constitutional claim sufficient to withstand a motion to dismiss.[28]

I respectfully dissent.

Notes

1 Georgia Code Ann. § 16-6-2 (1984) provides, in pertinent part, as follows:

   (a) A person commits the offense of sodomy when he performs or submits to any sexual act involving the sex organs of one person and the mouth or anus of another. . . .

   (b) A person convicted of the offense of sodomy shall be punished by imprisonment for not less than one nor more than 20 years. . . .

2 John and Mary Doe were also plaintiffs in the action. They alleged that they wished to engage in sexual activity

proscribed by § 16-6-2 in the privacy of their home, App. 3, and that they had been "chilled and deterred" from engaging in such activity by both the existence of the statute and Hardwick's arrest. Id. at 5. The District Court held, however, that, because they had neither sustained, nor were in immediate danger of sustaining, any direct injury from the enforcement of the statute, they did not have proper standing to maintain the action. Id. at 18. The Court of Appeals affirmed the District Court's judgment dismissing the Does' claim for lack of standing, 760 F.2d 1202, 1206-1207 (CA11 1985), and the Does do not challenge that holding in this Court.

The only claim properly before the Court, therefore, is Hardwick's challenge to the Georgia statute as applied to consensual homosexual sodomy. We express no opinion on the constitutionality of the Georgia statute as applied to other acts of sodomy.

3 See Baker v. Wade, 769 F.2d 289, rehearing denied, 774 F.2d 1285 (CA5 1985) (en banc); Dronenburg v. Zech, 239 U.S App.D.C. 229, 741 F.2d 1388, rehearing denied, 241 U.S.App.D.C. 262, 746 F.2d 1579 (1984).

4 Petitioner also submits that the Court of Appeals erred in holding that the District Court was not obligated to follow our summary affirmance in Doe. We need not resolve this dispute, for we prefer to give plenary consideration to the merits of this case rather than rely on our earlier action in Doe. See Usery v. Turner Elkhorn Mining Co., 428 U.S. 1, 14 (1976); Massachusetts Board of Retirement v. Murgia, 427 U.S. 307, 309, n. 1 (1976); Edelman v. Jordan, 415 U.S. 651, 671 (1974). Cf. Hicks v. Miranda, 422 U.S. 332, 344 (1975).

5 Criminal sodomy laws in effect in 1791: [. . .]

6 Criminal sodomy statutes in effect in 1868: [. . .]

7 In 1961, Illinois adopted the American Law Institute's Model Penal Code, which decriminalized adult, consensual, private, sexual conduct. Criminal Code of 1961, §§ 11 2, 11-3, 1961 Ill.Laws, pp.1985, 2006 (codified as amended at Ill.Rev.Stat., ch. 38,11-2, 11-3 (1983) (repealed 1984)). See American Law Institute, Model Penal Code §213.2 (Proposed Official Draft 1962).

8 Respondent does not defend the judgment below based on the Ninth Amendment, the Equal Protection Clause, or the Eighth Amendment.

9 Until 1968, Georgia defined sodomy as "the carnal knowledge and connection against the order of nature, by man with man, or in the same unnatural manner with woman." Ga.Crim.Code § 26-5901 (1933). In Thompson, v. Aldredge, 187 Ga. 467, 200 S.E. 799 (1939), the Georgia Supreme Court held that § 26-5901 did not prohibit lesbian activity. And in Riley v. Garrett, 219 Ga. 345, 133 S.E.2d 367 (1963), the Georgia Supreme Court held that § 26-5901 did not prohibit heterosexual cunnilingus. Georgia passed the act-specific statute currently in force "perhaps in response to the restrictive court decisions such as Riley," Note, The Crimes Against Nature, 16 J.Pub.L. 159, 167, n. 47 (1967).

10 In Robinson v. California, 370 U.S. 660 (1962), the Court held that the Eighth Amendment barred convicting a defendant due to his "status" as a narcotics addict, since that condition was "apparently an illness which may be contracted innocently or involuntarily." Id. at 667. In Powell v. Texas, 392 U.S. 514 (1968), where the Court refused to extend Robinson to punishment of public drunkenness by a chronic alcoholic, one of the factors relied on by JUSTICE MARSHALL, in writing the plurality opinion, was that Texas had not "attempted to regulate appellant's behavior in the privacy of his own home." Id. at 532. JUSTICE WHITE wrote separately:

Analysis of this difficult case is not advanced by preoccupation with the label "condition." In Robinson, the Court dealt with "a statute which makes the 'status' of narcotic addiction a criminal offense. . . ." 370 U.S. at 666. By precluding criminal conviction for such a "status," the Court was dealing with a condition brought about by acts remote in time from the application of the criminal sanctions contemplated, a condition which was relatively permanent in duration, and a condition of great magnitude and significance in terms of human behavior and values. . . . If it were necessary to distinguish between "acts" and "conditions" for purposes of the Eighth Amendment, I would adhere to the concept of "condition" implicit in the opinion in Robinson. . . . The proper subject of inquiry is whether volitional acts brought about the "condition" and whether those acts are sufficiently proximate to the "condition" for it to be permissible to impose penal sanctions on the "condition."

Id. at 550-551, n. 2.

Despite historical views of homosexuality, it is no longer viewed by mental health professionals as a "disease" or disorder. See Brief for American Psychological Association and American Public Health Association as Amici Curiae 8-11. But, obviously, neither is it simply a matter of deliberate personal election. Homosexual orientation may well form part of the very fiber of an individual's personality. Consequently, under JUSTICE WHITE's analysis in Powell, the Eighth Amendment may pose a constitutional barrier to sending an individual to prison for acting on that attraction regardless of the circumstances. An individual's ability to make constitutionally protected "decisions concerning sexual relations," Carey v. Population Services International, 431 U.S. 678, 711 (1977) (POWELL, J., concurring in part and concurring in judgment), is rendered empty indeed if he or she is given no real choice but a life without any physical intimacy.

With respect to the Equal Protection Clause's applicability to § 16-6-2, I note that Georgia's exclusive stress before this Court on its interest in prosecuting homosexual activity despite the gender-neutral terms of the statute may raise serious questions of discriminatory enforcement, questions that cannot be disposed of before this Court on a motion to dismiss. See Yick Wo v. Hopkins, 118 U.S. 356, 373-374 (1886). The legislature having decided that the sex of the participants is irrelevant to the legality of the acts, I do not see why the State can defend § 16-6-2 on the ground that individuals singled out for prosecution are of the same sex as their partners. Thus, under the circumstances of this case, a claim under the Equal Protection Clause may well be available without having to reach the more controversial question whether homosexuals are a suspect class. *See, e.g., Rowland v. Mad River Local School District*, 470 U.S. 1009 (1985) (BRENNAN, J., dissenting from denial of certiorari); Note, The Constitutional Status of Sexual Orientation: Homosexuality as a Suspect Classification, 98 Harv.L.Rev. 1285 (1985).

11 Even if a court faced with a challenge to § 16-6-2 were to apply simple rational basis scrutiny to the statute, Georgia would be required to show an actual connection between the forbidden acts and the ill effects it seeks to prevent. The connection between the acts prohibited by § 16-6-2 and the harms identified by petitioner in his brief before this Court is a subject of hot dispute, hardly amenable to dismissal under Federal Rule of Civil Procedure 12(b)(6). Compare, e.g., Brief for Petitioner 36-37 and Brief for David Robinson, Jr., as Amicus Curiae 23-28, on the one hand, with People v. Onofre, 51 N.Y.*2d* 476, 489, 415 N.E.2d 936, 941 (1980); Brief for the Attorney General of the State of New York, joined by the Attorney General of the State of California, as Amici Curiae 11-14; and Brief for the American Psychological Association and American Public Health Association as Amici Curiae 19-27, on the other.

12 Although I do not think it necessary to decide today issues that are not even remotely before us, it does seem to me that a court could find simple analytically sound distinctions between certain private, consensual sexual conduct, on the one hand, and adultery and incest (the only two vaguely specific "sexual crimes" to which the majority points, ante at 196), on the other. For example, marriage, in addition to its spiritual aspects, is a civil contract that entitles the contracting parties to a variety of governmentally provided benefits. A State might define the contractual commitment necessary to become eligible for these benefits to include a commitment of fidelity, and then punish individuals for breaching that contract. Moreover, a State might conclude that adultery is likely to injure third persons, in particular, spouses and children of persons who engage in extramarital affairs. With respect to incest, a court might well agree with respondent that the nature of familial relationships renders true consent to incestuous activity sufficiently problematical that a blanket prohibition of such activity is warranted. See Tr. of Oral Arg. 21-22. Notably, the Court makes no effort to explain why it has chosen to group private, consensual homosexual activity with adultery and incest, rather than with private, consensual heterosexual activity by unmarried persons or, indeed, with oral or anal sex within marriage.

13 The parallel between Loving and this case is almost uncanny. There, too, the State relied on a religious justification for its law. Compare 388 U.S. at 3 (quoting trial court's statement that "Almighty God created the races white, black, yellow, malay and red, and he placed them on separate continents. . . . The fact that he separated the races shows that he did not intend for the races to mix"), with Brief for Petitioner 20-21 (relying on the Old and New Testaments and the writings of St. Thomas Aquinas to show that "traditional Judeo-Christian values proscribe such conduct"). There, too, defenders of the challenged statute relied heavily on the fact that, when the Fourteenth Amendment was ratified, most of the States had similar prohibitions. Compare Brief for Appellee in Loving v. Virginia, O.T. 1966, No. 395, pp. 28-29, with ante at 192-194, and n. 6. There, too, at the time the case came before the Court, many of the States still had criminal statutes concerning the conduct at issue. Compare 388 U.S. at 6, n. 5 (noting that 16 States still outlawed interracial marriage), with ante at 193-194 (noting that 24 States and the District of Columbia have sodomy statutes). Yet the Court held not only that the invidious racism of Virginia's law violated the Equal Protection Clause, see 388 U.S. at 7-12, but also that the law deprived the Lovings of due process by denying them the "freedom of choice to marry" that had "long been recognized as one of the vital personal rights essential to the orderly pursuit of happiness by free men." Id. at 12.

14 The theological nature of the origin of Anglo-American antisodomy statutes is patent. It was not until 1533 that sodomy was made a secular offense in England. 25 Hen. VIII, ch. 6. Until that time, the offense was, in Sir James Stephen's words, "merely ecclesiastical." 2 J. Stephen, A History of the Criminal Law of England 429-430 (1883). Pollock and Maitland similarly observed that "[t]he crime against nature . . . was so closely connected with heresy that the vulgar had but one name for both." 2 F. Pollock & F. Maitland, The History of English Law 554 (1895). The transfer of jurisdiction over prosecutions for sodomy to the secular courts seems primarily due to the alteration of ecclesiastical jurisdiction attendant on England's break with the Roman Catholic Church, rather than to any new understanding of the sovereign's interest in preventing or punishing the behavior involved. Cf. 6 E. Coke, Institutes, ch. 10 (4th edn. 1797).

15 At oral argument, a suggestion appeared that, while the Fourth Amendment's special protection of the home might prevent the State from enforcing § 16-6-2 against individuals who engage in consensual sexual activity there, that protection would not make the statute invalid. See Tr. of Oral Arg. 10-11. The suggestion misses the point entirely. If the law is not invalid, then the police can invade the home to enforce it, provided, of course, that they obtain a determination of probable cause from a neutral magistrate. One of the reasons for the Court's holding in Griswold v. Connecticut, 381 U.S. 479 (1965), was precisely the possibility, and repugnancy, of permitting searches to obtain evidence regarding the use of contraceptives. Id. at 485-486. Permitting the kinds of searches that might be

necessary to obtain evidence of the sexual activity banned by § 16-6-2 seems no less intrusive or repugnant. Cf. Winston v. Lee, 470 U.S. 753 (1985); Mary Beth G. v. City of Chicago, 723 F.2d 1263,1274 (CA7 1983).

16 See Ga.Code Ann. § 16-6-2(a) (1984) ("A person commits the offense of sodomy when he performs or submits to any sexual act involving the sex organs of one person and the mouth or anus of another").

17 The Court states that the issue presented is whether the Federal Constitution confers a fundamental right upon homosexuals to engage in sodomy, and hence invalidates the laws of the many States that still make such conduct illegal, and have done so for a very long time.
Ante at 190. In reality, however, it is the indiscriminate prohibition of sodomy, heterosexual as well as homosexual, that has been present "for a very long time." *See* nn. 3, 4, and 5, *infra*. Moreover, the reasoning the Court employs would provide the same support for the statute as it is written as it does for the statute as it is narrowly construed by the Court.

18 See, e.g., 1 W. Hawkins, Pleas of the Crown 9 (6th ed. 1787) ("All unnatural carnal copulations, whether with man or beast, seem to come under the notion of sodomy, which was felony by the ancient common law, and punished, according to some authors, with burning; according to others, with burying alive"); 4 W. Blackstone, Commentaries *215 (discussing "the infamous crime against nature, committed either with man or beast; a crime which ought to be strictly and impartially proved, and then as strictly and impartially punished").

19 See 1 E. East, Pleas of the Crown 480 (1803) ("This offence, concerning which the least notice is the best, consists in a carnal knowledge committed against the order of nature by man with man, or in the same unnatural manner with woman, or by man or woman in any manner with beast"); J. Hawley & M. McGregor, The Criminal Law 287 (3d ed. 1899) ("Sodomy is the carnal knowledge against the order of nature by two persons with each other, or of a human being with a beast.... The offense may be committed between a man and a woman, or between two male persons, or between a man or a woman and a beast").

20 See J. May, The Law of Crimes § 203 (2d ed. 1893) ("Sodomy, otherwise called buggery, bestiality, and the crime against nature, is the unnatural copulation of two persons with each other, or of a human being with a beast.... It may be committed by a man with a man, by a man with a beast, or by a woman with a beast, or by a man with a woman – his wife, in which case, if she consent, she is an accomplice").

21 The predecessor of the current Georgia statute provided: Sodomy is the carnal knowledge and connection against the order of nature, by man with man, or in the same unnatural manner with woman.

Ga.Code, Tit. 1, Pt. 4, § 4251 (1861). This prohibition of heterosexual sodomy was not purely hortatory. *See, e.g., Comer v. State,* 21 Ga.App. 306, 94 S.E. 314 (1917) (affirming prosecution for consensual heterosexual sodomy).

22 See Thompson v. Aldredge, 187 Ga. 467, 200 S.E. 799 (1939).

23 A review of the statutes cited by the majority discloses that, in 1791, in 1868, and today, the vast majority of sodomy statutes do not differentiate between homosexual and heterosexual sodomy.

24 See Loving v. Virginia, 388 U.S. 1 (1967). Interestingly, miscegenation was once treated as a crime similar to sodomy. See Hawley & McGregor, The Criminal Law, at 287 (discussing crime of sodomy); id. at 288 (discussing crime of miscegenation).

25 Indeed, the Georgia Attorney General concedes that Georgia's statute would be unconstitutional if applied to a married couple. See Tr. of Oral Arg. 8 (stating that application of the statute to a married couple "would be unconstitutional" because of the "right of marital privacy as identified by the Court in Griswold"). Significantly, Georgia passed the current statute three years after the Court's decision in Griswold.

26 Ante at 198, n. 2 (POWELL, J., concurring). See also Tr. of Oral Arg. 4–5 (argument of Georgia Attorney General) (noting, in response to question about prosecution "where the activity took place in a private residence," the "last case I can recall was back in the 1930's or 40's").

27 It is, of course, possible to argue that a statute has a purely symbolic role. Cf. Carey v. Population Services International, 431 U.S. 678, 715, n. 3 (1977) (STEVENS, J., concurring in part and concurring in judgment) ("The fact that the State admittedly has never brought a prosecution under the statute . . . is consistent with appellants' position that the purpose of the statute is merely symbolic"). Since the Georgia Attorney General does not even defend the statute as written, however, see n. 10, supra, the State cannot possibly rest on the notion that the statute may be defended for its symbolic message.

28 Indeed, at this stage, it appears that the statute indiscriminately authorizes a policy of selective prosecution that is neither limited to the class of homosexual persons nor embraces all persons in that class, but rather applies to those who may be arbitrarily selected by the prosecutor for reasons that are not revealed either in the record of this case or in the text of the statute. If that is true, although the text of the statute is clear enough, its true meaning may be "so intolerably vague that evenhanded enforcement of the law is a virtual impossibility." Marks v. United States, 430 U.S. 188, 198 (1977) (STEVENS, J., concurring in part and dissenting in part).

26

Lawrence v. Texas

United States Supreme Court

Summary

The U.S. Supreme Court ruled that a Texas statute specifically criminalizing sexual conduct between people of the same sex was unconstitutional because it violated the privacy and liberty protections of the Fourteenth Amendment's Due Process Clause, was inconsistent with established privacy rulings, and singled out a particular class of persons for demeaning, stigmatizing, and criminal treatment. The Court overturned the Bowers v. Hardwick decision in the process, ruling that the Bowers decision was wrongly decided even in its own time because it appealed to overstated historical grounds, overstated the relevant legal history, ignored significant cases from the past 50 years, ignored the emerging recognition that private consensual sexual relations should not be criminalized, and ignored the importance of sexuality in the exercise of liberty. Dissenting opinion argued that the Court erred in its ruling because Texas did have a rational state interest in furthering the belief that certain sexual behaviors are immoral, the Texas statute did not single out any one group since both homosexuals and heterosexuals were prohibited from homosexual sex, and even if the statute did deny equal protection to homosexuals, that denial would still only need to be justified by the state's interest in enforcing traditional sexual morality.

Original publication details: Lawrence v. Texas 539 U.S. 558, No. 02–102 (2003). Public domain.

Sexual Ethics: An Anthology, First Edition. Edited by Patrick D. Hopkins.
© 2023 John Wiley & Sons, Inc. Published 2023 by John Wiley & Sons, Inc.

SUPREME COURT OF THE
UNITED STATES

No. 02-102

JOHN GEDDES LAWRENCE AND TYRON GARNER,
PETITIONERS v. TEXAS

ON WRIT OF CERTIORARI TO THE COURT OF
APPEALS OF

TEXAS, FOURTEENTH DISTRICT

[June 26, 2003]

JUSTICE KENNEDY delivered the opinion of the Court.

Liberty protects the person from unwarranted government intrusions into a dwelling or other private places. In our tradition the State is not omnipresent in the home. And there are other spheres of our lives and existence, outside the home, where the State should not be a dominant presence. Freedom extends beyond spatial bounds. Liberty presumes an autonomy of self that includes freedom of thought, belief, expression, and certain intimate conduct. The instant case involves liberty of the person both in its spatial and more transcendent dimensions.

I

The question before the Court is the validity of a Texas statute making it a crime for two persons of the same sex to engage in certain intimate sexual conduct.

In Houston, Texas, officers of the Harris County Police Department were dispatched to a private residence in response to a reported weapons disturbance. They entered an apartment where one of the petitioners, John Geddes Lawrence, resided. The right of the police to enter does not seem to have been questioned. The officers observed Lawrence and another man, Tyron Garner, engaging in a sexual act. The two petitioners were arrested, held in custody overnight, and charged and convicted before a Justice of the Peace.

The complaints described their crime as "deviate sexual intercourse, namely anal sex, with a member of the same sex (man)." App. to Pet. for Cert. 127a, 139a. The applicable state law is Tex. Penal Code Ann. §21.06(a) (2003). It provides: "A person commits an offense if he engages in deviate sexual intercourse with another individual of the same sex." The statute defines "[d]eviate sexual intercourse" as follows:

"(A) any contact between any part of the genitals of one person and the mouth or anus of another person; or

"(B) the penetration of the genitals or the anus of another person with an object." §21.01(1).

The petitioners exercised their right to a trial de novo in Harris County Criminal Court. They challenged the statute as a violation of the Equal Protection Clause of the Fourteenth Amendment and of a like provision of the Texas Constitution. Tex. Const., Art. 1, §3a. Those contentions were rejected. The petitioners, having entered a plea of nolo contendere, were each fined $200 and assessed court costs of $141.25. App. to Pet. for Cert. 107a–110a.

The Court of Appeals for the Texas Fourteenth District considered the petitioners' federal constitutional arguments under both the Equal Protection and Due Process Clauses of the Fourteenth Amendment. After hearing the case en banc the court, in a divided opinion, rejected the constitutional arguments and affirmed the convictions. 41 S. W. 3d 349 (Tex. App. 2001). The majority opinion indicates that the Court of Appeals considered our decision in Bowers v. Hardwick, 478 U. S. 186 (1986), to be controlling on the federal due process aspect of the case. Bowers then being authoritative, this was proper.

We granted certiorari, 537 U. S. 1044 (2002), to consider three questions:

"1. Whether Petitioners' criminal convictions under the Texas "Homosexual Conduct" law – which criminalizes sexual intimacy by same-sex couples, but not identical behavior by different-sex couples – violate the Fourteenth Amendment guarantee of equal protection of laws?

"2. Whether Petitioners' criminal convictions for adult consensual sexual intimacy in the home violate their vital interests in liberty and privacy protected by the Due Process Clause of the Fourteenth Amendment?

"3. Whether Bowers v. Hardwick, 478 U. S. 186 (1986), should be overruled?" Pet. for Cert. i.

The petitioners were adults at the time of the alleged offense. Their conduct was in private and consensual.

II

We conclude the case should be resolved by determining whether the petitioners were free as adults to engage in the private conduct in the exercise of their liberty under the Due Process Clause of the Fourteenth Amendment to the Constitution. For this inquiry we deem it necessary to reconsider the Court's holding in *Bowers*.

There are broad statements of the substantive reach of liberty under the Due Process Clause in earlier cases, including *Pierce* v. *Society of Sisters*, 268 U. S. 510 (1925), and *Meyer* v. *Nebraska*, 262 U. S. 390 (1923); but the most pertinent beginning point is our decision in *Griswold* v. *Connecticut*, 381 U. S. 479 (1965).

In *Griswold* the Court invalidated a state law prohibiting the use of drugs or devices of contraception and counseling or aiding and abetting the use of contraceptives. The Court described the protected interest as a right to privacy and placed emphasis on the marriage relation and the protected space of the marital bedroom. *Id.*, at 485.

After *Griswold* it was established that the right to make certain decisions regarding sexual conduct extends beyond the marital relationship. In *Eisenstadt* v. *Baird*, 405 U. S. 438 (1972), the Court invalidated a law prohibiting the distribution of contraceptives to unmarried persons. The case was decided under the Equal Protection Clause, *id.*, at 454; but with respect to unmarried persons, the Court went on to state the fundamental proposition that the law impaired the exercise of their personal rights, *ibid*. It quoted from the statement of the Court of Appeals finding the law to be in conflict with fundamental human rights, and it followed with this statement of its own:

> "It is true that in *Griswold* the right of privacy in question inhered in the marital relationship. . . . If the right of privacy means anything, it is the right of the *individual*, married or single, to be free from unwarranted governmental intrusion into matters so fundamentally affecting a person as the decision whether to bear or beget a child." *Id.*, at 453.

[. . .]

In *Carey* v. *Population Services Int'l*, 431 U. S. 678 (1977), the Court confronted a New York law forbidding sale or distribution of contraceptive devices to persons under 16 years of age. Although there was no single opinion for the Court, the law was invalidated. Both *Eisenstadt* and *Carey*, as well as the holding and rationale in *Roe*, confirmed that the reasoning of *Griswold* could not be confined to the protection of rights of married adults. This was the state of the law with respect to some of the most relevant cases when the Court considered *Bowers* v. *Hardwick*.

The facts in *Bowers* had some similarities to the instant case. A police officer, whose right to enter seems not to have been in question, observed Hardwick, in his own bedroom, engaging in intimate sexual conduct with another adult male. The conduct was in violation of a Georgia statute making it a criminal offense to engage in sodomy. One difference between the two cases is that the Georgia statute prohibited the conduct whether or not the participants were of the same sex, while the Texas statute, as we have seen, applies only to participants of the same sex. Hardwick was not prosecuted, but he brought an action in federal court to declare the state statute invalid. He alleged he was a practicing homosexual and that the criminal prohibition violated rights guaranteed to him by the Constitution. The Court, in an opinion by Justice White, sustained the Georgia law. [. . .]

The Court began its substantive discussion in *Bowers* as follows: "The issue presented is whether the Federal Constitution confers a fundamental right upon homosexuals to engage in sodomy and hence invalidates the laws of the many States that still make such conduct illegal and have done so for a very long time." *Id.*, at 190. That statement, we now conclude, discloses the Court's own failure to appreciate the extent of the liberty at stake. To say that the issue in *Bowers* was simply the right to engage in certain sexual conduct demeans the claim the individual put forward, just as it would demean a married couple were it to be said marriage is simply about the right to have sexual intercourse. The laws involved in *Bowers* and here are, to be sure, statutes that purport to do no more than prohibit a particular sexual act. Their penalties and purposes, though, have more far-reaching consequences, touching upon the most private human conduct, sexual behavior, and in the most private of places, the home. The statutes do seek to control a personal relationship that, whether or not entitled to formal recognition in the law, is within the liberty of persons to choose without being punished as criminals.

This, as a general rule, should counsel against attempts by the State, or a court, to define the meaning of the relationship or to set its boundaries absent injury to a person or abuse of an institution the law protects. It suffices for us to acknowledge that adults may choose to enter upon this relationship in the confines of their homes and their own private lives and still retain their dignity as free persons. When sexuality finds overt expression in intimate conduct with another person, the conduct can he but one element in a personal bond that is more enduring. The liberty protected by the

Constitution allows homosexual persons the right to make this choice.

Having misapprehended the claim of liberty there presented to it, and thus stating the claim to be whether there is a fundamental right to engage in consensual sodomy, the *Bowers* Court said: "Proscriptions against that conduct have ancient roots." *Id.*, at 192. In academic writings, and in many of the scholarly *amicus* briefs filed to assist the Court in this case, there are fundamental criticisms of the historical premises relied upon by the majority and concurring opinions in *Bowers*. [. . .]

At the outset it should be noted that there is no long-standing history in this country of laws directed at homosexual conduct as a distinct matter. Beginning in colonial times there were prohibitions of sodomy derived from the English criminal laws passed in the first instance by the Reformation Parliament of 1533. The English prohibition was understood to include relations between men and women as well as relations between men and men. See, *e.g., King* v. *Wiseman,* 92 Eng. Rep. 774, 775 (K. B. 1718) (interpreting "mankind" in Act of 1533 as including women and girls). Nineteenth-century commentators similarly read American sodomy, buggery, and crime-against-nature statutes as criminalizing certain relations between men and women and between men and men. See, *e.g.,* 2 J. Bishop, Criminal Law §1028 (1858); 2 J. Chitty, Criminal Law 47–50 (5th Am. ed. 1847); R. Desty, A Compendium of American Criminal Law 143 (1882); J. May, The Law of Crimes §203 (2d ed. 1893). The absence of legal prohibitions focusing on homosexual conduct may be explained in part by noting that according to some scholars the concept of the homosexual as a distinct category of person did not emerge until the late 19th century. See, *e.g.,* J. Katz, The Invention of Heterosexuality 10 (1995); J. D'Emilio & E. Freedman, Intimate Matters: A History of Sexuality in America 121 (2d ed. 1997) ("The modern terms *homosexuality* and *heterosexuality* do not apply to an era that had not yet articulated these distinctions"). Thus early American sodomy laws were not directed at homosexuals as such but instead sought to prohibit non-procreative sexual activity more generally. This does not suggest approval of homosexual conduct. It does tend to show that this particular form of conduct was not thought of as a separate category from like conduct between heterosexual persons.

Laws prohibiting sodomy do not seem to have been enforced against consenting adults acting in private. A substantial number of sodomy prosecutions and convictions for which there are surviving records were for predatory acts against those who could not or did not consent, as in the case of a minor or the victim of an assault. [. . .]

[. . .]

The policy of punishing consenting adults for private acts was not much discussed in the early legal literature. We can infer that one reason for this was the very private nature of the conduct. Despite the absence of prosecutions, there may have been periods in which there was public criticism of homosexuals as such and an insistence that the criminal laws be enforced to discourage their practices. But far from possessing "ancient roots," *Bowers,* 478 U. S., at 192, American laws targeting same-sex couples did not develop until the last third of the 20th century. The reported decisions concerning the prosecution of consensual, homosexual sodomy between adults for the years 1880–1995 are not always clear in the details, but a significant number involved conduct in a public place. See Brief for American Civil Liberties Union et al. as *Amici Curiae* 14–15, and n. 18.

It was not until the 1970s that any State singled out same-sex relations for criminal prosecution, and only nine States have done so. See 1977 Ark. Gen. Acts no. 828; 1983 Kan. Sess. Laws p. 652; 1974 Ky. Acts p. 847; 1977 Mo. Laws p. 687; 1973 Mont. Laws p. 1339; 1977 Nev. Stats, p. 1632; 1989 Tenn. Pub. Acts ch. 591; 1973 Tex. Gen. Laws ch. 399; see also *Post* v. *State,* 715 P. 2d 1105 (Okla. Crim. App. 1986) (sodomy law invalidated as applied to different-sex couples). Post-*Bowers* even some of these States did not adhere to the policy of suppressing homosexual conduct. Over the course of the last decades, States with same-sex prohibitions have moved toward abolishing them. [. . .]

In summary, the historical grounds relied upon in *Bowers* are more complex than the majority opinion and the concurring opinion by Chief Justice Burger indicate. Their historical premises are not without doubt and, at the very least, are overstated.

It must be acknowledged, of course, that the Court in *Bowers* was making the broader point that for centuries there have been powerful voices to condemn homosexual conduct as immoral. The condemnation has been shaped by religious beliefs, conceptions of right and acceptable behavior, and respect for the traditional family. [. . .]

Chief Justice Burger joined the opinion for the Court in *Bowers* and further explained his views as follows: "Decisions of individuals relating to homosexual conduct have been subject to state intervention throughout the history of Western civilization. Condemnation of those practices is firmly rooted in Judeo-Christian moral and ethical standards." 478 U. S., at 196. As with Justice White's assumptions about history, scholarship casts some doubt on the sweeping nature of the statement by Chief Justice Burger as it pertains to private homosexual conduct between consenting adults. See, *e.g.,* Eskridge, Hardwick and Historiography, 1999 U. Ill. L. Rev. 631, 656. In all events we think that our laws and traditions in the past half century are of most relevance here. These references show an emerging awareness that liberty gives substantial protection to adult persons in deciding how to conduct their private lives in matters pertaining to sex. "[H]istory and tradition are the starting point but not in all cases the ending point of the substantive due process inquiry." *County of Sacramento* v. *Lewis,* 523 U. S. 833, 857 (1998) (KENNEDY, J., concurring).

This emerging recognition should have been apparent when *Bowers* was decided. In 1955 the American Law Institute promulgated the Model Penal Code and made clear that it did not recommend or provide for "criminal penalties for consensual sexual relations conducted in private." ALI, Model Penal Code §213.2, Comment 2, p. 372 (1980). It justified its decision on three grounds: (1) The prohibitions undermined respect for the law by penalizing conduct many people engaged in; (2) the statutes regulated private conduct not harmful to others; and (3) the laws were arbitrarily enforced and thus invited the danger of blackmail. ALI, Model Penal Code, Commentary 277–280 (Tent. Draft No. 4, 1955). In 1961 Illinois changed its laws to conform to the Model Penal Code. Other States soon followed. Brief for Cato Institute as *Amicus Curiae* 15–16.

In *Bowers* the Court referred to the fact that before 1961 all 50 States had outlawed sodomy, and that at the time of the Court's decision 24 States and the District of Columbia had sodomy laws. 478 U. S., at 192–193. Justice Powell pointed out that these prohibitions often were being ignored, however. Georgia, for instance, had not sought to enforce its law for decades. *Id.,* at 197–198, n. 2 ("The history of nonenforcement suggests the moribund character today of laws criminalizing this type of private, consensual conduct").

The sweeping references by Chief Justice Burger to the history of Western civilization and to Judeo-Christian moral and ethical standards did not take account of other authorities pointing in an opposite direction. A committee advising the British Parliament recommended in 1957 repeal of laws punishing homosexual conduct. [. . .]

[. . .]

In our own constitutional system the deficiencies in *Bowers* became even more apparent in the years following its announcement. The 25 States with laws prohibiting the relevant conduct referenced in the *Bowers* decision are reduced now to 13, of which 4 enforce their laws only against homosexual conduct. In those States where sodomy is still proscribed, whether for same-sex or heterosexual conduct, there is a pattern of nonenforcement with respect to consenting adults acting in private. The State of Texas admitted in 1994 that as of that date it had not prosecuted anyone under those circumstances. *State* v. *Morales,* 869 S. W. 2d 941, 943.

Two principal cases decided after *Bowers* cast its holding into even more doubt. In *Planned Parenthood of Southeastern Pa.* v. *Casey,* 505 U. S. 833 (1992), the Court reaffirmed the substantive force of the liberty protected by the Due Process Clause. The *Casey* decision again confirmed that our laws and tradition afford constitutional protection to personal decisions relating to marriage, procreation, contraception, family relationships, child rearing, and education. [. . .]

[. . .]

The second *post-Bowers* case of principal relevance is *Romer* v. *Evans,* 517 U. S. 620 (1996). There the Court struck down class-based legislation directed at homosexuals as a violation of the Equal Protection Clause. *Romer* invalidated an amendment to Colorado's constitution which named as a solitary class persons who were homosexuals, lesbians, or bisexual either by "orientation, conduct, practices or relationships," *id.,* at 624 (internal quotation marks omitted), and deprived them of protection under state antidiscrimination laws. We concluded that the provision was "born of animosity toward the class of persons affected" and further that it had no rational relation to a legitimate governmental purpose. *Id.,* at 634.

As an alternative argument in this case, counsel for the petitioners and some *amici* contend that *Romer* provides the basis for declaring the Texas statute invalid under the Equal Protection Clause. That is a tenable argument, but we conclude the instant case requires us to address whether *Bowers* itself has continuing validity. [. . .] The central holding of *Bowers* has been brought in question by this case, and it should be addressed. Its continuance as precedent demeans the lives of homosexual persons.

The stigma this criminal statute imposes, moreover, is not trivial. The offense, to be sure, is but a class C misdemeanor, a minor offense in the Texas legal system. Still, it remains a criminal offense with all that imports for the dignity of the persons charged. The petitioners will bear on their record the history of their criminal convictions. [. . .]

[. . .]

The doctrine of *stare decisis* is essential to the respect accorded to the judgments of the Court and to the stability of the law. It is not, however, an inexorable command. *Payne* v. *Tennessee,* 501 U. S. 808, 828 (1991) ("*Stare decisis* is not an inexorable command; rather, it 'is a principle of policy and not a mechanical formula of adherence to the latest decision'") (quoting *Helvering* v. *Hallock,* 309 U. S. 106, 119 (1940)). In *Casey* we noted that when a Court is asked to overrule a precedent recognizing a constitutional liberty interest, individual or societal reliance on the existence of that liberty cautions with particular strength against reversing course. 505 U. S., at 855–856; see also *id.,* at 844 ("Liberty finds no refuge in a jurisprudence of doubt"). The holding in *Bowers,* however, has not induced detrimental reliance comparable to some instances where recognized individual rights are involved. Indeed, there has been no individual or societal reliance on *Bowers* of the sort that could counsel against overturning its holding once there are compelling reasons to do so. *Bowers* itself causes uncertainty, for the precedents before and after its issuance contradict its central holding.

The rationale of *Bowers* does not withstand careful analysis. In his dissenting opinion in *Bowers* JUSTICE STEVENS came to these conclusions:

"Our prior cases make two propositions abundantly clear. First, the fact that the governing majority in a State has traditionally viewed a particular practice as immoral is not a sufficient reason for upholding a law prohibiting the practice; neither history nor tradition could save a law prohibiting miscegenation from constitutional attack. Second, individual decisions by married persons, concerning the intimacies of their physical relationship, even when not intended to produce offspring, are a form of "liberty" protected by the Due Process Clause of the Fourteenth Amendment. Moreover, this protection extends to intimate choices by unmarried as well as married persons." 478 U. S., at 216 (footnotes and citations omitted).

JUSTICE STEVENS' analysis, in our view, should have been controlling in *Bowers* and should control here.

Bowers was not correct when it was decided, and it is not correct today. It ought not to remain binding precedent. *Bowers* v. *Hardwick* should be and now is overruled.

The present case does not involve minors. It does not involve persons who might be injured or coerced or who are situated in relationships where consent might not easily be refused. It does not involve public conduct or prostitution. It does not involve whether the government must give formal recognition to any relationship that homosexual persons seek to enter. The case does involve two adults who, with full and mutual consent from each other, engaged in sexual practices common to a homosexual lifestyle. The petitioners are entitled to respect for their private lives. The State cannot demean their existence or control their destiny by making their private sexual conduct a crime. Their right to liberty under the Due Process Clause gives them the full right to engage in their conduct without intervention of the government. 'It is a promise of the Constitution that there is a realm of personal liberty which the government may not enter." *Casey, supra,* at 847. The Texas statute furthers no legitimate state interest which can justify its intrusion into the personal and private life of the individual.

[. . .]

JUSTICE SCALIA, with whom THE CHIEF JUSTICE and JUSTICE THOMAS join, dissenting.

[. . .]

IV

I turn now to the ground on which the Court squarely rests its holding: the contention that there is no rational basis for the law here under attack. This proposition is so out of accord with our jurisprudence – indeed, with the jurisprudence of *any* society we know – that it requires little discussion.

The Texas statute undeniably seeks to further the belief of its citizens that certain forms of sexual behavior are "immoral and unacceptable," *Bowers, supra,* at 196 – the same interest furthered by criminal laws against fornication, bigamy, adultery, adult incest, bestiality, and obscenity. *Bowers* held that this *was* a legitimate state interest. The Court today reaches the opposite conclusion. The Texas statute, it says, "furthers *no legitimate state interest* which can justify its intrusion into the personal and private life of the individual," *ante,* at 18 (emphasis added). The Court embraces instead JUSTICE STEVENS' declaration in his *Bowers* dissent, that "the fact that the governing majority in a State has traditionally viewed a particular practice as immoral is not a sufficient reason for upholding a law prohibiting the practice," *ante,* at 17. This effectively decrees the end of all morals legislation. If, as the Court asserts, the promotion of majoritarian sexual morality is not even a *legitimate* state interest, none of the above-mentioned laws can survive rational-basis review.

V

Finally, I turn to petitioners' equal-protection challenge, which no Member of the Court save JUSTICE O'CONNOR, *ante,* at 1 (opinion concurring in judgment), embraces: On its face §21.06(a) applies equally to all persons. Men and women, heterosexuals and homosexuals, are all subject to its prohibition of deviate sexual intercourse with someone of the same sex. To be sure, §21.06 does distinguish between the sexes insofar as concerns the partner with whom the sexual acts are performed: men can violate the law only with other men, and women only with other women. But this cannot itself be a denial of equal protection, since it is precisely the same distinction regarding partner that is drawn in state laws prohibiting marriage with someone of the same sex while permitting marriage with someone of the opposite sex.

The objection is made, however, that the antimiscegenation laws invalidated in *Loving* v. *Virginia,* 388 U. S. 1, 8 (1967), similarly were applicable to whites and blacks alike, and only distinguished between the races insofar as the *partner* was concerned. In *Loving,* however, we correctly applied heightened scrutiny, rather than the usual rational-basis review, because the Virginia statute was "designed to maintain White Supremacy." *Id.,* at 6, 11. A racially discriminatory purpose is always sufficient to subject a law to strict scrutiny, even a facially neutral law that makes no mention of race. See *Washington* v. *Davis,* 426 U. S. 229, 241–242 (1976). No purpose to discriminate against men or women as a class can be gleaned from the Texas law, so rational-basis review applies. That review is readily satisfied here by the same rational basis that satisfied it in *Bowers* – society's belief that certain forms of sexual behavior are "immoral and unacceptable," 478 U. S., at 196. This is the same justification that supports many other laws regulating sexual behavior that make a distinction based upon the identity of the partner – for example, laws against adultery, fornication, and adult incest, and laws refusing to recognize homosexual marriage.

JUSTICE O'CONNOR argues that the discrimination in this law which must be justified is not its discrimination with regard to the sex of the partner but its discrimination with regard to the sexual proclivity of the principal actor.

> "While it is true that the law applies only to conduct, the conduct targeted by this law is conduct that is closely correlated with being homosexual. Under such circumstances, Texas' sodomy law is targeted at more than conduct. It is instead directed toward gay persons as a class." *Ante,* at 5.

Of course the same could be said of any law. A law against public nudity targets "the conduct that is closely correlated with being a nudist," and hence "is targeted at more than conduct"; it is "directed toward nudists as a class." But be that as it may. Even if the Texas law *does* deny equal protection to "homosexuals as a class," that denial *still* does not need to be justified by anything more than a rational basis, which our cases show is satisfied by the enforcement of traditional notions of sexual morality.

[. . .]

27

Therapies Focused on Attempts to Change Sexual Orientation (Reparative or Conversion Therapies): COPP Position Statement

American Psychiatric Association, Committee on Psychotherapy by Psychiatrists (COPP)

Summary

Argues that homosexuality per se is not a mental disorder and opposes any attempts to change a person's sexual orientation (reparative or conversion therapy) based on such beliefs. The issue of changing sexual orientation is highly politicized and is largely connected to fears that accepting homosexuality as a normal variant of human sexuality is morally wrong and socially harmful. As such, the scientific data (in which there are no rigorous studies of the efficacy or harm of reparative therapy) have been obscured. Reparative therapy techniques are at odds with the scientific position of the APA, incorporate older psychoanalytic theories, and link to religious beliefs condemning homosexuality. The APA recommends that therapists do not attempt to change individual's sexual orientation.

Original publication details: The American Psychiatric Association, "Therapies Focused on Attempts to Change Sexual Orientation (Reparative or Conversion Therapies) COPP Position Statement," APA Document Reference No. 200001 (2000). Reproduced with permission of American Psychiatric Association.

Therapies Focused on Attempts to Change Sexual Orientation (Reparative or Conversion Therapies) COPP POSITION STATEMENT
Approved by the Board of Trustees, March 2000
Approved by the Assembly, May 2000

"Policy documents are approved by the APA Assembly and Board of Trustees . . . These are . . . position statements that define APA official policy on specific subjects . . ." – *APA Operations Manual*.

Preamble
In December of 1998, the Board of Trustees issued a position statement that the American Psychiatric Association opposes any psychiatric treatment, such as "reparative" or conversion therapy, which is based upon the assumption that homosexuality per se is a mental disorder or based upon the a priori assumption that a patient should change his/her sexual homosexual orientation (Appendix 1). In doing so, the APA joined many other professional organizations that either oppose or are critical of "reparative" therapies, including the American Academy of Pediatrics, the American Medical Association, the American Psychological Association, The American Counseling Association, and the National Association of Social Workers (1).

The following Position Statement expands and elaborates upon the statement issued by the Board of Trustees in order to further address public and professional concerns about therapies designed to change a patient's sexual orientation or sexual identity. It augments rather than replaces the 1998 statement.

Position Statement
In the past, defining homosexuality as an illness buttressed society's moral opprobrium of same-sex relationships (2). In the current social climate, claiming homosexuality is a mental disorder stems from efforts to discredit the growing social acceptance of homosexuality as a normal variant of human sexuality. Consequently, the issue of changing sexual orientation has become highly politicized. The integration of gays and lesbians into the mainstream of American society is opposed by those who fear that such an integration is morally wrong and harmful to the social fabric. The political and moral debates surrounding this issue have obscured the scientific data by calling into question the motives and even the character of individuals on both sides of the issue. This document attempts to shed some light on this heated issue.

The validity, efficacy and ethics of clinical attempts to change an individual's sexual orientation have been challenged (3–6). To date, there are no scientifically rigorous outcome studies to determine either the actual efficacy or harm of "reparative" treatments. There is sparse scientific data about selection criteria, risks versus benefits of the treatment, and long-term outcomes of "reparative" therapies. The literature consists of anecdotal reports of individuals who have claimed to change, people who claim that attempts to change were harmful to them, and others who claimed to have changed and then later recanted those claims (7–9).

Even though there are little data about patients, it is still possible to evaluate the theories which rationalize the conduct of "reparative" and conversion therapies. Firstly, they are at odds with the scientific position of the American Psychiatric Association which has maintained, since 1973, that homosexuality per se, is not a mental disorder. The theories of "reparative" therapists define homosexuality as either a developmental arrest, a severe form of psychopathology, or some combination of both (10–15). In recent years, noted practitioners of "reparative" therapy have openly integrated older psychoanalytic theories that pathologize homosexuality with traditional religious beliefs condemning homosexuality (16–18).

The earliest scientific criticisms of the early theories and religious beliefs informing "reparative" or conversion therapies came primarily from sexology researchers (19–27). Later, criticisms emerged from psychoanalytic sources as well (28–39). There has also been an increasing body of religious thought arguing against traditional, biblical interpretations that condemn homosexuality and which underlie religious types of "reparative" therapy (40–46).

Recommendations:

1. APA affirms its 1973 position that homosexuality per se is not a diagnosable mental disorder. Recent publicized efforts to repathologize homosexuality by claiming that it can be cured are often guided not by rigorous scientific or psychiatric research, but sometimes by religious and political forces opposed to full civil rights for gay men and lesbians. APA recommends that the APA respond quickly and appropriately as a scientific organization when claims that homosexuality is a curable illness are made by political or religious groups.

2. As a general principle, a therapist should not determine the goal of treatment either coercively or

through subtle influence. Psychotherapeutic modalities to convert or "repair" homosexuality are based on developmental theories whose scientific validity is questionable. Furthermore, anecdotal reports of "cures" are counterbalanced by anecdotal claims of psychological harm. In the last four decades, "reparative" therapists have not produced any rigorous scientific research to substantiate their claims of cure. Until there is such research available, APA recommends that ethical practitioners refrain from attempts to change individuals' sexual orientation, keeping in mind the medical dictum to First, do no harm.

3. The "reparative" therapy literature uses theories that make it difficult to formulate scientific selection criteria for their treatment modality. This literature not only ignores the impact of social stigma in motivating efforts to cure homosexuality, it is a literature that actively stigmatizes homosexuality as well. "Reparative" therapy literature also tends to overstate the treatment's accomplishments while neglecting any potential risks to patients. APA encourages and supports research in the NIMH and the academic research community to further determine "reparative" therapy's risks versus its benefits.

References

1 National Association for Research and Treatment of Homosexuality (1999), American Counseling Association Passes Resolution to Oppose Reparative Therapy. NARTH Web site (www.narth.com/docs/acaresolution.html).

2 Bayer, R. (1981), *Homosexuality and American Psychiatry; The Politics of Diagnosis*. New York: Basic Books.

3 Haldeman, D. (1991), Sexual orientation conversion therapy for gay men and lesbians: A scientific examination. In *Homosexuality: Research Implications for Public Policy*, ed. J.C. Gonsiorek & J.D. Weinrich. Newbury Park, CA: Sage Publications, pp. 149–161.

4 Haldeman, D. (1994), The practice and ethics of sexual orientation conversion therapy. *J. of Consulting and Clin. Psychol.*, 62(2):221–227.

5 Brown, L.S. (1996), Ethical concerns with sexual minority patients. In: *Textbook of Homosexuality and Mental Health*, ed. R. Cabaj & T. Stein. Washington, D.C.: American Psychiatric Press, pp. 897–916.

6 Drescher, J. (1997), What needs changing? Some questions raised by reparative therapy practices. *New York State Psychiatric Society Bulletin*, 40(1):8–10.

7 Duberman, M. (1991), *Cures: A Gay Man's Odyssey*. New York: Dutton.

8 White, M. (1994), *Stranger at the Gate: To be Gay and Christian in America*. New York: Simon & Schuster.

9 Isay, R. (1996), *Becoming Gay. The Journey to Self-Acceptance*. New York: Pantheon.

10 Freud, S. (1905), Three essays on the theory of sexuality. *Standard Edition*, 7:123–246. London: Hogarth Press, 1953.

11 Rado, S. (1940), A critical examination of the concept of bisexuality. *Psychosomatic Medicine*, 2:459–467. Reprinted in *Sexual Inversion: The Multiple Roots of Homosexuality*, ed. J. Marmor. New York: Basic Books, 1965, pp. 175–189.

12 Bieber, I., Dain, R, Dince, P., Drellich, M., Grand, H., Gundlach, R., Kremer, M., Rifkin, A., Wilbur, C., & Bieber T. (1962), *Homosexuality: A Psychoanalytic Study*. New York: Basic Books.

13 Socarides, C. (1968), *The Overt Homosexual*. New York: Grune & Stratton.

14 Ovesey, L. (1969), *Homosexuality and Pseudohomosexuality*. New York: Science House.

15 Hatterer, L. (1970), *Changing Homosexuality in the Male*. New York: McGraw Hill.

16 Moberly, E. (1983), *Homosexuality: A New Christian Ethic*. Cambridge, UK: James Clarke & Co.

17 Harvey, J. (1987), *The Homosexual Person: New Thinking in Pastoral Care*. San Francisco, CA: Ignatius.

18 Nicolosi, J. (1991), *Reparative Therapy of Male Homosexuality: A New Clinical Approach*. Northvale, NJ: Aronson.

19 Kinsey, A., Pomeroy, W., & Martin, C. (1948), *Sexual Behavior in the Human Male*. Philadelphia, PA: Saunders.

20 Kinsey, A., Pomeroy, W., Martin, C., & Gebhard, P. (1953), *Sexual Behavior in the Human Female*. Philadelphia, PA: Saunders.

21 Ford, C. & Beach, F. (1951), *Patterns of Sexual Behavior*. New York: Harper.

22 Hooker, E. (1957), The adjustment of the male overt homosexual. *J Proj Tech*, 21:18–31.

23 Bell, A. & Weinberg, M. (1978), *Homosexualities: A Study of Diversity Among Men and Women*. New York: Simon and Schuster.

24 Bell, A., Weinberg, M. & Hammersmith S. (1981), *Sexual Preference: Its Development in Men and Women*. Bloomington, IN: Indiana University Press.

25 LeVay, S. (1991), A difference in hypothalamic structure between heterosexual and homosexual men. *Science*, 253:1034–1037.

26 Hamer, D., Hu, S., Magnuson, V., Hu, N. & Pattatucci, A. (1993), A linkage between DNA markers on the X-chromosome and male sexual orientation. *Science*, 261:321–327.

27 Bern, D. (1996), Exotic becomes erotic: A developmental theory of sexual orientation. *Psychol. Review*, 103(2): 320–335.

28 Marmor, J., ed. (1965), *Sexual Inversion: The Multiple Roots of Homosexuality*. New York: Basic Books.

29 Mitchell, S. (1978), Psychodynamics, homosexuality, and the question of pathology. *Psychiatry*, 41:254–263.

30 Marmor, J., ed. (1980), *Homosexual Behavior: A Modern Reappraisal*. New York: Basic Books.

31 Mitchell, S. (1981), The psychoanalytic treatment of homosexuality: Some technical considerations. *Int Rev. Psycho-Anal.*, 8:63–80.

32 Morgenthaler, F. (1984), *Homosexuality Heterosexuality Perversion*, trans. A. Aebi. Hillsdale, NJ: The Analytic Press, 1988.

33 Lewes, K. (1988), *The Psychoanalytic Theory of Male Homosexuality*. New York: Simon and Schuster. Reissued as *Psychoanalysis and Male Homosexuality* (1995), Northvale, NJ: Aronson.

34 Friedman, R.C. (1988), *Male Homosexuality: A Contemporary Psychoanalytic Perspective*. New Haven, CT: Yale University Press.

35 Isay, R. (1989), *Being Homosexual: Gay Men and Their Development*. New York: Farrar, Straus and Giroux.

36 O'Connor, N. & Ryan, J. (1993), *Wild Desires and Mistaken Identities: Lesbianism & Psychoanalysis*. New York: Columbia University.

37 Domenici, T. & Lesser, R., eds. (1995), *Disorienting Sexuality: Psychoanalytic Reappraisals of Sexual Identities*. New York: Routledge.

38 Magee, M. & Miller, D. (1997), *Lesbian Lives: Psychoanalytic Narratives Old and New*. Hillsdale, NJ: The Analytic Press.

39 Drescher, J. (1998), *Psychoanalytic Therapy and The Gay Man*. Hillsdale, NJ: The Analytic Press.

40 Boswell, J. (1980), *Christianity, Social Tolerance and Homosexuality*. Chicago, IL: University of Chicago Press.

41 McNeil, J. (1993), *The Church and the Homosexual*, 4th edn. Boston, MA: Beacon.

42 Pronk, P. (1993), *Against Nature: Types of Moral Argumentation Regarding Homosexuality*. Grand Rapids, MI: William B. Eerdmans.

43 Boswell, J. (1994), *Same-Sex Unions in Premodern Europe*. New York: Villard Books.

44 Helminiak, D. (1994), *What the Bible Really Says About Homosexuality*. San Francisco, CA: Alamo Press.

45 Gomes, P.J. (1996). *The Good Book: Reading the Bible with Mind and Heart*. New York: Avon.

46 Carrol, W. (1997), On being gay and an American Baptist minister. *The InSpiriter*, Spring, pp. 6–7, 11.

Appendix 1
APA Position Statement on Psychiatric Treatment and Sexual Orientation December 11, 1998

The Board of Trustees of the American Psychiatric Association removed homosexuality from the DSM in 1973 after reviewing the evidence that it was not a mental disorder. In 1987, ego-dystonic homosexuality was not included in the DSM-III-R after a similar review.

The American Psychiatric Association does not currently have a formal position statement on treatments that attempt to change a person's sexual orientation, also known as reparative or conversion therapy. There is an APA 1997 Fact Sheet on Homosexual and Bisexual Issues which states that there is no published scientific evidence supporting the efficacy of reparative therapy as a treatment to change one's sexual orientation.

The potential risks of reparative therapy are great, including depression, anxiety and self-destructive behavior, since therapist alignment with societal prejudices against homosexuality may reinforce self-hatred already experienced by the patient Many patients who have undergone reparative therapy relate that they were inaccurately told that homosexuals are lonely, unhappy individuals who never achieve acceptance or satisfaction. The possibility that the person might achieve happiness and satisfying interpersonal relationships as a gay man or lesbian is not presented, nor are alternative approaches to dealing the effects of societal stigmatization discussed. The APA recognizes that in the course of ongoing psychiatric treatment there may be appropriate clinical indications for attempting to change sexual behaviors.

Several major professional organizations including the American Psychological Association, the National Association of Social Workers and the American Academy of Pediatrics have all made statements against reparative therapy because of concerns for the harm caused to patients. The American Psychiatric Association has already taken clear stands against discrimination, prejudice and unethical treatment on a variety of issues including discrimination on the basis of sexual orientation.

Therefore, the American Psychiatric Association opposes any psychiatric treatment, such as reparative or conversion therapy which is based upon the assumption that homosexuality per se is a mental disorder or based upon the a priori assumption that the patient should change his/her sexual homosexual orientation.

28

(A) Can Some Gay Men and Lesbians Change Their Sexual Orientation? 200 Participants Reporting a Change from Homosexual to Heterosexual Orientation – Abstract; (B) Spitzer Reassesses His 2003 Study of Reparative Therapy of Homosexuality

Robert L. Spitzer

Summary

Argues in a 2003 study of self-selected individuals who reported some change from homosexual orientations to heterosexual orientations that such reports are credible. As such, there is evidence that sexual orientation can be changed. Argues in a 2012 Letter to the Editor of the same journal that after reassessing the 2003 study, the major critiques of that study are judged to be largely correct. The original study could not successfully answer the question it asked – Can some version of reparative therapy enable individuals to change from homosexual to heterosexual? Instead, it could only answer the question of how some individuals in reparative therapy describe their sexual orientation. The credibility of study participants could not be determined, however, and therefore the study did not provide evidence for the efficacy of reparative therapy.

Original publication details: Robert L. Spitzer, (A) "Can Some Gay Men and Lesbians Change Their Sexual Orientation?: 200 Participants Reporting a Change from Homosexual to Heterosexual Orientation – Abstract," p. 403 from Archives of Sexual Behavior 32 (2003); (B) "Spitzer Reassesses His 2003 Study of Reparative Therapy of Homosexuality," p. 757 from Archives of Sexual Behavior 41 (2012). Reproduced with permission of Springer Nature.

Can Some Gay Men and Lesbians Change Their Sexual Orientation? 200 Participants Reporting a Change from Homosexual to Heterosexual Orientation

Robert L. Spitzer, M.D.

Abstract

Position statements of the major mental health organizations in the United States state that there is no scientific evidence that a homosexual sexual orientation can be changed by psychotherapy, often referred to as "reparative therapy." This study tested the hypothesis that some individuals whose sexual orientation is predominantly homosexual can, with some form of reparative therapy, become predominantly heterosexual. The participants were 200 self-selected individuals (143 males, 57 females) who reported at least some minimal change from homosexual to heterosexual orientation that lasted at least 5 years. They were interviewed by telephone, using a structured interview that assessed same sex attraction, fantasy, yearning, and overt homosexual behavior. On all measures, the year prior to the therapy was compared to the year before the interview. The majority of participants gave reports of change from a predominantly or exclusively homosexual orientation before therapy to a predominantly or exclusively heterosexual orientation in the past year. Reports of complete change were uncommon. Female participants reported significantly more change than did male participants. Either some gay men and lesbians, following reparative therapy, actually change their predominantly homosexual orientation to a predominantly heterosexual orientation or some gay men and women construct elaborate self-deceptive narratives (or even lie) in which they claim to have changed their sexual orientation, or both. For many reasons, it is concluded that the participants' self-reports were, by-and-large, credible and that few elaborated self-deceptive narratives or lied. Thus, there is evidence that change in sexual orientation following some form of reparative therapy does occur in some gay men and lesbians.

Robert L. Spitzer

Spitzer Reassesses His 2003 Study of Reparative Therapy of Homosexuality
Robert L. Spitzer

Several months ago, I told the Editor of *Archives of Behavior that,* because of my revised view of my study of reparative therapy changing sexual orientation (Spitzer, 2003a),[1] I was considering writing something that would acknowledge that I now judged the major critiques of the study as largely correct. After discussing my revised view of the study with Gabriel Arana (see Arana, 2012), a reporter for *The American Prospect,* and with Malcolm Ritter, an Associated Press science writer, I decided that I had to make public my current thinking about the study. Here it is.

Basic Research Question

From the beginning, it was: Can some version of reparative therapy enable individuals to change their sexual orientation from homosexual to heterosexual? Realizing that the study design made it impossible to answer this question, I suggested that the study could be viewed as answering the question: How do individuals undergoing reparative therapy describe changes in sexual orientation? A not very interesting question.

The Fatal Flaw in the Study: There Was No Way to Judge the Credibility of Subject Reports of Change in Sexual Orientation

I offered several (unconvincing) reasons why it was reasonable to assume that the participants' reports of change were credible and not self-deception or outright lying. But the simple fact is that there was no way to determine if the participants' accounts of change were valid.

I believe I owe the gay community an apology for my study making unproven claims of the efficacy of reparative therapy. I also apologize to any gay person who wasted time and energy undergoing some form of reparative therapy because they believed that I had proven that reparative therapy works with some "highly motivated" individuals.

This letter refers to the article available at doi: 10.1023/A: 1025647527010.

Note

1   Editor's note. The Spitzer study was published as a "target article" with the understanding that it would be followed by a series of peer commentaries, followed by a reply by Spitzer (2003b). There were 26 commentaries published in the same issue (Zucker, 2003). Subsequent to the publication of the target article, the peer commentaries, and Spitzer's reply, they were reproduced in an edited volume by Drescher and Zucker (2006), which contained an additional five commentaries and an interview with Spitzer by Drescher.

References

Arana, G. (2012, April 11). My so-called ex-gay life. *The American Prospect.* Retrieved from http://prospect.org/article/my-so-called-ex-gay-life.

Drescher, J., & Zucker, K. J. (eds.). (2006). *Ex-gay research: Analyzing the Spitzer study and its relation to science, religion, politics, and culture.* New York: Harrington Park Press.

Spitzer, R. L. (2003a). Can some gay men and lesbians change their sexual orientation? 200 participants reporting a change from homosexual to heterosexual orientation. *Archives of Sexual Behavior, 32,* 403–417.

Spitzer, R.L. (2003b). Reply: Study results should not be dismissed and justify further research on the efficacy of sexual reorientation therapy. *Archives of Sexual Behavior, 32,* 469–472.

Zucker, K.J. (2003). The politics and science of "reparative therapy" [Editorial]. *Archives of Sexual Behavior, 32,* 399–402.

Welch v. Brown, Appellants' Opening Brief (Preliminary Injunction Appeal)

Kamala D. Harris, Douglas J. Woods, Tamar Pachter, Daniel J. Powell, Craig J. Konnoth, and Alexandra Robert Gordon

Summary

Argues in appealing an injunction blocking the implementation of California Senate Bill 1172 (which would prohibit mental health providers from engaging in sexual orientation change efforts with minors) that the US District Court erred in interpreting SB 1172 as interfering with free speech because it restricts "talk therapy." In ruling that the issue was with free speech, the Court wrongly applied strict scrutiny legal review to the case and concluded that the therapists requesting SB 1172 be blocked would likely succeed on First Amendment grounds. Instead, the issue is not the free speech of therapists but whether the state has the power to protect children from a discredited and harmful practice. Under established law, the state does have such power as long as it is reasonable and related to a legitimate government interest. While the First Amendment does protect political and religious speech, it does not extend to professional medical practices simply because those practices use speaking and writing. As such, the state has the right and responsibility to outlaw sexual orientation change therapies.

Original publication details: Kamala D. Harris, Douglas J. Woods, Tamar Pachter, Daniel J. Powell, Craig J. Konnoth and Alexandra Robert Gordon "Donald Welch, et al. v. Edmund G. Brown Jr., Governor of the State of California, et al., Appellants' Opening Brief (Preliminary Injunction Appeal)," pp. 1–76 in *The United States Court of Appeals for the Ninth Circuit*, Case No. 13-15023 (2013). Public Domain.

IN THE UNITED STATES COURT OF APPEALS FOR THE NINTH CIRCUIT

Case: 13-15023

(January 28, 2013)

DONALD WELCH, et al., Plaintiffs–Appellees, *v.* **EDMUND G. BROWN, JR., Governor of the State of California, et al.**, Defendants–Appellants

On Appeal from the United States District Court for the Eastern District of California

No. CIV. 2:12-2484 WBS KJN

The Honorable William B. Shubb, Judge

APPELLANTS' OPENING BRIEF (PRELIMINARY INJUNCTION APPEAL – NINTH CIRCUIT RULE 3-3)

KAMALA D. HARRIS
Attorney General of California
DOUGLAS J. WOODS
Senior Assistant Attorney General
TAMAR PACHTER
Supervising Deputy Attorney General
DANIEL J. POWELL
Deputy Attorney General
CRAIG J. KONNOTH
Deputy Solicitor General
ALEXANDRA ROBERT GORDON
State Bar No. 207650
Deputy Attorney General

Introduction

California Senate Bill (SB) 1172 prohibits state-licensed mental health providers from using a type of therapy known as "sexual orientation change efforts" with clients who are under 18 years old. The statute is based on a scientific and professional consensus reached decades ago that homosexuality is a normal expression of human sexuality and not a disease, condition, or disorder in need of a "cure." It is also based on the conclusions of every mainstream professional mental health organization that sexual orientation change efforts (SOCE) are both ineffective and harmful.

This is one of a pair of cases pending before this Court concerning the constitutionality of SB 1172. The cases appeal conflicting rulings from the Eastern District of California. In the other case, *Pickup v. Brown*, Case No. 12-17681, defendants urge affirmance of the order issued by the Honorable Kimberly J. Mueller, which *denied* a preliminary injunction on the grounds that there was no merit to the plaintiffs' First Amendment challenge. In this case, defendants appeal the order issued by the Honorable William B. Shubb *granting* a preliminary injunction on the grounds that the plaintiffs' First Amendment challenge was likely to succeed on the merits. The order granting a preliminary injunction should be reversed for legal error.

The Legislature enacted SB 1172 to protect the health and safety of California's children and teenagers. This prohibition of a discredited and unsafe practice is an ordinary exercise of the states' power to regulate professional conduct. Under established law, such regulation survives a constitutional challenge so long as it is reasonable and related to a legitimate government interest. Applying this standard, plaintiffs have no likelihood of success on the merits of their First Amendment free speech claims and the district court should have denied the plaintiffs' motion for a preliminary injunction.

Instead, the district court reasoned that because the law restricts a form of "talk therapy," it regulates speech protected by the First Amendment, is subject to strict scrutiny, and is unlikely to survive that exacting review. This analysis misapplied governing law. This Court and others uniformly have held that state regulation of professional conduct does not have to satisfy a more exacting standard just because professional services are provided by speaking, writing, or other use of language. At is core, the First Amendment protects against government regulation of speech that aims to suppress thoughts, ideas and the free exchange of truthful information. The First Amendment is not a shield for incompetent or harmful professional conduct and practices.

SB 1172 does not restrict expressive speech or otherwise protected communications between therapists and their patients; it only restricts therapists from using SOCE treatment on minors. The law leaves mental health professionals free to share with a child or his parent, information, opinions, and advice about SOCE, about the morality of homosexuality, about religious proscriptions, and about the changeability of same-sex attractions. Licensed mental health professionals also remain free to refer children to pastoral or other counselors, whose practice lies outside California's licensing scheme, for SOCE therapy.

Because SB 1172 is a reasonable regulation of professional conduct and not a restriction of protected speech, the district court erred in holding that the plaintiffs were likely to succeed on the merits of their claims. The preliminary injunction should be reversed.

[. . .]

Statement of The Case

SB 1172 prohibits licensed mental health professionals from treating children and teenagers with a discredited, ineffective, and unsafe therapy in a misguided effort to change their sexual orientation. For more than forty years, every mainstream mental health organization has agreed that same-sex attraction is not a disease in need of a cure. Nonetheless, the practice of SOCE persisted in the face of the evidence that SOCE does not work and may cause minors to suffer a range of harms, including suicidality, depression, and numerous other physical and psychological problems. Alarmed, the Legislature in 2012 made explicit that SOCE falls below the standard of care demanded of California's licensed mental health professionals by forbidding them to provide this therapy to minors.

Plaintiffs, two therapists who practice SOCE and a therapist-in-training who plans to practice SOCE, reject this scientific consensus and challenged SB 1172, claiming that they have a constitutional right to practice in a manner deemed ineffective and unsafe by the State. Plaintiffs alleged that SB 1172 violates: (1) the right to freedom of speech, association, and religion under the First and Fourteenth Amendments; and (2) the right to privacy and substantive due process under the Fifth and Fourteenth Amendments.[1] ER 335-357.

On, October 29, 2012, plaintiffs moved the district court to preliminarily enjoin the enforcement of SB 1172. By Order dated December 3, 2012, the district court granted the motion for a preliminary injunction as to the three named plaintiffs in this action. ER 1-38.

The district court concluded that plaintiffs were likely to succeed on the merits of their claim under the Free Speech Clause of the First Amendment. ER 34. First, the district court reasoned that while many SOCE treatments do not involve speech (and can therefore be regulated or banned by the State without triggering heightened scrutiny under the First Amendment), other forms, such as talk therapy, do involve speech, which is entitled to the highest level of First Amendment protection. ER 16-17. The district court then posited that because SB 1172 regulates speech, or at least has an "incidental effect on speech," that strict scrutiny would apply, unless SB 1172 was determined to be content- and viewpoint-neutral. ER 14-19.

The district court then concluded that the law is likely both an impermissible content and viewpoint-based regulation of speech. ER 19-26. The court did note that

SB 1172 does not preclude a mental health provider from talking with a minor patient about SOCE or about the changeability or morality of homosexuality, or from recommending or referring a minor to someone else who could legally provide SOCE therapy. ER 21. Nevertheless, the court decided that SB 1172 is a content-based regulation of speech because the Legislature "disagreed with the practice of SOCE," as evidenced by the Legislature's findings that SOCE is harmful and ineffective. ER 23-24. The court also ruled that SB 1172 discriminates on the basis of viewpoint because "messages about homosexuality can be inextricably linked with SOCE," and SB 1172 therefore "bans a mental health provider from expressing his or her viewpoints about homosexuality as part of SOCE treatment." ER26.

Consequently, the district court concluded that "it is likely that SB 1172 must ultimately be assessed under strict scrutiny." ER 26. Applying strict scrutiny, the court found that the State has a compelling interest in regulating to protect the physical and psychological well-being of minors and also to protect all of society from harmful, risky, or unproven mental health treatments. ER 29. Yet, the court reasoned that the evidence that SOCE causes harm to minors was "unlikely" to satisfy strict scrutiny. ER 30-33. The court therefore concluded that plaintiffs were likely to succeed on the merits of their free speech claims. ER 2.[2]

The district court further found that two of the plaintiffs, Welch and Duk, had established irreparable injury. The court held that SB 1172 would "likely infringe their First Amendment rights because it will restrict them from engaging in SOCE with their minor patients." ER 34-35. The court opined that any harm to plaintiff Bitzer "is more remote and less significant" because he is not currently a mental health provider and could still engage in SOCE with the various religious groups of which he is a part. ER 35. With respect to the balance of equities and the public interest, the district court acknowledged that any time the State is enjoined from enforcing a duly enacted statute, irreparable injury is presumed and stated that it "does not take lightly the possible harm SOCE may cause minors, especially when forced on minors who did not choose to undergo SOCE." ER 35, 37. However, the court concluded that these harms were outweighed by the interest in preserving the three plaintiffs' right to freedom of speech. ER 35-36. The court granted plaintiffs' motion, enjoining the state defendants from enforcing SB 1172 against the three plaintiffs. ER 37-38.

Defendants timely filed a notice of appeal from the district court's order on January 2, 2013. ER 39, 366.

Statement of Facts

I. Sexual Orientation Change Efforts Have Been Widely Discredited

SOCE, also commonly referred to as reparative or conversion therapy, encompasses a variety of mental health treatments, including techniques derived from psychoanalysis, behavioral therapy, and religious and spiritual counseling. "These techniques share the common goal of changing an individual's sexual orientation from homosexual to heterosexual." ER 378. Historically, SOCE included practices such as castration, lobotomy, hormone treatments, aversive conditioning with nausea-inducing drugs, and electroshock. ER379. These therapies take as their premise the (then accepted) view that homosexuality is a mental illness or disorder. ER 380. That understanding of homosexuality, however, was abandoned more than forty years ago.[3]

[. . .]

II. SB 1172 Is Part of a Comprehensive Scheme Regulating the Mental Health Professions to Protect Public Health and Safety

SB 1172 amends a comprehensive regulatory scheme that governs the professional conduct of state-licensed psychologists and other licensed mental health providers, including psychiatrists, clinical social workers, marriage and family therapists, and educational psychologists. California has long regulated the mental health professions based on legislative recognition of the "'actual and potential consumer harm that can result from the unlicensed or incompetent practice.'" *Nat'l Ass 'n for the Advancement of Psychoanalysis* v. *Cal. Bd. of Psychology*, 228 F.3d 1043, 1047 (9th Cir. 2000) ("*NAAP*") (quoting California Bd. of Psychology, *Sunset Review Report* at 1 (October 1, 1997)). State licensure and regulation of mental health professionals rests on a legislative determination that their practice "in California affects the public health, safety, and welfare." *Id*. (citing Cal. Bus. & Prof. Code § 2900). The Legislature has declared that "[p]rotection of the public shall be the highest priority" for the governing Boards "in exercising [their] licensing, regulatory, and disciplinary functions." Cal. Bus. & Prof. Code §§ 2001.1; 2920.1; 4990.16.

[. . .]

III. SB 1172 Prohibits Licensed Mental Health Professionals From Providing a Widely Discredited Therapy to Minors

A. The Legislature Enacted SB 1172 Based on the Professional Consensus That SOCE Has No Scientific Basis, Is Ineffective, and Is Potentially Harmful.

The Legislature included in SB 1172 a list of findings that explain the reasons for its adoption. In short, the mental health professions agree that: (1) SOCE has been obsolete since the 1970s, when the profession concluded that same-sex attractions are a normal variant of human sexuality, not a disorder in need of treatment; (2) no one has produced any reliable evidence that it is possible to change a person's sexual orientation; (3) there is evidence that SOCE causes psychological harm to patients because it reinforces feelings of societal rejection; and (4) some practitioners persist in treating children with SOCE despite wide-spread professional condemnation. Cal. Stats. 2012, ch. 835, § 1(a)-(m).

1. SOCE has been obsolete for more than forty years.

The Legislature found that "[b]eing lesbian, gay, or bisexual is not a disease, disorder, illness, deficiency, or shortcoming. The major professional associations of mental health practitioners and researchers in the United States have recognized this fact for nearly 40 years." *Id*. § 1(a).

2. Despite decades of practice, there is no reliable evidence that SOCE can reduce or eliminate same-sex attractions, or produce opposite-sex attractions.

The Legislature further determined, based on extensive research and study by the American Psychological Association, the American Psychiatric Association, and eight other respected professional psychological and counseling associations, that there is little or no empirical evidence that SOCE works. Cal. Stats. 2012, ch. 835, § 1(a)-(m).

The Legislature relied on the report of a task force convened by the American Psychological Association (APA), which concluded that there is little evidence that SOCE is an effective therapy, that is, that it can succeed in changing anyone's sexual orientation.

The APA task force conducted a "systematic review of peer-reviewed journal literature on SOCE." *Id*. § 1(b). It reviewed studies of SOCE aimed at: (1) decreasing interest in, sexual attraction to, and sexual behavior with same-sex partners; (2) increasing interest in, sexual attraction to, and sexual behavior with other-sex sexual partners; (3) increasing healthy relationships and marriages with other-sex partners; and (4) improving quality of life and mental health. Report of the American Psychological Association Task Force on Appropriate Therapeutic Responses to Sexual Orientation (2009) ("APA Task Force Report") ER 143-280. Overall, the APA task force determined that "the peer-refereed empirical research provides little evidence of efficacy . . . ." ER 185.

The only rigorous studies of SOCE – those evaluating aversion techniques such as electric shock – show that "enduring change to an individual's sexual orientation is uncommon"; that a "very small minority of people in these studies showed any credible evidence of reduced same-sex sexual attraction"; and there is a dearth of "strong evidence that any changes produced in laboratory conditions translated to daily life." ER 193; *see also* ER 379-386; 425, 428, 432.

More recent studies examined by the APA task force, including studies about the benefits of so-called reparative therapy, "have investigated whether people who have participated in efforts to change their sexual orientation report decreased same-sex sexual attractions . . . or how people evaluate their overall experiences of SOCE." ER187 (citations omitted). The APA found these studies used designs that do not permit cause-and-effect attributions to be made, and were incapable of addressing either the efficacy of SOCE or its promise as an intervention. ER 187, 189-191.

These findings – that there is no reliable scientific evidence that SOCE can change sexual orientation – are consistent with the assessments of every other mainstream association of mental health providers in the country. These include the American Psychiatric Association, which has determined that "'reparative' therapists have not produced any rigorous scientific research to substantiate their claims of cure." Cal. Stats. 2012, ch. 835§ 1(d). It also includes the National Association of Social Workers, which found that "[n]o data demonstrates that reparative or conversion therapies are effective." *Id.* § 1(h). *See also* ER 379-383, 385-386; 423-425, 432.

3. There is significant evidence that SOCE is harmful, and harmful to children who are already at risk.

In addition to the absence of any reliable evidence of efficacy, the Legislature noted that SOCE is particularly harmful to children who are already at high risk of suicide and other serious health problems. *Id.* § 1(m) (citing Caitlin Ryan et al., *Family Rejection as a Predictor of Negative Health Outcomes in White and Latino Lesbian, Gay, and Bisexual Young Adults*, 123 Pediatrics 346 (2009)). The evidence is that SOCE poses potentially severe risks of harm, including but not limited to depression; anxiety; problems in sexual and emotional intimacy; loss of faith; self-destructive behavior; alienation from family; and suicidality. *Id.* § 1(b) -(m).

The APA task force concluded that "attempts to change sexual orientation may cause or exacerbate distress and poor mental health in some individuals, including depression and suicidal thoughts. The lack of rigorous research on the safety of SOCE represents a serious concern, as do studies that report perceptions of harm." ER 192.

The APA's serious concern about the risk that SOCE causes harm reflects a widespread consensus in the mental health field. The American Psychiatric Association agrees that "the potential risks of reparative therapy are great." Cal. Stats. 2012, ch. 835, § 1(d). The American Psychoanalytic Association concurs that "purposeful attempts to 'convert,' 'repair,' 'change,' or shift an individual's sexual orientation . . . often result in substantial psychological pain by reinforcing damaging internalized attitudes." *Id.* § 1(j).

The American Academy of Child and Adolescent Psychiatry, which has a particular expertise and influence in evaluating mental health treatments for children, agreed and firmly discouraged practitioners against using SOCE. The Academy has stated that efforts by a therapist to change a minor's sexual orientation "may encourage family rejection and undermine self-esteem, connectedness and caring, important protective factors against suicidal ideation and attempts. Given that there is no evidence that efforts to alter sexual orientation are effective, beneficial or necessary, and the possibility that they carry the risk of significant harm, such interventions are contraindicated." *Id.* § 1(k).

[. . .]

B. The Statute.

SB 1172 defines SOCE and prohibits any licensed mental health provider from engaging in SOCE with patients under 18 years of age. Cal. Bus. & Prof. Code §§ 865.1, 865(a).[4] In addition, the law makes explicit that failure to observe the restriction on SOCE will result in professional discipline: "[a]ny sexual orientation change efforts attempted on a patient under 18 years of age by a mental health provider shall be considered unprofessional conduct and shall subject a mental health provider to discipline by the licensing entity for that mental health provider." *Id.* § 865.2.

SB 1172 defines SOCE as "[a]ny practices by mental health providers that seek to change an individual's sexual orientation. This includes efforts to change behaviors or gender expressions, or to eliminate or reduce sexual or romantic attractions or feelings toward individuals of the same sex." *Id.* § 865(b)(1). SOCE does not include "psychotherapies that: (A) provide acceptance, support, and understanding of clients or the facilitation of clients' coping, social support, and identity exploration and development, including sexual orientation-neutral interventions to prevent or address unlawful conduct or unsafe sexual practices; and (B) do not seek to change sexual orientation." *Id.* § 856(b)(2)).

Because they are exempt from the entire regulatory scheme that governs state-licensed mental health professionals, SB 1172 does not apply to duly ordained members of the clergy, or pastoral or other religious counselors who do not hold themselves out as licensed mental health professionals. *See* Cal. Bus. & Prof. Code §§ 2063, 2908, 4980.01(b), 4996.13.

Summary of Argument

SB 1172 prevents state-licensed mental health providers from administering SOCE, a discredited, inefficacious, and potentially harmful therapy, to children. SB 1172 is an ordinary exercise of the state's police power to protect the public health and safety by regulating professional conduct. As such, to survive a constitutional challenge, the State need only demonstrate that the regulation is a rational exercise of that police power. Given the State's unquestionable interest in protecting the physical and psychological well-being of minors and the evidence that SOCE lacks any scientific basis, cannot change anyone's sexual orientation, is unsafe, and is uniformly rejected by mainstream professional organizations, SB 1172 is constitutional.

The district court, however, did not apply the correct analytical framework. Instead, it misconstrued governing law and assumed that simply because some forms of SOCE involve talking, that this transformed SB 1172 from a regulation of professional conduct to be evaluated under a deferential standard into a restriction on speech protected by the First Amendment and subject to strict scrutiny. In so doing, the district court

failed to recognize that all not all regulations that in any way relate to, or affect speech implicate the First Amendment. In particular, the district court missed the critical distinction between a regulation of professional practice conducted through speech and an impermissible restriction on expressive or otherwise protected speech.

Apart from prohibiting SOCE treatment for minors, SB 1172 does not regulate the speech of licensed mental health professionals in any way. Thus, unlike in the cases relied upon by the district court, SB 1172 does not restrict protected speech. SB 1172 does not ban or compel the communication of particular messages or ideas, nor does it unreasonably interfere with the therapist–patient relationship, or arbitrarily restrict the exercise of professional judgment. SB 1172 enforces professional standards of competence to prevent minors from being harmed by a discredited and unsafe practice.

Contrary to the district court's understanding, the mere fact that a professional practice involves the use of language does not immunize it from the State's near plenary power to regulate for the public health and safety. Rather, courts recognize that regulating professional practice often involves an effect on speech and that such regulations generally do not raise First Amendment concerns so long as they are reasonable. This Court has held specifically that "talk therapy" is not speech entitled to special First Amendment protection, but treatment, and that regulations of licensed mental health professionals, even those engaged in the "talking cure," are subject only to rational basis review. Under this standard, SB 1172 is constitutional.

Accordingly, plaintiffs have no likelihood of success on the merits of their First Amendment free speech claims and the district court should have denied the plaintiffs' motion for a preliminary injunction. The order of the district court should thus be reversed.

Argument

[. . .]

2   The State's power to regulate professional conduct is not subject to more exacting scrutiny merely because professional services are rendered by means of speaking, writing, or other use of language.

The State's power to protect the public health and safety and proscribe harmful practices is in no way diminished where professional conduct takes place through speaking. "Limitations on professional conduct necessarily affect the use of language and association; accordingly, reasonable restraints on the practice of medicine and professional actions cannot be defeated by pointing to the fact that communication is involved." *Daly v. Sprague*, 742 F.2d 896, 899 (5th Cir. 1984). This Court has stated unequivocally that "[i]t has never been deemed an abridgment of freedom of speech or press to make a course of conduct illegal merely because the conduct was in part initiated, evidenced, or carried out by means of language, either spoken, written, or printed." *NAAP*, 228 F.3d at 1053 (quoting *Giboney v. Empire Storage & Ice Co.*, 336 U.S. 490, 502 (1949)).

Thus, government regulation of professional practice, including that of the "speaking professions" need only be reasonable. *See, e.g., Accountant's Soc'y of Va. v. Bowman*, 860 F.2d 602, 603-05 (4th Cir. 1988) ("Professional regulation is not invalid, nor is it subject to first amendment strict scrutiny, merely because it restricts some kinds of speech"); *see generally* Daniel Halberstam, *Commercial Speech, Professional Speech, and the Constitutional Status of Social Institutions*, 147 U. Pa. L. Rev. 771, 834-850 (1999).

Most legal practice, for example, involves speech in the broadest sense, but state bar regulations are permissible so long as they "have a rational connection with the applicant's fitness or capacity to practice [the profession]." *Schware v. Bd. of Bar Examiners*, 353 U.S. 232, 239 (1957). States regulate lawyers in a number of ways that restrict speech, including rules of evidence and procedure, bans on revealing grand jury testimony, prohibitions on counseling a client to commit perjury, restrictions on in person solicitation, and sanctions for frivolous pleadings. When a lawyer counsels her client to violate the law – including a law she believes to be unconstitutional or grossly unfair – she may be subject to professional discipline, notwithstanding that her advice was based on her personal views. [. . .]

Similarly, where speech is "part of the practice of medicine," it is "subject to reasonable licensing and regulation by the State." *Planned Parenthood of Southeastern Penn. V. Casey*, 505 U.S. 833, 884 (1992) (plurality opinion); *see also Gonzales v. Carhart*, 550 U.S. 124,157 (2007) (recognizing the state's "significant role . . . in regulating the medical profession"); *Shea v. Bd. Of Med. Exam'r*, 81 Cal. App. 3d 564, 577 (1978) (the First Amendment "does not insulate the verbal charlatan from responsibility for his conduct; nor does it impede the State in the proper exercise of its regulatory functions").

Indeed, "without so much as a nod to the First Amendment, doctors are routinely held liable for malpractice for speaking or for failing to speak. Doctors commit malpractice for failing to inform patients in a timely way of an accurate diagnosis, for failing to give patients proper instructions, for failing to ask patients necessary questions, or for failing to refer a patient to an appropriate specialist. In all these contexts, the regulation of professional speech is theoretically and practically inseparable from the regulation of medicine." Robert Post, *Informed Consent to Abortion: A First Amendment Analysis of Compelled Physician Speech*, 2007 U. Ill. L. Rev. 939, 949 (2007). As one court cogently explained, a recommendation by a medical practitioner "is a form of expression, since it can be conveyed only orally or in writing, but the First Amendment has never been thought to bar an action for medical malpractice based on such written or spoken expression in a medical context." *In re Factor VIII or IX Concentrate Blood Products Litigation*, 25 F. Supp. 2d 837, 845 (N.D. 111. 1998).

In keeping with these authorities, the Ninth Circuit has long held that the same reasonableness standard applies to regulations of licensed mental health professionals, even those engaged in the "talking cure." As this Court held in *NAAP*, 228 F.3d at 1054, "[t]hat psychoanalysts employ speech to treat their clients does not entitle them, or their profession, to special First Amendment protection." *See also Coggeshall v. Mass. Bd. Of Registration of Psychologists*, 604 F.3d 658, 667 (1st Cir. 2010) ("Simply because speech occurs does not exempt those who practice [psychology] from state regulation (including the imposition of disciplinary sanctions).") (citing *NAAP*, 228 F.3d at 1053-55). Thus, many valid regulations of mental health professionals restrict speech. *See, e.g.,* Cal. Bus. & Prof. Code § 2960(h) (unprofessional conduct for psychologist to disclose confidential information received from a patient); § 4982(w), (x) (unprofessional conduct for marriage and family therapist to fail to comply with child, elder, and dependent adult abuse reporting requirements); § 651(b) (7) (unlawful for licensed mental health professional to "[m]ake[] a scientific claim that cannot be substantiated by reliable, peer reviewed, published scientific studies"); § 4999.90(s) (unprofessional conduct for licensed clinical counsellor to hold oneself out as being able to perform professional services beyond the scope of one's competence); *see also Ewing v. Goldstein*, 120 Cal.App.4th 807, 820 (2004) (therapist has a duty to warn a potential victim if information communicated to the therapist leads the therapist to believe his or her patient poses a serious risk of grave bodily injury to another).

[...]

B. SB 1172 Satisfies Rational Basis Review Because the State Has a Strong Interest in Protecting the Physical and Psychological Health of Minors, and Prohibition of Practices Discredited and Renounced by Every Mainstream Organization of Mental Health Professionals Is Rationally Related to That Interest.

California's prohibition on treating children with SOCE is rationally related to its important interest in protecting the health and well-being of minors. Legislation subject to challenge survives rational basis review as long as the legislature is acting in pursuit of a permissible government interest that bears a rational relationship to the means chosen to achieve that interest. *Heller v. Doe*, 509 U.S. 312, 319 (1993). This review is deferential; courts do not sit in review of the wisdom of legislative policy judgments. Indeed, duly enacted laws are presumed to be constitutional. *NAAP*, 228 F.3d at 1050. "We do not require that the government's action actually advance its stated purposes, but merely look to see whether the government could have had a legitimate reason for acting as it did." *NAAP*, 228 F.3d at 1050 (quoting *Dittman v. California*, 191 F.3d 1020, 1031 (9th Cir. 2005)). Put another way, a legislative determination that a particular law or regulation is necessary will not be overturned provided it has a conceivable rational basis. *Id*. Measured against this deferential standard, SB 1172 is constitutional.

As the district court found, the State of California has a legitimate, indeed compelling, interest in protecting the physical and psychological well-being of minors. ER 29 (citing *Nunez by Nunez v. City of San Diego*, 114 F.3d at 946); *see also Sable Comm's of Cal. v. FCC*, 492 U.S. 115, 126 (1989). The State also has an interest in protecting all of society from harmful, risky, or unproven mental health treatments. *NAAP*, 228 F.3d at 1052, 1055 (California's interest in regulating mental health is compelling); *Watson v. Maryland*, 218 U.S.173, 176 (1910) ("It is too well settled to require discussion at this day that the police power of the States extends to the regulation of certain trades and callings, particularly those which closely concern the public health").

[...]

Under the proper governing standard, SB 1172 is thus constitutional.

C. The District Court Failed To Apply the Correct Legal Framework and Misapplied Ninth Circuit Law.

The district court, however, did not apply settled law regarding regulation of professional conduct. It held instead that rational basis review does not apply when "a law imposes restrictions on a professional's speech." ER 11. Although it noted that many forms of SOCE, such as electric shock treatment, emetics, "affection training," visualization, and sedative drugs, do not involve speech at all, ER 15-16, the district court reasoned that because "some forms of SOCE, such as 'talk therapy,' employ speech," this "communication" must receive a high level of protection under the First Amendment. ER 17.

The district court's error was in failing to distinguish between government regulation of speech, and government regulation of professional conduct that is carried out through speech. In so doing, the district court relied heavily on *Conant v. Walters*, 309 F.3d 629 (9th Cir. 2002), in which this Court invalidated a federal gag order on physician–patient communications regarding the potential benefits of medical marijuana. *Conant*, while instructive, is inapposite: it addressed a direct restriction of protected speech by a professional, not professional conduct. [...]

[...]

3 *The distinction drawn between regulation of health practices delivered by speaking, writing, or other use of language and direct regulation of expressive speech is necessary to avoid an over-broad application of the First Amendment that would obstruct the protection of the public health and safety.*

As set forth above, *Conant* does not support the district court's conclusion that all speech by a health professional, including that used to deliver treatment, is entitled to First Amendment protection.[5] Indeed, the Supreme Court has cautioned against the kind of rigid and reflexive application of the First Amendment at the heart of the district court's analysis. The "First Amendment embodies an overarching commitment to protect speech from government regulation through close judicial scrutiny, thereby enforcing the Constitution's constraints, but without imposing judicial formulas so rigid that they become a straitjacket that disables government from responding to serious problems." *Denver Area Educational Telecommunications Consortium, Inc. v. F.C.C., 518 U.S. 727, 741 (1996).*

Simply put, not all speech is treated the same for First Amendment purposes, and some does not implicate the First Amendment at all. "Because many, perhaps most, activities of human beings living together in communities take place through speech, and because speech-related risks and offsetting justifications differ depending upon context, [the Supreme] Court has distinguished for First Amendment purposes among different contexts in which speech takes place." *Sorrell v. IMS Health Inc.*, 131 S. Ct. 2653, 2673 (2011) (Breyer, J. dissenting). Therefore, while the First Amendment imposes "tight constraints" upon government efforts to restrict "core" political and expressive speech, the Supreme Court applies a far more "lenient approach to ordinary commercial or regulatory legislation that affects speech in less direct ways." *Id.* at 2673-74.[6]

Indeed, courts routinely distinguish between the regulation of expressive speech under the First Amendment (which must survive strict scrutiny) and the regulation of professional conduct carried out through speech (which need only have a rational basis). These distinctions are drawn because regulations that target expressions of opinion and/or "discourse on public matters" implicate the core values protected by the First Amendment. *See Brown v. Entm't Merchants Ass'n*, 131 S. Ct. 2729, 2733 (2011). In contrast, regulation of professional conduct does not "offend the First Amendment." *See, e.g., NAAP*, 228 F.3d at 1053; *Daly v. Sprague*, 742 F.2d at 899. The First Amendment protects speech related to the "intellect and spirit" and the "exposition of ideas" and political, social, and philosophical messages. *Wooley*

v. Maynard, 430 U.S. 705, 715 (1977); *Chaplinsky v. New Hampshire*, 315 U.S. 568, 572 (1942). Unlike such speech, mental health practices are not expressive and do not, per se, contribute to the "marketplace of ideas." *See Pickup v. Brown*, 2012 WL 6021465 at *10 (recognizing that courts reaching the question have found that "the provision of health care and other forms of treatment is not expressive conduct"); *O'Brien v. United States Dept. of Health & Human Servs.*, No. 12-476, 2012 WL 4481208, at*12 (E.D. Mo. Sept. 28, 2012) ("Giving or receiving health care is not a statement in the same sense as wearing a black armband or burning an American flag.") (internal citations omitted).[7]

SB 1172 does not regulate any idea, but instead regulates professional practice, and while the "First Amendment recognizes no such thing as a 'false idea,'" *Hustler Magazine, Inc. v. Falwell*, 485 U.S. 46, 51 (1988), there are false and dangerous practices and treatments that the State may regulate or ban to protect the public from harm. [. . .]

[. . .]

Conclusion

For the foregoing reasons, defendants respectfully request that this Court reverse the district court's order granting the motion for preliminary injunction, vacate the preliminary injunction, and grant such other relief as the Court deems just.

[. . .]

Notes

1 Defendants in this action include Governor Edmund G. Brown Jr., in his official capacity; Anna M. Caballero, in her official capacity as Secretary of the California State and Consumer Services Agency; Denise Brown, in her official capacity as Director of Consumer Affairs; Christine Wietlisbach, Patricia Dawson, Samara Ashley, Harry Douglas, Julia Johnson, Sarita Kohli, Renee Lonner, Karen Pines, and Christina Wong, in their official capacities as members of the California Board of Behavioral Sciences; and Sharon Levine, Michael Bishop, Silvia Diego, Dev Gnanadev, Reginald Low, Denise Pines, Janet Salomonson, Gerrie Schipske, David Serrano Sewell, and Barbara Yaroslavsky, in their official capacities as members of the California Medical Board.

2 The district court did not reach plaintiffs' remaining claims that SB 1172 violates the right to privacy, violates the Free Exercise and Establishment Clauses, and is unconstitutionally vague and overbroad. ER 2.

3 Homosexuality was listed as a mental disorder in the first edition of what came to be called the Diagnostic and Statistical Manual of Mental Disorders ("the DSM"), published in 1952, but was removed from the DSM in 1973. ER 372-73. Two years later, in 1975, the American Psychological Association (APA) affirmed that homosexuality is not a mental illness and urged its membership to work towards dispelling the stigma of mental illness associated with homosexuality. ER 373.

4 The term "mental health provider" is defined to include a "physician and surgeon specializing in the practice of psychiatry, a psychologist, a psychological assistant, intern, or trainee, a licensed marriage and family therapist, a registered marriage and family therapist, intern, or trainee, a licensed educational psychologist, a credentialed school psychologist, a licensed clinical social worker, an associate clinical social worker, a licensed professional clinical

counselor, a registered clinical counselor, intern, trainee, or any other person designated as a mental health professional under California law or regulation." Cal. Bus. & Prof. Code § 865(a).

5   The district court relied, in part, on a sentence from *Conant* stating that "professional speech may be entitled to 'the strongest protection our Constitution has to offer.'" 309 F.3d at 637 (quoting *Florida Bar v. Went For It, Inc.*, 515U.S. 618, 634 (1995)). However, in *Florida Bar* the Court stated that "[s]peech by professionals obviously has many dimensions." The Court noted that, for example, professional speech by attorneys may merit heightened protection when it concerns "public issues and matters of legal representation." 515 U.S. at 634. SB 1172 does not regulate speech by professionals on issues of public concern, but rather prohibits ineffective and unsafe practices. Accordingly, the district court's reliance on *Conant* and *Florida Bar* is misplaced.

6   *See also* Frederick Schauer, *The Boundaries of the First Amendment: A Preliminary Exploration of Constitutional Salience,* 117 Harv. L. Rev. 1765, 1769 (2004) ("Though many cases involve the First Amendment, many more do not. . . .. It is not that the speech is not protected. Rather, the entire event – an event that often involves 'speech' in the ordinary language sense of the word – does not present a First Amendment issue at all, and the government's action is consequently measured against no First Amendment standard whatsoever. The First Amendment just does not show up.").

7   Plaintiffs attempt to portray SOCE treatment itself as expressive speech, and profess that it conveys their values and beliefs about the morality and changeability of homosexuality. However, this argument fails. The Supreme Court has rejected the argument that "an apparently limitless variety of conduct can be labeled 'speech' whenever the person engaging in the conduct intends thereby to express an idea." *United States v. O'Brien*, 391 U.S. 367, 376 (1968); *City of Dallas v. Stanglin,* 490 U.S. 19, 25 (1989) (rejecting the idea that every activity with "some kernel of expression" is entitled to First Amendment protection). Therapy, and health care treatment generally, is not a forum for licensed professionals to engage in free expression, and licensed professionals do not have a constitutional right to provide treatment (especially to children) based on individually-held beliefs. [. . .]

Welch v. Brown, Brief Amicus Curiae of Foundation for Moral Law, in Support of Plaintiffs – Appellees Urging Affirmance

John A. Eidsmoe and Joshua M. Pendergrass

Summary

Argues that the injunction blocking SB 1172 was rightly decided because the counselors who practice conversion therapy believe it is sound counseling practice, are impelled by their moral and religious beliefs to deliver conversion therapy, and wish to publicly advocate the practice. As such, their promotion and practice of conversion therapy is protected by the free exercise of religion, free speech, free press, free association, and the privacy/liberty guarantees of the Fifth and Fourteenth Amendments. The rights of minors and their parents who want conversion therapy are likewise protected by these Amendments. Under the guise of protecting minors, the state is trying to establish by law the political position that sexual orientation cannot be changed, trying to affirm the homosexual lifestyle, and is being used by militant gay activists to suppress criticism of homosexuality. The State has not demonstrated a compelling interest in prohibiting conversion therapy nor has considered whether less restrictive means could achieve its aims. As such, SB 1172 should be blocked.

Original publication details: John A. Eidsmoe and Joshua M. Pendergrass, "Donald Welch, et al. v. Edmund G. Brown Jr., Governor of the State of California, et al., Brief Amicus Curiae of Foundation For Moral law, In Support Of Plaintiffs—Appellees Urging Affirmance," pp. 1–35 in *The United States Court of Appeals for the Ninth Circuit*, Case No. 13-15023 (2013). Public Domain.

Sexual Ethics: An Anthology, First Edition. Edited by Patrick D. Hopkins.
© 2023 John Wiley & Sons, Inc. Published 2023 by John Wiley & Sons, Inc.

John A. Eidsmoe and Joshua M. Pendergrass

IN THE UNITED STATES COURT OF APPEALS FOR THE NINTH CIRCUIT
Case: 13-15023
(February 26, 2013)
DONALD WELCH, et al., *Plaintiffs–Appellees*, v.
EDMUND G. BROWN, JR., Governor of the State of California, et al., *Defendants–Appellants*.

BRIEF AMICUS CURIAE OF FOUNDATION FOR MORAL LAW, IN SUPPORT OF PLAINTIFFS – APPELLEES URGING AFFIRMANCE

On Appeal From The United States District Court, Eastern District of California, Case No. CV-12-2484-WBS-KJN,
The Honorable William B. Shubb, Judge

JOHN A. EIDSMOE*
JOSHUA M. PENDERGRASS
FOUNDATION FOR MORAL LAW
One Dexter Avenue
Montgomery, Alabama 36104
Telephone: (334) 262-1245
Attorneys for Amicus Curiae
Foundation for Moral Law
[. . .]

Statement of Identity and Interests of *Amicus Curiae*, Foundation For Moral Law

Amicus Curiae Foundation for Moral Law (the Foundation), is a national public-interest organization based in Montgomery, Alabama, dedicated to defending the inalienable right to acknowledge God. The Foundation promotes a return in the judiciary (and other branches of government) to the historic and original interpretation of the United States Constitution, and promotes education about the Constitution and the moral foundation of this country's laws and justice system.

The Foundation has an interest in this case because it believes that this nation's laws should reflect the moral basis upon which the nation was founded, and that the ancient roots of the common law, the pronouncements of the legal philosophers from whom this nation's Founders derived their view of law, the views of the Founders themselves, and the views of the American people as a whole from the beginning of American history through the present, have held that homosexual conduct has always been and continues to be immoral and not protected by law.

* *Counsel of Record*

The Foundation also stands for freedom of expression of religious and moral beliefs and believes counselors should be free to counsel in accordance with their religious, moral, sociological, and scientific beliefs, including the belief that that homosexual conduct is wrong, immoral, unhealthy and destructive. The Foundation also stands for the authority of parents to make decisions for their children, including the decision to pursue conversion therapy, and for the right of children to pursue conversion therapy if they so desire.

[. . .]

Summary of Argument

Under the guise of protecting homosexual minors, SB 1172 actually prevents minors and their parents from seeking and finding the therapy they want and need. Under the guise of preventing the imposition of conversion therapy, SB 1172 actually establishes by law a rigid orthodoxy – that sexual preference is fixed genetically and cannot be changed – when in fact that is a much-disputed proposition both within and outside the counseling profession. Under the guise of affirming the homosexual lifestyle, SB 1172 actually establishes by law the religious and moral belief that homosexuality and homosexual acts are morally acceptable when in fact a large portion of the population and of the counseling community believe on religious, moral, and scientific grounds that homosexuality and homosexual acts are wrong. And under the guise of protecting minors at an age when they are vulnerable, SB 1172 actually prevents minors from obtaining therapy at the time when they need it most and can benefit from it most.

Make no mistake about it: SB 1172 is a blatant attempt to enforce the gay lobby's position that gender identity is fixed, to prohibit therapists from counseling otherwise, and to prevent minors and their parents from seeking counseling to change their homosexual orientation.

Counselors who practice conversion therapy do so because they believe it is a sound counseling practice and because their religious and moral convictions impel them to do so. Their right to believe in, advocate, and practice conversion therapy is protected by the guarantees of free exercise of religion, free speech, freedom of the press, freedom of association, and the privacy/liberty guarantees of the Fifth and Fourteenth Amendments to the U.S. Constitution as well as Article I, §§ 1, 2, and 4 of the California State Constitution. Equally, the rights of minors who want conversation therapy and of parents who want this therapy for their children are protected by the guarantees of free exercise, free speech, freedom of the press, freedom of association, and the privacy/liberty guarantees of the Fifth and Fourteenth amendments to the U.S. Constitution as well as Article I §§ 1, 2, and 4 of the California State Constitution. SB 1172 violates these rights of counselors, minors, and parents. The court below rightly ruled SB 1172 unconstitutional, and this Court should affirm that ruling.

Argument

These matters, involving the most intimate and personal choices a person may make in a lifetime, choices central to personal dignity and autonomy, are central to the liberty protected by the Fourteenth Amendment. At the heart of liberty is the right to define one's own concept of existence, of meaning, of the universe, and of the mystery of human life. Beliefs about these matters could not define the attributes of personhood were they formed under compulsion of the State.

Lawrence v. Texas, 539 U.S. 558, 574 (2003), quoting *Planned Parenthood v. Casey*, 505 U.S. 83, 851 (1992).

While claiming this "right to define one's own concept of existence" for themselves, advocates of SB 1172 would deny this freedom to others. They turn a deaf ear to those minors who do not want to define themselves as homosexuals and who want counseling to help them change from that orientation. They turn a deaf ear to those parents who want to help their children change from a lifestyle that they consider to be immoral, unhealthy, or undesirable for a host of other reasons. They turn a deaf ear to those counselors who believe sexual orientation is not fixed and who want to help those who want to change from homosexual orientation.

If the Constitution guarantees a liberty/privacy "right to define one's own concept of existence," does that right not belong equally to those who hold traditional values, to the person with homosexual inclinations who wants to define himself as an heterosexual, to the religious person who wants help in dealing with urges that he considers sinful, and to the counselor who wants to define his or her existence as that of a counselor who helps her clients live according to their traditional values? "Equal protection of the law" requires an affirmative answer to that question.

I. The Appellees Donald Welch, Anthony Duk, and Aaron Bitzer have a First and Fourteenth Amendment Right to Practice Conversion Therapy With Willing Patients.

The District Court below in its Memorandum and Order and Appellees in their Brief of Appellees masterfully and conclusively demonstrate that the First Amendment free speech guarantee applies to their counseling. *Amicus* will therefore not duplicate their analysis. [. . .]

[. . .]

Amicus argues that, in addition to the free speech guarantee, Appellees' right to engage in sexual orientation change efforts (SOCE) is protected by the Free Exercise of Religion guarantee of the First Amendment, the Freedom of Association guarantee of the First Amendment, and the liberty/privacy guarantee of the Fifth and Fourteenth Amendments.

A. *Free Exercise of Religion*

Free exercise of religion clearly involves much more than freedom of belief; the very term "exercise" demonstrates that the clause protects religious speech and action as well. As the Supreme Court said in *Cantwell v. Connecticut*, 310 U.S. 296 at 303-04 (1940):

The constitutional inhibition of legislation on the subject of religion has a double aspect. On the one hand, it forestalls compulsion by law of the acceptance of any creed or the practice of any form of worship. Freedom of conscience and freedom to adhere to such religious organization or form of worship as the individual may choose cannot be restricted by law. On the other hand, it safeguards the free exercise of the chosen form of religion. Thus the Amendment embraces two concepts – freedom to believe and freedom to act. The first is absolute but, in the nature of things, the second cannot be. Conduct remains subject to regulation for the protection of society. The freedom to act must have appropriate definition to preserve the enforcement of that protection. In every case the power to regulate must be so exercised as not, in attaining a permissible end, unduly to infringe the protected freedom.

The *Cantwell* Court recognized that religious actions do not have the same absolute protection that is accorded to religious beliefs, but religious actions are nevertheless protected. The government can infringe the free exercise of religion only "for the protection of society," and even then, "the power to regulate must be so exercised as not, in attaining a permissible end, unduly to infringe the protected freedom."

The Court clarified the protection afforded free exercise of religion in *Wisconsin v. Yoder*, 406 U.S.205 (1972). The Court held that if one can demonstrate that he or she has (1) a sincere religious belief and (2) a law or regulation imposes a substantial burden on the exercise of that sincere religious belief, then the burden shifts to the government to demonstrate that it has a compelling state interest that cannot be achieved by less restrictive means.

Appellees have clearly demonstrated that they hold sincere religious convictions concerning SOCE. Donald Welch is an ordained pastor who serves as Counseling Pastor for Skyline Wesleyan Church, which teaches that "human sexuality . . . is to be expressed only in a monogamous lifelong relationship between one man and one woman within the framework of marriage." He has demonstrated that his counseling ministry with Skyline Wesleyan Church will be jeopardized if he is forced to comply with SB 1172. Dr. Anthony Duk is a Roman Catholic medical doctor who conducts conversion therapy because his Roman Catholic religious convictions require him to do so, and he could not continue conducting SOCE if SB 1172 is upheld. Aaron Bitzer is an adult Christian who experienced same-sex attractions in childhood and was able to overcome these attractions through SOCE. He desires to become a therapist specifically to help others overcome same-sex attraction through SOCE, and if SB 1172 is upheld he will not be able to follow his plan (and, he believes, God's plan) for his life. Clearly, these plaintiffs have sincere religious convictions, and SB 1172 imposes a substantial burden upon the exercise of their convictions.

Before addressing the compelling interest / less restrictive means prong of the *Yoder* test, we need to note that in *Employment Division, Department of Human Resources of Oregon v. Smith*, 494 U.S. 872 (1990), the Court narrowed the *Yoder* ruling and held that the compelling interest / less restrictive means test applies only when the law (1) is directly aimed at religion, or (2) infringes not only free exercise of religion but also another right. Arguably, SB 1172 is directly aimed at religion. *Amicus* points to Appellants' proffered testimony of Dr. Beckstead, who claims that a major premise

underlying SOCE is that homosexuality is contrary to some counselors' religious and personal beliefs, that a problem with SOCE is that its practitioners do not seek to harmonize patients' religious beliefs with same-sex attraction or help patients to change their religious beliefs, and that the State should bar SOCE based on "the psychology of sexual orientation, the psychology of gender, and the psychology of religion." (Brief of Appellees 35–36). As the Supreme Court noted in *Church of the Lukumi Babalu Aye v. City of Hialeah*, 508 U.S. 520, 533 (1993), an ordinance may be directly aimed at religion either by its stated intent or by its practical effect.

[. . .]

C.   Liberty / Privacy

As noted earlier, Justice Kennedy stated in *Lawrence v. Texas*,

> These matters, involving the most intimate and personal choices a person may make in a lifetime, choices central to personal dignity and autonomy, are central to the liberty protected by the Fourteenth Amendment. At the heart of liberty is the right to define one's own concept of existence, of meaning, of the universe, and of the mystery of human life. Beliefs about these matters could not define the attributes of personhood were they formed under compulsion of the State.

539 U.S. 558, 574 (2003), quoting *Planned Parenthood v. Casey*, 505 U.S. 83, 851 (1992). *Lawrence* involved the right to engage in homosexual conduct, which, Justice Kennedy said, involves "the most intimate and personal choices a person may make in a lifetime" and "are central to the liberty protected by the Fourteenth Amendment."

If this liberty includes the right to choose to engage in homosexual conduct, it also includes the right not to so engage. If it includes the right to believe homosexual activity is acceptable, it also includes the right to believe the opposite. If Justice Kennedy's conclusion is taken as true, then the inverse must be true as well. It simply does not make sense, nor is it good law, to pick and choose when and by whom these "intimate and personal rights" may be exercised. The position espoused by the Appellants is the classic case of one "having his cake, and eating it too" – we have the right to make intimate and personal choices as to how we define our existence, but others do not have this right if their choices are different from ours.

This liberty also includes the right of minors who are troubled by homosexual urges to resist those urges and to seek help in doing so. It also includes the right of parents, who are responsible for their children's upbringing and training,[1] to guide them toward heterosexual rather than homosexual relationships and to seek help from counselors in doing so.[2]

This liberty/privacy right also includes the right of counselors to engage in SOCE. Assuming he or she is professionally qualified to do so, a lawyer has the right to define his/her existence by directing his/her practice toward protecting the environment, advancing the civil rights of minorities (including homosexuals), protecting the due process rights of those accused of crimes, prosecuting criminals to secure justice for victims, obtaining compensation for those injured by corporations, or a host of other causes. Similarly, Donald Welch and Anthony Duk have the right to define their existence by directing their counseling practice toward helping people avoid or leave a lifestyle which they believe to be harmful and immoral. Likewise Aaron Bitzer, having struggled with homosexual urges in his own childhood and having overcome them with the help of SOCE, has chosen to define his existence by dedicating his life toward helping others overcome homosexuality, and he has a liberty/privacy right to do so.

Ironically, some of the more strident gay rights activists who demand their right to live a certain lifestyle, are quick to deny those same rights to others. As Dr. D.A. Carson demonstrates in his book *The Intolerance of Tolerance* (Grand Rapids: Eerdmans 2012), many of the more militant activists are no longer willing to settle for the right to practice the homosexual lifestyle. Rather, they demand that the homosexual lifestyle be not only allowed but also accepted and approved, and they seek to use the force of law to silence and suppress those who make different choices for their lives and professions.

D. Compelling Interest/Less Restrictive Means

The right of Donald Welch, Anthony Duk, and (in the future) Aaron Bitzer and many others to engage in SOCE is a "hybrid right" combining free exercise of religion, free speech, freedom of association, and liberty/privacy. The State can infringe that right only if it can demonstrate that it has a compelling interest that cannot be achieved by less restrictive means.

[. . .]

Furthermore, even if the State could demonstrate a compelling interest, the State would also have to demonstrate that its interest cannot be achieved by less restrictive means. Without concluding that these means would pass constitutional muster or fully accommodate Appellees' constitutional rights, *Amicus* notes that the Legislature could have considered the following less restrictive means:

(a) Relying upon those who are critical of SOCE to inform the public about its alleged dangers through the free marketplace of ideas;

(b) Requiring counselors to inform their patients of the alleged dangers of SOCE before embarking upon a course of SOCE counseling;

(c) Prohibiting counselors from embarking upon a course of SOCE counseling with a minor, without that minor's and that minor's parents' informed written consent[3];

(d) Prohibiting some of the more extreme practices critics allege are associated with SOCE such as electroshock, lobotomies, castration, nausea, vomiting and rubber band snapping, without prohibiting oral counseling[4]; or

(e) Requiring counselors who undertake SOCE to have special training in that type of counseling[5].

The State has not demonstrated a compelling interest in prohibiting SOCE, nor has the State even considered whether these or other less restrictive means could satisfy the State's interest. The District Court therefore correctly enjoined the statute, and this Court should uphold the District Court's ruling.

II. SB 1172 Also Violates the Rights of Minors and to Receive Conversion Therapy and of Parents to Obtain Conversion Therapy for Their Children.

The District Court concluded that Appellees could not assert the third-party claims of minors and their parents who want conversion therapy. The Court explained that in order to assert a third-party claim, the litigant must satisfy three important criteria: (1) The litigant must have suffered an injury in fact, (2) The litigant must have a close relationship with the third party, and (3) There must exist some hindrance to the third party's ability to assert his or her own interests. The Court concluded that, even assuming Appellees can satisfy the first two criteria,

John A. Eidsmoe and Joshua M. Pendergrass

they cannot credibly assert the third, because minor children seeking SOCE and parents seeking SOCE for their minor children filed a case in the same court challenging SB 1172, referring to *Pickup v. Brown, op. cit.*

Amicus believes Appellees can satisfy this third criteria, *Pickup* notwithstanding. Even though the *Pickup* plaintiffs were willing to come forward and file suit, not many persons similarly situated would dare to do so, for two reasons: (1) They might be unwilling to disclose publicly that they or their children have homosexual urges because of peer pressure from friends, fellow students, members of the opposite sex, future military recruiters, and others; or (2) They might be unwilling to disclose publicly that they are seeking SOCE because of fear of criticism and reprisal from those elements of the gay community which abhor SOCE.

[. . .]

Amicus therefore urges this Court to consider the rights and interests of minors who want SOCE and parents who want SOCE for their children alongside the rights and interests of Appellees, especially because the *Pickup* case is also before this Court.

Conclusion

SB 1172 needs to be seen for exactly what it is – a raw attempt to establish one controversial point of view as the established orthodoxy and to silence opposing viewpoints by the force of law, and an equally raw attempt to

make the State take sides in a power struggle within and outside the counseling profession. The public debate over issues related to homosexuality and counseling is far from settled, yet militant activists seek to use the law to suppress their critics.

The State should not let itself be used in this power struggle by taking sides in this debate. As the Supreme Court said in *Gertz v. Robert Welch, Inc.*, 418 U.S. 323, 339 (1974), "Under the First Amendment, there is no 13-such thing as a false idea." And as the Court said in *West Virginia State Board of Education v. Barnette*, 319 U.S. 624, 642 (1943),

> If there is any fixed star in our constitutional constellation, it is that no official, high or petty, can prescribe what shall be orthodox in politics, nationalism, religion, or other matters of opinion or force citizens to confess by word or act their faith therein. If there are any circumstances which permit an exception, they do not now occur to us.

Nor would they occur here. SB 1172 is a blatant infringement upon the First and Fourteenth Amendment rights of counselors, minors, and parents. The District Court correctly enjoined SB 1172, and this Court should uphold the District Court's ruling.

Respectfully submitted, this the 26th day of February, 2013.

[. . .]

Notes

1 *Pierce v. Society of Sisters of the Holy Names of Jesus and Mary*, 268 U.S. 510 (1925): "The fundamental theory of liberty upon which all governments in this Union repose excludes any general power of the state to standardize its children by forcing them to accept instruction from public teachers only. The child is not the mere creature of the state; those who nurture him and direct his destiny have the right, coupled with the high duty, to recognize and prepare him for additional obligations."

2 The District Court below ruled that the Appellees as counselors are not entitled to third party standing to bring the claims of minors and their parents. As we will explain later in this brief, *Amicus* respectfully disagrees with this portion of the District Court's ruling. Furthermore, the parallel case of *Pickup v. Brown*, Civ. No. 2:12-2497 KJM EFB (E.D. Cal.) Compl. 2-6 (Docket No. 1), which is also before this

Court, involves minors seeking SOCE and parents seeking SOCE for their minor children.

3 Appellee Welch testified that he does not and will not engage in conversion therapy with an unwilling patient. Brief of Appellees 4–5.

4 Appellee Duk testified that he engages in only oral counseling and does not use any of these alternatives. Brief of Appellees 5.

5 Another irony of this case is that if SB 1172 is upheld and licensed counselors are not allowed to provide SOCE, people who want SOCE will seek it from others who may not have such training and licensing. Furthermore, if we accept Appellants' claim that SBG 1172 leaves counselors free to refer SOCE patients, whom could they refer them to? Obviously, to unlicensed counselors.

PART V

Transgender and Medicine

Introduction

While the nature of sexual attraction is a central concern of sexual ethics, the nature of sexual, or gender, identity is as well – though in a different way. In the debates about sexual attraction, the way a person sees someone else is typically what generates the attention. In debates around gender identity, the way a person sees themself is typically what generates the attention.

If a person is anatomically male, but feels that they are psychologically female, what is the best way to understand that situation and what options should be available to address it? Almost always, such a situation produces some sort of distress, frustration, discrimination, and confusion, and so *something* about the situation is wrong. But how we conceptualize what has gone wrong makes an important difference in how we deal with it. Should we think of what has gone wrong as a psychological problem – say, a delusion? That suggests we should treat it with psychotherapy. Should we think of it as a biological problem – say, an anatomical defect? That suggests we should treat it surgically. Should we think of what has gone wrong as a social problem – say, a cultural bigotry? That suggests we should treat it with education and anti-discrimination law. And what about the individual who might want to change their

anatomy? How should we understand that? If they are delusional, would they be self-harming? If they suffer from an anatomical defect, would they be correcting it? If they are victims of social bigotry, would they be internalizing culture's contempt, on par with homosexuals who seek out conversion therapy? And these kinds of questions apply to situations where anatomy is relatively clear. What about when anatomy itself is ambiguous, as when a child is born with genitalia neither distinctly female nor male? What should happen then, when the child is not cognitively capable of deciding what to do but whose life will be radically directed one way or another by others' decision to make them a certain sex or leave them ambiguous?

Part V examines issues of transgender, intersexed children, and medicine. Pulling in biology, psychology, identity politics, and aesthetics, these issues are explored here by focusing on concerns about medical classification and medical treatment.

Framing Questions

- *How should transgender be understood?*
- *How should we assess sex reassignment surgery?*
- *How should intersexed children be medically treated?*

Gender Identity Disorders in Childhood and Adolescence: A Critical Inquiry

Darryl B. Hill, Christina Rozanski, Jessica Carfagnini, and Brian Willoughby

Summary

Argues that while debates continue as to whether or not a diagnosis of gender identity disorder (GID) is wanted or needed by today's transgendered adult, there is increasing concern both in academic and lay literature regarding the diagnosis of children and adolescents with GID. Critically evaluates the diagnosis, assessment, and treatment of GID in children and adolescents in light of published controversies and urges a re-evaluation of the GID diagnosis. If the GID diagnostic category continues in the DSM-V, it should be rewritten to eliminate stereotyping and assumptions of gender dichotomy, should respect gender diversity, and should respect different cultures' notions of gender.

Original publication details: Darryl B. Hill, Christina Rozanski, Jessica Carfagnini, Brian Willoughby, "Gender Identity Disorders in Childhood and Adolescence: A Critical Inquiry," pp. 57–74 from *International Journal of Sexual Health* 19 (2007). Reproduced with permission of Taylor & Francis Group.

Darryl B. Hill, Christina Rozanski, Jessica Carfagnini, and Brian Willoughby

Introduction

Gender identity disorder (GID) is one of the more recent diagnoses to enter the *Diagnostic and Statistical Manual of Mental Disorders* (*DSM*), becoming a diagnosis in 1980 with the *DSM-III* (American Psychiatric Association, 1980). As it is currently described by the *DSM-IV-TR* (APA, 2000), GID is based on two main ideas: a strong and persistent cross-gender identification and discomfort about one's assigned sex or gender. In order to be diagnosed with GID, the individual must meet the four criteria listed in the Appendix. While debates continue as to whether or not GID is wanted or needed by today's *adult* transsexual (an issue *not* addressed by this paper), there is growing concern in both academic and lay literature regarding GID in children and adolescents. Recent published criticisms of GID in psychiatric and psychological journals, as well as book-length criticisms, target a wide range of problems with the conceptualization, assessment, and treatment of the diagnosis. These critiques build upon issues and positions that arose during a controversy in the late 1970s over using behavior modification techniques to alter gender identity in children and adolescents (e.g., Morin & Schultz, 1978; Newman, 1977; Nordyke, Baer, Etzel, & LeBlanc, 1977; Winkler, 1977; Wolfe, 1979).

[. . .]

This paper critically evaluates the diagnosis, assessment, and treatment of GID in children and adolescents in light of published controversies, evidence, and arguments in social science discourse since the publication of the *DSM-IV*. The heat has been rising on these debates in recent years, and the case against using the GID diagnosis with children and adolescents is strong. Yet, this discourse is full of twists and turns. Proponents of the diagnosis readily admit problems with the diagnosis, at least from a scientific point of view. And GID is not unusual in that sense: many diagnoses in the *DSM* are problematic, even controversial. As responsible scientists, they openly acknowledge the limitations of research on GID. Still, proponents persist with the diagnosis and treatment of children and adolescents, treatments that critics find offensive. There is often a moral tone to much of the discourse, reflecting conflicting ideologies and deeply held values, perhaps protecting vested interests or reflecting gender politics. The question facing many is whether to maintain a diagnosis in the face of critical rational scientific argument because it fits with traditional morals and values, many of which are increasingly out of step with quickly changing views on gender

and sexuality in the Western world. Ultimately, for some the appeal to morality fails to support this diagnosis. For, in a culture that widely supports the equality of the genders, and even (in many jurisdictions) legislates against discrimination on the basis of gender identity, critics argue that the best approach is to guide gender choices, but not enforce one gendered way of being on any young person solely because their gender violates social norms. Thus, those not swayed by the paucity of good science underlying the diagnosis of GID in children and adolescents are often moved by the humanistic arguments against it.

This review focuses on four broad debates: problems with the diagnostic criteria of GID, the validity and reliability of the diagnosis in clinical practice, whether GID is a "mental disorder" of youth, and the rationale for treatment (including the distress of the child and adult consequences of GID).

Problems with the Diagnostic Criteria

There are several basic challenges to the diagnostic criteria and whether the criteria lead to the proper diagnosis of youth suffering from their gender nonconformity. Debates focused on whether gender roles are clearly dichotomized, cultural and historical variations in gender role expectations, and making the criteria more exclusive.

Gender Roles Are Not Clearly Dichotomized. The "Diagnostic Features" section, the preamble to the disorder in the *DSM-IV-TR* (APA, 2000), describes boys and girls with GID. It specifies that boys with GID may prefer "traditionally feminine activities," "girls' or women's clothes," and they may reject stereotypical boys' activities (such as "rough-and-tumble" play) in favor of stereotypical girls' toys "such as Barbie" (p. 576). Boys might "insist on sitting to urinate" (p. 576). In contrast, girls diagnosed with GID shun dresses or other "feminine attire" for "boys' clothing and short hair" (pp. 576–577). They may find menstruation aversive. They usually have boys as playmates, enjoy "contact sports, rough-and-tumble play, and traditional boyhood games," and identify with "powerful male figures such as Batman or Superman" (p. 577). A girl with GID may "refuse to urinate in a sitting position" (p. 577).

These anachronistic depictions of gender rest on the assumptions that gender is highly dichotomous and uniform and that there is agreement about what is "stereotypical" for either gender. What exactly are "feminine" attire and activities according to youth today? Do we still live in a world where there are "boys' toys" and "girls' toys"? What are stereotypical games and pastimes for either sex? *Can't* boys urinate while sitting? *Must* girls sit? How much sense does it make to talk about length of hair, urinating position, preferences for playmates and activities as indicators of gender role? It seems increasingly difficult in modern Western culture to classify such a wide range of behaviors into neatly distinct forms. Even introductory texts on gender differences research in psychology are now clear that most psychological attributes and behaviors are normally distributed for each gender, with small differences emerging only for very specific abilities and limited contexts (Lips, 2005).

Of course there is a great deal of research in child development which finds sex-dimorphic preferences for behaviors in children, thus supporting the assertions of the DSM, at least in spirit. There are many reasons to be critical, however, of these findings. For one, many of the publications are based on 20- to 30-year-old studies, so it seems reasonable to expect that broad gender differences found between children in the 1970s might have lessened by the twenty-first century. Yet, there are recent studies that continue finding differences between young boys and girls in their behaviors. These studies typically find an average difference on some behavior (e.g., boys on average are more aggressive than girls), but this focus on averages belies the vast overlap in the behaviors of the genders. Is there any behavior that only boys do and not girls? So, yes, boys and girls may differ on average, but there are individual differences in these tendencies such that any boy and any girl may fall anywhere along most dimensions. Moreover, researchers who do these studies and look for the magnitude of the effect of gender on behavior find generally small effect sizes for gender. The differences are there, but they are small, and although statistically significant, may not support the view that the genders should be held to very different expectations.

In addition, it seems reasonable to expect that a child's own knowledge of gender expectations might influence their behavior in a laboratory (due to demand characteristics) or even under the watchful eye of parents. Yet, when these children are left alone, they may be much more flexible in their gendered choices. Lastly, while research may describe the two genders as at least somewhat different in childhood or adolescence, by adulthood, much of these differences lessen or disappear.

How many males reading this article are into "rough-and-tumble" play? How many women only engage in pastimes typical of their gender? The point is – why do we hold children and adolescents to rigid and dichotomous gender expectations, but relax these expectations for adults? What if children perceive the adults in their world as flexible in their gender and try to emulate this?

There Are Cultural and Historical Variances in Gender Role Expectations. An additional problem with the criteria is that whatever *is* appropriate *here and now* may not be appropriate for someone else in their community or in the future. The classification of "appropriate" feminine attire and activities obviously depends on historical and cultural context. Some of my neighbors believe that boys playing with dolls are disturbed; but some do not. Our parents might have; we may not. Complicating the matter is the assertion that different cultures and classes in North America may have different standards for gendered behavior. If different cultures have different standards for behavior, the gender prescriptions outlined in the *DSM* may be irrelevant to these other cultures (Davis, 1998), causing problems for those who immigrate to North America. Ideas like this led Newman (2002) to remind clinicians who work with gender disorders to explore the cultural background of the client and consider that gender nonconformity in one culture (e.g., American) may be a sign of a disorder, but not in another (e.g., Buddhist). Moreover, as gender expectations change over time, perhaps quite rapidly in the last 40 years, the language in the *DSM* does not reflect the spirit of these liberalizing attitudes about gender freedom. The language of this diagnostic category should be based on more sophisticated and contemporary conceptualizations of gender in which gender variance is statistically infrequent but nonpathological, and the standard is not conformity to stereotypical notions of gender differences in clothing, games, hairstyles, or urinating positions.

Cross-Sex Desire or Identification Must Be Present. A further problem centers on the issue that the *DSM* requires that a person meet only four of the five parts of criterion A. Part one – cross-gender identification or desire – is the most restrictive criterion. The other four parts refer to cross-gender activities and interests, which may be exhibited by children who are simply gender nonconformist. Therefore, it is pertinent to ask the question; Who might be exhibiting only parts two to five of criterion A? It is quite possible that healthy gender non-conformists may meet four of the five parts of criterion A and meet criteria B, C, and D. That is, some children may display obvious cross-gender preferences, but not cross-identify. For example, a girl may be drawn to stereotypically masculine activities, be uncomfortable with femininity, all the while knowing she is a female with no desire to change her sex. According to Zucker (1990a, 1992), clinicians with these cases should use the diagnosis "gender identity disorder – not otherwise specified."

However, basing diagnosis on cross-gender behavior and preferences alone, in the absence of a desire for a sex change, may lead, as Zucker (1992) admits, to an inflated false positive rate in diagnoses. On this issue, Bower (2001) hopes that the *DSM-V* will reflect the fact that a desire for hormones or surgery *must* be present *in addition to* an intense desire to be the other sex, a stipulation that would disqualify all but the very rare transsexual child or adolescent. In addition, critics like Richardson (1999) conclude that criterion A should require that the cross-gender behavior must not simply be present but be pathological (i.e., used maladaptively or distressing to the child). That is, a boy who happily cross-dresses, enjoys cross-gender role play, games and pastimes, along with a preference for cross-gender playmates (i.e., criterion A, parts 2–5), should be distinguished from boys who are extremely distressed about their masculinity or maleness, deploy their cross-gender interests maladaptively, and have strong desires to change their sex.

Distress Must Be Present. Criterion D, the experience of debilitating distress, has also been criticized. Indeed, the inclusion of distress as a criterion in the *DSM-IV* more generally has been criticized (e.g., Spitzer & Wakefield, 1999). Zucker, Bradley, and Sullivan (1992) state that they were not in favor of "distress" as a significant element of the *DSM-III* criteria, yet it remained in the *DSM-IV*. Elsewhere, there is general concern about how to operationalize distress and whether the distress of GID is ego-dystonic or syntonic. Richardson (1996) wonders if distress in youth diagnosed with GID may be a "mere epiphenomena of some other trouble" (p. 53), thus, suggesting that criterion D should state that the distress is *not* "attributable solely or principally to rejection or harassment because of his [sic] gender atypicality" (Richardson, 1999, p. 49). Richardson (1996) also worries that clinicians operationalize impairment differently from clinic to clinic. Zucker (1999), in response, agrees: "Very little empirical work preceded the introduction of this criterion (or any disorder), and virtually no guidelines exist with respect to how either distress or impairment is to be assessed" (p. 40). But there is a paradox; while distress is often less in younger children,

clinicians recommend beginning treatment with younger children so their gender nonconformity is less entrenched. Zucker (1999) concludes: "I hope that the vagaries of the distress/impairment criterion do not dissuade clinicians from providing early therapeutic intervention, because I believe that this would be a grave disservice to our child patients and their families" (p. 41).

Zucker's sentiments seem to be echoed by Bower (2001) who notes that distress is not present in every patient, and "its absence should not refute the diagnosis" (p. 2). For Bower, cross-gender identification and behavior, along with a stated desire for gender reassignment, are sufficient conditions for the GID diagnosis. This makes sense, but only if clinicians consider all five parts of criterion A. Moreover, a child who is not distressed by their gender variance should not be a candidate for reparative therapy (encouraging the youth to conform to their natal sex and associated gender), if only for purely humanistic reasons. Why force a happy gender-nonconforming child to go against their chosen gender? It seems this may only encourage them to suppress their cross-gender desires, and harbor hostility to those involved in the treatment, only to pursue their cross-gender wishes with renewed vigor once they become adults.

Reliability and Validity of GID Diagnosis

There have been increasing concerns over the reliability and validity of the GID diagnosis in children and adolescents. The central issues focus on the lack of evidence supporting diagnostic specificity for the existing criteria and the idea that cognitive maturity is a diagnostic confound.

There Is Little Evidence of Diagnostic Specificity. Can GID be consistently diagnosed, and can GID patients be differentiated from other similar patients? Past research has shown that approximately 20% of referrals for GID in adolescence (under the *DSM-III-R* criteria) fall into an "uncertain" classification (Bradley & Zucker, 1990). Zucker (2002) believes that there are three main paths into adulthood for boys diagnosed with GID: A few become transsexual adults, some become heterosexual without GID, but most become gay adults. The same may be true for girls. Considering these clinical reflections, the issue of diagnosis becomes whether the criteria can distinguish between these different phenomenologies. Concerns over diagnostic specificity have led

Richardson (1996) to wonder what differentiates gender nonconformist (e.g., "sissies" and "tomboys"), gay, lesbian, and bisexual and transsexual youth. There can be no question that the children clinicians see are often gender nonconformists, but Richardson wonders, should they be diagnosed with GID? Richardson contends, "We cannot yet conclude that gender identity disorder is categorically distinct from gender nonconformity" (p. 53). [. . .]

[. . .]

Cognitive Maturity Is a Diagnostic Confound. From studies in the last decade, it is becoming clear that future studies on the reliability and validity of the GID diagnosis must account for the age of the youth. It is commonly accepted amongst gender researchers and theorists that gender identity develops gradually in the early years (e.g., Lips, 2005). One's sense of masculinity or femininity, either applied to one's self or significant others, is something that emerges with one's ability to think in more complex ways. Thus, age, or more pointedly, cognitive maturity, seems like an obvious confound in the assessment of GID. Over a decade ago, Zucker (1990c) noticed that younger children were more likely to verbalize cross-gender wishes. Zucker and colleagues (1993), in a study to validate a clinical assessment interview, found that age negatively correlates with gender "deviance." That is, "cognitive gender confusion" is more common in children referred for gender identity problems, and as children age they are less likely to evaluate their own sex with ambivalence or negativity.

[. . .]

GID Is Not a Mental Disorder

Problems with validity and reliability of the diagnosis have led to questions as to whether or not GID is actually a valid "mental disorder" of the youth. Concerns on this issue in recent years have focused on how parents are implicated in their offspring's gender variations.

Parents of GID Youth Are Often Distressed. An interesting controversy in the literature focuses on the "location" of disorder: Are the youth disordered, or do they have disordered parents? Recent studies suggest that the parents play a crucial role in the young gender-variant child's life, often openly rejecting a gender-variant child, exacerbating the child's distress. Wren (2002) documented the extent to which parents might reject their trans-identified children. She interviewed 11 families with children or adolescents referred for gender identity

problems. She found that many parents believe their transgender child is gay because they simply can't understand the idea of transgenderism in youth. Parents especially reject their children's wishes to alter their bodies (e.g., sex changes), characterizing the child as immature, in no position to make such an important decision about their life, and resisting the child's chosen gender, greeting gender change with a sense of sadness and loss. Those parents who are dismayed by their child's transgenderism often "seek evidence for causal explanations that bolster their view that transsexuality is wrong for their child" (Wren, 2002, p. 389). In general, Wren finds that nonaccepting parents maintain secrecy about the problem, hope the problem will go away, and become preoccupied with the negative aspects of transgenderism.

Researchers are increasingly suspicious that GID in a child or adolescent might simply be an indication of family pathology manifesting in the child's gender. Zucker and Bradley (1995) note that several familial factors (e.g., marital discord), and specifically maternal factors (e.g., mother's social adaptation and affect regulation) are associated with GID diagnosis in children. Indeed, they test three different models to explain the connections between GID and family psychopathology. In their assessment, GID is an expression of family psychopathology since boys referred for gender problems often come from families with greater parental and familial dysfunction than normal controls. They also found that the strongest predictor of psychopathology (as measured by the *Child Behavior Check List* or *CBCL*) is maternal psychopathology (and often the mother is the parent rating the children on the *CBCL*).

Another study, Marantz and Coates (1991), found that compared with mothers of "normal" boys, mothers of boys diagnosed with GID were more likely to score in the clinical range for borderline personality and depression. Moreover, the mothers acted in ways that aggravated separation anxiety in their sons. Supporting these findings, Cohen-Kettenis and Van Goozen (2002) find that adolescents diagnosed with GID experience disagreements with their parents, as well as "serious relationship problems between parents, poor parenting skills or combinations of these factors" (p. 419).

Zucker (2000), in a review of the current state of GID theory and practice, speculates that parents may inadvertently create GID children by either tolerating or encouraging cross-gender behavior or by intentionally raising androgynous children, perhaps because the parents themselves have "pervasive conflict that revolves around gender issues" (p. 681). He describes one of his unpublished case studies in which a mother mourns the birth of a boy (she was hoping for a girl), and enacts gender ambivalence through child-rearing practices (e.g., active cross-dressing of the boy). Zucker also alleges that the fathers of children diagnosed with GID are more often suffering from alcohol abuse or depression. Consistent with these observations, Zucker and Bradley (1999) assert that the alleviation of marital discord and parental psychopathology will help a child's gender dysphoria. Specifically, parents need help carrying out the treatment plan which often discourages cross-gender behavior and encourages "gender-appropriate" behavior – mostly because "some of these parents find it difficult to believe that their child has a gender identity problem; others are reluctant to restrict their child's favorite fantasies or activities" (Zucker & Bradley, 1999, p. 383).

Meyer-Bahlburg (2002) goes one step further. In a report on treatment outcomes with children three to four years of age diagnosed with GID, the treatment is primarily directed at the *parents*. Reasoning that boys diagnosed with GID may have difficulties connecting with family and friends, and that boys diagnosed with GID typically "grow out of" their gender dysphoria, he hopes to "speed up the fading of the cross-gender identity which will typically happen in any case" (p. 361) by increasing same-sex socialization with his peers and father. He begins therapy by exploring the parent's understanding of gender, which is often too permissive in his eyes, convincing the parents that moderate sex-stereotyping "is required if the GID is to resolve" (p. 369). Then, parents are "sensitized" to encourage "gender-typical behaviors" in the boy by paying attention to desired actions, but discouraging cross-gender behaviors. In this study, directing therapy at the parents results in the elimination of GID in 10 of the 11 cases, with only occasional recurrence during the first year. Thus, Meyer-Bahlberg's "short-term parent-mediated peer-centered treatment," which amounts basically to parental gender dichotomization training, cures GID in preschool children. Of course, the change in the behavior of these cases might also be due to changes associated with the simple passage of time (i.e., aging). Further studies with controlled comparison groups are needed to assess any treatment effect.

Psychoeducational treatments directed at the parents seem to have an effect according to other initial reports. Rosenberg (2002) describes a parent-centered approach that encourages acceptance and support for the children just the way they are, helping parents cope with the sense of disappointment at not having a masculine boy or a feminine girl. She found that all the children remitted, accepting their natal gender. Menvielle and Tuerk (2002) provide similar treatments to parents, helping the children understand that they may simply be nonstereotypical boys and girls, preparing the parents to cope with having a gender-nonconformist child (e.g., handling embarrassing situations, using humor, enlisting the support of other adults, and advocating for their child). The goal here is not to convert the child back to a stereotypical gender, but rather to help the parents cope with their gender-variant child.

Parental Ratings of Children and Adolescents Are Biased. It seems reasonable to conclude that much of the attention to GID children comes from parents' intolerant of gender variance, not from the children themselves, as is the case with most childhood psychological problems. It has been noted repeatedly in the literature that almost all referrals of GID youth to gender treatment centers come from parents and other adults such as teachers (e.g., Zucker & Bradley, 1995; Rekers & Kilgus, 1995). Parents also figure prominently in the assessment of pathology. Upon referral to a clinician, usually the youth is interviewed and required to fill out a variety of psychometric tests. Zucker and Bradley (1999) report that assessments typically involve interviews with *both* the child and a parent, biomedical tests, the *Draw-A-Person* test, observations during free play, the *IT Scale*, and the *Rorschach Inkblot Test*. However, some of the best evidence of disorder in GID children and adolescents comes from parent and teacher ratings on the *CBCL* (Zucker & Bradley, 1995).

Parent ratings are typical in child developmental research, but several cautions should be raised when relying on observational data in the assessment of GID. First, observational ratings suffer from a wide range of problems including anchoring and contrast effects. Thus, a parent who is stereotypical in gender (i.e., gender-schematic) may assess their child's gender non-conformity as abnormal compared with their own or siblings' gender. Likewise, it has been noted regularly in psychometric literature that ratings of gendered behavior are biased by the beliefs of the rater (e.g., Cohen & Swederlik, 1999). Clinicians who work with children diagnosed with other disorders find that parents are often biased against their children (Johnston & Freeman, 1997) and parental attributions of the child's disordered behavior may indicate more about the parent than the child (Joiner & Wagner, 1996). Thus, ratings by parents and teachers who believe in rigidly distinct gender roles are clearly biased assessors of a child's behavior. [. . .]

[. . .]

Treatment Rationale

The treatment of GID in children and adolescents has been controversial for three decades, pre-dating even the listing of the diagnosis in 1980. Treatments documented by Rekers in the late 1970s were criticized for reinforcing sex-stereotyped patterns and the unproven link between nontraditional childhood gender behavior and later gender dysphoria or homosexuality (e.g., Nordyke et al., 1977; Winkler, 1977; Wolfe, 1979). Even now that there is better evidence for the link between atypical gender in youth and homosexuality (e.g., Bailey & Zucker, 1995), a risk of adulthood homosexuality is a very controversial rationale for treatment of childhood or adolescent gender dysphoria. These highly contentious and unresolved issues aside, since the *DSM-IV* three issues have dominated the discourse on treatment rationale: most GID youth are not pathological, most GID youth do not develop adult pathologies, and reparative therapies are harmful and contravene existing treatment standards.

There Is Little Evidence That GID Youth Are Pathological. The key rationale for treatment is that children who stray from the path of "normal" gender will not have a healthy happy life. Certainly some children, and their parents (see Griffiths, 2002), struggle and experience pain when the youth does not fit neatly into either the "boy" or the "girl" category. On one hand, some clinicians believe that children and adolescents diagnosed with GID are extremely pathological, typically exhibiting other disorders only alleviated by sex-reassignment surgery. On the other hand, even advocates of GID reform admit that gender-variant children are at risk for stigma and isolation (e.g., Minter, 1999) and need special support (Mallon, 1999). But what evidence is there to substantiate the idea that children and adolescents diagnosed with GID have a reduced capacity to live a successful and healthy life? Putting aside questions on the *meaning* of distress (which is a much bigger issue; see Zucker et al., 1992), researchers are only able to identify minor sources of distress in specific domains. Before reviewing these studies, it should be noted that this research often includes children who do

not meet the *DSM* criteria, considers only a narrow range of behaviors, and does not involve direct standardized assessments.

Zucker and Bradley (1995) are the most complete and authoritative source on the issue of psychopathology. Their assessments rely mostly on ratings provided by the *CBCL*. This scale, referred to earlier, broadly assesses disturbances in children as internalizing disorders (i.e., disturbances of emotion or behavior such as depression) and externalizing disorders (i.e., behavioral misconduct). Based on parent ratings, boys referred to a clinic for gender problems differed from their male siblings on several indexes, with a higher tendency toward internalizing disorders. When comparing these "gender-referred" boys with a matched clinical sample and sibling controls, the gender-referred boys were no different on *CBCL* mother ratings than boys in the clinical sample, but were more disturbed (but not falling in the "clinical" range) than their male siblings (according to their mother's ratings on the *CBCL*).

Zucker and Bradley (1995) also provide mother's *CBCL* ratings for girls with GID. They compared gender-referred girls with their siblings and found that on all five indices, gender-referred girls were rated higher than their siblings on behavioral disturbances. Controlling for age, however, they found that younger girls were less disturbed, with no differences between younger girls and their siblings on narrow-band scales. Older gender-referred girls had higher ratings on four of the nine scales.

The *CBCL* also has a section on social competence (the activities, social, and school subscales). On the activities, school, and total subscales, boys diagnosed with GID scored the same as their siblings and clinical controls, but lower than nonclinical boys. On the social subscale, there were no differences between the groups. Girls diagnosed with GID scored the same as their siblings on the activities and school scales, but lower on both the social and total score. Ultimately, Zucker and Bradley conclude that the *CBCL* data give "preliminary support to previous clinical observations that gender identity disorder in both boys and girls is, on average, associated with other behavioral difficulties" (p. 106).

A slightly different picture emerges with a more complete update on the children and adolescents referred to Zucker's clinic. Zucker, Owen, Bradley, and Ameeriar (2002) provide results on 358 child and 72 adolescent cases (346 male; 84 female) assessed by Zucker and his colleagues from 1975 to 2000. In this sample, 47% of the children and 85% of the adolescents fell within the clinical ranges of maternal ratings on the *CBCL*. Thus, older youth show more pathology, age being a significant factor in predicting pathology. Cohen-Kettenis and colleagues (2003) show that in both Toronto and Utrecht (Netherlands), the best predictors of *CBCL* pathology are three items that Zucker calls the "peer relations" ratings (i.e., maternal ratings on "Doesn't get along with other kids," "Gets teased a lot," and "Not liked by other kids"). Thus, judgments of a child's pathology associate with how well he gets along with others (in his mother's opinion), suggesting that perceptions of pathology are linked to maternal perceptions of the youth's rejection by peers.

Further evidence weakens the "distressed child" argument. Cohen, de Ruiter, Ringelberg, and Cohen-Kettenis (1997) compare Rorschach profiles of adolescent transsexuals with psychiatric outpatient and university student control groups. Finding few differences between the three groups (recalling Hooker's 1950s research comparing Rorschach profiles of heterosexual and homosexual men), they conclude that "adolescent transsexuals as a group do not show the marked degree of psychopathology encountered in psychiatric groups" (p. 194), and "the argument that gross psychopathology is a required condition for the development of transsexualism appears indefensible" (p. 195). [. . .]

[. . .]

Moreover, if these youth are distressed by having a condition deemed by society as unwanted, is this evidence of a disorder? Bartlett and colleagues (2000) note that the problem determining distress is aggravated in GID cases because it usually is not clear whether distress in the child is due to gender variance or secondary effects (e.g., due to ostracization or stigmatization). Overall, Bartlett and colleagues find little evidence for impairment in functioning. When boys with GID score below average in school and social functioning, are these indicators of psychological pathology or simply a sign that their peers reject them for their gender nonconformity? They observe that Zucker and Bradley (1995) find elevations on pathology scales, but these elevations are mostly not in the clinical range. Moreover, GID children are similar to other children who experience peer rejection and victimization.

Bartlett and colleagues (2000) also find contradictory results regarding the general mental health of children diagnosed with GID. They find that the reliance on parent ratings of the child's behavior is problematic because parent ratings tend not to correlate with children's self-reports, and parents tend to magnify problems with their children (i.e., children report fewer problems than the

adults observe), lending credence to the assertion that parents might exaggerate the child's problems. Furthermore, they find that the research on dysfunction among youth diagnosed with GID is equivocal: the only probable outcome of GID in children is homosexuality, but this can hardly be considered a symptom of dysfunction given that homosexuality is no longer a mental disorder.

Most GID Youth Do Not Develop Adult Pathologies. [. . .]

Comprehensive reviews of the literature by Zucker and Bradley (Zucker & Bradley, 1995, 1999; Bradley & Zucker, 1997) report that there are no definitive evaluations of interventions with children and adolescents diagnosed with GID. One study, often cited in discussions of the long-term implications of gender variance among youth is Green's (1987) report on "sissy boys." Very few discussions highlight the problematic findings of this study. Green conducted a follow-up on 66 feminine boys referred to his clinic and a control group of 56 masculine boys. He was able to contact only 44 of the feminine boys and 35 of the masculine boys for follow-up, representing a loss of approximately a third of both groups, raising concerns about biases among his remaining participants. Interestingly, of the feminine boys, only one was considering sex reassignment surgery at follow-up, but most reported same-sex or bisexual desires. Green concludes that most feminine boys eventually forgo the desire to change sex without therapy, suggesting that his sample largely consisted of "pre-homosexual" and not "pre-transsexual" boys. Green's study is a central cornerstone of early approaches to gender-variant youth, yet the study has been over-valued given its biases.

A better sense of what happened to Green's sissy boys was revealed in a recent report by one of the participants in Green's study. Bryant (2004), one of Green's "sissies," in a paper presented to the American Psychiatric Association, describes Green's treatments as a trauma. He reflected on Green's rejection of his femininity and said:

> I experienced this as a strong negative judgment about something I felt very deeply about myself, at my core. As a result, I think that the main thing that I took away from my years at [Green's gender clinic at] UCLA was a kind of self-hatred and a loss of a sense of who I really was. I learned to hide myself, to make myself invisible, even to myself. I learned that who I was, was wrong.

Bryant suggests that treatment protocols for these children and adolescents, especially those based on

converting the child back to a stereotypically gendered youth, may make matters worse, causing them to internalize their distress. In other words, treatment for GID in children and adolescents may have negative consequences.
[. . .]

There have been some recent studies on the effectiveness and success of gender reassignment. While this field of research is plagued by difficulties, it looks like most adults who gradually and slowly transition to another gender are satisfied with their lives, especially if therapists guide the client toward their own solution, assist in the transition, and address any coexisting psychological problems. An example of the empirical research on treatment effectiveness with adolescents is Meyenburg (1999). He reviews literature that suggests most children diagnosed with GID abandon gender-variant behavior by adolescence. Then, in an analysis of four case studies, he finds that a few adolescents with clear-cut symptoms of trans-sexualism will go on to have their gender surgically altered. Some will not, changing their minds without treatment. Overall, he urges caution when treating young patients who wish to transition because they may change their minds.

In contrast, many clinicians working with adolescent transsexuals support *early* reversible physical interventions (e.g., postponing puberty). An illustration of this position is argued by Cohen-Kettenis and Van Goozen (1997). They provide follow-up data on 22 adolescents (average age 17.5 years) who were given hormone therapy and sex reassignment surgery. At least one year later, they report improvements in their lives. However, most of their data were not subjected to statistical analysis, there was no control comparison group, and they were evaluated by the same staff that treated them (risking "faking good"). Moreover, the sample was, in their own words, the "best cases" for surgery (e.g., usually only "homosexual transsexuals" are recommended for this advance treatment). Smith (2001) also supports early intervention for adolescent transsexuals. She compares adolescents accepted for sex reassignment surgery with those who were rejected. She finds that treated adolescents were *less* pathological than the untreated adolescents, suggesting somewhat paradoxically that the most radical treatments are offered to the highest-functioning clients.

Reparative Therapies Are Harmful and Contravene Existing Treatment Standards. Zucker and Bradley (1995) believe that reparative treatments (encouraging the child to accept their natal sex and associated gender) can be therapeutic for several reasons. They believe that treatment can help reduce social ostracism by helping gender nonconforming children mix more readily with same-sex peers and prevent long-term psychopathological development (i.e., it is easier to change a child than a society intolerant of gender diversity). Reparative therapy is believed to reduce the chances of adult GID (i.e., transsexualism) which Zucker and Bradley characterize as undesirable. Thus, "nipping" gender disorder "in the bud" holds the promise of an easier life for the child in adulthood, something that resonates with some parents (Bauer, 2002). Zucker and Bradley (1995) believe these goals are clinically valid and provide sufficient justification for therapy which will "help children feel more secure about their gender identity as boys or as girls" (p. 270). Indeed, Zucker (1990b) points out that reducing peer ostracism and prevention of transsexualism alone are reason enough for treatment given the distress that adult transsexuals experience.

The above-mentioned rationale for treatment raises many concerns. Why do clinicians seek to align sex and gender instead of helping the child become comfortable with their gender variance and cope with threats? Reparative therapies disrespect the youth's subjective sense of gender (i.e., what if they *are* transsexual?) and often make both parents and therapists the "gender police." Furthermore, there is little controlled research supporting the idea that therapy can help these children accept their "born" sex and gender, weak evidence that treating children for gender variance assists in their comorbid conditions, no evidence that gender-variant children are at increased risk to grow up to be transsexual or transvestite, and no evidence that adult transsexuals or cross-dressers are worse off, psychologically, than others. The fact that children diagnosed with GID might have a more difficult life seems like a poor rationale for treating their gender. Analogously, there can be no doubt that being poor, black, and gay means a more difficult life, but that hardly justifies treatment to convert poor black gays and lesbians to wealthy white heterosexuals. Perhaps strategies for social change are a more suitable approach.

There are even more serious concerns about treatment for those who are below the age of consent (16 years). The current *Standards of Care for Gender Identity Disorders* (the widely accepted international professional guidelines for the treatment of GID), established by the *Harry Benjamin International Gender Dysphoria Association* (Meyer et al., 2001) recommends surgical gender reassignment procedures only when the youth becomes 18 (and has lived in their chosen gender for two years), partially reversible procedures (e.g., taking exogenous hormones) for those 16 and over, and only fully reversible interventions (e.g., pubertal delay) for those under 16. In guidelines for working with children and adolescents, the *Standards of Care* recommend that "irreversible physical interventions should be delayed as long as is clinically appropriate" (p. 7) since few youths diagnosed with GID become adult transsexuals (as noted elsewhere: APA, 2001; Meyenburg, 1999; Meyer et al., 2001). [. . .]

More questions about GID treatment remain unanswered. What is the rationale for the treatment of gender-variant children, if they will eventually grow out of it anyway, and their gender variance is an indication of their cognitive abilities to read and apply society's gender rules? If gender is a developmental accomplishment, is there any sustaining rationale for understanding GID as a psychopathology? If the children are too young to get treatment to change their sex or gender, then why are they old enough to get a diagnosis and receive reparative therapy to "correct" their chosen gender? While the *Standards of Care* are very hesitant to recommend treatment of children, and explicitly do not mention reparative therapy as an accepted practice, clinics continue creating "normally" gendered children.

[. . .]

Conclusion

There is much more evidence in support of GID now than there was in 1980 when the diagnosis was first proposed. However, far more overwhelming is the weight of 25 years of critique largely unaddressed by the current *DSM* criteria. While this paper reviewed material primarily since 1994, it should be apparent that there has been a lively and active debate over this extremely controversial diagnosis since inception, and critics have increased and broadened their challenges to GID. Many call for the complete removal of GID, especially for GID in children and adolescents. This is not to ignore those children and adolescents (and their families) who suffer greatly because they are the very rare case of the transsexual child. These children and adolescents should have access to suitable medical treatment, but the GID diagnosis is unnecessary for medical treatments that are appropriate for those under 16 years of age.

If the diagnosis of GID for children and adolescents remains in the *DSM-V*, we suggest a reconsideration of the language used to describe GID, especially in the 'Diagnostic Features" section, away from such a stereotypical and highly dichotomizing tone towards gender equality and respect for diversity in gender norms, especially among different cultures. Moreover, the diagnostic criteria should indicate that all of the five parts of criterion A need to be present for the diagnosis (thus only transsexual youth – so-called primary transsexuals – and not gender-variant youth, will be diagnosed), and that the cross-gender behaviors are maladaptive or pathological. Similarly, part one of criterion A should include desire for gender reassignment (e.g., hormones or surgery). Thus, a child diagnosed with GID would identify with the cross-gender, exhibit cross-gender behaviors and preferences (which is the source of their distress), and seek gender reassignment. The criteria should also clearly state that the diagnosis "GID–not otherwise specified" should *not* be used for children who meet all but part one of criterion A. Criterion D should be clarified such that children who are distressed due to harassment (but are ego-syntonic with respect to gender) *not* be subjected to reparative therapies.

[. . .]

References

American Psychiatric Association (1980). *Diagnostic and statistical manual of mental disorders* (3rd Ed.), Washington, DC: Author.

American Psychiatric Association (2000). *Diagnostic and statistical manual of mental disorders* (4th edn., Text Revised). Washington, DC: Author.

Bailey, J.M. & Zucker, K.J. (1995). Childhood sex-typed behavior and sexual orientation: A conceptual analysis and quantitative review. *Developmental Psychology, 21,* 43–55.

Bartlett, N.H., Vasey, P.L., & Bukowski, W.M. (2000). Is gender identity disorder in children a mental disorder? *Sex Roles, 43,* 753–785.

Bauer, G. (2002, November). Gender bender. *Saturday Night, 117*(6), 60–62, 64.

Bower, H. (2001). The gender identity disorder in the DSM–IV classification: A critical evaluation. *Australian and New Zealand Journal of Psychiatry, 35,* 1–8.

Bradley, S.J. & Zucker, K.J. (1990). Gender identity disorder and psychosexual problems in children and adolescents. *Canadian Journal of Psychiatry, 35,* 477–486.

Bradley, S.J. & Zucker, K.J. (1997). Gender identity disorder: A review of the past 10 years. *Journal of the American Academy of Child Adolescent Psychiatry, 36,* 872–880.

Bryant, K. (Speaker). (2004, May). *Diagnosing gender variant youth: A history of "Gender Identity Disorder"* (CD Recording No. 04APA/CD-S51A, Disk 2). Mobiltape Company.

Cohen, L., de Ruiter, C., Ringelberg, H., & Cohen-Kettenis, P.T. (1997). Psychological functioning of adolescent transsexuals: Personality and psychopathology. *Journal of Clinical Psychology, 53*, 187–196.

Cohen, R. & Swederlik, M. (1999). *Psychological testing and assessment: An introduction to tests and measurement* (4th edn.). Mountain View, CA: May-field Publishing.

Cohen-Kettenis, P.T. & Van Goozen, S.H.M. (1997). Sex reassignment of adolescent transsexuals: A follow-up study. *Journal of the American Academy of Child and Adolescent Psychiatry, 36*, 263–271.

Cohen-Kettenis, P.T. & Van Goozen, S.H.M. (2002). Adolescents who are eligible for sex reassignment surgery: Parental reports of emotional and behavioral problems. *Clinical Child Psychology and Psychiatry, 7*, 412–422.

Davis, D.L. (1998). The sexual and gender identity disorders. *Transcultural Psychiatry, 35*, 401–412.

Green, R. (1987). *The "Sissy Boy Syndrome" and the development of homosexuality*. New Haven, CT: Yale University Press.

Griffiths, M. (2002). Invisibility: The major obstacle in understanding and diagnosing transsexualism. *Clinical Child Psychology and Psychiatry, 7*, 493–496.

Johnston, C. & Freeman, W. (1997). Attributions for child behavior in parents of children without behavior disorders and children with attention deficit-hyperactivity disorder. *Journal of Consulting and Clinical Psychology, 65*, 636–645.

Joiner, T.E. & Wagner, K.D. (1996). Parental, child-centered attributions and outcome: A meta-analytic review with conceptual and methodological implications. *Journal of Abnormal Child Psychology, 24*, 37–52.

Lips, H. (2005). *Sex & Gender: An introduction* (5th edn.). New York, NY: McGraw-Hill.

Mallon, G.P. (ed.). (1999). *Social services with transgendered youth*. New York, NY: Harrington Park Press.

Marantz, S. & Coates, S. (1991). Mothers of boys with gender identity disorder: A comparison of matched controls. *Journal of the American Academy of Child and Adolescent Psychiatry, 30*, 310–315.

Menvielle, E.J. & Tuerk, C. (2002). A support group for parents of gender-nonconforming boys. *Journal of the American Academy of Child and Adolescent Psychiatry, 41*, 1010–1013.

Meyenburg, B. (1999). Gender identity disorder in adolescence: Outcomes of psychotherapy. *Adolescence, 34*, 305–313.

Meyer-Bahlburg, H.F.L. (2002). Gender identity disorder in young boys: A parent- and peer-based treatment protocol. *Clinical Child Psychology and Psychiatry, 7*, 360–377.

Minter, S. (1999). Diagnosis and treatment of gender identity disorder in children. In M. Rottnek (ed.), *Sissies & tomboys: Gender non-conformity & homosexual childhood* (pp. 9–33). New York, NY: New York University Press.

Morin, S.F. & Schultz, S.J. (1978). The gay movement and the rights of children. *Journal of Social Issues, 34*, 137–148.

Newman, L.E. (1977). Treatment for the parents of feminine boys. *Annual Progress in Child Psychiatry and Child Development, 10*, 230–239.

Newman, L.K. (2002). Sex, gender and culture: Issues in the definition, assessment and treatment of gender identity disorder. *Clinical Child Psychology and Psychiatry, 7*, 352–359.

Nordyke, N.S., Baer, D.M., Etzel, B.C., & LeBlanc, J.M. (1977). Implications of the stereotyping and modification of sex role. *Journal of Applied Behavior Analysis, 10*, 553–557.

Rekers, G.A. & Kilgus, M.D. (1995). Differential diagnosis and rationale for treatment of gender identity disorders and transvestism. In G.A. Rekers (ed.), *Handbook of child and adolescent sexual problems* (pp. 255–271). New York, NY: Lexington Books.

Richardson, J. (1996). Setting limits on gender health. *Harvard Review of Psychiatry, 4*, 49–53.

Richardson, J. (1999). Response: Finding the disorder in gender identity disorder. *Harvard Review of Psychiatry, 7*, 43–50.

Rosenberg, M. (2002). Children with gender identity issues and their parents in individual and group treatment *Journal of the American Academy of Child and Adolescent Psychiatry, 41*, 619–621.

Smith, Y.L.S. (2001). Adolescents with gender identity disorder who were accepted or rejected for sex reassignment surgery: A prospective follow-up study (Statistical Data included). *Journal of the American Academy of Child and Adolescent Psychiatry, 40*, 472–481.

Spitzer, R. & Wakefield, J.C. (1999). DSM-IV diagnostic criterion for clinical significance: Does it help solve the false positives problem? *The American Journal of Psychiatry, 156*, 1856–1864.

Winkler, R.C. (1977). What types of sex-role behavior should behavior modifiers promote? *Journal of Applied Behavior Analysis, 10*, 549–552.

Wolfe, B.E. (1979). Behavioral treatment of childhood gender disorders. *Behavior Modification, 3*, 550–575.

Wren, B. (2002). "I can accept my child is transsexual but if I ever see him in a dress I'll hit him": Dilemmas in parenting a transgendered adolescent. *Clinical Child Psychology and Psychiatry, 7*, 377–397.

Yunger, J.L., Carver, P.R., & Perry, D.G. (2004). Does gender identity influence children's psychological well-being? *Developmental Psychology, 40*, 572–582.

Zucker, KJ. (1982). Childhood gender disturbance: Diagnostic issues. *Journal of the American Academy of Child Psychiatry, 21*, 274–280.

Zucker, K.J. (1990a). Gender identity disorders in children: Clinical descriptions and natural history. In R. Blanchard & B.W. Steiner (Eds.), *Clinical management of gender identity disorders in children and adults* (pp. 1–23). Washington, DC: American Psychiatric Press.

Zucker, KJ. (1990b). Treatment of gender identity disorders in children. In R. Blanchard & B.W. Steiner (eds.), *Clinical management of gender identity disorders in children and adults* (pp. 25–47). Washington, DC: American Psychiatric Press.

Zucker, K.J. (1990c). Psychosocial and erotic development in cross-gender identified children. *Canadian Journal of Psychiatry*, 35, 487–495.

Zucker, KJ. (1992). Gender identity disorder. In S.R. Hooper, G.W. Hynd, & R.E. Mattison (eds.), *Child psychopathology: Diagnostic criteria and clinical assessment* (pp. 305–342). Hillsdale, NJ: Erlbaum.

Zucker, K.J. (1999). Commentary on Richardson's (1996) "Setting limits on gender health." *Harvard Review of Psychiatry*, 7, 37–42.

Zucker, K.J. (2000). Gender identity disorder. In A.J. Sameroff, M. Lewis, & S.M. Miller (eds.), *Handbook of developmental psychopathology* (2nd edn., pp. 671–686). New York, NY: Kluwer Academic/Plenum.

Zucker, K.J. (2002, November). *Gender identity disorder in children: Concepts, controversies, and conundrums.* Paper presented to the annual meeting of the Society for the Scientific Study of Sexuality, Montreal, QC.

Zucker, K.J. & Bradley, S.J. (1995). *Gender identity disorder and psychosexual problems in children and adolescents.* New York, NY: Guilford Press.

Zucker, K.J. & Bradley, S.J. (1999). Gender identity disorder and transvestic fetishism. In S.D. Netherton, D. Holmes, & C.E. Walker (eds.), *Child and adolescent psychological disorders: A comprehensive textbook* (pp. 367–396). New York, NY: Oxford University Press.

Zucker, K.J., Bradley, S.J., & Sullivan, C.L. (1992). Gender identity disorder in children. *Annual Review of Sex Research*, 3, 73–120.

Zucker, K.J., Owen, A., Bradley, S.J., & Ameeriar, L. (2002). Gender-dysphoric children and adolescents: A comparative analysis of demographic characteristics and behavioral problems. *Clinical Child Psychology and Psychiatry*, 7, 398–411.

Sexual and Gender Identity Disorders: Discussion of Questions for DSM-V (on GID)

Robert L. Spitzer

Summary

Argues that Hill et al.'s position on gender identity disorder is flawed because they seem to take the "social decon-structionist" position that no behavior is normal or pathological since all such things are merely social constructs. This position relies on faulty assumptions. The claim that gender is not dichotomous is overstated – gender identity does not follow a normal distribution pattern with a few male-identified males at one end and a few female-identified females at the other with the average person somewhere in between. In fact, the vast majority of people are very clear on being either male or female and there is virtually no overlap with clinical populations who have gender identity issues. This cross-cultural truth is consistent with evolutionary theory since there is obvious survival value in such identification. In addition, Hill et al. use the term "gender choice," which is a naive understanding of how gender identity is formed. Children do not choose their gender. For the rare child – such as a boy who has insisted since age 2 that he is a girl, will grow up to be a mommy, only plays with girls, wants to wear only dresses, and always sits to urinate – the belief that he is simply engaging in non-conforming behavior seriously ignores a more deeply-set condition.

Original publication details: Robert L. Spitzer, "Sexual and Gender Identity Disorders: Discussion of Questions for DSM-V," pp. 111–116 from *Journal of Psychology & Human Sexuality* 17:3–4 (2006). Reproduced with permission of Taylor & Francis Group.

[. . .]

The central issue for this symposium is Drs. Hill and Moser's remarkable proposal: that GID and all of the paraphilias should be eliminated from *DSM-V*. So the issue is not how the diagnoses of GID and the paraphilias can be better conceptualized or how the diagnostic criteria can be improved. The real issue is, are there any cases of kids or adults for which these diagnoses are appropriate.

Dr. Moser seems to believe that there is no such thing as pathological sexual behavior. This is rather remarkable. It is hard to think of any other kind of behavior or function that cannot go wrong, but for Dr. Moser, paraphilias are only statistically rare. Dr. Hill tells us that he does not want to eliminate GID from the *DSM*. He is willing to keep it in the *DSM* if the diagnosis was limited to children that ask for hormone or surgical change. Since kids with GID never make such a request – in essence he also wants to get rid of the category from the *DSM*.

The central issue then is how does one decide that something is just unusual (normal variation) or something is disordered (pathological)?

Consider this. Almost everybody who has eyes can see. Yet there are some people who have eyes that cannot see. Everybody intuitively knows that in such a case there is something wrong with the eyes. Being blind is not a normal variation because we have an intuitive sense that the eyes are designed to enable the individual to see. Some people would say the eye, like all parts of the body, are designed by God to function in a particular way. Other people, like me, would say, the body has been designed by natural selection, evolution. However you understand the concept of "design," it is clear that the eye has a certain function. When somebody has an eye that cannot see, there is some mechanism – which we may or not understand – that is not working. You can think of all kinds of other examples. Whenever you think of a medical disorder you are thinking of some biological function that is expected – that is part of being human – that is not working.

Does this concept of what is a medical disorder apply to human behavior? The answer is "yes." There are certain human qualities or behaviors that are part of being human, that are part of normal development. Here is an example. Humans tend to be social. They are not taught to be social. Kids are naturally interested in other kids. It is not because parents tell them that you will be better off if you are interested in other kids. Something is wrong with a child who has no interest in socializing with other kids. Another example: the ability to empathize, to sense what someone else is feeling. There is something wrong with a child who does not have that capacity.

What I have been presenting is sometimes referred to as essentialism – the view that some "things" (like being human) have properties or qualities that are invariable and represent the true essence of the "thing." As applied to human behavior, this means that there are human qualities or behaviors that are seen in all cultures, although the particular way in which it presents itself may vary in different cultures. In contrast to essentialism is another viewpoint: social deconstructionism – that seems to be the perspective of Drs. Hill and Moser. For them, no behavior is normal or pathological since such judgments are merely social constructs. One culture says masturbation is pathological, another says it is normal. Homosexuality prior to 1973 was a mental disorder – now it is normal variation.

[. . .]

Let us now consider gender identity disorder. Dr. Hill says that, contrary to *DSM-IV*, gender is not dichotomous – we are all somewhere in between. Are we all somewhere in between? That is news to me. Biologically, we are all male or and female – with very few exceptions. Biologically, there are a very small number of intersex – so we are not all in between biologically. Are we all in between in terms of gender identity? Is it a fact that there is a small number of males who are really sure they are male and then there is large number in the middle that are not quite sure what they are and then at the extreme there are men who think they are female? The fact is that almost all males know they are male and it is self-obvious to them. There is a very small number of males who feel uncomfortable being males. Ken Zucker[1] has noted that if you look at the behaviors that are in the *DSM* "A" criteria for gender identity disorder and you do a distribution of kids referred to his clinic because of gender identity problems and compare this with the distribution among a control group matched for age and sex, there is almost no overlap.

Very few young boys want to play with young girls. They want to play with boys. In all cultures, young boys want to play with boys. Young girls want to play with girls. This is not because they are taught or encouraged to do it. Again, interest in young children seems to be part of the human condition. If you are interested in evolutionary psychology, you ask yourself could that have some survival value? The answer is yes. Thousands of years ago when men were more likely to be in hunting and women were more likely to be in the nurturing role, if you were a young boy you would do better if you spent your time with other boys with whom, when you were older, you would go to the hunt.

Dr. Hill is correct when he notes that gender roles for males and females vary from culture to culture. But in all cultures, gender is recognized as a dichotomy and there are gender specific ways of identifying gender. In our culture, for example, very few men wear lipstick. There are some women who do not wear lipstick but almost all the lipstick wearers are women. And, of course, there are cultures where no one wears lipstick.

Children normally develop a sense of gender identity. It is not taught – it just happens. I would argue that by itself, the failure to develop a gender identity that is congruent with biological gender is a dysfunction. How severe it has to be to make a diagnosis and how and if you should treat it are separate issues.

For example, Dr. Kenneth Zucker has provided me with a case that he recently evaluated at his clinic. A two year and ten month old boy was referred for assessment. When asked his name, he says he is "Snow White." Since the age of 24 months, he has either insisted that he is a girl or that he wants to be a girl. He is adamant that he will grow up to be a mommy. When told by his parents

that he will grow up to be a daddy, he bursts into tears and is inconsolable. He wants to grow up to be a mommy. He likes to wear dresses in nursery school and have his hair put into a ponytail. He only plays with girls in his school and has no male playmates on his street. He sits to urinate. For the 10 months preceding the referral, and after the onset of the cross-gender behaviors, his parents had assumed the behavior was a phase out of which he would grow. His increasing distress about being told he was a boy led them to consult their family doctor who recommended a referral to Zucker's GID clinic.

I ask you: is this just non-conforming behavior? It seems rather obvious that there is something wrong in this child's gender identity.

Dr. Hill sometimes used the phrase "gender choice." This is rather naive. For these children, it is not a question of choice at all.

In conclusion, it interesting that Dr. Moser and Hill have not presented a single case of someone – child or adult – who was harmed by being given a diagnosis of a paraphilias or gender identity disorder. Their arguments for eliminating these categories in the *DSM* are weak at best.

Note

1 See Zucker, K. J. & Bradley, S. (1995). *Gender Identity Disorder and Psychosexual Problems in Children and Adolescents.* New York: Guilford Press.

Gender Dysphoria

American Psychiatric Association

Summary

Explains that the category of gender dysphoria in the new DSM-V (2013) will replace the previous classification of gender identity disorder (GID) and will distinguish between gender nonconformity (which is not necessarily a mental disorder) and the condition in which people see themselves as a different gender than their "assigned gender." The reason for these changes is in part to ensure that people have a diagnostic term they can use to gain access to psychiatric and medical care, will legally protect them from discrimination, and help to eliminate the idea that the patient is "disordered".

Original publication details: "American Psychiatric Association, "Gender Dysphoria," from Diagnostic and Statistical Manual of Mental Disorders (DSM–5). © 2013 American Psychiatric Association http://www.psychiatry.org/dsm5. Reproduced with permission of American Psychiatric Association"

Sexual Ethics: An Anthology, First Edition. Edited by Patrick D. Hopkins.
© 2023 John Wiley & Sons, Inc. Published 2023 by John Wiley & Sons, Inc.

Introduction

In the upcoming fifth edition of the *Diagnostic and Statistical Manual of Mental Disorders* (DSM-5), people whose gender at birth is contrary to the one they identify with will be diagnosed with gender dysphoria. This diagnosis is a revision of DSM-IV's criteria for gender identity disorder and is intended to better characterize the experiences of affected children, adolescents, and adults.

Respecting the Patient, Ensuring Access to Care

DSM not only determines how mental disorders are defined and diagnosed, it also impacts how people see themselves and how we see each other. While diagnostic terms facilitate clinical care and access to insurance coverage that supports mental health, these terms can also have a stigmatizing effect.

DSM-5 aims to avoid stigma and ensure clinical care for individuals who see and feel themselves to be a different gender than their assigned gender. It replaces the diagnostic name "gender identity disorder" with "gender dysphoria," as well as makes other important clarifications in the criteria. It is important to note that gender nonconformity is not in itself a mental disorder. The critical element of gender dysphoria is the presence of clinically significant distress associated with the condition.

Characteristics of the Condition

For a person to be diagnosed with gender dysphoria, there must be a marked difference between the individual's expressed/experienced gender and the gender others would assign him or her, and it must continue for at least six months. In children, the desire to be of the other gender must be present and verbalized. This condition causes clinically significant distress or impairment in social, occupational, or other important areas of functioning.

Gender dysphoria is manifested in a variety of ways, including strong desires to be treated as the other gender or to be rid of one's sex characteristics, or a strong conviction that one has feelings and reactions typical of the other gender.

The DSM-5 diagnosis adds a post-transition specifier for people who are living full-time as the desired gender (with or without legal sanction of the gender change). This ensures treatment access for individuals who continue to undergo hormone therapy, related surgery, or psychotherapy or counseling to support their gender transition.

Gender dysphoria will have its own chapter in DSM-5 and will be separated from Sexual Dysfunctions and Paraphilic Disorders.

Need for Change

Persons experiencing gender dysphoria need a diagnostic term that protects their access to care and won't be used against them in social, occupational, or legal areas.

When it comes to access to care, many of the treatment options for this condition include counseling, cross-sex hormones, gender reassignment surgery, and social and legal transition to the desired gender. To get insurance coverage for the medical treatments, individuals need a diagnosis. The Sexual and Gender Identity Disorders Work Group was concerned that removing the condition as a psychiatric diagnosis – as some had suggested – would jeopardize access to care.

Part of removing stigma is about choosing the right words. Replacing "disorder" with "dysphoria" in the diagnostic label is not only more appropriate and consistent with familiar clinical sexology terminology, it also removes the connotation that the patient is "disordered."

Ultimately, the changes regarding gender dysphoria in DSM-5 respect the individuals identified by offering a diagnostic name that is more appropriate to the symptoms and behaviors they experience without jeopardizing their access to effective treatment options.

[. . .]

The Psychopathology of "Sex Reassignment" Surgery: Assessing Its Medical, Psychological, and Ethical Appropriateness

Richard P. Fitzgibbons, Philip M. Sutton
and Dale O'Leary

Summary

Argues that sex reassignment surgery violates basic medical ethics principles of doing no harm by destroying and surgically altering functioning organs of healthy, non-diseased bodies, subjecting healthy patients to unnecessary risks, and uniquely treating a psychological disorder with surgery. Patients seeking sex reassignment have a disordered perception of self that properly requires psychological treatment, including learning to accept their masculinity or femininity as a good and addressing childhood trauma that led to the disorder. Sex reassignment surgery does not, in any case, change one's actual sex and therefore it simply collaborates in a mental illness rather than treats it.

Original publication details: Richard P. Fitzgibbons, Philip M. Sutton, and Dale O'Leary, "The Psychopathology of 'Sex Reassignment' Surgery," pp. 97–125 from *The National Catholic Bioethics Quarterly* 9 (2009). Reproduced with permission of The National Catholic Bioethics Center.

Sexual Ethics: An Anthology, First Edition. Edited by Patrick D. Hopkins.
© 2023 John Wiley & Sons, Inc. Published 2023 by John Wiley & Sons, Inc.

Introduction

The desire to imitate the other sex or to pass for the other sex is not new, nor is the amputation of healthy body parts. In many cultures, men were castrated for various reasons, in some cases to preserve the prepuberty boy-soprano voice, in others so that they could serve as guards of harems. Such practices are now considered barbaric. Individual women have at various times in history passed as men. Only when surgical skills advanced to the degree that surgeons could construct an artificial vagina and something resembling a penis or scrotum did sex reassignment surgery (SRS) develop as a surgical subspecialty. The materialist ethic of "If we can do something, we may do it" has created a climate where people see nothing wrong with surgeons destroying healthy reproductive organs and creating artificial organs for those who want them. Those who believe in the radically dualistic ethic of "It's my body, so I can manipulate it however I like," are offended if surgeons refuse to grant their demands.

Use of the term "sexual reassignment surgery" is in itself problematic, it implies that the sexual identity is assigned at birth and can actually be surgically reassigned. Sexual identity is observed at birth and, except in rare cases, matches the genetic structure. It is written on every cell of the body and can be determined through DNA testing. It cannot be changed. Calling men who have had SRS "women" does not change their genetic structure. It does not make them genetic women.

The use of "transsexual" is also problematic, since it also implies that a person can move from their true genetic sex to the other sex. At one time, the word "sex" was used to describe everything that was included in being male or female. The word "gender" was used in reference to language; words were masculine, feminine, or neuter in gender. Controversial psychologist, sexologist, and promoter of SRS John Money introduced the idea of "gender identity," defined as a person's own categorization of himself as male, female, or ambivalent. Radical feminists embraced the idea that sex – the biological reality – could be separated from gender, which they viewed as an artificial social construct imposed on male and female bodies. For them, sex may be a biological given, but gender is in the mind and because it is constructed by social interaction, it can be deconstructed.

Those calling themselves transsexuals took the separation of sex and gender in a different direction; for them, gender was natural and sex could be constructed – the body modified to fit the mind. Thus, a person could be male in sex (i.e., biologically, genetically) yet female in gender. This did not mean that a particular man simply had interests, talents, or other traits more likely to be found in women, but that at the core of his being he was essentially female and had been mis-assigned at birth. Therefore, his desire to be reassigned surgically and hormonally was reasonable and should be accommodated.

Persons seeking SRS experience a disharmony between their bodies and their self-image. The question is, should this disharmony be reconciled by changing the body or changing the mind? Those applying for SRS strongly resist psychological probing into the origins of their feelings, demanding instead a surgical solution to their problem.

Those publicly promoting SRS insist that once SRS procedures are completed, the patient is no longer the sex to which he or she was born, but has been surgically transformed into the other sex. However, SRS procedures create only an imitation of the organs involved in the sexual act which, in the case of women who wish to present themselves as men, are very poor, nonfunctional imitations. Surgery cannot change the DNA or reverse the effect of prenatal hormones on the brain. It can only create the appearance of the other sex. Persons who have undergone these procedures may engage in acts which simulate sexual intercourse between a male and female, but these acts are nonreproductive, since the surgical procedures cannot create fertility. In effect, SRS is the most radical form of sterilization, and according to Catholic moral teaching, it is unethical on that ground alone.

We argue that the desire for SRS generally results from an array of psychological disorders. In defense of this view, we provide information on the background of the SRS movement, a review of the procedures involved, and data on typical psychological problems suffered by these patients. There is a discussion of the three types of people who apply for SRS. We then address the ethical, religious, and other objections to SRS and the effect of general acceptance of SRS on freedom of religion, speech, and thought. We conclude that SRS does not serve the best interests of the patients and is a misuse of the skills of surgeons and psychiatrists.

Background

Johns Hopkins University in Baltimore, Maryland, was once a center for SRS. When Dr. Paul McHugh became psychiatrist-in-chief in 1975, however, he decided to investigate what he "considered to be a misdirection of psychiatry and to demand more information both before and after [the] operations." He asked for a follow-up on patients from psychiatrist and psychoanalyst Jon Meyer. Meyer found that "sex reassignment surgery confers no objective advantage in terms of social rehabilitation."[1] According to McHugh,

> most of the patients [Meyer] tracked down some years after their surgery were contented with what they had done and . . . only a few regretted it. But in every other respect, they were little changed in their psychological condition. They had much the same problems with relationships, work, and emotions as before. The hope that they would emerge now from their emotional difficulties to flourish psychologically had not been fulfilled. We saw the results as demonstrating that just as these men enjoyed cross-dressing as women before the operation, so they enjoyed cross-living after it. But they were no better in their psychological integration or any easier to live with.[2]

McHugh and others became convinced that SRS involved collaborating in mental disorder rather than treating it, and the SRS program at Johns Hopkins was discontinued.

[. . .]

Reassignment Process for Males

Sexual reassignment surgery is only one step in a long and expensive process. For *men* it involves dressing in public as a woman and undergoing electrolysis to remove facial hair, hormone treatment, electrolysis to remove hair on the genitals and prepare the genital tissue to be used to create a pseudo-vagina, removal of the penis and testes, creation of the pseudo-vagina, creation of an opening for the urethra, and cosmetic surgery – to decrease the size of the Adam's apple, insert breast implants, change other features, and insert silicone implants in the hips and buttocks.

Those who begin the process are often dissatisfied with the initial cosmetic results. Some of those seeking SRS not only want to be women, they want to be stunningly attractive women, and thus may become addicted to plastic surgery. Some also seek out back-alley practitioners for silicone injections and other changes, risking infection and even death.[3]

Some men present themselves in public as women but have not yet chosen to have surgery below the waist. These are sometimes referred to as "she-males," since with breast implants and cosmetic surgery above the waist they appear female, but below the waist they are physically male. Some she-males work as showgirls in clubs that specialize in this kind of entertainment or as prostitutes in order to save up the money needed for genital surgery. Certain men seek out the sexual services of she-males.[4]

Reassignment Process for Females

For *women* the reassignment process involves hormone treatments, removal of the breasts (often begun by binding them), total hysterectomy, and the creation of a pseudo-penis and testes. It is noteworthy that increasing testosterone levels in a woman – to stimulate facial hair growth and increase muscle – has the potential to cause a change in personality, including making the woman more aggressive. A hysterectomy is then performed to stop menstruation which, for many, removes the unwanted monthly evidence of womanhood and vulnerability. Relatively few women who undergo SRS, even those with severe gender dysphoria, choose to take the last step: the creation of a pseudo-penis and pseudo-testes. When this is done, the artificial organs are often small and are nonfunctional. A penis may be constructed to enable a mechanical erection and the simulation of sexual intercourse, but ejaculation is not possible. While the surgeons attempt to preserve sexual sensation in the pseudo-organs, they are not always successful.

[. . .]

Origins of the Desire for SRS

Ray Blanchard, of Clarke Institute of Psychiatry in Toronto (now part of the Centre for Addiction and Mental Health), has spent years studying and treating transsexuals. He identified two distinct syndromes: homosexual transsexuals (HT) and autogynephilic transsexuals (AT).[5] J. Michael Bailey's book *The Man Who Would Be Queen* explores the difference between the two.[6]

Homosexual Transsexual Males

According to the Blanchard analysis, HT males are men whose appearance, gestures, and speech are perceived as feminine and who are attracted to masculine men rather than other homosexual men. HT males believe that if they can appear to be real women and can "pass" as such, they will be able to attract these men.

Almost all HT males experienced gender identity disorder (GID) as children. They did not fully identify with their fathers, brothers, or peers and either believed that they were really female or wished to be female. They often expressed disgust at their male genitals, may have tried to hide them, refused to urinate standing, insisted on dressing in girls' clothes, and often chose only girls for playmates. These behaviors often resulted in rejection and teasing by male peers. Although some adult men with same-sex attraction (SSA) exhibit some of these symptoms before age five, in later childhood the symptoms commonly disappear. HT males, however, persist in their identification with females, often presenting an exaggerated image of womanhood in their gestures, speech, and dress.

Many HT males at some point become sexually intimate with males with SSA, but they do not find these relationships satisfying. This is in contrast with a boy who moves from GID to SSA and engages in relations with other men with SSA. The HT male wants a relationship with a heterosexual man and believes that by presenting himself as a very attractive woman he can fulfill this desire. It should be noted that in the gay community, masculinity is favored and very feminine males are not considered as desirable.

McHugh characterizes HT males as "conflicted and guilt-ridden homosexual men who [see] a sex-change as a way to resolve their conflicts over homosexuality by allowing them to behave sexually as females with men."[7] While HT males may insist that their only motivation is to become the women they always knew they were, Anne Lawrence, an autogynephile who has undergone SRS, believes that sexual desire plays a bigger part than many HTs are willing to admit:

> Homosexual transsexuals are not exactly devoid of sexual motivations themselves. Colleagues who have spent a lot of time interviewing homosexual transsexuals tell me that they can best be thought of as very effeminate gay men who do not defeminize in adolescence. Nearly all go through a "gay boy" period; and their decisions about whether or not to transition are often based in large part on whether they expect to be sufficiently passable in female role to attract (straight) male partners. Those who conclude they will not pass usually do not transition, no matter how feminine their behavior may be. Instead, they accept, perhaps grudgingly, a gay male identity, and remain within the gay male culture, where

they can realistically expect to find interested partners. This self-selection process explains the intriguing observation that transitioning homosexual transsexuals tend to be physically smaller and lighter than their autogynephilic sisters. The bottom line is that in homosexual transsexuality, too, a sexual calculus is often at work. Trans-sexualism is largely about sex – no matter what kind of transsexual one is.[8]

Gender Identity Disorder

There is general agreement that HT normally first manifests itself as childhood GID. Because the symptoms of GID (and therefore HT preceded by GID) appear very early in childhood, some assume that the condition is biological in its origin – either genetic or hormonal, and therefore unchangeable. But there is no scientific evidence to support this conclusion.[9]

A baby is conceived genetically male or female. Prenatal brain development is influenced by the same hormones that trigger the development of the reproductive organs. Babies discover there are two sexes, and to which sex they belong. This should lead to a positive self-awareness; "I am a boy. It is good to be a boy. I am like my daddy and brothers. My parents are happy that I am a boy." In the same way, a girl needs to feel that she is safe, accepted, and loved as a girl and that being a girl is a good thing.

Kenneth Zucker and Susan Bradley's book *Gender Identity Disorder and Psychosexual Problems in Children and Adolescents* represents years of work with patients with GID.[10] According to their clinical model for boys with GID, the disorder begins in early childhood with an insecure mother–child relationship and tends to affect boys who are emotionally vulnerable:

> The boy, who is highly sensitive to maternal signals, perceives the mother's feelings of depression and anger. Because of his own insecurity, he is all the more threatened by his mother's anger or hostility, which he perceives as directed at him. His worry about the loss of his mother intensifies his conflict over his own anger, resulting in high levels of arousal or anxiety.[11]

When anxiety occurs at such a sensitive developmental period, the child may choose behaviors common to the other sex, because in his mind these will make him more secure or more valued.

[. . .]

Zucker and Bradley explain a mother's positive reaction to cross-sex behavior in her baby: "The mother's need for nurturance and fear of aggression allow her to tolerate these behaviors, which may also be reinforced by her perception of her son as attractive; her tolerance may actually lead to a positive response to the initial cross-gender behaviors.[12] The mother may be unwilling to make the child "unhappy" by discouraging cross-dressing, while the father may be convinced that his son is going to become homosexual. It is only later, when identifying with the other sex leads to teasing and rejection, that the mother becomes concerned. Zucker and Bradley have found that many parents of these boys when confronted with obvious symptoms of GID "profess a rather marked ambivalence," ignoring the problem until it is impossible to do so.[13] Presumably, those with even more ambivalence never seek help.

Because of their own problems, parents are sometimes unable to meet their child's needs for security, acceptance, love, and a positive image of his or her own sex. In contemporary culture, fathers often bond with their sons through sporting activities and may not know how to help boys to incorporate their special creative, artistic, or other non-athletic talents into their masculinity. Fathers with creative or artistic sons need to learn how to support and affirm these interests as authentically masculine. Parents may also fail to appreciate the importance of helping these boys in early childhood to develop strong male friendships with boys who share their interests.

[. . .]

Richard Fitzgibbons has found that children – particularly boys – with GID often experience rejection, teasing, and mistreatment.[14] Boys who lack eye-hand coordination are often isolated or mercilessly teased because they cannot hit a pitch or properly kick a soccer ball. This rejection can cause an insecurely attached boy to believe that other people hate him. This in turn can lead to self-rejection that is focused on sex identity (e.g., "I hate being a boy" or "I hate being a girl!") or on particular body parts (e.g., boys may try to hide their genitals).

The experiences of girls with GID commonly differ from those of boys. Many girls with GID are noticeably *more* – not less – talented athletically and more temperamentally suited for competitive ("rough and tumble") sports than their female peers. This does not commonly lead to as much overt, peer rejection as boys who are *less* athletic and boys who are *less* competitive tend to experience. Yet to the extent that girls with GID, for other reasons, experience an inordinate vulnerability or dysphoria about being "female," they also may fear the biological hallmarks of their sex, such as the development of their breasts or the onset of menstruation. (See "Females Seeking SRS" below for further discussion of the causes and effects of a girl's rejection by female peers.)

Overall, Fitzgibbons believes that this rejection of one's natural body, accompanied by self-hatred and masochistic tendencies, can lead to the desire for SRS. According to Fitzgibbons, if psychotherapists would focus on helping children – and adult patients – learn how to resolve their anger with themselves and with those by whom they feel rejected, these children and adults can become happy with their birth sex.[15]

[. . .]

The failure to identify with the goodness of their own masculinity or femininity can lead to envying those who have the qualities which they perceive themselves to be lacking. One of the differences between persons whose GID is a path to SSA and those who are on a path to transsexuality is that persons moving toward SSA may envy and even covet the characteristics of their *own* sex which they see present in others but lacking in themselves, while those on the path to transsexuality envy or covet the characteristics of the *other* sex. Those developing transsexuality commonly believe that being – and becoming – the other sex would achieve their goal of feeling safe, accepted, and loved.

[. . .]

Autogynephilic Transsexuals

According to Ray Blanchard, who named the syndrome, AT males are men in love with the image of themselves as women. Blanchard writes:

1. All gender-dysphoric biological males who are not homosexual (erotically aroused by other males) are instead autogynephilic (erotically aroused by the thought or image of themselves as females)
2. Autogynephilia does not occur in women, that is, biological females are not sexually aroused by the simple thought of possessing breasts or vulvas.
3. The desire of some autogynephilic males for sex reassignment surgery represents a form of bonding to the love-object (fantasized female self) and is analogous to the desire of heterosexual men to marry wives and the desire of homosexual men to establish permanent relationships with male partners.

4. Autogynephilia is a misdirected type of heterosexual impulse, which arises in association with normal heterosexuality but also competes with it.
5. Autogynephilia is simply one example of a larger class of sexual variations that result from developmental errors of erotic target localization.[16]

Autogynephilia is classified with the paraphilia transvestism. Paraphilias are psychological disorders in which sexual excitement becomes obsessively associated with something other than the presence of a real, total person.

Some ATs object to the classification of their problem as a paraphilia because they are not (at least initially) restricted to enacting a single fantasy in order to achieve orgasm. Rather, the heterosexual ATs find that their fantasies compete with their sexual relationship with their partners. According to Anne Lawrence, a post-SRS AT:

What makes the issue complicated is that autogynephilia does not necessarily preclude attraction to other people. That is why one can say that some transsexuals are autogynephilic, and simultaneously categorize them as heterosexual, bisexual, or anallophilic [not attracted to other people]. (If autogynephilia completely precluded attraction to other people, all autogynephilic persons would be anallophilic.) But autogynephilic arousal often does seem to compete with arousal toward other people. For example, autogynephilic persons who are heterosexual or bisexual often report that when they first become involved with a new sexual partner, their autogynephilic fantasies tend to recede, and they become more focused on the partner. But as the relationship continues, and the novelty of the partner wears off, they more frequently return to autogynephilic fantasies for arousal. (Perhaps for biologic males, novelty is an important factor in determining which of several possible sources of arousal receives attention.)[17]

[. . .]

Most heterosexual transvestites remain content to engage in cross-dressing while others desire SRS. According to Bailey, Blanchard hypothesizes that a man who can "satisfy his urges by periodically cross-dressing in private or in the company of other transvestites" probably will not seek surgery, while a man "whose primary fantasy is having a vulva" eventually will.[18] Blanchard writes,

Autogynephilia takes a variety of forms. Some men are most aroused sexually by the idea of wearing women's clothes, and they are primarily interested in wearing women's clothes. Some men are most aroused sexually by the idea of having a woman's body, and they are most interested in acquiring a woman's body. Viewed in this light, the desire for sex reassignment surgery of the latter group appears as logical as the desire of heterosexual men to marry wives, the desire of homosexual men to establish permanent relationships with male partners, and perhaps the desire of other paraphilic men to bond with their paraphilic objects in ways no one has thought to observe.[19]

AT males commonly have decided to pursue surgery because they, according to McHugh,

found intense sexual arousal in cross-dressing as females. As they had grown older, they had become eager to add more verisimilitude to their costumes and either sought or had suggested to them a surgical transformation that would include breast implants, penile amputation, and pelvic reconstruction to resemble a woman. Further study of similar subjects in the psychiatric services of the Clark Institute in Toronto identified these men by the auto-arousal they experienced in imitating sexually seductive females. Many of them imagined that their displays might be sexually arousing to onlookers, especially to females.[20]

AT males are generally less convincing as women and less overtly "sexy" than HT males.[21]

AT in males generally begins with transvestic fetishes and masturbatory fantasies in adolescence. AT males, in general, did not suffer from GID as children; rather, during late childhood or early adolescence they began to secretly dress in women's clothing, particularly lingerie, and masturbate while looking at themselves in a mirror. Those seeking SRS are careful to deny their use of masturbation with fantasy. According to post-SRS AT Sandy Stone, "wringing the turkey's neck," the ritual of penile masturbation just before its surgical removal, "was the most secret of secret traditions" practiced by ATs.[22] To admit the habit of masturbation would be to risk being disqualified as a candidate for SRS.

Lawrence acknowledges the erotic aspects of autogynephilia but believes that focusing on the erotic misses other essential elements: "Autogynephilia can more accurately be conceptualized as a type of sexual orientation and as a variety of romantic love, involving both erotic and affectional or attachment-based elements."[23] For Lawrence, the AT desires to become what he loves. Lawrence views this desire as comparable to the heterosexual desire to become one with the beloved. [. . .]

[. . .]

Females Seeking SRS

Although the desire for SRS was once relatively rare among women, the number of those seeking partial or complete SRS has increased, almost all originally identifying themselves as lesbian.[24] Women with SSA can be divided into two groups: those with a strong masculine identification ("butch") and those without ("femmes"). The majority of those with a strong masculine identification experienced GID as children. As children, they tailed to identify with the goodness and beauty of their femininity and bodies. Like boys with GID, these girls often failed to establish close same-sex friendships. Many have a history of early insecure attachment to their mothers, whom they viewed as weak and vulnerable. They may have come to believe that if they were boys they could please their fathers or at least protect themselves and their mothers from male aggression. GID in girls differs from a more common "tomboyishness" in that GID girls vehemently resist wearing girls' clothing or engaging in typical girl play. Tomboyish girls on the other hand might be atypical in their interests, but are more flexible.

According to Zucker and Bradley, the girl who develops GID is a "temperamentally vulnerable child who easily develops high levels of anxiety," with a mother who has difficulty with feelings and who may have been depressed during the first year of the girl's life. There is often family conflict in which the father expresses a lack of respect for the mother or for women in general. The girl "perceives the marital conflict as a situation in which the mother is unable to defend herself." When the girl "tries out cross-gender behaviors in an initial effort to decrease anxiety," her mother reacts positively because the mother believes imitating males will protect her daughter. The father may also encourage cross-gender behavior. "This permits the child the fantasy of being the mother's protector through identification with the aggressor."[25] In some cases women with GID recalled that their fathers constantly demeaned women in general, but in particular their mothers.

Psychological Disorders Associated with the Desire for SRS

Persons who desire SRS typically experience serious emotional conflicts, often complicated by sexual self-rejection and depression. Because many therapists are not skilled in uncovering and addressing these serious conflicts, SRS is put forward as the best available solution – if not the only solution. The very availability of SRS motivates persons who see surgery as *the* answer to their problems to resist therapy. Those who desire SRS know that if they present themselves in a manner that meets the criteria set forth by SRS-affirmative therapists (i.e., if they claim they have always felt like women in men's bodies or vice versa and if they hide their SSA, their homosexual behavior, their compulsive masturbation, and their paraphilias), then they may be allowed to proceed with SRS. This does not encourage an honest therapeutic alliance. The availability of SRS effectively prevents the patient from revealing anything that might lead to nonsurgical (i.e., psychiatric and other psycho-therapeutic) resolution of underlying problems. Some therapists too readily accept a patient's "I feel trapped in the wrong body" explanation and do not probe – let alone help the patient to resolve – the patient's underlying narcissism, anger, and inability to embrace the reality of their sexual identity.

[. . .]

Do persons seeking SRS really believe that they have been mis-assigned, or have they learned that saying they are a woman in a man's body (or vice versa) is the only way they can qualify for SRS? Are therapists who evaluate such persons too willing to take these claims at face value? Sander Breiner, in an article titled "Transsexuality Explained," points out such a misperception is in itself a psychological problem:

When an adult who is normal in appearance and functioning believes there is something ugly or defective in their appearance that needs to be changed, it is clear that there is a psychological problem of some significance. The more pervasive and extensive is this misperception of himself, the more significant is the psychological problem. The more the patient is willing to do extensive surgical intervention (especially when it is destructive), the more serious is the psychological problem. It may not be psychosis. It may not require psychiatric hospitalization. But the significance of the psychological difficulty should not be minimized by a patient's seeming success socially and professionally in other areas.[26]

While those who make these claims may wish to believe that they are really trapped in the body of the wrong sex, it may be that what they actual [sic] believe is that if they were the other sex they would be happy, safer, more accepted, and more loved – which is not quite the same thing. The belief that one's problems would be solved if one undergoes SRS can be thought of as an *idée fixe* – an obsession that dominates thinking and resists evidence. For various reasons, rooted in their psychological history, these individuals believe that SRS will make them happy, and they are willing to do whatever is necessary to qualify for the treatment.

[. . .]

Childhood Sexual Abuse

Several studies have found that at least 40 percent of adults, both male and female, with SSA have a history that includes childhood sexual abuse (defined as sexual activity before age fourteen with a person five or more years older).[27] It should be noted that the "abuse" may be regarded as "consensual," with a troubled child accepting whatever kind of affection or attention is offered. Although some people think that SSA is caused by sexual abuse, all persons who are sexually abused do not develop SSA. While such abuse can be a primary or at least a contributing cause, in most instances the foundation for SSA is laid before the abuse. The early initiation into sexual activity, however, may set a pattern for subsequent behavior.

The percentage of HTs with a history of abuse may be even higher than 40 percent. A small study found that 55 percent of the transsexuals experienced unwanted sexual acts before age eighteen.[28] An article by Holly Devor explored the relationship between adult transsexualism and childhood sexual abuse. In one study of forty-five self-defined female-to-male transsexuals, 60 percent of the subjects reported physical, sexual, or emotional abuse:

> While an experience with at least one of the conventional adult psychopathological sequelae symptomatic of child abuse (e.g. fear, anxiety, depression, compulsive eating disorders, substance abuse, hyper-aggression, suicidal behavior) was often cited, the exact source of these behaviors may be a combination

of gender dysphoria and a history of child abuse. It is suggested that transsexualism may manifest in adulthood as an adaptive, extreme dissociative survival response in individuals with a past of severe child abuse.[29]

Childhood traumas can cause lasting damage. The extent of permanent damage depends not so much on the severity of the trauma as on the response of the adults around the child. If parents and other adults respond positively, they can help the child understand that whatever has happened (i.e., divorce, death, abuse) is not his or her fault. With positive adult input, a child's understandable sadness, anger, or feelings of guilt can be minimized. Unfortunately, the parents of children with GID are often unable to provide the support that their children need in order to deal with the trauma, forcing the child to develop his or her own strategy for coping.[30]

Whether motivated by a desire to resolve lingering distress resulting from acute trauma or other factors, an adolescent's (let alone a child's) request to be treated hormonally and altered surgically to appear more like his or her non-biological sex, needs to be viewed from the perspective of "competence to choose." SRS renders impossible a person's ever (again or initially) being able to function fully sexually or reproductively either as a member of his or her conceived (i.e., genetic) sex or as the sex which she or he would like to resemble. Research shows that brain development is affected by behavior and that areas of the brain critical for decision making, problem solving, and emotional management do not develop fully until persons are in their mid to late twenties.[31] Therefore, any child or teenager – let alone one who is suffering from gender dysphoria – is not mature enough or competent to decide on the use of sexual hormones or permanent SRS.

Humane parents do not support their child's persistent cutting – or other self-mutilating or self-injuring behaviors – even when such behaviors serve as emotion-regulating and distress-relieving activities. Likewise, parents, however well intended, ethically should not consent to a minor child's permanent sterilization or self-mutilation to ameliorate the psychological distress of a child's gender dysphoria. To the extent that parents or other guardians give consent for a minor to receive SRS rather than seek appropriate psychological and psychiatric care, these adults objectively are neglecting to protect their child from physical injury. Failure to protect children from seriously harming themselves or from being harmed by others – let alone enabling this to happen – objectively is abusive. Surgeons and other medical and mental health professionals, however motivated, ethically should not condone, provide, or otherwise cooperate in such disservice to youth.

[. . .]

Ethical Objection to SRS

The publicly promoted goal of SRS is to transform a person of one sex into the other sex. It is physiologically impossible to change a person's sex, since the sex of each individual is encoded in the genes – XX if female, XY if male. Surgery can only create the *appearance* of the other sex. George Burou, a Casablancan physician who has operated on over seven hundred American men, explained, "I don't change men into women. I transform male genitals into genitals that have a female aspect. All the rest is in the patient's mind."[32] Therapists may be unwilling to explore the erotic motivation of those seeking SRS: "Most therapists and surgeons would probably find it difficult to acknowledge that when they give approval for sex reassignment surgery, or perform it, they are sometimes simply helping a transsexual woman act out her own paraphilic sexual script"[33] Each person seeking SRS is a unique individual with his or her own history and particular psychological disorders and emotional problems.

The suffering of persons who desire SRS cannot be denied. In many cases, it began in early childhood. Many have been victims of various forms of abuse or neglect and of peer or parental rejection. Basic emotional needs for secure attachment relationships to same-sex peers and to the same-sex parent have often not been met. Gender dysphoria is rarely their only diagnosable psychological disorder. They are, however, united by the belief that SRS will solve their problems. They have created an erotic script in which, as persons of the other sex, they are able to overcome all difficulties. They may enlist the support of surgeons to make their fantasy come true, but such fantasies are not reality based. SRS may satisfy a fantasy wish but it cannot (re)create a person as a fully functioning member of the other sex, able to live honestly as the other sex in real-world situations. Such persons always will be living in their fantasy, trying ever harder to make it more perfect. Fantasies may sooth anxiety temporarily, but they cannot heal the wounds of childhood trauma and satisfy unmet early needs. Once persons receive SRS, they may be – and often are – even

more reticent to admit that they are still struggling with serious emotional conflicts.

Therapists are often unable to overcome patient resistance and uncover the underlying problems – serious emotional weaknesses of low self-esteem, sadness, and anger associated with the failure to develop secure attachment relationships in childhood and adolescence. Rather than admit this, they may surrender to the patient's self-analysis and disorder-driven demands. Authorizing SRS allows the medical team to feel that they are doing something – their patients are grateful. But the team overlooks the fact that SRS mutilates a healthy human body, results in significant pain and suffering, incurs real, unjustifiable risks to patients, and does not address the real psychological problems.

[. . .]

Religious and Other Objections

The Catholic Church has made it clear that, since it is not possible for a person to change their sex, "people who have undergone a sex-change operation cannot enter into a valid marriage, either because they would be marrying someone of the same sex in the eyes of the church or because their mental state casts doubt on their ability to make and uphold their marriage vows."[34] A woman who has undergone SRS cannot become a priest. The Church will not alter baptismal records to reflect the claim of a change of sex. Many other religious institutions also reject the claim of sex change as impossible and contrary to God's plan. In England, the Evangelical Alliance, an organization representing more than a million British Christians, submitted a strongly worded statement to the government opposing changing birth certificates to reflect SRS. It said, "We affirm God's love and concern for all humanity, including transsexual people, but believe that human beings are created by God as either male or female and that change from a given sex is not really possible."[35]

Arthur Goldberg, cofounder and codirector of JONAH (Jews Offering New Alternatives to Homosexuality), carefully documents and explains that the divinely created and revealed nature of humankind, as understood in the Old Testament and over thirty-eight hundred years of authoritative Judaic oral and written tradition, forbids the practice of SRS.[36] In brief, "no published opinion by any Orthodox [Jewish] scholar permits sex change surgery for reasons of gender dysphoria."[37] Also, this prohibition of SRS – as well as the prohibition of other forms of sexual immorality (e.g., fornication, adultery, promiscuity, masturbation, incest, bestiality, and homosexuality) – is understood by authoritative Jewish scholars as applying to all people, not just Jews.[38] In summary, Goldberg writes:

> SRS, for purposes of alleviating transsexual anxiety in a physically normal male or female, is forbidden, and no medical justification has yet been shown to exist. From so much as now is known, the procedure is dangerous, potentially harmful, of doubtful value or benefit, and emphatically contrary to medical ethics. Moreover, alternative and less drastic means of providing relief and a cure are available in gender-affirming processes (GAP) which . . . offer holistic approaches not only to resolving gender dysphoria but to fully reintegrating the shattered personality of the affected individual.[39]

Resistance to SRS is not limited to religious conservatives. Some lesbian and radical feminists, such as Janice Raymond, feel that men who have undergone SRS, who were not born female and so have never experienced growing up as women, have no right to claim to be women or, as they do in some cases, claim to be lesbian women.[40] Raymond is particularly offended that HT males who have undergone SRS promote demeaning stereotypes of women as sexual objects who exist for men's pleasure.[41] She is also offended that some HT males insist that they are better women than real women.[42] As the number of women with SSA seeking surgery has increased, their feminist and lesbian friends see these women as betraying the cause or going over to the enemy.[43] Some feminist and lesbian events are restricted to women born as women and living as women.[44]

Many women regard the transsexual males' description of what it means to be a woman – weak and dependent, wanting only to be cared for by a man, addicted to gossip and clothes – as insulting. McHugh reports on his impression of men who have undergone SRS:

> Those I met after surgery would tell me that the surgery and hormone treatments that had made them "women" had also made them happy and contented. None of these encounters were persuasive, however. The post-surgical subjects struck me as caricatures of women. They wore high heels, copious makeup, and flamboyant clothing; they spoke about how they found themselves able to give vent to their natural inclinations for peace, domesticity,

and gentleness – but their large hands, prominent Adam's apples, and thick facial features were incongruous (and would become more so as they aged). Women psychiatrists whom I sent to talk with them would intuitively see through the disguise and the exaggerated postures. "Gals know gals," one said to me, "and that's a guy."[45]
[...]

Freedom of Speech, Religion, and Thought

Those who believe that it is impossible to change a person's sex do not want to be insensitive to others, but neither should they be forced to lie by calling a man a woman or by calling a woman a man. Transsexual activists hope to force the public to use pronouns and designations of the sex the person wants to be rather than their true sex, even when the person has not undergone SRS. They want those who refuse to accept sex changes to be labeled as "transphobic" – and charged with discrimination. A flyer produced by a student group at the University of Massachusetts Amherst, lists attitudes condemned as transphobic, including

- Assuming that everyone is either male or female
- Continuing to use inappropriate gender pronouns for someone after being corrected or calling someone "it"
- Believing that transgender people cannot be "real women" or "real men"
- Considering transsexuality to be a mental illness or disorder
- Expecting all transgender people to be transsexual and want to transition completely or at all.
- Believing that transgender youths cannot be trusted to make decisions about their gender identities.[46]

Dignity USA has even issued guidelines for media coverage of transgender persons. They condemn "referring to transgendered persons using pronouns and possessive adjectives appropriate to their birth sex" as *"extremely offensive."*[47]

Colleges, including traditional women's colleges, are accommodating the demands of students who want to be treated as the other sex.[48] Activists are also pressuring schools to allow children with GID as early as kindergarten to cross-dress, change their names, and use the bathroom facilities of the other sex. Parents of these children's classmates often strenuously object to programs which force children – some as young as six or seven – to pretend that a fully biologically male child is a girl.[49]

[. . .]

Collaborating with Madness?

There is no question that SRS destroys healthy sexual organs, creates permanent sterility, and carries health risks. It cannot change sex but only creates the illusion of change. According to Anne Lawrence, "It is widely accepted that transsexualism represents a fundamental disorder in a person's sense of self."[50] SRS does not treat this disorder, it surrenders to it. The desire for SRS is a symptom of a number of psychological disorders. Since these serious problems are difficult to treat in

adolescents and adults, first priority should be given to prevention through education and early intervention. For the development of healthy masculinity and femininity, parents need to understand the critical importance of early secure attachment with each parent and siblings, positive support for sexual identity, encouragement for children with atypical talents and interests, and same-sex friendships in early childhood.

[. . .]

Efforts should be directed toward the development of effective therapy for adolescents and adults. The fact that such therapy is not described extensively in the literature and therefore is not widely available, and that these patients resist therapeutic interventions, does not justify giving in to the demand for surgical mutilation.

[. . .]

Notes

1 Jon Meyer and Donna Reter, "Sex Re-Assignment," *General Psychiatry* 36 (1979): 1010–1015.
2 Paul R. McHugh, "Surgical Sex," *First Things* 147 (November 2004): 35.
   [. . .]
3 "Silicone Death Leads to Prison," *Orlando Sentinel*, July 31, 2003.
4 J. Michael Bailey, *The Man Who Would Be Queen: The Science of Gender-Bending and Transsexualism* (Washington, D.C.: John Henry Press, 2003), 186–188.
5 Ray Blanchard, "Clinical Observations and Systemic Studies of Autogynephilia," *Journal of Sex and Marital Therapy*, 17.4 (Winter 1991): 235–251.
6 Bailey, *Man Who Would Be Queen*, 157–160
7 McHugh, "Surgical Sex," 35.
8 Anne Lawrence, "Men Trapped in Men's Bodies: An Introduction to the Concept of Autogynephilia," *Transgender Tapestry* 85 (Winter 1998).
9 J. Michael Bailey, Michael P. Dunne, and Nicholas G. Martin, "Genetic and Environmental Influences on Sexual Orientation and Its Correlates in an Australian Twins Sample," *Journal of Personality and Social Psychology* 78.3 (March 2000): 524–536; John de Cecco and David Parker, eds., *Sex, Cells, and Same-Sex Desire: The Biology of Sexual Preference* (New York: Harrington Park Press, 1995).
10 New York: Guilford Press, 1995. For an overview of Zucker's work on gender identity disorders, see National Association for Research and Therapy of Homosexuality (NARTH) Scientific Advisory Committee, "Gender Identity Disorders in Children and Adolescence: A Critical Inquiry and Review of the Kenneth Zucker Research," March 2007, http://www.narth.com/docs/GIDReviewKenZucker.pdf.
11 Kenneth J. Zucker and Susan J. Bradley, *Gender Identity Disorder and Psychosexual Problems in Children and Adolescents* (New York: Guildford Press, 1995), 262–263.
   [. . .]
12 Zucker and Bradley, *Gender Identity Disorder*, 263.
13 Ibid., 72–73.
   [. . .]
14 Richard P. Fitzgibbons, "Gender Identity Disorder," from the Institute for Marital Healing Web site, http://www.maritalhealing.com/conflicts/genderidentitydisorder.php.
15 Ibid.
   [. . .]
16 Ray Blanchard, "The Origins of the Concept of Autogynephilia," February 2004, http://www.autogynephilia.org/origins.htm.
17 Lawrence, "Men Trapped in Men's Bodies."
   [. . .]
18 Bailey, *Man Who Would Be Queen*, 165.
19 Blanchard, "Clinical Observations," 245–246, quoted in Lawrence, "Men Trapped in Men's Bodies."
20 McHugh, "Surgical Sex," 35.
21 *Sex Change Hospital*, a television series on the Women's Entertainment network, follows men through the procedure. Most of the clients are older men, who even after surgery are obviously not women.
22 Sandy Stone, "The 'Empire' Strikes Back: A Posttranssexual Manifesto," (2004), http://sandystone.com/empire-sdikes-back.
23 Anne Lawrence, "Becoming What We Love," *Perspectives in Biology and Medicine*, 50.4 (2007): 506.
   [. . .]

24 "'Gay' Group Sponsors Breast-Removal Workshop: 'Trans' Conference Seeks to Help Females Who Want to Be Men," WorldNetDaily.com, February 16, 2002, http://www.worldnetdaily.com/news/article.asp?ARTICLE_ID=26487; Paul Vitello, "The Trouble when Jane Becomes Jack," *New York Times*, August 20, 2006; and Yolanda Smith, Stephanie van Goozen, and Peggy Cohen-Kettenis, "Adolescents with Gender Identity Disorder Who Were Accepted or Rejected for Sex Reassignment Surgery: A Prospective Follow-Up Study," *Journal of the American Academy of Child and Adolescent Psychiatry* 40.4 (April 2001): 472–481, (of the twenty clients accepted, thirteen were female wanting to be male).

25 Zucker, *Gender Identity Disorder*, 263–264.
[. . .]

26 Sander Breiner, "Transsexuality Explained," *NARTH Bulletin* (March 27, 2008), http://www.narth.com/docs/transexpl.html.
[. . .]

27 Lynda Doll et al., "Self-Reported Childhood and Adolescent Sexual Abuse among Adult Homosexual and Bisexual Men," *Child Abuse & Neglect* 16.6 (November–December 1992): 8SS–864. Over 40 percent of adult homosexual and bisexual men in this study reported a history of sexual abuse. See also R.L. Johnson and D. K. Shrier, "Sexual Victimization of Boys: Experience at an Adolescent Medicine Clinic," *Journal of Adolescent Health Care* 6.5 (September 1985): 372–376; Judith Siegel et al., "The Prevalence of Childhood Sexual Assault: The Los Angeles Epidemiological Catchment Area Project," *American Journal of Epidemiology* 126.6 (December 1987): 1141; Gregory Dickson and Dean Byrd, "An Empirical Study of the Mother-Son Dyad in Relation to the Development of Male Homosexuality: An Object Relations Perspective," *Journal of the Association of Mormon Counselors and Psychotherapists* 30 (2006). The Dickson and Byrd study found that 49 percent of homosexual men (versus 2 percent of heterosexual men) had a history of sexual abuse.

28 Darlynne Gehring and Gail Knudson, "Prevalence of Childhood Trauma in a Clinical Population of Transsexual People," *International Journal of Transgenderism* 8.1 (2005): 23–30.

29 Holly Devor, "Transsexualism, Dissociation, and Child Abuse: An Initial Discussion Based on Nonclinical Data," *Journal of Psychology and Human Sexuality* 6.3 (1994): 49–72.

30 Jane Middelton-Moz, *Children of Trauma* (Deerfield Beach, FL: Health Communications, 1989).

31 J. N. Giedd et al., "Brain Development during Childhood and Adolescence: A Longitudinal MRI Study," *Nature Neuroscience* 2.10 (October 1999): 861–863.
[. . .]

32 Raymond, *Transsexual Empire*, 10.

33 Lawrence, "Men Trapped in Men's Bodies."
[. . .]

34 John Norton, "Vatican Says Sex Change Operation Does Not Change a Person's Gender," *Catholic News Service*, January 14, 2003.

35 Jonathan Petre and David Bamber, "Transsexual Weddings Are Condemned," May 14, 2000, http://www.telegraph.co.uk/htmlCotnent.html.

36 Arthur Goldberg, *Light in the Closet: Torah, Homosexuality and the Power to Change* (Los Angeles: Red Heifer Press, 2008), chapter 8, "Sexual Reassignment Surgery," 262–299.

37 Ibid., 299.

38 Ibid., chapter 6, "The Sexual Behavioral Prohibitions of the Torah," 175–233.

39 Ibid., 298–299.

40 Raymond, *Transsexual Empire*, 103.

41 Thomas Kando, *Sex Change: The Achievement of Gender Identity among Feminized Transsexuals* (Springfield, IL: Charles C. Thomas, 1973).

42 Ibid., 117.

43 Vitello, "When Jane Becomes Jack."

44 See, for example, "Womyn-Born-Womyn," http://en.wikipedia.org/wiki/Womyn-born-womyn.

45 McHugh, "Surgical Sex," 34.
[. . .]

46 What Does Transphobia Look Like?" Stonewall Center of the University of Massachusetts Amherst, www.umass.edu/stonewall.

47 Transgender Nation, "Transgender Persons: A Primer to Better Understanding," Dignity USA, July 2008, http://www.dignityusa.org/transgender/primer (original emphasis).

48 Fred A. Bernstein, "On Campus Rethinking Biology 101," *New York Times*, March 7, 2004.

49 Philadelphia Catholic Medical Association, press release, May 16, 2008, www.narth.com/docs/CMApressrelease.pdf.

50 Anne A. Lawrence, "Shame and Narcissistic Rage in Autogynephilic Transsexualism," *Archives of Sexual Behavior* 37 (April 23, 2008): 458, referencing Allan Beitel, "The Spectrum of Gender Identity Disturbances: An Intrapsychic Model," in Betty W. Steiner, ed., *Gender Dysphoric Development Research Management (Perspectives in Sexuality)*, (NY: Springer, 1985), 189–206; and U. Hartmann and H. Becker, C. Rueffer-Hesse, "Self and Gender: Narcissistic Pathology and Personality Factors in Gender Dysphoric Patients, Preliminary Results of a Prospective Study," *International Journal of Transgenderism* 1.1 (July-September 1997).
[. . .]

Transsexualism and Gender Reassignment Surgery

Heather Draper and Neil Evans

Summary

Argues that transsexualism is rightly understood as a complex and contested area of medical treatment given that psychiatrists are in the unusual position of seeking to be convinced by the patient's view of reality rather than convincing the patient of the accepted view of reality (what sex are you?). Thus, there is a question of whether transsexualism is a real condition that needs to be treated surgically. Whether the perception of the transsexual is true or false, however, the suffering produced by their condition may justify surgery "on-balance." In addition to the patient's beliefs and suffering, however, other important elements needed to justify surgery (since it creates risks and destroys healthy body parts) include surgical effectiveness, aesthetic success, realistic expectations, and adhering to HBIGDA guidelines. It must also be clear that no surgeon is responsible for creating an attractive or "passable" man or woman but only for doing what is surgically possible.

Original publication details: Heather Draper and Neil Evans, "Transsexualism and Gender Reassignment Surgery," pp. 97–110 from David Benatar (ed.), *Cutting to the Core: Exploring the Ethics of Contested Surgeries*. Rowman and Littlefield, 2006. Reproduced with permission of Rowman and Littlefield.

Introduction

The term *transsexual* is applied to people whose "gender identity is incongruent with their anatomical sex" (Herman-Jeglinska et al. 2002, 527), that is, they believe themselves to be trapped in a body that is of the opposite sex to the one they believe themselves to be.[1] Gender reassignment surgery (GReS)[2] in conjunction with hormone therapy – particularly for male-to-female (MF) transsexuals – has been the treatment of choice (for both individuals and their doctors) for many decades now. Transsexualism has been recognized as a psychiatric classification (DSMIV [1994] 302.85) since 1980. The surgery is obviously very radical: genitalia are removed and replaced with reconstructed genitalia, breasts are removed or implants given, and vocal cords, along with teeth, noses, lips, and so forth may be altered to align them with the appearance of the desired sex. The surgical process is generally – but not always – spread over a series of months, and the hormone therapy will continue for life.

Clearly, such radical – some might say mutilating – surgery would be difficult to justify, even with the consent of the patient, without certainty about the following: that the patient's assertion is real rather than delusional (or put another way, that transsexualism is a genuine condition); that the therapy is effective; that the therapy is the only means of resolving the patient's problems; and, finally that the correct diagnosis has been reached. After all, healthy, functioning organs are removed and replaced by largely dysfunctional ones, and loss of spontaneous reproductive capacity is also inevitable.[3] Yet there remains controversy about whether transsexualism is a genuine condition, and there can therefore be no certainty that this is the best way of resolving the patient's problem. There is no compelling evidence about the effectiveness of the therapy of choice; and mistakes in diagnosis – assuming the possibility of correct diagnosis – are made with disastrous consequences for those who wrongly receive the surgery (Batty 2004). Yet around 5,000 GReSs have already been performed in the United Kingdom and the leading U.K. clinic plans to perform around 150 more of these in 2005 at a cost of at least £3000 each (Batty 2004), though the total cost facing a health authority is likely to be considerably more than this.[4]

Ethical debate about transsexualism was reignited in Australia in 2004 when the Family Court of Australia gave permission for a 13-year-old girl to begin hormone therapy as a prelude to possible reassignment surgery when she reached the age of majority.[5] Some of the debate seems to have been caused by a misunderstanding of the effects of the treatment, namely, that it was thought to have included the surgery itself or to be permanent in nature – which was not the case. Nonetheless, the concern of many commentators centered on whether it was right to give treatment to a minor for a condition of uncertain validity. Although it is arguably permissible not to interfere with an adult's decision to do something that seems grossly harmful from another's point of view, it seems even more contestable to facilitate the same process in a minor. Spriggs (2004) noted, however, that the court decision "was not about giving in to the unstable preferences of an immature person," but was rather about determining how best to accommodate her development needs.

It is interesting to note that our reactions to issues tangentially related to the question of whether transsexualism is an actual medical disorder illustrate how important it is to decide this issue. For instance, objections to transsexuals taking part in competitive sports, or to becoming fellows of the all-woman Newnham College at Cambridge University, or to having their birth certificates or passports reissued, all come back to the issue of whether such women or men are really what they claim to be or are only ever surgically reconstructed versions of their original selves.

In this chapter we will explore some of the reasons GReS is contested surgery and offer some suggestions for how, given these constraints, the surgery should be conducted.

The Case of Sam Hashimi/Samantha Kane/ Charles Kane

The case of Sam Hashimi gained wide publicity in the United Kingdom during 2004, largely as a result of his own dealings with the media. Hashimi came to the United Kingdom as a student when he was 17. His first brush with publicity was in 1990 when, as a wealthy property developer, he made an unsuccessful takeover bid for a Sheffield football club. It is unclear from his various and inconsistent accounts whether he wrongly considered himself to be a transsexual as a result of losing his money, wife, and family or whether he always knew he was a transsexual. What is known is that Sam Hashimi became Samantha Kane during 1997.

As Samantha, Kane (1998) wrote a book about her experiences as an MF transsexual and, according to a subsequent documentary[6] also regained her wealth, though not her children's affections. Between 2003 and 2004 she was on a list of 12 patients whom colleagues of leading gender reassignment specialist Russell Reid claimed had been wrongly diagnosed and operated on. Reid was referred to the General Medical Council by these colleagues, and Kane made it known that she intended to sue Russell. The BBC documentary about Kane concerned his experiences as a wrongly diagnosed transsexual, which included following him through some of his therapies to be changed back to a man – Charles Kane.

Kane's case is unusual to the extent that Kane has been prepared to be a more public figure.[7] There are other reported instances, particularly of MF transsexuals seeking to get their surgery reversed.[8] The number of MF transsexuals seeking reversal is still only a small minority of all cases. The prevalence of MF requests for reversal probably reflects the fact that there appears to be somewhere between four and eight times more MF transsexuals than FM (female-to-male) ones (Raymond 1979, 24).

It is important to be sure about what such cases actually show. On the one hand, they have been used by critics of the whole notion of transsexualism to support the claim that it is a condition created by psychiatrists. On the other, all they may show is that doctors need to be extremely cautious in making a diagnosis and adhering to accepted guidelines before agreeing to perform surgery. For those concerned, undertaking surgery has left them suspended in a tragic limbo between male and female. It would be foolhardy in the extreme to assume that mistakes in diagnosis never occur, even in areas of medicine where there is absolutely no controversy about the condition misdiagnosed. However, when scalpels for hire undertake GReS, on the basis of only a short interview or basic physical appearance, it is unsurprising that mistakes – by both doctor and patient – are made.

Adhering to the strict guidelines, however, might not be acceptable to some transsexuals. Standard practice is for transsexuals to have at least three months of psychotherapy before beginning hormone therapy, and then to live as a member of their proclaimed sex for at least one year, full time and publicly – before undergoing any surgery (Harry Benjamin International Gender Dysphoria Association 2001). Given that transsexuals may wait for several years or even decades before presenting for help, a further wait can be frustrating. From the clinician's point of view, given that all there is to go on is the patient's sincere belief and ability to convince, the waiting period is an opportunity to be convinced over time, particularly when for a substantial period of this time the patient must experience the possible challenge to his/her beliefs of going public and facing the consequences in terms of negotiating new relationships with family, friends, and work colleagues. The waiting period is, then, also a test of resolve. However, from the point of view of the transsexual, particularly given that biomedical ethics and patient expectations are driven by patient autonomy and rights, this period can be viewed as unacceptably paternalistic. [. . .]

[. . .]

The Extent to which Transsexualism is a Medical/Surgical Problem

In the treatment of transsexualism, there is a convergence of three very different medical specialties: psychiatry, medicine, and surgery. The initial assessment, supervision, and monitoring fails to the psychiatrist; the patient is then referred to an endocrinologist, who takes responsibility for hormone and other therapies while a surgeon performs bodily reconstruction. This cooperation of specialties would appear to endorse the place of transsexualism within a medical model of disease or illness, but in each case there is a considerable divergence from normal practice in order to incorporate an ontological acceptance of transsexualism. We will focus particularly on psychiatry and surgery.

It is not unusual for psychiatrists to treat people who make claims that apparently challenge reality. For instance, in anorexia they would work on a woman's perception of herself as fat and try to realign her view of herself with the reality of her extreme thinness. Where transsexualism is unusual in psychiatry is that it is up to the patient to convince the psychiatrist that her view of herself, despite the "reality" of her body, is the correct one.[9] Thus, unlike the person with anorexia, the transsexual does not deny the facts of her male body: she is not trying to assert that her male penis is in fact a clitoris. Instead, she is arguing that it *ought* to be a clitoris. The transsexual's claim is based on some inner and unseen self that contradicts the facts about the external self. If there is a delusion operating here, then it is not a delusion about external appearances but about an inner self. In this respect, transsexualism is more like body dysmorphia.

In simple terms, then, in transsexualism the psychiatrist seeks to be convinced by the patient's view of reality, rather than the patient being convinced by the psychiatrist's, and it is only possible for the psychiatrist to be convinced if he has subscribed to the view that there *is* such a thing as transsexualism. Thus, the convincing that needs to be done centers around the sincerity and/or strength of the patient's own conviction, as measured against the psychiatrist's experience (either at first or second hand) with other transsexuals and their psychiatric histories. One aspect of this is the extent to which the patient is suffering as a result of her condition, which may take the form of suicidal tendencies, extreme unhappiness, and being unable to function socially (work, interact with family and friends, and so forth).

[. . .]

From the point of view of psychiatry, however, another general criticism is that the treatments on offer alter the *body* when the condition itself seems to have its origins in the *mind*. Of course, much of modern psychiatric practice involves altering the body, primarily the brain, using chemicals. So perhaps the challenge should be rephrased: if, as some psychiatrists hypothesize, transsexualism is caused by some malfunction in the wiring in the brain during fetal development, and if drugs were developed that could make good this wiring, would the treatment of preference continue to be the realignment of the body with the beliefs of the individual, or would it be to realign the perception with the body? Restoring the wiring to working order would be to cure transsexualism, whereas GReS concentrates only on the symptoms and thus could be argued to produce surgically constructed men and women (Raymond 1979, xvi n 5); put even more strongly, GReS turns "men into fake women and women into fake men" (Szasz 1980, 86–87).

Ironically, to argue that, given the choice, we should opt to treat the brain, and therefore the perception of the transsexual, suggests that the perception of the transsexual is actually a false one, which in turn undermines not the sincerity of the transsexuals claim but the truth of the claim, and therefore the validity of GReS. This does not mean that performing GReS is wrong: it could still be argued to be a pragmatic response to extreme suffering using what is currently available. So the current situation could be characterized in terms of what we can do technically determining treatment, which in turn determines diagnosis. If we accept that what is currently happening is a pragmatic approach, rather than one that accepts the truth of what is claimed, it makes sense for

psychiatrists to base a referral for radical surgery on proof of the extreme unhappiness of the patient and evidence that they are sincere in the beliefs about their gender and steadfast in their resolve to seek surgery. The extreme unhappiness might justify surgery within the current model of medical ethics, where no intervention should be given unless the harms outweigh the benefits. Thus surgery can be considered worthwhile on balance, even if the condition does not actually exist in quite the way that the transsexual believes.

Turning to surgery, this same on-balance justification could be employed, even though it could be contested when measured against the normal practice of surgery. Normally a surgeon would expect to remove or repair only diseased tissue, organs, or limbs, yet this is not what is happening in GreS where healthy, but undesired, organs are removed. However, there are other departures from normal practice that still fit comfortably with the surgical model, for instance, surgical sterilization or removal of healthy tissue for transplantation into another person. The "fit" seems to depend both on the acceptability to the surgeon of the existence of the condition and how extreme it is. Thus, removal of a healthy kidney for transplantation purposes is acceptable, but removal of a healthy heart would not be; likewise, GReS seems to be acceptable, while, in the United Kingdom at least, few surgeons would be comfortable removing two or more limbs in the case of body dysmorphia.

We have already looked at the question of how plausible the whole notion of transsexualism is, and clearly any surgeon performing the surgery must be prepared either to accept that transsexualism is a genuine condition or accept the "on balance justified" argument. But there are a series of other interrelated issues that arise for the surgeon. The first is how effective surgery is likely to be, since if it is not very effective this would affect the "on balance" judgment. Next is the question of whether the results have to be plausible – whether, for instance, the MF transsexual will pass readily as a woman. Finally there is the question of whether the surgery should be aimed solely at reconstruction or if it is necessary for the surgeon to create for the transsexual the woman or man he/she desires to become – the "ideal" or "perfect" man or woman.

There are two senses in which GReS can be judged to be effective or not: there is technical success, judged totally in terms of the surgical procedures, and success in terms of whether the patient feels better or more balanced as a result of having their gender reassigned. While the latter is in part dependent on the former, what is important from the point of view of the justification for performing the surgery is the latter: the surgery could be a success locally but fail in terms of the global project of improving the patient's quality of life. There is conflicting evidence of success taken globally. While there are papers purporting to have illustrated success, the Aggressive Research Intelligence Facility (ARIF) of the University of Birmingham, England, does not consider that the issue of effectiveness can be settled on the basis of the evidence currently available.[10] Moreover, there is much less evidence relating to FM transsexuals than to MF transsexuals. This is in part due to the smaller numbers but could also be due to a reluctance of FM transsexuals to draw any kind of attention to themselves (Raymond 1979, xxii). Lack of *conclusive* evidence of effectiveness does not, however, mean that it is not effective – especially as, in the current economic climate, it is not sufficient to show that an intervention is effective; it must also be *more* effective than other interventions in a randomized control trial. As ARIF observes, a trial aiming to randomize transsexuals in trial arms that would include psychotherapy only or doing nothing only as well as GReS are unlikely to recruit sufficient, if any, participants.

What we do know from retrospective research is that two factors seem to point to greater overall success. The first of these is the age at which surgery is performed (Lawrence 2003, 300) and the age at onset of the feelings of being a transsexual. The older one is, in each case, the less likely one is to be satisfied postsurgery. The second is the extent to which the surgery is un-problematic or successful in its own right. This brings in the two further related issues mentioned above: plausibility and conformity to desires.

The job of the surgeon here is to reassign gender, but for gender reassignment to be successful, it must also be plausible. The MF should be able to pass as a woman and the FM as a man, one aspect of which is being able to be attract sexual attention[11] from genetic men/women rather than reconstructed men/women, irrespective of sexual orientation. This might depend on physical characteristics that are not very amenable to surgical correction such as height and build. If the success of the surgery is based at least in part on how plausible the results are likely to be, then plausibility is likely, consciously or unconsciously, to become one criterion in the assessment of the suitability of transsexuals for GReS. This may, however, undermine other aspects of the assessment, such as testing the sincerity of the patient's belief or the resolve to continue.[12]

Plausibility is, however, quite a different goal from the one that the transsexual might set for him/herself. Many transsexuals seek not just to change sex but to end up as a conventionally attractive member of the opposite sex. The desire to be physically attractive is common, but in terms of GReS what might otherwise be classed as a cosmetic effect appears more fundamental. So, for instance, a typical MF transsexual is likely to want to be and appear to be more feminine than an average genetic woman (Herman-Jeglinska et al. 2002). Bound up with the conviction that he is truly female may be the desire to be an attractive female conforming to cultural norms of female beauty such as prettiness, thinness, femininity, desirability to the opposite sex, demureness, and provocativeness. For the transsexual, this means that cosmetic surgery might not be viewed as an optional extra to the GReS but part and parcel of changing gender. This can lead to differing expectations of what counts as success between the patients and their surgeons.

The surgeons could be defended for arguing that their role is to reassign sex, and so while they might not oppose cosmetic surgery in principle, they might argue that requests for what they perceive as cosmetic surgery should be judged alongside other (i.e., nontranssexual) patients' requests for enhancement and perhaps would not be available using public funds. Perhaps, then, all the surgeon contracts to do is to make a constructed woman/man rather than an *attractive* constructed woman/man.

This is important when considering how well a surgeon can be said to have done her job, or in a worst-case scenario, whether she can be considered negligent or to have in some other way failed her patient. Thus there might be two standards against which the surgery can be judged: the objective assessment of whether the surgery was carried out with due care (for example, avoiding unnecessary scarring, employing modern techniques competently, and so on), and the subjective judgment of the patient about whether the surgery has made her the kind of woman she wanted to be as opposed to simply making her a woman. We would argue that it is in the former that the duty of the surgeon lies, but this is not straightforward.

A transsexual person can be thought of, along with all others, as existing through three dimensions of the self: past, present, and future. The past self for the transsexual is the suffering self, the self that existed from earliest times as an isolated, estranged, unhappy, and dispossessed misfit. This past self often contemplated suicide and eventually sought medical help to alleviate the distress. The present self (now diagnosed as a transsexual) is a self on a journey, a transitional self moving forward. Nothing for this person is permanent because everything else in life is on hold, awaiting surgery. It is the future self exclusively that matters. It is the female self that is achieved following surgery that is the self that will know fulfillment, happiness, and recognition. This future self is to be revealed when all the surgical bandages are removed and she stands in front of a mirror for herself and all others to see. This is the moment of realization and of completion. This is the moment that life will begin for the first time and unhappiness will become a thing of the past.

In her autobiography *Conundrum,* Jan Morris writes of her response when she looked at herself in the mirror following surgery. Her physical appearance at last corresponded to the inner feelings that she had possessed for so long. In turn her new physicality impacted upon her inner experience in a way that was pleasing to her.

> It is not merely the loss of androgens that has made me more retiring, more ready to be led, more passive: the removal of the sex organs themselves has contributed; for there was to the presence of the penis something positive, thrusting and muscular. My body was then made to push and to initiate and it is now made to yield and accept and the outside change has had its inner consequences. (1974, 141)

This comment seems to demonstrate Morris's desire to conform to stereotypical views of femininity and the way in which surgery, especially as a result of the removal of the penis, accomplished this.

These divisions of the self are not absolute, as they coexist and overlap, but they provide a useful way of clarifying goals and concerns. To which self does the surgeon and psychiatrist owe a duty of care? Is it to the past suffering self – in which case, the motivation for performing GReS becomes one of alleviating and not creating further suffering? Or is it to the present self for whom surgery becomes a means or *the* means of achieving realization? Or is it to the future self – in which case, the surgeon may be agreeing to create a future self that brings about the dreams and wishes of the transsexual that include being sculpted into an attractive as well as plausible woman.

The pre-op transsexual has an unusually heavy investment in her future self. It could be argued that she is almost exclusively investing in her future self. Such investment is inherently problematic, though not only does it lead to a truncated appreciation of the present life

but it also carries with it the increased possibility that such investment will fail to bring the hoped-for returns (as it does for anyone living primarily in the future). To exclusively focus upon a future self in the belief that realizing that self will be the equivalent of entering the Promised Land is first to nurture false beliefs and second to create a condition in which disillusionment is a real possibility.

Thus, from this perspective, the transsexual may feel that it is legitimate to hold the surgeon responsible for any failure to make her an attractive woman because it is the surgeon who is constructing her as a woman. A genetic woman may regard herself as unattractive but, adverse incidents aside, has no one to blame for this. It seems to us, then, vital that it be made clear to the transsexual from the outset that the purpose of the surgery is to reassign gender and not to make an ideal (according to the patient) woman.

Proceeding with Treatment

What we have established so far is that although there could be grounds for suspecting that transsexualism is not a genuine condition in the sense that someone of one gender *is* trapped inside the body of the opposite gender, there are grounds for treating those that suffer as a result of their transsexual beliefs with GReS as a pragmatic response to an otherwise insoluble and debilitating condition. This justification is based on surgery being of benefit to the patient *on balance.* However, such a justification must require certain safeguards and precautions.

We have noted that in order to make a diagnosis, a psychiatrist has to be convinced of the sincerity of the transsexual's beliefs, and that in order to refer the patient for GReS, there must also be certainty about the resolve of the patient both to publicly live as a member of the opposite gender – with all the consequences that will flow for relationships with family, friends, and work colleagues – and to face repeated surgical procedures. It is clear from the Harry Benjamin guidelines that not all transsexuals require GReS; some are content with hormone therapy only, some do not even wish to live as a member of the opposite sex. Likewise, not all transsexuals want to undergo a complete gender reassignment: some FM transsexuals, while happy to live as a male, do not want to undergo penile construction but are content to go only as far as having breasts, ovaries, and uterus removed. So even though there is a sense in which, as we have explained, the possibility of GReS has facilitated the emergence of a diagnosis of transsexualism, this does not mean that GReS naturally follows from diagnosis. Thus, psychiatrists have an obligation to explore with the patient what is required for her to live a more balanced life. This is an unsurprising conclusion in the age of informed consent. However, if we also recall that the justification for surgery is an on-balance one, it is arguable that psychiatrists should be trying first and foremost to assess how *little* intervention is necessary to improve the patient's quality of life, rather than simply assessing whether they are informed about and prepared for the consequences of GReS.

Against this background and notwithstanding the arguments already outlined in relation to paternalism, the Harry Benjamin guidelines on both eligibility and readiness for GReS criteria are not just prudent in terms of defending negligence claims, but an ethical requirement. These require that the patient has reached the age of majority, has received hormone therapy for at least 12 months, has had 12 months successful *continuous* real-life experience (as opposed to real-life tests) of living as a member of the opposite sex, and has demonstrated progress in consolidating a gender identity and also that the continuous real-life experience has had an overall positive effect on his/her mental health. Although psychotherapy is not a requirement, given the criteria and the need for assessment, a therapeutic relationship of at least 12 months' standing seems to be built into the guidelines. Moreover, it seems to us that those seeking a reversal of GReS, too, should meet the same criteria. The Harry Benjamin guidelines also recommend long-term follow-up, though it is difficult to see how the psychiatrist can ensure the patient's cooperation with this.

[. . .]

Returning to the actual surgery, what are the obligations of the surgeon? Surgeons are not merely technicians; if they want to remain members of the medical profession, they have to abide by professional standards, and this means being more than surgically competent. The treatment of transsexuals is a team effort involving psychiatrists, endocrinologists, and surgeons. The psychiatrist takes the lead role in the diagnosis and assessment of the patient, and it is not unreasonable for the surgeon and endocrinologist to depend upon the psychiatrist's judgment. But this should not be an uncritical trust. As professionals, they must also be satisfied both ontologically and in terms of individual patients that intervention is necessary. This means that they should not be treating any patients who are not under the care of a psychiatrist (one who has experience of transsexualism) and they should not treat any patient who has not fulfilled the Harry Benjamin criteria of eligibility and readiness. While the surgeon cannot also be expected to undertake a psychiatric assessment, she can be expected to satisfy herself that such an assessment has been made by at least one, if not two, suitably qualified psychiatrists.

Further than this, the surgeon also has an obligation to ensure that her expectations for the surgery are in line with those of the patient. Based on our previous discussion, and again in line with conventional thinking about consent, this may involve explicit discussion with the patient about what can be realistically achieved with GReS and possibly later with cosmetic surgery.

A surgeon performing GReS cannot be held responsible for not constructing an attractive male or female, only for not performing with due skill and competence, but such a surgeon could be held responsible for holding out false promise or for not ensuring that the patient has realistic expectations of what they will look like when the bandages are removed and the scars heal.[13]

[. . .]

Notes

1 The ICD-10 judged transsexualism according to three criteria: "1. The desire to live and lie accepted as a number of the opposite sex, usually accompanied by the wish to make his or her body as congruent as possible with the preferred sex though surgery and hormone treatment; 2. The transsexual identity has been persistent for at least two years; 3. The disorder is not a symptom of another mental disorder or chromosomal abnormality" (Harry Benjamin International Gender Dysphoria Association 2001).

2 Sometimes also referred to as "sex reassignment surgery" or "sex-change operation."

3 Gametes can be stored, but it is difficult to see him useful they would be given that most transsexuals claim also to be heterosexual.

4 The Sulfolk Health Authority (1994) estimated this to be in the region of £50,000 more than 10 years ago.

5 *Be Alex: hormonal treatment far gender identity dysphoria* [2004] FamCA 297.

6 BBCI, "Make Me a Man Again," October 19, 2004.

7   Charles Kane is now reported to be writing a new book, *Back on Mars from a Long Trip to Venus*.

8   See, for instance, Batty 2004.

9   The assumption here is not that all transsexuals are male to female; the designation of he," etc., is used simply for reasons of style.

10 The available evidence reviewed and their reasons can be found online at http://www.ant.bham.ac.uk/Requests/g/genderreass.htm.

11 Which is not be the same thing as being generally sexually attractive, that is, conventionally beautiful or handsome.

12 Batty (2004) suggests that there is too much emphasis on plausibility in the history of those who consider that their surgery was a mistake.

13 For a summary of the British government policy, see http://www.dca.gov.uk/constitution/transsex/policy.htm.

References

Batty, D. 2004. Mistaken identity. *Guardian,* July 31. Available at http://society.guardian.co.uk/health/story/0,7890,1273045,00.html.

Harry Benjamin International Gender Dysphoria Association. 2001. Standards of care for gender identity disorders. 6th edn. Minneapolis: Harry Benjamin International Gender Dysphoria Association. Available at http://www.hbigda.org/soc.htm.

Herman-Jeglinska, A. et al. 2002. Masculinity, femininity, and transsexualism. *Archives of Sexual Behavior* 31 (6): 527–534.

Kane, S. 1998. *A two-tiered existence*. London: Writers and Artists.

Lawrence, A. 2003. Factors associated with satisfaction or regret following male–female sex reassignment surgery. *Archives of Sexual Behavior* 32 (4): 300.

Morris, J. 1974. *Conundrum*. London: Faber & Faber.

Raymond, J. G. 1979. *The transsexual empire*. London: Women's Press.

Spriggs, M. P. 2004. Ethics and the proposed treatment of a 13-year-old with atypical gender identity. *Medical Journal of Australia* 181 (6): 319–321.

Suffolk Health Authority. 1994. Transsexuals and sex reassignment surgery. Internal report. Available at "Press for Change," http://www.pfc.org.uk/medical/sulfolk.htm.

Szasz, T. 1980. *Sex: Facts, frauds and follies*. Oxford: Blackwell.

Surgical Progress is Not the Answer to Intersexuality

Cheryl Case

Summary

Argues that surgical sex assignment is not morally justified for intersexed children. While intersexed children should be labeled as male or female, those who undergo sex assignment surgery do not have better outcomes, surgical techniques are seriously flawed, and the primary harm described by former patients is the social stigma of intersexuality rather than poor surgical results. While intersexed adults should have access to cosmetic surgery, intersexed children (who are typically converted to anatomical girls because of aesthetic judgments) are harmed by the surgery and by the implication that they are not lovable unless surgically altered.

Original publication details: Cheryl Case, "Surgical Progress is Not the Answer to Intersexuality," pp. 385–392 from *The Journal of Clinical Ethics* 9:4 (1998). Reproduced with permission of Journal of Clinical Ethics.

Sexual Ethics: An Anthology, First Edition. Edited by Patrick D. Hopkins.

Introduction

Surgery's better *now! We're* rapidly *advancing!*
– Kenneth Glassberg, MD, in an interview about
intersex surgeries on *Dateline NBC* in 1997

The traditional model of medical treatment of intersexuality has been roundly challenged on ethical and empirical grounds.[1] While they have yet to respond to the ethical challenges, many holdouts for the traditional model insist that criticisms of former patients are irrelevant because "surgery is better now." Practically, there is no evidence to indicate that children operated on with current techniques will have better long-term outcomes than those operated on 10 or more years ago. What is more important, poor surgical outcomes are not the only – or even the primary – reason former patients feel harmed. The primary source of harm described by former patients is not surgery per se, but the underlying attitude that intersexuality is so shameful that it must be erased before the child can have any say in what will be done to his or her body. Early surgery is one means by which that message is conveyed to parents and to intersexed children.[2]

As the director of one of the most visible of the peer support/patient advocacy groups, I have been privileged to communicate with nearly 300 intersexed people and family members. I have seen firsthand hundreds of cases in which well-intentioned but misguided medicine has compounded, rather than alleviated, the difficulties of being born intersexed.[3] Some of this material is available on the internet (see <www.isna.org>).

Let me say outright that I believe that intersexed children should be labeled male or female,[4] that they should be provided with surgeries or drugs necessary for their *physical* health and well-being, and that for most families intersexuality is and will remain a painful issue. My primary concern is to make the world a safer place for intersexuals and their families. Enlightened doctors will have an important role in this endeavor. Intersexuals old enough to make *informed decisions* should have access to cosmetic surgeries.

A Surgical World-View

Surgery is good at removing structures, like infected appendices or localized tumors; it is much less useful for creating structures. When surgeons quip that they prefer to assign intersexed infants female rather than male because "you can dig a hole [that is, a vagina], but you can't build a pole [that is, a penis],"[5] they are acknowledging that theirs is essentially an obliterative, rather than a constructive, art (as well as revealing the crudest imaginable disregard for the complexities of female sexuality).[6]

When genital surgery is performed on an infant, the impact on sexual function cannot be evaluated until sexual maturity, many years later – but these follow-up studies have not been done.[7] For example, although the clitoroplasty technique used on large clitorises in intersex infants was first published over three decades ago, no long-term studies of its impact on sexual function have been done.[8] Surgeons concede that they do not know what impact these surgeries have on intersex children's future sexual function. Johns Hopkins University surgeon John Gearhart says, "We won't know until later whether these patients will be normal and sexually active. We cannot say that they will have orgasms when they are older."[9] A reporter covering a demonstration by former patients who had been sexually mutilated by "reconstructive" surgery related; "As for what happens 21 years later, Jeffs says he has no way of knowing. 'Is this going to be one that's satisfied or one that's out on the street: [protesting]? I don't know."[10]

In spite of a complete lack of data, many clinicians simply claim that surgeries do in fact preserve sexual function. In the pamphlet *Becoming a Boy or a Girl*, George Szasz tells parents who are asked to give consent for surgery on their intersexed child that "Female external genitalia will be constructed and reconstructed in a series of operations. A clitoris of appropriate size will be formed from the undeveloped 'penis.' The clitoris has normal sensation."[11] One author even elevated the article of faith "without loss of sensitivity" into his title,[12] and the accompanying commentary by Milton Edgerton[13] enthused that "For over 40 years, some form of clitorectomy or clitoroplasty has been used to treat little girls with adrenogenital syndrome. The only indication for performing this surgery has been to improve the body image of these children so that they feel 'more normal.' . . . *Not one has complained of loss of sensation even when the entire clitoris was removed* [emphasis in original]."[14] I wrote to complain to Edgerton about loss of sensation and absence of orgasmic response in myself and other intersexed women. He wrote back to acknowledge that even a tiny incision could damage sexual function.[15] Like other clinicians contacted by intersex patients mutilated by genital surgeries, he has not publicly corrected his assertion that genital surgery preserves sexual function. And, as Robert Crouch discusses in this issue, the silence and secrecy of the traditional medical model render former patients voiceless.[16] I believe that if Edgerton had never previously heard a complaint from a former patient, it is not because none has lost genital sensation, but because all were too filled with shame and rage to confront him.

Only careful follow-up data, not surgeons' faith, can show that a new technique is actually better than an old one. For example, until recently surgeons believed that "nerve-sparing" prostate surgery preserved sexual function in most men treated for cancer. Follow-up study, however, now reveals that "nerve sparing" surgery is just about as destructive of sexual function as the traditional surgery.[17] These sorts of results ought to be in the forefront of our thinking when considering claims that current "nerve-sparing" genital surgeries are vastly improved over any surgery performed during infancy or adolescence on an intersex person now old enough to voice a complaint.

Now that some intersexuals are finding a voice with which to complain, a new argument for discounting us has appeared. Gearhart and colleagues measured pudendal nerve latencies during clitoroplasty, and claimed that these electrical measurements, absent any investigation of the girl's actual experience of genital sensation, provided evidence that when grown she would enjoy good sexual function. The authors minimized the importance of a critical letter documenting identical nerve latency in a clitorectomized woman with no orgasmic response with a *non sequitur:* "In fact, some women who have never had surgery are anorgasmic."[18] Coincidental anorgasmia is an unlikely explanation, however, as many intersexed women, including those documented in the letter, are primarily sexual with women. In contrast to heterosexual women, anorgasmia is infrequent among women with extensive homosexual experience who have not had clitoral surgery. Kinsey's data reports that 17 percent of married women with five years of coital experience are anorgasmic, and that large numbers achieve orgasm only rarely. Of those women in his sample with extensive homosexual experience, none were anorgasmic, and four-fifths were orgasmic in most of their sexual contacts.[19] Intersexed women with a history of clitoral surgery who have extensive sexual experience with women and are inorgasmic can be fairly certain that the surgery is the cause.

How can surgeons justify the continued practice of surgery with demonstrated risks and no demonstrated benefits? A number of surgeons have expressed – in conversation and in private correspondence though not in

professional publications – the conviction that *any* surgical intervention, no matter how damaging to sexual function or how poor the cosmetic result, is better than leaving an intersexed child unaltered. One woman, searching for help to restore sensation destroyed by a clitorectomy, approached Judson Randolph, a well-known surgeon specializing in clitoroplasty. He told her that clitorectomy had been "all surgeons had to offer" when she was a child.[20] In another case, a man who had been mutilated by over a dozen genital reconstruction surgeries during childhood sought a minor surgery to smooth his surgically constructed penile urethra, which was causing debilitating urinary tract infections. The surgeon, at his own initiative and contrary to the expressed wishes of the anesthetized patient, performed a complete penile reconstruction, which left the man much worse off and motivated him to initiate a lawsuit. A surgeon recruited as an expert witness for the defense remarked that intersexuality was so rare and tragic that "any cutting, no matter how incompetently executed, is a kindness."[21] Again, one of the best-known pediatric endocrinologists in the field recently remarked in conversation that he had never in his career seen a good cosmetic result in intersex genital reconstructions, but "what can you do? The parents demand it."[22]

Catch-22

In this issue of *JCE*, Kipnis and Diamond discuss the "epistemological black hole" that precludes follow up of intersex surgeries: the purpose of surgery is to hide intersexuality, therefore intersexuals must be lied to about their histories and surgeries,[23] and thus follow up cannot be done because the patients would learn the truth.[24] Use of the claim "surgery is better now" is a strategy for silencing intersexed adults:[25] it relieves surgeons indefinitely of the responsibility of listening to any former patient.

If genital surgery is indeed "better now" and getting better all the time, that is actually a strong argument for allowing intersex children to be free of nonconsensual early surgery: when they are old enough, should they choose surgery, they will benefit from more than a decade surgical advances. Moreover, were genital surgery performed only on patients old enough to make informed decisions, surgeons could benefit from patient feedback on the outcome as soon as healing is complete. Imagine how quickly surgery might improve under such circumstances!

When is a Clitorectomy not a Clitorectomy?

Until the early 1970s, surgeons usually "feminized" intersex children via clitorectomy: they simply amputated the tip and part of the shaft of the clitoris. Today, surgeons use a more elaborate technique when "feminizing" intersex infants, and they bristle at any equation of their work with clitorectomy, which has come to be considered sexual mutilation and a violation of women's human rights. A wide variety of surgical techniques are used today – these are called clitoroplasty, or, more specifically, clitoral recession or clitoral reduction.

The distinction between "clitorectomy" and "clitoroplasty" is more political than technical. I have interviewed African women subjected to traditional clitorectomy and intersexed women subjected to medical clitorectomy. In both groups, some women are deprived of clitoral sensation and orgasm; some retain sensation in the clitoral stump; and some of these retain orgasmic response.

I have also interviewed women who have been subjected to a wide variety of clitoroplasty techniques: some retain some clitoral sensation; some retain orgasmic response; some are deprived of clitoral sensation and orgasm; and some are left with chronic pain. I see no trend for clitoroplasty to be less sexually mutilating than clitorectomy. If two women have been subjected to clitoral surgery and their sexual function damaged, ought the one whose surgery was labeled "clitoroplasty" feel less mutilated than the one whose surgery was labeled "clitorectomy"? African mothers, no less than American surgeons, act from a desire to care for their daughters. American surgeons, no less than African mothers, are misguided when they direct a knife at a child's clitoris.

[. . .]

Postcards Prom the Paradigm Shift

A number of clinicians have listened to the voices of intersex adults and are not only changing their practice, but working to re-educate their colleagues. One (who is not yet comfortable being identified) told me that after she had addressed a group of pediatric endocrinologists, one approached her to say, "I never thought we had any idea what the [expletive] we were doing with these kids, and now I know I was right." On another occasion, after she had shown the video *Hermaphrodites Speak!*[26] at a staff meeting, a nurse approached her to relate how saddened and moved she was. She had always wondered in private, she said, about "what we were doing to those children," but had kept her opinion to herself because "the doctors must have known what they were doing."[27]

One clinician told me that his colleague had presented a small follow up that indicated poor results in teenage girls subjected to early clitoroplasty. "I expected them to be embarrassed. Imagine my surprise," he wrote, when the audience at the pediatric endocrinology conference "turned on [his colleague] like vicious dogs."[28]

There are signs that even holdouts for the traditional model realize that it is indefensible. One prominent surgeon with many publications to his name agreed to be interviewed about his work on intersex children only under condition of anonymity, and with details changed to further protect his identity.[29] The guest editor of this issue of *JCE* told me that she was unable to recruit anyone to defend the ethics of the traditional model.

Two important books that investigate the medicalization of intersexuality and incorporate extensive coverage of the experiences of former patients have been published this year.[30] The silence with which these books have been greeted by the community of clinicians is deafening. When Dreger's book led to an editorial in the *New York Times* questioning the ethic of early genital surgeries,[31] a leader in pediatric endocrinology privately advised his colleagues that Dreger's goal was personal notoriety, and her work should be ignored.

Conclusion

Surgery does not produce "normal" looking genitals – a fact immediately obvious to anyone who glances at the "after" photos claimed as successes in surgery journals or surgical training tapes. [. . .] Rather, what surgery does is to convey the clear message that "abnormal" genitals (including surgically reconstructed ones) are unacceptable. Surgery inflicts emotional harm by legitimating the idea that the child is not lovable unless "fixed" with medically unnecessary plastic surgery carrying significant risks. For example, Martha Coventry told the *New York Times*, "I'd be considered one of the success stories. I still have clitoral sensation, and I'm orgasmic." Nonetheless, she said, "it's taken me my whole life to come to terms with my body and not to feel such terrible shame."[32]

Finally, as ethicists have noted repeatedly, the argument that "surgery is better now" ignores the lack of informed consent and patients' autonomy inherent in the old model. The argument "Surgery is better now," combined with an insistence on operating during infancy, gives surgeons a perpetual license to ignore patients' needs and voices. When we stop thinking of our

children born with atypical genitals as monsters, we will no longer risk their adult sexualities with nonconsensual, medically unnecessary genital surgeries.

Notes

1 S. Kessler, *Lessons from the Intersexed* (Piscataway, N.J.: Rutgers University Press, 1998); A.D. Dreger," 'Ambiguous Sex' – or Ambivalent Medicine? Ethical Issues in the Medical Treatment of Intersexuality," *Hastings Center Report* 28, no. 3 (1998): 24–35; RA. Crouch, "Betwixt and Between: Reflections on Intersexuality," in this issue of *JCE*; K. Kipnis and M. Diamond, "Pediatric Ethics and the Surgical Assignment of Sex," in this issue of *JCE*.

2 RA. Crouch, "Betwixt and Between," see note 1 above; S.E. Preves, "For the Sake of the Children: Destigmatizing Intersexuality," in this issue of *JCE*.

3 C. Chase, ed., "Special Issue on Intersexuality," *Chrysalis: The Journal of Transgressive Gender Identities* 2, no. 5 (Fall/Winter 1997); C. Chase, *Hermaphrodites Speak!* Intersex Society of North America (BNA), 26 minutes, 1997 videocassette. Copies may be obtained from ISNA, PO Box 31791, San Francisco, Calif. 94131; website <www.isna.org>.

4 M. Diamond and H.K. Sigmundson, "Management of Intersexuality: Guidelines for Dealing with Persons with Ambiguous Genitalia," *Archives of Pediatrics and Adolescent Medicine* 151 (1997): 1046–50.

5 M. Headricks, "Is It a Boy or a Girl?" *Johns Hopkins Magazine* (November 1993): 10–16.

6 Dreger, "'Ambiguous Sex'," see note 1 above.

7 Kipnis and Diamond, "Pediatric Ethics," see note 1 above; J.M. Schober, "Feminizing Genitoplasty for Intersex," in *Pediatric Surgery and Urology: Long-Term Outcomes*, eds. M.D. Stringer et al. (London: W.B. Saunders, 1998), 549–58.

8 J.K. Lattimer, "Relocation and Recession of the Enlarged Clitoris with Preservation of the Glans: An Alternative to Amputation," *Journal of Urology* 86, no. 1 (July 1961): 113–16.

9 Hendricks, "Is It a Boy," see note 5 above.

10 "Jeffs" in the quote is John Gearhart's co-author, Robert Jeffs. E. Barry, "United States of Ambiguity," *Boston Phoenix* (Styles section), 22 November 1996, 6–8.

11 G. Szasz and E. Durbach, "Becoming a Boy or a Girl," (Vancouver, B.C., Canada: British Columbia's Children's Hospital, 1995), 76.

12 N. Sagehashi, "Clitoroplasty for Clitoromegaly Due to Adrenogenital Syndrome without Loss of Sensitivity," *Plastic and Reconstructive Surgery* 91, no. 5 (1993): 950–56.

13 M.T. Edgerton, "Discussion: Clitoroplasty for Clitoromegaly Due to Adrenogenital Syndrome without Loss of

Sensitivity (by Nobuyuki Sagehashi)," *Plastic and Reconstructive Surgery* 91, no. 5 (1993): 956.

14 Sagehashi, "Clitoroplasty," see note 12 above; Edgerton, "Discussion: Clitoroplasty," see note 13 above.

15 M. Edgerton, personal communication with the author, 1994.

16 Crouch, "Betwixt and Between," see note 1 above.

17 J.A. Talcott et al., "Patient-Reported Impotence and Incontinence after Nerve-Sparing Radical Prostatectomy," *Journal of the National Cancer Institute* 89, no. 15 (1997): 1117–23.

18 C. Chase, "Re: Measurement of Evoked Potentials during Feminizing Genitoplasty: Techniques and Applications" (letter) *Journal of Urology* 156, no. 3 (1996): 1139–40.

19 A.C. Kinsey et al., *Sexual Behavior in the Human Female* (Philadelphia: W.B. Saunders, 1953).

20 Personal communication with the author by J. Randolph, 1993.

21 Personal communication with the author by a surgeon who asked to remain anonymous, 1998.

22 Personal communication with the author by a pediatric endocrenologist who asked to remain anonymous.

23 S.A. Groveman, "The Hannukah Bush," in this issue of *JCE*.

24 Kipnis and Diamond, "Pediatric Ethics," see note 1 above.

25 Crouch, "Betwixt and Between," see note 1 above.
   [...]

26 See note 3 above.

27 Personal communication with the author by a nurse who asked to remain anonymous.

28 Personal communication with the author by Nicholas Johnson.

29 E.H.-J. Lee, "Producing Sex: An Interdisciplinary Perspective on Sex Assignment Decisions for Intersexuals" (Senior thesis, Brown University, 1994).

30 Kessler, *Lessons from the Intersexed*, see note 1 above; A.D. Dreger, *Hermaphrodites and the Medical Invention of Sex* (Cambridge, Mass.: Harvard University Press, 1998).

31 A. Dreger, "When Medicine Goes Too Far in the Pursuit of Normality," *New York Times* (Science Times) 28 July 1998.
   [. . .]

32 N. Angier, "New Debate Over Surgery on Genitals," *New York Times*, 13 May 1997, B7.

The Ethics of Surgically Assigning Sex for Intersex Children

Merle Spriggs and Julian Savalescu

Summary

Argues that surgical sex assignment for intersexed children is a complicated issue involving questions of whether surgery should ever be performed, who should decide, and what criteria should be used to decide. While parents are usually in the best position to make decisions, several national courts have ruled that parents' authority should be restricted because they may be making decisions based on their own fears rather than the best interests of the child. Whoever decides, one argument against surgery is that it violates the autonomy of the child and their right to an open future. This line of thinking is faulty because autonomy is misunderstood as simply liberty, infants have no autonomy in the first place, and most importantly, either decision will affect the child's future. If surgery is performed, the child will have no choice later on about the surgical change. If the surgery is not performed, the child will have no choice to have avoided the social stigma affecting their childhood. While promoting understanding, openness, and positive attitudes toward intersexuality may be most indicated, neither promoting nor prohibiting early surgery is a clear moral answer.

Original publication details: Merle Spriggs and Julian Savalescu, "The Ethics of Surgically Assigning Sex for Intersex Children," pp. 79–96 from David Benatar (ed.), *Cutting to the Core: Exploring the Ethics of Contested Surgeries*. Rowman and Littlefield, 2006. Reproduced with permission of Rowman and Littlefield.

Introduction

Intersex conditions raise profound ethical issues for the children born with these conditions, for their parents and for clinicians. *Intersex* refers to conditions "in which chromosomal sex is inconsistent with phenotypic sex, or in which the phenotype is not classifiable as either male or female" (Sax 2002, 174). This means that a child with an intersex condition may be genetically female with external genitalia that appear to be male, or may be genetically male with external genitalia that appear to be female. In some rare cases the child has both male and female genitalia. The prevalence of these conditions is 1.8 in every 10,000 live births, and the most common of the "classic inter-sex conditions" are congenital adrenal hyperplasia (CAH) and complete androgen insensitivity syndrome (CAIS) (Sax 2002, 174–75). There is debate about the definition of *inter-sex*. Broader definitions, of course, will give a higher prevalence (Blackless et al. 2000).

In this chapter, our concern is with the contentious issue of early surgery – situations where the surgical assignment of sex or "corrective" surgery is an option. In the literature and in practice guidelines, intersex conditions are variously referred to as "developmental anomalies of the external genitalia" (American Academy of Pediatrics 2000), "atypical sexual differentiation" (Cohen-Kettenis and Pfäfflin 2003), and "ambiguous genitalia" (Rangecroft 2003; Low, Hutson, and Murdoch Childrens Research Institute Sex Study Group 2003), even though intersex children "may or may not be born with external genitals that are ambiguous" (Cohen-Kettenis and Pfäfflin 2003, 49). Some intersex conditions remain undetected until puberty or later.

Intersex conditions can be harmful in three ways. First, the condition itself can be harmful. The range of intersex condition may include recurrent urinary tract infections (Warne 2003), problems with infertility, precocious or delayed puberty, hormonal imbalance requiring medication, risk of cancer, problems with sexual functioning and satisfaction, and gender identity and relationship difficulties leading to social and psychological problems (Cohen-Kettenis and Pfäfflin 2003, 90–91). Second, openness about an infant's condition in an environment where people are not aware of, don't understand, and don't accept genital ambiguity can lead to the child being stigmatized. Third, not disclosing the child's condition creates "an atmosphere of secrecy" suggesting that the child suffers from "something shameful" (Cohen-Kettenis and Pfäfflin 2003, 87–88).

The attitude that ambiguous genitals are shameful is a "primary source of harm" for people with intersex conditions (Chase 1998).

Standard medical practice has been to make an early diagnosis and to perform early "corrective" genital surgery. The reasoning behind this is the need for a clear and unambiguous sex assignment to save intersex children from being ostracized and to enable parents to bond with their baby girl or baby boy (American Academy of Pediatrics 2000; Lawson Wilkins Pediatric Endocrine Society and European Society for Paediatric Endocrinology 2002). [. . .]

[. . .]

A growing number of objectors have argued against early genital surgery on the grounds that it is not necessary, is not reversible, and can cause harm (Intersex Society of North America 1998). Some commentators argue that surgery to normalize the infant is based on parents' fears and concerns rather than the best interests of the child and amounts to "the medical management of a psychological condition" performed on the child for the sake of the parents (Purves 2000, 30–37): "Cosmetic surgeries are performed without the subject's consent because of adults' discomfort with intersexuality" (Dreger 1999, 17).

The central questions in the management of intersex infants are:

- When, if ever, should surgery be carried out?
- Who should decide?
- On what criteria should decisions be based?

The focus of the above issues for some seems to be the child's future autonomy and the implications of parents or others making irrevocable decisions for young children. We will argue that the main ethical issue is not a question of autonomy but the question of whether surgery makes the child's life go better or worse. We begin by outlining the criticisms of the traditional treatment model and early surgery and then address the central questions.

The Challenge to the Traditional Treatment Model and Early Surgery

Since the 1990s the traditional treatment model has been challenged. Opposition to "normalizing" surgery for people with intersex conditions has been expressed by patient advocacy groups and through the personal testimony of patients who are not happy with the way their condition has been managed.

> Are medical professionals standing by with rulers and stamps of approval? To some extent they are, and we are all subject to their judgement. . . . We are not so quick to judge other parts of anatomy. We teach our children to respect diversity, yet adults create a "state of emergency" over the size and shape of genitals. The real phenomenon is that the prevalence of genital and reproductive variation is kept such a secret. Intersex variations are so quickly "disappeared" that we don't get a chance to know about them, or how they might mature. . . .
> At the age of 13, I was scheduled for surgery . . .. My body was altered to meet social values, but my values were never discussed. My puberty was focused on vaginal function before I had a chance to care (Morris 2004, 25–27).

One of the criticisms of the traditional treatment model is that it fails to recognize the experience of intersexed people and to recognize that they are experts in terms of their experience of intersex conditions (Dreger 1999, 19). Another factor in the opposition to early genital surgery is the failed sex reassignment of an infant whose penis was completely burned off in a circumcision accident – the much publicized "John-Joan case" (Aaronson 2004).

In this case, a biologically unambiguous male infant was reassigned to the female sex on the recommendation of psychologist John Money, who claimed that infants are sexually neutral, that nurture trumps nature, and that gender identity is determined by the prenatal environment (Daaboul and Frader 2001). In a series of publications, Money reported that the surgically reassigned male infant had been successfully reared as a girl – resulting in the wide dissemination of the view that gender is malleable. He wrote that "no one" would "ever conjecture" that the child was born a boy (Kipnis and Diamond 1998, 176). Ultimately, however, gender reassignment in this case proved unsuccessful. The child "never became a normal girl" and from the age of 14 lived as a male (Kipnis and Diamond 1998, 180). He underwent four rounds of reconstructive surgery and in 2004, at the age of 38, he committed suicide.[1] Many have taken this case as evidence that the claim that gender is socially constructed is wrong (Aaronson 2004).

In relation to the surgical assignment of sex, Kipnis and Diamond (1998, 186–88) make three recommendations which have wide support among those who oppose early surgery:

1. "That there be a general moratorium on such surgery when it is done without the consent of the patient." Kipnis and Diamond argue that doctors should not perform the surgery without the knowledge that "comparable patients generally do badly without the surgery." They also argue that the lack of evidence about benefits means that surgical assignment of sex is an "experimental procedure." Their objection is to the "*surgical* assignment of sex, not to gender assignment per se."
2. "That this moratorium not be lifted unless and until the medical profession completes comprehensive look-back studies and finds that the outcomes of past interventions have been positive." Kipnis and Diamond claim that retrospective outcome studies can be done with the thousands of grown intersexuals who have and have not had surgical and hormonal treatment
3. "That efforts be made to undo the effects of past deception by physicians."

Who Should Decide?

One of the controversies about early genital surgery focuses on the question of who should decide or who should have the authority to consent to surgery on behalf of children with intersex conditions. Should parents, doctors, or the courts decide, or should the decision be left to children themselves when they become old enough?

Parents are usually the best placed to judge what is in their children's best interests and ordinarily have authority to make medical decisions for them. However, there are some medical procedures for which parental consent is considered insufficient. These include interventions which are grave and irreversible, involve significant risk, involve difficult ethical issues, or are not for the purpose of treating an illness. Such interventions sometimes require court authorization.

In Australia there is a legal category of "special medical procedures" that require authorization. These procedures include nontherapeutic sterilization and hysterectomy, gender reassignment, and organ donation. The Australian High Court decided that some grave and irreversible medical procedures that may permanently affect a child's quality of life are not within the scope of parents' or guardians' powers and should be made by "an objective, independent umpire" such as the Family Court (Family Court of Australia 1998, vii).[2] The High Court thought that special medical procedures require special consideration because there is a significant risk of making a wrong decision and grave consequences for the child would follow if a wrong decision were made (2). Consideration of the child's best interests [. . .] was one of the key issues identified by the court.

Surgery for intersex newborns and infants falls into the category of special medical procedures requiring court authorization because it is irreversible, involves risk, and sometimes – namely, when the aim is for the genitals to match the assigned gender – is performed for cosmetic reasons rather than to treat an illness.

While it is generally assumed that parents will act in the best interests of their children, courts will scrutinize parents' decisions about their children's medical treatments when it seems they are not acting in their child's best interests or if they have a conflict of interest. Some people think that parents choosing surgery for their intersex infants involves a conflict of interest in the sense that it is difficult for parents to be sure that they are acting in their child's best interests when they are being pressured to make a quick decision.

The first high court in the world to consider the question of whether parents should or should not have the authority to choose surgery for their intersex children was the Constitutional Court of Colombia (Greenberg and Chase n.d.). The court decided in 1999 that "under the then existing medical practices in Colombia" parents might not be "in the best position" to make medical decisions for their intersex children for the following reasons:

1. parents typically lack information about intersexuality;
2. intersexuality is viewed as a disease that must be "cured"; and
3. the treating physicians convey a sense of urgency to provide a quick cure (Greenberg 2003, 283).

This suggests that the court was taking the view that intersexuality is not a disease and that there is no urgency to fix the problem surgically. The court also thought that parents "may be motivated by their own concerns and fears rather than the 'best interests' of their children" (283).

The court carried out "exhaustive consultations" for more than a year, hearing evidence in support of both the traditional treatment model and alternative treatment recommendations. After hearing all the evidence, the court concluded that

to prohibit surgeries until the children reach the age of consent would be engaging in social experimentation, but to allow the surgeries to continue under the standard protocol would not ensure that the best interests of the children are protected. (Greenberg 2003, 279)

While the court did not rule against surgery, it established rules *restricting* parents' authority to authorize surgery (Greenberg and Chase n.d.). It recommended a new category of consent in order to make parents "put their children's best interests ahead of their own fears and concerns about sexual ambiguity" (Greenberg 2003, 279). The court required consent to be "qualified and persistent" and required the development of procedures by legal and medical institutions to meet the following conditions:

1. The consent must be in writing.
2. The information provided must be complete. The parents must be informed about the dangers of current treatments, the existence of other paradigms, and the possibility of delaying surgeries and giving adequate psychological support to the child.
3. The authorization must be given on several occasions over a reasonable time period to make sure the parents have enough time to truly understand the situation.[3]

Some medical procedures are indeed special, requiring much thought and sometimes legal scrutiny. Based on these decisions, we should conclude that parents should ordinarily decide but the courts should be involved when a particular decision to perform surgery on an intersex child appears to be against that child's interests. This would involve someone seeking court intervention because of the belief that the child's best interests were not being served. Alternatively, surgery for intersex conditions could be classed as a "special medical procedure" requiring court authorization. Having to go to court to get authorization for surgical treatment could be traumatic for parents, but some parents may find welcome relief in sharing the weight of the decision. Next we summarize clinical guidance in these complex decisions.

The Clinical Perspective: Should Early Surgery be Carried Out?

Current Practice Guidelines for the Surgical Management of Intersex Newborns

American Academy of Pediatrics

The guidelines of the American Academy of Pediatrics (2000) famously begin with the statement: "The birth of a child with ambiguous genitalia constitutes a social emergency" (138). They emphasize the urgency of a prompt definitive diagnosis and treatment: "It is important that a definitive diagnosis be determined as quickly as possible so that an appropriate treatment plan can be established to minimize medical, psychological, and social complications" (138). The point is also made that most genital abnormalities are not ambiguous in appearance and "only a minority of intersex patients have genitalia that are so ambiguous that the sex is uncertain" (139).

According to the academy, decisions about the sex of rearing should be based on fertility potential, capacity for normal sexual function, endocrine function, and testosterone imprinting (140–41). "Ongoing counseling" of parents and affected children is recommended because of "remaining uncertainties with regard to the long-term psychological and physical aspects of treatment" (141). This document states that infants raised as girls "will usually require clitoral reduction" (141).

The type of evidence supporting the recommendations in this document is not stated.[4] This guideline is due to be reviewed.

British Association of Paediatric Surgeons

The guidance from the British Association of Paediatric Surgeons is meant to be an "evidence based summation of current thinking and suggested practice" (Paediatric Surgeons Working Party 2001). It notes the controversy relating to standard protocols, but claims that a policy of prohibiting surgery until the fully informed consent of the patient can be obtained – that is, when the child becomes "Gillick competent" (of sufficient maturity to be capable of giving independent consent during adolescence) – seems "too prescriptive" given that there are "so many specific issues related to the different diagnostic groups" (Rangecroft 2003, 799).

This guideline recommends referral to a multidisciplinary team (Rangecroft 2003) and recommends making "no assignment of gender" prior to referral (799).

It suggests that where continuing pressure from parents for early corrective surgery exists, "fully informed consent" for procedures would require parents being made aware of "the possibility of non-surgical management with psychological support for the child and family" (799).

[. . .]

Other Guidelines

Other guidelines and recommendations exist (Lawson Wilkins Pediatric Endocrine Society and European Society for Paediatric Endocrinology 2002; Frader et al. 2004; Eugster 2004; Daaboul and Frader 2001). The most striking conclusion from these guidelines is that recommendations are being made in the absence of long-term data about outcomes. Some evidence exists,[5] but there are serious problems with that evidence.

- The John-Joan case is not useful in terms of evidence. That case did not involve a child with an intersex condition and genital ambiguity. The child was harmed, but the real harm was caused by the botched circumcision (Mazur 2004; Bullough 2003).
- "Systematic prospective or even systematic retrospective overall outcome studies" are not available (Reiner 2004, 51).
- There are criticisms that the traditional treatment model fails to recognize the experience of intersexed people. This raises the question: "How do we know what the experience of intersexed people is?"
- It is not easy to obtain the experience of intersexed people. "Self-descriptions" of the long-term effects of reconstructive surgery and of the anomalies themselves are "rare" (Reiner 2004). According to W. G. Reiner, a urologist who has become a psychiatrist, while clinically useful studies that claim to provide overall outcomes such as health-related quality of life do exist, they are problematic – they are too narrow in scope and "too simplistic in their understanding of quality of life" and their data are difficult to interpret and not useful if there is a lack of systematization within research and clinical care (Reiner 2004, 51).
- There are doubts about the representativeness of individuals studied. Recruiting individuals from intersex support groups is thought to give a negative bias in terms of surgical management (Schober 2004, 701–2), while recruiting individuals from clinics gives a positive bias (Meyer-Bahlburg et al. 2004). [. . .]

[. . .]

The Threat to Future Autonomy

The threat to future autonomy is one of the reasons some people object to early surgery for intersex newborns. They are concerned about what happens when parents make irrevocable decisions for their children, and they worry that the intersex child's autonomy or developing autonomy will be affected by the way his or her condition is managed.

According to one commentator, "Intersexed people have their autonomy violated because their doctors and parents are allowed to make decisions about how their genitals should look" (Dreger 1999, 17). And, an adult who was born intersexed claims, "Intersexuals aren't encouraged to be autonomous. . . . Who we are is dictated to us" (Preves 1999, 56).

Intersex people who underwent surgery when they were young may have been harmed, but the harm is not to their autonomy. To begin with, very young children do not have autonomy – immaturity precludes autonomy. Nevertheless, that is not the focus of the concerns expressed above and will not eliminate worries about threats to children's autonomy. There is a need to make a distinction between two ideas:

1. The future autonomy of the child
2. The child's developing autonomy

Damage to cognitive abilities would harm the young person's developing autonomy, but the harm alluded to in the above quotes refers to a child's future autonomy and the idea that choices made by parents will close off certain options, thereby limiting the child's autonomy. This is what some commentators refer to as "a child's right to an open future" (Feinberg 1980).

Appealing to a child's future autonomy in this way is not useful. Autonomy is not just about the number of options a person has open. Although autonomy is sometimes used as a synonym for freedom or liberty, it is about more than that. A person's liberty or freedom can be affected by a reduction in options, but the availability and range of life options is not what makes a person autonomous. Autonomy is a richer concept. It is about self-rule and making decisions about how one's life should go. It is about acting or choosing in a way that reflects preferences and values and depends on a particular kind of thinking.

As long as there are basic opportunities to grow and learn, autonomy does not depend on the circumstances in which a person finds themselves. It is possible to be autonomous and make autonomous decisions within narrowed horizons and also when options are not to our liking. Autonomous decisions can be made in reduced circumstances, such as that brought about by illness (Spriggs 1998). Most important, whether or not surgery is performed, some options will be open while others irrevocably remain closed:

1. If surgery *is not* performed, the child will later have a choice of whether or not to have surgery, but no choice over whether he/she is stigmatized as an intersex child during early development.
2. If surgery *is* performed, the child will have choices opened as a result of having a more "accepted" appearance, but no choice later on whether to have surgery.

Someone with an intersex condition who has undergone surgery as an infant may be harmed by the surgery because sensation is affected, by the feeling of shame generated by having the surgery, or by being stigmatized because of their condition. That person may have different options available than if they had not had the surgery. Fertility may be affected, for example. However, their autonomy is not determined by these factors. Certainly the sex assigned will influence a person's plans and choices, but autonomy is characterized by a person's capacity to think critically about their preferences, desires, and wishes, and their "capacity to accept or attempt to change these in light of higher-order preferences and values" (Dworkin 1988, 20). In exercising that capacity, a person "defines their nature, gives meaning and coherence to their life and takes responsibility for their choices" (Spriggs 2005, 241). Ultimately, it is the result of these choices and the way they are made that determines the kind of person they become – and that may be an autonomous, mostly autonomous, sometimes autonomous, or never autonomous person.

[. . .]

Children's Developing Autonomy

Although it does not make sense to talk about harm to the intersex child's future autonomy, it may make sense to talk about harm to a child's developing autonomy. Autonomy is not something that appears fully developed. Training children to become autonomous requires practice. Therefore, it might be claimed that aspects of the traditional medical model undermine or harm developing autonomy by not allowing the child to exercise choice or practice decision making. John Stuart Mill's (1948) argument about individuality as one of the elements of well-being could be interpreted as an argument about why we should value autonomy and why preventing children from making decisions can thwart the development of their autonomy (LaFollette 1998). Mill argues that we express our individuality and our humanity when we make choices.

Qualities such as "perception, judgement, discriminative feeling, mental activity, and even moral preference" are, according to Mill, the distinctive endowment of a human being" and are exercised and developed only in the making of choices (51). The value is not in the choice but in Mill's idea of character or self-development (which we can interpret as autonomy) and in fully developing the necessary capacities:

> He who lets the world, or his own portion of it, choose his plan of life for him, has no need of any other faculty than the ape-like one of imitation. He who chooses his plan for himself, employs all his faculties (51–52).

Some adult intersexuals tell of childhoods in which they lacked information about their conditions (a basic requirement for meaningful decision making) and lacked choice in the sense that they were not able to refuse repeated genital examinations performed without their consent:

> Because [the hospital I went to] is a teaching hospital, they would line up shoulder to shoulder all the way around from one side of the bed at the head, all the way across to the front and back up the other side. And everybody got a peek and a poke between my legs. And along about nine [years of age] that started getting real uncomfortable for me. But I was not allowed the power to say, "No, I don't want to play this game anymore." (Preves 2003, 66).
>
> You know while you're laying there that you don't have the right to say, "No. Stop. I don't want you to do this." (Preves 2003, 72).

How would such an experience undermine developing autonomy? The capacities needed for autonomy and making autonomous decisions need to be developed, and as mentioned previously, that requires practice. To some extent, it means we need to treat children as though they are already autonomous (LaFollette 1998). Preventing

the exercise of choice may threaten developing autonomy, though it is not likely to undermine it entirely.

Helping intersexed children to develop autonomy is an important ethical consideration. But it is not clear that early surgery necessarily precludes that, as many opportunities for the exercise of choice in life still remain.

Does Early Surgery make an Intersex Individual's Life Go Better or Worse?

Though autonomy has been the main focus of ethical discussion, it is not the main ethical issue. The main ethical issue is the question, Does early surgery make the child's life go better or worse?

What is there about early surgery that can make the individual's life go worse?

- Poor surgical outcomes
- The attitude that intersexuality is shameful (Chase 1998, 385)

A poor surgical outcome is an obvious cause of harm, but it is not the only or the primary reason that former patients "feel harmed." Cheryl Chase (1998) argues that "the primary source of harm described by former patients is the underlying attitude that intersexuality is so shameful that it must be erased . . .. Early surgery is one means by which that message is conveyed to parents and to intersexed children." Another source of harm is the claim that "surgery is better now." This silences intersexed adults and "relieves surgeons indefinitely of the responsibility of listening to any former patient" (Chase 1998, 387).

The Intersex Society of North America (1998) refers to a "wealth of literature" expressing grief about the physical and emotional suffering caused by the surgery and anger toward the doctors who performed the surgery and the parents who consented to it. The society also places significance on the fact that there are no adults coming forward to say that they are grateful for having had early surgery performed.

The availability of literature about harm to intersex individuals who had early surgery is cause for concern, but it is not necessarily an indication that surgery made most intersex individuals lives go worse. It is possible that there is no audience for tales of successful surgery. Individuals who had surgery and are happy with it may not want to reveal their experience. What is more, unhappy outcomes would seem to be easier to name and describe, for example, in terms of grief and anger. How would we know if surgery made an individual's life go better? There is a need for information about the experience of those who feel that surgery was the right decision.

Parental Attitudes

There is some suggestion that parental attitude, rather than the decision to operate or not, has more influence on intersex children's successful development. In a study of children born with a small penis, "parental attitude" was reported to be the "strongest influence" on childhood experiences (Reilly and Woodhouse 1989). This study found that parents who were well informed and open with their children produced children who were "confident and well adjusted." Parents who were not open with their children, who focused on their abnormalities and told the child "to hide himself" produced shy, anxious, poorly adjusted children.

The importance of parental attitude is demonstrated further in the case of Ilizane Broks, a self-assured, seemingly well-adjusted 17-year-old with an intersex condition who has been brought up with full knowledge of her condition and "imbued" with a "healthy sense" of her "own identity and worth." She has been taught to "ignore the prejudice of the ignorant" and to be proud of her difference (Craig 2004). Ilizane has complete androgen insensitivity syndrome. She has both male and female genitalia. She looks like a girl, has a vagina but no uterus or ovaries, and has testes and XY chromosomes, which denote a boy. Ilizane overturns the image of the ostracized, cruelly teased intersex child. She delights in her father's story about her first day at school when she was a five-year-old. When each child was asked to stand on a chair and introduce themselves to the class, Ilizane climbed onto a chair and said: "Hello, my name is Ilizane. I'm not a girl and I'm not a boy . . . I'm an intersex!" Ilizane retains her early confidence, claiming she would like to be an actress: "I really like the idea of standing up in front of people and saying, 'Hey, this is me. Or rather, this isn't me. All is not as it seems.'"

In Ilizane's case, her parents resisted the suggestion to remove her testes and have left the decision to their daughter. Ilizane admits, however, that if she had congenital adrenal hyperplasia, the more common condition, she might have opted for surgery by now. The point being made here is that the child's environment

matters – not in the sense that environment determines gender – but in the sense that acceptance and openness regarding the child's condition influences how well or how badly the child's life will go.

Key Points in the Management Decisions about Intersex

The preceding discussion suggests a number of points to bear in mind in minimizing harm:

- Surgery is most justified when there is a clear health risk.
- An early decision to do surgery (when appropriate) does not have to be a quick or rushed decision.
- One can assign a gender without doing surgery to match.
- Promote the idea that parental attitude is important. Parents who are informed and open tend to produce confident well-adjusted children (Reilly and Woodhouse 1989).
- Rather than promoting surgery or a moratorium on surgery, we should promote the idea that education, information, and positive attitudes in relation to intersex conditions matter most.
- It is important to look at the reason why a significant minority are not happy with the management of their condition.

It is still not clear what we should or should not do. Sometimes surgery has caused harm. Sometimes surgery may be the right decision. We need criteria to guide decisions.

A decision whether or not to perform surgery has to be made. In addition to the relevant medical facts, we need criteria to guide decisions on behalf of intersex newborns. Deference to parents as the most suitable people to be making medical decisions on behalf of their children (with help from doctors and with the relevant information) is based on the belief that parents are the best placed and most likely people to seek the best interests of their children. Nevertheless, given the controversy about early surgery for intersex newborns, the idea that parents should (1) leave the decision until the child is old enough to decide or (2) try to decide as the child would decide when old enough may seem like attractive options. But there are difficulties. First, leaving the decision for the child to decide when old enough carries the possibility of harm. It amounts to a decision not to perform early surgery rather than a way to respect autonomy. Second, in trying to decide as the child would, parents may end up making a decision that they *think* is not in their child's best interests – and that turns out *is not* in the child's best interests – based on an assumption about what a child who has not attained competence would decide when older (Dworkin 1988). Getting it wrong would surely be worse when parents make a decision that they do not believe in.

Conclusion

[. . .]

We have argued that the critical ethical issue is whether early surgery benefits or harms a particular individual in the sense of making the person's overall life go better or worse. Strikingly, there is very little empirical evidence to answer this question. The management of intersex speaks to the moral imperative to conduct ethically informed scientific research. Only then will we know what we should do.

Notes

This paper benefited from discussions with Garry Warne, Mary Rillstone, and other members of the Murdoch Childrens Research Institute Sex Study Group (MCRISSG).

1   It is difficult to interpret this case, as this individual had a twin brother whose death from an overdose of medication was a suspected suicide. See Chalmers 2004 and *CBC News* 2004.

2   Secretary, Department of Health and Community Services v. J.W.B. and S.M.B. ("Marion's Case") [1992] HCA 15; (1992) 175 CLR 218 F.C. 92/010 (6 May 1992). Marion's case involved an application for the sterilization of a 14-year-old teenager with a severe intellectual disability for the purpose of "preventing pregnancy and menstruation with its psychological and behavioural consequences."

3   Sentencia SU-337/99, May 12, 1999, and T-551/00, Aug.2, 1999; quoted in Greenberg 2003, 279.

4   National Guideline Clearinghouse, available at www.guidehne.gov.

5   Studies supporting early corrective genital surgery include Warne et al. 2005; Meyer-Bahlburg et al. 2004; and Migeon, Wisniewski, Gearhart et al. 2002; Migeon, Wisniewski, Brown et al. 2002, Studies which do not support early surgery include Minto et al. 2003; Creighton, Minto, and Steele 2001; May, Boyle, and Grant 1996; Dittman, Kappes, and Kappes 1992; and Reilly and Woodhouse 1989.

References

Aaronson, I. 2004. Editorial. *Journal of Urology* 171:1619.

American Academy of Pediatrics, Committee on Genetics. 2000. Evaluation of the newborn with developmental anomalies of the external genitalia. *Pediatrics* 106 (1): 138–42.

Blackless, M., A. Charuvastra, A. Derryck, A. Fausto-Sterling, K. Lauzanne, and E. Lee. 2000. How sexually dimorphic are we? Review and synthesis. *American Journal of Human Biology* 12: 151–66.

Bullough, V. L. 2003. The contributions of John Money: A personal view. *Journal of Sex Research* 40 (3): 230–36.

CBC News. 2004. David Reimer: The boy who lived as a girl. *CBC News Online*. http://www.ibc.ca/news/background/reimer.May 10.

Chalmers, K. 2004. Sad end to boy/girl life: Subject of gender experiment. *Winnipeg Sun*. May 10. Available at http://wvw.canoe.ca/NewsStand/WinnipegSun/News/2004/05/10/453481.html.

Chase, C. 1998. Surgical progress is not the answer to intersexuality. *Journal of Clinical Ethics* 9 (4): 385–92.

Cohen-Kettenis, P. T., and F. Pfäfflin. 2003. *Transgenderism and intersexuality in childhood and adolescence: Making choices.* Vol. 46 of *Developmental clinical psychology and psychiatry*. Thousand Oaks, CA: Sage.

Craig, O. 2004. We are not what we seem. *Sunday Age*. Agenda section. March 28.

Creighton, S. M., C. L Minto. and S. J. Steele. 2001. Objective cosmetic and anatomical outcomes at adolescence of feminising surgery for ambiguous genitalia done in childhood. *Lancet* 358 (9276): 124–25.

Daaboul, J., and J. Frader. 2001. Ethics and the management of the patient with intersex: A middle way. *Journal of Pediatric Endocrinology & Metabolism* 14: 1575–83.

Dittman, R. W., M. E. Kappes, and M. H. Kappes. 1992. Sexual behaviour in adolescent and adult females with congenital adrenal hyperplasia. *Psychoneuroendocrinology* 117 (2/3): 153–70.

Dreger, A. D., ed. 1999. *Intersex in the age of ethics*. Hagerstown, MD: University Publishing Croup.

Dworkin, G. 1988. *The theory and practice of autonomy*. Cambridge: Cambridge University Press.

Eugster, E A. 2004. Reality vs recommendations in the care of infants with intersex conditions – invited critique. *Archives of Pediatric and Adolescent Medicine* 158: 428–29.

Family Court of Australia. 1998. A question of right treatment: The Family Court and special medical procedures for children – An introductory guide for use in Victoria. Available at http://www.familycourt.gov.au/papers/pdf/vicmedical.pdf.

Feinberg, J. 1980. The child's right to an open future. In *Whose Child? Children's rights, parental authority, and state power*, eds. W. Aiken and H. LaFollette, 124–53. Totowa, NJ: Rowman & Littlefield. Reprinted in Joel Feinberg, *Freedom and fulfillment*, 76–97. Princeton, NJ: Princeton University Press, 1992.

Frader, J., P. Alderson. A. Asch, C. Aspinall, D. Davis, A. Dreger, J. Edwards, E K. Feder, A. F, L A. Hedley, E. Kittay, J. Marsh, P. S. Miller, W. Mouradian, H. Nelson, and E. Parens, 2004. Health can-professionals and intersex conditions. *Archives of Pediatric and Adolescent Medicine* 158: 426–28.

Greenberg, J. 2003. Legal aspect of gender assignment. *Endocrinologist* 13 (3): 277–86.

Greenberg, J. A., and G. Chase. N.d. Background of Colombia decisions. Available at http://www.isna.org/drupal/book/view/21 (accessed September 7, 2004).

Intersex Society of North America. 1998. ISNA's amicus brief on intersex genital surgery. Available at http://www.isna.org/node/97.

Kipnis, K., and M. Diamond. 1998. Pediatric ethics and the surgical assignment of sex. *Journal of Clinical Ethics* 9 (4). Reprinted in Dreger 1999, 173–93.

LaFollette, H. 1998. Circumscribed autonomy. Children, care, and custody, in *Having and raising children*, ed. Uma Narayan and Julia J. Bartkowiak, 137–52. University Park: Pennsylvania State University Press.

Lawson Wilkins Pediatric Endocrine Society and European Society for Paediatric Endocrinology. 2002. Joint consensus statement on 21-hydroxylase deficiency from the Lawson Wilkins Pediatric Endocrine Society and the European Society for Paediatric Endocrinology. *J. Clin Endocrinol Metab* 87 (9): 4048–53.

Low, Y., J. Hutson, and Murdoch Childrens Research Institute Sex Study Croup. 2003. Rules for clinical diagnosis in babies with ambiguous genitalia. *J. Paediatr. Child Health* 39 (6): 406–13.

May, B., M. Boyle, and D. Grant. 1996. A comparative study of sexual experiences, *Journal of Health Psychology* 1 (4): 479–92.

Mazur, T. 2004. A lovemap of a different sort from John Money: *A first person history of pediatric psychoendocrinology* – book review, *Journal of Sex Research* 41 (1): 115–16.

Meyer-Bahlburg, H., C. Migeon, G. Berkovitz, J. Gearhart, C. Dolezal, and A. Wisniewski. 2004. Attitudes of adult 46,XY intersex persons to clinical management policies, *Journal of Urology* 171: 1615–19.

Migeon, C. J., A. B. Wisniewski, T. R. Brown, John A. Rock, Heino F. L. Meyer-Bahlburg, John Money, and Gary D. Berkovitz. 2002 46, XY intersex individuals: Phenotype and etiologic classification, knowledge of condition, and satisfaction with knowledge in adulthood. *Pediatrics* 110 (3): 32.

Migeon, C. J., A. B. Wisniewski, J. P. Gearhart, H. F. L. Meyer-Bahlburg, J. A. Rock, T. R. Brown. S. J. Casella, A. Maret, K. M. Ngai, J. Money, and G. D. Berkovitz. 2002. Ambiguous genitalia with perineoscrotal hypospadias in 46,XY individuals: Long-term medical, surgical, and psychosexual outcome. *Pediatrics* 110: 616–21.

Mill. J. S. 1948. On liberty. In *"On Liberty" and "Considerations on Representative Government."* ed. R. B. McCallum, 1–104. Oxford: Basil Blackwell.

Minto, C. L., L.-M. Liao, C. R. J. Woodhouse, P. C. Ransley, and S. M. Creighton. 2003. The effect of clitoral surgery on sexual outcome in individuals who have intersex conditions with ambiguous genitalia: A cross-sectional study. *Lancet* 361: 1252–57.

Morris, E. 2004. The self I will never know. *New Internationalist* 364: 25–27.

Paediatric Surgeons Working Party. 2001. Statement of the British Association of Paediatric Surgeons Working Party on the Surgical Management of Children Born with Ambiguous Genitalia. Available at http://www.bapsajrg.uk/documents/Intersex%20stateinent.htm.

Preves, S. E. 1999. For the sake of the children: Destigmatizing intersexuality. In Dreger 1999, 50–65.

Preves, S. E. 2003. *Intersex and identity: The contested self.* New Brunswick: Rutgers University Press.

Purves, B. S. 2000. Parental consent and the surgical management of intersexed newborns. *Monash Bioethics Review* 9 (1): 23–42.

Rangecroft, L., on behalf of the British Association of Paediatric Surgeons Working Party on the Surgical Management of Children Born with Ambiguous Genitalia. 2003. Surgical management of ambiguous genitalia. *Arch Dis Child* 88: 799–801.

Reilly, J. M., and C. R. J. Woodhouse. 1989. Small penis and male sexual role, *Journal of Virology* 142: 569–71.

Reiner, W. G. 2004. Mixed-method research for child outcomes in intersex conditions. *BJU* International 93, suppl. (3): 51–53.

Sax, L. 2002. How common is intersex? A response to Anne Fausto-Sterling. *Journal of Sex Research* 39 (3): 174–78.

Schober, J. M. 2004. Feminizing genitoplasty: A synopsis of issues relating to genital surgery in intersex individuals. *Journal of Pediatric Endocrinology & Metabolism* 17: 697–703.

Spriggs, M. 1998. Autonomy in the face of a devastating diagnosis, *Journal* of *Medical Ethics* 24 (2): 123–26.

Spriggs, M. 2005. *Autonomy and patients' decisions.* Lanham, MD: Lexington Books.

Warne, G. 2003. Ethical issues in gender assignment. *Endocrinologist* 13 (3): 182–86.

Warne, G. L., S. Grover, J. Hutson, A. H. Sinclair, S. Metcalfe, E Northam, J. Freeman E. Loughlin, M. Rillstone, P. Anderson, F. Hughes, J. Hooper, S. Todd, J. D. Zajac, and J. Savulescu. 2005. A long-term outcome study of intersex conditions, *Journal of Pediatric Endocrinology & Metabolism* 18 (6): 555–67.

PART VI

Commerce and Speech

Introduction

The judgment of some sexual acts is heavily influenced by the assumption that they involve private activities and private experiences and as such should be assessed with a relatively minimal weighting of other people's attitudes. Whether that is a good assumption is itself something that can be asked. However, some sexual acts are much more explicitly and deliberately public and directly involve commercial transactions. Played out in markets and media, they create concerns about public effects that cannot be avoided.

Dealing with sex in these arenas highlights two questions different than those already examined in other places in this book. While still asking about definitions (how is pornography different from erotic art?), tradition (why should we change?), and intrinsic character (does this treat someone wrongly?), the relatively public and absolutely commercial nature of pornography and prostitution also leads us to ask whether sex is the kind of thing that should not be commercialized at all and whether publicly consumable sex acts have harmful effects on consumers

and bystanders. Here, it becomes quickly apparent that this is a set of cases where consequentialist concerns (does this have bad effects?) come into direct conflict with deontological concerns (do people have a right to do this no matter what the results?). That leads to a mix of debates over empirical information about what commercial sex actually does and debates over whether rights such as free speech trump concerns about social consequences.

Part VI examines issues of commercial sex and rights of expression. Though such issues are part of numerous rights versus consequences debates, they are explored here by focusing on concerns about the evidence for social harm, the classification of pornography as speech, and the basic question of whether commercial sex is necessarily exploitative.

Framing Questions

- *Is pornography harmful?*
- *Should pornography be protected as free speech?*
- *Is prostitution necessarily immoral?*

38

The Question of Harm

Attorney General's Commission on Pornography, Final Report, 1986

Summary

Argues that sexually violent pornography increases sexual violence and antisocial acts, that non-violent but degrading pornography decreases how seriously people see sexual violence and increases the degree to which they hold rape victims responsible, that even non-violent and non-degrading pornography promotes promiscuity, immorality, and endangers children, and that all pornography damages the historically private nature of sex. These conclusions justify increased regulation.

Original Publication details: United States. Attorney General's Commission on Pornography, "Chapter 5, The Question of Harm," pp. 299–351 from *Attorney General's Commission on Pornography Final Report, Volume 1*. U.S. Department of Justice, 1986. Public domain.

Sexual Ethics: An Anthology, First Edition. Edited by Patrick D. Hopkins.
© 2023 John Wiley & Sons, Inc. Published 2023 by John Wiley & Sons, Inc.

5.1 Matters of Method

5.1.1 Harm and Regulation – The Scope of Our Inquiry

A central part of our mission has been to examine the question whether pornography is harmful. In attempting to answer this question, we have made a conscious decision not to allow our examination of the harm question to be constricted by the existing legal/constitutional definition of the legally obscene. [. . .] To address fully the question of government regulation, therefore, requires that an examination of possible harm encompass a range of materials broader than the legally obscene.

Moreover, the range of techniques of social control is itself broader than the scope of any form of permissible or desirable governmental regulation. We discuss in Chapter 8 of this Part many of these techniques, including pervasive social condemnation, public protest, picketing, and boycotts. It is appropriate here, however, to emphasize that we do not see any necessary connection between what is protected by law (and therefore protected from law), on the one hand, and what citizens may justifiably object to and take non-governmental action against, on the other. And if it is appropriate for citizens justifiably to protest against some sexually explicit materials despite the fact that those materials are constitutionally protected, then it is appropriate for us to broaden the realm of our inquiry accordingly.[1]

Most importantly, however, we categorically reject the idea that material cannot be constitutionally protected, and properly so, while still being harmful. All of us, for example, feel that the inflammatory utterances of Nazis, the Ku Klux Klan, and racists of other varieties are harmful both to the individuals to whom their epithets are directed as well as to society as a whole. Yet all of us acknowledge and most of us support the fact that the harmful speeches of these people are nevertheless constitutionally protected. That the same may hold true with respect to some sexually explicit materials was at least our working assumption in deciding to look at a range of materials broader than the legally obscene. There is no reason whatsoever to suppose that such material is necessarily harmless just because it is and should remain protected by the First Amendment. As a result, we reject the notion that an investigation of the question of harm must be restricted to material unprotected by the Constitution.

The converse of this is equally true. Just as there is no necessary connection between the constitutionally protected and the harmless, so too is there no necessary connection between the constitutionally unprotected and the harmful [. . .]

[. . .]

5.1.2 What Counts as a Harm?

[. . .]

We believe it useful in thinking about harms to note the distinction between harm and offense. Although the line between the two is hardly clear, most people can nevertheless imagine things that offend them, or offend others, that still would be hard to describe as harms. In Chapter 4 of this Part our discussion of laws and their enforcement will address the question of the place of governmental regulation in restricting things that some or many people may find offensive, but which are less plainly harmful, but at this point it should be sufficient to point out that we take the offensive to be well within the scope of our concerns.

In thinking about harms, it is useful to draw a rough distinction between primary and secondary harms. Primary harms are those in which the alleged harm is commonly taken to be intrinsically harmful, even though the precise way in which the harm is harmful might yet be further explored. Nevertheless, murder, rape, assault, and discrimination on the basis of race and gender are all examples of primary harms in this sense. We treat these acts as harms not because of where they will lead, but simply because of what they are.

In other instances, however, the alleged harm is secondary, not in the sense that it is in any way less important, but in the sense that the concern is not with what the act is, but where it will lead. Curfews are occasionally imposed not because there is anything wrong with people being out at night, but because in some circumstances it is thought that being out at night in large groups may cause people to commit other crimes. Possession of "burglar tools" is often prohibited because of what those tools may be used for. Thus, when it is urged that pornography is harmful because it causes some people to commit acts of sexual violence, because it causes promiscuity, because it encourages sexual relations outside of marriage, because it promotes so-called "unnatural" sexual practices, or because it leads men to treat women as existing solely for the sexual satisfaction of men, the alleged harms are secondary, again not in any sense suggesting that the harms are less important. The harms are secondary here because the allegation of harm presupposes a causal link between the act and the harm, a causal link that is superfluous if, as in the case of primary harms, the act quite simply is the harm.

Thus we think it important, with respect to every area of possible harm, to focus on whether the allegation relates to a harm that comes from the sexually explicit material itself, or whether it occurs as a result of something the material does. If it is the former, then the inquiry can focus directly on the nature of the alleged harm. But if it is the latter, then there must be a two-step inquiry. First it is necessary to determine if some hypothesized result is in fact harmful. In some cases, where the asserted consequent harm is unquestionably a harm, this step of the analysis is easy. With respect to claims that certain sexually explicit material increases the incidence of rape or other sexual violence, for example, no one could plausibly claim that such consequences were not harmful, and the inquiry can then turn to whether the causal link exists. In other cases, however, the harmfulness of the alleged harm is often debated. With respect to claims, for example, that some sexually explicit material causes promiscuity, encourages homosexuality, or legitimizes sexual practices other than vaginal intercourse, there is serious societal debate about whether the consequences themselves are harmful.

Thus, the analysis of the hypothesis that pornography causes harm must start with the identification of hypothesized harms, proceed to the determination of whether those hypothesized harms are indeed harmful, and then conclude with the examination of whether a causal link exists between the material and the harm. When the consequences of exposure to sexually explicit material are not harmful, or when there is no causal relationship between exposure to sexually explicit material and some harmful consequence, then we cannot say that the sexually explicit material is harmful. But if sexually explicit material of some variety is causally related to, or increases the incidence of, some behavior that is harmful, then it is safe to conclude that the material is harmful.

5.1.3   *The Standard of Proof*

In dealing with these questions, the standard of proof is a recurrent problem. How much evidence is needed, or how convinced should we be, before reaching the conclusion that certain sexually explicit material causes harm? The extremes of this question are easy. Whenever a causal question is even worth asking, there will never be conclusive proof that such a causal connection exists, if "conclusive" means that no other possibility exists. We note that frequently, and all too often, the claim that there is no "conclusive" proof is a claim made by someone who disagrees with the implications of the conclusion.

Few if any judgments of causality or danger are ever conclusive, and a requirement of conclusiveness is much more rhetorical device than analytical method. We therefore reject the suggestion that a causal link must be proved "conclusively" before we can identify a harm.

The opposite extreme is also easily dismissed. The fact that someone makes an assertion of fact to us is not necessarily sufficient proof of that fact, even if the assertion remains uncontradicted. We do not operate as a judge sitting in a court of law, and we require more evidence to reach an affirmative conclusion than does a judge whose sole function might in some circumstances be to determine if there is sufficient evidence to send the case to the jury. That there is a bit of evidence for a proposition is not the same as saying that the proposition has been established, and we do not reach causal conclusions in every instance in which there has been some evidence of that proposition.

Between these extremes the issues are more difficult. The reason for this is that how much proof is required is largely a function of what is to be done with an affirmative finding, and what the consequences are of proceeding on the basis of an affirmative finding. As we deal with causal assertions short of conclusive but more than merely some trifle of evidence, we have felt free to rely on less proof merely to make assertions about harm then [sic] we have required to recommend legal restrictions, and similarly we have required greater confidence in our assertions if the result was to recommend criminal penalties for a given form of behavior than we did to recommend other forms of legal restriction. [. . .]

[. . .]

5.1.4   *The Problem of Multiple Causation*

The world is complex, and most consequences are "caused" by numerous factors. Are highway deaths caused by failure to wear seat belts, failure of the automobile companies to install airbags, failure of the government to require automobile companies to install airbags, alcohol, judicial leniency towards drunk drivers, speeding, and so on and on? Is heart disease caused by cigarette smoking, obesity, stress, or excess animal fat in our diets? As with most other questions of this type, the answers can only be "all of the above," and so too with the problem of pornography. We have concluded, for example, that some forms of sexually explicit material bear a causal relationship both to sexual violence and to sex discrimination, but we are hardly so naive as to suppose that were these forms of pornography to disappear the problems of sex discrimination and sexual violence would come to an end.

If this is so, then what does it mean to identify a causal relationship? It means that the evidence supports the conclusion that if there were none of the material being tested, then the incidence of the consequences would be less. We live in a world of multiple causation, and to identify a factor as a cause in such a world means only that if this factor were eliminated while everything else stayed the same then the problem would at least be lessened. [. . .]

[. . .]

5.1.5   The Varieties of Evidence

We have looked at a wide range of types of evidence. Some has come from personal experience of witnesses, some from professionals whose orientation is primarily clinical, some from experimental social scientists, and some from other forms of empirical science. We have not categorically refused to consider any type of evidence, choosing instead to hear it all, consider it all, and give it the weight we believe in the final analysis it deserves. No form of evidence has been useless to us, and no form is without flaws. A few words about the advantages and disadvantages of various types of evidence may help to put into perspective the conclusions we reach and the basis on which we reach them.

Most controversial has been the evidence we have received from numerous people claiming to be victims of pornography, and reporting in some way on personal experiences relating to pornography. In later portions of this Report concerned with victimization and with the performers in pornographic material we discuss this evidence in more detail. We have considered this first-hand testimony, much of it provided at great personal sacrifice, quite useful, but it is important to note that not all of the first-hand testimony has been of the same type.

Some of the first-hand testimony has come from users of pornography, and a number of witnesses have told us how they became "addicted" to pornography, or how they were led to commit sex crimes as a result of exposure to pornographic materials. Although we have not totally disregarded the evidence that has come from offenders, in many respects it was less valuable than other victim evidence and other evidence in general. Much research supports the tendency of people to externalize their own problems by looking too easily for some external source beyond their own control. As with more extensive studies based on self-reports of sex offenders, evidence relying on what an offender thought caused his problem is likely to so overstate the external and so understate the internal as to be of less value to us than other evidence.

Most of the people who have testified about personal experiences, however, have not been at any point offenders, but rather have been women reporting on what men in their lives have done to them or to their children as a result of exposure to certain sexually explicit materials. As we explained in the introduction, we do not deceive ourselves into thinking that the sample before us is an accurate statistical reflection of the state of the world. Too many factors tended to place before us testimony that was by and large in the same direction and concentrated on those who testified about the presence rather than the absence of consequences. Nevertheless, as long as one does not draw statistical or percentage conclusions from this evidence, and we have not, it can still be important with respect to identification and description of a phenomenon. [. . .]

[. . .]

The problems of statistical generalization diminish drastically when we look to the findings of empirical social science. Here the attempt is to identify factors across a larger population, and thus many of the difficulties associated with any form of anecdotal evidence drop out when the field of inquiry is either an entire population, some large but relevant subset of a population, or an experimental group selected under some reliable sampling method.

Some of the evidence of this variety is correlational. If there is some positive statistical correlation between the prevalence of some type of material and some harmful act, then it is at least established that the two occur together more than one would expect merely from random intersection of totally independent variables. Some of the correlational evidence is less "scientific" than others, but we refuse to discount evidence merely because the researcher did not have some set of academic qualifications. For example, we have heard much evidence from law enforcement personnel that a disproportionate number of sex offenders were found to have large quantities of pornographic material in their residences. Pornographic material was found on the premises more, in the opinion of the witnesses, than one would expect to find it in the residences of a random sample of the population as a whole, in the residences of a random sample of non-offenders of the same sex, age, and socioeconomic status, or in the residences of a random sample of offenders whose offenses were not sex offenses. To the extent that we believe these witnesses, then there is a correlation between pornographic material and sex offenses. [. . .]

Correlational evidence suffers from its inability to establish a causal connection between the correlated phenomena. It is frequently the case that two phenomena are positively correlated precisely because they are both caused by some third phenomena.

We recognize, therefore, that a positive correlation between pornography and sex offenses does not itself establish a causal connection between the two. It may be that some other factor, some sexual or emotional imbalance, for example, might produce both excess use of pornographic materials as well as a tendency to commit sex offenses. But the fact that correlational evidence cannot definitively establish causality does not mean that it may not be some evidence of causality, and we have treated it as such.

[. . .]

The difficulty with experimental evidence [. . .] however, is that it is virtually impossible to conduct control group experiments outside of a laboratory setting. As a result, most of the experiments are conducted on those who can be induced to be subjects in such experiments, usually college age males taking psychology courses. Even a positive result, therefore, is a positive result only, in the narrowest sense, for a population like the experimental group. [. . .]

[. . .]

5.2 Our Conclusions About Harm

We present in the following sections our conclusions regarding the harms we have investigated with respect to the various subdividing categories we have found most useful. [. . .]

5.2.1 Sexually Violent Material

The category of material on which most of the evidence has focused is the category of material featuring actual or unmistakably simulated or unmistakably threatened violence presented in sexually explicit fashion with a predominant focus on the sexually explicit violence. Increasingly, the most prevalent forms of pornography, as well as an increasingly prevalent body of less sexually explicit material, fit this description. Some of this material involves sado-masochistic themes, with the standard accoutrements of the genre, including whips, chains, devices of torture, and so on. But another theme of some of this material is not sado-masochistic, but involves instead the recurrent theme of a man making some sort of sexual advance to a woman, being rebuffed, and then raping the woman or in some other way violently forcing himself on the woman. In almost all of this material, whether in magazine or motion picture form, the woman eventually becomes aroused and ecstatic about the initially forced sexual activity, and usually is portrayed as begging for more. There is also a large body of material, more "mainstream" in its availability, that portrays sexual activity or sexually suggestive nudity coupled with extreme violence, such as disfigurement or murder. The so-called "slasher" films fit this description, as does some material, both in films and in magazines, that is less or more sexually explicit than the prototypical "slasher" film.

[. . .]

When clinical and experimental research has focused particularly on sexually violent material, the conclusions have been virtually unanimous. In both clinical and experimental settings, exposure to sexually violent materials has indicated an increase in the likelihood of aggression. More specifically, the research, which is described in much detail later in this Report, shows a causal relationship between exposure to material of this type and aggressive behavior towards women.

Finding a link between aggressive behavior towards women and sexual violence, whether lawful or unlawful, requires assumptions not found exclusively in the experimental evidence. We see no reason, however, not to make these assumptions. The assumption that increased aggressive behavior towards women is causally related, for an aggregate population, to increased sexual violence is significantly supported by the clinical evidence, as well as by much of the less scientific evidence.[2] They are also to all of us assumptions that are plainly justified by our own common sense. This is not to say that all people with heightened levels of aggression will commit acts of sexual violence. But it is to say that over a sufficiently large number of cases we are confident in asserting that an increase in aggressive behavior directed at women will cause an increase in the level of sexual violence directed at women.

Thus we reach our conclusions by combining the results of the research with highly justifiable assumptions about the generalizability of more limited research results. Since the clinical and experimental evidence supports the conclusion that there is a causal relationship between exposure to sexually violent materials and an increase in aggressive behavior directed towards women, and since we believe that an increase in aggressive behavior towards women will in a population increase the incidence of sexual violence in that population, we have reached the conclusion, unanimously and confidently, that the available evidence strongly supports the hypothesis that substantial exposure to sexually violent materials as described here bears a causal relationship to antisocial acts of sexual violence and, for some subgroups, possibly to unlawful acts of sexual violence.

[. . .]

Sexual violence is not the only negative effect reported in the research to result from substantial exposure to sexually violent materials. The evidence is also strongly supportive of significant attitudinal changes on the part of those with substantial exposure to violent pornography. These attitudinal changes are numerous. Victims of rape and other forms of sexual violence are likely to be perceived by people so exposed as more responsible for the assault, as having suffered less injury, and as having been less degraded as a result of the experience. Similarly, people with a substantial exposure to violent pornography are likely to see the rapist or other sexual offender as less responsible for the act and as deserving of less stringent punishment.

These attitudinal changes have been shown experimentally to include a larger range of attitudes than those just discussed. The evidence also strongly supports the conclusion that substantial exposure to violent sexually explicit material leads to a greater acceptance of the "rape myth" in its broader sense – that women enjoy being coerced into sexual activity, that they enjoy being physically hurt in sexual context, and that as a result a man who forces himself on a woman sexually is in fact merely acceding to the "real" wishes of the woman, regardless of the extent to which she seems to be resisting. The myth is that a woman who says "no" really means "yes," and that men are justified in acting on the assumption that the "no" answer is indeed the "yes" answer. We have little trouble concluding that this attitude is both pervasive and profoundly harmful, and that any stimulus reinforcing or increasing the incidence of this attitude is for that reason alone properly designated as harmful.

[. . .]

5.2.2 Nonviolent Materials Depicting Degradation, Domination, Subordination, or Humiliation

Current research has rather consistently separated out violent pornography, the class of materials we have just discussed, from other sexually explicit materials. With respect to further subdivision the process has been less consistent. A few researchers have made further distinctions, while most have merely classed everything else as "non-violent." We have concluded that more subdivision than that is necessary. Our examination of the variety of sexually explicit materials convinces us that once again the category of "non-violent" ignores significant distinctions within this category, and thus combines classes of material that are in fact substantially different.

The subdivision we adopt is one that has surfaced in some of the research. And it is also one that might explain a significant amount of what would otherwise seem to be conflicting research results. Some researchers have found negative effects from non-violent material, while others report no such negative effects. But when the stimulus material these researchers have used is considered, there is some suggestion that the presence or absence of negative effects from non-violent material might turn on the non-violent material being considered "degrading," a term we shall explain shortly.[3] It appears that effects similar to although not as extensive as that involved with violent material can be identified with respect to such degrading material, but that these effects are likely absent when neither degradation nor violence is present.

An enormous amount of the most sexually explicit material available, as well as much of the material that is somewhat less sexually explicit, is material that we would characterize as "degrading," the term we use to encompass the undeniably linked characteristics of degradation, domination, subordination, and humiliation. The degradation we refer to is degradation of people, most often women, and here we are referring to material that, although not violent, depicts[4] people, usually women, as existing solely for the sexual satisfaction of others, usually men, or that depicts people, usually women, in decidedly subordinate roles in their sexual relations with others, or that depicts people engaged in sexual practices that would to most people be considered humiliating. Indeed, forms of degradation represent the largely predominant proportion of commercially available pornography.

With respect to material of this variety, our conclusions are substantially similar to those with respect to violent material, although we make them with somewhat less confidence and our making of them requires more in the way of assumption than was the case with respect to violent material. The evidence, scientific and otherwise, is more tentative, but supports the conclusion that the material we describe as degrading bears some causal relationship to the attitudinal changes we have previously identified. That is, substantial exposure to material of this variety is likely to increase the extent to which those exposed will view rape or other forms of sexual violence as less serious than they otherwise would have, will view the victims of rape and other forms of sexual violence as significantly more responsible, and will view the offenders as significantly less responsible. We also conclude that the evidence supports the conclusion that substantial exposure to material of this type will increase acceptance of the proposition that women like to be forced into sexual practices, and, once again, that the woman who says no really means "yes."

[. . .]

We should make clear what we have concluded here. We are not saying that everyone exposed to material of this type has his attitude about sexual violence changed. We are saying only that the evidence supports the conclusion that substantial exposure to degrading material increases the likelihood for an individual and the incidence over a large population that these attitudinal changes will occur. And we are not saying that everyone with these attitudes will commit an act of sexual violence or sexual coercion. We are saying that such attitudes will increase the likelihood for an individual and the incidence for a population that acts of sexual violence, sexual coercion, or unwanted sexual aggression will occur. Thus, we conclude that substantial exposure to materials of this type bears some causal relationship to the level of sexual violence, sexual coercion, or unwanted sexual aggression in the population so exposed.

[. . .]

5.2.3 Non-Violent and Non-Degrading Materials

Our most controversial category has been the category of sexually explicit materials that are not violent and are not degrading as we have used that term. They are materials in which the participants appear to be fully willing participants occupying substantially equal roles in a setting devoid of actual or apparent violence or pain. This category is in fact quite small in terms of currently available materials. There is some, to be sure, and the amount may increase as the division between the degrading and the non-degrading becomes more accepted; but we are convinced that only a small amount of currently available

highly sexually explicit material is neither violent nor degrading. We thus talk about a small category, but one that should not be ignored.

We have disagreed substantially about the effects of such materials, and that should come as no surprise. We are dealing in this category with "pure" sex, as to which there are widely divergent views in this society. That we have disagreed among ourselves does little more than reflect the extent to which we are representative of the population as a whole. In light of that disagreement, it is perhaps more appropriate to explain the various views rather than indicate a unanimity that does not exist, within this Commission or within society, or attempt the preposterous task of saying that some fundamental view about the role of sexuality and portrayals of sexuality was accepted or defeated by such-and-such vote. We do not wish to give easy answers to hard questions, and thus feel better with describing the diversity of opinion rather than suppressing part of it.

In examining the material in this category, we have not had the benefit of extensive evidence. Research has only recently begun to distinguish the non-violent but degrading from material that is neither violent nor degrading, and we have all relied on a combination of interpretation of existing studies that may not have drawn the same divisions, studies that did draw these distinctions, clinical evidence, interpretation of victim testimony, and our own perceptions of the effect of images on human behavior. Although the social science evidence is far from conclusive, we are on the current state of the evidence persuaded that material of this type does not bear a causal relationship to rape and other acts of sexual violence. We rely once again not only on scientific studies outlined later in the Report, and examined by each of us, but on the fact that the conclusions of these studies seem to most of us fully consistent with common sense. Just as materials depicting sexual violence seem intuitively likely to bear a causal relationship to sexual violence, materials containing no depictions or suggestions of sexual violence or sexual dominance seem to most of us intuitively unlikely to bear a causal relationship to sexual violence. [. . .]

That there does not appear from the social science evidence to be a causal link with sexual violence, however, does not answer the question of whether such materials might not themselves simply for some other reason constitute a harm in themselves, or bear a causal link to consequences other than sexual violence but still taken to be harmful. And it is here that we and society at large have the greatest differences of opinion.

One issue relates to materials that, although undoubtedly consensual and equal, depict sexual practices frequently condemned in this and other societies. In addition, level of societal condemnation varies for different activities; some activities are condemned by some people, but not by others. We have discovered that to some significant extent the assessment of the harmfulness of materials depicting such activities correlates directly with the assessment of the harmfulness of the activities themselves. Intuitively and not experimentally, we can hypothesize that materials portraying such an activity will either help to legitimize or will bear some causal relationship to that activity itself. With respect to these materials, therefore, it appears that a conclusion about the harmfulness of these materials turns on a conclusion about the harmfulness of the activity itself. As to this, we are unable to agree with respect to many of these activities. Our differences reflect differences now extant in society at large, and actively debated, and we can hardly resolve them here.

A larger issue is the very question of promiscuity. Even to the extent that the behavior depicted is not inherently condemned by some or any of us, the manner of presentation almost necessarily suggests that the activities are taking place outside of the context of marriage, love, commitment, or even affection. Again, it is far from implausible to hypothesize that materials depicting sexual activity without marriage, love, commitment, or affection bear some causal relationship to sexual activity without marriage, love, commitment, or affection. There are undoubtedly many causes for what used to be called the "sexual revolution," but it is absurd to suppose that depictions or descriptions of uncommitted sexuality were not among them.[5]

Thus, once again our disagreements reflect disagreements in society at large, although not to as great an extent. Although there are many members of this society who can and have made affirmative cases for uncommitted sexuality, none of us believes it to be a good thing. A number of us, however, believe that the level of commitment in sexuality is a matter of choice among those who voluntarily engage in the activity. Others of us believe that uncommitted sexual activity is wrong for the individuals involved and harmful to society to the extent of its prevalence. Our view of the ultimate harmfulness of much of this material, therefore, is reflective of our individual views about the extent to whether sexual commitment is purely a matter of individual choice.

Even insofar as sexually explicit material of the variety being discussed here is not perceived as harmful for the messages it carries or the symbols it represents, the very publicness of what is commonly taken to be private is cause for concern.[6] Even if we hypothesize a sexually explicit notion picture of a loving married couple engaged in mutually pleasurable and procreative vaginal intercourse, the depiction of that act on a screen or in a magazine may constitute a harm in its own right (a "primary harm" in the terminology introduced earlier in this Chapter) solely by virtue of being shown. Here the concern is with the preservation of sex as an essentially private act, in conformity with the basic privateness of sex long recognized by this and all other societies. The alleged harm here, therefore, is that as soon as sex is put on a screen or put in a magazine it changes its character, regardless of what variety of sex is portrayed. And to the extent that the character of sex as public rather than private is the consequence here, then that to many would constitute a harm.

[. . .]

Perhaps the most significant potential harm in this category exists with respect to children. We all agree that at least much, probably most, and maybe even all material in this category, regardless of whether it is harmful when used by adults only, is harmful when it falls into the hands of children. Exposure to sexuality is commonly taken, and properly so, to be primarily the responsibility of the family. Even those who would disagree with this statement would still prefer to have early exposure to sexuality be in the hands of a responsible professional in a controlled and guided setting. We have no hesitancy in concluding that learning about sexuality from most of the material in this category is not the best way for children to learn about the subject. There are harms both to the children themselves and to notions of family control over a child's introduction to sexuality if children learn about sex from the kinds of sexually explicit materials that constitute the bulk of this category of materials.

[. . .]

Perhaps the largest question, and for that reason the question we can hardly touch here, is the question of harm as it relates to the moral environment of a society. There is no doubt that numerous laws, taboos, and other social practices all serve to enforce some forms of shared moral assessment. The extent to which this enforcement should be enlarged, the extent to which sexual morality is a necessary component of a society's moral environment, and the appropriate balance between recognition of individual choice and the necessity of maintaining some sense of community in a society are questions that have been debated for generations. [. . .]

Thus, with respect to the materials in this category, there are areas of agreement and areas of disagreement. We unanimously agree that the material in this category in some settings and when used for some purposes can be harmful. None of us think that the material in this category, individually or as a class, is in every instance harmless. And to the extent that some of the materials in this category are largely educational or undeniably artistic, we unanimously agree that they are little cause for concern if not made available to children are [sic] foisted on unwilling viewers. But most of the materials in this category would not now be taken to be explicitly educational or artistic, and as to this balance of materials our disagreements are substantial. [. . .]

5.3   The Need for Further Research

Although we have mentioned it throughout this report, it is appropriate here to emphasize specially the importance of further research by professionals into the potential and actual harms we have discussed in this Chapter. We are confident that the quality and quantity of research far surpasses that available in 1970, but we also believe that the research remains in many respects unsystematic and unfocused. There is still a great deal to be done. In many respects research is still at a fairly rudimentary stage, with few attempts to standardize categories of analysis, self-reporting questionnaires, types of stimulus materials, description of stimulus materials, measurement of effects, and related problems.

[. . .]

Notes

1   With respect to the general issue of condemnation, and especially with respect to the condemnation of specific materials by name, our role as a government commission is somewhat more problematic. At some point governmental condemnation may act effectively as governmental restraint (see, Bantam Books, Inc. v. Sullivan, 372 U.S. 58 (1963), and we are therefore more cautious in condemning specific publications by name than citizens need be. This caution, however, does not mean that we feel that governmental agencies may not properly condemn even that which they cannot control. We feel that we have both the right and the duty to condemn, in some cases, that which is properly constitutionally protected, but we do so with more caution

2   For example, the evidence from formal or informal studies of self-reports of offenders themselves supports the conclusion that the causal connection we identify relates to actual sexual offenses rather than merely to aggressive behavior. For reasons we have explained in Section 5.1.5, the tendency to externalize leads us to give evidence of this variety rather little weight. But at the very least it does not point in the opposite direction from the conclusions reached here.

3   For example, the studies of Dr. Zillmann regarding nonviolent material, studies that have been particularly influential for some of us, use material that contain the following themes: "He is ready to take. She is ready to be taken. This active/passive differentiation that coincides with gender is stated on purpose." Women are portrayed as "masochistic, subservient, socially nondiscriminating nymphomaniacs." Dr. Zillmann goes on to characterize this material as

involving mutual consent and no *coercion*, but also describes the films as ones in which "women tend to overrespond in serving the male interest."

4   We restrict our analysis in large part to degradation that is in fact depicted in the material. It may very well be that degradation led to a woman being willing to pose for a picture of a certain variety, or to engage in what appears to be a non-degrading sexual act. It may be that coercion caused the picture to exist. And it may very well be that the existing disparity in the economic status of men and women is such that any sexually explicit depiction of a woman is at least suspect on account of the possibility that the economic disparity is what caused the woman to pose for a picture that most people in this society would find embarrassing. We do not deny any of these possibilities, and we do not deny the importance of considering as pervasively as possible the status of women in contemporary America, including the effects of their current status and what might be done to change some of the detrimental consequences of that status. But without engaging in an inquiry of that breadth, we must generally, absent more specific evidence to the contrary, assume that a picture represents what it depicts.

5   Nor, of course, do we deny the extent that the phenomenon, in part, also goes the other way. Sexually explicit materials in most cases seem both to reflect and to cause demand.

6   The concerns summarized here are articulated more fully in a statement that expresses the views of a number of individual members of this Commission.

The Findings and Recommendations of the Attorney General's Commission on Pornography: Do the Psychological "Facts" Fit the Political Fury?

Daniel Linz, Edward Donnerstein, and Steven Penrod

Summary

Argues that several of the Attorney General's Commission findings are flawed and relied on faulty extrapolations from social science research or relied on faulty research itself. Several studies are analyzed and in particular the claim that social harm is especially related to sexually explicit material (as distinct from non-sexual sexist and degrading images) is criticized.

Original publication details: Daniel Linz, Edward Donnerstein and Steven Penrod, "The Findings and Recommendations of the Attorney General's Commission on Pornography: Do the Psychological 'Facts' Fit the Political Fury?" pp. 946–953 from *American Psychologist* 42 (1987). Reproduced with permission of American Psychological Association.

[...]

The Attorney General's Commission on Pornography was charged by the President of the United States with the responsibility to "review . . . the available empirical evidence on the relationship between exposure to pornographic materials and antisocial behavior" and to explore "possible roles and initiatives that the Department of Justice and agencies of local, State, and federal government could pursue in controlling, consistent with constitutional guarantees, the production and distribution of pornography" (*Attorney General's Commission on Pornography*, 1986, p. 216).

During the course of several hearings at various locations across the country, the commission examined the nature of the pornography industry and the social, moral, political, and scientific implications of regulating that industry.

As a result of these hearings, the Commission recommended that existing obscenity statutes be expanded (for example, by amending the federal obscenity laws to prohibit the transmission of obscene material over the telephone and by eliminating the "utterly without redeeming social value" clause found in some state obscenity statutes). In all, the commission made 92 recommendations. These recommendations primarily involved changes in existing federal, state, and local obscenity laws, although some recommendations for mental health agencies and suggestions for future research were also included. Without exception, the recommendations for legal changes called for greater restrictions on sexually explicit material and more stringent enforcement of current obscenity law.

Compared to the 1970 Presidential Commission on Obscenity and Pornography (*Report of the Commission*, 1970), the 1986 commission was severely constrained by limited financial resources and time. Consequently, the final report is far from being a well-polished document reflecting a concise and unified point of view: It begins with a 200-page compendium of opinions by individual members of the commission, followed by a 210-page summary report that attempts to cover the main areas of inquiry and presumably represents the collective opinions of the commission members. The remaining 1,500 pages are devoted to legal recommendations; special sections on the victimization of women and children by pornography users; written descriptions of imagery found in magazines, books, and films in "adults only" pornographic outlets; and other topics.

Of greatest importance to psychologists is the summary report (pp. 215–429), especially chapter 5, "The Question of Harm" (pp. 299–351) and the detailed description of individual studies on the effects of pornography (pp. 901–1035) that accompany it. The commission relied heavily on this research in reaching conclusions about harm. The largest part of our commentary will focus on the commission's interpretation of this research.

[...]

Pornography and Harm

The commission attempted to distinguish between primary and secondary harms emanating from pornography, that is, between the alleged harm to consumers of pornography and the possibility that exposure to pornography will lead to harm of another person. In the commission's opinion, pornography's greatest potential for harm lies in the corruption of the individual.

> To a number of us, the most important harms must be seen in moral terms, and the act of moral condemnation of that which is immoral is not merely important but essential. From this perspective there are acts that need be seen not only as causes of immorality but as manifestations of it (p. 303).

Social science research can do little to inform decision makers about this issue other than to provide normative data (e.g., information obtained via public opinion polls) concerning beliefs and attitudes toward obscenity and pornography. The commission acknowledged that social science has relatively little to offer in this regard but reasserted that "issues of human dignity and human decency, no less real for their lack of scientific measurability, are for many of us central to thinking about the question of harm" (p. 303).

The commission considered four types of evidence for harmful effects other than immediate moral ones: individual accounts of victimization that was allegedly the result of pornography, clinical professional accounts of client victimization, correlational studies suggesting a relation between the prevalence of pornography and sexual assault arrest rates, and social psychological laboratory experiments. Despite reports to the contrary (e.g., Scott & Cuvelier; in press), the commission went to great lengths to enumerate the advantages and disadvantages of each source of information, was duly cautious about reliance on anecdotal evidence and individual case reports by clinicians, and was sensitive even to the problems of inferring causality from correlational evidence. The commission explicitly stated that it was most

Daniel Linz, Edward Donnerstein, and Steven Penrod

convinced by the findings of laboratory experiments that manipulated subjects' exposure to various forms of sexually explicit material, although the report made it dear that some of the conclusions were based on extrapolations from this form of social science research, bolstered by both the other forms of evidence and personal opinion. In the main, however, the commission contended that, to a significant extent, its conclusions were based on findings from the social sciences.

The commission divided pornography into four categories and attempted to assess the harms associated with each subtype, as follows: (a) sexually violent material; (b) nonviolent materials depicting degradation, domination, subordination, or humiliation; (c) nonviolent and non-degrading materials; and (d) nudity. We will discuss each of these categories, both in terms of the commission's interpretation of the applicable research findings and our assessment of these interpretations.

Sexually Violent Pornography

The Commission defined violent pornography as that which features actual or simulated violence within a sexually explicit context The commission placed its highest priority on regulating sexually violent materials, as follows:

> We would urge that prosecution of obscene materials that portray sexual violence be treated as a matter of special urgency. With respect to sexually violent materials the evidence is strongest, societal consensus is greatest, and the consequent harms of rape and other forms of sexual violence are hardly ones that this or any other society can take lightly. In light of this, we would urge that the prosecution of legally obscene material that contains violence be placed at the top of both state and federal priorities in enforcing the obscenity laws (pp. 376–377).

[. . .]

Causal Relation Between Pornography and Aggression

Irrespective of any alleged increase in violent pornography in recent years, the commission maintained that there is a "causal relationship" between exposure to sexually violent pornography and negative changes in certain attitudes toward and perceptions of women, as well as increased aggression toward women. This is an accurate

statement as long as we are referring to the results of laboratory studies examining sexually violent images. In the typical study male subjects are first exposed to depictions that show the female victim "enjoying" or reacting in a positive fashion to her mistreatment and then are asked to report on their attitudes and beliefs about rape victims and/or to administer electric shocks or other forms of "punishment" to a female victim. The results of these studies have generally indicated that male subjects exposed to sexual violence of this sort (a) show changes in the perception of a rape victim (e.g., seeing her as less injured and more responsible for her assault), (b) see a rapist as less responsible for his actions and as deserving less punishment, (c) show greater acceptance of certain "rape myths," and (d) behave more aggressively toward a female target than control subjects. Depictions involving victims who abhor their experience can often produce similar outcomes in a subpopulation of males exposed to these materials (for a review of these findings see Donnerstein & Linz, 1986; Donnerstein, Linz, & Penrod, 1987; Linz, Donnerstein, & Penrod, 1987; Malamuth & Donnerstein, 1982, 1984).

However, there are at least two important considerations that should be borne in mind when applying the results of these social psychological experiments to legal decision making about pornography and obscenity. The first involves the question of whether the changes in attitudes and behaviors following exposure to sexually violent material are a function of both the violence in depiction and the "pornographic" nature of the material per se (i.e., the fact that the material contains sexually explicit images), or are due primarily to messages about violence against women regardless of sexual explicitness. The second consideration is a methodological qualification and involves the familiar critiques of laboratory investigations of aggressive behavior.

Is Sexual Explicitness Necessary for the Effects to Occur?

Depictions of women "enjoying" the application of force and of women as the deserved victims of sexual and non-sexual violence are pervasive in the mass media. As we noted earlier at least one content analysis (Palys, 1986) has suggested that nonpornographic videos include more depictions in which at least one participant did not engage in sex freely or in which overt aggression was involved than did the X videos. There is also evidence from laboratory and field studies that these depictions need not be sexually explicit to have a negative impact.

Malamuth and Check (1981) have found that nonexplicit depictions of sexual violence contained in *The Getaway* (Foster & Brown, 1972), a popular film starring Ali McGraw and Steve McQueen, and another film with similar content negatively influenced the viewers' attitudes toward women. The study demonstrated that viewing the sexually aggressive films significantly increased men's but not women's acceptance of interpersonal violence and tended to increase men's acceptance of cultural stereotypes indicating that women deserve or secretly desire rape.

In a more recent pair of studies, Donnerstein, Berkowitz, and Linz (1986) systematically examined the relative contributions of the aggressive and sexual components of violent pornography. In the first study, male college students were angered by either a male or a female confederate and were then shown one of four different films. The first was similar to the aggressive pornography used in studies discussed earlier. The second was X-rated but contained no aggression or sexual coercion. Subjects rated it just as sexually and physiologically arousing as the first film. The third contained scenes of aggression against women but without any sexual content. Subjects rated it as less sexually and physiologically arousing than the previous two films. The final film contained neutral content.

After viewing the films, the men were given the opportunity to aggress against a male or a female confederate of the experimenter. The results showed that the men who viewed the aggressive pornographic film displayed the highest level of aggression against the woman, but the aggression-only film, which was devoid of explicit sex, produced more aggression against the woman than the sexually explicit film that contained no violence or coercion. In fact, there were no differences in aggression against the female target for subjects in the sex-only film condition and the neutral film condition. In the second study, subjects who viewed the combination of sex and violence showed higher levels of aggressive behavior than subjects in the sex-only group; under certain conditions (i.e., being angered), subjects exposed to the violence-only depiction also exhibited higher levels of aggression than the sex-only group.

These studies strongly suggest that the material shown to subjects need not attain a level of sexual explicitness anything like that which would be judged obscene or pornographic by virtually any standard in order to find harmful effects. This is not to say, of course, that exposure to violent pornography does not result in similar negative effects. The important point is that much of the

evidence for stating that sexually violent pornography is harmful is based on studies that have used materials that either confounded sexual explicitness and violence (e.g., Donnerstein & Borkowitz, 1981) or materials that were not sexually explicit (e.g., Malamuth & Check, 1981).

[. . .]

This would appear to make the commission's ultimate focus on pornography as a causal factor in sexually violent behavior and its subsequent recommendations for tighter legal control of pornography somewhat misplaced. Reliance on studies that have found harmful effects resulting from materials that would not be considered pornographic would seem to pose a logical dilemma for a commission devoted to the examination of the harmful effects that can be attributed uniquely to pornography. The results of these studies imply that both violent pornography *and* less sexually explicit depictions may produce nontrivial changes in attitudes and behaviors. To remain true to the specific stimuli used by experimenters and to the findings of their experiments, a more general emphasis on the potentially harmful effects of depictions of violence against women (sexually explicit or not) would have been more appropriate.

Generalizations From Laboratory Experiments

In addition to the problems associated with the fact that many of the experimental studies on which the commission based its findings did not employ obscene or pornographic stimuli, the commission also failed to exercise proper caution in generalizing the results of these studies to sexual violence outside the laboratory. Despite the higher level of causal certainty accorded the laboratory experiment relative to other forms of investigation, laboratory assessments of the media's effects on behavior, particularly in relation to the violence prevalent in mass media programming, are susceptible to many criticisms concerning external validity (Krattenmaker & Powe, 1978). Other authors have addressed these problems at length (see Freedman, 1984, 1986; Fredrich-Cofer & Huston, 1986), and we will not repeat their concerns here. We note only that the commission should at least have acknowledged a few of the most important of these criticisms, as follows: (a) Laboratory subjects may not really perceive themselves as inflicting harm when experimenters ask them to perform very artificial forms of aggression in their interactions with a confederate; (b) outside the laboratory people are sanctioned for violence, whereas in the laboratory aggression is condoned, even encouraged, after the subject has viewed violent material;

Daniel Linz, Edward Donnerstein, and Steven Penrod

(c) all the studies examined subjects from a very narrow segment of the general population; (d) laboratory experiments may be generally susceptible to what has been termed an "experimenter demand effect," wherein subjects attempt to guess and then confirm the experimenter's hypothesis; (e) usually only studies that obtain positive results are published; and (f) no one yet has been able to come up with either an acceptable operational definition of aggressive behavior on the part of the subject who is supposedly reacting to the film or other media event, or an acceptable definition of what actually constitutes violence in the media depiction itself.

[. . .]

Nonviolent and Degrading Pornography

This category of material, according to the commission, includes images that are nonviolent but depict (a) women in subordinate roles, (b) women existing just for the sexual satisfaction of others, or (c) sexual practices that most people would consider humiliating. With respect to the harmful effects of these materials, the commission asserted that the results of viewing this material are similar to those obtained from exposure to sexually violent depictions. To their credit, the commission drew these conclusions with "less confidence" because, as they pointed out, the scientific evidence is more tentative. We are compelled to say not only that the evidence is tentative with respect to these materials but also very inconsistent.

The commission stated that substantial exposure to this material will (a) lead individuals to view rape as less serious, (b) encourage individuals to view rape victims as more responsible for their plight and (c) increase the likelihood that men will say they would "force" women into sexual practices. We can find no consistent evidence for these specific conclusions. Only one study has found that long-term exposure to this type of material changes an individual's perceptions of a rape victim (Zillmann & Bryant 1982). But later studies with both male and female viewers have not replicated these findings (Krafka, 1985; Linz, 1985). Furthermore, only one study has found changes in subjects' willingness to say they would use force with a woman in order to have sex. This study, conducted by Check (1984), involved several methodological procedures that prevent us from placing as much confidence in the outcome of the experiment as we would like (e.g., subjects were recruited through newspaper advertisements rather than being sampled from some specified population; subjects in this experiment were told that the

evaluations of pornography they would be giving in the study would be used by the Parliament of Canada to help decide policy on the issue of pornography; and the time periods during which subjects viewed the stimulus material and the interval between the last pornographic film presentation and completion of the dependent measures varied nonrandomly across subjects). Finally, both Zillmann and Bryant's (1982) and Check's (1984) studies used a series of sexually explicit excerpts either taken from stag films or abstracted from feature-length X-rated films. The studies by Linz (1985) and Krafka (1985), which failed to produce similar findings, relied primarily on full-length film presentations.

In addition to changes in attitudes and perceptions, the commission also concluded that exposure to this type of material bears some causal relation to sexually violent behavior. Although it is not entirely clear from the text of the report, this conclusion is apparently based on the commission's interpretation of the research reported by Zillmann and Bryant (1982), described earlier, that suggested that exposure to degrading pornography results in callous attitudes about rape and research indicating a relation between certain rape-related attitudes and self-reported acts of sexual aggression (Malamuth, 1986). We will briefly describe the Malamuth experiment and then indicate what we feel is problematic about combining the results of these two independently conducted studies to arrive at the conclusion that sexually degrading pornography causes sexual violence.

Malamuth (1986) has conducted a study that suggests that certain callous attitudes about rape, sexual arousal to rape depictions, and other antisocial characteristics are predictive of self-reported sexual aggression. Male subjects in this study were assessed for dominance as a sexual motive, hostility toward women, the acceptance of interpersonal violence, and psychoticism (Eysenck & Eysenck, 1976). Next, Malamuth measured subjects' sexual arousal to both rape and consensual sex audio depictions. He then constructed a rape index from these measures (penile tumescence while listening to the rape story relative to a consenting story). Self-reports of sexual aggression assessed via an inventory developed by Koss and Oros (1982) were then regressed on all these measures. The results of this study indicated that nearly all of these, except antisocial characteristics, were correlated with self-reports of sexual aggression.

The commission appeared to make the assumption that because callous attitudes about rape are correlated with self-reported acts of aggression, and sexually degrading pornography results in callous attitudes about

352

rape, that there must be a *direct* relation between degrading pornography and acts of sexual aggression. As we have indicated earlier; the first problem with this reasoning is that it has not been consistently demonstrated that callous attitudes about rape result from exposure to degrading but nonviolent sexual material. However, even if there were an unequivocal relation between exposure to degrading pornography and negative attitudes about women in one study and evidence for a relation between similar attitudes and self-reported sexual violence in another study, we still could not conclude that degrading pornography increases violent behavior. Ideally, to conclude that degrading pornography influences negative attitudes, which then in turn affect behavior, we would need to show these relations in the same experimental study on a single sample of subjects. Such an experimental study is, of course, ethically impossible to conduct.

Barring this approach, at least a longitudinal study needs to be undertaken in which both attitudes and violent behaviors are measured in the same individuals. Even this approach would lack the causal certainty inherent in an experiment. Additional experimental studies of interventions designed to reduce violence against women and that would have implications for understanding the causes of violent behavior would need to be undertaken before any scientifically valid conclusions could be reached. These studies have not been conducted to date. (For further discussion of these issues see Malamuth & Briere, 1986.)

[. . .]

Summary

It seems to us that the legal recommendations made by the commission for strengthening obscenity laws do not follow from the data. We should be concerned about the detrimental effects of exposure to violent images both in pornography and *elsewhere* – particularly material that portrays the myth that women enjoy or in some way benefit from rape, torture, or other forms of sexual violence. The portrayal of this theme is not found only in pornography. To single out pornography for more stringent legal action is inappropriate, based on the empirical research. Many mass media depictions portray the same myth even though they contain little explicit sex or are only mildly sexually explicit.

These ideas about rape and sexual violence are so pervasive in our culture that it is shortsighted to call them the exclusive domain of violent pornography, much less the domain of the broader category of legally obscene materials. In fact, one would not have to search further than a local bookstore to find numerous violent murder mysteries that reinforce this point. It is interesting to note that in a recent content analysis of detective magazines, Dietz, Harry, and Hazelwood (1986) found that 76% of the covers depicted domination of women and 38% depicted women in bondage. These magazines are not generally the domain of adult bookstores and have never been considered pornographic or obscene.

Granted, the charter of the commission was to examine the pernicious effects of pornography on society. Granted also that time, money, and other resources of the commission were limited. But it seems appropriate to note that if the commissioners were looking for ways to curb the most nefarious media threat to public welfare, they missed it. It has now been fairly well documented that violent material, whether sexually explicit or not has the potential to promote violent behavior following exposure.

Unfortunately, legal remedies directed at suppressing even these materials would extend into every form of communication, and any laws devised to curb message of violence could be used to suppress other messages of questionable interpretation. Rather than call for stricter laws, we call for a more informed public. Based on the historical record (Penrod & Linz, 1984), we doubt that either pornography or violence is going to disappear from the mass media. Our own inclination has been to explore the possibility of developing educational programs that enable viewers to make wiser choices about the media to which they expose themselves.

[. . .]

References

Attorney General's Commission on Pornography: Final report (1986, July). Washington, DC: U.S. Department of Justice.

Check, J. V. P. (1984). *The effects of violent and nonviolent pornography* (Department of Supply and Services Contract No. 05SV 19200-3-0899). Ottawa. Ontario: Canadian Department of Justice.

Dietz, P. E, Harry, B., & Hazelwood, R. R. (1986). Detective magazines: Pornography for the sexual sadist? *Journal of Forensic Sciences, 31*(1), 197–211.

Donnerstein, E., & Berkowitz, L. (1981). Victim reactions in aggressive erotic films as a factor in violence against women. *Journal of Personality and Social Psychology, 41*, 710–724.

Donnerstein, E., Berkowitz, L., & Linz, D. (1986). *Role of aggressive and sexual images in violent pornography.* Unpublished manuscript, University of Wisconsin–Madison.

Donnerstein, E., & Linz, D. (1986). Mass media sexual violence and male viewers: Current theory and research. *American Behavioral Scientists, 29*(5), 601–618.

Eysenck, H. J., & Eysenck, S. B, G. (1976). *Psychoticism as a dimension of personality.* London: Hodder & Stoughton.

Foster, D., & Brown, M. (Producers), & Peckinpah, S. (Director). (1972). *The getaway* [Film]. Hollywood, CA: National General Pictures.

Fredrich-Cofer, L., & Huston, A. C. (1986). Television violence and aggression: The debate continues. *Psychological Bulletin, 100*, 364–371.

Freedman, J. L. (1984). Effect of television violence on aggressiveness. *Psychological Bulletin, 96*, 227–246.

Freedman, J. L. (1986). Television violence and aggression: A rejoinder. *Psychological Bulletin, 100*, 372–378.

Koss, M., & Oros, C. (1982). Sexual Experiences Survey: A research instrument investigating aggression and victimization. *Journal of Consulting and Clinical Psychology, 50*, 445–457.

Krafka, C. L. (1985). *Sexually explicit, sexually violent, and violent media: Effects of multiple naturalistic exposures and debriefing on female viewers. Unpublished doctoral dissertation. University of Wisconsin–Madison.*

Krattenmaker, T. G., & Powe Jr., L. A. (1978). Televised violence: First Amendment principles and social science. *Virginia Law Review, 64*, 1123–1297.

Linz, D. (1985). Sexual violence in the media: Effects on male viewers and implications for society. Unpublished doctoral dissertation, University of Wisconsin, Madison.

Linz, D., Donnerstein, E., & Penrod, S. (1987). Sexual violence in the mass media: Social psychological implications. In P. Shaver & C. Hendrick (eds.), *Review of Personality and Social Psychology*: Vol. 7. *Sex and gender* (pp. 95–123). Newbury Park, CA: Sage.

Malamuth, N. M. (1986). Predictors of naturalistic sexual aggression. *Journal of Personality and Social Psychology, 50*, 953–962.

Malamuth, N. M., & Briere, J. (1986). Sexual violence in the media: Indirect effects on aggression against women. *Journal of Social Issues, 42*(3), 75–92.

Malamuth, N. M., & Check, J. V. P. (1981). The effects of mass media exposure on acceptance of violence against women: A field experiment. *Journal of Research in Personality, 15*, 436–446.

Malamuth, N. M., & Donnerstein, E. (1982). The effects or aggressive-pornographic mass media stimuli. In L. Berkowitz (ed.), *Advances in Experimental Social Psychology* (Vol. 15, pp. 103–136). New York: Academic Press.

Malamuth, N. M., & Donnerstein, E. (eds.). (1984). *Pornography and sexual aggression,* New York: Academic Press.

Report of the Commission on Obscenity and Pornography (1970). Washington, DC: *U.S. Government Printing Office.*

Zillmann, D., & Bryant, J. (1982). Pornography, sexual callousness, and the trivialization of rape. *Journal of Communication, 32*, 10–21.

Pornography and the First Amendment

Cass R. Sunstein

Summary

Argues that pornography can be legitimately regulated within the existing accepted framework of constitutional free speech protections if the kind of speech it represents is properly understood. Pornography is identifiable as a specific type of speech, it produces significant harms in society, it is a form of "low-value" speech as a result of being far afield of governmental processes and being non-cognitive, it is not singled out for its content viewpoint but rather for its harmful consequences, and it has a chilling effect on others' speech. As low-value speech, pornography is less entitled to government protection than high-value speech in the first place. As harmful speech, government has a legitimate interest in regulating it, as with other forms of low-value and harmful speech such as bribes, threats, advertising, conspiracies, fighting words, slander, and libel.

Original publication details: Cass R. Sunstein, "Pornography and the First Amendment," pp. 589–627 from *Duke Law Journal* 1986: 4 (September). Duke University School of Law. Reproduced with permission of Cass R. Sunstein.

The problem of pornography has reappeared on the national agenda. Feminist approaches to the subject, based on novel arguments and rejecting traditional definitions of "obscenity,"[1] have resulted in legislation in Indianapolis[2] and significant efforts in other cities.[3] The Attorney General's Commission on Pornography has recently supported a national attack on pornography, adopting an amalgam of traditional and feminist objections to sexually explicit materials.[4] Particularly in light of the growth of the pornography industry,[5] the issue seems certain to produce controversy in coming years.[6]

It should not be surprising that discussions of antipornography regulation[7] often refer to Herbert Wechsler's famous essay on neutral principles.[8] Despite the essay's impact on first amendment theory, the notion of neutral principles has never been altogether clear.[9] It is possible, however, to distinguish weak and strong versions of the basic idea.

The weak version requires each judge to undertake an internal Socratic dialogue in order to ensure that a particular decision can be harmonized with other decisions that have been made and that might be made. Thus understood, the notion of neutrality is designed to ensure that judges do not simply implement whatever intuitions they happen to have, but that they order and make coherent those intuitions through reasoning by analogy. Although one might question whether this version of neutral principles imposes sharp constraints on judges, it has in fact been a basis for invalidating recent antipornography legislation.[10]

The strong version of neutral principles is associated, in Wechsler's own formulation, with severe doubt about the correctness of the result in *Brown v. Board of Education*.[11] Under the strong version, judges should not care "whose ox is gored" by a particular result; they should be indifferent to "who the loser is" in an important, substantive sense. Thus understood, the commitment to neutral principles is a commitment to abstraction or formality in the law. This version of neutral principles figures quite prominently in modern attacks on affirmative action.[12] It also plays an important role in recent discussions of pornography.[13] One court recently rejected the feminist argument for antipornography legislation on the ground that the legislation was an attempt to suppress a viewpoint on a public issue – a central first amendment evil.[14] This view has a powerful constitutional pedigree.[15]

This article will discuss the problem of pornography with special attention to the nature and desirability of "viewpoint neutrality" in first amendment adjudication.

In the process, it will touch on quite general themes associated with the constitutional guarantee of freedom of speech. Part I argues that pornography is a significant social problem that justifies legal concern.[16] Part II contends that pornography is "low-value" speech, entitled to less protection from government control than most forms of speech. This analysis, in conjunction with the analysis in Part I, supports the general position that pornography, narrowly defined, can be regulated consistently with the first amendment.[17] Part III examines and rejects the argument that antipornography regulation is unconstitutional because it regulates on the basis of "content" or "viewpoint."[18] Part IV analyzes the arguments of those who would defend antipornography legislation by attacking first amendment "neutrality" doctrine[19] and by asserting that antipornography regulation actually enhances free speech.[20] Part V explores some possible limitations of the reach of antipornography regulation.[21]

I.   Pornography, Obscenity, and Harms

Defining pornography is notoriously difficult; indeed, the difficulty of definition is a familiar problem in any attempt to design acceptable regulation. I will argue, however, that a definition can be framed so as to include only properly regulable materials. In short, regulable pornography must (a) be sexually explicit, (b) depict women as enjoying or deserving some form of physical abuse, and (c) have the purpose and effect of producing sexual arousal.

This definition draws on feminist approaches to the problem of pornography and represents a departure from current law, which is directed at "obscenity."[22] Though built-in ambiguities are inevitable in light of the limitations of language, the basic concept should not be obscure. The central concern is that pornography both sexualizes violence and women as sexually subordinate to men.[23] Pornographic materials feature rape, explicitly or implicitly, as a fundamental theme.[24] This definition differs from the approach urged by the Attorney General's Commission on Pornography, which operated within conventional obscenity law.[25] The definition is somewhat narrower than the one suggested by the Indianapolis ordinance, which created liability for graphic, sexually explicit subordination of women as "sexual objects."[26] The approach proposed here excludes sexually explicit materials that do not sexualize violence against women, and it ties the definition closely to the principal harms caused by pornography.[27] The definition, therefore, excludes the vast range of materials that are not sexually explicit but that do contain implicit rape themes. The requirement of sexual explicitness is thus a means of confining the definition.[28] Part of the definition, moreover, requires that the appeal of the materials be noncognitive[29] – hence the requirement that the purpose and effect be to produce sexual arousal.

[. . .]

The initial question is whether pornography, as defined here, is a cause for social concern. Until recently, it was common to dismiss the case against pornography as the product of prudishness or inhibition, a kind of aesthetic distaste not grounded in concrete showings of harm.[30] Regulation of sexually explicit material has thus been based on its offensiveness.[31] Under almost any view, regulation of speech merely because it is offensive is problematic under the first amendment.[32]

Only recently has pornography come to be regarded as posing any problem at all in terms of concrete harm – and that approach remains controversial in some circles.[33] Constitutional consideration of the pornography problem has almost always been obscured by the gender-neutral term "obscenity." Mirroring the aesthetic concerns referred to above, the Supreme Court treats "obscenity" as unprotected because it has nothing to do with underlying first amendment purposes and hence is not "speech" within the meaning of that amendment[34] Under the approach set forth in *Miller v. California*,[35] materials can be regulated as "obscene" when they: (1) taken as a whole, appeal to the prurient interest, (2) portray sexual conduct in a patently offensive way, measured by "contemporary community standards," and (3) taken as a whole, lack serious social value, whether literary, artistic, political, or scientific.[36] Under the Court's approach to obscenity, sexually explicit materials can be regulated merely because of environmental or aesthetic harms, and considerations of gender are irrelevant.[37]

An approach directed at pornography differs in important respects from one directed at obscenity. The term "obscenity" refers to indecency and filth; the term pornography – derived from the Greek word for "writing about whores" – refers to materials that treat women as prostitutes and that focus on the role of women in providing sexual pleasure to men.[38] The underlying rationale for regulation therefore differs depending on the definition involved, and the coverage of regulation will differ somewhat as well. In contrast to the vague basis of the obscenity doctrine, the

reasoning behind antipornography legislation is found in three categories of concrete, gender-related harms: harms to those who participate in the production of pornography, harms to the victims of sex crimes that would not have been committed in the absence of pornography, and harms to society through social conditioning that fosters discrimination and other unlawful activities.[39] Although it is not possible to describe all the available data here, some of the relevant evidence can be outlined.

First, pornography harms those women who are coerced into and brutalized in the process of producing pornography. Evidence of these harms is only beginning to come to light. But in many cases, women, mostly very young and often the victims of sexual abuse as children, are forced into pornography and brutally mistreated thereafter.[40] [. . .]

The second harmful effect that pornography produces is a general increase in sexual violence directed against women, violence that would not have occurred but for the massive circulation of pornography. To say that there is such a connection is not to say that pornography lies at the root of most sexual violence. Nor is it to say that most or even a significant percentage of men will perpetrate acts of sexual violence as a result of exposure to pornography. But it is to say that the existence of pornography increases the aggregate level of sexual violence. Pornography is at least as much a symptom as a cause; but it is a cause as well.

[. . .]

A third harmful effect of pornography stems from the role it plays as a conditioning factor in the lives of both men and women. Pornography acts as a filter through which men and women perceive gender roles and relationships between the sexes. Of course, pornography is only one of a number of conditioning factors, and others are of greater importance. If pornography were abolished, sexual inequality would hardly disappear. The connection between inequality unlawful discrimination, and pornography cannot be firmly established. But pornography undeniably reflects inequality, and through its reinforcing power, helps to perpetuate it.

All of these factors support the conclusion that pornography is a significant social problem – producing serious harm, mostly to women – and that substantial benefits would result if the pornography industry were regulated.[41] It is important to recognize that the various different harms point to different avenues for legal regulation. If the harm to women who participate in pornography is emphasized, regulation will depend on whether such harm has occurred. If the causal connection is emphasized, the question will be whether the material at issue is likely to cause sexual violence and subordination. I will return to these issues below.

II. Low-Value and High-Value Speech

Although the harms generated by pornography are serious, they are insufficient, standing alone, to justify regulation under the usual standards applied to political speech. After *Brandenburg v. Ohio*,[42] speech – not including obscenity – cannot be regulated because of the harm it produces unless it is shown that the speech is directed to produce harm that is both imminent and extremely likely to occur.[43] Moreover, the Court has rejected the notion that this showing can be made by linking a class of harm with a class of speech; it is necessary to connect particular harms to particular speech.[44] These doctrinal conclusions will not be questioned here, although they do have powerful adverse implications for antipornography legislation. If current standards are applied, a particular pornographic film or magazine might be beyond regulation unless the harms that result from the particular material are imminent, intended, and likely to occur. Demonstrating this, of course, will be hard to do.

But acceptance of these doctrinal conclusions does not resolve the question of the constitutionality of antipornography regulation. The Court has drawn a distinction between speech that may be banned only on the basis of an extremely powerful showing of government interest, and speech that may be regulated on the basis of a far less powerful demonstration of harm. Commercial speech, labor speech, and possibly group libel, for example, fall within the category of "low-value" speech.[45] Whether particular speech falls within the low-value category cannot be determined by a precise test, and under any standards there will be difficult intermediate cases. But in determining whether speech qualifies as low-value, the cases suggest that four factors are relevant.[46]

First, the speech must be far afield from the central concern of the first amendment, which, broadly speaking, is effective popular control of public affairs. Speech that concerns governmental processes is entitled to the highest level of protection;[47] speech that has little or nothing to do with public affairs may be accorded less protection.[48] Second, a distinction is drawn between cognitive and noncognitive aspects of speech.[49] Speech that has purely noncognitive appeal will be entitled to

less constitutional protection.[50] Third, the purpose of the speaker is relevant: if the speaker is seeking to communicate a message, he will be treated more favorably than if he is not.[51] Fourth, the various classes of low-value speech reflect judgments that in certain areas, government is unlikely to be acting for constitutionally impermissible reasons or producing constitutionally troublesome harms. In the cases of commercial speech, private libel, and fighting words, for example, government regulation is particularly likely to be based on legitimate reasons. Judicial scrutiny is therefore more deferential in these areas.[52]

The exclusion of obscene materials from first amendment protection, in contrast, stems largely from an act of definition. Obscene materials, to the Court, do not count as "speech" within the meaning of the first amendment.[53] But this definitional distinction can be viewed as reflecting the same considerations that define the low-value speech category. If the materials are defined narrowly, only nonpolitical and noncognitive material will be prohibited. The limitation of obscenity law to speech not having "serious literary, artistic, political, or scientific value"[54] fits comfortably with this understanding.

This four-factor analysis is, of course, controversial. The distinction between political and nonpolitical speech, for example, is often unclear and may ultimately depend on the political view of the decisionmaker.[55] The difficulty inherent in such line drawing, moreover, may support abandoning any attempt to do so. Perhaps more importantly, distinctions between cognitive and emotive aspects of speech are thin and in some respects pernicious.[56] Furthermore, approaches based on the purpose of the speaker are troublesome for familiar reasons.[57] Finally, freedom of speech might be thought to promote self-realization and, on that ground, attempts to make distinctions among categories of speech might be questioned.[58]

But it would be difficult to imagine a sensible system of free expression that did not distinguish among categories of speech in accordance with their importance to the underlying purposes of the free speech guarantee. A system that granted absolute protection to speech would be unduly mechanical, treading unjustifiably on important values and goals: consider laws forbidding threats, bribes, misleading commercial speech, and conspiracies.[59] [. . .]

Once it is accepted that distinctions should be drawn among different categories of speech, the question becomes one of identifying an appropriate basis for those distinctions. The issue is complex, and it will be possible only to outline some of the important considerations here. First, the distinction between political and nonpolitical speech is well-established, and properly so. The distinction protects speech that serves a central function of the first amendment and precludes regulation where it is most likely to be based on impermissible or disfavored justifications.[60]

The distinction between cognitive and noncognitive speech is more difficult to defend. This is so not only because of the existence of difficult intermediate cases, but also because the very concept of communication is badly misconceived if it is understood as an appeal to rational capacities alone.[61] But any attempt to distinguish among categories of speech must start with an effort to isolate what is uniquely important about speech in the first place. Speech that is not intended to communicate a substantive message or that is directed solely to noncognitive capacities may be wholly or largely without the properties that give speech its special status.[62] Subliminal advertising and hypnosis, for example, are entitled to less than full first amendment protection. Listeners or observers will frequently draw messages from speech or conduct, whether or not it has a communicative intent; the fact that a message may be drawn does not mean that the speech in question has the usual constitutional value.[63]

Under this approach, or any plausible variation, regulation of pornography need not be justified according to standards applicable to political speech. The effect and intent of pornography, as it is defined here, are to produce sexual arousal, not in any sense to affect the course of self-government. Though comprised of words and pictures, pornography does not have the special properties that single out speech for special protection; it is more akin to a sexual aid than a communicative expression.[64] In terms of the distinctions made among classes of speech, pornography is low-value speech not entitled to the same degree of protection accorded other forms of speech.

In one respect, however, the feminist case for regulation of pornography might seem, quite paradoxically, to weaken the argument for regulation. The feminist argument is that pornography represents an ideology, one that has important consequences for social attitudes.[65] Speech that amounts to an ideology, one might argue, cannot be considered low-value, for such speech lies at the heart of politics. If pornography indeed does amount

to an ideology of male supremacy, it might be thought to be entitled to the highest form of constitutional protection.[66]

But an argument along these lines is based on a misconception of what entitles speech to the highest form of protection. Child pornography, for example, may reflect an ideology, but this did not compel the Court to hold in *New York v. Ferber*[67] that child pornography is constitutionally protected. Indeed, most categories of low-value speech – fighting words, commercial speech, obscenity – amount in some respects to an ideology. In commercial speech, for example, there is an implicit ideology in favor of market-ordering, and perhaps some sort of ideology involving the product advertised. But that fact does not justify a conclusion that courts should accord such speech the highest level of constitutional protection.

Whether particular speech is low-value does not turn on whether the materials contain an implicit ideology;[68] if it did, almost all speech would be immunized. The question instead turns more generally on the speaker's purpose and on how the speaker communicates the message. The pornographer's purpose in disseminating pornographic material – to produce sexual arousal – can be determined by the nature of the material. And any implicit "ideology" is communicated indirectly and noncognitively.[69] A distinction along these lines has become an integral part of the Supreme Court's commercial speech doctrine. Paid speech addressed to social issues receives full first amendment protection; paid speech proposing specific commercial transactions receives less protection despite any implicit political statement such speech may contain.[70]

[. . .]

These considerations suggest a conventional, two-stage argument for the regulation of pornography. First, pornography is entitled to only a lower level of first amendment solicitude. Under any standard, pornography is far afield from the kind of speech conventionally protected by the first amendment. Second, the harms produced by pornographic materials are sufficient to justify regulation. Admittedly, there will be difficult intermediate cases and analogies that test the persuasiveness and reach of the argument. The crucial point, however, is that traditional first amendment doctrine furnishes the basis for an argument in favor of restricting pornography, and that such an argument can be made without running afoul of the weak version of the notion of neutral principles described above.[71]

Cass R. Sunstein

III. The Problem of Viewpoint Discrimination

The only federal court of appeals that has faced a challenge to anti-pornography legislation found it unnecessary to examine either the issue of low-value categorization or the issue of harms. *In American Booksellers Association v. Hudnut*,[72] the United States Court of Appeals for the Seventh Circuit invalidated antipornography legislation on the ground that it discriminated on the basis of viewpoint. In the court's view, the Indianapolis ordinance[73] amounted to "thought control," since it "establish[es] an approved view of women, of how they may react to sexual encounters, [and] . . . of how the sexes may relate to each other."[74] Under this decision, which the Supreme Court summarily affirmed,[75] neither the problem of low-value nor the problem of harm is relevant.

This basic approach is familiar in first amendment law.[76] Modern doctrine distinguishes among three categories of restrictions:[77] those that are based on viewpoint, or that single out and suppress particular opinions concerning a particular subject; those that are based on content, or that regulate any speech concerning a subject, regardless of viewpoint; and those that are both content- and viewpoint-neutral. The most intense constitutional hostility is reserved for measures that discriminate on the basis of viewpoint, even though such measures may suppress less speech than do other sorts of restrictions.[78] Thus, for example, a statute that prohibits all speech on billboards stands a far greater chance of constitutional success than a statute that prohibits speech on billboards that is critical of Republicans.[79]

[. . .]

The United States Court of Appeals for the Seventh Circuit concluded that the Indianapolis antipornography legislation was viewpoint-based and that its defenders failed to meet that burden of justification.[80] The legislation, in the court's view, singled out for suppression a particular point of view by aiming at the portrait of male–female relations reflected in some sexually graphic material. One portrait is ruled out; the other is permitted.[81] The issue of harm is irrelevant when restrictions based on viewpoint face a per se rule of illegality.

The initial response to a claim that antipornography legislation is viewpoint-based should be straightforward. The legislation aimed at pornography as defined here would be directed at harm rather than at viewpoint. Its purpose would be to prevent sexual violence and discrimination, not to suppress expression of a point of view. Only pornography – not sexist material in general or material that reinforces notions of female subordination – is regulated. Because of its focus on harm, antipornography legislation would not pose the dangers associated with viewpoint-based restrictions. The government, in effect, would have concrete data to back its legitimate purposes.

This approach is supported by a recent decision that was handed down by the Supreme Court in the same week that it summarily affirmed the Indianapolis case. In *City of Renton v. Playtime Theatres, Inc.*,[82] the Court was faced with a statute that prohibited the showing of sexually explicit motion pictures within 1000 feet of any residential zone, single- or multiple-family dwelling, church, park, or school. The Court concluded that the statute was content-neutral because it was aimed not at the substantive message of the speech, but at its secondary effects on crime rates, properly values, neighborhood quality, and retail trade. The statute's apparent content-based character, according to the Court, was not troubling because the statute could be justified by reference to these secondary effects. It might be said that *Renton* involves regulation on the basis of content rather than viewpoint – a point taken up below[83] – but it is not clear how that conclusion is relevant to the issue of whether harms rescue a statute from skepticism about government motivation. Although the *Renton* decision is questionable on its facts,[84] the Court's willingness to look at possible neutral justifications is sound and coexists uneasily with the outcome in *Hudnut*.

A response to this line of reasoning – and to the *Renton* analogy – would be to point out that viewpoint-based restrictions are frequently defended by reference to harm, and that the possibility of such defenses has not been thought to rescue the restrictions from severe constitutional scrutiny. For example, the government's defense of a law prohibiting people from criticizing a war effort in the presence of soldiers is not that it has any hostility toward the speaker's point of view, but that it is seeking to regulate something that could seriously prejudice the war effort. Despite this claim, the restriction is properly subject to the stringent standards applicable to viewpoint-based restrictions. The reason is straightforward: notwithstanding the possible invocation of harm, the government is attempting to bypass deliberative processes of the community. "More speech" and direct regulation of unlawful conduct should be the preferred remedy for harms. The risks of factional tyranny and self-interested representation are sufficient to justify imposing on government a heavy burden of showing that "more speech" and direct regulation of unlawful conduct are inadequate responses to the harm.

Harm-based justifications thus do not foreclose an attack on pornography legislation as viewpoint-based. Yet one may question the very applicability of the notion of "viewpoint discrimination" in this context. First amendment law contains several categories of speech that are subject to ban or regulation even though they are viewpoint-based in the same sense that antipornography legislation is said to be. The most obvious example can be found in labor law.

Courts have held that the first amendment permits the government to prohibit employers from speaking unfavorably about the effects of unionization in the period before a union election if the unfavorable statements might be interpreted as a threat.[85] In the leading case, the employer had suggested that the firm was not financially strong, that any strike would result in a plant closing, and that many employees would have a hard time finding alternative employment.[86] Regulation of such speech is unquestionably viewpoint-based, for employer speech favorable to unionization is not proscribed. Similarly, regulation of bribery turns not only on content but also on point of view; one may not offer $100 to tempt a person to commit murder, although a $100 offer to build a fence is permissible. Prohibitions of "fighting words" might he similarly understood.[87] False or misleading commercial speech, as well as television and radio advertisements for cigarettes and casinos, are regulable,[88] even though all are based on viewpoint.

[. . .]

These and other apparently viewpoint-based statutes are upheld because they respond, not to point of view, but to harms that the government has power to prevent. In regulating labor speech, the Court indicated that the government was aiming not at viewpoint but at coercion of employees.[89] The existence of genuine and substantial harm allayed concern about impermissible motivation. [. . .]

In the area of bribes, threats, and fighting words, the government is also attempting to combat obvious harms.[90] Analysis of suppression of speech advocating the immediate and violent overthrow of the government would be similar: the government is attempting to eradicate a harm, not attempting to impose a particular point of view. Bans on false or misleading commercial speech, cigarette advertising, or casino gambling are analyzed in

substantially the same way.[91] In the obscenity context, the reasoning is more obscure, but the central point remains: in some contexts, statutes that appear to be viewpoint-based are justified and accepted because of the harms involved. The harms are so obvious and immediate that claims that the government is attempting to silence one position in a "debate" do not have time even to register.[92]

[. . .]

All this suggests that the problem of identifying impermissible viewpoint regulation is far more complex than it at first appears. Regulation based on point of view is common in the law. The terms "viewpoint-based" and "viewpoint-neutral" often represent conclusions rather than analytical tools. In the easy cases, they serve as valuable simplifying devices. But in the hard cases, further analysis is needed. Specifically, three factors help identify impermissible viewpoint-based legislation.

The first factor is the connection between means and ends, a recurrent theme in constitutional law. If the harm invoked is minimal, or if it is implausible to think that the regulation will remedy the harm, it will be more likely that the regulation is in fact based on viewpoint.[93] The second factor is the nature of the process by which the message is communicated. Regulation of harms that derive from types of persuasion appealing to cognitive faculties is presumptively disfavored; more speech is the preferred remedy here. Regulation of antiwar speeches in the presence of soldiers is impermissible because any harm that results is derived from persuasion. More speech should be the solution. Finally, whether the speech is low- or high-value is also relevant.[94] The low-value issue, therefore, is not made irrelevant on the ground that antipornography legislation discriminates on the basis of viewpoint.[95] The viewpoint issue depends, in part, on whether the speech is low-value. Viewpoint-based regulation of high-value speech raises especially intense concerns about government motivation.

Under these criteria, antipornography legislation is defensible. First, the means-ends connection is quite close.[96] Such legislation could be tightly targeted to the cause of the harm: the production and dissemination of portrayals of sexual violence. Second, the "message" of pornography is communicated indirectly and not through rational persuasion. The harm it produces cannot easily be countered by more speech because it bypasses the process of public consideration and debate that underlies the concept of the marketplace of ideas.[97] Finally, pornography falls in the general category of low-value speech. Under these circumstances, antipornography legislation should be regarded not as an effort to exclude a point of view, but instead as an effort to prevent harm. In this respect, the best analogy is to labor speech – with the important caveat that labor speech, which touches public affairs, is far closer to the heart of first amendment concern than is pornography.

The task, in short, is to sort out permissible and impermissible viewpoint discrimination, and to explain the circumstances in which discrimination arguably on the basis of viewpoint should be permitted. It is important in this respect that efforts to regulate pornography, as defined here, do not interfere with deliberative processes at all. By hypothesis, pornography operates at a subconscious level, providing a form of social conditioning that is not analogous to the ordinary operation of freedom of speech. What is distinctive about pornography is its noncognitive character; though it amounts to words and pictures, its purposes and effects are far from the purposes and effects that justify the special protection accorded to freedom of speech. In these circumstances, the response to the claim of viewpoint discrimination is that antipornography legislation does not pose any of the dangers that make discrimination on the basis of viewpoint so troublesome. The three factors identified above – means-ends connection, nature of the process by which the "message" is communicated, and low-value – point in this direction.

[. . .]

IV. Substantivity, Formality, and the Free Speech Guarantee

The argument thus far has been somewhat technical, and it operates within the framework of traditional first amendment doctrine. But proponents of antipornography legislation argue not only that such legislation will combat related harms, but also that restrictions on pornography will promote freedom of speech. At first glance, the argument is mysterious. Conventional first amendment doctrine is based on the assumption that restrictions on speech cannot promote freedom of expression. As we shall see, that assumption ultimately stems from a belief that serious threats to free expression come mostly or exclusively from the public sphere, and that one should always distinguish the public and private spheres for purposes of first amendment analysis.[98]

The argument that antipornography legislation can promote free speech touches on more fundamental issues than have been discussed here thus far. Essentially, the claim is that an attack on antipornography legislation represents legal formalism akin to Professor Wechsler's attack on *Brown v. Board of Education*.[99] In both cases an abstract notion of equality is decisive, though a substantive examination of issues of power and powerlessness would lead to a conclusion that the abstract notion is untenable. Wechsler's view that *Brown* produced a conflict between two coequal sets of associational preferences now appears quite odd. The argument ignores issues of substantive power that make the social meaning – the purposes and effects – of the associational preferences of blacks altogether different from that of the associational preferences of whites. Similarly, first amendment doctrine that refuses to examine issues of substantive power and substantive powerlessness might be thought to generate an indefensible system of expression.[100]

More concretely, the argument goes, the pornography industry is so well-financed, and has such power to condition men and women, that it has the effect of silencing the antipornography cause in particular and women in general. The silencing involved is not the kind of silencing associated with totalitarian regimes. Instead, women who would engage in "more speech" to counter pornography are denied credibility, trust, and the opportunity to be heard – the predicates of free expression. The notion that "when she says no, she means yes" – a common theme in pornography – thus affects the social reception of the feminist attack on pornography. Understood in this way, the case for antipornography legislation is a version of the arguments derived from the famous footnote in *United States v. Carolene Products*.[101] Legal intervention is required because of a maldistribution of private power that interferes with a well-functioning political marketplace.[102] Akin to the view that correction of market failures is a valid basis for governmental intervention,[103] the argument might be understood as a variation of traditional justifications for affirmative action.[104]

[. . .]

V. Slippery Slopes, Vagueness, and Overbreadth

Some of the most powerful objections to antipornography legislation concern vagueness and overbreadth. Even if a definition of pornography identifies the specific class of materials with which one is most concerned, there remains the problem of overinclusion – regulating materials that have some social value and that are unlikely to produce the relevant harm. Three limiting strategies, therefore, might be helpful.

First, it might be desirable to limit antipornography legislation so that it applies to work "taken as a whole" or at the very least protects "isolated passages" in longer works.[105] Some materials that have pornographic components may on the whole generate little of the relevant harm. This might be the case, for example, where a motion picture contains pornographic scenes as part of a more general enterprise. In such circumstances the low-value argument is more difficult to make. Moreover, the resulting harm may be insufficient to justify regulation, and such materials are less likely to have a pernicious conditioning effect. They are thus less likely to produce sexual violence.

Second, as under current obscenity law, the regulation could be limited to material devoid of serious social value.[106] Matters having serious social value are, by definition, excluded from the category of low-value speech; their regulation is thus to be tested by more stringent standards which, for reasons suggested above, generally preclude regulation. There are costs as well as benefits associated with this limitation.[107] Without some such limitation, however, any argument for an antipornography legislation risks running afoul of competing analogies.

The costs arise in those cases in which pornography has been produced through coercive and abusive means. Distribution of such material may be regulable notwithstanding the value of the speech.[108] When regulation is based on harm, the social value of the material is ordinarily irrelevant; the speaker must excise the offending material, and is not given license to claim immunity on account of the general value of the communication.[109]

Third, it may be desirable to limit regulation to motion pictures and photography, and to exclude purely written materials. The evidence suggests that motion pictures and photography do the most to generate sexual violence; the data are more obscure with respect to written material.[110] Moreover, the harm to women participating in the production of pornography is, of course, limited to motion pictures and photography.

Strategies of this sort suggest that it should be possible to draft an antipornography ordinance that is sufficiently definite to withstand challenges of vagueness and overbreadth. But one final objection remains. That objection points to the familiar dangers posed by the "slippery slope" – dangers about which we are rightly concerned in the first amendment context.[111] The lines to which I have referred thus far are not so crisp as to alleviate all fear of misapplication. In light of these considerations, it might, be suggested that the disadvantages of suppression are simply too great to justify the acceptance of what has become a relatively elaborate and complex set of doctrinal distinctions.

Whether this argument, like others premised on slippery-slope concerns, is persuasive depends on two factors. The first is whether the problem at issue is a genuine one. If one believes that pornography is a legitimate source of concern, the possibility of misapplication will be relevant but not decisive. If one believes that pornography is not a serious social problem, or that the problem can be solved through "more speech," the dangers of misapplication support rejecting the argument entirely. The case for antipornography legislation thus depends on simultaneous beliefs that pornography produces significant harms and that those harms cannot be alleviated through public debate alone. I have offered arguments suggesting that both of these beliefs are true.[112]

The second factor is the possibility of holding the line. If one believes that pornography is genuinely indistinguishable from forms of speech that merit protection – either because of their value or because of their failure to produce harm – the argument premised on slippery-slope concerns will be quite powerful. But the rationale suggested here is designed to the likelihood of misapplication. Pornography has special characteristics with respect both to its effects and to the harm it produces. With art and literature generally, attempts to regulate would be unlikely to be justifiable by reference either to low-value analysis or to harms, and both justifications are necessary under the approach set out here. The traditional lawyers' facility in identifying the difficult intermediate case, or the seemingly contrary hypothetical, sometimes operates as an obstacle to legislation that is on balance highly desirable. In the first amendment setting, fears about difficult intermediate cases and misapplication are generally salutary. But at least in the context of pornography, they have proved a barrier to legislation that would in all likelihood do more good than harm.

VI. Conclusion

Antipornography legislation tests constitutional doctrine in unexpected ways – the difference between low- and high-value speech, the relationship between sexual

Cass R. Sunstein

equality and the first amendment, the distinction between viewpoint-based and viewpoint-neutral regulation, and the commitment to neutrality in both weak and strong senses are all drawn into question by the recent proposals.

It is possible, however, to defend such legislation within the confines of conventional doctrine. Pornography falls within the general class of low-value expression, and the harm it produces is sufficient to justify regulation of that expression. One can reach this conclusion without compromising other well-accepted doctrines. The most troubling issue is that of viewpoint-neutrality, but other seemingly viewpoint-based restrictions are sometimes upheld when sufficient harm is present. Antipornography legislation is based on harm rather than viewpoint. Furthermore, to the extent that

antipornography legislation might be deemed viewpoint-based, its status as such is less troubling in light of the peculiar character of the method by which the pornographic "message" is communicated.

I conclude that the skepticism about antipornography legislation is based on a simultaneous undervaluation of the harm pornography produces, a misapplication of conventional doctrines requiring viewpoint-neutrality, and – perhaps most important – an overvaluation of the dangers posed by generating a somewhat different category of regulable speech bound to have some definitional vagueness. At least as the notion is used here, antipornography legislation should produce important social benefits without posing significant threats to a well-functioning system of free expression.

Notes

[...]

1 *See* MacKinnon, Not a Moral Issue, 2 *Yale L, & Pol'y Rev.* 321, 322–24 (1984) (distinguishing "the male morality of liberalism and obscenity law from a feminist political critique of pornography"); *see also* A. Dworkin, *Pornography: Men Possessing Women* 9 (1981) ("Obscenity is not a synonym for pornography.").

2 *See* Indianapolis, Ind., City-County Gen. Ordinances ch. 16 (1984), *quoted in* Attorney General's Comm'n on Pornography, U.S. Dep't of Justice, Final Report 392 (1986) [hereinafter Final Report].

3 Antipornography legislation has been proposed in Cambridge, Los Angeles, and Minneapolis. *See* FINAL REPORT, *supra* note 2, at 392. The mayor of Minneapolis has twice vetoed antipornography measures passed by the Minneapolis City Council. *See The Proposed Minneapolis Pornography Ordinance: Pornography Regulation Versus Civil Rights or Pornography Regulation as Civil Rights?*, 11 *Wm. Mitchell L. Rev.* 39, 44 & n.6 (1985) (symposium).

4 FINAL REPORT, *supra* note 2. For a critique of the Commission's work, see Fields, ACLU Issues Critique of Pornography Commission, *Pub. Weekly*, Mar. 14, 1986, at 11.

5 The Commission concluded that "[t]here can be little doubt that there has within the last ten to twenty years been a dramatic increase in the size of the industry producing the kinds of sexually explicit materials that would generally be conceded to be pornographic." Final Report, *supra* note 2, at 284.

6 For examples of the popular debate; see The Place of Pornography, *Harper's*, Nov. 1984, at 31; Pornography: Love or Death?, *Film Comment*, Nov.–Dec. 1984, at 29; *The War Against Pornography*, NEWSWEEK, Mar. 18, 1985, at 58.

7 *See, e.g.*, MacKinnon, Pornography, Civil Rights, and Speech, 20 *Harv, C.R.-C.L. L. Rev.* 1, 4 n.6 (1985).

8 *See* Wechsler, Toward Neutral Principles of Constitutional Law, 73 *Harv. L. Rev.* 1 (1959).

9 *See* Bork, *Neutral Principles and Some First Amendment Problems*, 47 IND. L.J. 1, 20 (1977) (noting that requirement of neutral principles has not led the Supreme Court to accept any tenable, consistent theory regarding scope of constitutional protection office speech); Greenawalt, The Enduring Significance of Neutral Principles, 78 *Colum. L. Rev.* 982, 1001-13 (1978) (finding absence of definitive guidance for judges in resolving conflicts between adherence to neutral principles and fulfillment of other judicial responsibilities); Tushnet, *Following the* Rules Laid Down: A Critique of Interpretivism and Neutral Principles, 96 *Harv. L. Rev.* 781, 821-22 (1983) ("Each proposed definition [of neutral principles] left us with judges who could enforce their personal values unconstrained by the suggested version of the neutrality requirement.").

10 *See* American Booksellers Ass'n v. Hudnut, 771 F.2d 323, 327-32 (7th Cir. 1985) (pornography analyzed as protected speech through analogy to clearly protected speech such as political ideology), *aff'd*, 106 S. Ct. 1172 (1986); *see also* Stone, Anti-Pornography Legislation as Viewpoint-Discrimination, 9 *Harv. J.L. & Pub. Pol'y* 461, 463 (1986) (noting that Supreme Court applies stringent viewpoint-based standards even to legislation that is only indirectly viewpoint-based).

11 349 U.S. 294 (1955).

12 *See, e.g.*, Van Alstyne, Rites of Passage: Race, the Supreme Court, and the Constitution, 46 *U. Chi. L. Rev.* 775, 802 (1979) (only way to avoid giving Constitution an "accordianlike" quality is to refuse to allow discrimination on basis of race).

13 *See* Note, Effects of Violent Pornography, 8 *N.Y.U. Rev. L, & Soc. Change* 225, 236–37 (1979) (arguing that state must remain neutral about content of speech, including

pornography, if it is to adhere to moral rationale of first amendment).

14   *See* American Booksellers Ass'n v. Hudnut, 771 F.2d 323, 329–31 (7th Cir. 1985) (concluding that even though materials depict subordination of women, first amendment precludes restriction of pornographic "speech"), *aff'd*, 106 S. Ct. 1172 (1986).

15   *See infra* note 76.

16   *See infra* notes 22–41 and accompanying text.

17   *See infra* notes 42–71 and accompanying text.

18   *See infra* notes 72–97 and accompanying text.

19   *See infra* notes 98–104 and accompanying text.

20   *See infra* notes 105 and accompanying text.

21   *See infra* notes 105–112 and accompanying text.

22   *See* American Booksellers Ass'n v. Hudnut, 771 F.2d 323, 324–27 (7th Clr. 1985), *aff'd*, 106 S. Ct. 1172 (1986). The Supreme Court's obscenity doctrine has drawn heavy criticism from a Justice, *see* Ginzburg v. United States, 383 U.S. 463, 498 (1966) (Stewart, J., dissenting) (first amendment means that people should not be sent to prison "merely for distributing publications which offend a judge's aesthetic sensibilities"), as well as from commentators, *see* Henkin, Morals and the Constitution: The Sin of Obscenity, 63 *Colum. L. Rev.* 391, 395 (1963) (arguing that obscenity is suppressed not for the "protection of others," but merely for the "purity of the community" and the "salvation and welfare of the 'consumer'"); Richards, Free Speech and Obscenity Law: Toward a Moral Theory of the First Amendment, 123 *U. Pa. L. Rev.* 45, 73 (1974) (arguing that an understanding of moral function of first amendment would lead to protection of obscenity),

23   *See* MacKinnon, Pornography as Sex Discrimination, 4 *Law & Inequality* 38, 41 (1986).

24   Rape includes both sexual intercourse compelled by force and sexual intercourse with Impaired, unconscious, or underage females. *See Model Penal Code* § 213.1 (Proposed Official Draft 1962).

25   Final Report, *supra* note 2, at 376–77.

26   *See* Indianapolis, Ind., City-County Gen. Ordinances ch. 16 (1984), *quoted in* Final Report, *supra* note 2, at 392.

27   There is empirical support for drawing a distinction between violent and nonviolent sexually explicit materials. Edward Donnerstein, reviewing empirical studies, concludes that although drawing a "straightforward, definitive" conclusion about the relationship between pornography and aggression is "difficult to make," it appears that "the aggressive content of pornography . . . is the main contributor to violence against women." Donnerstein, Pornography: Its Effect on Violence Against Women, in *Pornography and Sexual Aggression* 53, 78–79 (N. Malamuth & E. Donnerstein eds. 1984) [hereinafter *Pornography and Sexual Aggression*]; *see also* H. Eysenck & D. Nias, *Sex, Violence and the Media* (1978) (concluding that link between violence in media and behavior is better established than link between portrayals of sex in media and behavior).

28   The requirement is justified as a rough and imperfect means of limiting the regulable category to speech that is of low first amendment value, *see infra* notes 42–71 and accompanying text, and that is likely to cause harm. *See infra* notes 33–41 and accompanying text. Furthermore, sexually explicit speech of the sort described here involves a highly distinctive relationship between speaker and user. *See infra* notes 61–64 and accompanying text.

29   *See Infra* notes 61–64 and accompanying text.

30   *See* Copp, Pornography and Censorship: An Introductory Essay, in *Pornography and Censorship* 15 (D. Copp & S, Wendell eds. 1983) [hereinafter *Pornography and Censorship*].

31   *See* L. Tribe, *American Constitutional Law* 661 (1977).

32   *See* T. Emerson, *The System of Freedom of Expression* 467, 499–501 (1970) (noting the difficulties inherent in reconciling "full protection" view of first amendment with social interests thought to be fostered by obscenity laws).

33   *See, e.g.*, Hertzberg, Big Boobs, *The New Republic*, July 14 & 21,1986 at 21–24 (attacking Final Report of Attorney General's Commission on Pornography for failing to demonstrate that pornography constitutes meaningful threat to public interest). The Supreme Court, of course, has said that the offensiveness of obscenity is a harm that the state may legitimately address in antiobscenity legislation. *Cf.* FCC v. Pacifica Found., 438 U.S. 726, 737–38 (1978) (holding that the FCC could regulate the broadcast of obscene, indecent, or profane language); *see also* Bethel School Dist. No. 403 v. Fraser, 106 S. Ct. 3159,3164 (1986) (ruling that the Constitution does not bar states from punishing the use of vulgar and offensive words in secondary schools). Furthermore, in New York v. Ferber, 458 U.S. 747, 756–64 (1982), the Court drew a connection between the production of child pornography and violence and held that the state may regulate child pornography.

34   *See, e.g.*, Paris Adult Theater I v, Slaton, 413 U.S. 49, 56 (1973) (holding that "obscene" material not protected by first amendment); Miller v. California, 413 U.S. 15, 23-24 (1973) (same); Roth v. United States, 354 U.S. 476, 481 (1957) (federal statute criminalizing "obscenity" was not violative of first amendment); Chaplinsky v. New Hampshire; 315 U.S. 568, 571-72 (1942) (certain classes of speech such as "the lewd and the obscene" not afforded first amendment protection).

35   413 U.S. 15 (1973).

36   *Id.* at 24.

37   *See* Emerson, Pornography and the First Amendment: A Reply to Professor MacKinnon, 3 *Yale L. & Pol'y Rev.* 130, 134 (1984) (aesthetic harms should not be the basis of suppressing acts of expression).

38   *See generally* A. Dworkin, *supra* note 1, at 199-202; MacKinnon, *supra* note 7, at 20-22.

39   *See* MacKinnon, *supra* note 7, at 32-60 (similarly categorizing the harms caused by pornography).

40   Numerous examples of abuse were reported to the Attorney General's Commission on Pornography. See Final Report, *supra* note 2, at 836-69.

41   The utilitarian "gains" from pornography, as defined here, should count little in the balance. *Cf.* Goodin, Laundering Preferences, in *Foundations of Social Choice Theory* 75 (J. Elster & A. Hylland eds. 1986).

42   395 U.S. 444 (1969) (per curiam) (overturning conviction of Ku Klux Khan leader for advocating violence at Klan gathering).

43   *Id.* at 447.

44   *See, e.g.,* Hess v. Indiana, 414 U.S. 105, 107-09 (1973) (overturning conviction for disorderly conduct on ground that defendant's speech was neither directed toward a particular person nor intended to incite specific act of violence).

45   *See* G. Stone, R. Seidman, C. Sunstein & M. Tushnet, *Constitutional Law* 1058–114(1986).

46   Because pornography and obscenity are obviously "speech," through of low-value, the rationale of Roth v. United States, 354 U.S. 476 (1957), and its progeny is highly questionable. The notion of "no value" speech is also questionable when applied to words and pictures. In general, however, the Supreme Court's approach to deciding what constitutes low-value speech is acceptable and is drawn on here.

47   *See* New York Times v. Sullivan, 376 U.S. 254,269 (1964) ("[The first amendment] was fashioned to assure unfettered interchange of ideas for the bringing about of political and social changes desired by the people." (quoting Roth v. United States, 354 U.S. 476,484 (1957))).

48   *See, e.g.,* Bethel School Dist. No. 403 v. Fraser, 106 S, Ct. 3159, 3166 (1986) (offensive student speech unrelated to public issues not entitled to first amendment protection).

49   The term "cognitive" as used here refers to whether the material is intended to or does in fact Impart knowledge in any sense. *See* Finnis, "Reason and Passion": The Constitutional Dialectic of Free Speech and Obscenity, 116 *U. Pa. L. Rev.* 222, 227 (1960) (obscenity regarded as lacking social utility because it appeals to realm of passion rather than to realm of intellect).

50   The Supreme Court has tied the level of constitutional protection afforded certain classes of speech to their ability to transmit ideology or ideas:

There are certain well-defined and narrowly limited classes of speech, the prevention and punishment of which has never been thought to raise any Constitutional problem. These include the lewd and obscene, the profane, the libelous, and the insulting or "fighting" words – those which by their very utterance inflict injury or tend to incite an immediate breach of the peace. It has been well observed that such utterances are no essential part of any exposition of ideas, and are of such slight social value as a step to truth that any benefit that may be derived from them is clearly outweighed by the social interest in order and morality. Chaplinsky v. New Hampshire, 315 U.S. 568, 571–72 (1942) (footnotes omitted).

The *Roth* Court's definition of "prurient interest" in obscenity doctrine fits comfortably into the cognitive/

noncognitive analytical framework. Justice Brennan, writing for the Court, defined material appealing to the "prurient interest" as "material having a tendency to excite lustful thoughts." Roth v. United States, 354 U.S. 476, 487 m20 (1957). Professor Schauer has suggested that the cognitive/noncognitive distinction underlies the Supreme Court's obscenity decisions: "[T]he Court's treatment of obscenity is consistent with a vision that emphasizes intellectual (and perhaps public) communication and not self-expression." Schauer, *Speech and "Speech" – Obscenity and "Obscenity": An Exercise in the Interpretation of Constitutional Language,* 67 GEO. L.J. 899, 932 (1979). Schauer ascribes to the Court an intention to formulate a definition of "obscenity" that functionally excludes noncognitive communication (with sexual content) from constitutional protection. *Id.* at 928. But cf. Perry, Freedom of Expression: An Essay on Theory and Doctrine, 78 *Nw. UX. Rev.* 1137, 1182 (1984) (contending that "there is no denying that obscene pornography constitutes a political-moral vision"). Note also that symbolic speech often has a significant cognitive content.

51   *See generally* Wright, A Rationale from J.S. Mitt for the Five Speech Clause, 1985 *Sup. Ct. Rev.* 149, 157 ("If one has sent a social message, however, even if none was received, or if an entirely different message was received, one has engaged in speech, even if imperfectly").

52   The adjustment of standards of review in accordance with the perception of the likelihood of impermissible government ends is a familiar constitutional theme; it underlies, for example, the various "tiers" of equal protection doctrine. *Compare* Korematsu v. United States, 323 U.S. 214, 219 (1944) (applying strict scrutiny in upholding executive order interning Americans of Japanese ancestry) *with* Craig v. Boren, 429 U.S. 190, 197 (1976) (applying intermediate scrutiny to gender classifications) *and* United States R.R. Retirement Bd. v. Fritz, 449 U.S. 166, 174–75 (1980) (applying rational basis standard in challenge to social and economic legislation).

53   *See* Roth v. United States, 354 U.S. 476, 481 (1957) ("[T]his Court has always assumed that obscenity is not protected by the freedoms of speech and press."); *see also* Schauer, *supra* note 50, at 926, 928.

54   Miller v. California, 413 U.S. 15, 24 (1973).

55   *See Infra* notes 93-95 and accompanying text.

56   For example; visceral and symbolic speech can challenge the listener, viewer, or reader by directly confronting basic beliefs and values. Such speech – consider flag banning – may have the purpose and effect of causing an emotional reaction. The confrontation, however, is ultimately intended to have a cognitive impact and to cause a reexamination of those values and beliefs. When visceral and symbolic speech is directed at public affairs, it falls well within the core of the first amendment and should receive the highest constitutional protection. *See* Cohen v. California, 403 U.S. 15, 26 (1971); *see also* Ely, Flag Desecration: A Case Study of Categorization and Balancing in First

Amendment Analysis, 88 *Harv. L. Rev.* 1482, 1482–83 (1975) ("At first glance, however, it is hard to see why [the Court finds the issue troubling]. Laws prohibiting flag desecration quite obviously inhibit political expression.. . .") This view can be associated with feminist attacks on distinctions between reason and emotion. *See* A. JAGGAR, *Feminist Politics and Human Nature* 367 (1983).

57 *See* Ackerman, Beyond Carotene Products, 98 *Harv. L. Rev.* 713 (1985).

58 *See, e.g.*, Redish, The Value of Free Speech, 130 *U. Pa. L. Rev.* 591, 625 (1982) ("Once one recognizes that the primary value of free speech is as a means of fostering individual development and aiding the malting of life-affecting decisions, the inappropriateness of distinguishing between the value of different types of speech becomes clear.").

59 *Cf.* Redish, *supra* note 58; Redish, The Content Distinction in First Amendment Analysis, 34 *Stan. L. Rev.* 113, 128–39 (1982). Professor Redish's position is that any speech that furthers a first amendment goal of self-realization – including obscenity and political speech – should be protected. This view differs from the well-known "absolutist" position, expressed most forcefully by Justice Black in Königsberg v. State Bar, 366 U.S. 36, 61 (1961) (Blade, J., dissenting). The criticisms of the absolutist position have, of course, carried the day. See generally Kalven, Upon Rereading Mr. Justice Black on the First Amendment, 14 *UCLA L. Rev.* 428, 441–47 (1967).

60 [Footnotes deleted]

61 *See, e.g.*, I. Balbus, *Marxism and Domination: A Neo-Hegelian, Feminist, Psychoanalytic Theory of Sexual, Political and Technology Liberation* 231 (1982) (criticizing J. Habermas, *Legitimation Crisis*(1975), for relying on a disembodied conception of reason and failing to account for "what might be called the psychodynamics of human communication").

62 *See* Schauer, *supra* note 50, at 920–28.

63 *See* United States v. O'Brien, 391 U.S. 367, 376 (1968) (rejecting contention that "an apparently limitless variety of conduct" intended to convey ideas merits constitutional protection). *But cf.* American Booksellers Ass'n v. Hudnut, 771 F.2d 323, 330 (7th Cir. 1985) (stating that failure to protect speech from which messages are drawn would invite government dictation of "which thoughts are good for us"), *aff'd*, 106 S. Ct. 1172 (1986).

64 *See* Schauer, *supra* note 50, at 923.

65 *See* S. Brownmiller, *Against Our Will: Men, Women and Rape* 394 (1975) ("Pornography is the undiluted essence of antifemale propaganda.").

66 *See* Stone, *supra* note 10, at 467 (arguing that legislation prohibiting portrayal of women as enjoying domination is viewpoint-based and thus constitutionally repugnant).

67 458 U.S. 747, 763–64 (1982).

68 *See* Pittsburgh Press Co. v. Human Relations Comm'n, 413 U.S. 376, 385 (1973) (although sex-designated employment advertisements may have expressed implicit ideology whether "certain positions ought to be filled by members of one or the other sex," ordinance forbidding such advertisements did not violate newspaper's first amendment rights because advertisements were commercial speech).

69 Even Justice Black, a first amendment "absolutist," believed that regulation of conduct that also touched associated speech could, in particular circumstances, be constitutional. *See* Königsberg v. State Bar, 366 U.S. 36,69 (1961) (Black, J., dissenting) (conceding that city ordinances intended to prevent unnecessary noise and traffic congestion that "incidentally" touch speech are permissible).

70 *Compare* New York Times v. Sullivan, 376 U.S, 254, 266 (1964) (paid political advertisement soliciting financial support for "right-to-vote" movement expressed opinion and communicated information on "matters of the highest public interest and concern") *with* Posadas de Puerto Rico Assocs. v. Tourism CO., 106 S. Ct. 2968, 2976–77 (1986) (regulations prohibiting advertising of casino gambling served substantial government interest).

71 *See supra* note 10 and accompanying text.

72 771 F.2d 323, 332 (7th Cir. 1985), *aff'd*, 106 S. Ct. 1172 (1986).

73 The Indianapolis ordinance used a somewhat different definition of pornography from that set out here. *See supra* note 26 and accompanying text. But those differences would not affect the applicability of the *Hudnut* reasoning to regulation using the definition I have proposed.

74 *Hudnut*, 771 F.2d at 328.

75 Chief Justice Burger, Justice Rehnquist, and Justice O'Connor dissented. Hudnut v. American Booksellers Ass'n, 106 S. Ct. 1172 (1986).

76 The Supreme Court, for example, reversed a New York Court of Appeals decision that upheld the prohibition of the showing on state property of a movie based on *Lady Chatterley's Lover. See* Kingsley Int'l Pictures Corp. v. Regents, 360 UB. 684 (1959). The New York decision was based on the explicit ground that the movie's subject matter – "adultery presented as being right and desirable for certain people" – permitted regulation. *Id.* at 687. In a concise summary of the basis of the presumption of unconstitutionality of viewpoint-based regulation, the Court stated:

What New York has done, therefore, is to prevent the exhibition of a motion picture because that picture advocates an idea – that adultery under certain circumstances may be proper behavior. Yet the First Amendment's basic guarantee is of freedom to advocate ideas. The State, quite simply, has thus struck at the very heart of constitutional protected liberty . . . . [The Constitution's] guarantee is not confined to the expression of ideas that are conventional or shared by a majority. It protects advocacy of the opinion that adultery may sometimes be proper, no less than advocacy of socialism or the single tax.

Id. at 688–89. *Kingsley* may be said to prohibit Antipornography legislation. *Yet Kingsley* deals with state suppression of a particular point of view that was not tightly connected to any demonstrable harm and that applied regardless of the value of the speech in the constitutional hierarchy. [. . .] In New York v. Ferber, 458 U.S. 747 (1982), the Court made it clear that narrowly-tailored harm-based regulation of low-value speech is constitutional *Kingsley* is thus distinguishable from a viewpoint-based challenge to antipornography legislation such as that made in *Hudnut*, 771 F.2d at 325.

77 *See* Cornelius v. NAACP Legal Defense & Educ. Fund, Inc., 105 S. Ct 3439, 3453–54 (1985) (distinguishing between content- and viewpoint-based regulation of access to public forums).

78 *See generally* Stone, Content Regulation and the First Amendment, 25 *Wm. & Mary L. Rev*, 189 (1983) (discussing use of stricter scrutiny for regulations based on content as compared to regulations not directed at content).

79 *See* Metromedia. Inc. v. City of San Diego, 453 U.S. 490, 514–15 (1981).

80 *See Hudnut*, 771 F.2d at 332–34.

81 *See id*. at 328.

82 106. S. Ct. 925 (1986). *Renton* may also represent the continuation of a trend in the Supreme Court to give increased deference to legislative fact-finding and balancing in the first amendment area. Both New York v. Ferber, 458 U.S. 747 (1982), and Kaplan v. California, 413 U.S. 115 (1973), are noteworthy in their deference to the legislature. Whether such deference will be extended outside the realm of low-value speech, *see supra* notes 42–71 and accompanying text, is unclear.

83 *See infra* notes 89–92 and accompanying text.

84 That harms can be invoked as a basis for regulation should not, as discussed below, be sufficient to rescue a statute from content or viewpoint scrutiny; harms can almost always be invoked to support statutes that exclude a point of view. Instead, the inquiry should require consideration of additional factors, such as whether the speech is low-value or high-value. Although it might be possible to distinguish between "primary" and "secondary" effects of regulation, such distinctions seem artificial. *See* Stone, Content-Neutral Restrictions, 54 *U. Chi. L. Rev*. (1987).

85 *See* NLRB v. Gissel Packing Co., 395 U.S. 575, 618–19 (1969).

86 *Id*.

87 *See* Chaplinsky v. New Hampshire, 315 U.S. 568 (1942).

88 *See* Posadas de Puerto Rico Assocs. v. Tourism Co., 106 S. Ct. 2968, 2976–79 (1986) (holding that state's power to bar gambling includes the lesser power to ban casino advertising, even where state has not banned casino gambling); Virginia State Bd. of Pharmacy v. Virginia Citizens Consumer Council, Inc., 425 U.S. 748, 771–73 & n.24 (1976) (state may suppress prescription drug advertisements that are false and misleading or that propose illegal transactions); Capitol Broadcasting Co. v. Mitchell, 333 F. Supp. 582, 584 (D.D.C. 1971) (upholding statute banning cigarette advertising on any medium subject to FCC jurisdiction), *aff'd* *sub nom*. Capitol Broadcasting Co. v. Kliendienst, 405 U.S. 1000 (1972).

89 *See* NLRB v. Gissel Packing Co., 395 U.S. 575, 618 (1969) ("[A] threat of retaliation based on misrepresentation and coercion [is] without the protection of the First Amendment").

90 The modern classification of obscenity as not being speech at all appeals to be based at least in part on a kind of judicial notice by the Supreme Court of harms perceived to flow from obscenity. *See* Roth v. United States, 3S4 U.S. 476, 484–85 (1957) (miniscule speech value of obscenity overcome by interest in preserving social order).

91 Technically, of course, the analysis differs. In the cases of fighting words and false or misleading advertising, the speech is beyond the first amendment if it fits the relevant definition. *Cf*. Posadas de Puerto Rico Assocs. v. Tourism Co., 106 S. Ct. 2968, 2976 (1986) ("[C]ommercial speech receives a limited form of First Amendment protection so long as it concerns a lawful activity and is not misleading or fraudulent"). On the other hand, the government cannot regulate casino advertising unless it shows a "substantial" state interest *See Posadas*, 106 S. Ct at 2977. In every case, however, the court is implicitly or explicitly weighing a perceived state interest against the perceived value of the speech involved. In any case, the requisite showing of harm does not appear to be difficult to satisfy. *See id*.

92 *See supra* notes 89–92 and accompanying text.

93 [Footnote deleted]

94 Whether the speech occupies a low position in first amendment hierarchy, however, should not he controlling. A statute forbidding commercial advertising unfavorable to Democrats could not be constitutional.

95 *See Hudnut*, 771 F.2d at 330–31; *see also* Stone, *supra* note 10, at 477.

96 [Footnote deleted]

97 It is thus incorrect to say, as have Professors Emerson and Dershowitz, that the appropriate remedy for the harms caused by pornography should rest solely on the power of "more speech." *See* . . . Emerson, *supra* note 37, at 142–43.

98 This point suggests the close connection between the antipornography debate and recent discussions involving the problem of "state action." *See* L. Tribe, *Constitutional Choices* 256–59 (1985).

99 *See* Wechsler, *supra* note 8, at 32–34.

100 *See* Dworkin, *Against the Male Flood: Censorship, Pornography and Equality*, 8 *Harv. Women's L.J.* 1, 13–17 (1985). The general attack on legal formalism described here resembles that set out in B. Ackerman, *Reconstructing American Law* 96–101, 110 (1984); Brest, State Action and Liberal Theory: A Casenote *on* Flagg Brothers v. Brooks 130 *U. Pa. L. Rev*. 1296 (1982); and Kennedy, Form and Substance In Private Law Adjudication, 89 *Harv. L, Rev*. 1685, 1776–78 (1976).

101 304 U.S. 144, 152 n.4 (1938).

102 *See* Olsen, *The Family and the Market: A Study of Ideology and Legal Reform,* 96 *Harv. L. Rev.* 1497, 1516–18 (1983).

103 *See, e.g.,* Hawaii Hous. Auth. v. Midkiff, 467 U.S. 229, 242 (1984).

104 For an exposition of those justifications, see Kaplan, Equal Justice In an Unequal World: Equality for the Negro – The Problem of Special Treatment, 60 *Nw. U.L. Rev.* 363, 364–67 (1966).

105 The absence of such a provision In the Indianapolis anti-pornography ordinance was identified as a constitutional defect by the United States Court of Appeals for the Seventh Circuit. *See* American Booksellers Ass'n v. Hudnut, 771 F.2d 323, 328 (7th Cir, 1985), *aff'd,* 106 S. Ct. 1172 (1986).

106 *See* Miller v. California, 413 U.S. 15, 24 (1973) (requiring that state prohibition be limited to materials that "do not have serious literary, artistic, political, or scientific value"). It is not altogether clear, however, that the "taken as a whole" and the "serious social value" limitations are constitutionally required. In other areas – consider libel – the unprotected speech is not immunized by surrounding high-value speech.

107 *See* MacKinnou, *supra* note 7.

108 This point was recognized in *Hudnut,* 771 F.2d at 332.

109 *Cf.* New York Times v. United States, 403 U.S. 713, 736–37 (1971) (White, J., concurring) (publication permitted despite the illegality of the transmittal of information in Pentagon Papers to newspaper).

110 *See supra* notes 25–29 and accompanying text.

111 *See* Blasi, The Pathological Perspective and the First Amendment, 85 *Colum. L. Rev.* 449, 474–80 (1985) (favoring outcome-determinative, mechanical standards and discouraging rules that would be vulnerable during "pathological" times).

112 [Footnote deleted]

41

Ashcroft v. Free Speech Coalition

United States Supreme Court

Summary

The U.S. Supreme Court ruled that the Child Pornography Prevention Act of 1996 (which criminalized computer-generated images of child pornography or "virtual child porn") is unconstitutional because the Act's inclusion of images that "appear to be" or "convey the impression" of children in sexual activity was overbroad and violated free speech protections. The Court argued that the Act prohibited speech that could have redeeming value, prohibited speech that was not itself a record of abuses (since producing virtual child pornography itself records no crimes and victimizes no children), and prohibited speech that adults have a right to hear (which may not be totally banned in an effort to protect children).

Original publication details: *Ashcroft v. Free Speech Coalition 535 U.S.* 234 No. 00-795 (2002). Public Domain.

Sexual Ethics: An Anthology, First Edition. Edited by Patrick D. Hopkins.
© 2023 John Wiley & Sons, Inc. Published 2023 by John Wiley & Sons, Inc.

SUPREME COURT OF THE UNITED STATES

No. 00-795
Syllabus

ASHCROFT, ATTORNEY GENERAL, et al. v.
FREE SPEECH COALITION et al.
CERTIORARI TO THE UNITED STATES
COURT OF APPEALS FOR THE NINTH
CIRCUIT

Argued October 30, 2001. Decided April 16, 2002.

[. . .]

Syllabus

The Child Pornography Prevention Act of 1996 (CPPA) expands the federal prohibition on child pornography to include not only pornographic images made using actual children, 18 U.S.C. § 2256(8)(A), but also "any visual depiction, including any photograph, film, video, picture, or computer or computer generated image or picture," that "is, or appears to be, of a minor engaging in sexually explicit conduct," § 2256(8)(B), and any sexually explicit image that is "advertised, promoted, presented, described, or distributed in such a manner that conveys the impression" it depicts "a minor engaging in sexually explicit conduct," § 2266(8)(D). Thus, § 2256(8)(B) bans a range of sexually explicit images, sometimes called "virtual child pornography," that appear to depict minors but were produced by means other than using real children, such as through the use of youthful-looking adults or computer-imaging technology. Section 2256(8)(D) is aimed at preventing the production or distribution of pornographic material pandered as child pornography. Fearing that the CPPA threatened their activities, respondents, an adult-entertainment trade association and others, filed this suit alleging that the "appears to be" and "conveys the impression" provisions are overbroad and vague, chilling production of works protected by the First Amendment. The District Court disagreed and granted the Government summary judgment, but the Ninth Circuit reversed. Generally, pornography can be banned only if it is obscene under *Miller v. California,* 413 U.S. 15, 93 S.Ct. 2607, 37 L.Ed.2d 419, but pornography depicting actual children can be proscribed whether or not the images are obscene because of the State's interest in protecting the children exploited by the production process, *New York v. Ferber,* 458 U.S. 747, 758, 102 S.Ct. 3348, 73 L.Ed.2d

1113, and in prosecuting those who promote such sexual exploitation, *id.,* at 761, 102 S.Ct. 3348. The Ninth Circuit held the CPPA invalid on its face, finding it to be substantially overbroad because it bans materials that are neither obscene under *Miller* nor produced by the exploitation of real children as in *Ferber.*

Held: The prohibitions of §§ 2256(8)(B) and 2256(8)(D) are over broad and unconstitutional. Pp. 1398–1406.

(a) Section 2256(8)(B) covers materials beyond the categories recognized in *Ferber* and *Miller,* and the reasons the Government offers in support of limiting the freedom of speech have no justification in this Court's precedents or First Amendment law. Pp. 1398–1405.

(1) The CPPA is inconsistent with *Miller.* It extends to images that are not obscene under the *Miller* standard, which requires the Government to prove that the work in question, taken as a whole, appeals to the prurient interest, is patently offensive in light of community standards, and lacks serious literary, artistic, political, or scientific value, 413 U.S., at 24, 93 S.Ct. 2607. Materials need not appeal to the prurient interest under the CPPA, which proscribes any depiction of sexually explicit activity, no matter how it is presented. It is not necessary, moreover, that the image be patently offensive. Pictures of what appear to be 17-year-olds engaging in sexually explicit activity do not in every case contravene community standards. The CPPA also prohibits speech having serious redeeming value, proscribing the visual depiction of an idea – that of teenagers engaging in sexual activity – that is a fact of modern society and has been a theme in art and literature for centuries. A number of acclaimed movies, filmed without any child actors, explore themes within the wide sweep of the statute's prohibitions. If those movies contain a single graphic depiction of sexual activity within the statutory definition, their possessor would be subject to severe punishment without inquiry into the literary value of the work. This is inconsistent with an essential First Amendment rule: A work's artistic merit does not depend on the presence of a single explicit scene. See, *e.g., Book Named "John Cleland's Memoirs of a Woman of Pleasure" v. Attorney General of Mass.,* 383 U.S. 413, 419, 86 S.Ct. 975, 16 L.Ed.2d 1. Under *Miller,* redeeming value is judged by considering the work as a whole. Where the scene is part of the narrative, the work itself does not for this reason become obscene, even though the scene in isolation might be offensive. See *Kois v. Wisconsin,* 408 U.S. 229, 231, 92 S.Ct. 2245, 33 L.Ed.2d 312 *(per curiam).* The CPPA cannot be read

to prohibit obscenity, because it lacks the required link between its prohibitions and the affront to community standards prohibited by the obscenity definition, Pp. 1398–1401.

(2) The CPPA finds no support in *Ferber*. The Court rejects the Government's argument that speech prohibited by the CPPA is virtually indistinguishable from material that may be banned under *Ferber*. That case upheld a prohibition on the distribution and sale of child pornography, as well as its production, because these acts were "intrinsically related" to the sexual abuse of children in two ways. 458 U.S., at 759, 102 S.Ct. 3348. First, as a permanent record of a child's abuse, the continued circulation itself would harm the child who had participated. See *id*, at 759, and n. 10, 102 S.Ct. 3348. Second, because the traffic in child pornography was an economic motive for its production, the State had an interest in closing the distribution network. *Id.*, at 760, 102 S.Ct. 3348. Under either rationale, the speech had what the Court in effect held was a proximate link to the crime from which it came. In contrast to the speech in *Ferber*, speech that is itself the record of sexual abuse, the CPPA prohibits speech that records no crime and creates no victims by its production. Virtual child pornography is not "intrinsically related" to the sexual abuse of children. While the Government asserts that the images can lead to actual instances of child abuse, the causal link is contingent and indirect. The harm does not necessarily follow from the speech, but depends upon some unquantified potential for subsequent criminal acts. The Government's argument that these in direct harms are sufficient because, as *Ferber* acknowledged, child pornography rarely can be valuable speech, see *id.*, at 762, 102 S.Ct. 3348, suffers from two flaws. First, *Ferber's* judgment about child pornography was based upon how it was made, not on what it communicated. The case reaffirmed that where the speech is neither obscene nor the product of sexual abuse, it does not fall outside the First Amendment's protection. See *id.*, at 764–765, 102 S.Ct. 3348. Second, *Ferber* did not hold that child pornography is by definition without value. It recognized some works in this category might have significant value, see *id.*, at 761, 102 S.Ct. 3348, but relied on virtual images – the very images prohibited by the CPPA – as an alternative and permissible means of expression, *id*, at 763, 102 S.Ct. 3348. Because *Ferber* relied on the distinction between actual and virtual child pornography as supporting its holding, it provides no support for a statute that eliminates the distinction and makes the alternative mode criminal as well. Pp. 1401–1402.

(3) The Court rejects other arguments offered by the Government to justify the CPPA's prohibitions. The contention that the CPPA is necessary because pedophiles may use virtual child pornography to seduce children runs afoul of the principle that speech within the rights of adults to hear may not be silenced completely in an attempt to shield children from it. See, *e.g., Sable Communications of Cal., Inc. v. FCC*, 492 U.S. 115, 130–131, 109 S.Ct. 2829, 106 L.Ed.2d 93. That the evil in question depends upon the actor's unlawful conduct, defined as criminal quite apart from any link to the speech in question, establishes that the speech ban is not narrowly drawn. The argument that virtual child pornography whets pedophiles' appetites and encourages them to engage in illegal conduct is unavailing because the mere tendency of speech to encourage unlawful acts is not a sufficient reason for banning it, *Stanley v. Georgia*, 394 U.S. 557, 566, 89 S.Ct. 1243, 22 L.Ed.2d 542, absent some showing of a direct connection between the speech and imminent illegal conduct, see, *e.g., Brandenburg v. Ohio*, 395 U.S. 444, 447, 89 S.Ct. 1827, 23 L.Ed.2d 430 *(per curiam)*. The argument that eliminating the market for pornography produced using real children necessitates a prohibition on virtual images as well is somewhat implausible because few pornographers would risk prosecution for abusing real children if fictional, computerized images would suffice. Moreover, even if the market deterrence theory were persuasive, the argument cannot justify the CPPA because, here, there is no underlying crime at all. Finally, the First Amendment is turned upside down by the argument that, because it is difficult to distinguish between images made using real children and those produced by computer imaging, both kinds of images must be prohibited. The overbreadth doctrine prohibits the Government from banning unprotected speech if a substantial amount of protected speech is prohibited or chilled in the process. See *Broadrick v. Oklahoma*, 413 U.S. 601, 612, 93 S.Ct. 2908, 37 L.Ed.2d 830. The Government's rejoinder that the CPPA should be read not as a prohibition on speech but as a measure shifting the burden to the accused to prove the speech is lawful raises serious constitutional difficulties. The Government misplaces its reliance on § 2252A(c), which creates an affirmative defense allowing a defendant to avoid conviction for nonpossession offenses by showing that the materials were produced using only adults and were not otherwise distributed in a manner conveying the impression that they depicted real children. Even if an affirmative defense can save a statute from First

Amendment challenge, here the defense is insufficient because it does not apply to possession or to images created by computer imaging, even where the defendant could demonstrate no children were harmed in producing the images. Thus, the defense leaves unprotected a substantial amount of speech not tied to the Government's interest in distinguishing images produced using real children from virtual ones. Pp. 1402–1405.

[. . .]

198 F.3d 1083, affirmed.

KENNEDY, J., delivered the opinion of the Court, in which STEVENS, SOUTER, GINSBURG, and BREYER, JJ., joined. THOMAS, J., filed an opinion concurring in the judgment, *post*, p. 1406. O'CONNOR, J., filed an opinion concurring in the judgment in part and dissenting in part, in which REHNQUIST, C.J., and SCALIA, J., joined as to Part II, *post*, p. 1407. REHNQUIST, C.J., filed a dissenting opinion, in which SCALIA, J., joined except for the paragraph discussing legislative history, *post*, p. 1411.

[. . .]

Justice O'CONNOR, with whom THE CHIEF JUSTICE and Justice SCALIA join as to Part II, concurring in the judgment in part and dissenting in part.
[. . .]

I disagree with the Court, however, that the CPPA's prohibition of virtual child pornography is overbroad. Before I reach that issue, there are two preliminary questions: whether the ban on virtual child pornography fails strict scrutiny and whether that ban is unconstitutionally vague. I would answer both in the negative.

The Court has long recognized that the Government has a compelling interest in protecting our Nation's children. See *Ferber, supra*, at 756–757, 102 S.Ct. 3348 (citing cases). This interest is promoted by efforts directed against sexual offenders and actual child pornography. These efforts, in turn, are supported by the CPPA's ban on virtual child pornography. Such images whet the appetites of child molesters, § 121, 110 Stat 3009-26, Congressional Findings (4), (10)(B), notes following 18

U.S.C. § 2251, who may use the images to seduce young children, id, Finding (3). Of even more serious concern is the prospect that defendants indicted for the production, distribution, or possession of actual child pornography may evade liability by claiming that the images attributed to them are in fact computer-generated. *Id,* Finding (6)(A). Respondents may be correct that no defendant has successfully employed this tactic. See, *e.g., United States v. Fox*, 248 F.3d 394 (CJL5 2001); *United States v. Vig*, 167 F.3d 443 (CA8 1999); *United States v. Kimbrough*, 69 F.3d 723 (C.A.5 1995); *United States v. Coleman*, 54 M.J. 869 (Army Ct.Crim.App. 2001). But, given the rapid pace of advances in computer-graphics technology, the Government's concern is reasonable. Computer-generated images lodged with the Court by *amici curiae* National Law Center for Children and Families et al. bear a remarkable likeness to actual human beings. Anyone who has seen, for example, the film Final Fantasy; The Spirits Within (H. Sakaguchi and M. Sakakibara directors, 2001) can understand the Government's concern. Moreover, this Court's cases do not require Congress to wait for harm to occur before it can legislate against it. See *Turner Broadcasting System, Inc. v. FCC*, 520 U.S. 180, 212, 117 S.Ct. 1174, 137 L.Ed.2d 369 (1997).

Respondents argue that, even if the Government has a compelling interest to justify banning virtual child pornography, the "appears to be . . . of a minor" language is not narrowly tailored to serve that interest. See *Sable Communications of Cal., Inc. v. FCC*, 492 U.S. 115, 126, 109 S.Ct. 2829, 106 L.Ed.2d 93 (1989). They assert that the CPPA would capture even cartoon sketches or statues of children that were sexually suggestive. Such images surely could not be used, for instance, to seduce children. I agree. A better interpretation of "appears to be . . . of" is "virtually indistinguishable from" – an interpretation that would not cover the examples respondents provide. Not only does the text of the statute comfortably bear this narrowing interpretation, the interpretation comports with the language that Congress repeatedly used in its findings of fact. [. . .]

42

What's Wrong with Prostitution?

Igor Primoratz

Summary

Argues that the four major arguments against prostitution fail and thus prostitution is morally permissible. The paternalistic argument is rejected for assuming the conventional moral condemnation of commercial sex and for interfering with potentially free, informed decisions. The "sex should not be for sale" argument is rejected for relying on either the Augustinian view that sex is a dangerous and necessary evil or the romantic view that sex is only valuable within loving relationships. The "degrading to women" argument is rejected for assuming that impersonal commercial exchanges are uniquely degrading in sex but not in other goods and services transactions. The "oppressing to women" argument is rejected for assuming that social meanings of sexual activity remain largely unchanged over time.

Original publication details: Igor Primoratz, "What's Wrong with Prostitution?" pp. 159–182 from *Philosophy: The Journal of the Royal Institute of Philosophy* 68 (1993). Reproduced with permission of Cambridge University Press.

Over the last three decades the sexual morality of many Western societies has changed beyond recognition. Most of the prohibitions which made up the traditional, extremely restrictive outlook on sex that reigned supreme until the fifties – the prohibitions of masturbation, pre-marital and extra-marital sex, promiscuity, homosexuality – are no longer seen as very serious or stringent or, indeed, as binding at all. But one or two traditional prohibitions are still with us. The moral ban on prostitution, in particular, does not seem to have been repealed or radically mitigated. To be sure, some of the old arguments against prostitution are hardly ever brought up these days; but then, several new ones are quite popular, at least in certain circles. Prostitution is no longer seen as the most extreme moral depravity a woman is capable of; but the view that it is at least seriously morally flawed, if not repugnant and intolerable, is still widely held. In this paper I want to look into some of the main arguments in support of this view and try to show that none of them is convincing.[1]

[. . .]

2. Paternalism

Paternalism is most commonly defined as 'the interference with a person's liberty of action justified by reasons referring exclusively to the welfare, good, happiness, needs, interests or values of the person being coerced.'[2] Philosophical discussions of paternalism have concentrated on paternalist legislation; for the most obvious, and often the most effective, kind of interference with an individual's liberty of action is by means of law. But paternalism can also be put forward as a moral position: it can be argued that the wrongness of doing something follows from the fact that doing it has serious adverse effects on the welfare, good, etc. of the agent and, having made that judgment, to exert the pressure of the moral sanction on the individuals concerned to get them to refrain from doing it. A popular way of arguing against prostitution is of this sort: it refers to such hazards of selling sex as (i) venereal diseases; (ii) unpleasant, humiliating, even violent behaviour of clients; (iii) exploitation by madams and pimps; (iv) the extremely low social status of prostitutes and the contempt and ostracism to which they are exposed. The facts showing that these are, indeed, the hazards of prostitution are well known; are they not enough to show that prostitution is bad and to be avoided?

A short way with this objection is to refuse to acknowledge the moral credentials of paternalism, and to say that

what we have here is merely a prudential, not a moral argument against prostitution.

However, we may decide to accept that paternalist considerations can be relevant to questions about what is morally right and wrong. In that case, the first thing to note about the paternalist argument is that it is an argument from *occupational* hazards and thus, if valid, valid only against prostitution as an *occupation*. For in addition to the professional prostitute, whose sole livelihood comes from mercenary sex, there is also the amateur, who is usually gainfully employed or married and engages in prostitution for additional income. The latter – also known as the secret prostitute – need not at all suffer from (iii) and (iv), and stands a much lower chance of being exposed to (i) and (ii). A reference to (iii) actually is not even an argument against professional prostitution, but merely against a particular, by no means necessary way of practising it; if a professional prostitute is likely to be exploited by a madam or pimp, then she should pursue the trade on her own.

But it is more important to note that the crucial, although indirect cause of all these hazards of professional prostitution is the negative attitude of society, the condemnation of prostitution by its morality and its laws. But for that, the prostitute could enjoy much better medical protection, much more effective police protection from abusive and aggressive behaviour of clients and legal protection from exploitation by pimps and madams, and her social status would be quite different. Thus the paternalist argument takes for granted the conventional moral condemnation of prostitution, and merely gives an additional reason for not engaging in something that has already been established as wrong. But we can and should refuse to take that for granted, because we can and should refuse to submit to positive morality as the arbiter of moral issues. If we do so, and if a good case for morally condemning commercial sex has still not been made out, as I am trying to show in this paper, then all these hazards should be seen as reasons for trying to disabuse society of the prejudices against it and help to change the law and social conditions in general in which prostitutes work, in order radically to reduce, if not completely eliminate, such hazards.

However, there is one occupational hazard that has not been mentioned so far: one that cannot be blamed on unenlightened social morality, and would remain even if society were to treat prostitution as any other legitimate occupation. That is the danger to the sex life of the prostitute. As Lars Ericsson neatly puts it, 'Can one have a well-functioning sexual life if sex is what one lives by?'[3]

One way of tackling this particular paternalist objection is to say, with David A. J. Richards, that perhaps one can. Richards claims that there is no evidence that prostitution makes it impossible for those who practice it to have loving relationships, and adds that 'there is some evidence that prostitutes, as a class, are more sexually fulfilled than other American women.'[4] The last claim is based on a study in which 175 prostitutes were systematically interviewed, and which showed that 'they experienced orgasm and multiple orgasm more frequently in their personal, "non-commercial" intercourse than did the normal woman (as defined by Kinsey norms).'[5] Another, probably safer response is to point out, as Ericsson does, that the question is an empirical one and that, since there is no conclusive evidence either way, we are not in a position to draw any conclusion.[6]

My preferred response is different. I would rather grant the empirical claim that a life of prostitution is liable to wreck one's sex life, i.e. the minor premise of the argument, and then look a bit more closely into the major premise, the principle of paternalism. For there are two rather different versions of that principle. The weak version prevents the individual from acting on a choice that is not fully voluntary, either because the individual is permanently incompetent or because the choice in question is a result of ignorance of some important facts or made under extreme psychological or social pressure. Otherwise the individual is considered the sole qualified judge of his or her own welfare, good, happiness, needs, interests and values, and the choice is ultimately his or hers. Moreover, when a usually competent individual is prevented from acting on a choice that is either uninformed or made under extreme pressure, and is therefore not fully voluntary, that individual will, when the choice-impairing conditions no longer obtain, agree that the paternalist interference was appropriate and legitimate, and perhaps even be grateful for it. Strong paternalism *is* meant to protect the individual from his or her voluntary choices, and therefore will not be legitimized by retrospective consent of the individual paternalized. The assumption is not that the individual is normally the proper judge of his or her own welfare, good, etc., but rather that someone else knows better where the individual's true welfare, good, etc. lie, and therefore has the right to force the individual to act in accordance with the latter, even though that means acting against his or her fully voluntary choice, which is said to be merely 'subjective' or 'arbitrary'. Obviously, the weak version of paternalism does not conflict with personal liberty, but should rather be seen as its corollary; for it does not protect the

individual from choices that express his or her considered preferences and settled values, but only against his or her 'non-voluntary choices', choices the individual will subsequently disavow. Strong paternalism, on the other hand, is essentially opposed to individual liberty, and cannot be accepted by anyone who takes liberty seriously. Such paternalism smacks of intellectual and moral arrogance, and it is hard to see how it could ever be established by rational argument.[7]

Accordingly, if the argument from the dangers to the prostitute's sex life is not to be made rather implausible from the start, it ought to be put forward in terms of weak rather than strong paternalism. When put in these terms, however, it is not really an argument that prostitution is wrong because imprudent, but rather that it is wrong if and when it is taken up imprudently. It reminds us that persons permanently incompetent and those who still have not reached the age of consent should not (be allowed to) take up the life of prostitution and thereby most likely throw away the prospect of a good sex life. (They should not (be allowed to) become prostitutes for other reasons anyway.) As for a competent adult, the only legitimate paternalist interference with the choice of such a person to become a prostitute is to make sure that the choice is a free and informed one. But if an adult and sane person is fully apprised of the dangers of prostitution to the sex life of the prostitute and decides, without undue pressure of any sort, that the advantages of prostitution as an occupation are worth it, then it is neither imprudent nor wrong for that person to embark on the line of work chosen.[8] In such a case, as Mill put it, 'neither one person, nor any number of persons, is warranted in saying to another human creature of ripe years that he shall not do with his life for his own benefit what he chooses to do with it.[9]

3. Some Things Just Are Not for Sale

In the eyes of many, by far the best argument against prostitution is brief and simple: some things just are not for sale, and sex is one of them.

It would be difficult not to go along with the first part of this argument. The belief that not everything can or should be bought and sold is extremely widespread, if not universal. The list of things not for sale is not exactly the same in all societies, but it seems that every society does have such a list, a list of 'blocked exchanges'.

The term is Michael Walzer's, and a discussion of such exchanges is an important part of his theory of justice. The central thesis of the theory is that there are several spheres of personal qualities and social goods, each autonomous, with its own criteria, procedures and agents of distribution. Injustice occurs when this autonomy is violated, when the borders are crossed and a sphere of goods becomes dominated by another in that the goods of the former are no longer distributed in accordance with its own criteria and procedures, but in accordance with those of the other sphere. The market is one such sphere – actually, the sphere with the strongest tendency to expand into, and dominate, other spheres of goods, at least in a modern capitalist society. But even this kind of society has an impressive list of things not for sale. The one Walzer offers as 'the full set of blocked exchanges in the United States today', but which would be valid for any contemporary liberal and democratic society, includes the sale of human beings (slavery), political power and office, criminal justice, freedom of speech, various prizes and honours, love and friendship, and more.[10] This is, obviously, a mixed lot. In some cases, the very nature of a good rules out its being bought and sold (love, friendship; in others, that is precluded by the conventions which constitute it (prizes); in still others, the dominant conception of a certain sphere of social life prohibits the sale, as, for instance, our conception of the nature and purpose of the political process entails that political power and office must not be bought and sold. (To be sure, some of the things listed as a matter of fact are bought and sold. But that happens only on the black market, and the fact that the market is 'black', and that those who buy and sell there do so in secret, goes to show both the illegitimacy and the secondary, parasitic character of such transactions.) There is, thus, no single criterion by reference to which one could explain why all these items appear on the list, and why no other does.

What of sex? It is not on the list; for sex, unlike love, can, as a matter of fact, be bought and sold, and there is no single, generally accepted conception of sex that prohibits its sale and purchase. 'People who believe that sexual intercourse is morally tied to love and marriage are likely to favour a ban on prostitution . . .(. . .) Sex can be sold only when it is understood in terms of pleasure and not exclusively in terms of married love . . .'[11].

This is helpful, for it reminds us that the 'Not for sale' argument is elliptic; the understanding of sex that is presupposed must be explicated before the argument can be assessed. But the remark is also inaccurate, since it conflates two views of sex that are both historically and theoretically different: the traditional view, which originated in religion, that sex is legitimate only within

marriage and as a means to procreation, and the more modern, secular, 'romantic' view that sex is to be valued only when it expresses and enhances a loving relationship. Let me look briefly into these two views in order to see whether a commitment to either does, indeed, commit one to favouring a ban on prostitution.

The first views sex as intrinsically inferior, sinful and shameful, and accepts it only when, and in so far as, it serves an important extrinsic purpose which cannot be attained by any other means: procreation. Moreover, the only proper framework for bringing up children is marriage; therefore sex is permissible only within marriage. These two statements make up the core of the traditional Christian understanding of sex, elaborated in the writings of St. Augustine and St. Thomas Aquinas, which has been by far the most important source of Western sexual ethics. To be sure, modern Christian thought and practice have broadened this view in various ways, in order to allow for the role of sex in expressing and enhancing conjugal love and care. Within the Catholic tradition this has been recognized as the 'unitive' function of sex in marriage; but that is a rather limited development, for it is still maintained that the two functions of sex, the unitive and the procreative, are inseparable.

Do those who are committed to this view of sex – and in contemporary Western societies, I suppose, only practising Catholics are – have to endorse the ban on prostitution? At a certain level, they obviously must think ill of it; for, as has often been pointed out, theirs is the most restrictive and repressive sexual ethics possible. It confines sex within the bounds of heterosexual, monogamous, exclusive, indissoluble marriage, and rules out sexual relations between any possible partners except husband and wife (as well as masturbation). Moreover, it restricts the legitimate sexual relations between the spouses to those that are 'by nature ordained' toward procreation. Prostitution or, more accurately, common prostitution, which is both non-marital and disconnected from procreation, would seem to be beyond the pale.

But then, even the legitimacy of marital and procreative sex is of a rather low order: as sex, it is intrinsically problematic; as marital and procreative, it is accepted as a necessary evil, an inevitable concession to fallen human nature. As St. Augustine says, 'any friend of wisdom and holy joys who lives a married life' would surely prefer to beget children without 'the lust that excites the indecent parts of the body', if it only were possible.[12] Therefore, if it turns out that accepting sex within marriage and for the purpose of procreation only is not concession enough, that human sexuality is so strong and unruly that it cannot be confined within these bounds and that attempts to confine it actually endanger the institution of marriage itself, the inevitable conclusion will be that further concession is in order. That is just the conclusion reached by many authors with regard to prostitution: it should be tolerated, for it provides a safety valve for a force which will otherwise subvert the institution of marriage and destroy all the chastity and decency this institution makes possible. My favourite quotation is from Mandeville, who, of course, sees that as but another instance of the general truth that private vices are public benefits:

> If Courtezans and Strumpets were to be prosecuted with as much Rigour as some silly People would have it, what Locks or Bars would be sufficient to preserve the Honour of our Wives and Daughters? For 'tis not only that the Women in general would meet with far greater Temptations, and the Attempts to ensnare the Innocence of Virgins would seem more excusable to the sober part of Mankind than they do now: But some Men would grow outrageous, and Ravishing would become a common Crime. Where six or seven Thousand Sailors arrive at once, as it often happens at *Amsterdam,* that have seen none but their own Sex for many Months together, how is it to be supposed that honest Women should walk the Streets unmolested, if there were no Harlots to be had at reasonable Prices? (. . .). . . There is a Necessity of sacrificing one part of Womankind to preserve the other, and prevent a Filthiness of a more heinous Nature.[13]

That prostitution is indispensable for the stability and the very survival of marriage has not been pointed out only by cynics like Mandeville, misanthropes like Schopenhauer,[14] or godless rationalists like Lecky[15] and Russell;[16] it was acknowledged as a fact, and as one that entails that prostitution ought to be tolerated rather than suppressed, by St. Augustine and St. Thomas themselves.[17] Moreover, it has been confirmed by sociological study of human sexual behaviour, which shows that the majority of clients of prostitutes are married men who do not find complete sexual fulfillment within marriage, but are content to stay married provided they can have extramarital commercial sex as well.[18] Accordingly, even if one adopts the most conservative and restrictive view of sex there is, the view which ties sex to marriage and procreation, one need not, indeed should not condemn prostitution. One should rather take a tolerant attitude to it, knowing that it is twice removed from the ideal state of affairs, but that its demise would bring about something incomparably worse.

Another view which would seem to call for the condemnation of prostitution is the 'romantic' view of sex as essentially tied to love; for mercenary sex is normally as loveless as sex can ever get. The important thing to note is that whatever unfavourable judgment on prostitution is suggested by this view of sex, it will not be a judgment unfavourable to prostitution as such, but rather to prostitution as a type of loveless sex. It is the lovelessness, not the commercial nature of the practice that the 'romantic' objects to.

One response to this kind of objection would be to take on squarely the view of sex that generates it. One could, first, take a critical look at the arguments advanced in support of the view that sex should always be bound up with love; second, bring out the difficulties of the linkage, the tensions between love and sex which seem to make a stable and fruitful combination of the two rather unlikely; finally, argue for the superiority of loveless, noncommittal, 'plain sex' over sex that is bound up with love. All this has already been done by philosophers such as Alan Goldman and Russell Vannoy,[19] and probably by innumerable non-philosophers as well.

Another response would be to grant the validity of the 'romantic' view of sex, but only as a personal ideal, not a universally binding moral standard. This is the tack taken by Richards,[20] who points out that it would be signally misguided, indeed absurd, to try to enforce this particular ideal, based as it is 'on the cultivation of spontaneous romantic feeling.'[21] My preferred response to the 'romantic' objection is along these lines, but I would like to go a bit further, and emphasize that it is possible to appreciate the 'romantic, ideal and at the same time not only grant that sex which falls short of it need not be wrong, but also allow that it can be positively good (without going as far as to claim that it is actually better than sex with love).

The 'romantic' typically points out the difference between sex with and without love. The former is a distinctively human, complex, rich and fruitful experience, and a matter of great importance; the latter is merely casual, a one-dimensional, barren experience that satisfies only for a short while and belongs to our animal nature. These differences are taken to show that sex with love is valuable, while loveless sex is not. This kind of reasoning has the following structure:

A is much better than B.

Therefore, B is no good at all.

In addition to being logically flawed, this line of reasoning, if it were to be applied in areas other than sex, would prove quite difficult to follow. For one thing, all but the very rich among us would die of hunger; for only the very rich can afford to take *all* their meals at the fanciest restaurants.[22]

Of course, B can be good, even if it is much less good than A. Loveless sex is a case in point. Moreover, other things being equal, it is better to be able to enjoy both loving and loveless sex than only the former. A person who enjoyed sex as part of loving relationships but was completely incapable of enjoying plain sex would seem to be missing out on something. To be sure, the 'romantic' rejection of plain sex often includes the claim that other things are not equal: that a person who indulges in plain sex thereby somehow damages, and ultimately destroys, his or her capacity for experiencing sex as an integral part of a loving relationship. This is a straightforward empirical claim about human psychology; and it is clearly false.

[. . .]

4. The Feminist Critique (a): Degradation of Women

[. . .]

One might want to take issue with the whole feminist approach to the question of prostitution as a question about women; for, after all, not all prostitutes are women, But this is not a promising tack; for, if not all, most of them are and always have been. So if prostitution involves either degradation or oppression, the great majority of those degraded or oppressed are women. But does it?

There is no denying that the belief that prostitution degrades those who practise it is very widespread. But this belief may be wrong. The question is: *Just why* should prostitution be considered degrading? There are four main answers: (i) because it is utterly impersonal; (ii) because the prostitute is reduced to a mere means; (iii) because of the intimate nature of the acts she performs for money; (iv) became she actually sells her body, herself. Let me look into each of these claims in turn.

(i) Prostitution is degrading because the relation between the prostitute and the client is completely impersonal. The client does not even perceive, let alone treat the prostitute as the person she is; he has no interest, no time for any of her personal characteristics, but relates to her merely as a source of sexual satisfaction, nothing more than a sex object.

One possible response to this is that prostitution need not be impersonal. There is, of course, the streetwalker who sells sex to all comers (or almost); but there is also the prostitute with a limited number of steady clients, with whom she develops quite personal relationships. So if the objection is to the impersonal character of the relation, the most that can be said is that a certain kind of prostitution is degrading, not that prostitution as such is. I do not want to make much of this, though. For although in this, as in many other services, there is the option of personalized service, the other, impersonal variety is typical.

My difficulty with the argument is more basic: I cannot see why the impersonal nature of a social transaction or relation makes that transaction or relation degrading. After all, the personal relations we have with others – with our family, friends and acquaintances – are just a small part (although the most important part) of our social life. The other part includes the overwhelming majority of our social transactions and relations which are, and have to be, quite impersonal. I do not have a personal relationship with the newspaper vendor, the bus driver, the shop assistant, and all those numerous other people I interact with in the course of a single day; and, as long as the basic decencies of social intercourse (which are purely formal and impersonal) are observed, there is nothing wrong with that. There is nothing wrong for me to think of and relate to the newspaper vendor as just that and, as far as I am concerned, nothing more. That our social relations must for the most part be impersonal may be merely a consequence of the scarcity of resources we invest in them. But it is inescapable in any but the smallest and simplest, so-called face-to-face society.

[. . .]

(ii) Prostitution is said to degrade the prostitute because she is used as a means by the client. The client relates to the prostitute in a purely instrumental way: she is no more than a means to his sexual satisfaction. If so, is he not reducing her to a mere means, a thing, a sex object, and thereby degrading her?

If he were to rape her, that would indeed amount to treating her without regard to her desires, and thus to reducing, degrading her to a mere means. But as a customer rather than a rapist, he gets sexual satisfaction from her for a charge, on the basis of a mutual understanding, and she does her part of the bargain willingly. It is not true that he acts without regard to her desires. He does not satisfy her sexual desire; indeed, the prostitute does not desire that he should do so. But he does satisfy the one desire she has with regard to him: the desire for money. Their transaction is not 'a mutual delight, entered into solely from the spontaneous impulse of both parties', but rather a calculated exchange of goods of different order. But it does not offend against the principle of respect for human beings as such as long as it is free from coercion and fraud, and both sides get what they want.[23]

[...]

(iii) Sex is an intimate, perhaps the most intimate part of our lives. Should it not therefore be off limits to commercial considerations and transactions? And is it not degrading to perform something so intimate as a sex act with a complete stranger and for money?

It is not. As Ericsson points out,

> we are no more justified in devaluating the prostitute, who, for example, masturbates her customers, than we are in devaluating the assistant nurse, whose job it is to take care of the intimate hygiene of disabled patients. Both help to satisfy important human needs, and both get paid for doing so. That the harlot, in distinction to the nurse, intentionally gives her client pleasure is of course nothing that should be held against her![24]

It might be objected that the analogy is not valid, for there is an important asymmetry between pain and pleasure: the former has significantly greater moral weight than the latter. While it may be morally acceptable to cross the borders of intimacy in order to relieve pain or suffering, which is what the nurse does, that does not show that it is permissible to do so merely for the sake of giving pleasure, which is what the prostitute provides. But if so, what are we to say of a fairly good looking woman who undergoes plastic surgery and has her breasts enlarged (or made smaller) in order to become even more attractive and make her sex life richer and more pleasurable than it already is? Is she really doing something degrading and morally wrong?

(iv) Prostitution is degrading because what the prostitute sells is not simply and innocuously a service, as it may appear to a superficial look; actually, there is much truth in the old-fashioned way of speaking of her as a woman who 'sells herself'. And if *that* is not degrading, what is?

This point has been made in two different ways.

David Archard has recently argued that there is a sense in which the prostitute sells herself because of the roles and attitudes involved in the transaction;

Sexual pleasure is not . . . an innocent commodity. Always implicated in such pleasure is the performance of roles, both willing and unwilling. These roles range from the possibly benign ones of doer and done-to, through superior and subordinate to abaser and abased. Thus, when a man buys 'sex' he also buys a sexual role from his partner, and this involves the prostitute in being something more than simply the neutral exchanger of some commodity.

More specifically,

> if I buy (and you willingly sell) your allegiance, your obsequiousness, your flattery or your servility there is no easy distinction to be made between you as 'seller' and the 'good' you choose to sell. Your whole person is implicated in the exchange. So it is too with the sale of sex.[25]

However, commercial sex need not involve obsequiousness, flattery or servility, let alone allegiance, on the part of the prostitute. These attitudes, and the 'role' they might be thought to make up, are not its constitutive parts; whether, when, and to what degree they characterize the transaction is an empirical question that admits of no simple and general answer. Indeed, those who, knowingly or not, tend to approach the whole subject of sex from a 'romantic' point of view often say that sex with prostitutes is an impoverished, even sordid experience because of the impersonal, quick, mechanical, blunt way in which the prostitute goes about her job.

Moreover, some services that have nothing to do with sex tend to involve and are expected to involve some such attitudes on the part of the person providing the service. Examples would vary from culture to culture; the waiter and the hairdresser come to mind in ours. Now such attitudes are undoubtedly morally flawed; but that does not tell against any particular occupation in which they may be manifested, but rather against the attitudes themselves, the individuals who, perhaps unthinkingly, come to adopt them, and the social conventions that foster such attitudes.

Another way to try to show that the prostitute sells herself, rather than merely a service like any other, is to focus on the concept of self-identity. This is the tack taken by Carole Pateman. She first points out that the service provided by the prostitute is related in a much closer way to her body than is the case with any other service, for sex and sexuality are constitutive of the body, while the labour and skills hired out in other lines of work are not. 'Sexuality and the body are . . . integrally connected to conceptions of femininity and masculinity, and all these are constitutive of our individuality, our sense of self-identity.'[26] Therefore, when sex becomes a commodity, so do bodies and selves.

But if so, what of our ethnic identity? When asked to say who they are, do not people normally bring up their ethnic identity as one of the most important things they need to mention? If it is granted that one's ethnic identity is also constitutive of one's individuality, one's sense of self-identity, what are we to say of a person who creates an item of authentic folk art and then sells it, or of a singer who gives a concert of folk music and charges for attendance? Are they also selling themselves, and thus doing something degrading and wrong?

[. . .]

5. The Feminist Critique (b): Oppression of Women

The other main feminist objection to prostitution is that it exemplifies and helps to maintain the oppression of women. This objection is much more often made than argued. It is frequently made by quoting the words of Simone de Beauvoir that the prostitute 'sums up all the forms of feminine slavery at once';[27] but de Beauvoir's chapter on prostitution, although quite good as a description of some of its main types, is short on argument and does nothing to show that prostitution as such must be implicated in the oppression of women.

An argument meant to establish that with regard to our society has recently been offered by Laurie Shrage. She expressly rejects the idea of discussing commercial sex in a 'cross-cultural' or 'trans-historical' way, and grants that it need not be oppressive to women in every conceivable or, indeed, every existing society. What she does claim is that in our society prostitution epitomizes and perpetuates certain basic cultural assumptions about men, women and sex which provide justification for the oppression of women in many domains of their lives, and in this way harm both prostitutes and women in general.[28]

There are four such cultural assumptions, which need not be held consciously but may be implicit in daily behaviour. A strong sex drive is a universal human trait. Sexual behaviour defines one's social identity, makes one a particular 'kind' of person: one is 'a homosexual', 'a prostitute', 'a loose woman'. Men are 'naturally' dominant. In this connection, Shrage points out that the sex industry in our society caters almost exclusively to men, and 'even the relatively small number of male prostitutes at work serve a predominantly male consumer group.'[29] Finally, sexual contact pollutes and harms women.

The last claim is supported by a three-pronged argument. (i) In a woman, a history of sexual activity is not taken to suggest experience in a positive sense, expertise, high-quality sex. On the contrary, it is seen as a negative mark that marks off a certain kind of woman; women are valued for their 'innocence'. (ii) That sex with men is damaging to women is implicit in the vulgar language used to describe the sex act: 'a woman is "fucked", "screwed", "banged", "had", and so forth, and it is a man (a "prick") who does it to her.'[30] (iii) The same assumption is implicit in 'the metaphors we use' for the sex act. Here Shrage draws on Andrea Dworkin's book *Intercourse,* which invokes images of physical assault and imperialist domination and describes women having sexual intercourse with men as being not only entered or penetrated, but also 'split', 'invaded', 'occupied' and 'colonized' by men.

These cultural assumptions define the meaning of prostitution in our society. By tolerating prostitution, our society implies its acceptance of these assumptions, which legitimize and perpetuate the oppression of women and their marginality in all the main areas of social life. As for prostitutes and their clients, whatever their personal views of sex, men and women, they imply by their actions that they accept these assumptions and the practice they justify.

Now this argument is unobjectionable as far as it goes; but it does not go as far as Shrage means it to. In order to assess its real scope, we should first note that she repeatedly speaks of 'our' and 'our society's' toleration of prostitution, and refers to this toleration as the main ground for the conclusion that the cultural assumptions prostitution is said to epitomize in our society are indeed generally accepted in it, But toleration and acceptance are not quite the same; actually, toleration is normally defined as the putting up with something we *do not* accept, Moreover, prostitution is not tolerated at all. It is not tolerated legally: in the United States it is legal only in Nevada and illegal in all other states, while in the United Kingdom and elsewhere in the West, even though it is not against the law as such, various activities practically inseparable from it are. Some of these restrictions are quite crippling; for instance, as Marilyn G. Haft rightly says, 'to legalize prostitution while prohibiting solicitation makes as much sense as encouraging free elections but prohibiting campaigning.'[31] It certainly is not tolerated morally; as I pointed out at the beginning, the condemnation of prostitution is one of the very few prohibitions of the traditional sexual morality that are still with us. It is still widely held that prostitution is seriously morally wrong, and the prostitute is subjected to considerable moral pressure, including the ultimate moral sanction, ostracism from decent society. That the practice is still with us is not for want of trying to suppress it, and therefore should not be taken as a sign that it is being tolerated.

Furthermore, not all the cultural assumptions prostitution in our society allegedly epitomizes and reinforces are really generally accepted. The first two – that human beings have a strong sex drive, and that one's sexual behaviour defines one's social identity – probably are. The other two assumptions – that men are 'naturally' dominant, and that sex with men harms women – are more important, for they make it possible to speak of oppression of women in this context. I am not so sure about the former; my impression is that at the very least it is no longer accepted quite as widely as it used to be a couple of decades ago. And I think it is clear that the latter is not generally accepted in our society today. The evidence Shrage brings up to show that it is far from compelling.

(i) It is probably true that the fact that a woman has a history of sexual activity is not generally appreciated as an indicator of experience and expertise, analogously to other activities. But whatever the explanation is – and one is certainly needed – I do not think that entails the other half of Shrage's diagnosis, namely that women are valued for their 'innocence'. That particular way of valuing women and the whole 'Madonna or harlot' outlook to which it belongs are well behind us as a society, although they characterize the sexual morality of some very traditional communities. A society which has made its peace with non-marital sex in general and adolescent sex in particular to the extent that ours has could not possibly have persisted in valuing women for their 'innocence'.

(ii) Shrage draws on Robert Baker's analysis of the language used to refer to men, women and sex. Baker's point of departure is the claim that the way we talk about something reflects our conception of it; be looks into the ways we talk about sex and gender in order to discover what our conceptions of these are. With regard to sexual intercourse, it turns out that the vulgar verbs used to refer to it such as 'fuck', 'screw', 'lay', 'have' etc. display an interesting asymmetry: they require an active construction when the subject is a man, and a passive one when the subject is a woman. This reveals that we conceive of male and female roles in sex in different ways: the male is active, the female passive. Some of these verbs – 'fuck', 'screw', 'have' – are also used metaphorically to indicate deceiving, taking advantage of, harming someone. This shows that we conceive of the male sexual role as that of harming the person in the female role, and of a person who plays the female sexual role as someone who is being harmed.[32]

This is both interesting and revealing, but what is revealed is not enough to support Shrage's case. Why is 'the standard view of sexual intercourse'[33] revealed not in the standard, but in the vulgar, i.e. substandard way of talking about it? After all, everybody, at least occasionally, talks about it in the standard way, while only some use the vulgar language too. Baker justifies his focusing on the latter by pointing out that the verbs which belong to the former, and are not used in the sense of inflicting harm as well, 'can take both females and males as subjects (in active constructions) and thus *do not pick out the female role*. This demonstrates that we conceive of sexual roles in such a way that only females are thought to be taken advantage of in intercourse.'[34] It seems to me that the 'we' is quite problematic, and that all that these facts demonstrate is that some of us, namely those who speak of having sex with women as fucking or screwing them, also think of sex with them in these terms. Furthermore, the ways of talking about sex may be less fixed than Baker's analysis seems to suggest. According to Baker, sentences such as 'Jane fucked Dick', 'Jane screwed Dick' and 'Jane laid Dick', if taken in the literal sense, are not sentences in English. But the usage seems to have changed since his article was published; I have heard native speakers of English make such sentences without a single (linguistic) eyebrow being raised. The asymmetry seems to have lost ground. So the import of the facts analysed by Baker is much more limited than he and Shrage take it to be, and the facts themselves are less clear-cut and static too.

(iii) Shrage's third argument for the claim that our society thinks of sex with men as polluting and harmful to women is the weakest. Images of physical assault and imperialist domination certainly are not 'the metaphors we use for the act of sexual intercourse'; I do not know that anyone except Andrea Dworkin does. The most likely reason people do not is that it would be silly to do so.

What all this shows, I think, is that there is no good reason to believe that our society adheres to a single conception of heterosexual sex, the conception defined by the four cultural assumptions Shrage describes, claims to be epitomized in, and reinforced by, prostitution, and wants to ascribe to every single case of commercial sex in our society as its 'political and social meaning', whatever the beliefs and values of the individuals concerned. Some members of our society think of heterosexual sex in terms of Shrage's four assumptions and some do not. Accordingly, there are in our society two rather different conceptions of prostitution, which in this context are best termed (a) prostitution as commercial screwing, and (b) prostitution as commercial sex *simpliciter*. What is their relative influence on the practice of prostitution in our society is a question for empirical research. Shrage rightly objects to the former for being implicated in the oppression of women in our society, and one need not be a feminist in order to agree. But that objection is not an objection to prostitution in our society as such.

6. Conclusion

I have taken a critical look at a number of arguments advanced to support the claim that prostitution stands morally condemned. If what I have been saying is right, none of these arguments is convincing.[35] Therefore, until some new and better ones are put forward, the conclusion must be that there is nothing morally wrong with it.[36] [. . .]

Notes

1 I am concerned only with prostitution in its primary, narrow sense of 'commercial' or 'mercenary sex', 'sex for money', and not with prostitution in the derived sense of 'use of one's ability or talent in a base or unworthy way'. The question I am asking is whether prostitution in the former, original sense is a case of prostitution in the latter, secondary sense.

2 G. Dworkin, 'Paternalism', *The Monist* 56 (1972), 65.

3 L. Ericsson, 'Charges against Prostitution: An Attempt at a Philosophical Assessment', *Ethics* 90 (1979/80), 357.

4 D. A. J. Richards, *Sex, Drugs, Death, and the Law: An Essay on Human Rights and Overcriminalization* (Totowa, NJ: Rowman and Littlefield, 1982), 113.

5 Ibid., 146 n. 251. The study referred to is described in W. B. Pomeroy, 'Some Aspects of Prostitution', *Journal of Sex Research* 1 (1965).

6 L. Ericsson, loc. cit.

7 For an analysis of the two kinds of paternalism, see J. Feinberg, 'Legal Paternalism', *Canadian Journal of Philosophy* 1 (1971).

8 Many authors who have written on prostitution as a 'social evil' have claimed that it is virtually never a freely chosen occupation, since various social conditions (lack of education, poverty, unemployment) force innumerable women into it. This argument makes it possible for Mrs Warren (and many others) to condemn prostitution, while absolving the prostitute. But even if the empirical claim were true, it would not amount to an argument against prostitution, but only against the lack of alternatives to it.

9 J. S, Mill, *On Liberty*, C. V. Shields (ed.) (Indianapolis: Bobbs-Merrill, 1956), 93.
It was clear to Mill that his rejection of paternalism applied in the case of prostitution just as in any other case, but the way he says that is somewhat demure; see ibid., 120–122.

10 M. Walzer, *The Spheres of Justice* (New York: Basic Books, 1983), 100–103.

11 Ibid., 103, (The parts of the quotation I have deleted refer to religious prostitution, which is not the subject of this paper.)

12 Augustine, *Concerning the City of God*, trans. H. Bettenson (Harmonds-worth: Penguin, 1972), Bk. 14, Ch. 16, 577.

13 B. Mandeville, *The Fable of the Bees*, F. B. Kaye (ed.) (Oxford University Press, 1957), Remark (H.), I, 95–96, 100.
Mandeville discusses prostitution in detail in *A Modest Defence of Publick Stews: or, an Essay upon Whoring, As it is now practis'd in these Kingdoms* (London: A. Moore, 1724) (published anonymously). The argument I have quoted from the *Fable* is elaborated on pp. ii–iii, xi–xii, 39–52.

14 A. Schopenhauer, 'On Women', *Parerga and Paralipomena*, trans. E. F. J. Payne (Oxford: Oxford University Press, 1974), I, 623.

15 W. E. H. Lecky, *History of European Morals* (London: Longmans, Green & Co., 1869), II, 299–300.

16 B. Russell, *Marriage and Morals* (London: George Allen & Unwin, 1958), 116.

17 St. Augustine, *De ordine*, II, 4; St. Thomas Aquinas, *Summa theologiae*, 2a2ae, q. 10, art. 11.

18 H. Benjamin and R. E. L. Masters, *Prostitution and Morality* (London: Souvenir Press, 1965), 201.

19 See A. Goldman, 'Plain Sex', *Philosophy of Sex*, A. Soble (ed.) (Totowa, NJ: Littlefield, Adams & Co., 1980); R. Vannoy, *Sex without Love: A Philosophical Exploration* (Buffalo: Prometheus Books, 1980).

20 op. cit., 99–104.

21 Ibid., 103–104.

22 For examples of this kind of reasoning and a detailed discussion of its structure, see J. Wilson, *Logic and Sexual Morality* (Harmondsworth: Penguin, 1965), 59–74.

23 Here I find Russell's version of the principle of respect for human beings as such more helpful than the classic, Kantian one (H. J. Paton, *The Moral Law: Kant's Groundwork*

of the Metaphysic of Morals (London: Hutchinson, 1969), 90–93); for Russell puts it forward as an independent principle, while in Kant it cannot function on its own, but only when accepted together with other tenets of Kant's ethical theory, which one may well find problematic (cf, H. E. Jones, *Kant's Principle of Personality* (Madison: The University of Wisconsin Press, 1971)).

24 L. Ericsson, op. cit., 342.

25 D. Archard, 'Sex for Sale: The Morality of Prostitution', *Cogito* 3 (1989), 49–50.

26 C. Pateman, 'Defending Prostitution: Charges against Ericsson', *Ethics* 93 (1982/3), 562.

27 S. de Beauvoir, *The Second Sex*, trans. and ed. H. M. Parabley (London: Pan Books, 1988), 569.

28 By 'our society' Shrage most of the time seems to mean contemporary American society, but toward the end of the paper claims to have discussed 'the meaning of commercial sex in modern Western culture' (L. Shrage, 'Should Feminists Oppose Prostitution?', *Ethics* 99 (1989/90), 361).

29 Ibid. 354.

30 Ibid. 355.

31 M. G. Haft, 'Hustling for Rights', *The Civil Liberties Review* 1 (1973/4), 20, quoted in A. M. Jaggar, 'Prostitution', *Philosophy of Sex*, A. Soble (ed.), 350.

32 See R. Baker, '"Pricks" and "Chicks": A Plea for "Persons"', *Philosophy and Sex*, R. Baker and P. Elliston (eds.) (Buffalo: Prometheus Books, 1975).

33 Ibid. 50.

34 Ibid. 61.

35 I have not discussed those arguments against prostitution which I think have been effectively refuted by others. See L. Ericsson, op. cit., on the arguments that prostitution exemplifies and reinforces commercialization of society, that it is an extreme case of the general inequality between men and women, that sex is much too basic and elementary in human life to be sold, and on the marxist critique of prostitution in general, and L. E. Lomasky, 'Gift Relations, Sexual Relations and Freedom', *The Philosophical Quarterly* 33 (1983), on the argument that commercial sex devalues sex given freely, as a gift.

36 That is, there is nothing morally wrong with it as long as the term 'morally wrong' is used in its robust sense, nicely captured e.g. by Mill: 'We do not call anything wrong unless we mean to imply that a person ought to be punished in some way or other for doing it – if not by law, by the opinion of his fellow creatures; if not by opinion, by the reproaches of his own conscience' (*Utilitarianism*, G. Sher (ed.) (Indianapolis: Hackett, 1979), 47). This is the sense the term usually has in everyday moral discourse. When we say, e.g., that stealing is wrong, we normally do not mean to say merely that stealing falls short of the ideal way of relating to other people's property, or is not part of the good life, the best use one can put one's fingers to, or something one would recommend as a career to one's teenage daughter; we rather express our condemnation of stealing and imply that it is appropriate to apply the pressure of the moral sanction on those who steal. Of course, those given to using the term in some wider, watered-down sense may well come to the conclusion that prostitution is wrong after all.

43

Moral Reflections on Prostitution

Yolanda Estes

Summary

Argues that liberal and libertarian accounts of the moral innocence of prostitution are flawed. Taking a Kantian perspective, argues that prostitution is immoral because it always involves taking a disrespectful objectifying attitude toward another human as a mere means to achieve a bodily goal – a position supported by the phenomenal description of prostitution as degrading and manipulative.

Original publication details: Yolanda Estes, "Moral Reflections on Prostitution," pp. 73–83 from *Essays in Philosophy* 2:2 (2001). Reproduced with permission of Philosophy Documentation Center.

Sexual Ethics: An Anthology, First Edition. Edited by Patrick D. Hopkins.

Yolanda Estes

Introduction

Many "liberal," or libertarian, accounts of prostitution assert that prostitution is no more intrinsically wrong or harmful than any other type of service work.[1] I believe that prostitution violates the Kantian "principle of humanity," because it reflects a disrespectful attitude, which is expressed in the nonchalant use of the human body as a mere means to achieve some goal.[2] I hope to convince my readers, who may not share my moral presuppositions, that prostitution defies the limits of respectful sexual relations, because it proffers a monetary substitute for mutual desire and concern and, hence, that it is a morally questionable and harmful activity.[3] In support of these claims, I offer: 1) a discussion of Kantian morality and sexual ethics, 2) an explanation of the minimum criteria for respectful sexual relations, 3) a description of the general dynamic of prostitution, 4) an analysis of the client's objective, and 5) a phenomenology of prostituted sex.

I. Kantian Morality and Sexual Ethics

Kantian moral theory identifies subjectivity and dignity with a self-determining will located within the limited willing activity of embodied individuals. The individual knows itself as a subject only by means of the recognition of another subject within a particular social context.[4] Sexuality is one way in which individuals express their subjectivity. Each empirical subject is partly determined by its choices with regard to sexual expression and its mode of integrating sex, gender, and sexuality within its life as a whole.

All sexual activities express subjectivity, but not all sexual activities involve mutual respect. Some sexual activities reflect a person's attempt to determine another subject, by receiving the other's recognition of the person's will, without yielding to the other's influence, recognizing the other's will, and thus without incurring an obligation to them. The wrongfulness of actions, sexual or not, resides in this affront to another person's human dignity. This account of sexual morality may not satisfy every moral theory, but most moral theories would allow that sexual relations should involve some type of mutual respect, so I shall outline some minimum criteria for mutually respectful sexual relations that do not bind the reader to an explicitly Kantian position.

II. Mutually Respectful Sex

Mutually respectful sex occurs within a context of mutual consent, desire, and concern. Mutual respect requires that potential sexual partners give an explicit, or at least an implicit, expression of their willing participation in the sexual act. Verbal consent is the most obvious expression of a person's free decision to participate in an activity, but consent alone provides no immunity to moral reproach. Insofar as one shows a respectful regard for a potential sexual partner, one cannot ignore her desires.[5] While one need not accommodate others' desires, one ought to take their desires and aversions into account.[6] Moreover, one should exhibit concern for the other's interests, needs, and general well being.[7]

Without mutual consent, desire, and concern, potentially pleasing, bodily acts become sexual intrusions that obscure the distinction between a human body and a thing.[8] Other standards might be necessary to determine that a sexual encounter is morally right, personally satisfying, or prudent, but respect for persons in the sexual context requires these minimum criteria. If the motivations for sexual activity preclude treating either sexual partner with respect, sexual activity objectifies the participants and violates their human dignity. Although such acts can damage or destroy the human body, the relevant issue is that they appropriate it without concern for its subjectivity.[9] The following description shows that the general dynamic of prostitution presumes the absence of mutual desire and concern and thus, that prostitution fails to meet minimum criteria of mutually respectful sexual relations.

III. The General Dynamic of Prostitution

The prostitute uses her body as a means for monetary gain. Money is her primary objective and not merely a deciding factor.[10] This factor would be secondary only if the prostitute were willing to engage in the act without it. She engages in the act for reasons other than her own sexual desire and hence, her toleration of sex in the prostitution encounter occurs without expressing a desire to relate to her client sexually. Do these conditions imply anything significant about prostitution? I believe so, but in order to expose those implications, I must first consider the client, his objective, and certain arguments for prostitution.

The client uses the prostitute's body as a means for sexual gratification. Sexual pleasure is his primary motivation. The client understands that something other than sexual desire motivates her actions. Regardless of attempts to convince himself otherwise, only a very stupid man believes a woman desires him when she rejects his sexual advances without monetary compensation. The client's lack of concern for her is equally obvious insofar as he accepts her terms. Nonetheless, many outlets for sexual expression exist, so what motivates a man to buy the services of a prostitute rather than to seek the company of unpaid lovers or his own right hand? The general dynamic of prostitution fails to answer this question. The client's secret objective hides between the cracks in a common liberal account of prostitution. Exposing this objective will show that not only does prostitution fail to meet minimum criteria of respectful sexual relations but that it also raises profound concerns for almost any moral theory.

IV. The Client's Objective

Many liberal accounts of prostitution compare sexual desires to physical needs, like hunger, and sexual work to service work, like the restaurant industry. If this comparison were strong then an analogy of buying sex and dining out would illuminate the client's objectives. A man buys a meal in a restaurant because he is hungry and does not like, know how, or have time to cook.

Presumably, a man uses a prostitute to sate his sexual appetite. At this point, however, the analogy between the motivations of the client and the diner weakens. After all, masturbation offers a form of immediate sexual relief that most people readily enjoy and grasp.

Lest I be accused of oversimplifying the liberal account, I shall consider a more refined version of the analogy by comparing the prostitute's client and the gourmet diner. A full stomach fails to satisfy the gourmet who craves a meal prepared by an expert chef. Perhaps the client seeks sexual expertise. This seems most unlikely. If men sought prostitutes because they wanted sexual skill, prostitutes would possess some type of unique sexual training or talent. Very few, if any, prostitutes undergo any sort of unique sexual training, and although prostitutes accumulate a certain level of experience; experience, as disappointed diners and lovers know, does not necessarily produce good cooks or lovers.[11] The prostitute's client is no more like a gourmet diner than he is like a hungry man.

The liberal analogy fails because it reflects the misconception that prostitution exists to relieve sexual needs. The prostitute's client wants something other than a mere orgasm or even an especially good orgasm.

He wants sexual relations with a woman. This, however, does not explain why he buys the sexual services of a woman. Perhaps, he is homely, loathsome, shy, or in some way unappealing to most women and therefore unable to find willing sexual partners. Although few people are that repugnant, most people meet obstacles in their pursuit of sexual satisfaction.[12] It is, however, usually possible to overcome these difficulties by altering one's expectations, improving oneself, and in general, trying harder. Furthermore, most men who seek prostitutes have, or could obtain, willing, unpaid sexual partners.[13] In other words, finding a sexual partner is not the issue; perhaps, he wants a particular sort of woman.

What sort of woman does the client want? He might want a more comely, obliging, or sexually adventurous woman. Why not seek relationships with beautiful, accommodating, or innovative women with whom he can share his desires? I reply, in a word: expedience. Initiating, building, and working for the type of sexual relationships that he desires involve an inconvenient, time-consuming, and arduous endeavor. Sexual activity offers potential delight but also potential rebuff, chagrin, and feelings of inadequacy. Moreover, even so-called "casual" relationships require some work, time, and obligations. Sexual partners may fulfill our desires, but they usually have desires that they want obliged too. Maintaining sexual relationships burdens the client with responsibilities and demands, which he would prefer to avoid.[14]

The prostitute does not satisfy the need for a woman or even the demand for a particular sort of woman. She accommodates the client's desires for a woman who ceases to exist when she is no longer wanted.[15] A man seeks a prostitute in order to avoid the inconvenience of sexual relations with another subject. Indeed, he pays her to disguise the subjectivity expressed through her individual needs, interests, and desires.[16] With a prostitute, a man can have sex when and how he wants it. The client can choose a woman on the basis of almost any criteria without exerting himself to attract her attention and arouse her desire. The consequences she bears for their sexual encounter need not concern him.

The prostitute's client wants to be like a restaurant patron or a gourmet diner. He *wants* to "taste" a woman with the same casual sensuality displayed in consuming a well-prepared rump-roast.[17] But what he wants in addition to this, the most demanding gourmet never asked from any piece of meat. Good manners, sexual skill, and convenience will not suffice. The prostitute must attend to her client as would a desiring lover. Her sexual performance must exhibit recognition of his individuality, his person.[18] As noted by John Start Mill and Immanuel Kant and more recently seconded by Carol Pateman:

> Their masters require something more from them than actual service. Men do not want solely the obedience of women, they want their sentiments. All men, except the most brutish, desire to have, not a forced slave but a willing one, not a slave merely, but a favorite.[19]

Here, the liberal account of prostitution as a mutually beneficial, morally neutral, rational agreement between consenting equals disintegrates. The client stands in the absurd position of desiring a contradiction. Moreover, his desire expresses morally suspect objectives; for what 'more than actual service' could one rightfully demand from a professional, an employee, a servant, or, even, a "forced" slave? If the reader would imagine how these objectives influence the participants' sexual interplay, he or she might see that prostitution is scarcely beneficial for the prostitute or her client.

V. A Phenomenology of Prostitution

In prostitution, as in slavery, the "master's" desires remain unfulfilled, for obedience is bought rather than given.[20] The prostitute's consent to engage in sexual relations need not express her sentiments and indeed; her client has every reason to suspect that it does not. Her sexual identity and desires are entangled in a web of familial and social ties, personal interests and activities that constitute her life beyond prostitution. He cannot tap her passions without enmeshing himself therein.

The prostitute's role as "willing" slave demands that she exclude her sexual individuality from the encounter. She wants to preserve the integrity of her subjectivity and personal life without jeopardizing her agreement with the client. An indifferent attitude might insulate her individual subjectivity, but he expects more than a skilled automaton. Passionate reference to the richness of her personal life or solicitations for recognition of her desires and interests might force him to view her as a subject. Nonetheless, these modes of disclosing her subjectivity jeopardize her privacy and exceed the scope of her agreement with the client. A compromise more aptly preserves both her professional role and her sense of self and, thus, she might present an image of sexual desire by means of small talk, flirtation, and other theatrical devices.

Their sexual activity evokes feelings, emotions, and autonomic reactions that threaten the illusion. Every visible reaction evinced by the handling of her body must address the client's desires rather than her own. Her repugnance must not appear to him as disgust. Submitting to any pleasurable sensation threatens the integrity of her bonds with others, her sense of control, and the pretended irrelevance of her own bodily needs. In order to attend to her client's pleasure, without succumbing to her own responses, she must detach herself from the bodily event without separating herself from her body.

The repeated desensitization required by prostitution nullifies every emotion or sensible reaction threatening to engage the prostitute in the bodily event. The prostitute attempts to annihilate her very presence within sexual activity by extinguishing her reaction to it. Mindful of the threat posed by potentially intense sensations and emotions, she alienates herself from her prostituted flesh, presenting the specter of a subject with a sensibility that she cannot permit herself to possess. A profound fragmentation of self allows her to believe that her body, which feels the corporeal presence of the client within itself, is not her "real" self. She creates a living mirage, simulating sexual involvement, but when the illusion dissolves, she expects to reintegrate her "real" untouchable self and her body. However, this is impossible, because her alienation is not a separation from her body, so it is not difficult to imagine that she might become conditioned to respond similarly to all sexual stimulation.

The client's conflicting demands mirror the prostitute's self-fragmentation. The client expects the hidden subject to recognize his subjectivity, but that would require acknowledging her subjectivity as well. A genuine interest in her individual needs and desires compromises the bargain and hence, the contradictory nature of his demands precludes a happy coincidence of his desires. His attempt to obtain her recognition without incurring any obligation perpetuates her self-dissolution. He must reunite the fragments in order to obtain her recognition, but his endeavor to do so embroils him in mimicry of seduction or rape.

Attempts to seduce the prostitute, by coaxing her into dropping her defenses, produce an illusion of trust, understanding, and mutual recognition, which the mercenary nature of their encounter renders impossible. In order to see the prostitute as someone with whom he identifies, the client might "normalize" their encounter by making disarming compliments with regard to her appearance, but even more so, to her intelligence, charm, and qualities of character. Concerned sounding questions about her personal life or attempts to perform the sex act in a diligent, gentle manner, as would a "good lover," might create the appearance of a connection based on mutual desire, concern, and respect. Indeed, the need to maintain this illusion might inspire the client to manifest his courtesy by frequently asking what pleases her, showing great interest to avoid causing distress, or making the most determined efforts to bring her to climax. From outward appearance, his seduction of the reluctant mistress appears to be the model for considerate lovemaking.

Seduction is only one of many possibilities. He might instead attempt to provoke a genuine response by degrading her. He might demonstrate his disregard for her needs and desires by making a show of doing exactly what seems to revolt or injure her. Stressing the mercenary nature of their encounter, he might insist on "getting his money's worth." After making it clear that her entire worth rests on her sexual performance, he might denigrate her services by claiming she is not worth the price he paid. In short, he might present a model for brutal sexual intercourse that resembles rape in every respect other than her pre-consent.

Of course, the client might do something else to reach her, but unless he is willing to forgo his original objectives, everything he does is destined to fail. Although savageness denies the prostitute's subjectivity in a more cruel way, tenderness might interfere with her endeavor to extricate herself from the situation in a more disconcerting manner. On the one hand, brutality undermines her sense of self-respect and composure. As his intrusions become more persistent, her effort to separate herself from the encounter becomes more desperate. On the other hand, kindly gestures compel her to view him as a person. Her task might be easier if the client left her the option of viewing him as nothing more than a vicious animal that relieves itself in her body. By avoiding feelings of compassion or respect for the client, she denies his capacity to touch her.

One can easily imagine that she resents any attempt to engage her. In other contexts, those to whom the prostitute is bound by more complex patterns of emotions, loyalties, and responsibilities touch her body. How dare this man, who merely paid for a service, attempt to arouse her, as would a lover, as if he expected a genuine response? By what right does he pretend to recognize her humanity, thereby seeking to integrate himself within the context of a life she has so carefully abstracted from this encounter? How dare this other man, who bought her obedience, attempt to hurt, anger, or shame

her in order to steal the sentiment he could not buy? It is plausible that she might re-integrate herself, but she has solid grounds to doubt the veracity of her self-perception, since she has disowned its reports and ignored its advice.

One can imagine that the client also feels somewhat cheated. While expecting to buy sex, he expects to buy sex with a woman, albeit one over whom he has temporary control. She, however, denies him what he most desires: recognition of his subjectivity through an authentic surrender of body and soul. The client seeks to control the prostitute's sexual expression without stifling the candid spontaneity of her responses. He wants for her to get caught up in the moment despite herself, to elicit from her a genuine, but predictable, response. It is conceivable that he might penetrate her defense, but if so, he has good reason to suspect the authenticity of her response, for while predictable responses can be genuine, one cannot require that genuine responses be predictable.

Conclusion

Both the client and the prostitute attempt to use the other as a mere means to an end, but neither achieves his or her original objective, because their ends are self-contradictory. Each intends to leave with something gained, but each loses more than was counted in the bargain. Sex in such a context may be consenting, but it demonstrates a callous insensitivity to the interests of the participants. This disdain for persons makes prostitution wrong from a Kantian moral perspective. Moreover, prostitution ensnares the participants in a web of deception and contradiction from which neither is likely to emerge unharmed, which should raise serious questions about its moral permissibility regardless of one's moral presuppositions.

While neither the client nor the prostitute is innocent, I do not call for the vilification or legal censure of those who bear an immediate and commensurate penalty for their mistakes. The relationship between prostitutes and their clients reflects a form of destructive interaction present in many other sexual and non-sexual human relationships. As an extreme example of this general form of injurious behavior, it highlights wrongful features of other sexual or labor relationships. Consequently, prostitution points to the need for amending a social vision that reduces morality to consent, contract, and fair market price and for revising human interactions that resemble prostitution.[21]

Notes

1 Common usage defines prostitution as selling oneself for sexual hire or an unworthy cause. According to this definition, many forms of prostitution are legal, condoned, or even encouraged. In order to narrow the scope of this critique, I focus on the most overt form of sexual prostitution: the explicit, verbally consensual, voluntary exchange of a sexual act involving direct physical contact for money. I consider only the sexual relations between female prostitutes and male clients. I address the experience of prostitution in contemporary western society rather than presenting "origin stories," cross-cultural comparisons, socioeconomic analyses, or theories of prostitution. I do not discuss the present legal status of prostitution, because I deny that the essential problematic aspect of prostitution depend on its illegality. I am well aware of the division among feminists on this issue and do not wish to deny that some harmful aspects of prostitution stem from its illegality. Strong argument could be offered in defense of decriminalizing prostitution, but this argument will not be offered within the context of this paper. On the origins of prostitution and the need for a theory of prostitution see, Alison M. Jaggar, "Prostitution," in *Philosophy of Sex*, ed. Alan Soble (Totowa, NJ: Rowman and Littlefield, 1980), 348–368. For a comparison of prostitution in different societies see, Laurie Shrage, *Moral Dilemmas of Feminism: Prostitution, Adultery, and Abortion* (New York, NY: Routledge, 1994). For a discussion on the role of prostitution and marriage in patriarchal, capitalist society see, Carole Pateman, The Sexual Contract (Stanford: Stanford University Press, 1988). For a discussion of the need for prostitutes to assume a subject position in philosophical discourse on prostitution see, Shannon Bell, *Reading, Writing, and Rewriting the Prostitute Body* (Bloomington and Indianapolis: Indiana University Press, 1994).

2 I appeal to Kant's "principle of humanity," which states: "Act in such a way that you always treat humanity, whether in your own person or in the person of any other, never simply as a means, but always at the same time as an end." See, Immanuel Kant, *Groundwork of the Metaphysic of Morals*, trans. H.J. Paton (New York, NY: Harper and Row, 1964), 96.

   In appealing to the principle of humanity, I assert that my argument presupposes basic Kantian principles, but I make no claims about Kant's views of prostitution. Consequently this essay represents a "Kantian" reflection on prostitution rather than Kant's reflections on prostitution. My argument depends on several features of Kant's philosophy that tend to be minimized by contemporary critics. First, despite accusations to the contrary, Kant showed a remarkable understanding of our carnal, finite nature. Consequently, many of his claims about sexual relations are based on his cognizance that sexuality is inseparable from empirical subjectivity. Sexual relations involve the human subject in its entirety. Second, according to Kant's interpretation of the

Categorical Imperative, actions should not merely maintain humanity as an end in itself but should actively promote this end. Consequently, one has a meritorious duty to adopt the ends of others, with regard to their greater moral perfection, general human development, and their self-determined projects. For a discussion of this meritorious duty to others, see Ibid. 96–7.

3 This essay is based on an earlier essay, "The Myth of the Happy Hooker," in *Violence Against Women*, edit. Stanley French, Laura Purdy, and Wanda Teays (Ithaca, NY: Cornell University Press, 1998). In the earlier essay, my cowriter, Clelia Smyth Anderson and I argued that prostitution is also inherently violent, but I think that the wrongful nature of prostitution can be established independent of that claim.

4 This concept of human subjectivity originates with Kant and exerts profound influence on the tradition of German Idealism and on Continental Philosophy in general. Fichte assumes Kant's notion of an intelligible subject or "moral will" and argues that the intelligible I only appears in consciousness through the empirically determined, limited, embodied individual members of a social whole. According to both the Kantian and Fichtean theories of morality, human beings possess dignity because they are "ends in themselves," i.e., willing beings capable of determining their own goals and projects. We show deference to the dignity of others by respecting their individual concerns, desires, and projects. The notion of "recognition" was introduced by Fichte through the doctrine of *Aufforderung*, the summons, but the reader is probably more familiar with the Hegelian and Sartrean concepts of recognition.

5 We might imagine a society in which a specifically sexual desire plays little or no role in intercourse, but in contemporary western society, sexual desire is a very relevant feature of sexual relations. To say, "I do not care if my sexual partner desires me," is equivalent to saying "Her needs and wishes for pleasure, comfort, and contentment do not concern me." How could one say this if one held one's partner in high regard and possessed even a slight concern for her general well-being?

6 It should be self-explanatory that we violate a person's freedom when we involve them in activities without their obvious agreement to engage in those activities. For this reason, consent is a necessary condition of sexual relations according to the implications of most moral theories. Nonetheless, to assume that consent is a sufficient condition for morally acceptable sexual relations seems a reckless moral attitude. People often consent to have sexual relations without desire. For instance, some people are afraid of hurting their potential partner's feelings, of appearing "frigid," or of failing some imaginary obligation. Although I am inviting a good deal of criticism by saying so, I suspect the feelings of uneasiness, bad faith, and guilt aroused by such "altruistic"

sexual acts probably indicates something problematic. Moreover, when one imagines the complex and often tragic consequences of even so-called "casual" sexual encounters, requiring no more than consent seems unconscionably lenient. Human beings suffer when they engage in undesired activities just as they suffer when our desires are unfulfilled. Sometimes, suffering is unavoidable or morally necessary, such as when our desires are unreasonable or morally objectionable, but inflicting unnecessary suffering on another or on oneself is morally questionable at best.

7 In this context, "concern" does not denote a type of emotional sympathy but simply a moral regard for others' interests, which include their needs, desires, and projects as well as their psychological and moral well-being. This claim might seem paternalistic, but demonstrating concern for others' interests and acting in a paternalistic manner are not the same. Most moral theories acknowledge that one should consider others' interests as well as one's own. It is paternalistic to force or coerce a person into promoting her own interests, but it is only morally proper to refrain from actions that undermine another person's interests. With regard to the case at hand, it is paternalistic to force or coerce a prostitute to give up her trade on the grounds that doing so is in her best interest. On the other hand, it is not paternalistic to refrain from purchasing her services because it is not in her best interest even if she consents to sell her services.

8 Many sexual abusers attempt to justify their actions by claiming that their victims "really" wanted, needed, or enjoyed the sexual encounter. Some sexual abusers claim to feel genuine concern and affection for their victims. This does not show that desire or concern justify sexual abuse, but it reveals that even the sexual abuser recognizes the significance of concern and desire within sexual relations. People who have been disillusioned by their sexual partner's lack of concern or desire often report feeling dirtied or violated. This does not show that mutual concern and desire provides sufficient basis for a sexual relationship, but it does reveal that these factors affect our interpretation of our sexual relationships.

9 This attitude makes blatant physical violence possible, because it cultivates an image of others that permits more obvious forms of assault, such as rape, battery, and murder. Assuming an attitude of callous insensitivity towards human beings and viewing them as if they were mere means makes it easier to treat them like things that one can buy, waste, or break.

10 A woman considers this way of earning a living for a variety of reasons. I can imagine some very practical considerations that might make prostitution appealing to some women. Women often experience difficulty earning a living wage and prostitution offers rather significant returns for the investment of time and money. Because many women are often family care-givers, they need flexible working schedules. Prostitution generally allows for a more flexible schedule than other jobs. Nonetheless, each particular act of prostitution occurs on condition that the prostitute receives money for the sexual services she provides. This exchange defines the sexual interaction as prostitution.

11 The myth of the sexual expertise does not wash when we remember that many clients will pay extra for a "new girl" or a supposed virgin. Furthermore, if experience were the relevant issue, it seems to be a fact of common knowledge that experienced lovers do not usually become so by playing hard to get. It is true that many prostitutes receive a type of "training" at the hands of pimps, proprietors of "escort" agencies, or "massage" parlors, but this type of "education" mainly focuses on etiquette, appearance, and overcoming aversions to particular sexual acts. This may indeed make a prostitute more successful, but it does not endow her with any special sexual skills. Furthermore, it does not distinguish prostitutes from other polite, attractive, uninhibited women. For an indication of the training through exposure to pornography, etc. that many prostitutes receive see, Evelina Giobbe, "Confronting the Liberal Lies about Prostitution," in *Living with Contradictions: Controversies in Feminist Social Ethics*, ed. Alison M. Jaggar (Boulder: Westview Press, 1994), 125. See also, Sunny Carter, "A Most Useful Tool," in *Living with Contradictions: Controversies in Feminist Social Ethics*, p. 114 for a discussion of the extent of unique skills and sexual education of one former prostitute: "I went shopping for what I imagined to be proper "hooker clothes": a long, flowing dressing gown, garter belts and stockings, ridiculously high heels. I practiced walking the length of my apartment until I felt confident that I could wear the damn things without falling down. I felt I had to call attention to my only good feature – my legs. The rest of me was twenty pounds overweight, I had no waist at all, my breasts were big, but droopy. My face was passing, but nothing to write home about. Still, nobody had ever kicked me out of bed, so, as I waited for my very first client, a fellow named Harold, I walked back and forth to make sure I had the shoes down pat, smoked one cigarette after another and made several trips to the john to check my make-up and hair."

12 It was recently suggested to me that a plausible and morally acceptable reason for having sexual relations with a prostitute would be that one's "beloved" but infirm wife could not participate in conjugal relations. Presumably, seeking a prostitute would spare the "beloved" sexual advances that she could not reciprocate and emotional infidelity that an extramarital lover could present. While there are surely situations in which performing the sexual act might be painful, repugnant, or dangerous, one might ask oneself if a devoted spouse ought not concern himself with something other than his own sexual needs in such a case. One might ask as well, if the "beloved" wife ought to be overcome by gratitude for his "consideration."

13 A recent talk-show interview with a man who claimed he was unable to find willing sexual partners sheds some light

on this issue. After "confessing" to thousands of television viewers and the live audience that he was "forced" to pay for sex, the rather ordinary, but by no means physically repugnant individual revealed that his problem had developed during middle age. He was no longer able to attract the sort of woman who attracted him. Indeed, he said he was unwilling to have sex with a woman whose "sexual standards were low enough to be attracted to me."

14 In this respect, the prostitute's client differs from the pedophile, the zoophile, and the necrophile only in degree. The fact that he attempts to accomplish his end by means of a live, adult, homo sapien provides him with a socially acceptable varnish that belies his perverse avoidance of human contact.

15 A recent article in *Playboy* concurs with this analysis. In "The Rules of the Game," *Playboy*, 42 (10), p. 52, October 1995, James R. Peterson cites Al Goldstein's explanation of why men seek the services of prostitutes. "Of all the commentators, Screw publisher Al Goldstein was most honest, reporting a story about the night he spent $1000 on an escort. 'It was splendid, rollicking sex. When it was over I felt like willing my body to science. And then she left. As the supreme final act in our opera of fucking, her leaving was like a cherry on a sundae, a sumptuous dessert after a seven course meal, a plunge into cool water after running a marathon. That's when I had my glistening realization. I realized I wasn't paying this woman for sex. I was paying her for the luxury of her leaving after sex.'"

16 Every individual's sexual "personality" is a unique, complex combination of physical and emotional needs and responses. The same basic sexual acts may arouse feelings or pleasure, discomfort, or repugnance depending on the particular context, the participant's bodily states, and the manner in which the acts are performed. The prostitute cannot yield to her particular sexual personality, because she must exhibit the personality that he desires. Mature sexual partners understand that sex is that it is an exploration in which one is permitted to fail. Prostitution forbids her this luxury. Moreover, even if she feels pleasure, she must express her pleasure in a manner that is pleasurable for him.

17 He wants to make of her "a thing on which another satisfies his appetite, just as he satisfies his hunger on a steak." (Immanuel Kant, *The Philosophy of Law,* trans. W. Hastie, in Morality and Moral Controversies, ed. John Arthur, Englewood Cliffs, NJ: Prentice Hall, 1993, p. 254.)

18 See Carole Pateman, "What's Wrong with Prostitution," in *Living with Contradictions: Controversies in Feminist Social Ethics,* ed. Alison M. Jaggar (Boulder: Westview Press, 1994), p. 131. Pateman points out that the complaints of most clients of prostitutes concern the prostitutes' cold, disinterested, and mercenary attitudes. In other words, a pretty appearance, sexual expertise, and good manners are not the only issues. Men who seek prostitutes expect a degree of warmth and personal interest. They expect to be treated as something more than a party to a mercenary arrangement. To be sure, a restaurant patron expects a little more than tasty food, but if the food is good, the establishment is clean, and the service is polite and efficient, he would have no grounds to complain that the waiter was mechanical and impersonal or that the chef did not "really care."

19 John Stuart Mill, "The Subjection of Women," in *Essays on Sex Equality,* ed. A. S. Rossi (Chicago: University of Chicago Press, 1970), p. 141. Compare this passage to Immanuel Kant: "For love out of inclination cannot be commanded." See *Groundwork of the Metaphysic of Morals,* trans. H.J. Paton (New York, NY: Harper and Row, 1964), p. 67.

20 Of course, we do not mean to suggest that slavery, prostitution, and marriage are identical. Generally speaking, women do not choose to be sold as slaves, but they do often choose to become wives or prostitutes. Nonetheless, the attitudes of some husbands and all clients towards wives and prostitutes resemble the attitudes of masters towards slaves in many respects. See also on the relations between contract laborers and employers versus slaves and masters, Immanuel Kant: "It may however appear that one man may bind himself to another by a contract of hire, to discharge a certain service that is permissible in its kind, but is left entirely undetermined as regards its measure or amount; and that as receiving wages or board or protection in return, he thus becomes only a servant subject to the will of a master (subditus) and not a slave (servus). But this is an illusion.. . . [T]his would imply that they had actually given themselves away to their masters as property; which, in the case of persons, is impossible. A person can, therefore, only contract to perform work that is defined both in quality and quantity, either as a day-labourer or as a domiciled subject." The relationship between sexual partners is something quite different for Kant, sexual partners give themselves over wholly in an exchange of like for like, which is not at all the same as a contract of money for service. See Immanuel Kant, *The Science of Right,* trans. W. Hastie, in *Great Books of the Western World,* V. 42 (Chicago: IL, Encyclopaedia Britannica, Inc., 1952), p. 419–45.

21 I would like to thank the following people for valuable advice and support in preparing the final version of this essay: Michael Clifford, Melanie Eckford-Prosser Clifford, Michael Goodman, Clelia Smyth Anderson, and the anonymous reviewer of *Essays in Philosophy*.

PART VII

Paraphilia and Pathology

Introduction

More than most applied ethics topics, sexual ethics involves reactions of disgust. In medical ethics, environmental ethics, and business ethics, people debating the issues might get angry, or frustrated, or resolute, or horrified, or dumbfounded, or unsettled, but rarely do they get disgusted. For various reasons (experimentally explored in psychology), discussing euthanasia, or protecting endangered species, or giving corporations personal rights might result in some strong feelings – but not feelings of visceral revulsion. People might think of their opponents as willful, or mistaken, or even evil, but not mentally ill, sick, or perverted.

In sexual ethics, however, it is not uncommon for some actions to be cast in terms of perversion and pathology. In some ways, an action might be thought of as morally impermissible *because* it is perverse or sick and in other ways it might be thought of as both morally impermissible and *additionally* so abnormal that it indicates a diseased mind. The notions of perversion and pathology add an important element to the debate. If someone's sexual desire is perverse, then it is very difficult (though not impossible) to argue that their desire is not also immoral. If someone's sexual desire is pathological, then it calls into question their competency to be held responsible as well as the methods by which medicine and psychology determine

what counts as pathological and healthy. It is certainly the case that some desires and behaviors have at times been categorized as diseased (such as homosexuality) only to later be reclassified as acceptable variations. This leads some to argue that all desires and behaviors classified as sexual pathologies are merely socially disapproved of and the rhetoric of pathology is merely used to justify mistreatment of sexual minorities. Others argue that this claim is far too sweeping and poorly thought out, indicating as it would that sexuality is somehow uniquely immune among human characteristics to pathology and that no one, no matter what they desire or do, could be considered to have anything sexually wrong with them.

Part VII examines issues of sexual pathology and paradigm cases of aberrant behavior. Though such issues involve concepts of health, normality, perversion, and dignity that can be applied to various cases, they are explored here by focusing on concerns about sex involving violence, animals, and children.

Framing Questions

- *Are some sexual desires a type of disease?*
- *Is sadomasochism necessarily immoral?*
- *Is bestiality necessarily immoral?*
- *Is pedophilia necessarily immoral?*

44

DSM-IV-TR and the Paraphilias: An Argument for Removal

Charles Moser and Peggy J. Kleinplatz

Summary

Argues that the concept of Paraphilia disorders as set forth in the DSM-IV-TR (2000) fails to meet the text's own definitional standards. The Paraphilia diagnostic category lacks consistency, clarity, and empirical evidence. Healthy sexuality is not defined, so pathological sexuality has no clear boundaries. As such, there is no reason to think that Paraphilia is actually a distinct mental disorder and the entire category should be removed from the next DSM. However, this does not imply all sexually deviant behaviors are permissible. For example, sexual acts between adults and children should still be criminalized, although there is no reason to classify pedophilia as a mental illness.

Original publication details: Charles Moser and Peggy Kleinplatz, "DSM-IV-TR and the Paraphilias: An Argument for Removal," pp. 91–109 from *Journal of Psychology & Human Sexuality* 17: 3–4 (2006). Reproduced with permission of Taylor & Francis Group.

Charles Moser and Peggy J. Kleinplatz

All societies attempt to control the sexual behavior of their members. One mechanism of exercising this control is to define a specific sexual interest as pathognomonic for a mental disorder. Historically and cross-culturally, even an accusation of interest in specific sexual practices could result in death, imprisonment, loss of civil rights, and other social sanctions. Similarly, being classified as mentally ill could result in death, imprisonment, loss of civil rights, and other social sanctions. Thus, the confounding of mental illness with unusual sexual desires is understandable.

Which sexual interests are proscribed often changes; masturbation, oral sex, anal sex, and homosexuality were once considered mental disorders or symptoms of other mental disorders but are now typically accepted as part of the spectrum of healthy sexual expression. Similarly there are conditions that were accepted as "normal" in the past, but are now classified as mental disorders (e.g., hypoactive sexual desire, sexual aversion disorder, and female orgasmic disorder). It is exceedingly difficult to eliminate historical and cultural factors from the assessment of unusual sexual interests. Empirically based, scientific definitions of healthy and pathological sexual behavior continue to elude us.

Cross-culturally, sexual activity considered "acceptable" in the United States is viewed as "stigmatized" in other cultures; similarly, sexual activity considered "unacceptable" in other countries is not "stigmatized" in the United States. For example, non-marital coitus is accepted in the US, but is stigmatized harshly in many Moslem countries; topless sunbathing among women at public beaches is accepted in Western Europe, but illegal and condemned in most of the United States. Violation of these cultural norms often results in strong negative reactions. Given the socio-cultural context in which such beliefs are embedded, it is not surprising that the lay public and even many sex experts cannot understand how unusual sexual interests can signify anything but mental disorders. Nevertheless, it is the assumption that unusual sexual interests constitute symptoms of or are mental disorders per se, that we are questioning.

The American Psychiatric Association (APA) publishes the *Diagnostic and Statistical Manual* (*DSM*); it describes the diagnostic criteria and defining features of all formally recognized mental disorders. It serves as a definitive resource for mental health professionals. Although its primary influence is in the United States, its impact is global. A psychiatric diagnosis is more than shorthand to facilitate communication among professionals or to standardize research parameters. Psychiatric diagnoses affect child custody decisions, self-esteem, whether individuals are hired or fired, receive security clearances, or have other rights and privileges curtailed. Criminals may find that their sentences are either mitigated or enhanced as a direct result of their diagnoses. The equating of unusual sexual interests with psychiatric diagnoses has been used to justify the oppression of sexual minorities and to serve political agendas. A review of this area is not only a scientific issue, but also a human rights issue. The power and impact of the *DSM* should not be underestimated.

The *DSM* is revised at regular intervals. Diagnoses can be added or eliminated, and diagnostic criteria reformulated with each new edition. There have been six editions to date (APA, 1952, 1968, 1980, 1987, 1994, 2000). The current edition is designated *DSM-IV-TR* (APA, 2000) and will be the focus of this paper.

With the publication of *DSM-III* (1980), the focus of the *DSM* changed from a theoretically based, psychoanalytic model of illness to an evidence-based and descriptive model. The *DSM* is currently intended ". . . to be neutral with respect to theories of etiology" (APA, 2000, p. xxvi), based on objective observation, and able to support its statements with empirical research. With this transition, the nomenclature of these disorders changed from "Sexual deviation" to "Paraphilia," a supposedly atheoretical, non-pejorative descriptor.

In the text of the latest edition of the *DSM*, it is asserted that a "comprehensive and systematic" (APA, 2000, p. xxvi) review of the literature was conducted in preparation of the *DSM*. "The utility and credibility of the DSM-IV require that it . . . be supported by an extensive empirical foundation" (APA, 2000, p. xxiii). The text indicates, ". . . the majority of paragraphs in the DSM-IV have not been revised, indicating that, even after the literature review, most of the information in the original text remains up-to-date" (APA, 2000, p. 829). Our own, extensive review found no literature to support most of the assertions made in the Paraphilia section of the *DSM* and several studies were found that contradict the text (discussed below). Objective data to support the classification of the Paraphilias as mental disorders is lacking.

When the APA removed homosexuality from the *DSM* approximately 30 years ago, some observers thought that the other Paraphilias would also be removed from subsequent editions. The argument for removal of homosexuality was bolstered by the lack of objective research supporting its inclusion and research that failed to support the theory that homosexuals fit specific psychiatric stereotypes. Nevertheless, some observers believe the removal of homosexuality was primarily a political act (Bayer, 1981). The situation of the Paraphilias at present parallels that of homosexuality in the early 1970s. Without the support or political astuteness of those who fought for the removal of homosexuality, the Paraphilias continue to be listed in the *DSM*.

The term "paraphilia" will be employed here in keeping with its use in the literature, even though we have serious reservations about the validity of the diagnosis and the applicability of this term. The rationale for the inclusion of the Paraphilia diagnostic category as it is constituted in the *DSM-IV-TR* (APA, 2000) will be addressed and challenged. We will suggest that the construct of the Paraphilias is ambiguous and does not describe a diagnosable, distinct mental disorder. A review of the scientific literature does not support the inclusion of this diagnostic category in the *DSM*.

Are the Paraphilias Mental Disorders?

[. . .]

The assumption that Paraphilias are a form of psychopathology has been questioned and each subsequent edition has attempted to address some of the perceived weaknesses in this diagnostic category. Nevertheless, the bulk of serious criticism (Davis, 1996; McConaghy, 1999; Rubin, 1992; Silverstein, 1984; Suppe, 1984) has not been addressed fully.

In the *DSM*, it is indicated that it is difficult to define a mental disorder as well as mental health. Nonetheless, the text defines a mental disorder as being ". . . associated with present distress . . . or disability . . . or significantly increased risk of suffering death, pain, disability, or an important loss of freedom" (APA, 2000, p. xxxi). Individuals who engage in many common activities (scuba divers, gun owners, mountain climbers, inhabitants of many large cities, and criminals) also incur increased risks of death, pain, disability, or loss of freedom, but are not diagnosed with mental disorders. This apparent contradiction demonstrates that social context can affect the application of this definition.

To clarify the definition, the *DSM* further states, "Neither deviant behavior (e.g., political, religious, or sexual) nor conflicts that are primarily between the individual and society are mental disorders unless the deviance or conflict is a symptom of a dysfunction in the individual, as described above" (2000, p. xxxi). There is concern that psychiatric diagnoses can be used

inappropriately to discredit dissenters; at least in some venues, criminals have more rights and credibility than psychiatric patients do. The above statement was added to protect the labeling of unpopular or illegal activities as mental illnesses, but the last clause allows the clinician to disregard this distinction.

The *DSM* does not define healthy sexuality, much less healthy mood, thoughts, or personalities. Unfortunately, the range of "healthy" human sexual behavior is not known, thus creating potential pitfalls in the diagnostic process. The *DSM* is meant to be interpreted by an experienced and objective clinician. Without consensus from the scientific literature, however, clinicians are often forced to rely on their own subjective evaluations.

The problem here is that engaging in "Paraphilic" behavior qualifies the participant a priori as a candidate for diagnosis. In addition, when individuals have unusual sexual interests, there is often speculation that any presenting problems are related to their sexuality. When a behavior per se signifies a diagnosis, then by definition the behavior is symptomatic of the disorder. This confound obscures the possibility that for at least some individuals, their specific sexual behaviors are healthy expressions of sexuality and beneficial to them. The fact that specific sexual behaviors are socially unacceptable or illegal is, and should be, irrelevant to the diagnostic process.

[. . .]

The *DSM* has been organized with a "categorical" approach to classification of mental disorders since the third edition (APA, 1980). This approach works best ". . . when there are clear boundaries between classes, and when the different classes are mutually exclusive" (APA, 2000, p. xxxi). Although the text acknowledges problems with the categorical approach, these problems are particularly evident with the Paraphilias. The Paraphilia disorders do not have clear boundaries (Laws & O'Donohue, 1997). Non-clinical studies of individuals with unusual sexual interests demonstrate that these individuals are indistinguishable from those with "normophilic" (i.e., conventional) sexual interests (Brown et al., 1996; Wise, Fagan, Schmidt, Ponticas, & Costa, 1991). The clinical studies do not identify a discernible group who have anything more in common than their shared sexual interest. The existing empirical research does not distinguish individuals with Paraphilias from those with other mental disorders. That is, there is no demonstrable and distinct class of "paraphiliacs," except as created by defining specific sexual interests, a priori, as evidence of psychopathology. The inability to define "healthy" sexuality or to distinguish the characteristics of individuals with a paraphilia from those without one, suggests that the distinction does not exist and the category is invalid.

Individuals can and do experience psychiatric problems related to their sexual interests and behavior. Problems related to normophilic sexual interests or behaviors, associated with distress or dysfunctions, are dealt with differently and given non-sexual diagnoses. We can find no logical or scientific reason why some sexual behaviors and interests have been designated as Paraphilias and others have not.

The DSM Definition of a Paraphilia

"The essential features of a Paraphilia are recurrent, intense sexually arousing fantasies, sexual urges, or behaviors . . . that occur over a period of at least 6 months. . ." (APA, 2000, p. 566). The definition of intense is the issue; otherwise this statement in isolation describes healthy, sexually active individuals. The DSM already defines terms such as compulsive, impulsive, and obsessive; so intense in this situation must have a different implication. Even trained clinicians have difficulty distinguishing strong "unhealthy" sexual interests from strong "healthy" sexual interests, as demonstrated by previous, failed attempts to define promiscuity (having more partners than the evaluator) and excessive masturbation (engaging in the act more often than the evaluator). Conversely, individuals lacking intense sexual arousal may be subject to diagnosis with a Sexual Arousal Disorder or Hypoactive Sexual Desire Disorder.

The editors further qualify their paraphilia definition by stating, ". . . generally involving (1) nonhuman objects, (2) the suffering or humiliation of oneself or one's sex partner, or (3) children or other nonconsenting persons . . ." (p. 566). The implication is that the distinction between a mental disorder and a healthy sex interest is based in the nature of the specific sexual interest rather than in its intensity.

[. . .]

The tradition of identifying specific sexual behaviors as pathological predates the *DSM-1* (1952), possibly originating with Krafft-Ebing (1965/1886). It is a remnant of the reclassification of sexual sin to sexual pathology in the 19th century (Bullough & Bullough, 1977). The specifying of behaviors creates problems for at least six reasons:

1. A behavior in and of itself is not evidence of psychopathology. Even when a behavior is construed as a

symptom of a mental disorder, we do not classify the mental disorder by the symptom or the behavior. Paranoia may be a symptom of several psychiatric diagnoses (e.g., schizophrenia, paranoid personality disorder, delusional disorder, psychoactive substance use, bipolar disorder), but paranoia by itself is not a diagnosis. Compulsive hand washing may be a symptom of obsessive-compulsive disorder, but it is not a hand-washing disorder.

2. The act of specifying particular, sexual behaviors as pathological leads to discrimination against all practitioners of those behaviors, even when their behavioral expressions are appropriate and benign. Furthermore, at present, the urges may be construed as pathological even if one never acts upon them.

3. Specifying particular behaviors allows for the inference that other (i.e., unclassified) behaviors are unlikely to be the source of difficulties. As most practitioners in the field know, normative heterosexual behaviors can be problematic as well (cf., Kafka & Hennen, 1999).

4. Specifying the behavior focuses the evaluation and treatment on that behavior. Some individuals do experience problems related to their sexual interests and these may be an appropriate focus of therapy. However, the clinician may be diverted from any underlying concerns and attend unduly to controlling the specified behavior (Moser & Kleinplatz, 2002).

5. Social, political, religious and historical factors affect the inclination to see certain behaviors or sexual proclivities as pathological (Bullough, 1988; Davis, 1996, 1998). As acknowledged in the *DSM* (APA, 2000), these cultural values are a confounding influence and are contrary to the supposedly objective perspective of the *DSM*.

6. The therapist's own socialization or theoretical perspective is likely to affect judgments of health or pathology. This adds an unwelcome and inevitably, subjective component to an allegedly objective process.

[. . .]

The "B" Criterion: Distress and Dysfunction and the "Paraphilias"

An essential criterion for making the diagnosis of paraphilia is that the behavior, urges, or fantasies cause distress or dysfunction. These two symptoms will be analyzed separately.

Distress

It is acknowledged in the *DSM* that, "These individuals are rarely self-referred and usually come to the attention of mental health professionals only when their behavior has brought them into conflict with sexual partners or society" (APA, 2000, p. 566). Possibly for emphasis, the *DSM* includes the statement: "Many individuals with these disorders assert that the behavior causes them no distress and that their only problem is social dysfunction as a result of the reaction of others to their behavior" (p. 567). One must conclude that distress is rarely a problem for those individuals diagnosed with a paraphilia.

Consider the minority of individuals diagnosed with a paraphilia who are distressed because of their sexual interests. Although one's sexual interests "tend to be chronic and lifelong" (APA, 2000, p. 568), there is no indication that the distress is chronic. This distinction has been overlooked in the diagnostic criteria. If the distress can be mitigated, would these individuals cease to be diagnosable as having Paraphilias? Support groups can alleviate social stigma and isolation. Although they are helpful to mitigate this distress, they are rarely mentioned in the clinical literature in regard to the treatment of the Paraphilias (Moser, 1988, 1999). A strict reading of the definition of a mental disorder suggests that the distress must be "present distress" (APA, 2000, p. xxxi), which implies that if the distress is mitigated, the individual no longer meets the criteria for the diagnosis.

[. . .]

Dysfunction

The "B" criterion allows for the diagnosis if there is ". . . impairment in social, occupational, or other important areas of functioning" (APA, 2000, p. 566). The implication is that the dysfunction results from the paraphilia per se, rather than social reactions to the sexuality. Theoretically, the paraphilia diagnosis might be justified if the patient was fired for being habitually late as a result of engaging in the paraphilic behavior. However, if one is fired solely due to the discomfort of others, it does not signify dysfunction on the part of the employee.

Suppose an individual is functioning in society without difficulty and also has an interest in a Paraphilia, thereby satisfying the "A" but not the "B" criterion. Theoretically, that person would not be diagnosed with a Paraphilia. Now assume that an employer, spouse, or parent discovers this interest. This revelation leads to termination of employment, discord in the couple or family, etc. Is it appropriate to conclude that the "paraphilia" is the cause of the "dysfunction" and the person now meets the diagnostic criteria? Is the distinction between health and psychopathology being able to keep unusual sexual interests hidden?

Whether the nature of the problem is a psychiatric dysfunction or practical difficulty is particularly murky. Social isolation may lead to depression; participating in support groups and in a subculture surrounding the specific sexual interest may lead to resolution of the alienation and associated depression without psychotherapy or anti-depressants.

[. . .]

The *DSM* contains the statement, "There is often impairment in the capacity for reciprocal, affectionate sexual activity" (APA, 2000, p. 567). The theme of reciprocal, affectionate sexual activity is repeated through several editions. In the *DSM-III* (1980), this phrase was used in conjunction with Ego-dystonic Homosexuality. Although this diagnosis was technically abandoned with the publication of *DSM-III-R* (1987), essentially the same wording remains in the description of Sex Disorder, Not Otherwise Specified in *DSM-III-R* (1987), *DSM-IV* (1994), and *DSM-IV-TR* (2000). The judgment of what constitutes reciprocal, affectionate sexual activity is clearly value laden and suggests an underlying, implicit, theoretical orientation. There are no data to suggest that individuals diagnosed with a paraphilia have any more difficulty maintaining relationships than "normal" heterosexuals, who have staggering divorce rates.

When do "Paraphilic" Sexual Behaviors Become Pathological?

The *DSM* is intended to help the clinician distinguish between healthy functioning and mental disorders. The *DSM* cautions, "A paraphilia must be distinguished from the *nonpathological use of sexual fantasies, behaviors, or objects as a stimulus for sexual excitement*" (APA, 2000, p. 568, emphasis in the original). The statement implies, but does not state explicitly that the stimuli can include the paraphilic "fantasies, behaviors, or objects." Guidance on how the clinician is to make this distinction is not given in the text.

[. . .]

Statements of Fact?

The Paraphilia section contains a number of purportedly factual statements that do not appear to be supported by the research literature. For example, ". . . for Sexual Masochism. . . the sex ratio is estimated to be 20 males for each female" (APA, 2000, p. 568). No studies were found to support the 20:1 statement. Several studies were found that reported a significant number of women in the S/M subculture (Breslow, Evans, & Langley, 1985; Gosselin, Wilson, & Barrett, 1991; Levitt, Moser, & Jamison, 1994). By combining the data of Breslow et al. (1985) and Levitt et al. (1994), a ratio of four male masochists to each female masochist was found. Even if clinical samples are overwhelmingly male, no study supports the naming of a specific ratio.

The *DSM-IV-TR* states, "Approximately one-half of the individuals with Paraphilias seen clinically are married" (APA, 2000, p. 568). One study (Wise et al., 1991) appears to support that statement. That study involved 50 men, comprised of 24 "transvestitic fetishists" and 26 "other paraphiliacs." The "other" types of paraphilias were not specified. However, only by combining the divorced, separated, and married category could one conclude that one-half the individuals were married. It is not clear if the "finding" that half are married is higher or lower than expected. Of interest, the Paraphilias were the only diagnostic section to include information about marital status. The rationale for inclusion of this poorly substantiated "fact" is not clear.

The purpose of many of the statements made in the Paraphilia section is nebulous. Some statements, while correct, are equally true for both those with a Paraphilia diagnosis as those judged to be normophilic. For example, "Frequent, unprotected sex may result in infection with, or transmission of, a sexually transmitted disease" (APA, 2000, p. 567) or, "The behaviors may increase. . . with increased opportunity" (p. 568). The implication is that those diagnosed with Paraphilias are more likely to have sexually transmitted diseases or difficulty engaging or refraining from their sexual interests than those with more conventional interests. Neither point is supported by data nor is the reason for their inclusion in the *DSM* apparent.

Another misleading statement is, "Sadistic or masochistic behaviors may lead to injuries ranging in extent from minor to life threatening" (APA, 2000, p. 567). Although any sexual activity can lead to injury, there is no data to suggest that the practitioners of "sadistic or masochistic behaviors" frequent emergency departments more often than practitioners of other sexual behaviors. A review of the sports medicine and emergency medicine literature reveals numerous studies of specific injuries related to various sports and other activities. If unusual sexual acts resulted in a significant number of injuries, presumably they, too, would appear prominently in the medical literature.

Another erroneous statement is evident in the confusion of hypoxyphilia with sexual masochism. The *DSM* contains the following statement: "One particularly dangerous form of Sexual Masochism, called 'hypoxyphilia,' involves sexual arousal from oxygen deprivation . . ." (APA, 2000, p. 572). In fact there is no empirical data correlating hypoxyphilia to masochism. In their study of 117 fatal cases of autoerotic asphyxia, Blanchard and Hucker conclude, "In contrast to transvestism, bondage during the fatal asphyxial episode was not differentially associated with any specific erotic object or interest that we examined, even bondage pornography" (1991, p. 375).

[. . .]

The Special Case of Pedophilia

The politics and moral outage surrounding the diagnosis of pedophilia are so pervasive that specific comments about this sexual interest must be explicit. Pedophiles occupy a particularly odious position in our society and suggestions that these individuals do not suffer from a mental disorder may be interpreted as support for their activities. We wish to clarify that our suggestion to remove the paraphilias, which includes pedophilia, from the *DSM* does not mean that sexual acts with children are not crimes. We would argue that the removal of pedophilia from the *DSM* would focus attention on the criminal aspect of these acts, and not allow the perpetrators to claim mental illness as a defense or use it to mitigate responsibility for their crimes. Individuals convicted of these crimes should be punished as provided by the laws in the jurisdiction in which the crime occurred. Any interpretation of our work as supporting adult-child sexual interactions is misguided and wrong.

Discussion

[...]

The premise of the *DSM* is that diagnoses should be based upon objective science and not on political or social motivations. Therefore, objective research is needed to substantiate statements that some forms of sexual expression are healthy and other forms constitute mental disorders. Although it may be tempting to generalize from one's clinical experiences, it is contrary to the premise and stated goals of the APA in the *DSM*. Without data to suggest that a behavior pattern is dysfunctional, one should either suspend judgment or assume the behavior pattern signifies a healthy, normal variation. Although that statement also has political ramifications, it is correct from a scientific perspective.

The *DSM* criteria for diagnosis of unusual sexual interests as pathological rests on a series of unproven and more importantly, untested assumptions. Given the explicit intent to produce an empirically valid document,

the *DSM* must provide supporting documentation. Even if future research should verify their current assumptions, they have been inserted into the *DSM* inappropriately at this time. In the interim, these untested assumptions can be and are being misused.

The text of the *DSM* states, "... all changes proposed for the text had to be supported by empirical data" (2000, p. xxix). Although this goal is laudable, it can be interpreted as setting up an impossible burden for the removal of a diagnosis or category. If health cannot be defined, then it is impossible to prove that individuals currently subject to a specific diagnosis are actually "healthy" and not pathological. It is logically impossible to prove a negative. Diagnoses should be removed if they cannot be shown to meet the definition of a mental disorder unambiguously and be substantiated by appropriate research. Failing that, the diagnosis in question should be either considered experimental or removed from the *DSM* completely.

[...]

References

American Psychiatric Association. (1952). *Diagnostic and statistical manual: Mental disorders*. Washington, DC: Author.

American Psychiatric Association. (1968). *Diagnostic and statistical manual of mental disorders* (2nd edn.). Washington, DC: Author.

American Psychiatric Association. (1980). *Diagnostic and statistical manual of mental disorders* (3rd edn.). Washington, DC: Author.

American Psychiatric Association. (1987). *Diagnostic and statistical manual of mental disorders* (3rd edn., Revised). Washington, DC: Author.

American Psychiatric Association. (1994). *Diagnostic and statistical manual of mental disorders* (4th edn.). Washington, DC: Author.

American Psychiatric Association. (2000). *Diagnostic and statistical manual of mental disorders* (4th edn., Text Revised). Washington, DC: Author.

Bayer, R. (1981). *Homosexuality and American psychiatry: The politics of diagnosis*. New York: Basic Books.

Blanchard, R., & Hucker, S.J. (1991). Age, transvestism, bondage, and concurrent paraphilic activities in 117 fatal cases of autoerotic asphyxia. *British Journal of Psychiatry, 159*, 371–377.

Brown, G.R., Wise, T.N., Costa, P.T., Herbst, J.H., Fagan, P.J., & Schmidt, C.W. (1996). Personality characteristics and sexual functioning of 188 cross-dressing men. *The Journal of Nervous and Mental Disease, 184*, 265–273.

Bullough, V. (1988). Historical perspective. In D. Dailey (ed.), *The sexually unusual: Guide to understanding and helping* (pp. 15–24). New York: The Haworth Press, Inc.

Bullough, V., & Bullough, B. (1977). *Sin, sickness, and sanity: A history of sexual attitudes*. New York: New American Library.

Davis, D.L. (1996). Cultural sensitivity and the sexual disorders of the DSM-IV: Review and assessment. In J.E. Mezzich, A. Kleinman, H. Fabrega, & D. L. Parron (eds.), *Culture and psychiatric diagnosis: A DSM-IV perspective* (pp. 191–208). Washington, DC: American Psychiatric Press.

Davis, D. L. (1998). The sexual and gender identity disorders. *Transcultural Psychiatry, 35*, 401–412.

Kafka, M.P., & Hennen, J. (1999). The paraphilia-related disorders: An empirical investigation of nonparaphilic hypersexuality disorders in outpatient males. *Journal of Sex & Marital Therapy, 25*, 305–320.

Krafft-Ebing, R. von (1965). *Psychopathia sexualis*. (F. S. Klaf, Trans.). New York: Bell Publishing Company, Inc. (Translated from the 12th German edition; original work published 1886).

Laws, D.R., & O'Donohue, W. (1997). Introduction: Fundamental issues in sexual deviance. In D.R. Laws & W. O'Donohue (Eds.), *Sexual deviance: Theory, assessment, and treatment* (pp. 1–21). New York: Guilford Press.

McConaghy, N. (1999). Unresolved issues in scientific sexology. *Archives of Sexual Behavior, 28*, 285–302.

Moser, C. (1988). Sadomasochism. *Journal of Psychology and Human Sexuality, 7*, 43–56. Also published in D. Dailey (Ed.), *The sexually unusual: Guide to understanding and helping*, (pp. 43–56). New York: The Haworth Press, Inc.

Moser, C. (1999). The psychology of sadomasochism (S/M). In S. Wright (ed.), *SM Classics* (pp. 47–61). New York: Masquerade Books.

Moser, C., & Kleinplatz, P.J. (2002). Transvestic fetishism: Psychopathology or iatrogenic artifact? *New Jersey Psychologist, 52* (2), 16–17.

Rubin, G. (1992). Thinking sex: Notes for a radical theory of the politics of sexuality. In C. S. Vance (ed.), *Pleasure and danger: Exploring female sexuality* (pp. 267–319). London, UK: Pandora Press.

Silverstein, C. (1984). The ethical and moral implications of Sexual Classification: A Commentary. *Journal of Homosexuality, 9* (4), 29–37.

Suppe, F. (1984). Classifying sexual disorders: The *Diagnostic and Statistical Manual* of the American Psychiatric Association. *Journal of Homosexuality, 9* (4), 9–28.

Wise, T.N., Fagan, P.J., Schmidt, C.W., Ponticas, Y., & Costa, P.T. (1991). Personality and sexual functioning of transvestitic fetishists and other paraphilics. *The Journal of Nervous and Mental Disease, 179,* 694–698.

Sexual and Gender Identity Disorders: Discussion of Questions for DSM-V (on Paraphilia)

Robert L. Spitzer

Summary

Argues that Moser's and Kleinplatz's position against paraphilia is weak because it provides no way to conceive of any pathological sexual behavior and provides no evidence that people have been harmed by paraphilia diagnoses. The central issue is how to decide whether something is just unusual or something is disordered. An essentialist view takes it that behavioral and biological properties have functions and if those properties fail to fulfill their functions, they are disordered. The position that there are no sexual interest or sexual behavior pathologies would mean that although an adult man's desire to have sex with children would be have to be resisted for legal reasons, there is nothing psychologically wrong with him.

Original publication details: Robert L. Spitzer, "Sexual and Gender Identity Disorders: Discussion of Questions for DSM-V," pp. 111–116 from *Journal of Psychology & Human Sexuality* 17:3–4 (2006). Reproduced with permission of Taylor & Francis Group.

[. . .]

The central issue for this symposium is Drs. Hill and Moser's remarkable proposal: that GID and all of the paraphilias should be eliminated from *DSM-V*. So the issue is not how the diagnoses of GID and the paraphilias can be better conceptualized or how the diagnostic criteria can be improved. The real issue is, are there any cases of kids or adults for which these diagnoses are appropriate.

Dr. Moser seems to believe that there is no such thing as pathological sexual behavior. This is rather remarkable. It is hard to think of any other kind of behavior or function that cannot go wrong, but for Dr. Moser, paraphilias are only statistically rare. [. . .]

The central issue then is how does one decide that something is just unusual (normal variation) or something is disordered (pathological)?

Consider this. Almost everybody who has eyes can see. Yet there are some people who have eyes that cannot see. Everybody intuitively knows that in such a case there is something wrong with the eyes. Being blind is not a normal variation because we have an intuitive sense that the eyes are designed to enable the individual to see. Some people would say the eye, like all parts of the body, are designed by God to function in a particular way. Other people, like me, would say, the body has been designed by natural selection, evolution. However you understand the concept of "design," it is clear that the eye has a certain function. When somebody has an eye that cannot see, there is some mechanism – which we may or not understand – that is not working. You can think of all kinds of other examples. Whenever you think of a medical disorder you are thinking of some biological function that is expected – that is part of being human – that is not working.

Does this concept of what is a medical disorder apply to human behavior? The answer is "yes." There are certain human qualities or behaviors that are part of being human, that are part of normal development. Here is an example. Humans tend to be social. They are not taught to be social. Kids are naturally interested in other kids. It is not because parents tell them that you will be better off if you are interested in other kids. Something is wrong with a child who has no interest in socializing with other kids. Another example: the ability to empathize, to sense what someone else is feeling. There is something wrong with a child who does not have that capacity.

What I have been presenting is sometimes referred to as essentialism – the view that some "things" (like being human) have properties or qualities that are invariable and represent the true essence of the "thing." As applied to human behavior, this means that there are human qualities or behaviors that are seen in all cultures, although the particular way in which it presents itself may vary in different cultures. In contrast to essentialism is another viewpoint: social deconstructionism – that seems to be the perspective of Drs. Hill and Moser. For them, no behavior is normal or pathological since such judgments are merely social constructs. One culture says masturbation is pathological, another says it is normal. Homosexuality prior to 1973 was a mental disorder – now it is normal variation.

How does this apply to GID and the paraphilias? . . .

What are paraphilias all about ? Dr. Moser said it is about sexual "interest." It is not interest – it is about what we are attracted to – what we find sexually arousing. In every culture, almost all boys and girls show an interest in sex and a capacity for sexual arousal. That is part of being human. Does sexual arousal have a function? We say the heart pumps blood and the eye sees. Why do we have sexual arousal? It is obvious. Sexual arousal brings people together to have that interpersonal sex. Sexual arousal has the function of facilitating pair bonding which is facilitated by reciprocal affectionate relationships. There is a normal development of sexual arousal and sometimes it can go wrong. Dr. Moser says that paraphilic interests are not inherently different from normative interests – except in their frequency. Not true. If one turned on by undergarments, and one is more interested in undergarments than in people, I think it reasonable to assume that something has gone wrong with that individual's sexual development.

I have a fantasy. It is the year 2023 and my grandson comes up to me and says, "Grand Dad, I understand you were once a famous psychiatrist. So I've got a problem. I can have sex with Judy, my wife, but what really turns me on is 7 to 10 year-old girls and I'm so turned on by this that when I see these girls I get the thought – maybe I should really grab one of them." What should I tell my grandson? I guess that according to Dr. Moser I should say: "We used to think that what you describe was pathological. However, we have known since *DSM-V* in 2010 that it is just normal variation. But if you give in to the impulse, that is a criminal offense. But it has nothing to do with psychology."

That would be ridiculous. It is true that the diagnostic criteria for the paraphilias change in minor ways from time to time and the boundary with normal sexual arousal is not always clear. For example, somebody finds sex a little bit more fun if they fantasize a little rough stuff or maybe being humiliated. I do not know at what point it becomes pathological. But certainly at some point it does.

It is interesting to realize that very few men struggle with the issue of being attracted to children. It is not because of social sanctions against having sex with children. It is just that most men have no sexual interest in children. Now why is that? Evolutionary psychologists say that probably it has evolutionary significance because being interested in children is not going to have survival value. There are probably normal inhibitory mechanisms in most men against sexual attraction to children.

What are the consequences if we go the route that Drs. Moser and Kleinplatz suggest and remove the paraphilias from the *DSM?* First of all, it is not going to happen because it would be a public relations disaster for psychiatry. There was already a little disaster when the initial *DSM-IV* put in the "clinical significance" criterion that had the effect of requiring distress or impairment before pedophilia could be diagnosed. The APA wisely corrected that in *DSM-IV-TR*.

[. . .]

In conclusion, it interesting that Dr. Moser and Hill have not presented a single case of someone – child or adult – who was harmed by being given a diagnosis of a paraphilias or gender identity disorder. Their arguments for eliminating these categories in the *DSM* are weak at best.

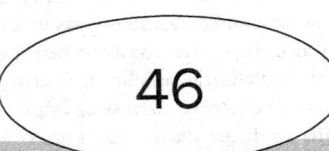

46

Paraphilic Disorders

American Psychiatric Association

Summary

Explains that the category of Paraphilic Disorders in the new DSM-V (2013) distinguishes between atypical human behavior and behavior that causes mental distress to a person or makes the person a threat to others. Legal implications were considered in the DSM-V revisions. The new category does not pathologize atypical sexual desire or behavior unless they cause distress or could harm others. There are eight recognized paraphilic disorders.

In the *Diagnostic and Statistical Manual of Mental Disorders* (DSM), paraphilic disorders are often misunderstood as a catch-all definition for any unusual sexual behavior. In the upcoming fifth edition of the book, DSM-5, the Sexual and Gender Identity Disorders Work Group sought to draw a line between atypical human behavior and behavior that causes mental distress to a person or makes the person a serious threat to the psychological and physical well-being of other individuals. While legal implications of paraphilic disorders were considered seriously in revising diagnostic criteria, the goal was to update the disorders in this category based on the latest science and effective clinical practice.

Through careful consideration of the research as well as of the collective clinical knowledge of experts in the field, several important changes were made to the criteria of paraphilic disorders, or paraphilias as they have been called in previous editions of the manual.

Characteristics of Paraphilic Disorders

Most people with atypical sexual interests do not have a mental disorder. To be diagnosed with a paraphilic disorder, DSM-5 requires that people with these interests:

- feel personal distress about their interest, not merely distress resulting from society's disapproval; or
- have a sexual desire or behavior that involves another person's psychological distress, injury, or death, or a desire for sexual behaviors involving unwilling persons or persons unable to give legal consent.

To further define the line between an atypical sexual interest and disorder, the Work Group revised the names of these disorders to differentiate between the behavior itself and the disorder stemming from that behavior

(i.e., Sexual Masochism in DSM-IV will be titled Sexual Masochism Disorder in DSM-5).

It is a subtle but crucial difference that makes it possible for an individual to engage in consensual atypical sexual behavior without inappropriately being labeled with a mental disorder. With this revision, DSM-5 clearly distinguishes between atypical sexual interests and mental disorders involving these desires or behaviors.

The chapter on paraphilic disorders includes eight conditions: exhibitionistic disorder, fetishistic disorder, frotteuristic disorder, pedophilic disorder, sexual masochism disorder, sexual sadism disorder, transvestic disorder, and voyeuristic disorder.

Additional Changes to Paraphilic Disorders

Other changes to diagnostic criteria for two DSM-5 paraphilic disorders also should be noted.

The first concerns transvestic disorder, which identifies people who are sexually aroused by dressing as the opposite sex but who experience significant distress or impairment in their lives – socially or occupationally – because of their behavior. DSM-IV limited this behavior to heterosexual males; DSM-5 has no such restriction, opening the diagnosis to women or gay men who have this sexual interest. While the change could increase the number of people diagnosed with transvestic disorder, the requirement remains that individuals must experience significant distress or impairment because of their behavior.

In the case of pedophilic disorder, the notable detail is what wasn't revised in the new manual. Although proposals were discussed throughout the DSM-5 development process, diagnostic criteria ultimately remained the same as in DSM-IV TR. Only the disorder name will be changed from pedophilia to pedophilic disorder to maintain consistency with the chapter's other listings.

47

Rethinking Sadomasochism: Feminism, Interpretation, and Simulation

Patrick D. Hopkins

Summary

Argues that sadomasochistic practices have been sharply criticized (especially by feminists) as immoral because they replicate sexist relationships, eroticize dominance and submission in a way that cannot be genuinely consented to, and validate and reinforce sexism. However, these criticisms do not succeed because SM culture eroticizes the simulation of sexist and other abusive actions, not sexist and abusive actions themselves. SM participants are not typically attracted to genuinely abusive activities, but only to superficial versions of those activities understood as play and theatre. As such, SM is not necessarily immoral because it lacks the intent, desire, and consequences of real sexist and abusive relationships.

Original publication details: Patrick D. Hopkins, "Rethinking Sadomasochism: Feminism, Interpretation, and Simulation," pp. 116–141 from *Hypatia* 9 (1994). Reproduced with permission of Cambridge University Press.

Sadomasochism has often been considered by feminists to be a major epistemological and behavioral structure of male dominated societies.[1] Most often, this structure has manifested itself in the form of dominant males coercing and controlling females for their own aims.

[. . .]

It was then both shocking and horrifying for many radical and politically active feminists in the late 1970s and early 1980s to discover that there were women who called themselves both feminists *and* sadomasochists. These were not women who believed that male domination was a good thing. They were not reactionary anti-feminists. These women were lesbians and radicals and feminist activists and scholars who claimed that one could be *both* a radical feminist committed to the liberation of women *and* a sadomasochist who enjoyed sexual activity based on the dominant/submissive model.

An unusual kind of altercation ensued – a battle among feminists about what feminism meant and what sadomasochism meant, with tremendous anger and hostility and incredulity on both sides.

[. . .]

In what follows, I want to engage the original criticisms of sadomasochism put forth by radical anti-SM feminists, assessing their relevance for dealing with contemporary SM epistemology and ethics as I see them. My premise in this paper is not that current SM activists have developed stunning new defenses of SM which sweep away the former radical critiques. Rather, my premise is that with the increased radicalization and communitization of SM, it becomes apparent that SM activity must be interpreted with a greater degree of subtlety and attention to context, both internal and external, than has previously been employed. To that end I will first look at the arguments against traditional concepts of SM. I will reinterpret SM in light of its recent articulation, and in turn, question the applicability of established counterarguments.

I. Anti-SM Feminist Oppositional Strategies

Generally, radical feminist opposition to lesbian SM can be characterized in terms of three primary strategies: 1. Lesbian SM replicates patriarchal relationships; 2. Consent to activities which eroticize dominance, submission, pain, and powerlessness is structurally impossible or ethically irrelevant; 3. Lesbian SM validates and supports patriarchy, though perhaps unintentionally.

First: The claim with which most anti-SM feminists begin, and which is probably the first reaction to hearing about the practice of lesbian "feminist" SM, is that SM replicates patriarchy. It seems an obvious inference to make, at least at first. Patriarchal society allows or encourages the sexual, economic, and psychological abuse of women, largely at the hands of men and for men's purposes. Lesbians who derive pleasure from humiliating or causing pain to other women seem blatantly to be reproducing the implicit values of patriarchal cultures, probably as a result of having internalized the view that women are sexual objects to be used for pleasure. Pleasure is to be had at the expense of women's pain.

The emphasis in this criticism is clear. Sadomasochism is a core structure of male-dominated culture. The fact that women engage in SM with other women does not obscure this fact. Indeed, it brings it into greater relief. Women, lesbians, even purported feminists, can internalize the degradation of women into sexual objects as a value without realizing that they have bought into patriarchal culture.

Bat Ami Bar-on:

> The primary claim of [feminist opposition] is that the erotization of violence or domination, and of pain or powerlessness, is at the core of sadomasochism and, consequently, that the practice of sadomasochism embodies the same values as heterosexual practices of sexual domination in general and sexually violent practices like rape in particular. (Bar-On 1982, 75)

[. . .]

Second: SM advocates often claim that since participants in an SM activity consent to the act, they are not doing anything wrong. It is something that they themselves desire, even seek out. But radical feminists disagree. They claim that consent has long been used to justify treating women as lesser creatures, and the fact that women often say that they consent to certain patterns of male domination does not prove that they are acting freely. Women, like men, typically learn and internalize patriarchal values and think of them as natural. Consent to abuse cannot be considered justification of abuse. The purported "consent" is just an example of how deeply the internalization of oppression goes. In fact, even if a certain woman's assent to engage in a painful sexual activity can be considered consent, this does not mean that it can be considered a feminist activity, nor even can it be considered non-oppressive. The fact that an activity is merely consensual does not suggest that it should be considered morally permissible, non-pathological, and certainly not politically practical. Consent, therefore, can be seen as either a structural impossibility in the context of eroticized dominance/submission or as a hopelessly conflated irrelevancy.

Diana Russell:

> Women have been reared to be submissive, to anticipate and even want domination by men. But wanting or consenting to domination and humiliation does not make it nonoppressive. It merely demonstrates how deep and profound the oppression is. Many young Brahmin women in the nineteenth century "voluntarily" jumped into the funeral pyres of their dead husbands. What feminist would argue that these women were not oppressed? . . . such consent does not mean that power has not been abused. (Russell 1982, 177)
>
> [. . .]

Third: As a result of replicating patriarchal values, desires, and behaviors, and by employing a naive conception of consent as defense, promoting and practicing sadomasochism actually ends up supporting patriarchy. SMists validate patriarchy's activities and undercut the power of feminist opposition by claiming that enjoying women's pain and humiliation can be conjoined with feminism itself This is stronger than merely the claim that SM replicates patriarchy; this is the claim that SM actually furthers patriarchy, promotes patriarchy, and as such, inhibits the development of feminism and actively interferes with the liberation of women. Lesbian "feminist" SM reinforces the oppression of women.

[. . .]

Audre Lorde:

> Sadomasochism is an institutionalized celebration of dominant/subordinate relationships. And, it *prepares* us either to accept subordination or to enforce dominance. *Even in play,* to affirm that the exertion of power over powerlessness is erotic, is empowering, is to set the emotional and social stage for the continuation of that relationship, politically, socially and economically. (Lorde and Star 1982, 68)
>
> [. . .]

I thus find that the charges of replicating patriarchy, the irrelevancy or impossibility of consent, and the validation

of patriarchy are recurring argument strategies. But are these charges accurate? Are they even applicable? Are radical critics even talking about the same things that the SM advocates are talking about?

Before making any interpretive sense of these questions or indeed of the supposed object of interest – SM – it will be necessary to explore the internal interpretive context of sadomasochistic activity. This will be critical in answering the question of whether or not SM replicates patriarchy and will situate questions of the relevancy of consent and the validation of patriarchy. In terms of the question of replication, I find two parallel, apparently similar, but largely discontinuous discourses operating regarding SM – one interpreting the "internal" context of SM encounters from the perspective of non-participating spectator, the other interpreting the "internal" context of SM encounters from the perspective of participant.

II. Replication Versus Simulation: Interpretive Contexts of SM

Radical critics often treat SM activities as if they were contextually and performatively identical with any other "sadistic" or "masochistic" act occurring anywhere, anytime. The working assumption seems to be that within patriarchal context' (and perhaps beyond it), certain behaviors possess an "essence" of their own, an intrinsic meaning, that cannot genuinely be altered by participant consent, community specification, or conscious negotiation.

[. . .]

Activities that eroticize submission and dominance are interpreted as operating exactly on the model of submission/dominance characteristic of male-dominated cultures. Any such activity, therefore, is thought to replicate patriarchal value, patriarchal desire, patriarchal behavior. That such activity might include the participation of lesbians does nothing to alter the interpretation – it still replicates the structure of masculinist desire. SM behavior is essentially no different from any other occurrence of the rape, beating, humiliation, exploitation, or degradation of women.

Sarah Hoagland writes: "What I've found quite jolting in several communities is the impulse to silence and ostracize Lesbian batterers while at the same time providing a forum for Lesbian sadists. This is significant because most batterers do not think that beating and humiliating another Lesbian is a positive thing to do, while sadists not only think it is alright but advocate it in the name of feminism, sisterhood and trust" (Hoagland 1982, 156). But is it the case that SM thinking and activity is really indistinguishable from apparently similar behavior in coercive, patriarchal context? Is it really even "apparently similar"? Is the meaning of the activities the same in SM and lesbian battery? Sarah Hoagland seems to think so, and by implication suggests that SM lesbians are encouraging the *kind* of activity that occurs in lesbian domestic violence.

[. . .]

The oft-repeated defense of SM that is supposed to demonstrate that SM activity is not just like patriarchal violence is that SM activity is consensual. Consent to beating, humiliation, or role-playing is thought to justify such activity. Radicals question both the existence or relevance of consent. But is consent the only defense? I think not. I think that SM practitioners, as well as their radical critics, have not read with sufficient subtlety the dynamics of SM encounters. The interpretive context of SM has much more to offer as a defense.

That defense is this: SM sexual activity does not replicate patriarchal sexual activity. It simulates it. Replication and simulation are very different. Replication implies that SM encounters merely reproduce patriarchal activity in a different physical area. Simulation implies that SM selectively replays surface patriarchal behaviors onto a different contextual field. That contextual field makes a profound difference.

SM participants do not rape, they do rape scenes. SMists do not enslave, they do slave scenes. SMists do not kidnap, they do capture and bondage scenes. The use of the term "scenes" exposes a critical, central aspect of SM culture. SM is constructed as a performance, as a staging, a production, a simulation in which participants are writers, producers, directors, actors, and audience. Importantly, this is a simulation recognized as such. Participants know they are doing a scene. They have sought out other performers.

As with other kinds of performances, other kinds of simulations, there appear to be many similarities between the "real" activity and the staged activity. In the case of SM, there is strong emotion. There is tension. And there may be real, genuine pain.[2]

But similarity is not sufficient for replication. Core features of real patriarchal violence, coercive violence, are absent. In real rapes, the victim is not a participant. She is not a subject. She is object, sport, commodity, disposable. She has little or no power. In an SM rape scene, however, the "victim" of a "rapist" is no replication of the victim of a rapist. This "victim" has

negotiated with her "rapist" ahead of time to establish the design, production, duration, and performance of the "rape." She might establish "safe words" she can use during the scene to slow down or stop the action if it gets too intense, or too fast, or if it's just not stimulating enough. Often, safe words like "yellow" for slow down, or "red" for stop, are used (Weinberg, Williams, and Moser 1984, 385). True to the context of performance and simulation however, sometimes the safe word is simply "safe word," a self-reflective signification of simulation (Truscott 1991, 19).

In real slavery, the slave is commodity and possession; the master may need fear, but not approval. The slave is capital resource, and often a threat – to be purchased, or bred, and acted upon. In SM "slave" and "master" scenes, however, the "slave" may reject the "master" (or "mistress") because she is not dominant enough, not experienced enough, not skillful enough to satisfy the "slave's" desires.[3] The "slave" may establish a time limit on her "slavery" because she has to get up and go to work at six o'clock the next morning. The "slave" may compliment (or criticize) the "master's" whipping technique and set up a time to meet her again next weekend.

It is certainly not absurd that critics of SM see replication of patriarchal roles and activities in SM. The surfaces seem similar to out-group observers. But though patriarchal violence may appear to parallel SM "violence," the parallel is unstable. The interpretive context is different. The material conditions are different. All the behaviors I mentioned – negotiation, safe words, mutual definition – take place in a self-defined community. SM communities, in their diversity – lesbian, gay, bisexual, heterosexual – have their own gathering places, their own publications, their own rules, their own senses of identity. This context of community is one aspect of SM that makes the charge of replicating patriarchal activity contestable.

In fact, SM scenes gut the behaviors they simulate of their violent, patriarchal, defining features. What makes events like rape, kidnapping, slavery, and bondage evil in the first place is the fact that they cause harm, limit freedom, terrify, scar, destroy, and coerce. But in SM there is attraction, negotiation, the power to halt the activity, the power to switch roles, and attention to safety. Like a Shakespearean duel on stage, with blunted blades and actors' training, violence is simulated, but is not replicated.

But what about another level of the problem of possible replication? Even if some critics of SM might agree that the material conditions and the interpretive context of SM are significantly different from genuine violence, perhaps they would suggest that this in no way eliminates the initial problem that the SM practitioner is attracted to violence, revels in the dominant/submissive model of sexuality, and derives pleasure from the suffering of women (herself or others). Even if such suffering is only simulated, not actually replicated, the sadomasochist still exhibits false consciousness, still engages in anti-feminist behavior, and still takes pleasure in abusing women or in being abused (albeit simulated).

But this criticism would fail to take the power of simulation into account. Certainly some people who enjoy the genuine suffering of women may make forays into the SM community before they are ferreted out. But it is not obvious that taking pleasure in the simulation of violence, domination, and submission is the same as or even indicative of taking pleasure in genuine violence, domination, and submission. Sexual desires do not always, perhaps not even predominantly, take as their objects isolated acts or isolated bodies. The context of the body and the act in an environment establishes the erotic interpretation. Thus, desire is not simply directed at certain specifiable bodies, but also at certain relatively specifiable environments. An entire context can be the "object" of desire. Not just an act, not just a body, not just a physiological reaction, but rather the entirety of bodies and circumstance and interpretation is desired. One can lust after a scene.[4]

In the case of SM therefore, it should not be assumed that SM participants actually find pleasure in the torture of slaves, nor in the cries of a rape victim, nor in the humiliation of women, nor in the relentless assault of an attacker. In fact, it is a central ethical and political value of those SMists who also profess to be feminists that such events are indeed evil, deplorable, and repugnant. At the same time however, it is possible to desire the *simulation* of those events, to lust after the context of a negotiated and consensual "submission" or "domination." This does not mean that simulation is the closest the SM practitioner can get to her real desires. This does not mean that the simulation of rape is a legal stand-in for the real thing. Neither should it be taken for granted that the participants get their pleasure by getting so far into the fantasy that they feel like it is the real thing. Rather, the sadomasochist can *desire the simulation itself*, not as inferior copy of the real thing, not as copy of anything at all, but as simulation qua simulation. There is a specific sexual context. The real events of rape and attack may be the object of intense hatred, intense sorrow, intense resistance. Lesbian sadomasochists march

in Take Back The Night marches, volunteer in rape crisis centers, and may even be victims of sexual assault themselves and speak out against it, bringing charges against their assailants. But this is not contradiction. For the actual desire of the SM participant may not be any form of real abuse. The desire may be for the simulation itself. Without limits, consent, ethical codes, safe words and community connection, the simulation would not be simulation. It would be replication or imitation – not the desired experience, and thus not erotic.

In significant ways, SM scenes parallel the experience of being on a roller coaster. There is intense emotion – fear, tension, anticipation, thrill. There is physiological arousal – adrenaline rush, headiness, gut twisting, a body high. All this because one has placed herself in the position of simulating plummeting to her death, of simulating flying off into space, of simulating the possibility of smashing into trees or metal railings. But is the best interpretation of the roller coaster rider's desire that she really would like to plummet to her death or collide with another train? Is it the case that she genuinely desires to be crushed against the ground, but because the law and conventional morality attempt to prevent it, alas, she is not able? Is riding a roller coaster just a matter of settling for the weaker imitation, for the copy of plummeting to her death?[5]

Of course not. In fact, the experience desired by the roller coaster rider is *precisely the simulation* of those lethal experiences – not because simulation is all she can get, but because *the simulation itself* is thrilling and satisfying. There is no actual desire to die, or fall, or crash. The simulation itself is the goal, not a lesser copy of the goal. So in the same way the roller coaster rider may find actually falling to her death repugnant and horrible, but finds simulation of that event thrilling and exciting, the SM practitioner may find actual violence and humiliation repugnant and horrible, but finds the simulation of that event thrilling and exciting – not as stand-in but as a goal in itself. It is simply not justified to assume that an SM participant finds real violence, real sexism, or real domination and submission desirable. As the lesbian feminist SM advocacy/support group Samois's Ministry of Truth put it: "Calling an S/M person sexist is like calling someone who plays Monopoly a capitalist" (Samois 1987, 151).

III. Consent and Content

For many SM practitioners, the belief that SM is not or cannot be genuinely consensual is part of a pervasive and false psychological stereotype of SM participants and encounters – an example of the kind of false stereotypes often attributed to minority groups. Experiences of their own autonomy and assertiveness in sexual scenes prove to SMists that they do in fact consent to SM activity and that their consent is not problematic. Gayle Rubin (herself a feminist scholar and sadomasochist) says: "The silliest arguments about S/M have been those which claim that it is impossible that people really consent to do it. . . . [T]he overwhelming coercion with regard to S/M is the way in which people are prevented from doing it. We are fighting for the freedom to consent to our sexuality without interference, and without penalty" (Rubin 1987, 224–25).

Rubin does not provide an argument defending the presence of consent in SM activities; she seems to think that she does not have to. Rubin largely treats the SM community like any other cultural minority, and suggests that the problem of questioning consent in SM lies not with SM practitioners, who experience the fullness of consent in every sought-after scene, but rather with radical feminist critics who are intent on attributing a set of unwarranted psychological traits to SMists. For Rubin, the case is no different from that of heterosexuals who claim that lesbians and gays can never be truly happy, even if they say they are.

[. . .]

In addition to the defense of personal experience in which masochists and sadists both have complete trust in their own consent, some SMists have claimed that the contractual nature of SM not only ensures consent but allows it to flourish. In fact, SM is thought to provide a radically honest, democratic model of consent that can be beneficially applied to other situations. Carol Truscott states:

The starting point of all S/M relationships, then, is talk of the most intimate kind. The talk is about what S/M play gets the potential partners off; who will assume which role; whether other people may be included . . .; what each person's limits are; whether or not "safe words" are allowed or required, and if so, what they are; the health of the partners . . .; and, more mundanely, whether one or the other has to leave for work at five the next morning . . . traditional relationships don't usually begin with this intimate a discussion. Most couples never talk openly about what they want and what they are prepared to give in their sexual relationships. Communication about sexual activities is largely nonverbal: incoherent

sounds combined with one partner seeking to move parts of the other's body in the hope that the "offending" partner will understand that something is amiss. . . . It is this, the negotiation preparatory to the new S/M relationship, that is the most important gift of contemporary consensual sadomasochism to the larger society. (Truscott 1991, 19)

[. . .]

But though this talk about consent sounds honest and arises from the kind of context feminists normally value – personal experience – there is still strong, gut-level resistance. A feminist cannot listen to claims about the joys of consenting to be tied down, whipped or urinated on, and claims that pretending to be a slave or a rape victim help teach independence and assertiveness, without remembering – remembering images of Chinese mothers "consenting" to have their daughters' feet bound, images of young girls "consenting" to be married to older men, images of women "consenting" unquestioningly to their husbands' will out of religious conviction, images of battered wives "consenting" to stay with their abusive husbands, images of fashion-conscious women "consenting" to endless and dangerous diets. Personal experience, while a powerful source of feminist insight and political truth, is also a potent site for the twisting of women's desires. Domination is not always achieved through physical and economic coercion alone. The imagination can be colonized as well. The personality can be coerced into constructing desires that serve other's interests. For some radical critics, the structure of certain choices themselves suggest that consent is doubtful.

Bat Ami Bar-On says: "The erotization of violence or domination and pain or powerlessness *necessarily* involves a violation of the right to determine what can be done with and to one's body" (Bar-On 1982, 76) [italics added]. It seems that for Bar-On, violence, domination, pain, and powerlessness are such clear and present evils that any notion of one "consenting" to such events must be read as the colonization of desires, not as the expression of autonomous attraction.

[. . .]

Perhaps in light of what I have said about SM as simulation, a challenge can be brought forth. If it is possible, or maybe even probable, that SM participants desire the simulation itself, then the derivative eroticization would not be of "violence or domination and of pain or powerlessness" but of simulated violence, simulated domination, and simulated powerlessness. I leave out the term

Patrick D. Hopkins

"pain" in this speculation because the pain experienced in SM can be very real indeed. While some role-playing activities use soft cloth "whips" or loose bondage, many activities involve real whips, restrictive bondage, and genuine pain (see footnote 2).

If the eroticization of *simulated* violence, domination, and submission is what is going on in SM scenes, then Bar-On's claim would not seem to apply. Although the SM theorists whom I have read appear not to have thought about their sexual activities explicitly in terms of simulation, I think much of their rhetoric suggests that they would agree with Bar-On that eroticizing violence, domination, and submission necessarily involves a violation of the right of bodily determination. However, many reject the claim that what goes on in SM relationships is violence.

[. . .]

It is thus crucial in considering claims about consent in SM to ask the following question: What is a sado-masochist consenting to? If the characterization of SM scenes as simulation is accurate, then one cannot claim that a sadomasochist consents to genuine powerlessness, genuine domination, or genuine submission. The SMist is instead consenting to particular simulative performances negotiated beforehand among performers with equal power and equal say. As such, the radicals' critique of consent fails to apply to the claims of consent employed in consensual SM relationships. This is not a circular argument – consensual SM is by consent so it is consensual. This is instead a re-cognition of the context of SM as a practice of simulation in a specific and knowledgeable community.[6] It may be true that one cannot genuinely consent to powerlessness and domination, but this is not an argument against consenting to simulated powerlessness and domination. The practices are different, the contexts are different, the participants are different.

IV. Validation, Assimilation, and Public Relations

But even if we are to understand SM activity in terms of simulation and recognize that consent to simulation is less problematic than consent to genuine violence or powerlessness, SM still occurs in a patriarchal culture and cannot be uncomplicatedly extracted from that culture and analyzed or experienced strictly in its own terms. The fact remains that genuine violence and domination do occur, and most representations of such are not subject to the kind of consent ethics present in the SM community. [. . .] There is a larger context to think about in regard to the presence of SM, a context which affects all women.

The fear, and often primary criticism, of most radical critics is that SM actually validates and supports the degradation of, and violence against, women. It is not obvious that this claim has been challenged by characterizing SM as consensual performances in contexts of simulation. The validation of violence against women, of seeing women as fantasy fodder and sexual fodder for heterosexual men, does not rest in any internal interpretation of an SM scene, but rather in the situatedness of that "scene" in broader patriarchal cultural context. Lesbian SM, like any other SM, still operates within the relatively uncritical larger field of sexism and the oppression of women. Can't it therefore still *function*, even unintentionally, as a representation, and thus validation, of the non-consensual domination model? This could occur in at least two ways. First, even if SM is primarily simulative rather than replicative, SM could validate patriarchy by condoning (perhaps unwittingly) the ideology of coercive sexual domination. Second, SM could be a destabilizing force within feminism itself, interfering with relations among feminists by scattering energy needed for specific projects and presenting feminism to the world as a movement of infighting and dissension.

In the first case, that of condoning a patriarchal ideology leading to violence against women, it should be made clear that this does not have to mean that any SM participant deliberately does this. Rather, just by taking place in patriarchal culture/context, SM will be seen as condoning the objectification of women's bodies, even if the dominant is herself a woman. It makes no difference if it really is simulation, even self-characterized subversive simulation.

[. . .]

The radicals' claim is that such imagery is not seen by viewers as rigidly compartmentalized into a self-conscious fantasy, separated from male-dominated culture, but is instead an uncritical reinforcement of the fetishization of female submission and powerlessness central to the structures of patriarchal sexual desire. Lesbian SM provides a particularly insidious reinforcement of that desire – it provides an image of assertive, even "feminist" women, who say that it really is their desire to be dominated, and that sex based on dichotomies of power is what really turns them on. Perhaps in a world where feminist critical insights abounded and where a robust notion of simulation was active, a contextual interpretation of such claims would not be so dangerous, in the sense of validating sexual desire focused on coercive or manipulative sex. But in a world where feminist critical insights and self-conscious cinematic metaphoricity are the possession of a relatively small group, lesbian SM functions merely as a dumping of images into masculinist context. One can easily imagine that those masculinist men who might have access to such images will have little more critical insight than to defend their sexual desires or their version of women's sexual desires by grunting "Well, she's a woman and *she* likes it" or "Well, she's a feminist and *she* likes it."

The second way that lesbian SM is purported to validate patriarchy is by hurting feminists and feminist projects. Again, this is not a charge of deliberate harm, but of inevitable harm.

[. . .]

In her short narrative *A Letter of the Times*, Alice Walker describes a class in feminist theology in which students have been studying slave narratives. Students are encouraged to imagine what it would be like to be enslaved or to be a mistress. Near the end of the class a television special on sadomasochism airs in which a white "mistress" and her black "slave" are presented. Walker's character writes: "All I had been teaching was subverted by that one image, and I was incensed to think of the hard struggle of my students to rid themselves of stereotype, to combat prejudice, to put themselves into enslaved women's skins, and then to see their struggle mocked, and the actual enslaved *condition* of literally millions of our mothers trivialized – because two ignorant women insisted on their right to act out publicly a 'fantasy' that still strikes terror in black women's hearts" (Walker 1982, 207). Again, the chief indictment of lesbian SM is that it has the result of interfering with feminist projects and reinforces a patriarchal worldview.

I think it is clear, historically, that the presence of lesbian SM has created dissension and animosity among feminists. It has not, however, been demonstrated that SM, if accepted as an ethically permissible form of sexual activity, would in fact reinforce patriarchal beliefs about women's sexuality in the way radical critics claim it would. After all, sadomasochists who advocate understanding of and tolerance for the free exercise of their sexuality are constantly making it clear that consent, playfulness, safety, and the option of "role reversal" are central to their sexuality. But for purposes of this essay, let us assume that acknowledged SM sexuality *does* reinforce patriarchal beliefs in a significant number of persons as well as create problems for

interfeminist relations – in spite of feminist SMists' attempts to prevent these effects. What political stance should feminist SMists take as a result of this knowledge? I do not think the answer is obvious.

Certainly the option radicals offer is that SMists renounce SM and stop living out their fantasies.[7] But this answer is politically, personally, and theoretically problematic, particularly for women informed by the critical insights of lesbian/radical feminism itself. In general, it sounds like SMists are being admonished to renounce, or at least hide, their sexual/political activities because they hurt "the movement" or because they "make things worse" by being so blatant and weird. For many SMists such a claim sounds suspiciously like the admonishments made by so-called "assimilationists" – admonishments radical feminists, and particularly lesbian feminists, typically reject.

Consider the advice given in the book *After the Ball*, which maps out a marketing/advertising strategy by which lesbians and gay men can achieve equality and acceptance in the US. The strategy focuses primarily on public relations for lesbians and gays and calls for the withdrawal of "fringe groups" that disturb the unity of the gay rights movement and reinforce harmful stereotypes. In describing a media campaign directed toward the goal of gay rights, Marshall Kirk and Hunter Madsen state:

> Persons featured in the media campaign should be wholesome and admirable by straight standards, and completely unexceptional in appearance; in a word, they should be indistinguishable from the straights we'd like to reach. In practical terms, this means that cocky mustachioed leathermen, drag queens, and bull dykes would not appear in gay commercials and other public presentations . . . . One could also argue that lesbians should be featured more prominently than gay men in the early stages of the media campaign. Straights generally have fewer and cloudier preconceptions about lesbians and may feel less hostile toward them. And *as women* (generally seen as less threatening and more vulnerable than men), lesbians may be more credible objects of sympathy. (Kirk and Madsen 1989, 183–184)[8]

Of course, most radical feminists and especially lesbian separatist feminists vociferously reject the notion that they want to join mainstream (malestream) U.S. culture (especially by making lesbians seem less threatening) and that SMists are interfering with that goal. But this is

Patrick D. Hopkins

not my claim. Instead, I want to suggest a parallel between the kind of emotional/political reaction SMists have to claims that they hurt feminism and reinforce patriarchal culture, and the emotional/political reaction separatists and other radicals have to the claim that they hurt the cause of lesbian and gay liberation by disrupting the unity of "the movement." In both cases, members of the impugned groups feel that their experiences, identities, and political aims will be ignored, repressed, or co-opted for the "greater good," with little or no good for them. And in the way that a mainstream, "assimilationist" gay rights movement would not serve the political goals of radical lesbian feminists, an "assimilationist" radical lesbian feminist movement may not serve the goals of sadomasochist feminists.

It is not by accident that the leading lesbian SM activist group Samois chose as their slogan "The Leather Menace." The slogan is a play on words of the phrase "The Lavender Menace" that was used to describe the presence of lesbians in the National Organization for Women when NOW was trying to purge lesbians from its membership (Califia 1987, 264). The parallel for SMists is obvious. NOW members thought that lesbians were hurting feminism and feminist projects and sought to expurgate them for purposes of political expediency. And of course, NOW was not merely being reactionary. There was a contemporary political reality to face. Lesbians really did pose more of a threat than straight, liberal feminist women and really did possess the potential to disrupt NOW's political goals and public relations campaigns. But the question for lesbians at the time was whether or not it was somehow their "feminist duty" to shut up and get out, at least until society had been changed enough to permit their presence later on. Obviously, many lesbians did not take it as their feminist duty to shut up and get out. Many lesbians did not simply interpret their own situation as that of being feminists who happened to like having sex with other women, and thus did not feel that they were merely positing a liberal claim to sexual freedom somewhat beyond that of NOW. Instead, they saw their sexuality intimately entwined with their polities, identity and culture. They formed radical political associations of their own because they no longer saw that the "feminist movement" was particularly benefiting them and realized they had to form their own theories and practices. Sadomasochists have been and are in a similar position.[9]

[. . .]

Hearing feminists decry SMists is strikingly similar, for feminist sadomasochists, to hearing feminists decry lesbians. And although many sadomasochists strongly feel that they are feminists, just like lesbians in NOW felt that they were feminists, many SMists have come to see radical feminists as agents of oppression.[10]

[. . .]

It appears that in the context of an interpretation of SMists as a sexual minority developing and expressing their own culture, an appropriate response for SMists to the claim that SMists are hurting feminism is not necessarily to renounce SM, but to develop a politics which addresses their own needs and perspectives, including the continued identification as both feminists and sadomasochists. Part of such a politics, as in other movements, would be the continuing education of the public. SMists can provide information on the nature of consent, the nature of sexual play and fantasy, and information regarding stereotypes of SMists, thereby assuring that information about SM from SMists would be reflective of actual, considered practice, and not easily interpreted by others as a reinforcement, validation, or replication of patriarchal practice.

[. . .]

Notes

1 One passionate and eloquent example of this is certainly Mary Daly's *Gyn/Ecology: The Metaethics of Radical Feminism* (1978), particularly in her descriptions of Sado-Ritual Syndrome, Goddess Dismemberment, and of the "necrophilic" attraction males have for females.

2 Carol Truscott wants to make it very clear that real pain does occur in some SM situations. However, she also notes that an essential component of SM is the reconceptualizing of pain as "sensations of changing, sometimes increasing intensity, rather than considering it something to be avoided as we do under ordinary circumstances" (Truscott 1991, n. 24).

3 Pat Califia discusses the way in which tops' sexual and emotional needs are often ignored by thoughtless bottoms. She admonishes tops to "stop acting like a bunch of victimized codependents held hostage by rapacious bottoms" (Califia 1992, 19). It is revealing of the internal context of SM relations that bottoms can be considered manipulative, assertive, or insensitive, while tops, can be considered inadequately assertive or inattentive to their own sexual satisfaction.

4 See Gilles Deleuze and Félix Guattari (1977). Also see Alphonso Lingis (1985). Lingis describes Deleuze and

Guattari's position as one in which "sexual desire does not have as its objects persons or things at all. It is invested in whole environments, in vibrations and fluxes of all kinds; it is essentially nomadic. It is always with worlds that we make love" (Lingis 1985, 90).

5   My thanks go to Perry Stevens for this illuminating analogy.

6   The notion of community as applied to SM may be empirically somewhat problematic, at least in non-urban areas, for the simple reason that SM is still extremely vilified and as such, community visibility is dangerous. It is not, however, theoretically more problematic than any other community that serves persons whose "identifying" traits are stigmatized, unobvious behavioral and emotional interests, such as lesbians, gays, bisexuals etc. Having said that, the very presence of a person in an SM community setting (provided it is not accidental) suggests a mutual recognition of desire. This is not to say that mere presence implies consent to any specific act, but a presence does suggest community affinity.

7   Sandra Bartky has an interesting, but I think ultimately unsatisfactory analysis of this option. She believes that sadomasochistic desire is incompatible with feminist principles but that it is extremely difficult to teach women how to "decolonize the imagination." She seems to think that women who have SM desires but want to remain consistent with feminist principles are doomed to living out a life of "existential unease" (Bartky 1990, 60–62).

8   I do not intend to make any judgment in this paper whatsoever regarding the desirability or undesirability of Kirk's and Madsen's position. Such a discussion is worthy of, at the very least, a separate and lengthy paper. I only use their work as an example of what radical lesbians/gays/feminists often consider assimilationist.

9   It may be claimed that this analogy only holds in the end if SM really is harmless for feminism. The problem with such a claim is knowing what should and should not be considered to "harm feminism." One could make the claim that the presence of lesbians really did harm the kind of feminism NOW was promoting at the time by giving conservatives support for their claims that feminism threatened the traditional family, promoted homosexuality, etc. NOW's eventual move was not to defend their particular brand of feminism forever, but to alter their feminism to include the struggle for lesbian visibility and rights. Sadomasochists, not surprisingly, could call for the same sort of inclusion, or at least a halt to resistance, by claiming that their sexuality is no more harmful to a certain kind of inclusive feminism than lesbian sexuality was harmful to a certain kind of inclusive feminism.

10   Gayle Rubin's claim concerning "one best way to do sex" may be a straw person, but only in the sense that she might be attributing the notion of the "one best way" to all radicals. Certainly there are some radicals who would allow a variety of sexual activity while still rejecting SM as an ethically permissible sexual activity. However, Rubin is responding to radicals who have chosen to publicly renounce her sexuality and fight its acceptance. Some of these radicals do seem to claim that the only ethically/politically permissible sexual activity for a feminist is egalitarian sex with another woman – where "egalitarian" is specified in terms of necessary, formal, physical requirements, ruling out the possibility of consensual SM activity regardless of the participants' interpretations of such activities.

References

Bar-On, Bat Ami. 1982. Feminism and sadomasochism: Self-critical notes. In *Against sadomasochism: A radical feminist analysis.* See Linden et al. 1982.

Bartky, Sandra. 1990. *Femininity and domination.* New York: Routledge.

Califia, Pat. 1987. A personal view of the history of the lesbian S/M community and movement in San Francisco. In *Coming to power: Writings and graphics on lesbian S/M.* See Samois 1987.

Califia, Pat. 1992. The limits of the S/M relationship, or Mr. Benson doesn't live here anymore. In *Leatherfolk: Radical sex, people, politics, and practice.* See Thompson 1991.

Daly, Mary, 1978. *Gyn/Ecology: The metaethics of radical feminism.* Boston: Beacon Press.

Hoagland, Sarah Lucia. 1982. Sadism, masochism and lesbian-feminism. In *Against sadomasochism: A radical feminist analysis.* See Linden et al. 1982.

Kirk, Marshall and Hunter Madsen. 1989. *After the ball: How America will conquer its fear of gays in the 1990s.* New York: Doubleday.

Linden, Robin Ruth, Darlene R. Pagano, Diana E. H. Russell, and Susan Leigh Star. 1982. *Against sadomasochism: A radical feminist analysis.* San Francisco: Frog In The Well.

Lingis, Alphonso. 1985. *Libido: The French existential theories.* Bloomington: Indiana University Press.

Lorde, Audre and Susan Leigh Star. 1982. Interview with Audre Lorde. In *Against sadomasochism: A radical feminist analysis.* See Linden et al. 1982.

Meredith, Jesse. 1982. A Response to Samois. In *Against sadomasochism: A radical feminist analysis*. See Linden et al. 1982.

Rian, Karen. 1982. Sadomasochism and the social construction of desire. In *Against sadomasochism: A radical feminist analysis*. See Linden et al. 1982.

Rubin, Gayle. 1987. The leather menace: Comments on politics and S/M. In *Coming to power: Writings and graphics on lesbian S/M*. See Samois 1987.

Russell, Diana E. H. 1982. Sadomasochism: A contra-feminist activity. In *Against sadomasochism: A radical feminist analysis*. See Linden et al. 1982.

Samois. 1987. *Coming to power: Writings and graphics on lesbian S/M*. Boston: Alyson Publications, Inc.

Thompson, Mark, ed. 1991. *Leatherfolk: Radical sex, people, politics, and practice*. Boston: Alyson Publications, Inc.

Truscott, Carol. 1991. S/M: Some questions and a few answers. In *Leatherfolk: Radical sex, people, politics, and practice*. See Thompson 1991.

Walker, Alice. 1982. A letter of the times, or should this sadomasochism be saved? In *Against sadomasochism: A radical feminist analysis*. See Linden et al. 1982.

Weinberg, Martin S., Colin J. Williams, and Charles Moser. 1984. The social constituents of sadomasochism. *Social Problems* 31(4): 379–389.

48

Naughty Fantasies

John Corvino

Summary

Argues that sexual fantasizing about immoral activities (whether just imagined or played out) is itself immoral. This rules out rape fantasies, humiliation fantasies, or sadomasochistic role-playing as morally permissible. Contra Hopkins, a person can only eroticize the content of depictions, not depictions themselves and so it is not psychologically possible to eroticize simulations. Rejecting consequentialist arguments, neither can naughty fantasies be defended by consent because finding such activities erotic is dependent on actual immoral activities and as such is incompatible with being a virtuous person.

Original publication details: John Corvino, "Naughty Fantasies," from David Boonin (ed.), The Palgrave Handbook of Sexual Ethics. Palgrave Macmillan, 2022. Reproduced with permission of John Corvino. This is a slightly modified version (with a new postscript) of an article that appeared in *Southwest Philosophy Review: The Journal of the Southwestern Philosophical Society* 18:1 (January 2002), pp. 213–220.

Is it wrong to eroticize activities that are themselves wrong? Consider the following scenarios:

1. Sally is a feminist who enjoys light sadomasochism, including spanking, whipping, and slave-master roleplaying. Sometimes she is the "top" in such activities, and sometimes her boyfriend is, but in all cases the activities am consensual and mutually pleasurable.
2. Fred is a gay man who finds himself aroused by stories of fraternity hazing, particularly those involving stripping and humiliation. He is against such activity in "real life," and indeed he discourages college-age friends from joining fraternities because of these and other troubling practices. Nevertheless, he occasionally visits websites that contain such stories for the purpose of erotic stimulation.
3. Ramona, who was raped as a teenager, occasionally fantasizes about rape while masturbating or having sex with partners. Given her serious opposition to rape and to exploitation of women more generally, she feels guilty about such fantasies. Nevertheless, she finds that her sexual experiences are intensified when she recalls her own rape or imagines others.

Some (notably certain feminists) have argued that actively entertaining the sorts of fantasies described above is always wrong, insofar as these fantasies depend on models of domination and exploitation. Others (including other feminists) have defended such practices on grounds of personal freedom and privacy. In this paper I would like to revisit this debate by clarifying and evaluating one of the core arguments within it. Although my conclusions will be somewhat tentative, I hope at least to elucidate some of the ethical and conceptual issues raised by these practices, which are not merely controversial but also rather common.

[. . .]

By "naughty fantasies" I mean any sexual fantasy, *either imagined or acted out*, involving the eroticization of an activity that is itself morally wrong. (Notice that the three examples above represent a range of such fantasies.) By "eroticization," I mean actively regarding the activity with sexual desire (although as I shall explain below, I think the phenomenon of eroticization is itself in need of better analysis). The argument I wish to clarify and evaluate is as follows:

1. It is wrong to eroticize activities that are themselves wrong.

2. Naughty fantasies eroticize activities that are themselves wrong.

Therefore, it is wrong to pursue naughty fantasies.

Let us call this the "naughty-fantasies argument." Note that the first premise is intended *a priori*. One could, of course, make the consequentialist argument that those who pursue naughty fantasies are more likely to engage in *actual* exploitation than those who do not, or that they are more likely to be violent or callous or incapable of intimacy – but this is not the argument under consideration here. Rather, the question is whether it is wrong in *itself* to eroticize wrongful activities.

One way to rebut the argument is to attack the second premise. Patrick Hopkins takes this approach in his defense of sadomasochism.[1] According to Hopkins, sadomasochism does not eroticize a wrongful activity, it eroticizes the *simulation* of a wrongful activity:

> In the case of SM . . . it should not be assumed that SM participants actually find pleasure in the torture of slaves, nor in the cries of a rape victim, nor in the **humiliation** of women, nor in the relentless assault of an attacker. In fact, it is a central ethical and political value of those SMists who also profess to be feminists that such events are indeed evil, deplorable, and repugnant. At the same time, however, it is possible to desire the *simulation* of those events, to lust after the context of a negotiated and consensual "submission" or "domination.".. . .[T]he sadomasochist can *desire the simulation itself,* not as an inferior copy of the real thing, not as a copy of anything at all, but as simulation qua simulation.[2]

In one sense, Hopkins is correct when he claims that SM participants do not find pleasure in the torture of slaves and so on: the typical naughty fantasizer is as horrified by *actual* atrocities as anyone else. But during fantasy, the distinction between the fictional and the actual is not so clear. When Fred reads a fraternity-hazing story on the internet, does it matter for erotic purposes whether the story is true or not? Suppose Fred discovers that a favorite story that he had believed to be "fictional" is actually a biographical account. He might feel guilty about continuing to eroticize the story, but will he find it less erotic? Might he not even find it *more* erotic?

The answers to these questions depend on Fred's particular situation. But whatever the answers, the question remains whether it is psychologically possible for Fred (or anyone else) to eroticize a *simulation qua simulation*.

In order to understand this question, put aside the issue of eroticization and consider first what it means to *attend to* a simulation qua simulation. Take barn facades, for example. One can attend to these qua barns, in which case one might notice their charming architecture, their idyllic settings, their bright red siding. Or one can attend to them qua simulations, in which case one might notice their apparent three-dimensionality, their realistic stature, or their propensity for appearing in Gettier-type counterexamples. Note that the features noticed when attending to the barn facade qua simulation are largely exclusive of those noticed when attending to it qua barn: indeed, when attending to it qua simulation, one is **mindful** of precisely those features that make the object *not* a real barn.

The case is somewhat different in naughty fantasies. True, SM participants frequently attend to the pleasure of their partners, and to that extent, they are mindful of features that distinguish their activities from actual violence. But they are also mindful of features that occur in the "real" case: the spanking, the quickened heartbeat, the gasps and groans. When they eroticize these features, SM participants (and other naughty fantasizers) seem to be eroticizing not simulations qua simulations, but domination and its **manifestations**. The simulation is not the object of arousal; rather, it is the vehicle for the object of arousal.

To see this point more clearly, let us suppose that Fred is watching a porn film depicting fraternity-hazing. If Fred were to focus on the film qua simulation, what features would he notice? Presumably, he would attend to things like the convincingness (or lack thereof) of the actors' humiliation, the realistic nature of the dorm-room sets, or the level of detail in the storyline. Such attention would be more appropriate to the film critic than the sexual participant. Indeed, it is not even clear what it would mean to *eroticize* such features (although someone who did would possess a most interesting fetish). What turns people on in naughty fantasies is not depiction, but rather what is being depicted.

This is not to say that the object of a naughty fantasy – that is, the part that "turns on" the fantasizer – is typically clear or well-defined. Fred may not know why he enjoys fraternity-hazing scenes, and he will likely find that over-analysis of this issue serves merely to spoil his fun. Lacking a developed "phenomenology of arousal," we may find that it is harder to explain what the object of arousal *is* than to explain what it is *not*. In any case, we must reject Hopkins' claim that the object is simulation qua simulation and consider a different approach to the naughty-fantasies argument.

Perhaps it would be more promising to grant the second premise of the naughty-fantasies argument and instead attack the first, which states that it is always wrong to eroticize wrongful activities. Hopkins employs this approach briefly when he writes,

> In fact, SM scenes gut the behaviors they simulate of their violent, patriarchal, defining features. What makes events like rape, kidnapping, slavery and bondage evil in the first place is the fact that they cause harm, limit freedom, terrify, scar, destroy, and coerce. But in SM there is attraction, negotiation, the power to halt the activity, the power to switch roles, and attention to safety. Like a Shakespearean duel on stage, with blunted blades and actors' framing, violence is simulated, but is not replicated.[3]

Hopkins is correct that the central wrong-making features of rape are absent from rape fantasies. Moreover, one could argue that rape fantasies not only lack the wrong-making features but also add a good-making one, namely the pleasure of the fantasizer. But this argument misreads the first premise of the naughty-fantasies argument as being consequentialist in nature. Recall that proponents of the argument are not (or at least, not *here*) concerned with whether such fantasies have good or bad consequences. The fact that people take pleasure in such fantasies is precisely the problem, according to this argument: some pleasures are bad because their objects are inappropriate as objects of pleasure.

There are at least two non-consequentialist ways to understand the first premise of the naughty-fantasies argument. One might adopt a virtue-ethics approach and argue that naughty fantasies are incompatible with good character, particularly if they are pursued habitually. The idea here is not that regular pursuit of such fantasies might cause one to be more violent, or callous, or indifferent to human suffering; that argument would be consequentialist. Rather, the idea is that naughty fantasies are incompatible with some virtue or set of virtues that has some *non-instrumental* value in a well-lived life.[4] Someone lacking such virtues would be missing something, even if neither she nor anyone else is less happy as a result. Alternatively, one might argue that actively entertaining naughty fantasies is wrong in itself, apart from any connection with virtue. I will focus on this latter claim, though much of what I say will apply to the virtue-ethics version as well.[5]

The intuition that drives this claim is that any seriously wrongful activity merits an attitude of disapproval, and eroticization of such an activity is inconsistent with this attitude. I suggest that the best way to defend this intuition is dialectically, through the use of further examples.

Consider Raymond, who collects and studies newspaper accounts of *actual* rapes in older to enhance his erotic life. Suppose that he, like Ramona, is deeply against rape and would never commit it. Now one might have trouble accepting this supposition, mainly because it seems incompatible with Raymond's enjoyment of real-life rape stories. In other words, there seems to be some incoherence involved in being against rape while deriving sexual pleasure from reading about real rapes. Yet notice that on consequentialist grounds, Raymond is in the clear. (We are assuming that Raymond is sincere in his opposition and that he is no more inclined to be violent or callous because of his predilections.) His pleasure in reading such accounts results in a net gain in utility.

Or consider Charlie, married with grown children, who sometimes fantasies about having sex with underage girls. He is deeply opposed to child abuse and would never engage in such activity himself. On a few occasions he has purchased magazines with erotic images of females who are in fact over eighteen but who appear to be as young as twelve, and he has privately begun writing (and via the internet, sharing) fictional stories about forcible sex with these girls. His relationships with his wife and others appear unaffected by this activity, which occupies very little of his time and which he would abandon entirely were it not for the sexual charge it brings him. Or if Charlie's case does not trouble you, consider Chester, who is like Charlie in every respect except that the stories he shares are *actual accounts* of adult–child rape. Consequentialist concerns aside, there is a strong intuition that in Chester's case (if not in Charlie's as well) the eroticization of child abuse represents a failure to exhibit the appropriate attitude toward a deeply wrongful activity.

One might object in the cases of Raymond and Chester, who seek real-life accounts rather than fictional ones, on the grounds that their predilections are *causally dependent* on the existence of actual atrocities. The problem is that the same seems true in the case of Ramona, Fred, and Charlie. Presumably, naughty fantasies give them a sexual charge in large part because of the intense emotions associated with *actual* domination and **humiliation**. Thus, if causal dependence on real atrocities tarnishes Raymond's and Chester's fantasies, it tarnishes all

naughty fantasies. (Indeed, a major thrust of **feminist** ethics is that human actions cannot be evaluated apart from the social context that imbues them with meaning.)

The point about inappropriate attitudes can be illustrated with non-sexual examples as well. Some years ago I attended a large Southern university where one of the local fraternities annually held an "Old South Ball." The fraternity, which was notorious for its white-only membership, would hire black students to pose as "slaves" at the ball for the sake of verisimilitude. Needless to say, this event regularly provoked a serious outcry within the campus community. While some defended the fraternity on the grounds that the black actors were willfully (though, to many minds, inexplicably) participating, most thought that the event involved a serious failure on the part of all participants to adopt an appropriate attitude toward slavery. The fact that these actors were paid well was beside the point.

This is not to say that any and all depictions of wrongful practices are bad. Compare the Old South Ball to the mini-series *Roots* and the difference is immediately apparent: those who watch *Roots* should (and typically do) sympathize with the slaves; those fraternity members who participated in the ball simply enjoyed themselves at the "slaves'" expense. On the other hand, if someone were to watch *Roots* and smile or cheer during a lynching scene, others might reasonably balk. Similar points can be made about war movies. A person who watches a World War II film, for example, and fails to sympathize with the Jews is missing something – a point that was made humorously during a Seinfeld episode, when Jerry was chided mercilessly by his parents after being caught making out with his girlfriend during *Schindler's List*.

Video games may provide an even better analogy because of their more clearly participatory nature. Suppose Victor enjoys games in which he assumes the role of a fighter pilot bombing various military targets. Such games are quite common and are widely regarded as harmless (the familiar objections to violent toys notwithstanding). Now suppose the game is based on an *actual war* – say, the civil war in Bosnia – and Victor assumes the role of a Serb targeting Muslim civilians. Further, suppose that although Victor is opposed to the "ethnic cleansing" in Bosnia, he really enjoys his video game and cheers loudly every time a Slavic Muslim in the game is killed. Even if we were convinced that Victor would never behave this way toward ethnic minorities in "real life," would we not find his behavior during the games problematic?

The analogy is, needless to say, imperfect. For one thing, eroticizing something is not the same as cheering for it (more on this below). But the example does capture the concern that anti-SM feminists and others have about naughty fantasies: rape, humiliation, and exploitation are real and all-too-common evils. To seek out their depictions for the purpose of pleasuring oneself is to fail to acknowledge that evil properly.

Having done my best to defend this intuition, let me conclude by noting a few points that militate against it. (I acknowledged at the outset that my conclusions in this paper are tentative.) The naughty-fantasies argument (in particular, the first premise) depends upon the assumption that eroticization involves a kind of pro-attitude which, as such, is incompatible with condemnation of the depicted activity. Yet the truth of that assumption is by no means clear, for several reasons. First, as noted above, the object of eroticization is often non-specific. Just as one can enjoy a movie (say, Schindler's list) without endorsing particular characters, perhaps one can eroticize a wrongful behavior while remaining fully cognizant of its wrongfulness. This again points to the need for a more developed phenomenology of eroticization.

Second, eroticization may not be fully voluntary. If Ramona recalls her own rape experience while daydreaming, and she subsequently becomes aroused, has she really adopted an attitude? Isn't it more accurate to say that she has experienced a *reaction* to a stimulus (and an uninvited stimulus at that)? Insofar as the reaction is involuntary, Ramona cannot be held morally accountable for it. Of course, the matter is somewhat different when she is not merely daydreaming but instead perusing her local adult bookstore. There seem to be various possible degrees of participation in erotic arousal, ranging from the involuntary to the deliberate. It is toward the latter end of the spectrum that one begins to suspect a pro-attitude.

Yet even if Ramona's arousal is deliberate, there is still another defense she can marshal — especially given her status as a survivor of rape. Is it not possible that in eroticizing wrongful activities, those who pursue naughty fantasies thus rob these activities of their wrongfulness? I have in mind the kind of transformation intended when (for example) gays use the word "queer" or Jews make jokes about the Holocaust — Mel Brooks's musical comedy *The Producers* being a brilliant example of the latter. Of course, these sorts of reclamations raise troubling questions of their own. But they also raise the helpful suggestion that the solution to the naughty-fantasies dilemma lies in areas having very little to do with sex.

[. . .]

Notes

1 Patrick Hopkins, "Rethinking Sadomasochism: Feminism, Interpretation, and Simulation," *Hypatia* 9:1 (1994), pp. 116–41.
2 Ibid., p. 198.
3 Ibid., p. 197.
4 For a defense of a non-instrumentalist understanding of the virtues see Walter Schaller, "Are Virtues No More Than Dispositions to Obey Moral Rules?" *Philosophia* 20 (July 1990).
5 Notice that if one adopts the virtue-ethics understanding of the first premise it is no longer true *a priori*, since the virtues are learned through experience.

49

What (if Anything) Is Wrong with Bestiality?

Neil Levy

Summary

Argues that none of the standard moral objections to bestiality succeed. Analyzes and rejects the arguments that bestiality is a perversion, that animals are unable to consent to sexual activity, that animals are necessarily harmed, that using animals as mere means is wrong, and that bestiality necessarily inculcates vices in human beings. As such, bestiality is not immoral for consequentialist, deontological, or virtue-ethical reasons. Why then is there such a strong taboo against it? Some have argued that it is merely a leftover belief in human superiority from pre-evolutionary worldviews. This position is too narrow. Instead, the taboo is part of a wider view of the value of human life that recognizes certain limits on human activity as definitive of our human identity and human community. As such, the taboo is rational and protects human identity.

Original publication details: Neil Levy, "What (if Anything) Is Wrong with Bestiality?" pp. 444–456 from *Journal of Social Philosophy* 34:3 (2003). Reproduced with permission of John Wiley & Sons.

Peter Singer is used to controversy – indeed, he seems to court it – but nothing could have prepared him for the reaction which followed his recent review of Midas Dekker's *Dearest Pet* for the on-line version of *Nerve* magazine.[1] Dekker's book is a social, historical, and psychological examination of bestiality, and Singer's review has been widely perceived as condoning the practice. The horrified reaction from the mass media was almost immediate. Singer was denounced in the editorial pages of newspapers across the United States and beyond. Condemnation came from the right and the left alike: "Animal Crackers," the opinion piece in *The Wall Street Journal* was entitled,[2] while the *Village Voice* declared that it was Singer himself who was the animal.[3]

Singer claims that he was not in fact defending bestiality, merely examining the reasons for the taboo against it.[4] But this is a little disingenuous. Clearly Singer believes that the taboo is irrational,[5] the product of our superstitious belief that "a wide, unbridgeable gulf" separates us humans from other animals. In fact, Singer points out, we are very much like them, and nowhere more so in than in our sexuality: "We copulate as they do." Since with this realization the usual supports of the taboo fall away, we must look elsewhere for reasons supporting the banning of bestiality – or give up the prohibition altogether. From Singer's utilitarian viewpoint, to establish that bestiality is wrong we would have to be able to show that it would have harmful consequences, for the participants or for others. But it is difficult to believe that such harms will characterize all acts of bestiality. Hence, Singer clearly implies, there is nothing wrong with bestiality.

Of course, Singer's critics are far from conceding the point. Interestingly, many of them do not seem to think that the taboo against bestiality needs any defense at all (for *The Wall Street Journal*, for instance, the mere fact that Singer was defending the practice ought to "come as a tremendous embarrassment to professional ethicists"). But some of Singer's critics do put forward arguments. In what follows, I will examine the arguments against bestiality, from newspapers and philosophers alike. As we shall see, none of them are very convincing. Nevertheless, I am not willing to conclude, with Singer, that the taboo against bestiality is simply the last residue of a fundamentally superstitious worldview. I therefore devote the last part of the paper to a reconsideration of the taboo. As we shall see, though Singer is right in thinking that bestiality is not immoral, it does not follow from this fact that giving up the taboo is rational.

I. Standard Objections to Bestiality

Bestiality and Perversion

Before turning to the agenda I have set myself, however, I will briefly sketch and dismiss a quick line which might be taken on the matter. We might argue, simply, that bestiality is a perversion, and for that reason it ought to be prohibited. It is certainly the case that bestiality will qualify as perverse, on the everyday concept of perversion. It also qualifies on at least some standard philosophical conceptions. Thus, for example, on Nagel's view, in which a sexual activity counts as a perversion if it does not possess the right sort of multilayered desire and arousal structure, bestiality will be a perversion since nonhuman animals do not possess the cognitive faculties requisite for this kind of intentionality.[6] On Solomon's view, according to which perversions are sexual activities which are not communicative in the right kind of way, bestiality will be perverse because one of the conversation partners does not possess much in the way of communicative resources: a little "like discussing Spinoza with a moderately intelligently sheep," in Solomon's memorable phrase.[7] Other views of perversion, those that identify their target in terms of statistical frequency, or reproductive fitness, for instance, will concur.

Nevertheless, we cannot conclude from the fact that these accounts entail that bestiality is a perversion that bestiality is wrong, even if these accounts of perversion turn out to be correct. All these accounts of perversion identify as perverse some acts which are clearly unobjectionable (masturbation is a paradigm upon some views). Worse, on all these accounts some acts which are clearly paradigmatically immoral pass the perversion test. If these accounts are accurate, then it is clear that the category of perversion is not extensionally equivalent to the category of immoral acts in the sexual realm. Many accounts of perversion will identify consensual sado-masochism as perverse, but rape as nonperverse. Since rape is clearly much more objectionable than the perversions, the notion of perversity is irrelevant when it comes to the question whether or not a certain practice is wrong. The fact that shoe fetishism qualifies as perverse on most accounts gives us no reason to ban it, or, perhaps, even to condemn it; therefore the fact that bestiality will also probably qualify does not tell us whether or not it is permissible.[8]

Bestiality and Consent

Most of Singer's critics concentrate upon just one issue: consent. At first sight, this seems a promising line of enquiry. After all, what distinguishes licit from illicit sexual activity between human beings is, first and foremost, consent. Almost any sexual activity to which people freely give informed consent is permissible. Thus we might think that consent will be at the heart of the question of the permissibility of bestiality as well.

Some critics claim that animals cannot consent to sexual activity with human beings. Thus, for Raymond Belliotti, "bestiality is inherently nonconsensual."[9] On at least some analyses of consent, this claim is true. According to these analyses, consent is an intentional act of a quite complicated kind, well beyond the cognitive capacities of most animals. Indeed, if the "identity thesis" is correct, a necessary condition of consent is that the consenter intends quite precisely the same act as is intended by her partner. Clearly, this requires that the consenting party cannot be greatly inferior in cognitive ability to her partner.[10]

However, though this analysis of consent may be appropriate to sexual relations between adult persons, it is very far from obvious that it is equally appropriate where we are concerned with animals. Failure to meet the very high standard demanded by the identity thesis renders bestiality impermissible only if the standard is the appropriate one to apply in this context.

[: : :]

[W]e must ask why it is normally appropriate to demand that consent be informed before sexual activity is legitimate. In general, the demand is appropriate only when the subject who is to give or withhold consent is normally, or at some time in the future will be, able adequately to understand the psychosocial significance of sexual activity. When the subject is, or will be, capable of such understanding, we hold that he is unable to consent to sexual activity unless or until he is in fact in this state. Thus children are unable to consent to sexual activity because they are not yet in possession of their full cognitive abilities; people who are badly affected by drugs or alcohol are unable to give consent because their cognitive abilities are temporarily impaired. In these cases, consent is insufficient to render sexual activity permissible. Now, why do we demand this higher standard of consent where such people are concerned? I suggest it is because we know that if they merely consent in their cognitively impaired or undeveloped state, there is a high probability that they will, when they come to possess full cognitive ability, regret their consent; indeed, they may be traumatized or psychically damaged by the memory. Thus it is appropriate to apply the high standard of informed consent to sexual relations between (normal)

human beings; since children are incapable of such informed consent, pedophilia is impermissible.[11]

Adult nonhumans typically possess less in the way of cognitive ability than normal human children. Hence if such children are incapable of informed consent, so are nonhuman animals. These animals are even less capable of understanding human sexuality and its psychosocial significance than are children. However, such animals will not go on to possess the cognitive abilities of adult human beings. Hence they will not be damaged or traumatized by the memory of sexual activity. Thus it is inappropriate to apply the standard of informed consent to sexual activity with them. Such a standard is in place only when we can contrast the current cognitive state of the subject with the state that it will come, at some future time, to possess, or that it normally possesses; in the absence of this contrast, the standard has no application.

[: : :]

Does Bestiality Wrongfully Use Animals as a Means?

An opponent of bestiality could accept that the question of informed consent is irrelevant to the question of its permissibility and instead argue that bestiality is wrong because it uses an animal as a mere means. Thus, for instance, Raymond Belliotti argues that bestiality is "typically immoral: it typically uses an animal as a mere instrument for human purposes."[12]

To this line of attack, the defender of bestiality can reply by herself sketching a dilemma, structurally identical to the one utilized earlier by the opponent of bestiality:

Either it is permissible to use nonhuman animals as a mere means or it is not. If it is, then (so far as this argument is concerned) bestiality is permissible. If it is not, then bestiality is impermissible = but so are hunting, raising animals for food, using them for transport, and many other activities besides.

On the first horn of the dilemma, the fact (if it is a fact) that bestiality uses animals as a mere means does not render it impermissible; on the second, it is ruled out only by considerations which also entail that many other seemingly innocuous activities are also impermissible. Thus, the second horn functions as a reductio ad absurdum of the general claim that it is impermissible to use nonhuman animals as a mere means.

How might the opponent of bestiality reply to this line of argument? Two courses seem open to her. On the one hand, she might deny that these apparently innocuous activities really utilize animals as a mere means. She might, for instance, point out that animals raised for food are brought into existence, fed and sheltered, given veterinary care, and so on, in exchange for their milk. Even when they are slaughtered, their life might have been "paid for," by giving them sufficient care for a long enough time. Similar claims could be made concerning the use of animals for transport, and so on.

The problem with this response is that exactly the same line is open to the defender of bestiality. If animals used in farming or in transport are not generally treated as mere means, then it is hard to see why animals kept for sex should be. Indeed, as the examples given by Singer suggest, the sexual activity could be mutually pleasurable, in which case the animal would be treated as an end, as well as a means.

On the other hand, the opponent of bestiality could bite the bullet and accept that the use of animals in farming, for transport, and so on, is impermissible on the same grounds as bestiality. Some radical animal activists hold just this view. Of course, if this move is to be persuasive, we need an argument as to *why* it is always wrong to treat animals as a mere means (when so doing does not involve cruelty). Kantian arguments will be of no help here, since Kant grounds the respect we owe to all persons on the fact that they are rational beings. And even if it could be established that it was so impermissible, this leaves untouched the reply that some acts of bestiality could be reciprocal.

[. . .]

The opponent of bestiality could press a related objection here: if it is wrong to use human beings as mere means only on Kantian grounds – that is, because they are rational – then it is not wrong to use such handicapped children as mere means. If we are to defend bestiality, then, we need some principled way of distinguishing between the consensual use of nonhuman animals for sexual gratification and consensual sexual relations between normal human adults and the permanently mentally handicapped – or bite a rather unpalatable bullet.

[. . .]

I suggest virtue-ethical grounds: though it is possible to imagine situations in which there is no direct harm to the children in question, nor any harmful consequences, we will object to the use of the handicapped for sex on the grounds that engaging in such sexual activity would tend to inculcate undesirable habits and dispositions in the agent. That is, the agent would tend to acquire the disposition to treat persons beings as mere objects, or to apply a standard lower than that of informed consent to sexual relations with persons. On these grounds, we can find a principled way to distinguish between (for all that has been said so far) permissible bestiality and impermissible consensual sexual relations between normal adult human beings and the permanently mentally handicapped.

Of course, the invocation of virtue ethics will immediately suggest to the opponent of bestiality another line of attack: does bestiality inculcate vices in human beings? I suggest that we have nothing to fear from bestiality on these grounds (so long as it is consensual, cruelty-free, and so on). Bestiality does not inculcate any attitudes toward animals that are inappropriate. On the contrary, it is consistent with our justifiable behavior toward nonhuman animals in other spheres.

Thus, all the more plausible objections to bestiality based on the standard moves in moral philosophy fail. Bestiality does not appear to be objectionable on consequentialist, deontological, or virtue-ethical grounds. In fact, we have our answer to the question we posed: there is nothing wrong with bestiality, morally speaking. And yet, as the hysterical reaction to the Singer article makes abundantly clear, most people continue to find bestiality objectionable, and it continues to be illegal in most jurisdictions.[13] What accounts for this reaction? Is it merely a remnant of a religious worldview that has long since lost its power to convince? Or is there some more rational basis for it? I turn now from the standard moral arguments against bestiality to the explanation of the taboo against it.

II. The Taboo against Bestiality

For Singer, the taboo against bestiality is fundamentally a relic of a now-discredited metaphysics. We in the West have, as a legacy of the Judeo-Christian tradition, inherited a view of ourselves as fundamentally different from, and superior to, nonhuman animals. But the apparent boundary between us and them required policing, and nowhere more so than with regard to sex. For nowhere does our claim to be essentially different from other animals look weaker than with regard to sexuality:

there are many way [sic] in which we cannot help behaving just as animals do – or mammals anyway – and sex is one of the most obvious ones. We copulate, as they do. They have penises and vaginas, as we do.[14]

Sex across the species line had to be prohibited, because it threatened to demonstrate how hollow are our claims to fundamental difference.

For Singer, of course, the view that we are essentially different from nonhuman animals has been shown to be false by evolutionary theory, and the idea that we have a special dignity that makes us morally different in kind cannot be sustained. Thus the entire metaphysics which prohibited bestiality falls away, and with it should go the taboo.

[. . .]

Since science has shown that the gap between humans and animals is small, we should "take the plunge and recognize that there are now no good reasons for protecting this particular boundary."[15]

The suggestion that the prohibition upon bestiality is the product of an attempt to shore up the boundaries between rational humanity and the threatening brute is plausible.[16] However, I want to resist the suggestion that the taboo is no more than a residue from a discredited metaphysical view of the world. If we think of the prohibition upon bestiality as part of a wider view concerning the source of value and significance in human life, we might be able to discover defensible foundations for it.

The Significance of Limits in Human Life

How ought we to think of the limits of human capabilities, the boundaries beyond which we cannot go? Some philosophers regard them as merely contingent restrictions which can and ought to be tested. For Gregory Pence, for instance, accepting our de facto limits as moral boundaries, beyond which we ought not to go, is the way of "defeat and fatalism."[17] Crossing such limits does not threaten our carefully constructed view of humanity; on the contrary, refusing to accept such limits and taking our destiny in our own hands is what *distinguishes* us from other animals. As Pence's great inspiration, Joseph Fletcher, put it, with regard to the limit crossed by new reproductive technologies:

> Laboratory reproduction is radically human compared to conception by ordinary heterosexual intercourse. It is willed, chosen, purposed and controlled, and surely those are among the traits that distinguish Homo Sapiens from others in the animal genus, from the primates on down.[18]

Other philosophers, however, suggest that such limits are crossed at our peril. For John Haldane, for example,

use of these same new reproductive technologies is "a breach of the philosophical responsibility to live within human limits."[19]

Much of this debate, as it has played itself out in bioethics, seems confused. Too often, the argument that such boundaries ought not to be transgressed relies upon an equivocation between a descriptive and a prescriptive sense of the word "limit." From the premise that human life *is*, currently, subject to certain limits, the conclusion is drawn that we *ought not* to attempt to cross those limits. Haldane, for instance, points out that a virtuous life is a life lived within limits and concludes that there are certain things we must never do – clone a human being, for instance. But this is fallacious. We can agree with him that some limits are necessary to virtue yet point out that however new technologies might redraw the map, they will not and cannot efface limits altogether. Moving the boundaries is not eliminating them: limits we might need, but limits we shall have, whatever we do.

[...]

These considerations. . .concern crossing our upper limits: "playing God," as the opponents of new technologies often have it, or even becoming one. Nevertheless, I think that they can be fruitfully transposed to the problem with which we are here concerned. Repugnance toward bestiality is, as Morriss suggests, itself a horrified reaction to a kind of boundary crossing, this time, not at our upper limits, but at our lower. Morriss, Pence, and Singer believe that the notion that there are limits which we ought not to cross is a mere hangover from a discarded and discredited worldview. I want to suggest, against them, that respect for such limits is not mere superstition but can be given a rational foundation.

[. . .]

But to say that the limit that bestiality represents does not play the same sort of role in human life as do our upper limits is not to say that it does not play a role at all. In fact, both sets of limits, upper and lower, are in part definitive of humanity. My suggestion is this: the set of limits definitive of human life contains elements from many different sources. Some of them, like the limit represented by human mortality and by our physical bodies in general, are given by nature. Though we can press against them, push them back in various ways, we cannot will them away. They are a permanent feature of life, altered even in minor ways only with great effort. Others, however, are cultural limits. They are the products of the collective imagining of a people. They are, however, no less identity constituting for all that. These two sets of limits are nicely captured by the word "humanity." What makes us human is at once a set of physical and psychological features that are natural (a certain genetic endowment, opposable thumbs, the ability to learn a language, and so on) and a set of characteristics that are, at least in part, cultural (the disposition to think of the needs of other people, sympathy, and so on). When we speak of someone's inhumanity, it is invariably the latter set of characteristics with which we are concerned.

Our upper limits are largely given by nature; thus they play an especially important role in our sense of who we are. We share these limits, more or less, with all human beings everywhere. But our lower limits, which are largely culturally defined, are also identity constituting. They are conditions, not of excellent human life, but of a life which counts as human at all. If we cross our upper bounds, we will cease to be human, becoming something different and not necessarily (by our lights) better. If we cross our lower limits, a similar fate threatens. To transgress this boundary might be to move to another form of life, in which characteristic human activities have no place or are transformed in ways unimaginable from here. This might be a limit we cannot cross while yet retaining our sense of who we are.

Thus, though there is nothing *immoral* about bestiality, it might nevertheless be irrational for us to cross this

boundary. It would be difficult to do so while yet retaining a strong grip on our identity. This is not to say, of course, that people who engage in isolated acts of bestiality remove themselves from the moral community at a stroke. To say that bestiality is *identity-threatening* is not to say that it is instantaneously corrosive of identity. My claim is weaker: to the extent that someone engages in bestiality, she will find it harder to retain a grip on her identity as a full member of our community, and we will find it harder to admit her to full membership. It is because bestiality is identity-threatening in this way, I submit, that we suspect those people who do decide to cross this boundary of psychological illness. They have chosen to remove themselves from our community, as it currently defines itself. Crossing the species boundary is a significant act, at least for us, here and now, as we currently define ourselves.

[. . .]

If this picture is correct, then Singer is, at least partially, correct: there is nothing wrong with bestiality, at least from the point of view of morality understood narrowly. Nevertheless, the repugnance that we, most of us, feel with regard to it is not irrational. It is not merely the residue of a superstitious worldview but reflects the culturally defined conditions of our sense of who we are.

[. . .]

Notes

1 Peter Singer, "Heavy Petting," *Nerve,* March 13, 2001 (unpaginated). Available online at (http://www.nerve.com/Opinions/Singer/heavyPetting/main.asp).

2 *Wall Street Journal, March 30, 2001.*

3 Norah Vincent, "You're an Animal," *Village Voice,* March 26, 2001.

4 In a statement released in April 2001 and posted on the Internet at (http://arwww.asairs.com/singer.html).

5 The contention that a taboo is irrational might strike some as oxymoronic. Taboos are the kinds of prohibitions for which it is generally thought that the giving of reasons is unnecessary. Nevertheless, though I shall be concerned with examining the morality and rationality of the prohibition upon bestiality, I shall retain the word "taboo," since it seems to capture the almost instinctive repulsion that the subject often seems to provoke.

6 Thomas Nagel, "Sexual Perversion," in *Mortal Questions* (Cambridge: Cambridge University Press, 1979), 39–52.

7 Robert Solomon, "Sexual Paradigms," in *The Philosophy of Sex: Contemporary Readings,* ed. Alan Soble (Lanham, Md.: Rowman & Littlefield, 1997), 21–29, at 28.

8 Here I am in agreement with Alan Goldman: "no conduct otherwise immoral should be excused because it is sexual

conduct, and nothing in sex is immoral unless condemned by rules which apply elsewhere as well." Alan Goldman, "Plain Sex," in *The Philosophy of Sex: Contemporary Readings,* ed. Alan Soble (Lanham, Md.: Rowman & Littlefield, 1997), 39–55, at 50. Of course, it might be thought that we should revise our notion of perversion, adopting a conception according to which all and only immoral acts count as perverse. Obviously, however, adopting such a conception will leave the question of the morality of bestiality untouched: all the work of determining whether it is perverse, on this revisionist conception, remains to be done.

9 Raymond A. Belliotti, *Good Sex: Perspectives on Sexual Ethics* (Lawrence: University Press of Kansas, 1993), 230.

10 For the analysis of consent as an intentional act, and the elaboration of the identity thesis, see Heidi M. Hurd, "The Moral Magic of Consent," *Legal Theory* 2 (1996): 121–46.

11 This cannot be a full account of the wrongness of pedophilia. If it were, we would have to think that sexual experimentation by children with other children is as wrong as pedophilia (I thank Igor Primoratz for this point). Nevertheless, it seems to me to capture an essential component of our attitudes toward children and sexuality. This is

manifested in the fact that though we do not regard childhood sexual experimentation as *wrong*, we do think that it might be *dangerous*. We discourage little Johnny and Mary from exploring each other's bodies *too much*. To be sure, the wrongness of pedophilia goes far beyond such exploration, involving, as it does, problems of exploitation of vulnerability and abuse of trust, for instance, which are absent from such sexual play.

12 Belliotti, *Good Sex*, 232.

13 The 1984 recommendations of the English Criminal Law Revision Committee (CLRC) are, I suspect, representative of the most widely held attitudes toward bestiality in Western countries. Bestiality is currently punishable by life imprisonment in England; the CLRC recommended that bestiality should remain an offense, but that the punishment be reduced to a maximum of six months' imprisonment (Criminal Law Revision Committee, *Fifteenth Report: Sexual Offences* [London: HMSO, 1984], 88–9).

14 Singer, "Heavy Petting."

15 Ibid., 281.

16 Kant's remarks on bestiality are suggestive in this context. For him, sexuality is a product of our "animal nature," and therefore "the sexual impulse puts humanity in peril of being equated with animality" (*Lectures on Ethics*, trans. Peter Heath [Cambridge: Cambridge University Press, 1997], 156). But if sexuality risks debasing humanity to the level of animals, then acts of bestiality "degrade humanity *below* the animal level, for no animal turns away from its own species" (161, italics added).

17 Gregory E. Pence, *Who's Afraid of Human Cloning?* (Lanham, Md.: Rowman & Littlefield, 1998), 7.

18 Quoted in ibid., 125.

19 John Haldane, "Being Human: Science, Knowledge and Virtue," in *Philosophy and Public Affairs*, ed. John Haldane (Cambridge: Cambridge University Press, 2000), 189–202, at 200.

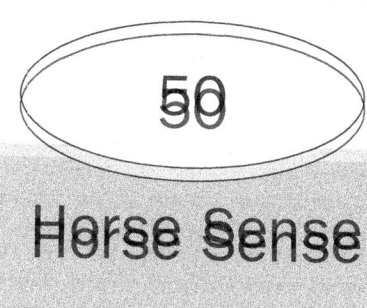

50

Horse Sense

Wesley J. Smith

Summary

Argues that the issue in bestiality is not consent or cruelty or taboo but rather "human exceptionalism" – the position that humans are in fact unique, special, and of the highest moral worth in the known universe. While human exceptionalism used to be taken for granted, movements in bioethics, animal rights, and post-Darwinian science are pushing to see humans as just another kind of animal. Since humans are not simply other animals but have an exalted moral status, laws should not only criminalize bestiality but explicitly state that one reason to do so is that it subverts human dignity and humanity's inherent moral status.

Original publication details: Wesley J. Smith, "Horse Sense," from *The Weekly Standard* (August 31, 2005) https://web.archive.org/web/20150906222530/http://www.weeklystandard.com/Content/Public/Articles/000/000/005/985pgwjh.asp. Reproduced with permission of The Weekly Standard LLC.

Sexual Ethics: An Anthology, First Edition. Edited by Patrick D. Hopkins.
© 2023 John Wiley & Sons, Inc. Published 2023 by John Wiley & Sons, Inc.

A WASHINGTON MAN died recently from internal injuries he sustained while having sex with a horse. After his body was dropped off at a hospital, police discovered that out-of-towners had rented a rural farm and then made local animals available for use in bestiality. Yes, video taping was involved.

This disgusting story should have had a quick ending with the arrests of the operators of the human/animal sex farm and their swift punishment. However, police discovered that there is no law against bestiality in Washington. So, even though a man is dead from a very intimate injury, even though police confiscated hundreds of graphic videotapes of people having sex with animals, apparently nothing is to be done about it.

Enter Republican state Senator Pam Roach, who announced plans to introduce legislation in the next legislative session to make it a felony in Washington to commit bestiality. "I found out that Washington is one of the few states in the country that doesn't outlaw this activity," she told me. "This has made Washington a Mecca for bestiality. People know it isn't against the law and so they come from other states to have sex with animals."

Roach told me she is receiving cooperation from the Democratic leaders of the legislature, but to her surprise, the proposed bill has stirred some controversy. The most prominent voice so far against outlawing bestiality is the Seattle Post Intelligencer's liberal columnist, Robert L. Jamieson Jr. In a July 23 column, Jamieson ridiculed Roach's proposal, writing that practices such as masturbation, oral sex, and gay sex were once considered wrong, too, and so why worry now about human/animal copulation if the animal isn't injured? "Human sex with animals remains a towering taboo, booty and the beast. But as Princeton University philosopher Peter Singer, the father of the animal rights movement, has put it, 'Sex with animals does not always involve cruelty.'"

In a follow-up column, Jamieson accused Roach of engaging in "knee-jerk lawmaking and moral hysteria" in order to pander politically to "animal-loving voters, of which there are many." Responding to Roach's condemnation of the bestiality videotapes found at the sex farm as "pornography with animals," Jamieson countered, "Isn't pornography of the human variety legal so long as children aren't involved?" As to Roach's argument that having sex with animals is wrong because they can't consent to sex, Jamieson noted that animals also don't consent to "being ground into all-beef patties," and accused Roach of "taking animal love to extremes," for seeking to outlaw bestiality.

BOTH JAMIESON AND ROACH (and a very mild Post Intelligencer editorial supporting Roach) miss the true nub of what makes this repugnant issue so important. Bestiality is so very wrong not only because using animals sexually is abusive, but because such behavior is profoundly degrading and utterly subversive to the crucial understanding that human beings are unique, special, and of the highest moral worth in the known universe – a concept known as "human exceptionalism."

And this brings us back to Peter Singer, the world's most famous bioethicist and philosopher, who clearly does understand that the crucial moral issue of our time is whether human life has intrinsic value simply – merely – because it is human. Indeed, Singer is an avowed enemy of human exceptionalism.

Thus, it is no surprise that when he was asked in 2000 to review a book extolling bestiality for an online pornography magazine, he leaped at the chance to bestow his approval. In "Heavy Petting" Singer, in often vulgar language, asserted that since both humans and animals copulate and both have the same sex organs, the continuing "taboo" against bestiality merely reflects "our desire to differentiate ourselves, erotically and in every other way, from animals."

In support of his thesis that this distinction is irrational, Singer writes of attending a conference and speaking to a woman who had been sexually assaulted by an orangutan while visiting an animal rehabilitation center. When she called out for help, the operator of the facility, a woman named Birute Galdikas, told the distraught woman not to worry because orangutans are not well endowed. (The animal lost interest before completing the assault.)

This lack of concern deeply impressed Singer. "Galdikas understands very well that we are animals, indeed more specifically, we are great apes. This does not make sex across the species barrier normal, or natural, whatever those much-misused words may mean, but it does imply that it ceases to be an offense to our status and dignity as human beings." In other words, bestiality is fine, for those who are attracted to that sort of thing, because it merely constitutes two animals rubbing body parts.

IT ISN'T JUST PETER SINGER. There is apparently a deep and growing yearning across an alarmingly wide swath of public advocacy to destroy the wall of moral distinction that separates animals and humans. In the bioethics movement, for example, to assert that humans have special value is denigrated as "speciesism," that is, discrimination against animals. This concept is taught in most of our major colleges and universities.

Similarly, the animal liberation movement claims that it is the ability to feel pain, rather than humanhood, which bestows equal moral value. "We are all animals," a PETA advocacy slogan asserts, by which they are not merely stating a biological fact but espousing an explicit moral equality between man and beasts. Thus, since both cows and humans can feel pain, PETA claims cattle ranching to be as evil as human slavery. The London Zoo has actually put a herd of humans on display to "demonstrate the basic nature of man as an animal and examine the impact that Homo sapiens have on the rest of the animal kingdom."

We even see this theme popping up in the ongoing controversy over high school science curricula. Thus, Verlyn Klinkenborg, a member of the New York Times editorial board, savaged critics of materialistic Darwinism in part on philosophical grounds, because (he believes) they seek "to preserve the myth that there is a separate, divine creation for humans," that separates us from animals. "But there is a destructive hubris, a fearful arrogance to this myth," Klinkenborg writes. "It sets us apart from nature, except to dominate it. It misses both the grace and moral depth of knowing that humans have only the same stake, the same right, in the Earth as every other creature that has ever lived here."

MOST PEOPLE take human exceptionalism for granted. They can no longer afford to do so. The great philosophical question of the 21st Century is going to be whether we will knock humans off the pedestal of moral exceptionalism and instead define ourselves as just another animal in the forest. The stakes of the coming debate couldn't be more important: It is our exalted moral status that both bestows special rights upon us and imposes unique and solemn moral responsibilities — including the human duty not to abuse animals.

Nothing would more graphically demonstrate our unexceptionalism than countenancing human/animal sex. Thus, when Roach's legislation passes, the law's preamble should explicitly state that one of the reasons bestiality is condemned through law is that such degrading conduct unacceptably subverts standards of basic human dignity and is an affront to humankind's inestimable importance and intrinsic moral worth.

51

Pedophilia

Igor Primoratz

Summary

Argues that true pedophilia (as distinguished from the less problematic pederasty and ephebophilia) has been strongly condemned in three ways – as perversion, as non-consensual, and as harmful. The perversion argument is entirely unhelpful as a conceptual matter. The harm argument relies on claims that are not clearly established in the research literature – such research often relies on biased samples of children in clinical and legal contexts that are not representative of the population, has difficulty distinguishing between the harm of the sexual activity and the harm of parents' or law's fierce reaction of anger and disgust, and has difficulty distinguishing between the direct harm of sex and the harm of feeling guilty over violating a social norm. The argument that children cannot consent to sex with adults, however, is a very strong argument because children cannot fully understand sex, cannot be fully educated to understand it while still children, are always under the power of adults, and attach different meanings to sex than adults. As such, pedophilia is justly condemned morally and legally.

Original publication details: Igor Primoratz, "Pedophilia," pp. 99–110 from *Public Affairs Quarterly* 13:1 (1999). Reproduced with permission of University of Illinois Press.

I

While debates on quite a few questions in sexual morality sometimes arouse strong feelings, the issue discussed in this paper almost invariably does so, and the feelings aroused are usually very strong indeed. It is understandable why that should be so. It is less clear why contemporary philosophers who have written on sexuality and sexual morality have tended to neglect the subject. This paper is meant as a step towards remedying this neglect.

The discussion must be prefaced by a few words of clarification. Most instances of pedophilia that have recently received much media attention in the United States, some European countries, and Australia, have been cases of pedophilia within the family or in a child care or educational institution. Many have involved physical or psychological abuse of the minor. In this paper, however, I focus on pedophilia as such. For if we are to be in a good position to understand and judge cases of pedophilia compounded by child abuse or violation of a relationship of parental responsibility, care, trust, or authority, we must first come to an understanding of pedophilia not aggravated by additional wrongdoing: pedophilia in itself.

Another clarification concerns terminology. We need to distinguish between "pederasty," "ephebophilia," and "pedophilia," as well as between the wide and narrow senses of the last term.

"Pederasty" refers to sexual attraction of an adult male to boys and sex between an adult male and a boy in his mid-teens. It has been the characteristic form of male homosexuality in many societies; its best known type, of course, is the "love of boys" among the ancient Greeks. What is distinctive about pederasty is best described in contrast to the dominant type of male homosexuality in modern Western societies, in which both sides are adults. [. . .]

Ephebophilia, too, is a variety of male homosexuality. But unlike pederasts, ephebophiles are attracted to post-pubertal, sexually mature youths. An ephebophile finds sexually attractive the very thing that puts off a pederast: the fully developed, vigorous maleness of adolescence.[1]

Both pederasty and ephebophilia are varieties of pedophilia in the wide sense of the term, i.e., types of sexual attraction to, and sex with, minors (of the same or different sex). To be sure, ephebophilia would not count as pedophilia, if there were a single age of consent [. . .].

In the narrow sense, "pedophilia" refers only to sexual attraction of adults to pre-pubescent and pubescent children and sex with them. When the term is used in this sense, ephebophilia is not included as one of its varieties, but rather distinguished from it, the end puberty providing the line of demarcation.

II

In our type of society, pedophilia is considered both a grave moral offense and a crime deserving serious punishment. In purely moral contexts, it tends to be condemned as a sexual perversion. I will not discuss this particular point here, as I have argued elsewhere that the concept of sexual perversion is quite unhelpful and should be discarded altogether.[2] There are two further arguments against pedophilia that constitute the standard rationale behind both its moral condemnation and legal proscription: first, sex with minors is wrong because it is non-consensual; second, it is harmful to them. But however straightforward and even obvious this rationale might seem, it bears looking into. Indeed, both arguments have been questioned.

Before discussing them, however, a few words may be in order on the way pedophilia tends to be conceived by the general public. The pedophile is often envisaged as "a dirty old man," a stranger to his victims, who forces himself on children and has full-fledged sexual intercourse with them, thus putting them through a frightening and painful experience and inflicting serious long-term psychological damage on them. This popular notion explains why pedophiles are colloquially called child molesters, and why pedophilia seems to be "the most hated of all the sexual variations."[3] But, for the most part, it is not borne out by the known facts. What is true is that most pedophiles are men. But the majority are young or middle-aged. More often than not, they are not strangers; they are more likely to be family, lodgers, neighbors, or other adults from the immediate social environment of the minor. Nor is it true that pedophiles typically use force, or engage in full-fledged sexual intercourse. Summarizing the findings of a number of studies, Peter Righton writes that "the most characteristic paedophile activities are cuddling, caressing and genital fondling," and that "when full intercourse takes place, it occurs most commonly when the child is well into adolescence."[4] Finally, the harmful effects of pedophilia on the minor's sexual, emotional, and general personality development are still a matter of research and debate, rather than of well-established fact.[5]

To point out the inaccuracies and simplifications involved in the popular notion of pedophilia does nothing to show that its conventional condemnation is not justified. It merely helps clear the ground for a more rational discussion of the subject. Most importantly, it suggests that it may not be very fruitful to discuss pedophilia in its wider sense of sex with minors. [. . .]

III

This leaves us with pedophilia in the narrow sense of sexual attraction of adults to pre-pubescent and pubescent children and sex with them. In the rest of this paper I discuss only pedophilia in this sense, or pedophilia proper.

It clearly presents a much more controversial issue. The best way to approach it is by looking into the arguments of its defenders. I will leave aside discussions limited to the "Greek love" of boys,[6] and focus on two recent apologies of pedophilia in general, i.e., of its male *and* female, heterosexual *and* homosexual varieties: Tom O'Carroll's book *Paedophilia: The Radical Case,* and Robert Ehman's paper "Adult–Child Sex."[7]

Both O'Carroll and Ehman point out that pre-pubescent children are not asexual creatures. The idea that they are and their consequent exclusion from all discourse about, and experience of, sex are not mandated by their nature and thus universal, but rather a comparatively recent development. Both authors draw on the well-known thesis first advanced by Philippe Aries that the understanding of children as sexually innocent was brought about by the far-reaching change in the Western conception of childhood that took place in the seventeenth and eighteenth centuries. According to the Aries thesis, in earlier periods, children were in many respects part of the same social world as adults: they wore the same type of clothes, played the same games, worked together with adults – and were not sheltered from manifestations of adult sexuality, nor denied sexual interests and activities of their own. By the end of eighteenth century, however, the "discovery of childhood" was completed. Children came to be thought of as having a distinctive nature of their own, a set of characteristics significantly unlike those of adults that enjoined their systematic exclusion from many areas of adult experience and activity. In particular, they came to be considered innocent of sexual knowledge, interest, or desire, and in need of protection from all manifestations of adult sexuality.[8]

As O'Carroll and Ehman see it, our own unwillingness to acknowledge the facts of child sexuality shows that we still subscribe to this view of childhood, which sees all sexual contact between an adult and a child as molestation and defilement of the innocent and defenseless child.[9] It also suggests a suspicion of sex in general. In the words of Robert Ehman, "there is, of course, a remnant of sexual puritanism in this reaction toward adult–child sex, since unless there were something morally problematic and impure about sex, how could it corrupt the child? The attitude toward adult–child sex is the last unquestioned bastion of sexual puritanism."[10]

But the facts of child sexuality cannot be denied. They have been pointed out by Freud and some of his followers, and described in some detail in a number of empirical studies of human sexuality, including those by Alfred C. Kinsey and associates. These studies show that from a very early age, children of both sexes tend to engage in sex play and are capable of various types of sexual experience, including orgasm.[11] Not only do children enjoy such experiences; they also need them for their normal sexual development.[12]

Defenders of pedophilia argue that the harms widely believed to be typically inflicted on children by sexual contact with adults are by no means an established fact. Research that has been done on the subject has serious limitations, and its findings do not support the popular view in a clear and compelling way. For one thing, much research is based on clinical or legal data. But such data cannot be representative of the entire relevant child population; they relate only to children who were troubled, distressed, or harmed by their encounters with pedophiles, while leaving out those who were not. Furthermore, researches [sic] do not always differentiate clearly enough, if at all, between instances where the adult employed force or exerted pressure and those where that was not the case. Nor do they separate consistently enough, if at all, the harm caused by the sexual encounter or relationship itself, from that caused by the response of parents and others to such an encounter or relationship, and the harm attendant on the legal proceedings against the adult in which the child is made to play a part.

Both O'Carroll and Ehman are extremely suspicious of the overwhelming majority of research; indeed, each finds only one study of the effects of pedophilia on children reliable enough. O'Carroll singles out Lindy Burton's book *Vulnerable Children – a* study of children, mostly girls, most of whom had sexual encounters with adults before the age of ten.[13] Burton's general conclusion is that the experience "does not appear to have an excessively unsettling effect on the child's personality development"[14] Ehman's preferred piece of research is that of Marvis Tsai and associates, who studied the effects of childhood sexual contacts with adults on psychosexual functioning in adult women.[15] On the basis of that study Ehman draws the following conclusions concerning the issue of harm:

> The two main causes, according to Tsai et al., of adult psychosexual problems on the part of sexually molested children are the negative feelings of the children toward their adult partner and their feeling of responsibility for, and guilt from, the violation of a social norm. There is nothing in the study to indicate that there would be a negative impact apart from an aversion to the adult and a violation of a norm. For this reason, the study does not provide the least evidence in favor of a norm prohibiting sexual contact between a child and adult when the child is not averse. On the contrary, the fact that the negative impact of the perceived violation of the norm is a large contributor to the harmful effects of adult–child sex is an argument *against* the norm.[16]

Not only authors who set out to defend pedophilia, such as O'Carroll or Ehman, but also some of those who define their task solely in terms of scientific research, have reached conclusions of this sort. Thus Kenneth Plummer writes that in cases of the child's willing participation in sexual contact with an adult "studies point to the experience being without trauma and frequently mutually pleasurable . . . unless, and this is an important proviso, it is 'discovered' by the family or the community. When this happens, it appears that the child can become shocked by the engulfing anger and outrage of the adult."[17] Graham E. Powell and A. I. Chalkley offer a critical review of over forty studies of the impact on children of their sexual contacts with adults. Having emphasized the methodological limitations of the research done so far, which make interpretation of data difficult and any conclusion reached "somewhat muted," they say that the evidence does not bear out the popular belief that pedophile attention has long-term and wholly harmful effects on the child. Specifically, they point out that children who were disturbed after sexual contact with adults tended to be those who were disturbed beforehand, and that incidents of such contact do not seem to have long-term negative effects on the development of children.[18]

The other standard argument for the immorality of pedophilia is that from consent: children are incapable of valid consent to sex with adults, and such sex is therefore impermissible.[19] But Ehman claims that the argument from consent adds nothing to that from harm. Why, he asks, should a child's incapacity to give valid consent to *sex* with an adult be grounds enough for a prohibition of such sex, when we do not insist on such consent with regard to many other sorts of acts? The only reply seems to be that sex with adults is harmful to children. We are thus taken back a full circle to the argument from harm, which has been shown to be unconvincing.[20]

O'Carroll adopts a similar line. Children are said to be lacking knowledge and understanding of the various aspects and ramifications of sex; therefore they are considered incapable of giving valid consent to sex with adults. But then, do all adults really have that sort of knowledge and understanding?

> Even adults, in embarking on a sexual encounter or relationship, cannot be sure "where it will all end"; nor do most people enter adulthood with a fixed idea as to the activities, and people, that might turn them on – the scope for experiment and discovery is a lifelong one. . . . The usual mistake is to believe that sexual activity, especially for children, is so alarming and dangerous that participants need to have an absolute, total awareness of every conceivable ramification of taking part before they can be said to give valid consent. What there most definitely needs to be, is the child's *willingness* to take part in the activity in question. . . . But there is no need whatever for the child to know "the consequences" of engaging in harmless sex play, simply because it is exactly that: harmless.[21]

Since "the vast majority of sexual acts between children and adults are not aggressively imposed, any more than those between adults,"[22] in many cases the child is indeed willing. When it is, adult–child sex should be neither prevented nor condemned. The current moral rejection and legal prohibition of all sexual contact between children and adults is part and parcel of an unjustified, undiscerning and oppressive paternalism towards children. Children should have rights too, including the right to make their own sexual choices. The age of consent laws should be abolished, and the issues relating to sex between adults and children should for the most part be dealt with by means of civil, rather than criminal law.[23]

IV

In assessing these arguments in defense of pedophilia, a good starting point are the remarks of Marilyn Frye in response to Ehman's discussion of the question of harm:

> I would have more questions: How was it for [the child]? Not: Did this, or is it likely to, result in life-long psychosexual dysfunction? but: Was it nice? Did she have fun? Was it not soured by ambivalence, confusion, pain, feelings of powerlessness, anxiety about displeasing a partner on whom she is emotionally and materially dependent . . .? And if it is not good, can she, will she, would she dare, make this clear to him? . . . An experience can be horrible without precipitating bedwetting or causing "maladjustment." Are we to say it is harmless if it is merely wretched but does not demonstrably cause behavior that parents or clinical psychologists identify as "problematic"?[24]

Frye is making two separate but related points. If we are operating with a notion of harm that focuses on consequences and accordingly entails a distinction between harm and hurt, we need to look into the question of hurt too. An experience may not be bad in the sense of being harmful, and still be very bad indeed in that it hurts; that is, it may be bad in itself. And whether it is likely to be much more difficult to know than whether it has bad consequences, because of an important asymmetry of the situation in which it takes place.

This asymmetry is significant for the question of consent, or whatever type of a child's willingness to participate in a sex act with an adult Ehman and O'Carroll propose to substitute for full-fledged consent. It is true that the consent of some adults to sex might be thought flawed because of their insufficient knowledge of relevant facts and poor appreciation of various ramifications of their decisions and actions. But this is surely not reason enough for discarding the requirement of valid consent altogether. For in the case of adults this flaw is normally contingent, in that the adult could attain to more specific knowledge and better comprehension of such matters, if he or she made an effort to do so. The position of a child is importantly different. Owing to the child's limited experience and limited psychological resources, both cognitive and emotional, its knowledge and understanding of self and the world is inevitably limited too. Because of that, a child does not merely *happen to have*, but *cannot help having* a very limited

comprehension of the physical, psychological, and social aspects of serf. Accordingly, *all* children are at a considerable and *inescapable* disadvantage on this count.

This is compounded by the fact that pedophiles and children involved with them tend to attach significantly different meaning to their actions and experiences. As Sandor Ferenczi pointed out in a lecture given in 1932, adult–child sexual contact is liable to generate much misunderstanding because of a fundamental difference between adult erotic experience and that of children. The former is characterized by sexual passion, whereas the latter usually amounts to nothing more than playfulness, tenderness, and affection. What often happens is that the adult "mistakes the child's playfulness for wishes of a sexually mature person," and then acts on the basis of this misperception.[25] This warning has been echoed by more recent research on children who willingly participate in sexual contact with adults. What such a child typically looks for in its relation with the adult is sympathy and affection, rather than sexual gratification. The actions which the adult interprets as sexually suggestive or even provocative are not meant as such by the child, but are rather expressions of curiosity or playfulness, Thus the whole interaction takes on sexual import for the adult, but not for the child.[26]

For consent to be morally (and legally) valid, it must be informed and given freely. In view of the asymmetry of knowledge and comprehension, compounded by the difference of meaning the interaction has for the adult and the child, it can be maintained that the willing child is not reasonably informed, and therefore its willingness cannot legitimize an adult's sexual involvement with it. It is also not free enough. David Finkelhor explains the child's lack of freedom by the fact that "adults control all kinds of resources that are essential to [children] – food, money, freedom, etc. In this sense, the child is exactly like the prisoner who volunteers to be a research subject. The child has no freedom in which to consider the choice."[27] I think that the main cause of the child's predicament should be sought elsewhere: in the far-reaching asymmetry of physical and psychological maturity and power, as well as the consequent social standing, between a child and an adult. Because of this asymmetry and of the way it is acknowledged and reinforced in the course of bringing up children, a child tends to see an adult as something of an authority figure merely by virtue of being adult. It tends to defer to adults, and often finds it very difficult to assert itself against an adult, to say no to an adult's requests and advances. Therefore it can be maintained that a child's willingness to go along is not free enough to license an adult's sexual involvement with it.

To be sure, not every sexual involvement among adults takes place on an equal footing. An adult's consent to sex may be morally (and perhaps also legally) invalid, or flawed, because it is extorted by a threat, or procured by a coercive or exploitative offer, against a background of significant power inequality. But again, while only *some* adults are in a position of gross inequality in relation to others, *all* children are in a position of greatly unequal power in relation to adults.

[. . .]

It seems to me, then, that although it must be granted that the harmfulness of pedophilia is still very much a moot point, other arguments against it are valid. They provide sufficient ground for both its moral condemnation and legal prohibition.

[. . .]

Notes

1   See Stephen Donaldson, "Ephebophilia," in W. R. Dynes, ed., op. cit., vol. 1.

2   See Igor Primoratz, "Sexual Perversion," *American Philosophical Quarterly* 34 (1997).

3   Ken Plummer, "'The Paedophile's' Progress: A View from Below," In Brian Taylor, ed., *Perspectives on Paedophilia* (London: Batsford, 1981), p. 130.

4   Peter Righton, "The Adult," in B. Taylor, ed., op. cit., p. 27.

5   On the stereotypes of pedophilia see K. Plummer, "Pedophilia: Constructing a Sociological Baseline," in M. Cook and K. Howells, eds., *Adult Sexual Interest in Children* (London: Academic Press, 1981), pp. 224–228; P. Righton, op. cit.

6   Such as J. Z. Eglinton, *Greek Love* (London: Neville Spearman, 1971).

7   T. O'Carroll, *Paedophilia: The Radical Case* (London: Peter Owen, 1980); R. Ehman, "Adult–Child Sex," in R. Baker and F. Elliston, eds., *Philosophy and Sex*, 2nd edn. (Buffalo: Prometheus Books, 1984).

8   See Philippe Aries, *Centuries of Childhood: A Social History of Family Life*, trans. R. Baldick (New York: Vintage Books, 1962), in particular part I, chap. V: From Immodesty to Innocence. For a good account of the main problems plaguing the Aries thesis, see David Archard, *Children: Rights and Childhood* (London: Routledge, 1993), chaps. 2–3.

9   Roger Scruton has recently endorsed the idea of sexual innocence of children: "We desire that [sexual] initiation should not occur before the 'age of innocence' has expired, since we desire sexual expression to be withheld until it can exist as an interpersonal response. Our perception of the moral innocence of the child is therefore combined with a powerful interdiction: not to awaken in the child an interest in these things which are forbidden to him" (R. Scruton, op.cit., p. 297).

10   R. Ehman, op.cit., p. 433.

11   See A. C. Kinsey, W. B. Pomeroy, and C. E. Martin, *Sexual Behavior in the Human Male* (Philadelphia: W. B. Saunders, 1948), chap. 5; A. C. Kinsey, W. B. Pomeroy, C. E. Martin and P. H. Gebhard, *Sexual Behavior in the Human Female* (Philadelphia: W. B. Saunders, 1953), chap. 4.

12   See T. O'Carroll, op.cit., chaps. 2 and 5.

13   L. Burton, *Vulnerable Children* (London: Routledge and Kegan Paul, 1967).

14   Quoted in T. O'Carroll, op.cit., p. 64.

15   M. Tsai, S. Feldman-Summers, and M. Edgar, "Childhood Molestation: Variables Related to Differential Impacts on Psychosexual Functioning in Adult Women," *Journal of Abnormal Psychology* 88 (1979).

16   R. Ehman, op.cit., pp. 435–436.

17   K. Plummer, op.cit., p. 227.

18   G. E. Powell and A. J. Chalkley, "The Effects of Paedophile Attention on the Child," in B. Taylor, ed., op.cit.

19   See David Finkelhor, "What's Wrong with Sex between Adults and Children?" *American Journal of Orthopsychiatry* 49 (1979).

20   R. Ehman, op.cit., pp. 439–441.

21   T. O'Carroll, op.cit., p. 153.

22   Ibid., p. 56.

23   For a detailed proposal of legal reform along these lines, see T. O'Carroll, op.cit., chap. 6. On children's rights in general, see David Archard, op.cit., chaps. 4–7.

24   M. Frye, "Critique," in R. Baker and F. Elliston, eds., op.cit., pp. 450–451.

25   S. Ferenczi, "Sprachverwirrung zwischen den Erwachsenen und dem Kind (Die Sprache der Zaertlichkeit und der Leidenschaft)," *Bausteine zur Psychoanalyse*, 2. Aufl., Bd. III (Bern: Verlag Hans Huber, 1964), p. 518.

26   See, e.g., Michael Ingram, "Participating Victims: A Study of Sexual Offenses with Boys," in Larry L. Constantine and Floyd M. Martinson, eds., *Children and Sex: New Findings, New Perspectives* (Boston: Little, Brown and Co., 1981).

27   D. Finkelhor, op.cit., p. 695.

52

What Really Is Wrong with Pedophilia?

Robert Ehman

Summary

Argues that the two main arguments used to condemn adult/child sex are flawed and have little evidence behind them. The argument that children are necessarily harmed by sex with adults has been called into question by reviews of the psychological literature. The argument that children cannot consent to sex is specious because children are capable of some consent (depending on the age), children do have goals and desires that can be taken into account, parameters of sexual activity can be explained, and the child could retrospectively affirm the experience after becoming an adult if measures were taken to respect the child. The key issue, however, is determining why such strong emphasis is placed on children's consent to sexual activity when no such emphasis is placed on other activities. Children are regularly required by adults to participate in religious services, sports activities, educational programs, and medical treatments with no regard to their consent. Uniquely condemning sex for non-consent is inconsistent.

Original publication details: Robert Ehman, "What Really Is Wrong with Pedophilia?" *Public Affairs Quarterly* 14:2 (2000). Reproduced with permission of University of Illinois Press.

Sexual Ethics: An Anthology, First Edition. Edited by Patrick D. Hopkins.
© 2023 John Wiley & Sons, Inc. Published 2023 by John Wiley & Sons, Inc.

Introduction

Philosophers tend to neglect pedophilia even though it raises fundamental questions about the justification of the actions of adults toward children. The neglect appears in part to be a result of the radically negative attitudes toward pedophilia in our society. These attitudes are perhaps the final bastion of Puritan sexual ethics. But in part, the neglect might also be accounted for by the assumption that the standard arguments against pedophilia are persuasive. These are, first, the argument that pedophilia is psychologically harmful to children and, second, the argument that since children cannot validly consent to sex, sex with children is a violation of their rights.

I believe that there are serious questions about both of these arguments. The case for a causal connection between a child's sex with an adult and psychological harm is at best inconclusive. Those not negatively affected often remain invisible to clinical observation. Moreover, much of the harm from pedophilia arises from the negative social reaction to it, and to the extent that the harm arises from the social reaction, it provides only a limited argument against pedophilia. For harm arising from negative attitudes does nothing to show that the negative attitudes themselves are justified. Moreover, if the harm from pedophilia depends on a negative social reaction alone, it provides an argument against pedophilia only when it cannot be successfully concealed from public view.

Since there have been a number of recent extensive reviews of the psychological literature regarding the harmfulness of child–adult sex putting these claims into question, I shall focus in this paper on the argument from consent.[1] I shall argue that the inability of a child to consent in a full sense to sexual interactions is not sufficient to rule out pedophilia. However, I shall attempt to show that if we take the argument from consent one step further and consider the issue in the light of the child's retrospective consent as an adult to the earlier encounter, the argument points to a fundamental constraint on any child–adult sex.

[. . .]

In considering the capacity for consent, there is a tendency to assume that an agent is either capable of full consent or not capable of consent at all. But since children mature gradually, they increasingly become capable of consent. The assumption that there is a hard and fast boundary between consent and the absence of consent appears to arise from the usefulness of clear legal criteria for consent rather than from an actual examination of the capacities of the agents in question. Moreover, as we shall see, there are at least two distinct dimensions of consent: informed consent and free consent. The one is based on the agent's level of knowledge of the nature and consequences of his choices; the other on the degree to which the agent is free of subordination to others. These not only in each case admit of degrees but also might vary independently of one another. The complexity and variability of a child's capacity for consent make arguments that appeal to a child's lack of consent more problematic than often supposed.

I

In a recent article in *Public Affairs Quarterly*. Professor Igor Primoratz advances the most recent version of the argument that pedophilia is impermissible because of the child's inability to consent to sex.[2] In making his case, Primoratz provides an account of the necessary conditions of consent to sex. The first of these conditions is a knowledge of the physical, psychological, and social aspects of sex. For Primoratz, the inescapable limitation of a child's knowledge of these aspects of sex means that a child cannot consent to sex. While Primoratz admits that adults might in some cases be as naive and mistaken with regard to the ramifications of their sexual affairs as are children, he maintains that because these limitations are not applicable generally to adult sexual choices and result for the most part from the adult's decision not to examine his sexual choices as fully as he might, they do not put the validity of adult consent to sex in general into question as they do in the case of sex with children.

There is clearly an age at which a child does not have sufficient knowledge of sex to be capable of informed consent to it. However, Primoratz and others who reject pedophilia because the child cannot consent to it fail to explain why a child must be capable of informed consent to engage in sex with adults and not to engage in a wide range of other activities for which the child is equally incapable of informed consent.[3] Children are typically less informed than adults about the physical, psychological, and social consequences of many of their activities. They do not appear to be less informed of the consequences of sex with adults than of the consequences of athletics, courses of study, religion, and many non-sexual social relationships. I take it that Primoratz and other critics of child–adult sex would hardly prohibit all of these activities on the ground that the child has insufficient knowledge and experience to make possible informed consent to them.

For Primoratz children are not only incapable of informed consent to sex with adults, they are also incapable of free consent because of their dependence upon adults and the superior social position of adults. Primoratz introduces his argument for the inability of children to freely consent to sex with adults by considering David Finkelbor's contention that "adults control all kinds of resources that are essential to (children) – food, money, freedom etc. In this sense the child is exactly like the prisoner who volunteers to be a research subject. The child has no freedom in which to consider the choice."[4]

[. . .]

However, while the social and economic asymmetry between adults and children puts free consent into question, it does nothing to explain why this rules out sex between children and adults but not other active ties that adults encourage children to pursue. The same asymmetry between children and adults is present in many other cases as well as sex. Why is free consent necessary for the permissibility of sex and not for the permissibility of participation in sports or religious activities? These too might involve the exercise of authority over the child to motivate the child to participate in activities that the child might not otherwise participate in.

The asymmetry in social status between the adult and child is in any case far more complex and variable than Primoratz appears to recognize. As a child grows older, the child's dependence and inferiority are reduced in many domains. Hence, an early adolescent is far less subject to the authority of adults in general than a preschool child. When we consider very young children, it is doubtful that they have any real freedom from their adult caretakers. However, this is by no means generally the case even in older preadolescents. The asymmetry between child and adult is likewise affected by the relationship in which the younger person stands to the adult in question. In the case of parents and teachers who have authority over the child, the freedom of the child to reject the requests of the adults is typically less than their freedom to reject the requests of adults who have no authority over the child. A ten-year-old child's eighteen-year-old second cousin, for example, has far less control and authority over the child than the child's parents or teachers. By the time a child is school age, the child can normally distinguish between those who have authority over him or her and those who do not and can recognize the domain and extent of the authority. Primoratz's

argument that a child cannot freely consent to activities that adults encourage is more plausible the younger the child and the greater the authority the adult in question exercises over the child.

Primoratz appeals to studies by Sandor Ferenczi in 1932 and Michael Ingram in 1981 showing that in typical cases of child–adult sex, the activity has different meanings for the child and for the adult. He argues that this further puts into question the legitimacy of adult–child sexual interaction.[5] For the child according to Ferenczi the sexual act is simply playfulness, tenderness, and affection. The adult often "mistakes the child's playfulness for wishes of a sexually mature person" and acts on the basis of this misperception.

One might question whether it is indeed generally the case that children misinterpret sexual activity as non-sexual in the light of the fact that, as most observers admit, children have genuine sexual desires. If they are not asexual, why do they typically fail to recognize sexual activity? But even if we admit that the child typically interprets sexual activity in a non sexual manner, what does this show? In adult sex, the two parties often interpret the meaning of the act differently. One of the parties might take the sexual act as an expression of love and the other simply as erotic play. If one party misleads the other, this indeed undermines consent and puts the legitimacy of the interaction into doubt. But a difference in interpretation alone does not by itself undermine consent. If the absence of consent is sufficient to rule out sex with children, the difference in interpretation of the act is not needed to condemn it. If the absence of consent is not sufficient to rule out sex with children, it hardly seems that a mere difference of interpretation of the meaning of the act is a stronger basis for condemnation. For children and adults interpret almost every activity in a somewhat different light. Certainly this does not put into question the legitimacy of all such activities. If a difference in interpretation does not put into question other activities in which adults participate with children, why does it put sexual activities into question?

One reason why we might require consent for sex and not for such activities as religion, courses of study, or even the decision as to the parent with whom the child is to live might be that sex involves an intimate physical interaction in a manner in which these other activities do not. Hence, one might argue that nonconsensual sex involves a violation of a child's right to bodily privacy and to a control of his or her body. From this perspective, sexual interaction with a child is a trespass in a sense in which nonsexual activities are not.

I find it hard to understand this claim for a special status for sexual interaction. Medical treatment, sports, and nonsexual displays of physical affection involve bodily contact with children. There are nonsexual demonstrations of affection, e.g., the comforting of a child who is ill, that might be more physically intimate than some sexual acts such as masturbation in the presence of a child. One would hardly prohibit all physical interactions between adults and children on the ground that children are not capable of free informed consent to them. In order to prohibit sexual interaction on the ground that it involves physical intimacy, one must make a case that there are physical or psychological features of sexual interaction that justify the ruling out of nonconsensual sex but not other nonconsensual bodily interactions. If, as I suspect, one cannot make such a case, one can rule out nonconsensual sexual interactions between adults and children without ruling out all nonconsensual interactions only if one shows that sexual interactions typically fail to meet the general condition of any legitimate comportment toward children.

II

I shall argue that the condition of legitimate nonconsensual interactions with children is that the children be justified in retrospectively consenting to the interaction once they become capable of mature judgment. The first step in this argument is to answer the question as to why we require consent as distinct from a mere willingness as a condition of the legitimacy of certain actions of adults toward one another. Consent imposes more stringent conditions on an action than willingness. In order for an act to be willing, it is necessary only that an agent perform an act apart from coercion or threat. The agent need not understand what he is choosing or be prepared to take responsibility for the outcome. Nor must an agent be free of subordination to the authority of others in choosing the action. By contrast, when an agent consents to perform an action, he must recognize what he chooses and recognize the risks and rewards of the choice and be an independent agent. Hence, consent involves a knowledge of the nature of the act and its significant costs and benefits as well as the freedom to make a decision free from subordination to others.

If an action fails to fulfill these conditions of consent, an agent will rightly look back upon the action itself and its consequences as incidental to himself as an agent, and he will therefore be justified in disclaiming responsibility for the act and its outcome. Since he will not understand what he is choosing or the consequences of his choice, he cannot be said in a strict sense to choose the act at all. He will for this reason not regard it as his own in a full sense.

If a child is incapable of consent to sex, he will to that extent see the act from the future perspective of an agent capable of consent as something for which he was not himself responsible. The fact that he was willing to engage in the act or that he derived satisfaction from it at the time does not take away from his failure to understand what he was doing, to recognize its risks or rewards, or from his subordination to the adults with whom he interacted. If from the perspective of mature judgment, he finds that the act is one that he would not have consented to at the time, he will be justified in affirming that he was taken advantage of for ends other than his own even when he was not harmed by the encounter. He will therefore be justified in condemning the adults for their conduct toward him regardless of whether or not it harmed him.

For a child to understand the nature of a sexual interaction with an adult in our society poses a substantial challenge to the child. For in the same manner as most other human acts, sexual acts are defined by the rules that apply to them. Just as in order to understand what it is to buy a bond or an option, an agent must understand the rules that govern these investments, so must those who engage in a sexual interaction understand the rules of the relationship. These are often complex. The fact our society generally forbids child sexual activity means that there are no established positive rules that prescribe the expectations that children might reasonably entertain as to the character of their sexual interactions with adults. For this reason, children and the adults who participate in sexual interaction with them must in each case formulate and communicate to each other the rules of the relationship. These include entry and exit rules, rules prescribing the sort of acts permitted and forbidden, rules regarding sexual relationships with others, rules regarding the scheduling of the activity, rules of the disclosure of the affair and so forth. The younger and less experienced the child, the more likely the child will fail to understand some or all of these rules. The fact that an adult cannot appeal to established social rules means that adults too might fail to have a clear conception of the rules of their sexual interaction with a child. Insofar as adults fail to understand the rules of the interaction, they too fail to meet a necessary condition of informed consent.

The existence of established rules in the cases of those activities that we typically find acceptable for children marks an important distinction between these and sex. The existence of these rules in these cases make it more likely that a child will be able to understand the nature of his interactions with others. For example, children typically understand the rules of the sports in which they participate and therefore to that extent understand the nature of the activity even though they might lack an adequate understanding of the benefits and risks. However, children often fail to understand other rules governing the sport. Hence, they might not understand the rules and practices of the adults who coach and supervise the sport or the rules and expectations of the parents and other adults who are involved in the sport as spectators or in other roles. If they fail to understand the full range of rules that govern an activity, their consent is not fully informed in spite of their understanding of certain of the rules of the activity.

In order to be capable of informed consent, an agent must, as we have pointed out, not only understand the nature of the act that he chooses but also recognize the significant risks and benefits of the act. In the case of sex, this involves understanding the risks of disappointment, abandonment, sexual competition, the chance of humiliating or offending the other and of the other's humiliating and offending oneself, and in certain cases, the risk of pregnancy. The younger and less experienced the child, the less likely it is that the child will be able to understand these risks at the time of his action and as a result will experience these as a mere fate that befalls him rather than as a consequence of his own choices.

In order to minimize a child's ignorance of the risks of his or her actions, adults must clearly communicate the parameters of their interaction with the child so that the child understands what sort of commitment the adult is making to the child. If a sexual interaction is to be brief and casual, the adult must make this clear to the child and have evidence that the child understands and accepts this. If the child has expectations of a further commitment, it is essential that the adult make an effort to understand these expectations and be prepared to meet them if he decides in this case to have a sexual relationship with the child. If a child is too young to understand the parameters of an encounter or if the adult is not prepared to meet the expectations of the child, he must refrain from the act since he otherwise takes a high risk of disappointing the child.

Children, as Primoratz points out, are typically subordinate to adults in a manner that limits their freedom of choice in relation to the requests of adults. This limitation is, as we have seen, a matter of degree. To the degree that a child's willingness to engage in a sexual relationship with an adult is a result of the superior authority of the adult, to that degree it is unfree and nonconsensual. In order to make the choice of the child as free as possible, adults must make clear to the child that they will do nothing to punish the child because of the child's refusal to engage in the interaction.

While adults typically cannot bring a child to the point where the child is capable of full consent, they can take actions that make a child's interactions with them as consensual as possible. If they do this, and have good reason to suppose that the action will be accord with the child's reasonable goals and values, the person will be justified in retrospectively affirming the relationship as he becomes capable of full consent.

This appeal to appeal to future consent as a surrogate for present consent might appear open to the objection that since future consent is based on the values and goals of the adult, not those of the child, it is therefore not a justifiable basis for an assessment of an action toward a child. But the consent in this case is not based on the adult's present values and goals but on the values and goals of the child. In order to be justified in retrospectively consenting to the action, the person must have reason to affirm that the adult took care to assure that the action met the conditions of legitimate actions toward children. In order to be legitimate, these actions need not accord with all the goals and values that the person might acquire as an adult. If this were a requirement of legitimacy, it would be hard to justify any action toward children. For it is just about impossible to know during childhood what the goals and values of a person as an adult will turn out to be. What adults who interact with children can be expected to know is whether or not an action is in accord with the reasonable goals and values of the child.

For example, it is legitimate for an adult to encourage a child to attend a church when the activity is as consensual as possible, enjoyable to the child, and the adult has reason to believe that it will have no harmful effects on the child. The adult need not have reason to suppose that the person will remain religious as an adult. In the same manner, the fact that a person might reject a certain sort of sexual interaction as an adult does not justify a condemnation of that interaction as a child when the interaction is as consensual as possible, enjoyable, and appears at the time likely to have no harmful consequences for the child's well-being.

The justification of sex between adults and children does not demand meeting the impossible condition that an adult be certain of the child's retrospective assessment of the interaction. It implies only that the adult has good reason to affirm that as the child matures into an adult, he will have no good reason for not consenting to the relationship. For example, social pressures and prejudices might cause a person to condemn a past relationship simply because it violates a common social norm, not because it was manipulative, uncaring, or irresponsible. If a person condemns a past relationship for no good reason, this does not invalidate the relationship; it invalidates the negative judgment.

The requirement of justified retrospective consent does not depend on the presence of psychological harm in the absence of such consent. While the duty toward the child in this case is a duty to demonstrate a concern for the child's future welfare, a failure to fulfill the duty might not lead to psychological harm. The moral wrong of a violation of this duty is as independent of actual psychological harm as is the moral wrong from the violation of other duties. No more than a person must suffer demonstrable psychological harm from being defrauded or betrayed in order to claim that he has been wronged by these acts need a person suffer such harm in order to claim that he was wronged in a childhood sexual encounter. Those who condemn adult–child sex because of psychological harm to the child are as mistaken as those who condemn other moral wrongs on the basis of psychological harm to the victim rather than because of a failure to fulfill one's duties to the victim.

[. . .]

Those adults who remain too inexperienced and naive to become informed of what is relevant to their sexual decisions must be treated in the same manner as children are treated. Others must act toward them in such a way that they have good reason to believe that the ill-informed agents would endorse the action once they become capable of informed consent. Those who take advantage of childlike adults are not morally superior to those who take advantage of children. For these adults will retrospectively rightly regard themselves as having been taken advantage of just as children do when treated in this manner.

Sexual interactions between adults in a superior position toward adults subject to their authority raise issues similar to those raised by adult–child sex. There are two conditions under which adults have legitimate authority over other adults. In the one, subordinates give free informed consent to the authority; in the other,

superiors exercise authority apart from free consent in military or other emergency situations where there may be justification for nonconsensual exercise of authority. When the authority is not consensual, superiors must appeal to retrospective consent to justify the nonconsensual imposition of authority in the same manner as adults must appeal to retrospective consent to justify their interactions with children.

The authority of adults over other adults does not legitimately extend to sexual demands. For legitimate sexual interaction between superiors and subordinates, it is necessary that they be as consensual as sexual interaction between equals. This requires that the authority of the superior play no role in the choice of the subordinate to participate in the interaction. Superiors who engage in sexual interactions with subordinates must accept the burden of proof in justifying the relationship because there is typically a reasonable doubt as to whether a subordinate freely consents in this case. In the same manner that in the case of adult–child sex we must ask whether the child would consent as an adult, in the case of sexual interactions between superiors and subordinates we must ask whether the subordinate would consent as an equal. Unless we have good reason for an affirmative answer, we cannot justify the sexual interaction in either case.

The appeal to retrospective consent to justify actions toward children is not distinctive of sex. When an adult leads a child into a sport or a social interaction that the adult does not have good reason to suppose that the child will consent to as an adult, he violates his responsibility toward the child just as he does when he leads a child into a sexual affair that he does not have good reason to suppose that the child will consent to as an adult. The adult's encouragement of a child to engage in a sport might indeed be even worse than encouraging the child into a sexual interaction if the child is less willing at the time to participate in the sport than to participate in the sex. This means that unless we are prepared to impose harsh sanctions for these nonsexual infractions of a child's autonomy, we cannot consistently impose harsh sanctions for sex when the failure to take into account the subsequent consent of the child to the sexual activity is the sole offense against the child.

In conclusion, let me summarize the basic distinction between my position and the position that pedophilia is impermissible because of the inability of the child to consent to sex. I argue that the absence of valid consent alone is not sufficient to prohibit sex since it is arbitrary to require consent for sex and not for other activities with children. However, I hold that the inability of children to consent imposes a constraint on all adult interaction with children. The adult's interaction with children is legitimate absent full consent only when the adult has reason to suppose the child will have good reason to consent to the interaction when the child becomes an adult capable of free informed consent. When adults constrain their actions toward children in this manner, they can defend their conduct toward them regardless of the nature of the activity. For the most part, adults cannot make the case that children will consent to adult–child sex when they assess it as mature agents. If they cannot make this case, adult–child sex is illegitimate.

Notes

1 For a critical review of the literature on the psychological affect on children of child–adult sex, see T. O. O'Carroll, *Pedophilia: The Radical Case* (London: Peter Owen, 1980), and R. Ehman, "Adult–Child Sex," in *Philosophy and Sex,* 2d edn, eds. R. Baker and F Elliston (Buffalo: Prometheus Books, 1984).

2 "Pedophilia," *Public Affairs Quarterly*, vol. 13 (1999), pp. 99–109.

3 For a further discussion of this point see Ehman, "Adult–Child Sex."

4 David Finkelhor, "What's Wrong with Sex between Adults and Children?" *American Journal of Orthopsychiatry*, vol. 49 (1979).

5 S. Ferenczi, "Sprachverwirrung zwischen den Erwachsenen and Dem Kind (Die Sprache der Zaertlichkeit and der Leildenschaft)," *Bausteine zur Psychoanalyse*, 2 Aufl., Bd. III (Bern: Verlag Hans Huber, 1964), p. 518; Michael Ingram, "Participating Victims: A Study of Sexual Offenses with Boys," in *Children and Sex: New Findings, New Perspectives*, ed. Larry L Constantine and Floyd M Martinsom (Boston: Little Brown and Co., 1981).

Index

Please note that References to Notes will contain the letter 'n' following the Note number

Index

Index

Index

Index

Index